The Thomas Guide®

G000292993

Pacific Northwest
roadatlas

We want to hear from you!
Give us your feedback at:
http://go.randmcnally.com/comments

Help us keep your road atlas
more accurate than online maps.
If you find an error, report it here:
http://go.randmcnally.com/report

The paper used inside this book is manufactured using an elemental chlorine-free method and is sourced from forests that are managed responsibly through forest certification programs such as the Sustainable Forestry Initiative.®

If you have questions, concerns, or even a compliment, contact us by visiting our website at consumeraffairs@randmcnally.com

or write to:
Rand McNally Consumer Affairs
P.O. Box 7600
Chicago, Illinois 60680-9915

 RAND M℃NALLY   NAVTEQ ON BOARD

Contents
Contenidos

Introduction
Introducción

Maps
Mapas

Lists and Indexes
Lista e índices

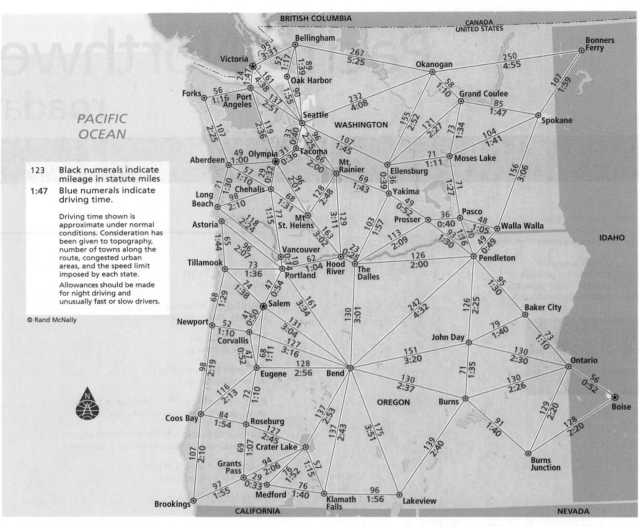

123   Black numerals indicate mileage in statute miles

1:47   Blue numerals indicate driving time.

Driving time shown is approximate under normal conditions. Consideration has been given to topography, number of towns along the route, congested urban areas, and the speed limit imposed by each state.

Allowances should be made for night driving and unusually fast or slow drivers.

© Rand McNally

Legend

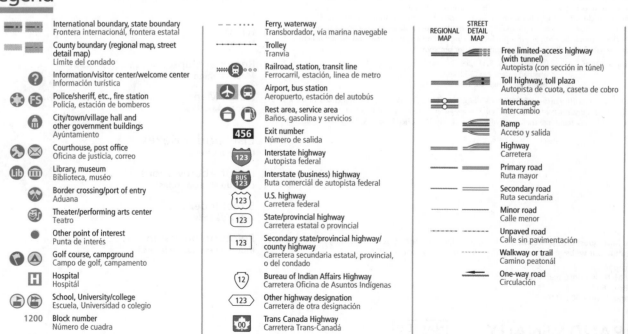

International boundary, state boundary	Frontera internacionál, frontera estatal
County boundary (regional map, street detail map)	Límite del condado
Information/visitor center/welcome center	Información turística
Police/sheriff, etc., fire station	Policía, estación de bomberos
City/town/village hall and other government buildings	Ayúntamiento
Courthouse, post office	Oficina de justicia, correo
Library, museum	Biblioteca, múseo
Border crossing/port of entry	Aduana
Theater/performing arts center	Teatro
Other point of interest	Punta de interés
Golf course, campground	Campo de golf, campamento
Hospital	Hospitál
School, University/college	Escuela, Universidad o colegio
1200 Block number	Número de cuadra

Ferry, waterway	Transbordador, vía marina navegable
Trolley	Tranvia
Railroad, station, transit line	Ferrocarril, estación, linea de metro
Airport, bus station	Aeropuerto, estación del autobús
Rest area, service area	Baños, gasolina y servicios
456 Exit number	Número de salida
123 Interstate highway	Autopista federal
BUS 123 Interstate (business) highway	Ruta comerciál de autopista federal
123 U.S. highway	Carretera federal
123 State/provincial highway	Carretera estatal o provincial
123 Secondary state/provincial highway/county highway	Carretera secundaria estatal, provincial, o del condado
12 Bureau of Indian Affairs Highway	Carretera Oficina de Asuntos Indigenas
123 Other highway designation	Carretera de otra designación
00 Trans Canada Highway	Carretera Trans-Canadá

REGIONAL MAP   STREET DETAIL MAP

Free limited-access highway (with tunnel)	Autopista (con sección in túnel)
Toll highway, toll plaza	Autopista de cuota, caseta de cobro
Interchange	Intercambio
Ramp	Acceso y salida
Highway	Carretera
Primary road	Ruta mayor
Secondary road	Ruta secundaria
Minor road	Calle menor
Unpaved road	Calle sin pavimentación
Walkway or trail	Camino peatonál
One-way road	Circulación

RAND MCNALLY

Mileage Chart

	Astoria, OR	Bellingham, WA	Bend, OR	Boise, ID	Bonners Ferry, ID	Burns, OR	Coos Bay, OR	Corvallis, OR	Ellensburg, WA	Eugene, OR	Grants Pass, OR	Hood River, OR	Lakeview, OR	Medford, OR	Moses Lake, WA	Newport, OR	Oak Harbor, WA	Olympia, WA	Pasco, WA	Port Angeles, WA	Portland, OR	Prosser, WA	Salem, OR	Sea-Tac Airport, WA	Seattle, WA	Spokane, WA	The Dalles, OR	Vancouver, BC	Victoria, BC	Yakima, WA
Aberdeen, WA	77	197	296	564	474	415	364	225	196	252	386	196	516	414	266	213	142	49	315	143	142	279	188	98	109	367	218	249	167	231
Albany, OR	152	331	123	498	526	253	157	11	289	44	179	131	281	207	354	63	331	183	285	299	71	265	27	232	242	420	153	383	323	254
Anacortes, WA	254	40	404	575	456	548	472	334	178	360	495	305	624	523	248	385	20	138	297	86	250	262	296	92	78	350	315	92	63	213
Ashland, OR	368	546	186	485	742	297	182	222	505	178	42	346	159	13	569	274	547	398	500	514	286	480	243	447	458	635	368	598	538	469
Astoria, OR		265	250	518	546	370	231	166	268	193	328	151	443	356	338	133	209	121	305	211	96	284	129	170	181	440	173	317	235	222
Baker City, OR	392	460	230	128	405	150	524	386	271	412	475	242	289	442	235	437	460	409	164	495	303	187	348	383	377	299	221	511	519	236
Bellingham, WA	265		415	586	468	559	484	345	189	371	506	316	635	534	260	396	52	149	308	118	261	273	307	103	89	361	326	52	95	224
Bend, OR	250	415		318	491	130	253	127	253	128	241	143	175	216	318	179	416	267	250	383	161	229	131	316	327	384	130	467	407	218
Boise, ID	518	586	318		487	188	570	512	398	445	524	368	327	498	361	564	587	535	290	621	429	314	475	510	504	425	347	638	646	362
Bremerton, WA	148	153	324	548	429	443	392	254	151	280	415	225	544	443	221	305	74	58	270	76	170	235	216	56	64	323	247	204	100	186
Burns, OR	370	559	130	188	505		382	257	371	257	338	262	139	310	334	308	560	386	264	502	281	287	261	436	446	398	250	611	526	336
Chehalis, WA	92	177	240	508	453	359	308	169	175	196	331	140	460	359	245	221	178	29	232	145	86	196	132	78	88	347	162	228	169	148
Cheney, WA	427	348	372	412	123	386	560	421	160	448	582	277	525	610	92	473	349	307	123	383	338	157	384	272	266	16	256	401	408	189
Coeur d'Alene, ID	472	394	417	412	78	431	605	466	205	493	628	323	570	655	136	518	394	352	168	428	383	201	429	317	311	34	301	446	453	234
Coos Bay, OR	231	484	253	570	679	382		160	442	116	142	284	341	170	506	98	484	335	438	451	224	417	180	384	395	572	306	535	476	407
Corvallis, OR	166	345	127	512	540	257	160		303	47	182	145	284	210	368	52	345	197	299	313	85	278	41	245	256	434	167	396	337	268
Crater Lake, OR	361	540	137	439	626	252	210	215	389	172	94	278	127	76	454	267	540	391	385	507	280	364	236	440	451	520	266	591	532	354
Ellensburg, WA	268	189	253	398	279	371	442	303		330	464	159	428	492	71	354	190	148	120	224	220	85	266	113	107	172	138	241	249	36
Eugene, OR	193	371	128	445	567	257	116	47	330		138	171	268	166	394	99	372	223	326	339	111	305	68	272	282	460	193	423	363	294
Everett, WA	209	61	355	525	407	499	423	284	129	311	445	255	575	473	199	336	62	89	248	87	201	212	247	42	28	300	266	113	156	164
Florence, OR	183	432	193	510	628	322	49	84	391	61	162	233	306	212	456	49	433	284	387	400	173	366	129	333	344	522	254	484	425	356
Forks, WA	184	174	403	671	559	522	471	333	281	359	494	304	623	522	351	321	123	156	400	56	249	364	295	186	193	452	326	226	80	316
Gold Beach, OR	310	562	331	648	758	461	79	238	520	194	124	362	324	153	585	177	562	414	516	530	302	496	258	463	473	651	384	614	554	485
Grand Coulee, WA	388	271	369	434	192	408	557	418	121	445	579	274	546	607	73	470	271	268	144	345	335	164	380	233	227	85	253	323	369	151
Grants Pass, OR	328	506	241	524	702	338	142	182	464	138		306	198	29	529	233	506	358	460	474	246	440	202	407	417	595	328	558	498	429
Hillsboro, OR	78	278	181	448	476	299	229	91	239	117	252	80	381	280	304	106	279	131	235	247	18	214	53	179	190	370	102	331	271	203
Hood River, OR	151	316	143	368	397	262	284	145	159	171	306		347	334	224	196	316	168	155	284	62	134	107	216	227	290	23	367	308	124
Kennewick, WA	302	308	246	287	247	260	434	296	120	322	457	152	399	485	77	347	309	267	6	343	213	36	258	232	226	140	130	360	367	84
Klamath Falls, OR	362	540	137	422	627	234	245	216	390	172	102	279	96	76	454	268	541	392	386	508	280	366	237	441	452	520	266	592	532	355
La Grande, OR	348	416	292	170	361	193	480	342	227	368	503	198	332	464	191	393	416	365	120	451	259	143	304	339	333	254	177	467	475	192
Lake Oswego, OR	104	269	160	437	465	279	216	78	228	104	239	69	368	267	293	129	270	121	224	237	10	203	40	170	180	358	91	321	261	192
Lewiston, ID	433	397	377	300	192	378	565	427	209	453	588	283	517	616	162	478	398	356	128	432	344	162	389	321	315	104	261	450	457	211
Long Beach, WA	19	259	274	547	536	398	248	187	258	214	349	180	478	377	328	150	204	111	334	205	112	313	150	160	171	429	202	311	229	245
Long View, WA	50	216	202	470	492	322	270	132	214	158	293	103	422	321	284	183	216	68	257	184	48	236	94	116	127	386	125	267	208	167
McMinnville, OR	101	299	159	466	494	288	206	46	257	94	229	99	358	256	322	75	299	151	253	267	39	233	28	200	210	388	121	350	291	222
Medford, OR	356	534	216	498	730	310	170	210	492	166	29	334	172		557	261	534	386	488	502	274	468	230	435	445	623	356	586	526	457
Milton-Freewater, OR	327	361	271	243	274	226	460	321	172	347	482	177	364	443	123	372	362	344	55	411	238	88	283	318	312	167	155	414	435	137
Moses Lake, WA	338	260	318	361	210	334	506	368	71	394	529	224	474	557		419	260	218	71	294	285	105	330	183	177	104	202	311	319	100
Mount St. Helens, WA	113	244	262	530	520	381	330	192	221	218	353	163	482	381	312	243	244	96	273	212	109	238	154	144	155	414	185	296	236	189
Mount Vernon, WA	242	28	388	559	440	532	456	318	162	344	479	289	608	507	232	369	29	122	281	95	234	246	280	76	62	334	299	80	123	197
Mt. Rainier, WA	160	182	305	431	374	404	374	235	102	261	396	129	525	424	166	286	182	114	153	186	152	118	197	87	96	268	149	233	211	69
Newport, OR	133	396	179	564	592	308	98	52	354	99	233	196	336	261	419		397	248	351	364	136	330	83	297	307	485	218	448	388	319
Newport, WA	487	408	432	472	61	446	620	481	220	507	642	337	584	670	152	532	409	367	182	443	398	216	443	332	326	47	316	461	467	249
Oak Harbor, WA	209	52	416	587	468	560	484	345	190	372	506	316	636	534	260	397		150	309	67	262	274	308	103	90	361	327	104	91	225
Okanogan, WA	393	267	409	474	250	447	597	458	155	485	620	315	583	648	112	510	267	273	184	350	376	215	421	238	232	143	293	298	374	191
Olympia, WA	121	149	267	535	426	386	335	197	148	223	358	168	487	386	218	248	150		267	119	113	232	159	50	61	319	190	201	144	183
Ontario, OR	464	531	260	56	434	130	512	457	343	387	468	314	269	440	306	509	532	480	236	567	374	259	420	455	449	370	292	583	591	308
Pasco, WA	305	308	250	290	242	264	438	299	120	326	460	155	403	488	71	351	309	267		343	216	36	262	232	226	135	134	360	368	85
Pendleton, OR	298	365	242	221	311	196	430	292	177	318	453	148	335	481	140	343	366	314	70	401	209	93	254	289	283	204	126	417	425	142
Port Angeles, WA	211	118	383	621	502	502	451	313	224	339	474	284	603	502	294	364	67	119	343		229	308	275	129	137	396	306	170	24	260
Portland Airport, OR	96	261	158	426	454	278	233	94	217	121	256	59	385	284	282	146	262	113	213	229	12	192	57	162	172	348	81	313	253	182
Portland, OR	96	261	161	429	457	281	224	85	220	111	246	62	375	274	285	136	262	113	216	229		196	47	162	172	351	84	313	253	185
Prosser, WA	284	273	229	314	275	287	417	278	85	305	440	134	426	468	105	330	274	232	36	308	196		241	197	190	169	113	325	332	49
Richland, WA	315	284	259	300	252	273	447	308	95	335	470	165	412	498	81	360	284	242	12	319	225	28	271	207	201	145	143	336	343	77
Roseburg, OR	261	439	208	526	635	338	84	115	397	72	69	239	231	97	462	166	440	291	394	407	179	373	135	340	350	528	261	491	431	362
Salem, OR	129	307	131	475	503	261	180	41	266	68	202	107	332	230	330	83	308	159	262	275	47	241		208	219	396	129	359	299	230
Sea-Tac Airport, WA	170	103	316	510	391	436	384	245	113	272	407	216	536	435	183	297	103	50	232	129	162	197	208		14	284	238	154	154	148
Seattle, WA	181	89	327	504	385	446	395	256	107	282	417	227	546	445	177	307	90	61	226	137	172	190	219	14		278	249	141	161	142
Shelton, WA	113	170	285	553	446	404	354	215	168	242	376	186	505	404	238	266	97	22	287	98	132	252	178	70	81	340	208	222	122	204
Spokane, WA	440	361	384	425	107	398	572	434	172	460	595	290	537	623	104	485	361	319	135	396	351	169	396	284	278		268	413	420	202
St. Helens, OR	66	240	190	458	486	309	251	112	242	138	273	91	402	301	312	163	241	92	245	208	28	224	74	141	152	379	112	292	233	195
Tacoma, WA	151	122	296	518	399	416	365	226	120	252	387	197	516	415	191	277	122	31	240	106	142	204	188	23	33	292	219	174	130	156
The Dalles, OR	173	326	130	347	375	250	306	167	138	193	328	23	335	356	202	218	327	190	134	306	84	113	129	238	249	268		378	330	103
Tillamook, OR	65	333	206	503	530	335	166	90	294	141	275	135	404	303	358	68	334	186	289	279	73	269	74	247	257	424	157	385	303	258
Vancouver, BC	317	52	467	638	520	611	535	396	241	423	558	367	687	586	311	448	104	201	360	170	313	325	359	154	141	413	378		68	276
Vancouver, WA	88	253	166	434	462	285	231	92	225	119	254	67	383	282	290	144	253	105	221	221	9	200	55	156	164	356	88	304	245	190
Victoria, BC	235	95	407	646	527	526	476	337	249	363	498	308	627	526	319	388	91	144	368	24	253	332	299	154	161	420	330	68		284
Walla Walla, WA	331	354	281	253	263	236	470	331	166	358	492	181	375	520	116	382	355	313	48	390	242	82	293	278	272	156	159	406	414	131
Wenatchee, WA	309	182	324	427	276	400	512	374	70	400	535	230	498	563	68	425	183	188	137	265	291	127	336	153	148	169	208	234	289	106
Yakima, WA	222	224	218	362	308	336	407	268	36	294	429	124	392	457	100	319	225	183	85	260	185	49	230	148	142	202	103	276	284	

Mileages in this chart are based upon the routes usually followed by motorists. Highway systems involved include interstate, U.S., and state highways.

General Information

HIGHWAY PATROL

British Columbia . . . . In case of emergency, call 911

Washington State . . . . In case of emergency, call 911

Oregon State. In case of emergency, call 911

Idaho State . . . . In case of emergency, call 911

ROAD CONDITIONS

British Columbia . . . . DriveBC: (800) 550-4997
www.drivebc.ca

Washington State . . . . Washington State Department of Transportation: 511, (800) 695-7623
www.wsdot.wa.gov/traffic/

Oregon State. Oregon Department of Transportation: 511, (800) 977-6368, (503) 588-2941
www.tripcheck.com

Idaho State . . . . Idaho Transportation Department: 511, (888) 432-7623
511.idaho.gov

DEPARTMENT OF TRANSPORTATION

British Columbia . . . . BC Ministry of Transportation & Infrastructure:
www.gov.bc.ca/tran/

Washington State . . . . Washington State Department of Transportation: (360) 705-7000
www.wsdot.wa.gov

Oregon State. Oregon Department of Transportation: (888) 275-6368
www.odot.state.or.us

Idaho State . . . . Idaho State Tourism & Transportation:
www.state.id.us/tourism_transport/

FERRY CROSSING

British Columbia . . . . BC Ferries: (888) 223-3779
www.bcferries.com

Washington State . . . . Washington State Ferries:
Seattle: (206) 464-6400,
Toll free in state: (888) 808-7977 or (800) 843-3779
www.wsdot.wa.gov/ferries

CROSSING THE BORDER

British Columbia . . . . Canada Border Services Agency:
www.cbsa-asfc.gc.ca

Washington State . . . . U.S. Customs and Border Protection:
www.cbp.gov

WEATHER CONDITIONS

British Columbia . . . . www.weatheroffice.gc.ca

Washington State . . . . www.weather.com

Oregon State. www.weather.com

Idaho State . . . . www.weather.com

VISITOR'S INFORMATION

Tourism British Columbia . . . . (800) 435-5622
www.hellobc.com

Washington State Tourism . . . . (800) 544-1800
www.experiencewashington.com

Travel Oregon . . . . (800) 547-7842
www.traveloregon.com

Idaho Division of Tourism Development (800) 847-4843, (208) 334-2470
www.visitidaho.org

You can also get tourism information and road construction updates at RandMcNally.com.

Volcanic *Legacy*

A Best of the Road® trip

Crater Lake

The Cascade Range runs the length of Oregon, from the Washington border and fingering south into state parks, national wildlife refuges, and national forests that lie just shy of California. It's where rivers run fast and wild, lakes deep and clear. From the peaks of Crater Lake National Park to the pear orchards in the Rogue River valley and small towns in between, southern Oregon's mountains and valleys rival the better-known beach destinations. ▶

The trip begins just south of Eugene, on OR 58 heading straight into the Willamette National Forest. Rivers hug the roadside, and a covered bridge at **Lowell State Recreation Site** serves as a reminder of days when horses trod these routes. Continue southeast until

Lowell Covered Bridge, built in 1945, spans the Willamette River

the road hooks up with US 97 and then west again at OR 138 towards the north entrance (open only during summer) of **Crater Lake National Park**.

The road climbs south through a pumice "desert." It meets up with the scenic rim drive along the top of the volcanic caldera, offering views of the amazing blue lake, deepest in the U.S. at 1,943 feet. The energetic can climb the Mt. Scott trail, but a Crater Lake boat ride (accessible from the Cleetwood Trail) remains a highlight for most visitors. Boats run only in summer, however. (The park receives an average of 533 inches of snow each year from October to June.)

Continue out the south end of Crater Lake on OR 62, making a stop at **Fort Klamath Museum**, on the grounds of a fort that stood here from 1863-1890. While original buildings are gone, military artifacts and an excellent museum staff fill in the history.

Connect back with US 97 and go north just past the Chiloquin exit to **Happy Trails Cowboy Campground**. Here, horses, people, even the family dog are welcome. (And owner Bob Lafferty prefers dogs off-leash, as they tend to be less aggressive.) If you don't have your own mount or an RV, don't worry. Bob will set you up with a friendly steed for a personal trail ride into the adjacent forest preserve, hustle up a delicious steak dinner by the fire, and make up a comfy bed in a platform tent for the night.

Come daybreak, pack up and head south along Klamath Lake to Klamath Falls and breakfast at **Nibbley's Cafe**. Don't let the strip mall location fool you: you'll find friendly waitresses and tasty, creative dishes for breakfast or lunch. The house specialty is oatcakes, a substantial pancake that can be topped with blueberries, pecans, or bananas. The daily specials might include local salmon omelettes, salads, and wraps, accompanied by fresh baked oat bread, wheat bread, or other bakery offerings.

In town you can rent canoes or kayaks at The Ledge. Put in south of town at Lake Ewauna, where pelicans and other fowl flock, or south at **Lower Klamath Lake Wildlife Reserve** along the California border in Tulelake. It's a scenic drive and well worth it for birders as this is a flyway. Another option is driving north on OR 140 to traverse the other side of Upper Klamath Lake, stopping at **Rocky Point Resort**. Campers can spend the night, and a few motel rooms and cabins accommodate other guests. But the real joy here is the **Upper Klamath National Wildlife Reserve canoe trail**. Put in your craft (canoes are available for rent onsite) and paddle through marsh and open water. Wildlife abounds, with the opportunity to see bald eagles fishing, white pelicans and osprey nesting, and other waterfowl.

From Rocky Point, drive east on OR 140 to Central Point and OR 99. Central Point is the home of **Rogue Creamery**, which has been making cheese since the 1930s. They branched into blue cheese in 1957, and the varieties of blues continue to rank among customer favorites. Cheeses for sale include Oregon Blue, Smokey Blue, Crater Lake Blue, and other Rogue specialties, like Oregonzola. It's all made from

Cheeses and samples in creamery store

hormone- and antibiotic-free milk from grass-fed cows. While you cannot actually tour the creamery, employees will demonstrate how the cheese is made, and you can watch some of the production from behind a glass window in the store.

Just across the parking lot from Rogue is **Lillie Belle Farms**. The custom-chocolate shop sells artisan chocolates handmade from primarily organic ingredients. Unusual samplings include chocolate with local lavender, and fresh fruits such as strawberries, raspberries, and marionberries. Each piece is a work of art: dark ganache with white paisley design, marzipan fig, or blue cheese and chocolate balls wrapped in lavender-colored foil.

The National Historic Landmark town of **Jacksonville** lies southeast of Central Point. In the center of this former gold rush town, the **Jacksonville Inn** offers fine dining, bed-and-breakfast lodging, and a wine shop. It's an easy stroll from the inn to see some of the 100 19th-century buildings, now converted into shops and other businesses. Stop in at the Beekman House for a visit with the costumed docents who recall lives of the wealthy 19th-century merchant class.

From Jacksonville, swing down to Medford for a stop at **Harry & David Country Village** and tour. There's something about the climate here that pears love. That is why Harry & David still sells more pears than any other delicious fruit or candy in their vast catalog complex. The country village is a retail venue (with lots of in-store specials) to buy fresh produce or start a tour of the production facility. The tour costs $5, redeemable at the store if you purchase $40 worth of merchandise. You'll be taken past rows of chocolate dippers (Harry & David calls the process "enrobing"), and fruit and basket packers. The walking tour takes about one hour.

Volcanic Legacy (cont.)

If there's time, continue on south to Ashland, home of the famed Shakespeare Festival. Stroll through Lithium Park and spend the night at the golden-hued **Ashland Springs Hotel**. Built in 1925, the hotel offers 70 boutique rooms with full-service hotel amenities. It is on the National Register of Historic Places and is one of the Historic Hotels of America.

Across the street, Chef Neil Clooney—named Oregon's best chef in 2008—creates Latin and Asian fusion dishes daily at the **Dragonfly Cafe**. Inspired dishes range from coconut French toast and avocado scramble for breakfast to ahi tuna plates and big bowls of udon noodles, Portobello mushrooms, and peanut sauce for dinner.

Drive north and back through Jacksonville, then east along the Applegate River to US 199. A fun stop in Kirby is **It's a Burl**, where artisans carve craft tables, chairs, porch swings,

and more from gnarly burled wood. Continue up the twisting hairpin curves of OR 46 en route to **Oregon Caves National Monument**. Most visitors take the guided cave tour that features amazing formations of stalactites, stalagmites, curtains, and more. For those with extra energy, a two- to three-hour hike with a more than 1,000-foot elevation gain along the Big Tree trail leads to the widest Douglas fir in the state of Oregon. Views of the Siskiyou mountains surrounding the park make the trek rewarding. Along the trail you may see the Oregon Caves forest snail, a striped-shell creature that lives only in or near the monument.

Return back to US 199 and north to Grants Pass. It's a bustling town worth exploring, but first stop for a jetboat ride at **Hellgate Jetboat Excursions**. It doesn't take athletic skill to sit in a jetboat and ride the wild and scenic Rogue River, but it sure feels adventurous. Excursions ($37-$62 for adults) range from two-hour blasts

Jetboat near dock

to four-hour power rides with lunch or dinner to five-hour white-water adventures. The boat's captain revs up the motor of the hydro-jet and roars downstream. This fast pace slows only for guests to check out the osprey nests, beaver dams, and other wildlife along the route. If another boat is nearby, the two captains might enact a chase scene through rapids and spin 360 degrees a few times just for screams. It's a wild end to a southern Oregon vacation.

—By Laurie D. Borman

Additional Information

Lowell State Recreation Site
Hwy. 58 and Pengra Rd.
Lowell, OR 97452
(541) 937-1173
www.oregonstateparks.org

Crater Lake National Park
Crater Lake, OR 97604
(541) 594-3000
www.nps.gov/crla

Fort Klamath Museum
51400 OR 62
Chiloquin, OR 97624
(541) 381-2230
www.co.klamath.or.us/museum/Profile%20
FKM.htm

Happy Trails Cowboy Campground
46925 US 97 North
Chiloquin, OR 97624
(541) 783-3559
www.happytrailscowboycampground.com

Nibbley's Cafe
2650 Washburn Way, Ste. 120
Klamath Falls, OR 97601
(541) 883-2314

Klamath Lake National Wildlife Reserve and Rocky Point Resort
28121 Rocky Point Rd.
Klamath Falls, OR 97601
(530) 667-2230
www.fws.gov/klamathbasinrefuges/index.html

Rogue Creamery
311 N. Front St.
Central Point, OR 97502
(541) 664-1537
www.roguecreamery.com

Lillie Belle Farms
211 N. Front St.
Central Point, OR 97502
(541) 664-2815
www.lilliebellefarms.com

Jacksonville Chamber of Commerce & Visitor Center
185 N. Oregon St.
Jacksonville, OR 97530
(541) 899-8118
www.jacksonvilleoregon.org

Jacksonville Inn
175 E. California St.
Jacksonville, OR 97530
(541) 899-1900
www.jacksonvilleinn.com

Harry & David Country Village
1314 Center Dr.
Medford, OR 97501
(877) 322-8000
www.harryanddavid.com/

Ashland Springs Hotel
212 East Main St.
Ashland, OR 97520
(541) 488-1700
www.ashlandspringshotel.com

Dragonfly Cafe and Gardens
241 Hargadine St.
Ashland, OR 97520
(541) 488-4855
www.dragonflyashland.com

It's a Burl
24025 Redwood Hwy.
Kerby, OR 97523
(541) 592-2141
www.itsaburl.com

Oregon Caves National Monument
19000 Caves Hwy.
Cave Junction, OR 97523
(541) 592-2100
www.nps.gov/orca

Hellgate Jetboat Excursions
966 SW 6th St.
Grants Pass, OR 97526
(800) 648-4874
www.hellgate.com

Oregon Tourism Commission
(800) 547-7842
www.traveloregon.com

H

State and National Park Information

CAMPING & LODGING RESERVATIONS

British Columbia... Campgrounds * Campings Canada
www.campcanada.com

Washington ...... Washington State Parks
(888) 226-7688
www.parks.wa.gov/reserve.asp

Oregon .... Oregon Parks and Recreation Department
(800) 452-5687
www.reserveamerica.com

Idaho............ State of Idaho Parks and Recreation
(208) 630-5050

NATIONAL & STATE PARK INFORMATION

British Columbia... BCParks
(800) 689-9025
www.env.gov.bc.ca/bcparks/

Washington ...... Washington State Parks & Recreation Commission:
www.parks.wa.gov

Oregon .... Oregon Parks and Recreation Department
www.oregon.gov/OPRD/index.shtml

Idaho............ State of Idaho Parks and Recreation
http://parksandrecreation.idaho.gov/index.aspx

Selected National & State Parks including Recreation Areas, Forests, and National Monuments

Province	Parks	Page	Camping	Trailer/RV	Picnicking	Swimming	Fishing	Hiking	Boating	Beach
BC	**NATIONAL PARKS**									
	Pacific Rim National Park	12	•	•	•	•	•	•	•	•
	PROVINCIAL PARKS									
	Carmanah Pacific Provincial Park	12	•	•	•			•		
	Cathedral Provincial Park	8	•	•	•		•	•	•	
	Cultus Lake Provincial Park	5	•	•	•		•	•	•	•
	Desolation Sound Provincial Marine Park	1	•			•	•	•	•	
	Garibaldi Provincial Park	2	•	•	•	•	•	•	•	
	Golden Ears Provincial Park	5	•	•	•	•	•	•	•	•
	Manning Provincial Park	7	•	•	•	•	•	•	•	
	Skagit Valley Provincial Park	6	•	•	•		•	•	•	
	Strathcona Provincial Park	110	•	•	•	•	•	•	•	
STATE	PARK									
WA	**NATIONAL PARKS**									
	Mount Rainier National Park	36	•	•	•		•	•	•	
	North Cascades National Park	17	•	•	•		•	•	•	
	Olympic National Park	23	•	•	•		•	•	•	
	NATIONAL/STATE FORESTS									
	Colville National Forest	10	•	•	•	•	•		•	•
	Gifford Pinchot National Forest	36	•	•	•	•	•	•	•	•
	Kaniksu National Forest	11	•	•	•	•	•	•	•	•
	Mount Baker-Snoqualmie National Forest	16	•	•	•	•	•	•	•	•
	Okanogan National Forest	18	•	•	•	•	•	•	•	
	Olympic National Forest	23	•	•	•	•	•	•	•	
	Wenatchee National Forest	27	•	•	•	•	•	•	•	
	PARKS/RECREATION AREAS/MONUMENTS									
	Beacon Rock State Park	45	•	•	•		•	•	•	
	Birch Bay State Park	5	•	•	•	•	•	•	•	•
	Bogachiel State Park	13	•	•	•		•	•		
	Brooks Memorial State Park	47	•	•	•		•	•		
	Cape Disappointment State Park	33	•	•	•		•	•	•	•
	Fort Flagler State Park	15	•	•	•	•	•	•	•	•
	Fort Worden State Park	119	•	•	•	•	•	•	•	•
	Kanaskat-Palmer State Park	26	•	•	•		•	•		
	Lake Chelan State Park	18	•	•	•		•	•	•	
	Lake Roosevelt National Recreation Area	20	•	•	•	•	•	•	•	
	Larrabee State Park	15	•	•	•		•	•	•	•
	Millersylvania State Park	34	•	•	•		•	•	•	
	Mount Saint Helens National Volcanic Monument	35	•					•		
	Mount Spokane State Park	21	•		•			•		
	Ocean City State Park	23	•	•	•	•	•		•	•
	Pacific Beach State Park	23	•	•	•	•	•			•
	Potholes State Park	39	•	•	•	•	•		•	•
	Ross Lake National Recreation Area	7	•	•	•	•	•	•	•	
	Schafer State Park	24	•	•	•		•	•		
	Seaquest State Park	34	•	•	•			•		
	Sequim Bay State Park	14	•	•	•		•	•	•	
	Sun Lakes State Park	28	•	•	•	•	•	•	•	
	Twanoh State Park	24	•	•	•	•	•	•	•	
	Wenberg State Park	15	•	•	•	•	•		•	
	Yakima Sportsman State Park	37	•	•	•		•			
OR	**NATIONAL PARKS**									
	Crater Lake National Park	88	•	•	•					
	NATIONAL/STATE FORESTS									
	Clatsop State Forest	43	•	•	•	•	•	•	•	
	Deschutes National Forest	77	•	•	•	•	•	•	•	
	Elliott State Forest	74	•	•	•	•	•	•		

State	Parks	Page	Camping	Trailer/RV	Picnicking	Swimming	Fishing	Hiking	Boating	Beach
OR (cont.)	Fremont National Forest	89	•	•	•	•	•	•	•	•
	Malheur National Forest	69	•	•	•	•	•	•	•	•
	Mount Hood National Forest	56	•	•	•	•	•	•	•	•
	Ochoco National Forest	67	•	•	•	•	•	•	•	•
	Rogue River National Forest	98	•	•	•	•	•	•	•	•
	Santiam State Forest	55	•	•	•	•	•	•	•	•
	Siskiyou National Forest	96	•	•	•	•	•	•	•	•
	Siuslaw National Forest	63	•	•	•	•	•	•	•	•
	Tillamook State Forest	43	•	•	•	•	•	•	•	•
	Umatilla National Forest	59	•	•	•	•	•	•	•	•
	Umpqua National Forest	76	•	•	•	•	•	•	•	•
	Wallowa National Forest	51	•	•	•	•	•	•	•	•
	Willamette National Forest	76	•	•	•	•	•	•	•	•
	Winema National Forest	77	•	•	•	•	•	•	•	•
	PARKS/RECREATION AREAS/MONUMENTS									
	Beachside State Park	63	•	•	•		•			•
	Beverly Beach State Park	53	•	•	•		•			•
	Bullards Beach State Park	73	•	•	•		•		•	•
	Cape Blanco State Park	85	•	•	•		•	•		•
	Cape Lookout State Park	53	•	•	•		•	•		•
	Champoeg State Park	54	•	•	•		•	•	•	
	Collier Memorial State Park	88	•	•	•		•	•		
	Detroit Lake State Park	55	•	•	•	•	•		•	•
	Emigrant Springs State Park	18	•	•	•			•		
	Fort Stevens State Park	33	•	•	•	•	•	•	•	•
	Harris Beach State Park	96	•	•	•		•	•		•
	Hells Canyon National Recreation Area	62	•	•	•	•	•	•	•	•
	Humbug Mountain State Park	85	•	•	•		•	•		•
	Jessie M Honeyman Memorial State Park	63	•	•	•	•	•	•	•	•
	John Day Fossil Beds National Monument	57, 68			•			•		
	Joseph Stewart State Park	87	•	•	•		•	•	•	•
	Lake Owyhee State Park	82	•	•	•		•		•	
	Lewis & Clark National Historical Park	82			•			•		
	McDonald State Park	54	•	•	•			•		
	Memaloose State Park	46	•	•						
	Milo McIver State Park	55	•	•	•		•	•	•	
	Nehalem Bay State Park	43	•	•	•		•	•	•	•
	Newberry National Volcanic Monument	77	•	•	•	•	•	•	•	
	Oregon Cascades Recreation Area	76	•	•	•	•	•	•	•	
	Oregon Caves National Monument	97			•			•		
	Oregon Dunes National Recreation Area	73	•				•	•		•
	Silver Falls State Park	55	•	•	•	•	•	•	•	
	South Beach State Park	53	•	•	•		•	•	•	•
	Sunset Bay State Park	73	•	•	•	•	•	•	•	•
	The Cove Palisades State Park	66	•	•	•	•	•	•	•	•
	Umpqua Lighthouse State Park	74	•	•	•	•	•	•	•	•
	Valley of the Rogue State Park	87	•	•	•		•	•	•	
	Viento State Park	46	•	•	•			•		
	Wallowa Lake State Park	61	•	•	•	•	•	•	•	•
	William M Tugman State Park	74	•	•	•	•	•	•	•	•
ID	**NATIONAL/STATE FORESTS**									
	Coeur d'Alene National Forest	32	•	•	•	•	•	•	•	•
	Kaniksu National Forest	21	•	•	•	•	•	•	•	•
	Nez Perce National Forest	52	•	•	•	•	•	•	•	•
	Payette National Forest	72	•	•	•	•	•	•	•	•
	Saint Joe National Forest	32	•	•	•	•	•	•	•	•
	PARKS/RECREATION AREAS/MONUMENTS									
	Farragut State Park	22	•	•	•	•	•	•	•	
	Heyburn State Park	32	•	•	•	•	•	•	•	
CA	**NATIONAL PARKS**									
	Redwood National Park	97	•	•	•		•	•	•	•
	NATIONAL/STATE FORESTS									
	Klamath National Forest	99	•	•	•	•	•	•	•	•
	Modoc National Forest	101	•	•	•	•	•	•	•	•
	Siskiyou National Forest	96	•	•	•	•	•	•	•	•
	Six River National Forest	97	•	•	•	•	•	•	•	•
	PARKS/RECREATION AREAS/MONUMENTS									
	Del Norte Coast Redwoods State Park	96	•	•	•		•	•		•
	Lava Beds National Monument	100	•	•	•			•		
	Smith River National Recreation Area	97			•		•	•	•	•
NV	**NATIONAL/STATE FORESTS**									
	Humboldt National Forest	105	•	•	•		•	•	•	•
MT	**NATIONAL/STATE FORESTS**									
	Kootenai National Forest	22	•	•	•	•	•	•	•	•

Using Your Road Atlas Como usar su Road Atlas

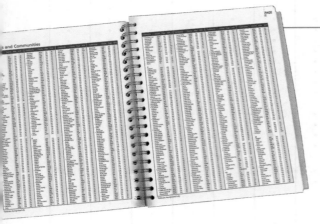

City Listings

- The Cities and Communities Index includes all communities large or small. State, page number, and grid location for each are listed.
- Find the community you're looking for in the list, then turn to the page number indicated.

El Índice de las Ciudades

- El Índice de las Ciudades y Comunidades incluye todas las comunidades grandes o pequeñas. El estado, el número de página, y la ubicación de cuadrícula para de cada uno se enumeran.
- Encontrar la comunidad que está buscando en la lista y, a continuación, a su vez, el número de la página indicada.

The Index

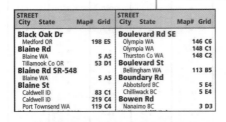

STREET City State	Map#	Grid
Black Oak Dr		
Medford OR	198	E5
Blaine Rd		
Blaine WA	5	A5
Tillamook Co OR	53	D1
Blaine Rd SR-548		
Blaine WA	5	A5
Blaine St		
Caldwell ID	83	C1
Caldwell ID	219	C4
Port Townsend WA	119	C4

STREET City State	Map#	Grid
Boulevard Rd SE		
Olympia WA	146	C6
Olympia WA	148	C1
Thurston Co WA	148	C2
Boulevard St		
Bellingham WA	113	B5
Boundary Rd		
Abbotsford BC	5	E4
Chilliwack BC	5	E4
Bowen Rd		
Nanaimo BC	3	D3

FEATURE NAME Address City State	MA
Optimist Youth Sports Complex, Ada Co, ID	
Oregon Ballet Theatre, 818 SE 6th Av, Portland, OR	
Oregon Convention Center, 777 NE Martin Luther King Jr Bl - Portland, OR	
Oregon State Fair & Expo Center, 1330 17th St NE, Salem, OR	
Oregon Theater, 3530 SE Division St, Portland, OR	
Oregon Zoo, 4001 SW Zoo Parking Rd, Portland, OR	
Orpheum Theatre, 601 Smithe St, Vancouver, BC	
Pacific Coliseum, Vancouver, BC	
Pacific Northwest Ballet, 301 Mercer St, Seattle, WA	
Pacific Theatre, 1440 W 12th Av, Vancouver, BC	
Pantages Theatre, 901 Broadway, Tacoma, WA	

- The Road Atlas includes separate indexes for streets, schools, parks, shopping centers, golf courses, and other points of interest.
- In the street listings, information is presented in the following order: city, state, map page number, and grid reference.
- A grid reference is a letter-number combination (B6 for example) that tells you precisely where to find a particular street or point of interest on a map.

El Índice

- Esta guía incluye índices para calles, escuelas, parques, centros de comercio, campos de golf, y otros lugares de interés.
- En el índice de calles, información esta representada en forma de: nombre de la calle, ciudad, estado, página, y cuadrícula.
- La cuadrícula es una combinación de letra y números (por ejemplo "B6") que le indica precisamente donde se halla una calle o punto de interés en la página del mapa indicado.

The Maps

- Each map is divided into a grid formed by rows and columns. These rows and columns correspond to letters and numbers running horizontally and vertically along the edges of the map.
- To use a grid reference from the index, search horizontally within the appropriate row and vertically within the appropriate column. The destination can be found within the grid square where the row and column meet.
- Adjacent map pages are indicated by numbers that appear at the top, bottom, and sides of each map.
- The legend explains symbols that appear on the maps.

Los Mapas

- Cada mapa está dividido en una cuadrícula de columnas y filas. Estas columnas y filas corresponden a las letras y números que se encuentran por las orillas del mapa.
- Para localizar una cuadrícula representada en el índice, busca la letra de la columna y el número de la fila por las orillas del mapa indicado y sigue la fila y la columna hasta que se encuentren. La calle o punto de interés que busca se encontrará en la cuadra donde la fila y la columna se encuentren.
- Los mapas de continuación se encontrarán en las páginas indicadas por las orillas de los mapas.
- La leyenda explica la mayoría de los símbolos representados en los mapas.

Using Three Types of Maps

You will find white boxes on many different types of maps in this atlas. Each box indicates an area covered in greater detail on a subsequent page. If your area of interest falls within one of these boxes, turn to the indicated page to view in greater detail.

Va a encontrar recuadros de color blanco en muchos tipos diferentes de mapas en este guía. Cada recuadro indica una área con más detalle en una página posterior. Si su área de interés pertenece a una de estos recuadros, dar la vuelta a la página indicada para ver con mayor detalle.

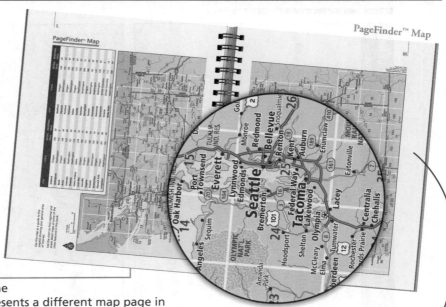

PageFinder™ Map

The PageFinder™ Map

- Turn to the PageFinder™ Map. Each of the small squares outlined on this map represents a different map page in the Road Atlas.

- Locate the specific part of the Road Atlas coverage area that you're interested in.

- Note the appropriate map page number. Turn to that map page.

El PageFinder™ Map

- Refiérese al PageFinder™ Map. Cada una de las cuadras enumeradas en este mapa representan una página de mapa distinta de este guía.
- Identifica el área del mapa PageFinder que le interesa.
- Hágase cuenta del número en la cuadra representada.
- Ese número es la página del guía donde se representa el mapa de esa área.

Regional Map

Regional Maps

- Regional maps offer a general view of your area of interest.
- Use Regional maps for long distance planning and navigation.

Mapas Regionales

- Mapas de Regionales ofrecen una vista general de su área de interés.
- Utilice los Mapas de Regionales para planificación y navegación de viajes de larga distancia.

Detail Map

Detail Maps

- Detail maps offer street detail as well as multiple points of interest.
- Use Detail maps for local planning and navigation and for locating many points of interest.

Mapas de Detalles

- Los Mapas de Detalle ofrecen detalles de la calle, así como puntos de interés múltiples.
- Utilice Mapas de Detalle para planificación y de navegación local y para la localización de muchos puntos de interés.

L

PageFinder™ Map

Use this map as a guide to the page(s) showing your general area of interest.

Use the chart to find regional and street detail maps of some of the cities featured in this book.

1:3,550,000
1 in. = 56 mi.
0   25   50
miles

CITY	STATE	DETAIL PAGE	REGIONAL PAGE
Ashland	Oregon	199	87
Bellingham	Washington	113	5
Bend	Oregon	189	66
Boise	Idaho	224	84
Centralia	Washington	151	34
Chehalis	Washington	152	34
Coeur d'Alene	Idaho	218	32
Coos Bay	Oregon	193	73
Corvallis	Oregon	177	64
Eugene	Oregon	185	64
Everett	Washington	120	15
Grants Pass	Oregon	197	87
Klamath Falls	Oregon	201	89
Longview	Washington	155	44

CITY	STATE	DETAIL PAGE	REGIONAL PAGE
Medford	Oregon	198	87
Olympia	Washington	145	24
Portland	Oregon	166	45
Richland	Washington	203	39
Salem	Oregon	173	54
Seattle	Washington	132	25
Spokane	Washington	209	31
Springfield	Oregon	188	64
Tacoma	Washington	141	25
Tumwater	Washington	147	34
Vancouver	Washington	159	45
Vancouver	British Columbia	110	4
Victoria	British Columbia	111	14
Walla Walla	Washington	208	50

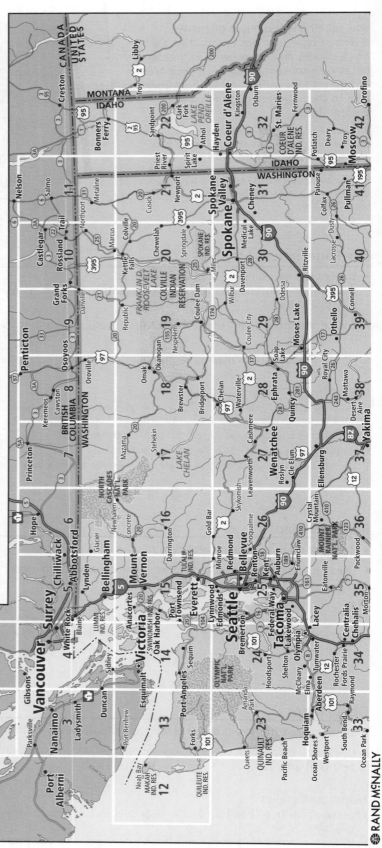

PageFinder™ Map
U.S. Patent No. 5,419,586
Canadian Patent No. 2,116,425
Patente Mexicana No. 188186

PACIFIC OCEAN

RAND M?NALLY

Moscow 42
Pullman 41
Lewiston
Orofino
Troy
Clarkston
Craigmont
Cottonwood
Grangeville 52
Craigmont
NEZ PERCE IND. RES.
New Meadows
McCall
Cascade
Council 62
Weiser 72
Payette
Fruitland
Ontario 71
Boise
Nampa
Caldwell 83
IDAHO
OREGON
Mountain Home
Murphy
95
106
105
Orovada
McDermitt
FORT McDERMITT IND. RES.
DUCK VALLEY IND. RES.
Owyhee

Connell 39
Pasco
Kennewick
Richland
Pendleton 49
WASHINGTON
OREGON
Enterprise
Joseph
51
61
Halfway
Richland
Baker City 60
La Grande
82
81
94
93
95
Jordan Valley
Adrian
Vale
Huntington
Unity
70
Burns Junction
Crane
Denio
104
140

Mattawa
Yakima 38
Sunnyside
Prosser
Umatilla 48
Arlington
Condon 58
Fossil 57
Spray
Dayville
Mount Vernon
Long Creek
Ukiah 59
Pilot Rock
John Day 69
Prairie City
Seneca
80
Hines
Burns
Riley
79
91
Alkali Lake Station
Paisley
Adel
NEVADA
OREGON
CALIFORNIA
102
GOOSE LAKE
Willow Ranch
101
395

Yakima 37
Wapato
Toppenish
YAKAMA INDIAN RESERVATION
Grandview
White Salmon
The Dalles 47
Wasco
Grass Valley
Antelope 57
Madras
Prineville 67
Redmond 66
Bend
68
78
Summer Lake
90
Bly
Lakeview
New Pine Creek
395
Newell
139
100

Packwood 36
MT. ST. HELENS NAT'L VOLCANIC MON.
Trout Lake
Hood River 46
Government Camp
WARM SPRINGS IND. RES.
Maupin
Durfur
56
Terrebonne
La Pine 77
Gilchrist
Diamond Lake Junction
Chiloquin 89
UPPER KLAMATH LAKE
Klamath Falls
Merrill
Tulelake
Macdoel
LAVA BEDS NAT'L MON.

Cougar 35
Morton
Amboy
Battle Ground
Vancouver 45
Gresham
Portland
Oregon City
McKenzie Bridge
Sweet Home 65
Oakridge
NEWBERRY NAT'L VOLCANIC MON.
76
Steamboat
Union Creek
CRATER LAKE NAT'L PARK
Prospect
Shady Cove 88
White City
CASCADE-SISKIYOU NAT'L MON.
99
Keno
97

Kalama
Longview 34
St. Helens
Woodburn 55
Keizer
Stayton
Mill City
Lebanon
Brownsville
Springfield
Eugene
64
Cottage Grove
Sutherlin 75
Roseburg
Green
Canyonville
87
Medford
Ashland
Hilt
98
Yreka

Fords Prairie
Centralia 35
Chehalis
Winlock
Clatskanie
Banks
Cornelius
Beaverton
Tigard
Newberg
McMinnville
Sheridan 53
Salem 54
Albany
Corvallis
Junction City
Drain
74
Winston
Coquille
Myrtle Point
Grants Pass 86
Cave Junction
Happy Camp
REDWOOD NAT'L PARK
97

South Bend 33
Ocean Park
Long Beach
Raymond
Astoria 33
Seaside
Cannon Beach
Rockaway Beach
Bay City
Tillamook 43
Pacific City
Lincoln City 53
Lincoln Beach
Newport
Waldport 63
Florence
Dunes City
Reedsport
Lakeside
North Bend 73
Coos Bay
Bandon
Port Orford 85
Gold Beach
Brookings
Crescent City 96

Cities and Communities

Community	State	Map#	Grid
A			
* Abbotsford	BC	5	C4
* Aberdeen	WA	33	D1
Academy	WA	31	B4
Acme	WA	5	D7
ADA CO	ID	224	C4
* Adair Village	OR	54	B7
* Adams	OR	50	A5
ADAMS CO	ID	62	C4
Adamsview Park	WA	37	D6
Ada Station	OR	63	B6
Addy	WA	20	D3
Adel	OR	102	C1
Adelma Beach	WA	14	E6
Admiral's Cove	WA	15	B5
Adna	WA	34	D4
* Adrian	OR	82	E1
Aeneas	WA	19	C2
Agassiz	BC	6	B3
Agate Bay	WA	5	C7
Agness	OR	86	A4
Agnew	WA	14	C5
Ahsahka	ID	42	C5
Ahtanum	WA	37	C5
Ainsworth Corner	CA	100	B2
Airlie	OR	54	A6
* Airway Heights	WA	31	A2
* Albany	OR	175	C1
Albee	OR	59	D2
ALBERNI-CLAYOQUOT	BC	3	A3
* Albion	WA	41	C2
Alder	WA	35	C3
Aldergrove	BC	5	B4
Alderton	WA	25	D6
Alderwood	WA	5	B6
Alderwood Manor	WA	25	D1
Alexander Beach	WA	114	A6
Alfalfa	OR	67	A5
Alger	WA	15	C1
Algoma	ID	22	B4
* Algona	WA	25	C5
Alicel	OR	60	D1
Alkali Lake Station	OR	91	B1
Allegany	OR	74	B3
Allen	WA	15	C2
Allentown	WA	137	B5
Allyn	WA	24	E5
Alma	OR	63	E7
* Almira	WA	29	C2
Aloha	WA	23	B6
Aloha	OR	44	D7
Alpental	WA	26	C4
Alpha	WA	35	A4
Alpine	OR	64	A3
Alsea	OR	63	E2
Alston	OR	44	D2
Altamont	OR	202	B7
Altoona	WA	33	E7
* Alturas	CA	101	D7
Alvadore	OR	64	A4
Amanda Park	WA	23	D4
Amber	WA	30	E5
Amboy	WA	45	B3
American Lake	WA	25	B7
* Amity	OR	54	B3
* Anacortes	WA	114	C4
Anatone	WA	51	D1
Anderson Island	WA	25	A6
Anlauf	OR	75	B1
* Anmore	BC	5	A2
Annex	OR	72	A3
* Antelope	OR	57	B5
Applegate	OR	87	B7
Appleton	WA	46	D4
Apple Valley	ID	72	A7
Arago	OR	74	A6
Arcadia	WA	24	D6
Arch Cape	OR	43	C4
Arden	WA	20	D2
Ardenvoir	WA	27	E2
Ariel	WA	45	A3
Arletta	WA	25	A5
* Arlington	OR	48	A5
* Arlington	WA	15	D5
Arlington Heights	WA	15	E4
Armar	WA	15	D6
Arock	OR	94	C1
Arrowhead Beach	WA	15	C4
Artic	WA	33	E2
Artondale	WA	25	A5
Ashford	WA	35	E3
* Ashland	OR	199	D3
Ashwood	OR	57	B7
Asotin	WA	41	E6
ASOTIN CO	WA	51	C1
* Astoria	OR	153	C2
* Athena	OR	50	A4
* Athol	ID	22	A6
* Auburn	WA	25	D6
* Aumsville	OR	54	D5
* Aurora	OR	54	E2
Austin	OR	70	A1
Avon	ID	42	B2
Avon	WA	15	C2
Ayer	WA	40	B4
Ayock Beach	WA	24	D3
Azalea	OR	87	A2
Azwell	WA	18	B7
B			
Baby Island Heights	WA	15	B5
Baileysburg	WA	40	D7
* Bainbridge Island	WA	25	B2
BAKER CO	OR	61	C5
* Baker City	OR	60	E6
Baker Heights	WA	15	D3
Ballston	OR	54	A3
* Bandon	OR	73	D6
* Banks	OR	44	C6
Barberton	WA	45	A5
Baring	WA	26	C1
* Barlow	OR	54	E2
Barstow	WA	10	B6
Barton	OR	55	B1
Barview	OR	73	E4
Barview	OR	43	C6
Basin City	WA	39	B4
Basque	OR	94	A5
Bates	OR	70	A1
Battin	OR	45	A7
* Battle Ground	WA	45	B4
Bay Center	WA	33	C4
Bay City	WA	33	C2
* Bay City	OR	43	C6
Bayshore	OR	179	B2
Bay Shore	WA	24	D6
Bayside Garden	OR	43	C5
Bay View	WA	15	C6
Bayview	ID	22	A6
Bayview	WA	15	B2
Bazinet Edition	WA	34	D4
Beachcombers Hdn Bch	WA	15	B5
Beachcrest	WA	25	A7
Beacon Hill	WA	44	D1
Bear	ID	62	B4
Beatty	OR	89	D5
* Beaux Arts Village	WA	134	C2
Beaver	WA	13	B5
Beaver	OR	53	C1
Beaver Creek	OR	55	A2
Beaverdell	BC	9	B1
Beaver Marsh	OR	77	A6
* Beaverton	OR	44	D7
Beaver Valley	WA	15	A7
Beckett Point	WA	14	E6
Beech Creek	OR	59	B7
* Belcarra	BC	4	E2
Belfair	WA	24	E4
Belknap Springs	OR	65	D4
* Bellevue	WA	130	D6
Bellevue	OR	54	A3
Bellfountain	OR	64	A2
* Bellingham	WA	113	C3
Belmont	ID	22	A7
Belmont	WA	31	C7
Belvidere	WA	19	B6
* Bend	OR	189	E7
BENEWAH CO	ID	32	B6
Benge	WA	40	C2
Benson Hill	WA	25	D4
BENTON CO	OR	177	D4
* Benton City	WA	38	E7
Bertsch Terrace	CA	96	E4
Bethany	OR	44	D6
Bethel	WA	25	A4
Beverly	WA	38	B2
Beverly Beach	WA	15	B6
Beverly Beach	OR	53	B6
Bickleton	WA	47	E3
Biggs	OR	47	B6
Big Lake	WA	15	D3
* Bingen	WA	46	C5
Bingham Springs	OR	50	B5
Birch Bay	WA	5	A5
Birdsview	WA	16	A2
Birkenfeld	OR	44	B2
Biz Point	WA	15	A2
Blachly	OR	63	E4
Black Butte Ranch	OR	66	A3
* Black Diamond	WA	25	E5
Blaine	OR	53	D1
* Blaine	WA	5	A5
Blanchard	ID	21	D6
Blanchard	WA	15	C1
Blockhouse	WA	47	A4
Blodgett	OR	53	E7
Blubber Bay	BC	1	A4
Bluecreek	WA	20	D3
Blue Lake	WA	28	E3
Blue River	OR	65	B4
Blueslide	WA	21	B1
Bly	OR	89	E6
Blyn	WA	14	D6
* Boardman	OR	48	C4
* Boise	ID	222	C7
Boise	WA	25	E6
BOISE CO	ID	84	B1
* Bonanza	OR	89	C7
BONNER CO	ID	22	B4
Bonneville	OR	45	E6
* Bonney Lake	WA	25	D6
Bonny Slope	OR	44	E6
Boring	OR	45	B7
Bossburg	WA	10	C7
Boston Harbor	WA	24	E7
* Bothell	WA	25	D1
Boulevard Park	WA	136	D5
BOUNDARY CO	ID	22	B1
* Bovill	ID	42	C2
Bow	WA	15	C1
Bowen Island	BC	4	C1
Bowmont	ID	83	D3
Boyd	OR	46	E7
Boyds	WA	10	B7
Brackendale	BC	2	D5
Bradwood	OR	44	A1
Brady	WA	34	A1
Bray	CA	99	D5
Breidablick	WA	25	A1
Breitenbush	OR	55	E6
* Bremerton	WA	122	B4
Brentwood Bay	BC	14	B1
* Brewster	WA	18	C5
Briarwood	OR	170	A6
Briarwood	WA	25	D4
Brickerville	OR	63	C5
Bridal Veil	OR	45	D6
Bridesville	BC	9	A4
Bridge	OR	74	B7
Bridgeport	OR	71	A1
* Bridgeport	WA	18	C6
Bridgeport	OR	54	A5
Bridgeview	OR	97	D1
Brief	WA	17	D7
* Brier	WA	25	C1
Brighton	OR	43	C5
Brightwood	OR	55	E1
Brinnon	WA	24	E2
Britannia Beach	BC	2	C6
Broadbent	OR	74	A7
Brogan	OR	71	B3
Bronx	ID	22	B3
Brookdale	WA	25	C7
* Brookings	OR	96	D1
Brooks	OR	54	D4
Brothers	OR	67	C7
Brownlee	OR	62	A5
Brownsmead	OR	34	A7
Browns Point	WA	25	B5
Brownstown	WA	37	C6
Brownsville	WA	25	A2
* Brownsville	OR	64	C2
Brush Prairie	WA	45	A5
Bryant	WA	15	D4
Bryn Mawr	WA	138	A4
Buchanan	OR	81	A2
Buckhorn	WA	4	E7
* Buckley	WA	25	E7
* Bucoda	WA	34	E3
Buena	WA	37	E6
Buena Vista	OR	54	B6
Bullards	OR	73	D6
Bunker	WA	34	C4
Bunker Hill	OR	74	A4
Burbank	WA	49	C1
Burbank Heights	WA	49	C1
* Burien	WA	139	C1
Burley	WA	25	A4
Burlington	OR	44	E5
* Burlington	WA	115	B5
* Burnaby	BC	4	E2
Burnett	WA	25	E7
* Burns	OR	80	C2
Burns Junction	OR	94	A2
Burnt Woods	OR	53	E7
Burton	WA	25	B4
Bush Point	WA	15	B5
Butler Acres	WA	156	C1
* Butte Falls	OR	88	A4
Butteville	OR	54	E2
Buxton	OR	44	C5
BZ Corner	WA	46	C4
C			
Cabin Creek	WA	26	D6
Cabinet	ID	22	D5
Cairo	OR	72	A5
Calder	ID	32	D5
* Caldwell	ID	219	B3
California Pines	CA	101	B7
Camaloch	WA	15	B4
Camano	WA	15	B5
Camano City	WA	15	B5
Camano Country Club	WA	15	C5
* Camas	WA	45	B6
Camas Valley	OR	74	D7
* Cambridge	ID	62	B7
Camelot	WA	25	C5
Cameron	ID	42	B4
Campbell's Glen	WA	15	C6
Camp Murray	WA	25	A7
Camp Sherman	OR	66	B2
Camp Twelve	OR	53	C6
Camp Union	WA	24	E3
Canal Tract	WA	24	E2
* Canby	OR	54	E2
Canby	CA	101	A7
* Cannon Beach	OR	43	C3
Cannon Beach Junc	OR	43	C3
CANYON CO	ID	220	C4
* Canyon City	OR	69	C3
* Canyonville	OR	87	A1
Cape George	WA	14	E5
Cape Meares	OR	43	C7
CAPITAL	BC	111	D4
* Carbonado	WA	25	E7
Care Free Loop	WA	13	B6
Careywood	ID	22	A6
Carlisle	WA	23	C6
Carlsborg	WA	14	C5
Carlton	WA	18	A4
* Carlton	OR	54	B1

*Indicates incorporated city

Community	State	Map#	Grid	Community	State	Map#	Grid	Community	State	Map#	Grid	Community	State	Map#	Grid
* Carnation	WA	26	A2	Clagstone	ID	21	E6	* Council	ID	62	D6	DEL NORTE CO	CA	97	C6
Carpenterville	OR	85	D7	CLALLAM CO	WA	117	C3	Country Homes	WA	31	B1	Delphi	WA	34	D1
Carrick Addition	CA	99	B7	Clallam Bay	WA	13	B4	Countryside Beach	WA	24	D7	Delphi Country Club	WA	34	D1
Carrolls	WA	44	E2	Claquato	WA	34	D4	* Coupeville	WA	15	A4	* Delta	BC	4	D4
Carson	OR	61	D4	CLARK CO	WA	159	C7	Cove	WA	25	B4	Delta	ID	32	E2
Carson	WA	46	A5	* Clark Fork	ID	22	D4	* Cove	OR	60	E1	Deming	WA	5	D6
Carus	OR	55	A2	Clarkia	ID	32	D7	Cove Orchard	OR	54	C1	Denio	NV	104	A2
Carylon Beach	WA	24	E6	* Clarkston	WA	41	D6	* Covington	WA	25	D5	Denison	WA	21	B7
Cascade Gorge	OR	88	A3	Clarkston Heights	WA	41	D6	Cowichan Bay	BC	4	A7	Denmark	OR	85	D1
* Cascade Locks	OR	46	A5	Clarksville	ID	32	A1	COWICHAN VALLEY	BC	3	C5	Denny Park	WA	126	A1
* Cascade Park	WA	160	A6	* Clatskanie	OR	44	C1	Cowiche	WA	37	C4	Dent	ID	42	D4
Cascade Summit	OR	76	D2	CLATSOP CO	OR	153	C2	COWLITZ CO	WA	155	C3	* Depoe Bay	OR	53	B5
Cascade Terrace	WA	25	D6	Clay City	WA	35	D1	Crabtree	OR	54	D7	Deroche	BC	5	E3
Cascade Vista	WA	25	D4	Clayton	WA	21	A6	* Craigmont	ID	42	C7	DESCHUTES CO	OR	190	C5
Cascadia	OR	65	B2	Clearbrook	BC	5	C4	Crane	OR	81	A4	Deschutes Junction	OR	66	D4
* Cashmere	WA	27	D4	Clear Creek	CA	97	E4	Crawfordsville	OR	64	D3	Desert Aire	WA	38	B4
Cassidy	BC	3	E4	Clear Lake	WA	35	C1	Crescent	OR	77	A4	De Smet	ID	31	E6
* Castlegar	BC	10	D2	Clear Lake	WA	15	D2	Crescent Bar	WA	28	B6	* Des Moines	WA	139	D7
* Castle Rock	WA	34	D7	Clear Lake	WA	30	E3	* Crescent City	CA	96	E4	* Detroit	OR	55	D6
Cataldo	ID	32	C3	Clearview	WA	25	D1	Crescent Lake	OR	76	D3	Devereaux Lake	WA	24	E4
Cathcart	WA	25	E1	Clearwater	WA	23	B2	Crescent Valley	BC	10	E1	Dewatto	WA	24	D4
* Cathlamet	WA	44	B1	CLEARWATER CO	ID	42	D4	* Creston	WA	29	E1	Dewdney	BC	5	D3
* Cave Junction	OR	86	D7	* Cle Elum	WA	27	A6	* Creswell	OR	64	C6	Dewey	WA	15	B3
Cavelero Beach	WA	15	B5	Cleveland	WA	47	E3	Crockett Lake Estates	WA	15	A5	Dexter	OR	64	D6
Cavendish	ID	42	C4	Cliffdell	WA	36	E1	Crofton	BC	4	A6	Dexter by the Sea	WA	33	C3
Cawston	BC	8	C3	Clinton	WA	15	C6	Cromwell	WA	25	A5	Diablo	WA	6	E7
Cayuse	OR	49	E5	Clipper	WA	5	D7	CROOK CO	OR	67	C3	Diamond	OR	80	E7
Cecil	OR	48	B6	Cloverdale	BC	5	A4	Crooked River Ranch	OR	66	D2	Diamond	WA	41	A1
Cedar	BC	3	E3	Cloverdale	OR	53	C2	Crow	OR	64	A6	Diamond Lake	OR	76	D6
Cedar Dale	OR	55	A3	* Clyde Hill	WA	130	B4	Crowfoot	OR	64	D1	Diamond Lake	WA	21	C5
Cedardale	WA	15	C3	Coal Creek	WA	44	D1	Crystal Mountain	WA	36	C1	Diamond Lake Junction	OR	76	E7
Cedar Falls	WA	26	A4	Coalfield	WA	25	D4	Crystal Village	WA	26	B7	Dickey Prairie	OR	55	A3
Cedar Grove	WA	25	E4	Cobble Hill	BC	4	A7	* Culdesac	ID	42	B6	Dillard	OR	74	E6
Cedar Hills	OR	44	E7	* Coburg	OR	64	C4	Culp Creek	OR	75	D1	Dilley	OR	44	C7
Cedarhome	WA	15	C4	Cocolalla	ID	22	A5	Cultus Lake	BC	5	E4	Dines Point	WA	15	B6
Cedarhurst Park	OR	55	B1	* Coeur d'Alene	ID	218	C6	* Culver	OR	66	D1	Disautel	WA	19	A3
Cedar Mill	WA	44	E6	Colbert	WA	21	B7	Cumberland	WA	25	E6	Discovery Bay	WA	14	E6
Cedar Mountain	WA	25	E4	Colburn	ID	22	A2	Cunningham	WA	39	D2	Disston	OR	75	E1
Cedarville	WA	34	B2	Colby	WA	25	B3	Cuprum	ID	62	B3	Dixie	WA	50	C1
Cedarville	CA	102	A6	Colchester	WA	25	B3	Curlew	WA	9	D6	Dixonville	OR	75	A6
Cedonia	WA	20	B5	Coles Corner	WA	27	C2	Currinsville	OR	55	C1	Dockton	WA	25	B5
Celilo	OR	47	A6	* Colfax	WA	41	B2	CURRY CO	OR	85	D1	Dodge	WA	40	E5
Center	WA	15	A7	* College Place	WA	207	B6	Curtin	OR	75	B1	Dodson	OR	45	E6
Centerville	WA	47	A5	Colton	OR	55	B3	Curtis	WA	34	C4	Doe Bay	WA	15	A1
* Centralia	WA	151	C4	* Colton	WA	41	D4	Cushman Dam	WA	24	C4	Dollar's Corner	WA	45	A4
CENTRAL KOOTENAY	BC	11	B2	COLUMBIA CO	OR	155	A7	* Cusick	WA	21	B3	* Donald	OR	54	E2
Central Park	WA	33	E1	Columbia Beach	WA	15	C7	Custer	WA	5	B5	Donald	WA	37	D5
Central Point	OR	55	A1	* Columbia City	OR	44	E3					Dorena	OR	75	D1
* Central Point	OR	198	A1	Columbia Heights	WA	155	D1	**D**				* Dorris	CA	99	E2
* Central Saanich	BC	14	B1	* Colville	WA	20	D1	Dairy	OR	89	B7	Doty	WA	34	B4
Central Valley	WA	25	A2	* Colwood	BC	14	B2	Daisy	WA	20	B3	Douglas	WA	28	B3
Chapman	OR	44	D4	COMOX VALLEY	BC	1	A7	Dale	OR	59	C4	DOUGLAS CO	OR	195	B4
Charleston	OR	73	E4	* Conconully	WA	18	C2	Dalkena	WA	21	B4	Douglas Park	CA	97	A3
Charleston Beach	WA	25	A3	Concord	OR	55	A1	* Dallas	OR	54	B5	* Dover	ID	22	A4
Chatcolet	ID	32	A4	* Concrete	WA	16	B2	Dallesport	WA	46	E6	Downing	WA	18	C6
Chattaroy	WA	21	B7	* Condon	OR	58	A2	* Dalton Gardens	ID	217	C7	* Drain	OR	75	A2
Cheeseville	CA	98	C6	* Connell	WA	39	C4	* Damascus	OR	45	B7	Draper Springs Camp	WA	46	D2
Chehalis	WA	152	C4	Conway	WA	15	C3	Danner	OR	94	D1	Draperville	OR	176	E1
* Chelan	WA	28	A1	Cook	WA	46	C5	Danville	WA	9	E5	Drew	OR	87	C1
CHELAN CO	WA	27	C3	Coolin	ID	21	E2	Daphnedale Park	CA	101	C6	Drewsey	OR	70	B7
Chelan Falls	WA	28	B1	Coombs	BC	3	B2	* Darrington	WA	16	B4	Driftwood Acres	WA	26	E6
Chelatchie	WA	45	C3	Cooper Point	WA	24	D7	Dash Point	WA	25	B5	Driftwood Point	WA	25	D6
Chemainus	BC	3	E5	COOS CO	OR	193	C4	* Davenport	WA	30	C2	Driftwood Shores	WA	15	B4
Chemult	OR	77	A6	* Coos Bay	OR	193	C4	Davis Creek	CA	101	E4	Dryad	WA	34	B4
* Cheney	WA	31	A3	Cooston	OR	194	D4	Day Creek	WA	15	E2	Dryden	WA	27	C3
Chenoweth	OR	46	D6	Copalis Beach	WA	23	B7	Days Creek	OR	75	B7	* Dufur	OR	46	E7
Cherry Grove	WA	45	A4	Copalis Crossing	WA	23	C7	* Dayton	WA	40	D7	* Duncan	BC	4	A6
Cherry Grove	OR	44	B7	Copco	CA	99	B2	Dayton	WA	24	C6	* Dundee	OR	54	D2
Cherry Point	WA	5	A6	* Coquille	OR	74	A5	* Dayton	OR	54	C2	* Dunes City	OR	63	A6
Chesaw	WA	9	B5	* Coquitlam	BC	5	A2	* Dayville	OR	68	E2	Dungeness	WA	14	D5
Cheshire	OR	64	B4	Corbett	OR	45	C7	Deadwood	OR	63	D5	Dunthorpe	OR	170	A5
* Chewelah	WA	20	E4	* Cornelius	OR	44	C7	* Deary	ID	42	B2	* Dupont	WA	25	A4
Chico	WA	25	A3	Coronado Shores	OR	53	B5	Decatur	WA	15	A2	* Durham	OR	54	E1
Chilco	ID	22	A7	* Corvallis	OR	177	D4	Dee	OR	46	B6	Durkee	OR	61	B7
* Chilliwack	BC	6	A3	* Cosmopolis	WA	33	D1	Deep Creek	WA	30	E2	Dusty	WA	41	A2
* Chiloquin	OR	88	E4	* Cottage Grove	OR	64	B7	Deep River	WA	33	E6	* Duvall	WA	25	E2
Chimacum	WA	15	A6	Cottage Lake Bridle Tr	WA	25	E1	Deer Harbor	WA	14	D1	Duwamish	WA	137	A3
Chinook	WA	33	C7	* Cottonwood	ID	52	C2	Deer Island	OR	44	D3				
Christina Lake	BC	10	B4	Cottonwood Beach	WA	5	A5	Deer Island	WA	25	D6	**E**			
Christmas Valley	OR	78	C5	Cottrell	OR	45	C7	Deer Lake	WA	21	A5	* Eagle	ID	83	E1
Cinebar	WA	35	B4	Cougar	WA	45	C2	* Deer Park	WA	21	A6	Eagle Creek	OR	55	B1
Clackamas	OR	55	A1	* Coulee City	WA	29	A3	Delano Beach	WA	25	A6	* Eagle Point	OR	87	D5
CLACKAMAS CO	OR	169	C6	* Coulee Dam	WA	19	C7	Dellwood	OR	74	B4	East Everett	WA	15	D6

*Indicates incorporated city

Cities and Communities

Community	State	Map#	Grid
East Farms	WA	31	D1
East Gardiner	OR	74	B1
Eastgate	WA	25	D3
East Heights	WA	19	C7
* East Hope	ID	22	C4
East Hoquiam	WA	13	D6
Eastmont	WA	15	D7
East Olympia	WA	148	E6
Easton	WA	26	E6
East Port Orchard	WA	25	A3
East Quilcene	WA	24	E1
East Raymond	WA	33	E4
East Selah	WA	37	D4
Eastsound	WA	4	E7
Eastview Hills	WA	15	D7
* East Wenatchee	WA	27	E4
Eaton	ID	71	E3
* Eatonville	WA	35	C2
* Echo	OR	49	B5
Echo Dell	OR	55	B1
Eckman Lake	OR	179	D6
Eddyville	ID	32	A2
Eddyville	OR	53	D7
* Edgewood	WA	25	C6
Edgewood	CA	99	A7
Edison	WA	15	C1
* Edmonds	WA	25	C1
Edwall	WA	30	D3
Eglon	WA	15	B7
Egmont	BC	1	E5
Elbe	WA	35	D3
Elberton	WA	41	C1
Eldon	WA	24	D3
Eldorado Hills	WA	25	A2
* Electric City	WA	19	B7
* Elgin	OR	50	D6
Elk	WA	21	C6
Elk City	OR	53	C7
Elkhorn	OR	55	B6
Elk Lake	OR	66	A6
ELKO CO	NV	106	C4
Elk Plain	WA	25	C7
* Elk River	ID	42	D2
* Elkton	OR	74	E2
* Ellensburg	WA	37	C1
Ellisforde	WA	8	E7
Ellisport	WA	25	C4
Ellsworth	WA	159	D7
* Elma	WA	34	B1
* Elmer City	WA	19	C6
Elmira	ID	22	B2
Elmira	OR	64	A5
ELMORE CO	ID	84	D4
Elsie	OR	43	E3
Eltopia	WA	39	C6
Emida	ID	32	B6
* Emmett	ID	72	D6
* Endicott	WA	40	E1
Enetai	WA	122	E3
Englewood	OR	169	C4
* Enterprise	OR	51	C7
* Entiat	WA	28	A2
* Enumclaw	WA	25	E6
Eola	OR	54	C5
Eola Village	OR	54	C5
* Ephrata	WA	28	D5
Erlands Point	WA	121	C2
Errington	BC	3	B2
Eschbach	WA	37	C4
Espanola	WA	30	E2
* Esquimalt	BC	111	B4
* Estacada	OR	55	C2
Ethel	WA	35	A5
* Etna	CA	98	C7
Eufaula Heights	WA	44	D1
* Eugene	OR	181	C5
Eureka	WA	39	E7
Evans	WA	10	C7
* Everett	WA	120	C3
Evergreen Estates	WA	35	A1
Evergreen Shores	WA	34	D1
* Everson	WA	5	C5
Ewan	WA	30	E7

Community	State	Map#	Grid
F			
Fairfax	WA	35	E1
* Fairfield	WA	31	C4
Fair Harbor	WA	24	E5
Fair Oaks	OR	170	A6
Fair Oaks	OR	75	B4
Fairview	OR	74	A5
Fairview	WA	25	A2
* Fairview	OR	45	B6
Fairview	OR	43	D7
Fairwood	WA	25	D4
Falcon Heights	OR	100	A1
Fall City	WA	26	A3
Fall Creek	OR	64	D6
* Falls City	OR	54	A5
Fargher Lake	WA	45	B3
* Farmington	WA	31	D7
Faubion	OR	55	E1
Fawn Lake	WA	24	D6
* Federal Way	WA	25	C5
Felida	WA	45	A5
Felterwood	CA	96	E3
Fenn	ID	52	D2
* Ferdinand	ID	52	C1
* Fernan Lake Village	ID	218	E6
* Ferndale	WA	5	B6
Fern Hill	OR	43	E1
Fern Prairie	WA	45	B6
Fernwood	ID	32	C6
FERRY CO	WA	19	D4
Fields	OR	93	A7
* Fife	WA	142	E6
Fife Heights	WA	25	C6
Finley	WA	49	B1
Finn Rock	OR	65	B5
* Fircrest	WA	141	A7
Fircrest Eddition	WA	34	E4
Firgrove	WA	15	D7
Firlock	WA	44	E7
Fir Villa	OR	54	B5
Fisher	WA	164	D2
Fishers Corner	OR	55	A2
Fish Lake Resort	OR	88	B5
Five Corners	OR	101	D1
Flora	OR	51	C3
* Florence	OR	63	A5
Florence	WA	15	C4
Fobes Hill	WA	15	D7
Foothill	WA	31	C1
Ford	WA	20	E7
Fordair	WA	29	A2
Fords Prairie	WA	34	D3
Forest	WA	34	E4
Forest Beach	WA	25	A5
Forest Glen	WA	34	E1
* Forest Grove	OR	44	C7
Forest Hills Addition	WA	31	A1
Forfar	OR	63	B1
* Forks	WA	13	A6
Fort Bidwell	CA	102	A3
Fort Dick	CA	96	E3
* Fort Jones	CA	98	C5
Fort Klamath	OR	88	D3
Fort Langley	BC	5	B3
Fort Rock	OR	77	E4
Fort Stevens	OR	33	C7
Fortune Branch	OR	87	A2
* Fossil	OR	58	A4
Four Corners	OR	174	C2
Four Lakes	WA	31	A3
Fourmile	OR	73	D7
Fox	OR	59	B7
Fragaria	WA	25	B4
Frances	WA	34	A5
Franklin	OR	64	A4
FRANKLIN CO	WA	204	C4
FRASER VALLEY	BC	6	C3
Frederickson	WA	25	C7
Freeland	WA	15	B6
Freeman	WA	31	C3
Frenchglen	OR	92	D2
* Friday Harbor	WA	14	D1
Fruitdale	OR	197	E6

Community	State	Map#	Grid
* Fruitland	ID	72	A5
Fruitland	WA	20	B6
Fruitvale	ID	62	D5
Fruitvale	BC	11	A4
Furport	WA	21	C4
Furry Creek	BC	2	C6
G			
Gabriola	BC	3	E3
Gales Creek	OR	44	B6
Galiano	BC	4	B5
Galice	OR	86	D4
Galvin	WA	34	D3
Gamblewood	WA	25	B1
Gardena	WA	49	E2
Garden Bay	BC	1	D6
* Garden City	ID	221	C4
Garden City	WA	24	B7
Gardiner	OR	74	A1
Gardiner	WA	14	E6
* Garfield	WA	41	D1
GARFIELD CO	WA	41	B5
* Garibaldi	OR	43	C6
Garibaldi Highlands	BC	2	D5
Garrett	WA	207	A5
Garwood	ID	21	E7
Gasquet	CA	97	A3
* Gaston	OR	44	C7
Gate	WA	34	C2
* Gates	OR	55	B6
Gateway	OR	56	E6
Gaylord	OR	74	A7
Gazelle	CA	99	A6
* Gearhart	OR	154	C2
GEM CO	ID	72	D6
Genelle	BC	10	E3
* Genesee	ID	41	E4
Geneva	WA	5	C7
* George	WA	28	C7
Georgetown	WA	132	C6
* Gervais	OR	54	D3
Getchell	WA	15	E6
Gibbon	OR	50	B5
Gibraltar	WA	15	B2
Gibsons	BC	4	B1
Gifford	ID	42	B5
Gifford	WA	20	B4
* Gig Harbor	WA	25	A5
Gilberton	WA	25	B2
Gilchrist	OR	77	A3
GILLIAM CO	OR	58	A3
Gillies Bay	BC	1	A5
Gilmer	WA	46	C4
Givens Hot Springs	ID	83	B3
Glacier	WA	6	A6
* Gladstone	OR	55	A1
Glasgow	OR	74	A3
Gleed	WA	37	C4
Glen Acres	WA	25	B4
Glenada	OR	63	A6
Glen Cove	WA	119	A6
Glencove	WA	25	A5
* Glendale	OR	86	E2
Glendale	WA	15	C7
Gleneden Beach	OR	53	B5
Glengary	ID	22	B4
Glengary	OR	75	A6
Glenoma	WA	35	D5
Glenrose	WA	31	B2
Glenwood	OR	43	C1
Glenwood	WA	46	D2
Glenwood	WA	25	A4
Glenwood	OR	186	D2
Glenwood	OR	44	B5
Glide	OR	75	B5
Goble	OR	44	D2
* Gold Bar	WA	26	B1
* Gold Beach	OR	85	D5
* Goldendale	WA	47	B4
* Gold Hill	OR	87	B5
Goodrich	ID	62	C7
Gooseberry Point	WA	5	A7
Goose Prairie	WA	36	D2

Community	State	Map#	Grid
Gorst	WA	25	A3
Goshen	OR	64	C6
Govan	WA	29	D2
Government Camp	OR	56	A1
Graham	WA	25	C7
Graham Point	WA	24	E6
* Grand Coulee	WA	19	B7
* Grand Forks	BC	10	A4
Grand Mound	WA	34	D2
Grand Ronde	OR	53	E3
Grand Ronde Agency	OR	53	E3
* Grand View	ID	84	B7
* Grandview	WA	38	B7
* Granger	WA	38	A7
* Grangeville	ID	52	E3
* Granite	OR	60	B6
* Granite Falls	WA	15	E5
GRANT CO	WA	29	B4
Granthams Landing	BC	4	B1
Grant Road Addition	WA	27	E4
* Grants Pass	OR	197	C4
Grapeview	WA	24	E5
Grassmere	WA	16	A2
* Grass Valley	OR	57	B1
Gravelford	OR	74	A6
Grayland	WA	33	C2
GRAYS HARBOR CO	WA	149	C4
Grays Harbor City	WA	33	C1
Grays Landing	WA	21	B6
Grays River	WA	33	E6
GREATER VANCOUVER	BC	109	C4
Green	OR	75	A6
Green Acres	OR	73	E5
Green Acres	OR	74	C1
Greenbank	WA	15	B5
Greenbank Estates	WA	15	B5
Greenberry	OR	64	B2
Green Bluff	WA	21	C7
Greencreek	ID	52	D1
Green Hills	OR	44	E7
Greenhorn	OR	60	A7
* Greenleaf	ID	83	B1
* Greenleaf	OR	63	D5
Greens Landing	WA	18	A7
Greenview	CA	98	C6
Greenwater	WA	26	B7
Greenwood	WA	34	B1
* Greenwood	BC	9	D4
Greenwood	WA	5	C5
Greer	ID	42	D6
Grenada	CA	99	A5
* Gresham	OR	168	E7
Grisdale	WA	24	A5
Gromore	WA	37	B4
Grotto	WA	26	C2
Guemes	WA	15	A2
H			
* Haines	OR	60	D5
Halfmoon Bay	BC	1	D7
* Halfway	OR	61	D5
* Halsey	OR	64	C2
Hamburg	CA	98	B4
Hamilton	OR	59	A7
* Hamilton	WA	15	E2
Hampton	OR	79	A2
Hampton	ID	41	E1
Hansville	WA	15	B7
Happy Camp	CA	97	E4
* Happy Valley	OR	45	B7
Harbor	OR	96	E1
Harbor Center	WA	15	B6
Hardman	OR	58	D3
Harlan	OR	63	D1
Harmon Heights	WA	26	A4
HARNEY CO	OR	80	C4
Harper	WA	25	B3
Harper	OR	71	B7
* Harrah	WA	37	D6
* Harrington	WA	30	B4
* Harrisburg	OR	64	B3
* Harrison	ID	32	A4
* Harrison Hot Springs	BC	6	B2

*Indicates incorporated city

Community	State	Map#	Grid	Community	State	Map#	Grid	Community	State	Map#	Grid	Community	State	Map#	Grid
Harrison Mills	BC	6	A2	Hoskins	OR	54	A7	Kangley	WA	26	A5	Lake Cowichan	BC	3	D6
*Hartline	WA	29	B2	Hot Springs	OR	100	D1	Kapowsin	WA	35	D1	Lakecreek	OR	87	E5
Hartstene	WA	24	E5	*Hubbard	OR	54	E3	Keasey	OR	44	B3	Lake Crescent	WA	13	E5
Harvard	ID	42	A1	*Huetter	ID	31	E1	*Keizer	OR	171	D2	Lakedale	WA	27	A6
Harwood	WA	37	C5	HUMBOLDT CO	NV	105	C5	Keller	WA	19	D6	Lake Dolloff	WA	25	C5
*Hatton	WA	39	D3	Humptulips	WA	23	D6	*Kellogg	ID	32	D3	Lake Earl	CA	96	E3
Hauser	OR	73	E3	Hunters	WA	20	B5	Kellogg Marsh	WA	15	D6	Lake Errock	BC	5	E3
*Hauser	ID	31	D1	*Huntington	OR	71	D3	Kellys Korner	WA	34	E1	*Lake Forest Park	WA	25	C1
Havillah	WA	9	A6	*Hunts Point	WA	130	A3	Kelso	OR	55	C1	Lake Heights	WA	134	D5
Hawk Acres	WA	24	E7	Huston	ID	83	B2	*Kelso	WA	156	C4	Lake Howard	WA	15	C5
Hawkinsville	CA	98	E4	Husum	WA	46	C4	Kendall	WA	5	D5	Lake Joy	WA	26	A2
Hay	WA	40	D4	Hyak	WA	26	D5	*Kendrick	ID	42	A4	Lake Kachees	WA	26	D5
*Hayden	ID	217	B3					*Kenmore	WA	25	D2	Lake Kathleen	WA	25	E4
*Hayden Lake	ID	217	D3	**I**				Kennard Corner	WA	25	D1	Lake Ki	WA	15	D5
Hayesville	OR	172	C3	IDAHO CO	ID	52	D3	*Kennewick	WA	206	B3	Lake Loma	WA	15	D5
Hayford	WA	31	A2	*Idanha	OR	55	D7	Keno	OR	99	E1	Lake Martha	WA	15	C5
Hazel	WA	16	A4	Idaville	OR	43	C6	Kenroy	WA	27	E4	Lake McDonald	WA	25	E4
Hazel Dell	WA	45	A5	Idleyld Park	OR	75	C5	*Kent	BC	6	B2	Lake of the Woods	OR	88	C6
Hazelwood	WA	134	C6	Illahee	WA	25	B3	*Kent	WA	140	D6	*Lake Oswego	OR	169	E6
Hebo	OR	53	C2	Illinois Valley	OR	97	C1	Kent	OR	57	C2	Lake Pattison	WA	34	E1
Heceta Beach	OR	63	A5	*Ilwaco	WA	33	B7	Kerby	OR	86	C7	Lake Retreat	WA	25	E5
Heceta Junction	OR	63	A5	Image	WA	159	B7	Keremeos	BC	8	C3	Lakeridge	WA	137	E4
Hedley	BC	8	A2	*Imbler	OR	50	D7	Kernville	OR	53	B5	*Lakeside	OR	74	A2
Heisson	WA	45	B4	Imnaha	OR	52	A6	*Kettle Falls	WA	20	C1	*Lake Stevens	WA	15	E6
*Helix	OR	49	E4	Inchelium	WA	20	B3	Keuterville	ID	52	C2	Lakeview	ID	22	B6
Helmer	ID	42	C2	*Independence	OR	54	B5	Kewa	WA	20	B4	*Lakeview	OR	101	E1
Helvetia	OR	44	D6	*Index	WA	26	C1	Key Center	WA	25	A5	Lakeview Park	WA	28	D5
Hemlock	OR	53	D1	Indian Beach	WA	15	B5	Keyport	WA	25	B2	Lakeview Terrace	WA	19	C7
Henley	OR	100	A1	Indian Cove	ID	84	E7	Keystone	WA	15	A5	*Lakewood	WA	143	A5
Henley	CA	99	A3	Indianola	WA	25	B1	Kimberly	OR	58	D6	Lamb Creek	ID	21	D2
Henrici	OR	55	A1	Indian Valley	ID	62	D7	KING CO	WA	124	C4	Lamoine	WA	28	B2
*Heppner	OR	58	D1	Indian Village	WA	15	B1	*King City	OR	54	E1	Lamona	WA	30	A5
Hereford	OR	70	D1	Inglis	OR	44	C1	Kings Corner	ID	83	D3	*Lamont	WA	30	D6
*Hermiston	OR	49	A4	Ioco	BC	4	E2	Kingsgate	WA	25	D2	Lancaster	WA	31	A7
Heron	MT	22	E5	*Ione	OR	48	C7	Kings Lakeside	WA	45	B3	LANE CO	OR	183	C4
Herron Island	WA	24	E5	*Ione	WA	11	A7	Kingston	WA	25	B1	Langell Valley	OR	100	D2
Hidden Valley	WA	35	E3	Irby	WA	29	C5	Kingston	ID	32	C3	*Langford	BC	14	B2
Highland Estates	WA	24	C6	Irondale	WA	15	A6	Kings Valley	OR	54	A6	*Langley	BC	5	B4
Highland Heights	WA	23	B6	Ironside	OR	70	E3	Kinton	OR	44	D7	*Langley	WA	15	C6
Highlands	BC	14	B2	Iron Springs	WA	23	B6	Kiona	WA	38	E7	Langlois	OR	85	D1
High Point	WA	25	E3	*Irrigon	OR	48	E3	*Kirkland	WA	126	C5	Lantzville	BC	3	D2
High Valley	WA	25	E4	Isabella Lake	WA	24	C6	KITSAP CO	WA	122	C4	La Pine	OR	77	C2
Hilgard	OR	60	C1	ISLAND CO	WA	14	E4	Kitsap Lake	WA	121	B3	La Push	WA	12	E7
*Hillsboro	OR	44	D6	*Island City	OR	60	D1	*Kittitas	WA	37	D1	*Lapwai	ID	42	A6
Hilltop	WA	25	D3	Island Lake	WA	25	A2	KITTITAS CO	WA	27	B6	Larimers Corner	WA	15	D7
Hilt	CA	98	E2	*Issaquah	WA	25	E3	Klaber	WA	34	C5	Larwood	OR	54	E7
*Hines	OR	80	C3					Klamath	CA	97	A6	*Latah	WA	31	C5
Hiouchi Valley	CA	97	A3	**J**				KLAMATH CO	OR	202	C4	LATAH CO	ID	42	B2
Hobart	WA	25	E4	JACKSON CO	OR	198	C4	Klamath Agency	OR	88	D4	Latham	OR	75	C1
Hobsonville	OR	43	C6	*Jacksonville	OR	87	C6	*Klamath Falls	OR	201	C5	Latourell Falls	OR	45	C6
Hockinson	WA	45	B5	Jamieson	OR	71	C4	Klamath Glen	CA	97	A6	Laurel	OR	44	D7
Hogans Corner	WA	23	B7	Jasper	OR	64	D6	Klamath River	CA	98	D3	Laurel	WA	5	B6
Holcomb	WA	33	E4	Jeffers Garden	OR	153	A5	Klaus	WA	34	E4	Laurelwood	OR	44	C7
Holden Village	WA	17	B5	*Jefferson	OR	54	C6	Klickitat	WA	46	E4	Laurier	WA	10	B5
Holley	OR	64	E3	JEFFERSON CO	WA	119	C3	KLICKITAT CO	WA	47	C4	Lawen	OR	80	D4
Holly	WA	24	D3	Jennings Lodge	OR	55	A1	Klipsan Beach	WA	33	C5	Lawrence	WA	5	D6
Hollywood	WA	25	D2	Jerome Prairie	OR	86	E5	Knappa	OR	43	E1	Lazy C	WA	24	E2
Hollywood Beach	WA	18	A7	Jewell	OR	44	A3	Koksilah	BC	4	A6	Leaburg	OR	64	E5
Holman	WA	33	B6	Jimtown	OR	61	D5	Kooskooskie	WA	50	C2	Leadpoint	WA	10	E5
Holmes Harbor Ests	WA	15	B5	Joel	ID	41	E3	*Kootenai	ID	22	B3	*Leavenworth	WA	27	C3
Home	WA	25	A5	*John Day	OR	69	C2	KOOTENAI CO	ID	216	C4	Lebam	WA	34	A4
*Homedale	ID	83	A2	Johnson	WA	41	D4	KOOTENAY BOUNDRY	BC	9	C3	*Lebanon	OR	64	D1
Homestead	OR	62	A4	*Johnson City	OR	55	A1	*Krupp	WA	29	C4	Ledgewood Beach	WA	15	B5
Home Valley	WA	46	A5	*Jordan Valley	OR	83	A7	*Kuna	ID	83	E3	Lee's Camp	OR	43	E6
Honeymoon Bay	BC	3	C6	*Joseph	OR	61	C1					Leland	WA	14	E7
Honeymoon Vista Bay	WA	15	B6	JOSEPHINE CO	OR	197	C4	**L**				Leland	OR	86	E3
Honeysuckle Hills	ID	32	B1	Joyce	WA	13	E5	Labish Village	OR	54	D4	Leland	ID	42	B4
Hood	WA	46	B5	*Juliaetta	ID	42	A4	*La Center	WA	45	A4	Lemolo	WA	25	B2
*Hood River	OR	46	B5	Junction City	WA	33	E1	*Lacey	WA	148	E2	Lenore	ID	42	B5
HOOD RIVER CO	OR	46	A6	*Junction City	OR	64	B4	Laclede	ID	21	E4	Letha	ID	72	C6
Hoodsport	WA	24	C4	Juniper Beach	WA	15	C4	Lacomb	OR	64	E1	LEWIS CO	WA	151	C4
Hoogdal	WA	15	D1	Juntura	OR	81	D1	*La Conner	WA	15	B3	Lewisburg	OR	54	B7
Hooper	WA	40	C3					*Lacrosse	WA	40	D2	*Lewiston	ID	41	E6
*Hope	ID	22	C4	**K**				Ladner	BC	4	D4	Lexington	WA	44	D1
*Hope	BC	6	C1	Kachees Ridge	WA	26	D5	Ladysmith	BC	3	E4	*Lexington	OR	48	D7
Hope	WA	25	A6	*Kahlotus	WA	39	E4	*Lafayette	OR	54	C2	Libby	OR	73	E4
*Hoquiam	WA	33	D1	Kalaloch	WA	23	A2	Lagoon Point	WA	15	A6	Liberal	OR	55	A2
Hornbrook	CA	99	A3	*Kalama	WA	44	E2	La Grande	WA	35	C2	Liberty	WA	27	C6
Hornby Island	BC	1	A7	Kala Point	WA	15	A6	*La Grande	OR	60	C1	*Liberty Lake	WA	31	D2
Horse Creek	CA	98	E3	Kaleden	BC	8	D1	LAKE CO	OR	90	C4	Lilliwaup	WA	24	C4
Horseshoe Bay	BC	4	C1	Kamela	OR	50	B7	Lake Alice	WA	26	A3	Lincoln	OR	99	A1
Horseshoe Lake	WA	25	A4	Kamilche	WA	24	C7	Lakebay	WA	25	A6	Lincoln	WA	30	A1
Horton	OR	63	E4	Kanaskat	WA	26	A5	Lake City	CA	102	A5	LINCOLN CO	OR	179	C4

*Indicates incorporated city

Cities and Communities

Community	State	Map#	Grid	Community	State	Map#	Grid	Community	State	Map#	Grid	Community	State	Map#	Grid
Lincoln Beach	OR	53	B5	Marblemount	WA	16	C2	* Midvale	ID	72	B1	Murphy	ID	83	D5
* Lincoln City	OR	53	B4	Marcola	OR	64	D4	Midvale Corner	WA	15	C6	Mushroom Corner	WA	24	E7
* Lind	WA	39	E1	* Marcus	WA	10	C7	Midway	WA	25	C5	Myrtle	ID	42	A5
Lindberg	OR	44	D2	Marietta	WA	5	B6	Midway	BC	9	D4	* Myrtle Creek	OR	75	A7
Lindell Beach	BC	5	E4	Marion	OR	54	D6	Midway	OR	44	D7	* Myrtle Point	OR	74	A7
LINN CO	OR	176	B4	MARION CO	OR	173	C4	Mikkalo	OR	47	E7				
Lions Bay	BC	2	C7	Marion Forks	OR	55	E7	Milan	WA	21	B6	**N**			
Little Albany	OR	63	C2	Marketown	WA	15	A3	Miles	WA	20	B7	* Naches	WA	37	C3
Little Boston	WA	15	B7	Markham	WA	33	C1	Miles Crossing	OR	153	C5	Nahcotta	WA	33	C5
Little Falls	WA	30	D1	Marlene Village	OR	44	E7	Mill A	WA	46	B5	Nahwatzel Lake	WA	24	B6
Littlerock	WA	34	D2	Marmot	OR	55	D1	Mill Bay	BC	4	A7	* Nampa	ID	220	C3
Little Shasta	CA	99	A5	Marquam	OR	54	E3	* Mill City	OR	55	B6	* Nanaimo	BC	3	D2
Lochsloy	WA	15	E6	Marshall	WA	31	A3	* Mill Creek	WA	15	D7	NANAIMO	BC	3	B3
Locke	WA	21	B2	Marshland	OR	44	B1	Millersburg	OR	176	B1	Nanoose Bay	BC	3	C2
Lofall	WA	25	A1	* Marsing	ID	83	B2	Millington	OR	74	A4	* Napavine	WA	34	D5
Logsden	OR	53	D6	Maryhill	WA	47	B5	Mill Plain	WA	160	D4	Naples	ID	22	B1
Lone Lake Shores	WA	15	B6	* Marysville	WA	15	D6	Milltown	ID	32	B5	Naselle	WA	33	D6
Lone Pine	WA	19	C6	MASON CO	WA	24	D5	Millwood	OR	74	D4	Nashville	OR	53	E7
* Lonerock	OR	58	B3	Matlock	WA	24	B6	* Millwood	WA	213	C1	Natal	OR	44	C3
* Long Beach	WA	33	B6	* Mattawa	WA	38	B3	Milner	BC	5	B3	National	WA	35	E3
Longbranch	WA	25	A6	Maud	WA	20	C3	Milo	OR	87	C1	Navy Yard City	WA	121	E7
* Long Creek	OR	59	B7	* Maupin	OR	56	E3	* Milton	WA	25	C6	Neah Bay	WA	12	E3
Long Lake	WA	25	A4	Maxwelton	WA	15	B7	* Milton-Freewater	OR	50	B3	Neahkahnie Beach	OR	43	C4
Long Lake	WA	30	D1	Mayger	OR	44	C1	* Milwaukie	OR	170	B4	Nedonna	OR	43	C5
Longmire	WA	36	A3	Mayne	BC	4	C6	Milwaukie Heights	OR	170	C5	* Nehalem	OR	43	C5
Long Point Manor	WA	15	A4	Mays Pond	WA	25	D1	Minam	OR	51	A6	Neilton	WA	23	D4
* Longview	WA	155	C3	Maytown	WA	34	D2	Mineral	WA	35	D3	Nemah	WA	33	D5
Lookingglass	OR	74	E6	Mayville	OR	58	A4	Minnehaha	WA	45	A5	Neotsu	OR	53	C4
Loomis	WA	8	D6	* Maywood Park	OR	163	D5	* Mission	BC	5	D3	Nesika Beach	OR	85	D4
Loon Lake	WA	20	E5	Mazama	WA	17	D1	Mission	OR	49	E5	Neskowin	OR	53	B3
Lopez	WA	14	E2	* McCall	ID	62	E4	Mission Beach	WA	15	C6	* Nespelem	WA	19	B5
Lorane	OR	64	B7	* McCleary	WA	24	B7	Mist	OR	44	B2	Netarts	OR	43	C7
Lorella	OR	100	D1	McCoy	OR	54	B4	Misty Meadows	WA	25	D1	Newaukum	WA	25	D6
* Lostine	OR	51	B7	McDermitt	NV	105	B2	* Mitchell	OR	68	A1	* Newberg	OR	54	D1
Lost Lake	WA	15	B5	McDonald	WA	29	A7	Moclips	WA	23	B5	New Bridge	OR	61	D5
Loveland	WA	25	B7	McGinnis Lake	WA	19	C6	MODOC CO	CA	101	C5	* Newcastle	WA	138	D1
Lowden	WA	49	E2	McGuires	ID	215	A5	Modoc Point	OR	88	E5	Newell	CA	100	C3
* Lowell	OR	64	E6	McKee Bridge	OR	98	B1	Mohawk	OR	64	D4	Newhalem	WA	16	E1
Lucerne	WA	17	C5	McKees Beach	WA	15	C5	Mohler	WA	30	A4	New Hope	OR	86	E6
Lucile	ID	52	D6	Mckenna	WA	35	B1	Mohler	ID	42	D6	New London	WA	23	D7
Lummi Island	WA	5	A7	McKenzie Bridge	OR	65	D4	Mohler	OR	43	D5	Newman Lake	WA	31	C1
Lyle	WA	46	D5	McKinley	OR	74	B5	* Molalla	OR	55	A3	* New Meadows	ID	62	E4
* Lyman	WA	15	E2	McMillin	WA	25	D7	Molson	WA	9	A5	New Pine Creek	OR	101	E2
* Lynden	WA	5	C5	* McMinnville	OR	54	B2	Mondovi	WA	30	C2	* New Plymouth	ID	72	B6
* Lynnwood	WA	25	C1	McMurray	WA	15	D4	Monitor	WA	27	D4	* Newport	OR	53	B7
* Lyons	OR	55	A6	McNulty	OR	44	E4	Monitor	OR	54	E3	* Newport	WA	21	C4
				Meacham	OR	50	A7	* Monmouth	OR	54	B5	New Princeton	OR	81	A5
M				Mead	WA	31	B1	* Monroe	OR	64	B3	Newton	BC	5	A3
Mabana	WA	15	C5	Meadowbrook	OR	55	A3	* Monroe	WA	25	E1	Newton	WA	23	C7
* Mabton	WA	48	B1	Meadowdale	WA	25	A2	Monse	WA	18	C5	Newton Creek	OR	195	B4
Macdoel	CA	99	D4	Meadow Glade	WA	45	A5	* Montague	CA	99	A4	* New Westminster	BC	4	E3
Machias	WA	15	E6	Meadows	ID	62	E4	* Montesano	WA	24	A7	* Nezperce	ID	42	D7
Madeira Park	BC	1	D6	* Medford	OR	198	C4	Montrose	BC	10	E4	NEZ PERCE CO	ID	42	B4
* Madras	OR	56	E7	* Medical Lake	WA	30	E3	* Monument	OR	58	E6	Nighthawk	WA	8	C5
Madrona Beach	WA	15	B4	Medical Springs	OR	61	A4	Mora	ID	83	E3	Nimrod	OR	65	B5
Malaga	WA	28	A5	Medimont	ID	32	A3	Moran Prairie	WA	212	E7	Nine Mile Falls	WA	31	A1
Malahat	BC	14	A1	* Medina	WA	129	E5	Morgan Acres	WA	31	B1	Nisson	WA	23	D7
* Malden	WA	31	B6	Mehama	OR	55	A6	* Moro	OR	47	B7	Nonpareil	OR	75	B4
MALHEUR CO	OR	94	C4	* Melba	ID	83	D4	MORROW CO	OR	48	C6	* Nooksack	WA	5	C5
* Malin	OR	100	C2	Melbourne	WA	33	E1	* Morton	WA	35	C5	Nordland	WA	15	A6
Malo	WA	9	E6	Melrose	OR	74	E5	Moscow	ID	41	E3	Nordman	ID	11	D7
Malone	WA	34	B1	Melville	OR	43	D2	* Moses Lake	WA	29	A7	Norma Beach	WA	15	C7
Malott	WA	18	C4	Menlo	WA	33	E4	* Mosier	OR	46	C5	* Normandy Park	WA	139	B3
Maltby	WA	25	E1	* Mercer Island	WA	134	B3	Mossyrock	WA	35	B5	North Beach	WA	4	E7
Manchester	WA	25	B3	* Meridian	ID	83	E2	* Mountain Home	ID	84	D6	* North Bend	OR	193	E2
Manito Club Estates	WA	212	C7	Merlin	OR	86	E4	Mountain View Beach	WA	15	B5	* North Bend	WA	26	A4
Manitou Beach	WA	25	B2	* Merrill	OR	100	B2	* Mt Angel	OR	54	E3	* North Bonneville	WA	45	E6
Manning	OR	44	C5	Merritt	WA	27	B1	Mount Hebron	CA	99	D4	North Cowichan	BC	3	E6
Manning Park	BC	7	C4	Mesa	ID	62	D7	Mount Hood	OR	46	B7	North Lake	WA	25	C5
* Mansfield	WA	28	D1	* Mesa	WA	39	C5	Mount Hope	WA	31	C4	North Lynnwood	WA	15	C7
Manson	WA	18	A7	Mesachie Lake	BC	3	C6	Mount Idaho	ID	52	E3	* North Plains	OR	44	D6
* Manzanita	OR	43	C5	* Metaline	WA	11	A6	* Mountlake Terrace	WA	25	C1	* Northport	WA	10	D5
Maple Beach	WA	4	D4	* Metaline Falls	WA	11	A6	* Mt Vernon	OR	69	B2	* North Powder	OR	60	A4
Maple Falls	WA	5	E5	* Metchosin	BC	14	A3	* Mt Vernon	WA	116	C4	North Prosser	WA	48	C1
Maple Grove	WA	13	E5	Methow	WA	18	A5	* Moxee	WA	37	D5	North Puyallup	WA	25	C6
Maple Hills	WA	25	E4	* Metolius	OR	66	E1	Mugginsville	CA	98	C6	* North Saanich	BC	4	B7
* Maple Ridge	BC	5	B2	Metzger	OR	44	E7	* Mukilteo	WA	15	C7	North Santiam	OR	54	D6
Mapleton	OR	63	C5	Mica	ID	31	E2	Mulino	OR	55	A2	Northside	ID	72	D6
* Maple Valley	WA	25	E5	Mica	WA	31	C3	MULTNOMAH CO	OR	162	C4	North Umpqua Village	OR	75	C5
Maple Valley Heights	WA	25	D4	Midas	ID	22	B4	Munson Point	WA	24	D6	* North Vancouver	BC	108	D5
Maplewood	WA	25	D4	* Middleton	ID	83	C1	Murdock	WA	46	E6	Northwood	WA	5	C5
Maplewood Heights	WA	25	D4	Midland	OR	99	E1	Murphy	OR	87	A6	Northwoods	WA	45	D2
Marble Creek	ID	32	E5	Midland	WA	144	C7					Nortons	OR	53	D7

*Indicates incorporated city

Community	State	Map#	Grid	Community	State	Map#	Grid	Community	State	Map#	Grid	Community	State	Map#	Grid
Norway	OR	74	A6	**P**				Pleasant Valley	OR	86	E4	Ramsdell	ID	32	A4
Norwood	OR	54	E1	* Pacific	WA	25	D6	Pleasant Valley	OR	53	D1	Rand	OR	86	D4
Noti	OR	64	A5	PACIFIC CO	WA	33	D5	* Plummer	ID	31	E5	Randle	WA	35	E5
* Notus	ID	83	B1	Pacific Beach	WA	23	B6	Plush	OR	91	C6	* Rathdrum	ID	31	E1
Nugents Corner	WA	5	C6	Pacific City	OR	53	C2	Plymouth	WA	49	A3	Ravensdale	WA	25	E5
* Nyssa	OR	72	A6	Packwood	WA	36	B4	Pocahontas	OR	60	D6	* Raymond	WA	33	E3
				Page	ID	32	D3	Pocahontas Bay	WA	21	B6	* Reardan	WA	30	D2
O				Painted Hills	WA	31	C2	Point Roberts	WA	4	D5	Redland	OR	55	B1
* Oak Bay	BC	112	C5	* Paisley	OR	90	D3	POLK CO	OR	171	D6	* Redmond	OR	66	E4
* Oakesdale	WA	31	C6	Palisades	WA	28	B4	Pollock	ID	62	D1	* Redmond	WA	25	D2
Oak Grove	OR	170	B6	Palmer	WA	26	A5	* Pomeroy	WA	41	A5	* Reedsport	OR	74	A1
* Oak Harbor	WA	15	A4	Palmer Junction	OR	50	E5	Pomona Heights	WA	37	D4	Rees Corner	WA	15	E7
* Oakland	OR	75	A4	* Palouse	WA	41	D1	* Ponderay	ID	22	B3	Reintree	WA	25	E1
* Oakridge	OR	76	B1	Panhandle Lake	WA	24	B6	Ponderosa Estates	WA	25	D7	Remote	OR	74	B7
* Oakville	WA	34	C2	Paradise Estates	WA	35	E3	Pondosa	OR	61	A4	* Renton	WA	138	B7
O'Brien	OR	97	C1	Paradise Park	OR	55	B1	Portage	WA	25	B4	* Republic	WA	19	D1
Obstruction Pass	WA	15	A1	Paradise Valley	NV	105	C6	* Port Angeles	WA	117	C3	Requa	CA	97	A5
Ocean City	WA	23	B7	Park	ID	42	C3	* Port Coquitlam	BC	5	A2	Retsil	WA	122	E7
Ocean Grove	WA	23	B6	Park	WA	5	D7	Porter	WA	34	B1	* Reubens	ID	42	B6
Ocean Park	WA	33	C5	Parkdale	OR	46	B7	Port Gamble	WA	15	B7	Reynolds	ID	83	C5
* Ocean Shores	WA	149	C4	Parker	WA	37	D5	* Portland	OR	165	E3	Rhodesia Beach	WA	33	C4
Oceanside	OR	43	C7	Parkland	WA	25	C7	Port Ludlow	WA	15	A7	Rhododendron	OR	55	E1
Ocosta	WA	33	C2	Parkline	ID	32	A5	Port Mellon	BC	2	B7	Rhododendron Park	WA	25	D7
Odell	OR	46	B6	Park Orchard	WA	25	D4	* Port Moody	BC	4	E2	Rice	WA	20	B2
Odessa	OR	89	E5	* Parksville	BC	3	B1	* Port Orchard	WA	122	C7	* Richland	OR	61	D6
* Odessa	WA	29	D5	Parkwood	WA	25	A3	* Port Orford	OR	85	C2	* Richland	WA	203	D5
Offutt Lake	WA	34	E2	* Parma	ID	72	A7	Port Renfrew	BC	13	A1	* Richmond	BC	4	D3
Ohanapecosh	WA	36	C3	Pasadena Park	WA	31	C2	Port Stanley	WA	14	E2	Rickreall	OR	54	B5
Okanagan Falls	BC	8	D2	* Pasco	WA	204	C4	* Port Townsend	WA	119	C3	* Riddle	OR	87	A1
OKANAGAN-SIMLKMN	BC	8	C3	Pataha City	WA	41	A5	Possession	WA	15	C7	* Ridgefield	WA	44	E4
* Okanogan	WA	18	D3	* Pateros	WA	18	B6	Possession Shores	WA	15	C7	Rieth	OR	49	D5
OKANOGAN CO	WA	18	C3	Paterson	WA	48	D3	Post	OR	67	D4	* Riggins	ID	52	D7
Ola	ID	72	E4	Patrick Creek	CA	97	B3	* Post Falls	ID	215	C4	Riley	OR	79	E3
Olalla	WA	25	B4	Patterson Junction	OR	48	D3	Potlatch	OR	54	E1	Rimrock	WA	36	E4
Oldport	WA	145	C1	Paulina	OR	68	B5	* Potlatch	ID	41	E1	Ritter	OR	59	B5
* Oldtown	ID	21	D5	* Payette	ID	72	A5	Potlatch	WA	24	C5	* Ritzville	WA	30	A7
Old Town	OR	75	A3	PAYETTE CO	ID	72	B4	Potlatch Junction	ID	41	E1	Riverbend	WA	27	C3
Old Willapa	WA	33	E3	Pearcot	WA	27	E5	* Poulsbo	WA	25	A1	Rivercrest	WA	15	D7
Olene	OR	100	B1	Pearson	WA	25	A2	Poverty Bay	WA	25	C5	Riverdale	OR	45	A7
Olex	OR	48	A7	* Peck	ID	42	C5	Powell Butte	OR	67	A4	* Rivergrove	OR	54	E1
Olga	WA	14	E1	Pecwan	CA	97	B7	* Powell River	BC	1	A4	River Jordan	BC	13	C2
Oliver	BC	8	D3	Pedee	ID	32	A5	POWELL RIVER	BC	1	B4	Riverside	OR	54	C7
Olney	OR	43	D1	Pedee	OR	54	A6	Power City	OR	49	A3	Riverside	OR	81	D3
* Olympia	WA	145	C4	Peel	OR	75	C5	* Powers	OR	86	A1	* Riverside	WA	18	D2
Olympic View	WA	25	A2	* Pe Ell	WA	34	B4	Prairie	WA	15	D1	Riverton	OR	73	E6
Olympus Ocean Ests	WA	23	A6	Pender Island	BC	4	C6	* Prairie City	OR	69	E2	Riverton	WA	137	A6
* Omak	WA	18	D3	* Pendleton	OR	49	D5	Pratum	OR	54	D4	Riverton Heights	WA	140	A1
Onalaska	WA	35	A5	PEND OREILLE CO	WA	21	C3	* Prescott	OR	44	D2	Riverview Hills	WA	31	B1
* Ontario	OR	72	A5	Pend Orielle Village	WA	11	A5	* Prescott	WA	40	B7	Riverwood	OR	170	A4
Ophir	OR	85	D4	Penn Cove Park	WA	15	A4	Preston	WA	26	A3	Roads End	OR	53	B4
Orcas	WA	14	E1	* Penticton	BC	8	D1	Prichard	ID	32	E2	Robe	WA	16	A6
Orchard Prairie	WA	31	B1	Peone	WA	31	C1	* Priest River	ID	21	E4	Roberts Creek	BC	4	A1
Orchards	WA	159	D1	Peoria	OR	64	B2	Princeton	ID	42	A1	Robson	BC	10	D1
Oreana	ID	83	E6	Perry	OR	60	C1	Princeton	BC	7	D1	Roche Harbor	WA	14	D1
* Oregon City	OR	55	A1	Perrydale	OR	54	B4	Prindle	WA	45	D6	Rochester	WA	34	C2
Oretown	OR	53	C3	Peshastin	WA	27	C3	* Prineville	OR	67	B3	* Rockaway Beach	OR	43	C6
Orient	WA	10	B6	Petersburg	OR	46	E6	Proebstel	WA	45	B5	Rock Creek	OR	60	D5
Orient	OR	45	C1	* Philomath	OR	177	A7	Prospect	OR	88	A2	Rock Creek	BC	9	B4
Orin	WA	20	D2	* Phoenix	OR	87	D7	Prosper	OR	73	D6	* Rockford	WA	31	D4
* Orofino	ID	42	D5	Picnic Point	WA	25	B5	* Prosser	WA	48	C1	Rockford Bay	ID	31	E3
Oro Fino	CA	98	C5	PIERCE CO	WA	141	C4	Puget Island	WA	44	A1	Rockie Four Corners	OR	54	E4
Orondo	WA	27	C3	Pillar Rock	WA	33	E7	* Pullman	WA	41	C3	* Rock Island	WA	28	A5
Orovada	NV	105	B6	* Pilot Rock	OR	49	D7	Purdy	WA	25	A5	Rockport	WA	16	B2
* Oroville	WA	8	E5	Pine	OR	61	E5	* Puyallup	WA	25	C6	Rockville	OR	82	E4
* Orting	WA	25	D7	Pine City	WA	31	A6					Rockwood	OR	168	E3
* Osburn	ID	32	E3	Pinecliff	WA	37	A2	**Q**				Rocky Point	ID	32	A4
Osceola	WA	25	E6	Pine Glen	WA	26	E6	Qualicum Beach	BC	3	A1	Rocky Point	WA	15	B4
Oso	WA	16	A4	Pine Grove	OR	56	C3	Queets	WA	23	B3	Rocky Point	OR	88	D5
Osoyoos	BC	8	E4	Pinehurst	ID	62	D1	Quilcene	WA	24	E1	Rocky Point	WA	121	E2
Ostrander	WA	44	E1	Pinehurst	OR	99	B1	Quinaby	WA	54	D4	Rocky Woods	WA	35	C1
* Othello	WA	39	B2	* Pinehurst	ID	32	D3	Quinault	WA	23	D4	Rodena Beach	WA	15	B4
Otis	OR	53	C4	Pine Ridge	ID	62	D1	Quincy	OR	44	C1	* Rogue River	OR	87	B5
Otis Orchards	WA	31	C2	Pine Ridge	OR	88	E4	* Quincy	WA	28	C6	Rolling Hills	WA	15	A4
Otter Rock	OR	53	B6	Pioneer	WA	45	A4	Quines Creek	OR	87	A2	Rome	OR	94	B2
Outlet Bay	ID	21	E2	Pistol River	OR	85	D6					Ronald	WA	27	A6
Outlook	OR	55	B1	* Pitt Meadows	BC	5	A3	**R**				Roosevelt	WA	48	A5
Outlook	WA	38	A7	Pittsburg	OR	44	C3	Rainbow	OR	65	C4	Roosevelt	WA	15	E7
Owyhee	OR	71	E7	Plain	WA	27	C1	* Rainier	OR	155	B7	Roosevelt Beach	WA	23	B6
OWYHEE CO	ID	95	C4	Plaza	WA	31	B5	* Rainier	WA	35	A2	* Rosalia	WA	31	B6
Oyhut	WA	23	B7	Pleasant Harbor	WA	24	E2	Rainier Terrace	WA	25	C7	Rosario	WA	14	E1
Oysterville	WA	33	C4	Pleasant Hill	WA	34	E7	Raleigh Hills	OR	44	E7	Rosario Beach	WA	15	A3
Ozette	WA	12	E4	Pleasant Hill	OR	64	D6	Ralston	WA	40	B1	Rosburg	WA	33	E6
				Pleasant Valley	OR	61	A7	Rambler Park	WA	37	C4	* Roseburg	OR	196	B4
								Ramey	ID	72	A5				

*Indicates incorporated city

Cities and Communities

Community	State	Map#	Grid
Rosedale	BC	6	A3
Rosedale	WA	25	A5
Rose Lake	ID	32	B3
Rose Lodge	OR	53	C4
Rose Valley	WA	44	E2
Rosewood	WA	209	E2
*Roslyn	WA	27	A6
*Rossland	BC	10	D4
Roswell	ID	83	A1
Rowena	OR	46	D6
*Roy	WA	35	B1
Royal Camp	WA	38	E2
*Royal City	WA	38	D2
Ruch	OR	87	C7
Ruff	WA	29	C6
*Rufus	OR	47	B5
Ruggs	OR	58	D2
*Ruston	WA	25	B5
Ryderwood	WA	34	D6
S			
*Saanich	BC	111	D1
Saanichton	BC	14	B1
Saginaw	OR	64	C7
Sagle	ID	22	B4
St. Andrews	WA	28	E2
*St. Helens	OR	44	E4
St. Joe	ID	32	C5
*St. John	WA	31	A7
*St. Maries	ID	32	B5
*St. Paul	OR	54	D2
*Salem	OR	173	C4
Salishan	OR	53	B5
Salkum	WA	35	A5
Salmo	BC	11	B3
Salmon Creek	WA	45	A5
Saltspring Island	BC	4	B6
Samish Island	WA	15	B1
Samish Lake	WA	5	C7
*Sammamish	WA	25	E3
Sams Valley	OR	87	C5
Samuels	ID	22	B2
San de Fuca	WA	15	A4
Sanders	ID	32	A7
SANDERS CO	MT	22	E5
Sand Lake	OR	53	C1
*Sandpoint	ID	22	A3
*Sandy	OR	55	C1
Sandy Hook	WA	15	C7
Sandy Hook Park	WA	25	B2
Sandy Point	WA	15	C6
SAN JUAN CO	WA	14	E2
San Marine	OR	63	B2
Santa	ID	32	C6
Santiago Beach	WA	23	B5
Sappho	WA	13	B5
Sara	WA	44	E5
Saratoga Beach	WA	15	B5
Saratoga Heights	WA	15	B5
Saratoga Shores	WA	15	B5
Sardis	BC	6	A4
Satsop	WA	34	A1
Saturna	BC	4	D6
Satus	WA	38	A7
Sauk River Estates	WA	16	C3
Saunders Lake	OR	74	A2
Sawyer	WA	37	E6
Scandia	WA	25	A2
*Scappoose	OR	44	D5
Scatchet Head	WA	15	B7
Schawana	WA	38	B3
Schneiders Prairie	WA	24	D7
Scholls	OR	44	D7
*Scio	OR	54	D7
Scofield	OR	44	B5
Scott Bar	CA	98	C4
Scott Lake	WA	34	D1
Scottsburg	OR	74	C2
*Scotts Mills	OR	55	A4
Sea Acres	WA	15	A1
Seabeck	WA	24	E2
Seal Rock	WA	24	E2
Seal Rock	OR	63	B1
Seamount Estates	WA	24	D2
*Seaside	OR	154	C5
*Seatac	WA	140	B5
Seatons Grove	WA	19	C6
*Seattle	WA	128	C7
Seaview	WA	33	B6
Sechelt	BC	2	A7
*Sedro-Woolley	WA	15	D2
Seekseequa	OR	56	D7
Seghers	OR	44	C7
Seiad Valley	CA	98	A3
Sekiu	WA	13	B4
*Selah	WA	37	D4
Selleck	WA	26	A5
Selma	OR	86	D6
*Seneca	OR	69	C5
*Sequim	WA	118	C5
Service Creek	OR	58	B6
Setters	ID	31	D4
Seven Bays	WA	20	A3
Seven Mile	WA	31	A1
Shadowood	OR	55	A1
*Shady Cove	OR	87	D4
Shana Park	WA	148	D3
Shangri-La Shores	WA	15	B5
*Shaniko	OR	57	B4
Shaw	OR	54	D5
Shaw Island	WA	14	E1
Shawnigan Lake	BC	4	A7
Shedd	OR	64	C2
Shelburn	OR	54	D6
*Shelton	WA	24	D6
*Sheridan	OR	54	A3
SHERMAN CO	OR	47	C6
*Sherwood	OR	54	E1
Sherwood Beach	ID	21	E2
Shine	WA	15	A7
Shore Acres	WA	25	A5
*Shoreline	WA	25	C1
Shorewood	OR	73	E3
Shorewood	WA	136	C4
Shorewood Beach	WA	25	A6
SHOSHONE CO	ID	32	D4
Shrine Beach	WA	18	A7
Shuwah	WA	13	A6
*Sidney	BC	4	B7
Sierra Division	WA	15	A4
Sifton	WA	45	A5
Silcott	WA	41	D6
*Siletz	OR	53	C6
Siltcoos	OR	63	B6
Silvana	WA	15	D5
Silver Beach	ID	21	E6
Silver Brook	WA	35	E5
Silver City	ID	83	C7
Silver Creek	WA	35	A5
Silverdale	WA	25	A2
Silver Lake	WA	34	E7
Silver Lake	OR	77	E6
Silver Lake	WA	15	D7
Silver Lake	WA	30	E3
*Silverton	OR	54	E4
Silverton	ID	32	E3
Silverton	WA	16	C6
Similk Beach	WA	15	B2
Simnasho	OR	56	C4
Sirdar	BC	11	E1
Sisco Heights	WA	15	E5
SISKIYOU CO	CA	98	C5
*Sisters	OR	66	B3
Sitkum	OR	74	C6
Sixes	OR	85	D1
SKAGIT CO	WA	115	C3
Skagit Country Club	WA	15	C2
Skamania	WA	45	D6
SKAMANIA CO	WA	45	D3
Skamokawa	WA	34	A7
*Skykomish	WA	26	D2
Skyway	WA	137	D5
Slate Creek	ID	52	D5
*Smelterville	ID	32	D3
Smith River	CA	96	E2
Smyrna	WA	38	D2
Snee Oosh	WA	15	B3
*Snohomish	WA	15	E7
SNOHOMISH CO	WA	120	C4
*Snoqualmie	WA	26	A3
Snoqualmie Pass	WA	26	D4
*Soap Lake	WA	28	E5
*Sodaville	OR	64	D2
Somes Bar	CA	97	D7
Sooke	BC	13	E3
South Bay	WA	146	E1
South Beach	WA	4	D5
*South Bend	WA	33	D3
South Colby	WA	25	B3
South Elma	WA	34	B1
Southern Heights	WA	136	D4
South Junction	OR	56	E5
South Point	WA	25	A1
*South Prairie	WA	25	D7
South Slocan	BC	11	A1
South Snohomish	WA	15	E7
South Union	WA	34	D1
South Wenatchee	WA	27	E5
Southwick	ID	42	C4
Southworth	WA	25	B3
Spalding	ID	42	A5
Spanaway	WA	25	B7
*Spangle	WA	31	B4
*Spirit Lake	ID	21	E6
*Spokane	WA	211	E1
SPOKANE CO	WA	214	C4
*Spokane Valley	WA	214	A4
*Sprague	WA	30	D5
Sprague River	OR	89	B5
*Spray	OR	58	C6
Spring Creek	WA	27	A6
Springdale	OR	45	C7
*Springdale	WA	20	E6
*Springfield	OR	187	C2
Spring Glen	WA	26	A3
Springwater	OR	55	B2
*Squamish	BC	2	D5
SQUAMISH-LILLOOET	BC	2	C3
Stabler	WA	45	E4
Stafford	OR	54	E1
*Stanfield	OR	49	B4
*Stanwood	WA	15	C4
*Star	ID	83	D1
*Starbuck	WA	40	C5
Starkey	ID	62	D5
Starkey	OR	60	A2
Startup	WA	16	B7
*State Line	ID	31	D1
*Stayton	OR	54	E6
Steamboat	OR	75	E4
Stehekin	WA	17	C4
*Steilacoom	WA	25	A6
Steptoe	WA	41	B1
Sterling	WA	15	D2
STEVENS CO	WA	20	D5
*Stevenson	WA	45	E5
Stewart Springs	CA	99	A7
Stillwater	WA	26	A2
Stimson Crossing	WA	15	D5
Stratford	WA	28	E4
Streeters	WA	34	E7
Stringtown	WA	33	C7
*Sublimity	OR	54	E6
Sudden Valley	WA	5	C7
*Sultan	WA	16	A7
*Sumas	WA	5	D5
Summer Lake	OR	90	B1
Summer Lake Hot Spr	OR	90	C3
*Summerville	OR	50	D7
Summerwood	WA	31	B1
Summit	OR	53	E7
Summit	WA	25	C6
Summit Lake	WA	24	C7
Summit Park	WA	15	B2
Sumner	WA	74	A5
*Sumner	WA	25	D6
*Sumpter	OR	60	C6
Suncrest	WA	31	A1
Sundale	WA	47	E5
Sundins Beach	WA	15	C4
Sun Island	WA	26	E6
Sunland Estates	WA	28	B7
Sunlight Beach	WA	15	B6
Sunlight Shores	WA	15	B6
Sunny Bay	WA	25	A5
Sunnyside	ID	22	B3
Sunnyside	OR	45	A7
Sunnyside	WA	15	D6
Sunnyside	OR	50	A3
*Sunnyside	WA	38	B7
Sunnyside Beach	WA	25	A6
Sunnyslope	WA	27	E4
Sunnyslope	WA	25	A4
Sunny Valley	OR	87	A3
Sunrise	WA	36	B2
Sunrise Point	WA	15	C5
Sunriver	OR	66	C7
Sunset	WA	31	A7
Sunset Bay	WA	20	E7
Sunset Beach	OR	43	C1
Sunset Beach	WA	23	B6
Sunset Beach	WA	15	B4
Sunset Beach	WA	24	E4
Sunset Beach	WA	25	A6
Sunset West	WA	34	D4
SUNSHINE COAST	BC	1	C6
Sunwood Lakes	WA	34	E1
Suquamish	WA	25	B2
*Surrey	BC	5	A4
*Sutherlin	OR	75	A4
Suver	OR	54	B6
Svensen	OR	43	E1
Swan Trail	WA	15	D7
Swedetown	OR	44	C2
Sweet	ID	72	E5
*Sweet Home	OR	64	E2
Sweetwater	ID	42	A6
Swisshome	OR	63	C5
T			
Table Rock	OR	87	C5
*Tacoma	WA	142	A4
Tacoma Point	WA	25	D6
Tahlequah	WA	25	B5
Taholah	WA	23	A5
Tahuya	WA	24	D5
Takilma	OR	97	D1
Talache	ID	22	B5
*Talent	OR	87	D7
Tamarack	ID	62	D4
Tampico	WA	37	A5
*Tangent	OR	64	B1
Tanglewilde	WA	24	E7
Tanglewilde East	WA	25	A7
Tanner	WA	26	B4
Taylorville	OR	44	A1
Teanaway	WA	27	B7
*Tekoa	WA	31	D6
Telma	WA	27	B1
Telocaset	OR	60	E3
*Tenino	WA	34	E2
Tenmile	ID	83	E2
Tenmile	OR	74	A2
Tennant	CA	99	E6
*Tensed	ID	31	E6
Teronda West	WA	15	B5
Terrace Heights	WA	37	D4
Terrebonne	OR	66	D3
Terrill Beach	WA	4	E7
*The Dalles	OR	46	D6
Thetis Island	BC	4	A4
Thomas	WA	25	D5
Thompson Place	WA	24	E7
Thornhollow	OR	50	A5
Thornton	WA	31	B7
Thorp	WA	27	C7
Three Lakes	WA	15	E7
Three Lynx	OR	55	D3
Thrift	WA	25	D6
THURSTON CO	WA	148	C5
Tide	OR	63	C5
Tidewater	OR	63	C2

*Indicates incorporated city

Community	State	Map#	Grid	Community	State	Map#	Grid	Community	State	Map#	Grid	Community	State	Map#	Grid
Tiernan	OR	63	B5	*Vale	OR	71	D6	Wauconda	WA	9	B7	Winema Beach	OR	53	B3
Tierra Del Mar	OR	53	C2	Valley	WA	20	E5	Waukon	WA	30	D3	Wingville	OR	60	D5
*Tieton	WA	37	B4	VALLEY CO	ID	72	E3	Wauna	WA	25	A5	*Winlock	WA	34	D5
*Tigard	OR	44	D7	Valley Falls	OR	90	E5	Wautauga Beach	WA	25	B3	Winona	WA	40	E1
Tiger	WA	11	A7	Valleyford	WA	31	C3	*Waverly	WA	31	C5	*Winston	OR	74	E6
*Tillamook	OR	43	D7	Valley Junction	OR	53	E3	Wedderburn	OR	85	D5	Winterville	OR	73	D6
TILLAMOOK CO	OR	43	D7	Valley View	WA	13	A6	*Weed	CA	99	B7	*Winthrop	WA	18	A2
Tiller	OR	87	C1	Valley View Heights	ID	41	E6	*Weiser	ID	72	A3	Wishkah	WA	23	E7
Tillicum Beach	WA	15	C5	Valsetz	OR	53	D5	Welches	OR	55	E1	Wishram	WA	47	A6
Timber	OR	44	B5	Van Anda	BC	1	A5	Welcome	WA	5	D6	Wishram Heights	WA	47	A5
Timber Lakes	WA	24	D6	*Vancouver	WA	158	A4	Wellpinit	WA	20	C7	Withrow	WA	28	C2
Tionesta	CA	100	C5	*Vancouver	BC	110	A4	*Wenatchee	WA	27	D5	Wocus	OR	88	E7
Tokeland	WA	33	C3	Van Horn	WA	16	B2	Wenatchee Heights	WA	27	E5	Wolf Creek	OR	86	E3
Toketee Falls	OR	76	A5	Vantage	WA	38	B1	West Beach	WA	4	E7	Wolf Lodge	ID	32	A2
*Toledo	OR	53	C7	Van Zandt	WA	5	D6	Westbridge	BC	9	B3	Wollochet	WA	25	A6
*Toledo	WA	34	E6	Vashon	WA	25	B4	West Clarkston	WA	41	D6	Wonder	OR	86	D6
Tollgate	OR	50	C4	Vashon Center	WA	25	B4	Westfall	OR	71	A6	*Woodburn	OR	54	E3
*Tonasket	WA	8	E7	Vashon Heights	WA	25	B3	*Westfir	OR	76	A1	*Woodinville	WA	25	D1
Top	OR	58	E5	Vaughn	OR	64	A5	West Haven-Sylvan	OR	44	E6	*Woodland	WA	44	E3
Tophill	OR	44	C5	Vaughn	WA	25	A5	Westholme	BC	4	A6	Woodland	ID	42	E6
*Toppenish	WA	37	E6	Vedder Crossing	BC	5	E4	Westlake	OR	63	A6	Woodland Beach	WA	15	B5
Touchet	WA	49	E2	Venersborg	WA	45	B4	*West Linn	OR	55	A1	Woodland Creek	WA	24	E7
Toutle	WA	34	E7	*Veneta	OR	64	A5	Westmond	ID	22	A5	Woodland Park	WA	45	B2
Tracyton	WA	122	A1	Verboort	OR	44	C6	Westmont Acres	WA	28	D5	Woods	OR	53	C2
Trafton	WA	15	E4	Verlot	WA	16	A6	*Weston	OR	50	A4	Woodsmuir	WA	148	C3
Trail	OR	87	D3	*Vernonia	OR	44	C4	Westport	OR	44	B1	Woodson	OR	44	B1
*Trail	BC	10	D4	*Victoria	BC	111	E5	*Westport	WA	150	C3	*Wood Village	OR	45	B6
Trask	OR	43	E7	Vida	OR	65	A4	*West Richland	WA	203	A6	*Woodway	WA	25	C1
Treasure Island	WA	24	E5	View Park	WA	25	B4	West Scio	OR	54	D6	Worden	OR	99	E2
Treharne	OR	44	B4	*View Royal	BC	111	A1	West Side	OR	101	D1	*Worley	ID	31	E4
Trestle Creek	ID	22	C3	Villa Beach	WA	25	A6	West Slope	OR	44	E7	Wren	OR	54	A7
Triangle Lake	OR	63	E4	Vinland	WA	25	A1	West Sound	WA	14	E1	Wye Lake	WA	25	A4
Tri-City	OR	75	A7	Viola	OR	55	B2	West Stayton	OR	54	D6				
TRINITY CO	CA	98	E7	Viola	ID	41	D2	West Tapps	WA	25	D6	**Y**			
Triton	WA	24	D3	Virginia	WA	25	A2	West Union	OR	44	D6	*Yachats	OR	63	B3
Trout Creek	OR	46	B6	Vision Acres	WA	44	E2	*West Vancouver	BC	107	C3	*Yacolt	WA	45	B4
*Troutdale	OR	45	B7	Vya	NV	102	C6	Weyerhaeuser Twnsite	OR	99	E1	*Yakima	WA	37	D4
Trout Lake	WA	46	C3					Whalley	BC	5	A3	YAKIMA CO	WA	37	C5
*Troy	MT	22	E2	**W**				WHATCOM CO	WA	113	C2	Yale	WA	45	B3
*Troy	ID	42	A3	Wagontire	OR	79	C5	Wheeler	WA	29	B7	*Yamhill	OR	54	B1
Troy	OR	51	B3	Waha	ID	42	A7	*Wheeler	OR	43	C5	YAMHILL CO	OR	54	B2
Tsawwassen	BC	4	D4	Wahkiacus	WA	46	E4	WHEELER CO	OR	58	B6	Yankton	OR	44	D4
*Tualatin	OR	54	E1	WAHKIAKUM CO	WA	34	A7	*Whistler	BC	2	E2	*Yarrow Point	WA	130	B2
*Tukwila	WA	140	D1	*Waitsburg	WA	40	C7	*White Bird	ID	52	D4	*Yelm	WA	35	A1
Tulalip	WA	15	D6	Waitts Lake	WA	20	D4	White Center	WA	136	A2	Ymir	BC	11	B2
*Tulelake	CA	100	B3	Wakonda Beach	OR	63	B2	White City	OR	87	D5	Yokeko Point	WA	15	B3
Tumalo	OR	66	C5	Walden	WA	75	C1	White Pass	WA	36	D4	*Yoncalla	OR	75	A2
Tumtum	WA	20	E7	*Waldport	OR	179	C5	*White Rock	BC	5	A4	Youbou	BC	3	C5
*Tumwater	WA	147	D3	Waldron	WA	4	D7	Whites	WA	24	B7	*Yreka	CA	98	E4
Turner	WA	40	D6	Walker	OR	64	C7	*White Salmon	WA	46	C5				
*Turner	OR	54	D5	*Walla Walla	WA	208	B3	Whiteson	OR	54	B3	**Z**			
Turner Corner	WA	25	D1	WALLA WALLA CO	WA	207	B3	White Swan	WA	37	C6	Zigzag	OR	55	E1
Twinlow	ID	21	E7	*Wallowa	OR	51	B6	WHITMAN CO	WA	41	C2	*Zillah	WA	37	E6
Twin Rocks	OR	43	C6	WALLOWA CO	OR	51	C5	Whitney	OR	60	B7				
*Twisp	WA	18	A3	Wallowa Lake Resort	OR	61	D1	Whitney Esttes	WA	34	D4				
Tygh Valley	OR	56	D2	Wallula	WA	49	C2	Whitstran	WA	48	D1				
Tyler	WA	30	E4	Wallula Junction	WA	49	C2	Wickersham	WA	15	D1				
				Walnut Grove	WA	45	A5	Wilbur	WA	75	A4				
U				Walterville	OR	64	D5	*Wilbur	WA	29	D1				
Ubc	BC	4	C2	Walton	OR	63	E5	Wildcat Lake	WA	25	A3				
*Ukiah	OR	59	C3	Wamic	OR	56	D2	*Wilder	ID	83	A1				
Umapine	OR	50	A3	Wanapum Village	WA	38	B2	Wilderness	WA	148	D2				
*Umatilla	OR	49	A3	*Wapato	WA	37	D6	Wilderville	OR	86	E5				
UMATILLA CO	OR	49	C5	Wapato	OR	44	C7	Wildwood	OR	55	E1				
Umpqua	OR	74	E4	Wapinitia	OR	56	D3	Wiley City	WA	37	C5				
Underwood	WA	46	C5	*Warden	WA	39	B1	Wilhoit	OR	55	A4				
Union	WA	24	C5	Warfield	BC	10	D4	*Wilkeson	WA	25	E7				
*Union	OR	60	E2	Warm Beach	WA	15	C5	*Willamina	OR	54	A3				
UNION CO	OR	60	C2	Warm Springs	OR	56	D6	Willapa	WA	33	E3				
Union Creek	OR	88	B1	Warren	OR	44	E4	Willard	WA	46	B4				
Union Gap	WA	37	D5	Warren	WA	25	A5	Williams	OR	87	A7				
Union Mill	WA	34	E1	*Warrenton	OR	153	A4	Willowcreek	OR	71	C5				
Union Mills	OR	55	A2	*Wasco	OR	47	C6	Willowdale	OR	57	A6				
*Uniontown	WA	41	D5	WASCO CO	OR	56	C4	Willow Grove	WA	44	C1				
Unionvale	OR	54	C3	WASHINGTON CO	ID	72	B2	Willow Ranch	CA	101	E3				
*Unity	OR	70	C2	Washoe	ID	72	A5	Wilson Beach	OR	43	E3				
University Place	WA	143	A2	WASHOE CO	NV	102	D5	Wilson Creek	WA	29	B4				
Upper Preston	WA	26	A4	*Washougal	WA	45	C6	*Wilsonville	OR	54	E1				
Upper Soda	OR	65	C2	*Washtucna	WA	40	A3	Wimer	OR	87	B4				
Useless Bay Ctry Club	WA	15	B6	*Waterloo	OR	64	E1	Winchester	OR	75	A4				
Usk	WA	21	B3	Waterman	WA	25	B3	Winchester	WA	28	C6				
Utsalady	WA	15	B4	*Waterville	WA	28	A2	*Winchester	ID	42	B7				
*Vader	WA	34	D6	Watseco	OR	43	C6	Winchester Bay	OR	74	A1				

*Indicates incorporated city

MAP
1

1:380,160
1 in. = 6 mi.

0   4   8
miles

MAP
1

50°13'39"
50°15'17"

EAST REDONDA ISLAND

STRATHCONA

SECHELT INDIAN GOVERNMENT DISTRICT

50°06'43"
50°08'21"

DESOLATION SOUND PROVINCIAL MARINE PARK

GOAT ISLAND

POWELL LAKE

49°59'48"
50°01'26"

SECHELT INDIAN GOVERNMENT DISTRICT

SLIAMMON INDIAN RESERVE 1

101

49°52'52"
49°54'30"

Powell River

HARWOOD ISLAND

POWELL RIVER

SEE
2
MAP

ABBITUS AV
MARINE PT
MANSON AV

POWELL RIVER-LITTLE RIVER FY

JOYCE AV
TANNER AV

Powell River Airport

49°45'57"
49°47'34"

Blubber Bay

101

SECHELT INDIAN GOVERNMENT DISTRICT

101

Egmont

Van Anda

SECHELT INDIAN GOVERNMENT DISTRICT

NELSON ISLAND

101

Gillies Bay

49°39'01"
49°40'38"

TEXADA ISLAND

SUNSHINE COAST

Garden Bay

COMOX VALLEY

Madeira Park

BELLINGHAM PRINCE RUPERT FY
BELLINGHAM KETCHIKAN FY

49°32'06"
49°33'42"

101

Hornby Island

STRAIT OF GEORGIA

Halfmoon Bay

SUNSHINE COAST HWY

TRAIL AV

101

49°25'10"
49°26'47"

124°38'25"   124°27'47"   124°17'10"   124°06'32"   123°55'55"   123°45'16"

A   B   C   D   E

SEE
3
MAP

MAP
2

MAP
2

1:380,160
1 in. = 6 mi.
0   4   8
miles

N

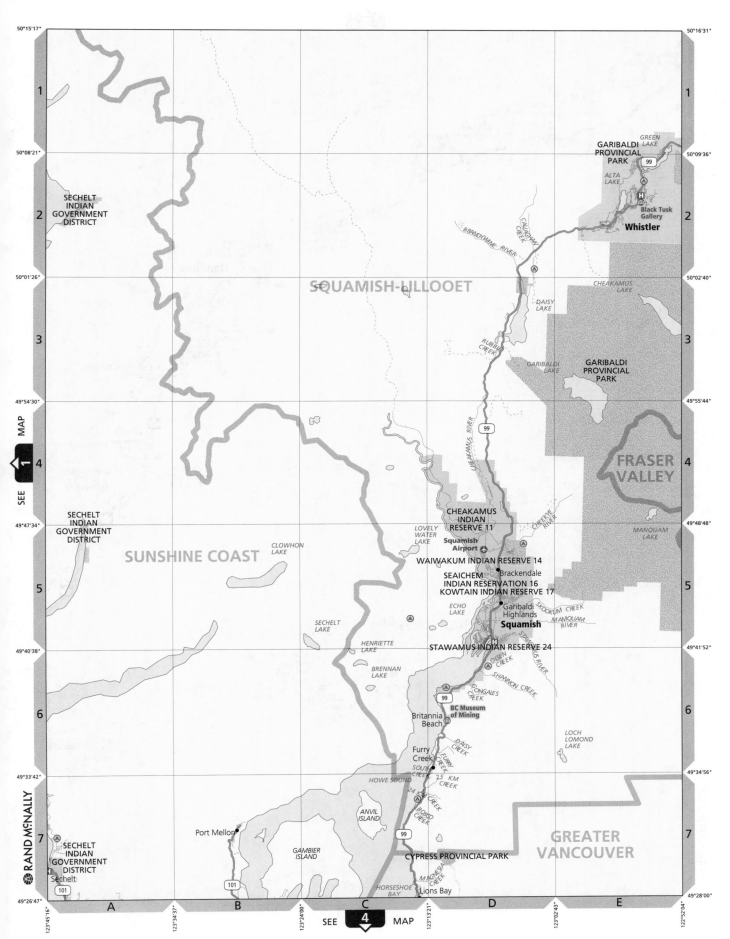

GARIBALDI
PROVINCIAL
PARK

GREEN
LAKE

99

ALTA
LAKE

Black Tusk
Gallery

Whistler

CALICHAN CREEK

BRANDYWINE RIVER

CHEAKAMUS
LAKE

SQUAMISH-LILLOOET

DAISY
LAKE

RUBBLE CREEK

GARIBALDI
LAKE

GARIBALDI
PROVINCIAL
PARK

99

CHEAKAMUS RIVER

FRASER
VALLEY

SECHELT
INDIAN
GOVERNMENT
DISTRICT

SECHELT
INDIAN
GOVERNMENT
DISTRICT

SEE MAP 1

CHEAKAMUS
INDIAN
RESERVE 11

CHEEKYE RIVER

MANQUAM
LAKE

LOVELY
WATER
LAKE

Squamish
Airport

SUNSHINE COAST

CLOWHON
LAKE

WAIWAKUM INDIAN RESERVE 14

Brackendale

SEAICHEM
INDIAN RESERVATION 16
KOWTAIN INDIAN RESERVE 17

SKOOKUM CREEK

ECHO
LAKE

Garibaldi
Highlands

MAMQUAM
RIVER

SECHELT
LAKE

Squamish

HENRIETTE
LAKE

STAWAMUS INDIAN RESERVE 24

STAWAMUS RIVER

BRENNAN
LAKE

OLSEN CREEK

SHANNON CREEK

GONGALES CREEK

99

LOCH
LOMOND
LAKE

BC Museum
of Mining

Britannia
Beach

DAISY
CREEK

Furry
Creek

FURRY CREEK

SOUTH
CREEK

25 KM
CREEK

HOWE SOUND

24 KM CREEK

ANVIL
ISLAND

BOSCO
CREEK

GREATER
VANCOUVER

99

Port Mellon

RAND McNALLY

SECHELT
INDIAN
GOVERNMENT
DISTRICT

Sechelt

101

GAMBIER
ISLAND

CYPRESS PROVINCIAL PARK

MAGNESIA CREEK

101

HORSESHOE
BAY

Lions Bay

50°15'17"
50°08'21"
50°01'26"
49°54'30"
49°47'34"
49°40'38"
49°33'42"
49°26'47"

50°16'31"
50°09'36"
50°02'40"
49°55'44"
49°48'48"
49°41'52"
49°34'56"
49°28'00"

123°45'16"
123°34'37"
123°24'00"
123°13'21"
123°02'43"
122°52'04"

1   2   3   4   5   6   7

A   B   C   D   E

SEE 4 MAP

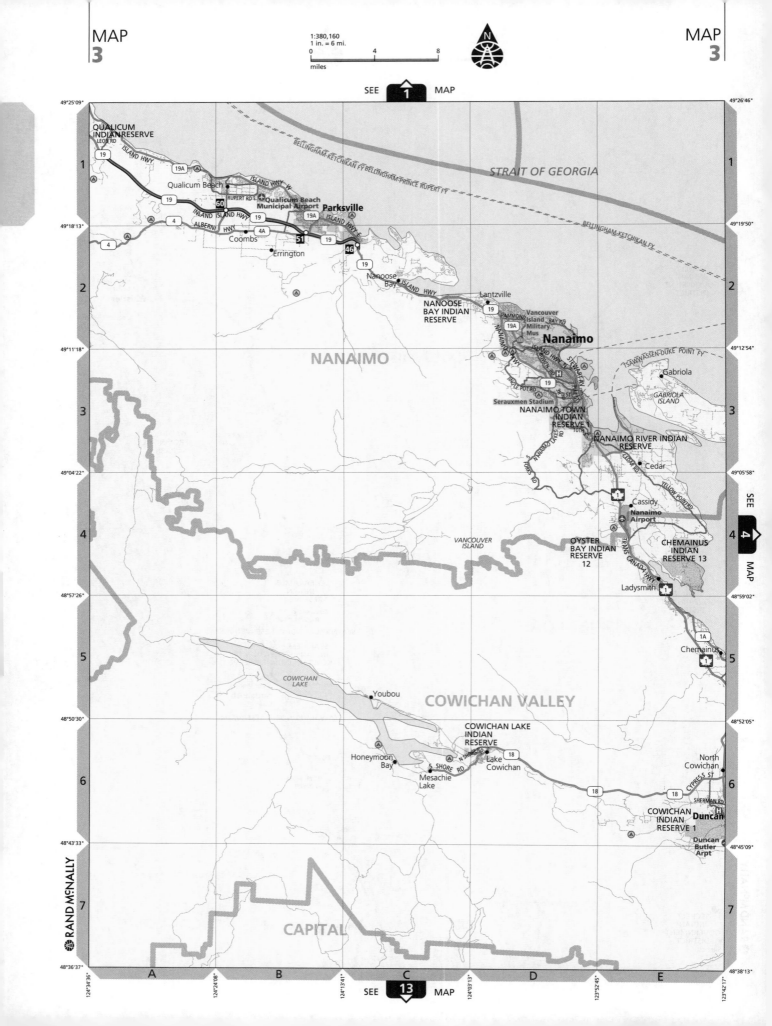

MAP
3

MAP
3

1:380,160
1 in. = 6 mi.

0   4   8

miles

N

SEE 1 MAP

49°25'09"

QUALICUM
INDIAN RESERVE
LEON RD

19   ISLAND HWY

19A

Qualicum Beach

19

60

RUPERT RD E

Qualicum Beach
Municipal Airport

ISLAND HWY W

Parksville

INLAND ISLAND HWY

49°18'13"

4   ALBERNI HWY

4A

19

19A

ISLAND HWY E

Coombs

4

51   46

Errington

19

Nanoose
Bay   ISLAND HWY

NANOOSE
BAY INDIAN
RESERVE

Lantzville

19

HAMMOND

Vancouver
Island
Military
Mus.

BAY RD

Nanaimo

NANAIMO

19A

19

JINGLE POT RD

H

3RD ST

STEWART AVE

ISLAND HWY N

Serauxmen Stadium

NANAIMO TOWN
INDIAN
RESERVE 1

10TH

49°11'18"

NANAIMO LAKES RD

S NANAIMO LAKES RD

NANAIMO RIVER INDIAN
RESERVE

Cedar

S FORKS RD

CEDAR RD

YELLOW POINT RD

49°04'22"

1

Cassidy

Nanaimo
Airport

VANCOUVER
ISLAND

OYSTER
BAY INDIAN
RESERVE
12

TRANS CANADA HWY

CHEMAINUS
INDIAN
RESERVE 13

Ladysmith   1

SEE 4 MAP

1A

Chemainus

1

48°57'26"

COWICHAN LAKE

Youbou

COWICHAN VALLEY

48°50'30"

COWICHAN LAKE
INDIAN
RESERVE

N SHORE RD

18

North
Cowichan

Honeymoon
Bay

S SHORE RD

Lake
Cowichan

CYPRESS ST

Mesachie
Lake

18

18

SHERMAN RD

COWICHAN
INDIAN
RESERVE 1

Duncan

48°43'33"

Duncan
Butler
Arpt

RAND MCNALLY

CAPITAL

48°36'37"

A   B   C   D   E

STRAIT OF GEORGIA

BELLINGHAM-KETCHIKAN FY BELLINGHAM-PRINCE RUPERT FY

BELLINGHAM-KETCHIKAN FY

49°26'46"

49°19'50"

TSAWWASSEN-DUKE POINT FY

Gabriola

GABRIOLA
ISLAND

49°12'54"

49°05'58"

48°59'02"

48°52'05"

48°45'09"

48°38'13"

124°34'36"   124°24'08"   124°13'41"   124°03'13"   123°52'45"   123°42'17"

SEE 13 MAP

MAP 4

1:380,160
1 in. = 6 mi.
0   4   8
miles

N

MAP 4

SEE 2 MAP

49°26'46"
49°27'59"

SECHELT INDIAN GOVERNMENT DISTRICT
SUNSHINE COAST
Sunshine Coast Hwy
101
Roberts Creek
Granthams Landing
Gibsons
CHEKWELP INDIAN RESERVE 26
KEATS ISLAND
GOWER POINT
PRATT RD
STEWART RD
Bowen Island
Bowen Island Historians Museum
BOWEN ISLAND
HOWE SOUND
GAMBIER ISLAND
Langdale
HORSESHOE BAY-LANGDALE FY
Horseshoe Bay
Lions Bay
99
SEA TO SKY HWY
CYPRESS PROVINCIAL PARK
CHARLES CREEK
GREATER VANCOUVER
CAPILANO LAKE
KENNEDY CREEK
MT SEYMOUR PROVINCIAL PARK
North Vancouver District
Mt Seymour
BUNTZEN LAKE

1

49°19'50"
49°21'03"

HORSESHOE BAY-DEPARTURE BAY FY
Ski Cypress Bowl Area
West Vancouver
MARINE DR
PARK ROYAL SOUTH
LYNN VALLEY CENTRE
DEMPSEY RD
Capilano College
BURRARD INLET INDIAN RESERVE
BEDWELL BAY
Belcarra
Port Moody
loco
BARNET RD
7A

BURRARD INLET
107
108
North Vancouver
1A 99
23
22
25
BARNET HWY
SIMON FRASER UNIV
Burnaby
LOUGHED TOWN CENTRE
Coquitlam

2

49°12'54"
49°14'07"

NW MARINE DR
Museum of Anthropology
UBC-MY Williams Geological Museum
UNIVERSITY OF BRITISH COLUMBIA
Vancouver Museum
BC Golf Museum & Library
109
110
99
Pacific Coliseum
Labour Heritage Centre Project
29
32
Burnaby Lake Nature House
Swangard Stad
H
37
Queens Park
40
116 AV
116A AV

MUSQUEAM INDIAN RESERVE 2
Vancouver
NAT BAILEY STADIUM
99A
METROPOLIS AT METROTOWN
IMPERIAL ST
Japanese Canadian National Mus
MARINE DR
New Westminster
91A
Bug Lab Invertebrate Zoo
104 AV
90 AV
NORDEL WY

3

49°05'58"
49°07'11"

NANAIMO
GABRIOLA ISLAND
STRAIT OF GEORGIA
TSAWWASSEN-DUKE POINT FY
BELLINGHAM-KETCHIKAN FY BELLINGHAM-PRINCE RUPERT FY
Vancouver International Airport
River Rock Casino Resort
KWANTLEN UNIVERSITY COL-RICHMOND
38
91
36
RICHMOND CENTRE
BLUNDELL RD
FRANCIS RD
STEVESTON HWY
99
LULU ISLAND
RIVER RD
DERWENT WY
11
SCOTT RD
96 AV
80 AV
Gulf of Georgia Cannery National Site
32
29
28
Delta
72 AV
64 AV
58 AV
MUD BAY
3

MONCTON
Steveston Post Office Museum
Richmond
Delta Museum & Archives
Ladner
10
99
LADNER TRUNK RD
20
10
16
99
124 ST
96A AV

4

49°00'14"
48°59'02"

COWICHAN VALLEY
THETIS ISLAND
Thetis Island
GALIANO ISLAND INDIAN RESERVE 9
KUPER ISLAND
KUPER ISLAND INDIAN RESERVE 7
MUSQUEAM INDIAN RESERVE 4
WESTHAM ISLAND
TSAWWASSEN INDIAN RESERVE
Tsawwassen
17
DELTAPORT WY
28 AV
17
12 AV
BOUNDARY BAY AIRPORT
BOUNDARY BAY
Maple Beach
TSAWWASSEN TOWN CENTRE MALL
Delta Air Park
Surrey
124 ST
24 AV
16 AV
MARINE DR

Point Roberts
South Beach
JOHNSON RD
APA RD
TYEE RD
WHATCOM

5

48°52'05"
48°53'18"

CHEMAINUS-THETIS ISLAND FY
CAPITAL
Chemainus Valley Museum
SQUAW-HAY-ONE INDIAN RESERVE 11
TSUSSIE INDIAN RESERVE 6
HALALT INDIAN RESERVE 2
Westholme
GALIANO ISLAND
Galiano
MAYNE ISLAND INDIAN RESERVE 6
Mayne
BELLINGHAM-PRINCE RUPERT FY BELLINGHAM-KETCHIKAN FY
WASHINGTON
BRITISH COLUMBIA

MAP 3
SEE 3
MAP 5
SEE 5

6

48°45'09"
48°46'21"

Crofton
1A
HERD RD
MAPLE BAY RD
LAKES RD
PENDER ISLAND-LONG HARBOUR FY
Saltspring Island
SALTSPRING ISLAND
Mayne
MAYNE ISLAND
Pender Island
NORTH PENDER ISLAND
SATURNA ISLAND-LONG HARBOUR FY
Saturna
SATURNA ISLAND
SUCIA ISLAND STATE PARK
ECHO BAY

Duncan
Koksilah
COWICHAN INDIAN RESERVE 1
THEIK INDIAN RESERVE 2
KIL-PAH-LAS INDIAN RESERVE 3
Cowichan Bay
SALTSPRING ISLAND
SWARTZ BAY-LONG HARBOUR FY SALTSPRING ISLAND-PENDER ISLAND FY
SOUTH PENDER ISLAND
CANADA
UNITED STATES
Waldronaire Airport
North Beach
Orcas Island Airport
Terrill Beach
Buckhorn
Eastsound

7

48°38'13"
48°39'25"

RAND McNALLY
Duncan Butler Arpt
1
VANCOUVER ISLAND
Cobble Hill
Shawnigan Lake
MILL BAY RD
TRANS CANADA HWY
MILL BAY
SAANICH INLET
LANDS END
North Saanich
17A
UNION BAY INDIAN RESERVE 4
Sidney
17
Sidney Museum
Victoria Int'l Arpt
HARO STRAIT
SWARTZ BAY-SATURNA ISLAND FY
BOUNDARY PASS
Waldron
WALDRON ISLAND
JOHN PASS
REID HARBOR
PRESIDENT CHANNEL
ORCAS ISLAND
EAST SOUND
Orcas Island Historical Mus
SAN JUAN
MORAN STATE PARK

SEE 14 MAP

123°42'16"   123°31'47"   123°21'19"   123°10'51"   123°00'22"   122°49'53"

A   B   C   D   E

MAP
5

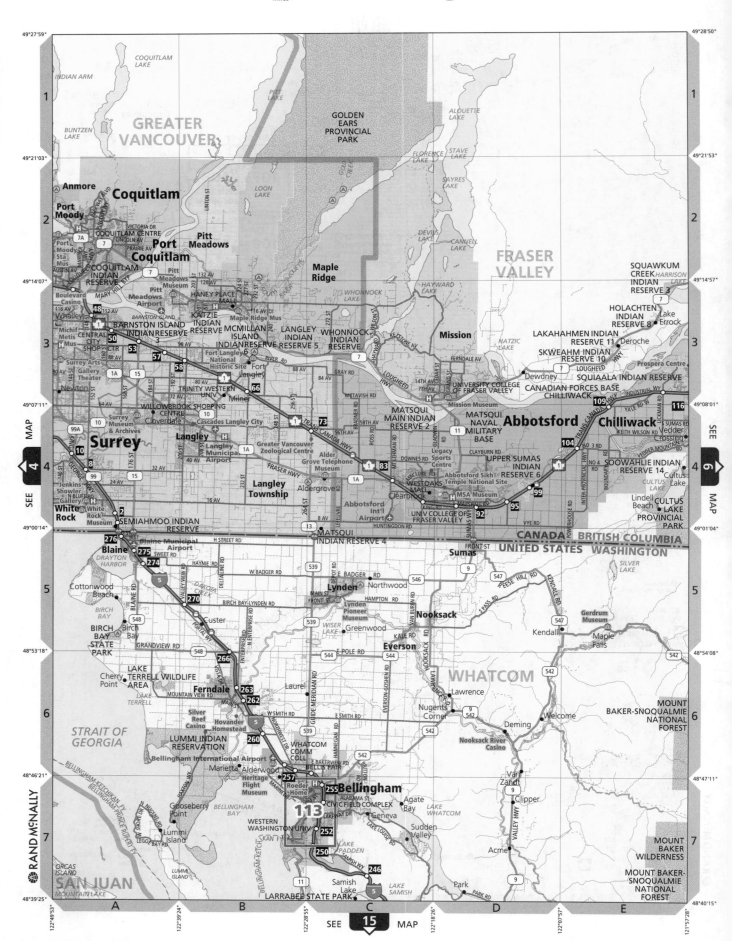

MAP
5

1:380,160
1 in. = 6 mi.

0   4   8
miles

MAP
6

MAP
6

1:380,160
1 in. = 6 mi.
0   4   8
miles

N

MAP 6

49°28'50"

STULLAWHEETS INDIAN RESERVE 8

PUCKATHOLETCHIN INDIAN RESERVE 11

SWAHLISEAH INDIAN RESERVE 14

195

192

5

TRANS CANADA HWY

COQUIHALLA HWY

183

SCHKAM INDIAN RESERVE 2

AYWAWWIS INDIAN RESERVE 15

Hope

CHAWATHIL INDIAN RESERVE

SKAWAHLOOK INDIAN RESERVE 1

7

170

173

5

Hemlock Valley Resort

RUBY CREEK INDIAN RESERVE 2

LUKSEETSISSUM INDIAN RESERVE 9

165

168

Hope Museum

3

1

49°21'53"

49°22'20"

HARRISON LAKE

OHAMIL INDIAN RESERVE 1

160

1

3

Harrison Hot Springs

7

PETERS INDIAN RESERVE 1

153

CHEHALIS INDIAN RESERVE 5

PINE AV

9

SEABIRD ISLAND INDIAN RESERVE

151

3

HOPE-PRINCETON HWY

1

Kent

Agassiz-Harrison Museum

7

146

FRASER VALLEY

3

49°14'57"

49°15'24"

Harrison Mills

HAIG HWY

MANNING PROVINCIAL PARK

SCOWLITZ INDIAN RESERVE 1

7

Agassiz

TSEATAH INDIAN RESERVE 2

SKWALI INDIAN RESERVE 3

Pickwick's Pie Shop-British Mus

CHEAM INDIAN RESERVE 1

POPKUM INDIAN RESERVE 1

ALE RD E

SCHELOWAT INDIAN RESERVE 1

Rosedale

138

Chilliwack Mun Arpt

135

PRAIRIE CENTRAL RD

ANNIS RD

1

129

1

49°08'01"

49°08'28"

123

Artisan Gallery

YAKWEAKWIOOSE INDIAN RESERVE 12

Sardis

SKAGIT VALLEY PROVINCIAL PARK

TZEACHTEN INDIAN RESERVE 13

Chilliwack

CANADIAN FORCES BASE CHILLIWACK

SOOWAHLIE INDIAN RESERVE 14

CHILLIWACK LAKE

CULTUS LAKE PROVINCIAL PARK

49°01'04"

49°01'31"

CANADA
UNITED STATES

BRITISH COLUMBIA
WASHINGTON

ROSS LAKE NATIONAL RECREATION AREA

ROSS LAKE

MOUNT BAKER-SNOQUALMIE NATIONAL FOREST

542

48°54'08"

48°54'35"

Glacier

542

Mount Baker Ski Resort

NORTH CASCADES NATIONAL PARK

WHATCOM

MOUNT BAKER WILDERNESS

ROSS LAKE NATIONAL RECREATION AREA

48°47'11"

48°47'38"

MOUNT BAKER-SNOQUALMIE NATIONAL FOREST

BAKER LAKE

ROSS LAKE NATIONAL RECREATION AREA

Diablo

DIABLO LAKE

NOISY-DIOBSUD WILDERNESS

GORGE LAKE

SKAGIT RIVER

20

48°40'15"

48°40'41"

A   B   C   D   E

121°57'27"   121°46'58"   121°36'29"   121°26'00"   121°15'31"   121°05'02"

SEE **16** MAP

MAP SEE 5

SEE 7 MAP

RAND McNALLY

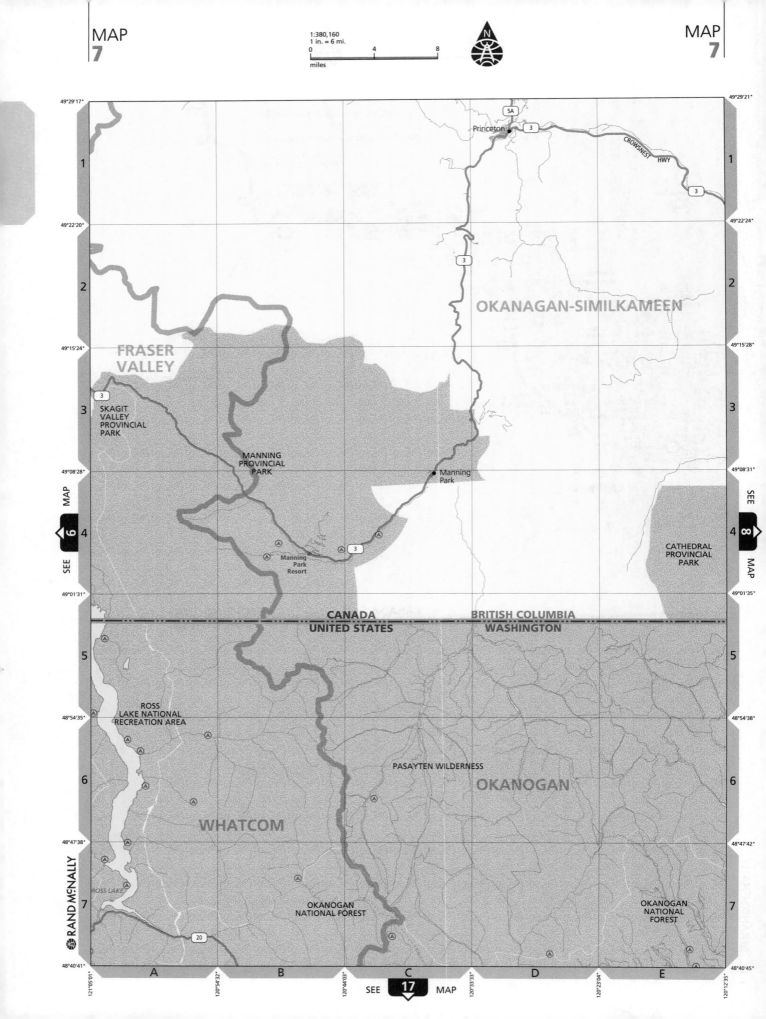

MAP
7

MAP
7

1:380,160
1 in. = 6 mi.
0   4   8
miles

N

49°29'17"
49°22'20"
49°15'24"
49°08'28"
49°01'31"
48°54'35"
48°47'38"
48°40'41"

49°29'21"
49°22'24"
49°15'28"
49°08'31"
49°01'35"
48°54'38"
48°47'42"
48°40'45"

1
2
3
4
5
6
7

5A
Princeton
3
CROWSNEST HWY
3

3

3

OKANAGAN-SIMILKAMEEN

FRASER
VALLEY

3
SKAGIT
VALLEY
PROVINCIAL
PARK

MANNING
PROVINCIAL
PARK

Manning
Park

3

Manning
Park
Resort

CATHEDRAL
PROVINCIAL
PARK

CANADA
UNITED STATES

BRITISH COLUMBIA
WASHINGTON

ROSS
LAKE NATIONAL
RECREATION AREA

PASAYTEN WILDERNESS

OKANOGAN

WHATCOM

ROSS LAKE

OKANOGAN
NATIONAL FOREST

OKANOGAN
NATIONAL
FOREST

20

RAND MCNALLY

121°05'01"
120°54'32"
120°44'03"
120°33'33"
120°23'04"
120°12'35"

MAP
8
MAP
8

1:380,160
1 in. = 6 mi.

0   4   8
miles

N

49°29'21"
49°29'01"

SEE 7 MAP
SEE 9 MAP
SEE 18 MAP

Leir House Cultural Center
Penticton Regional Airport
CHERRY LANE SHOPPING CENTRE
PENTICTON INDIAN RESERVE 1
Penticton
97
SKAHA LAKE

Apex Mountain Resort

49°22'24"
49°22'05"

CHUCHUWAYHA INDIAN RESERVE 2
3
Hedley

Kaleden
3A
Okanagan Falls
MAIN ST

2

49°15'28"
49°15'09"

ASHNOLA INDIAN RESERVE 10
3

OKANAGAN-SIMILKAMEEN

3A
3A

ALEXIS INDIAN RESERVE 9
KEREMEOS BYP
BLIND CREEK INDIAN RESERVE 6
Keremeos
3
Cawston
Oliver
97
OSOYOOS INDIAN RESERVE 1
Mt Baldy Ski Area

3

49°08'31"
49°08'12"

LOWER SIMILKAMEEN INDIAN RESERVE 2

CATHEDRAL PROVINCIAL PARK

CROWSNEST HWY
97
97

OSOYOOS LAKE

3

49°01'35"
49°01'16"

CHOPAKA INDIAN RESERVE 7 & 8
Osoyoos
MAIN ST
97 TH ST
3
CROWSNEST HWY

BRITISH COLUMBIA   CANADA
WASHINGTON   UNITED STATES

97
Dorothy Scott Airport
CHESAW RD

Nighthawk

Molson School Museum
Oroville
CENTRAL AV

PASAYTEN WILDERNESS

PALMER LAKE
WANNACUT LAKE

OKANOGAN NATIONAL FOREST

48°54'38"
48°54'19"

5

OKANOGAN

6

97

Loomis
SPECTACLE LAKE

48°47'42"
48°47'23"

OKANOGAN NATIONAL FOREST

Ellisforde

TONASKET-HAVILLAH RD

7

4TH ST
6TH ST
Tonasket
97
20

48°40'45"
48°40'26"

A   B   C   D   E

120°12'34"
120°02'05"
119°51'36"
119°41'06"
119°30'38"
119°20'08"

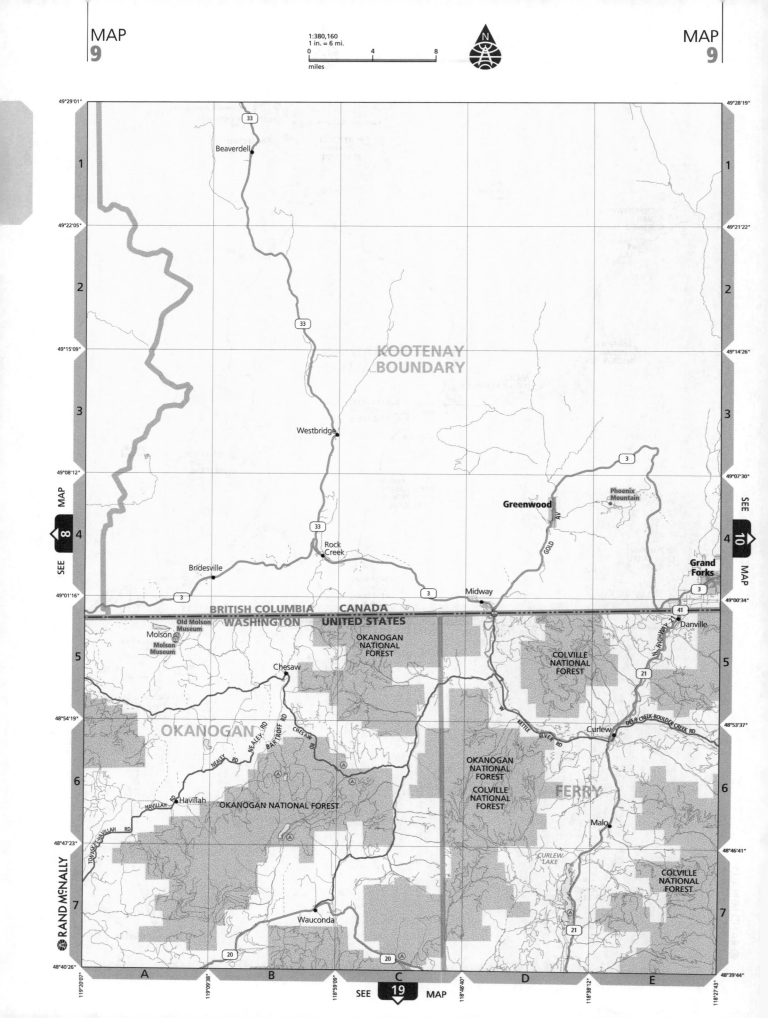

MAP
9

MAP
9

1:380,160
1 in. = 6 mi.

0   4   8
miles

N

SEE MAP 8
SEE MAP 10
SEE 19 MAP

KOOTENAY
BOUNDARY

Beaverdell

Westbridge

Greenwood

Phoenix
Mountain

GOLD AV

Grand
Forks

Rock
Creek

Bridesville

Midway

Danville

BRITISH COLUMBIA   CANADA
WASHINGTON   UNITED STATES

Old Molson
Museum
Molson
Molson
Museum

OKANOGAN
NATIONAL
FOREST

COLVILLE
NATIONAL
FOREST

N. HIGHWAY

Chesaw

NEALEY RD

BARTROFF RD

CHESAW RD

NEALEY RD

KETTLE RIVER RD

Curlew

DEER CREEK-BOULDER CREEK RD

OKANOGAN

OKANOGAN
NATIONAL
FOREST

COLVILLE
NATIONAL
FOREST

FERRY

Havillah

HAVILLAH RD

OKANOGAN NATIONAL FOREST

TOROD-CHAVILLAH RD

Malo

CURLEW
LAKE

COLVILLE
NATIONAL
FOREST

Wauconda

20

20

21

21

RAND MCNALLY

49°29'01"
49°22'05"
49°15'09"
49°08'12"
49°01'16"
48°54'19"
48°47'23"
48°40'26"

49°28'19"
49°21'22"
49°14'26"
49°07'30"
49°00'34"
48°53'37"
48°46'41"
48°39'44"

119°20'07"
119°09'38"
118°59'09"
118°48'40"
118°38'12"
118°27'43"

A   B   C   D   E

33

41

MAP
10

MAP
10

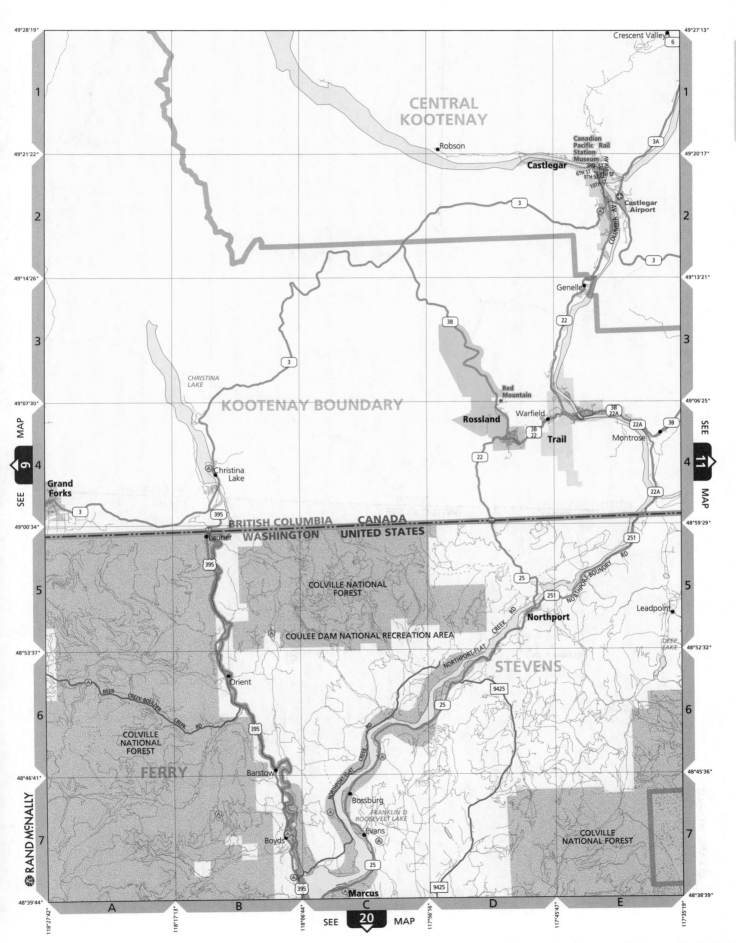

N

CENTRAL
KOOTENAY

Robson

Canadian
Pacific Rail
Station
Museum
3RD ST
6TH ST
9TH 8TH ST
10TH ST

Castlegar

Castlegar
Airport

3A

3

3

Genelle

22

KOOTENAY BOUNDARY

CHRISTINA
LAKE

3B

Red
Mountain

Warfield

3B
22A

Rossland

3B
22

Trail

22A

3B

Montrose

22

22A

SEE
9
MAP

SEE
11
MAP

Grand
Forks

Christina
Lake

251

3

BRITISH COLUMBIA   CANADA
WASHINGTON   UNITED STATES

Laurier

251

RD

395

25

NORTHPORT-BOUNDRY

COLVILLE NATIONAL
FOREST

251

Leadpoint

COULEE DAM NATIONAL RECREATION AREA

CREEK RD

Northport

DEEP
LAKE

STEVENS

NORTHPORT-FLAT

Orient

9425

DEER CREEK-BOULDER

CREEK RD

25

COLVILLE
NATIONAL
FOREST

395

CREEK RD

FERRY

Barstow

NORTHPORT-FLAT

Bossburg

FRANKLIN D
ROOSEVELT LAKE

COLVILLE
NATIONAL FOREST

Boyds

Evans

395

25

9425

Marcus

SEE
20
MAP

RAND MCNALLY

A   B   C   D   E

MAP
11

1:380,160
1 in. = 6 mi.

0   4   8

miles

MAP
11

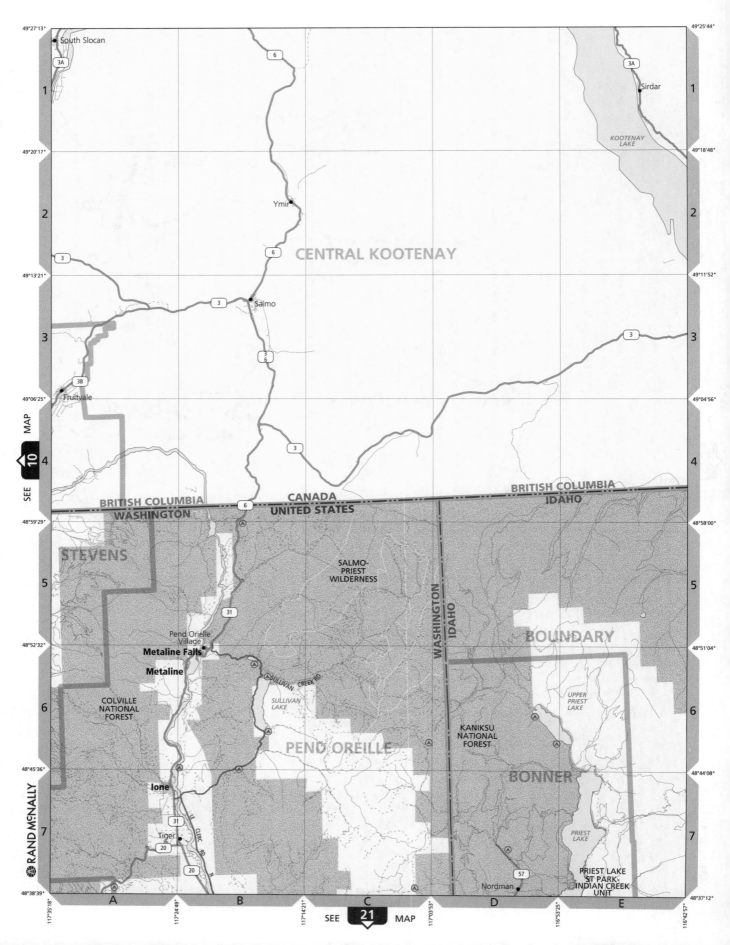

South Slocan

3A

Sirdar

3A

KOOTENAY
LAKE

Ymir

CENTRAL KOOTENAY

3

3

Salmo

3
6

3B

Fruitvale

3

3

SEE MAP 10

CANADA
BRITISH COLUMBIA
BRITISH COLUMBIA
WASHINGTON
IDAHO
UNITED STATES

STEVENS

SALMO-
PRIEST
WILDERNESS

BOUNDARY

31

WASHINGTON   IDAHO

Pend Orielle
Village

UPPER
PRIEST
LAKE

Metaline Falls

Metaline

SULLIVAN CREEK RD

COLVILLE
NATIONAL
FOREST

SULLIVAN
LAKE

KANIKSU
NATIONAL
FOREST

PEND OREILLE

BONNER

Ione

PRIEST
LAKE

31

31

LE CLERC RD

Tiger

20

20

57

Nordman

PRIEST LAKE
ST PARK-
INDIAN CREEK
UNIT

RAND MCNALLY

A   B   C   D   E

SEE 21 MAP

MAP
12

1:380,160
1 in. = 6 mi.

0   4   8
miles

MAP
12

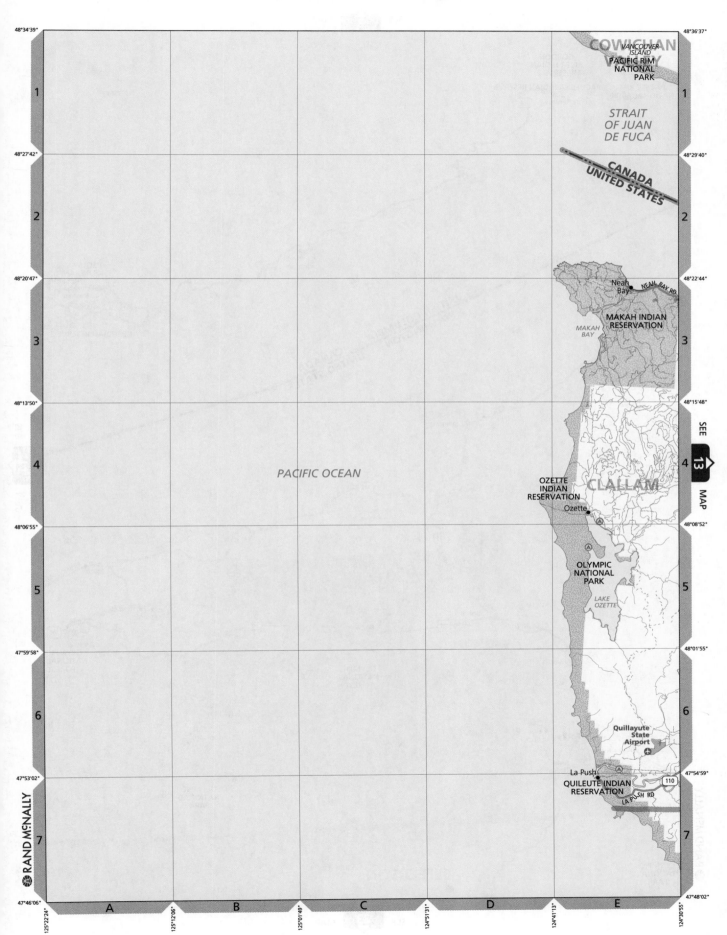

COWICHAN VALLEY

VANCOUVER ISLAND

PACIFIC RIM NATIONAL PARK

STRAIT OF JUAN DE FUCA

CANADA
UNITED STATES

Neah Bay

NEAH BAY RD.

MAKAH INDIAN RESERVATION

MAKAH BAY

SEE 13 MAP

CLALLAM

OZETTE INDIAN RESERVATION

Ozette

OLYMPIC NATIONAL PARK

LAKE OZETTE

PACIFIC OCEAN

Quillayute State Airport

La Push

QUILEUTE INDIAN RESERVATION

LA PUSH RD.

110

48°34'39"
48°27'42"
48°20'47"
48°13'50"
48°06'55"
47°59'58"
47°53'02"
47°46'06"

48°36'37"
48°29'40"
48°22'44"
48°15'48"
48°08'52"
48°01'55"
47°54'59"
47°48'02"

1
2
3
4
5
6
7

A   B   C   D   E

125°22'24"
125°12'06"
125°01'49"
124°51'31"
124°41'13"
124°30'55"

RAND MCNALLY

MAP
13

MAP
13

1:380,160
1 in. = 6 mi.

0   4   8
miles

N

SEE 3 MAP

GORDON
RIVER INDIAN
RESERVE 2
PACHEENA INDIAN RESERVE 1

PACIFIC RIM
NATIONAL PARK

Port Renfrew 14

1

VANCOUVER
ISLAND

CAPITAL

2

STRAIT
OF JUAN
DE FUCA

River
Jordan

T'SOU-
KE INDIAN
RESERVE
1

MAKAH INDIAN
RESERVATION

112

BRITISH COLUMBIA CANADA
WASHINGTON UNITED STATES

Sooke Region
Museum

Sooke

W COAST RD

14

OTTER POINT RD

T'SOU-
KE INDIAN RESERVE 2

3

Sekiu
Airport

Sekiu CLALLAM BAY

Clallam
Bay

112 112

113

CRESCENT
BAY

112 Joyce PIEDMONT RD

4

DICKEY
LAKE

CLALLAM

OLYMPIC
NATIONAL
FOREST

Lake
Crescent

E BEACH RD

Maple
Grove 101

LAKE
SUTHERLAND

OLYMPIC
NATIONAL
FOREST

5

LAKE
PLEASANT

BURNT MOUNTAIN RD

Sappho

Beaver 101

LAKE CRESCENT

OLYMPIC HWY

Shuwah

101

110

Care
Free
Loop

Forks
Forks Airport

Valley
View

LA PUSH RD

101

Forks
Timber
Museum

East
Hoquiam

OLYMPIC
NATIONAL
PARK

6

OLYMPIC
NATIONAL
PARK

101

JEFFERSON

7

SEE 23 MAP

SEE 12 MAP
SEE 14 MAP

RAND M?NALLY

A B C D E

MAP
14

MAP
14

1:380,160
1 in. = 6 mi.

0   4   8
miles

N

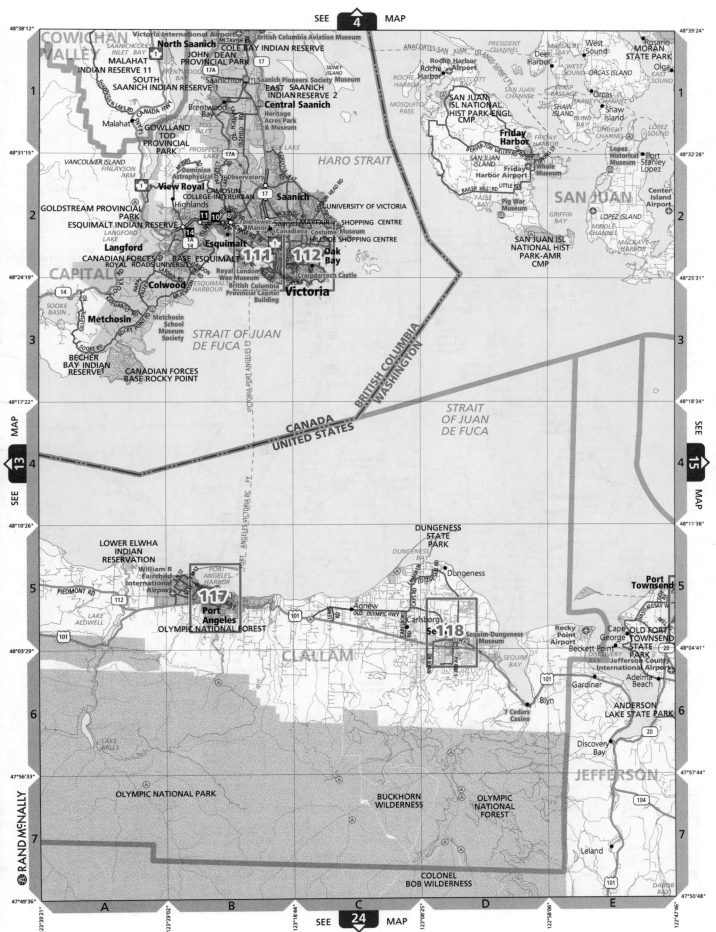

SEE 4 MAP

48°38'12"

COWICHAN
VALLEY

Victoria International Airport
North Saanich
MALAHAT
INDIAN RESERVE 11
SOUTH
SAANICH INDIAN RESERVE 1
Malahat
GOWLLAND
TOD
PROVINCIAL
PARK
VANCOUVER ISLAND
FINLAYSON
ARM

JOHN DEAN
PROVINCIAL PARK
Saanichton
Brentwood
Bay
TOD
INLET
PROSPECT
LAKE

COLE BAY INDIAN RESERVE
British Columbia Aviation Museum

SIDNEY

Saanich Pioneers Society Museum
EAST SAANICH
INDIAN RESERVE 2
Central Saanich

Heritage
Acres Park
& Museum
ELK LAKE

HARO STRAIT

ANACORTES-SAN JUAN ISLANDS-SIDNEY FY

Roche Harbor
Airport
Roche
Harbor
WESTCOTT
SAN JUAN
ISL NATIONAL
HIST PARK-ENGL
CMP

PRESIDENT
CHANNEL
West
Sound

Deer
Harbor
MASSACRE
BAY
WEST
SOUND
ORCAS ISLAND
Orcas
HARNEY CHANNEL
SHAW
ISLAND

MORAN
STATE PARK
Olga
EAST
SOUND

Rosario

Shaw
Island

48°39'24"

1

48°31'15"

View Royal
Dominion
Astrophysical
Observatory
CAMOSUN
COLLEGE-INTERURBAN
Highlands

Saanich

UNIVERSITY OF VICTORIA

Friday
Harbor
SAN JUAN
ISLAND
Friday
Harbor Airport
BAILER HILL RD
False
Bay
Pig War
Museum

FRIDAY
HARBOR
Whale
Museum
LITTLE RD

LOPEZ
SOUND

Lopez
Historical
Museum

Port
Stanley
Lopez

SAN JUAN

Center
Island
Airport

48°32'28"

48°24'19"

GOLDSTREAM PROVINCIAL
PARK
ESQUIMALT INDIAN RESERVE
LANGFORD
LAKE
Langford
CANADIAN FORCES
ROYAL ROADS UNIVERSITY
Colwood

CAPITAL

11 10 8
Craigflower
Manor
Esquimalt
BASE ESQUIMALT
ESQUIMALT
HARBOUR
14
1A
14

Canadiana Costume Museum
HILLSIDE SHOPPING CENTRE
111
112
Royal London
Wax Museum
British Columbia
Provincial Capitol
Building

MAYFAIR SHOPPING CENTRE

Oak
Bay
Craigdarroch Castle
Victoria

SAN JUAN ISL
NATIONAL HIST
PARK-AMR
CMP

GRIFFIN
BAY
MIDDLE
CHANNEL

LOPEZ ISLAND
MACKAYE
HARBOR

48°25'31"

2

Metchosin
Metchosin
School
Museum
Society

STRAIT OF JUAN
DE FUCA

48°17'22"

BECHER
BAY INDIAN
RESERVE1
CANADIAN FORCES
BASE ROCKY POINT

SOOKE
BASIN

CANADA
UNITED STATES

BRITISH COLUMBIA
WASHINGTON

STRAIT
OF JUAN
DE FUCA

48°18'34"

SEE 13 MAP

4

SEE 15 MAP

48°10'26"

LOWER ELWHA
INDIAN
RESERVATION
William R
Fairchild
International
Airport
PIEDMONT RD
112
LAKE
ALDWELL
101
OLYMPIC NATIONAL FOREST

DUNGENESS
STATE PARK
DUNGENESS
BAY
Dungeness

Agnew
OLD OLYMPIC HWY
101
Carlsborg
Se 118
CLALLAM

Rocky
Point
Airport
Sequim-Dungeness
Museum
SEQUIM
BAY

Port
Townsend

OLD FORT
TOWNSEND
STATE
PARK
20

48°11'38"

Port
Angeles
117

48°03'29"

Blyn

7 Cedars
Casino

Cape
George
Beckett Point
DISCOVERY
BAY
101
Gardiner

Jefferson County
International Airport
Adelma
Beach

ANDERSON
LAKE STATE PARK

20

48°04'41"

6

LAKE
MILLS

OLYMPIC NATIONAL PARK

BUCKHORN
WILDERNESS

OLYMPIC
NATIONAL
FOREST

JEFFERSON

Discovery
Bay

47°57'44"

47°56'33"

COLONEL
BOB WILDERNESS

Leland

104

101
DABOB
BAY

47°50'48"

47°49'36"

A   B   C   D   E

SEE 24 MAP

123°39'21"   123°29'02"   123°18'44"   123°08'25"   122°58'06"   122°47'46"

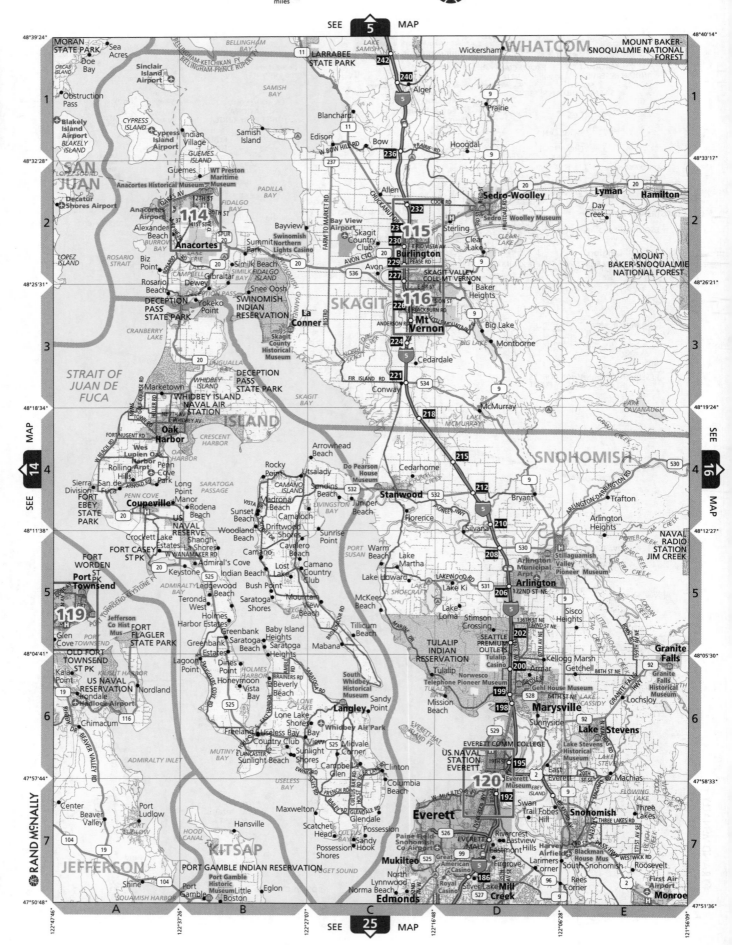

MAP
15

1:380,160
1 in. = 6 mi.
0   4   8
miles

MAP
15

SEE MAP 5

MAP
16

1:380,160
1 in. = 6 mi.

0   4   8
miles

N

MAP
16

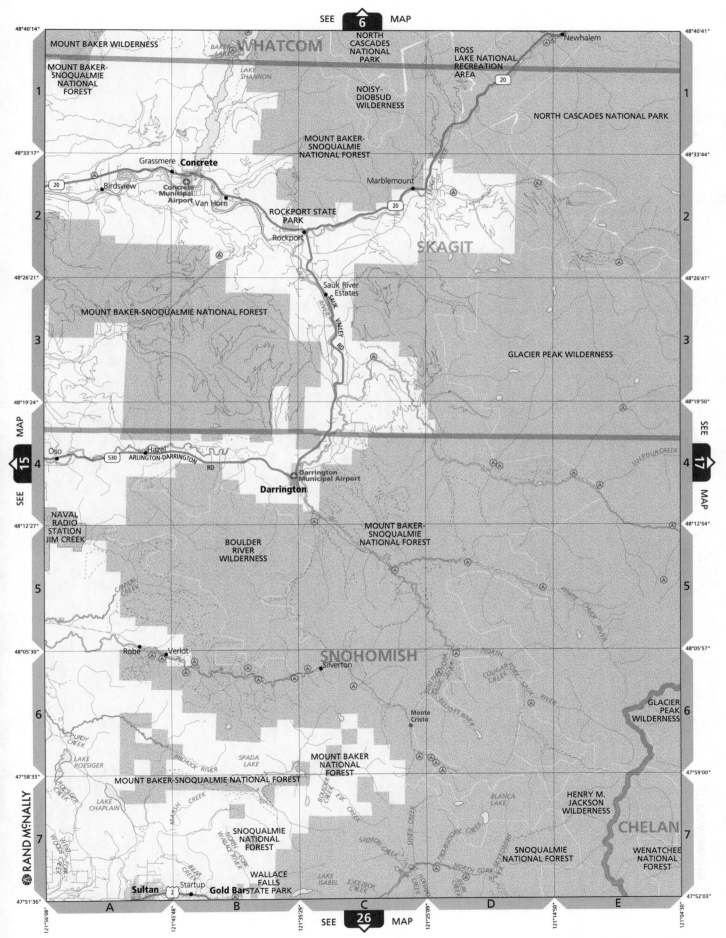

SEE **6** MAP

MOUNT BAKER WILDERNESS

WHATCOM

NORTH CASCADES NATIONAL PARK

ROSS LAKE NATIONAL RECREATION AREA

Newhalem

20

1

MOUNT BAKER-SNOQUALMIE NATIONAL FOREST

LAKE SHANNON

NOISY-DIOBSUD WILDERNESS

NORTH CASCADES NATIONAL PARK

MOUNT BAKER-SNOQUALMIE NATIONAL FOREST

Grassmere   Concrete

20   Birdsview

Concrete Municipal Airport

Van Horn

Marblemount

20

SKAGIT

2

ROCKPORT STATE PARK

Rockport

Sauk River Estates

SAUK RIVER

SAUK VALLEY RD

MOUNT BAKER-SNOQUALMIE NATIONAL FOREST

3

GLACIER PEAK WILDERNESS

SEE **15** MAP   SEE **17** MAP

Oso   Hazel

530   ARLINGTON-DARRINGTON RD

Darrington Municipal Airport

Darrington

SULPHUR CREEK

4

NAVAL RADIO STATION JIM CREEK

BOULDER RIVER WILDERNESS

MOUNT BAKER-SNOQUALMIE NATIONAL FOREST

5

CANYON CREEK

WHITE CHUCK RIVER

Robe   Verlot

SNOHOMISH

Silverton

SOUTH FORK SAUK RIVER

NORTH FORK SAUK RIVER

COUGAR CREEK

6

Monte Cristo

ELLIOTT RIVER

GLACIER PEAK WILDERNESS

PURDY CREEK

LAKE ROESIGER

PILCHUCK RIVER

SPADA LAKE

MOUNT BAKER NATIONAL FOREST

BOULDER CREEK   ELK CREEK

BLANCA LAKE

HENRY M. JACKSON WILDERNESS

CHELAN

7

MOUNT BAKER-SNOQUALMIE NATIONAL FOREST

LAKE CHAPLAIN

MARCH CREEK

SNOQUALMIE NATIONAL FOREST

NORTH FORK WALLACE RIVER

WALLACE FALLS STATE PARK

LAKE ISABEL

EXCELSIOR CREEK

SALMON CREEK

SILVER CREEK

TROUBLESOME CREEK

HOWARD CREEK

NORTH FORK SKYKOMISH RIVER

BEAR CREEK

SNOQUALMIE NATIONAL FOREST

WENATCHEE NATIONAL FOREST

Sultan   Startup

2

Gold Bar

WEST FORK WOODS CREEK

ROSS FORK CREEK

RAND McNALLY

SEE **26** MAP

MAP
17

1:380,160
1 in. = 6 mi.

0   4   8
miles

N

MAP
17

SEE 7 MAP

48°40'41"
DIABLO LAKE ROSS LAKE NATIONAL RECREATION AREA
WHATCOM
48°40'44"

SKAGIT

PASAYTEN WILDERNESS

20

Lost River Resort Airport

1

OKANOGAN NATIONAL FOREST

20

Mazama

1

48°33'44"
48°33'48"

20

NORTH CASCADES NATIONAL PARK

2

LAKE CHELAN-SAWTOOTH WILDERNESS

OKANOGAN

2

48°26'47"
48°26'51"

3

LAKE CHELAN NATIONAL RECREATION AREA

3

Stehekin State Airport

48°19'50"
48°19'54"

Stehekin

MAP
16

SEE

SULPHUR CREEK

GLACIER PEAK WILDERNESS

4

SEE
18
MAP

4

48°12'54"
48°12'57"

Holden Village

Lucerne

SNOHOMISH

DOMKE LAKE

5

CHELAN

5

SUIATTLE RIVER

48°05'57"
48°06'00"

6

LAKE CHELAN

6

WENATCHEE NATIONAL FOREST

TWENTY FIVE MILE CREEK STATE PARK

47°59'00"
47°59'03"

HENRY M. JACKSON WILDERNESS

7

TWIN LAKES

LAKE CHELAN

7

RAND McNALLY

Brief

47°52'03"
47°52'07"

A   B   C   D   E

SEE 27 MAP

121°04'29"   120°54'09"   120°43'50"   120°33'30"   120°23'11"   120°12'51"

MAP
18

MAP
18

1:380,160
1 in. = 6 mi.

0   4   8
miles

N

SEE **8** MAP

48°40'44"

48°40'25"

1

20

97

48°33'48"

Conconully

CONCONULLY
LAKE

CONCONULLY
RESERVOIR

48°33'29"

OKANOGAN
NATIONAL
FOREST

2

Riverside

97

48°26'51"

PEARRYGIN
LAKE

PEARRYGIN
LAKE
STATE PARK

CHEWUCK RIVER

METHOW RIVER

Winthrop

20

Omak

OMAK AVE
4TH AV

Okanogan
County
Historical
Museum

97

48°26'32"

3

OKANOGAN

20

2ND AV N

St.
Mary's
Mission

155

Twisp

Twisp
Municipal
Airport

20

Methow Valley
State Airport

Okanogan

48°19'54"

20

48°19'35"

153

4

SEE **17** MAP

SEE **19** MAP

Carlton

Malott

OMAK
LAKE

97

COLVILLE
INDIAN
RESERVATION

48°12'57"

48°12'38"

5

Monse

Methow

OKANOGAN
NATIONAL
FOREST

153

RUFUS
WOODS
LAKE

48°06'00"

Brewster

97

LAKE
PATEROS

48°05'42"

97

173

CHIEF JOSEPH
STATE PARK

Pateros

6

ALTA
LAKE

ALTA
LAKE
STATE
PARK

Downing

17

BRIDGEPORT
STATE
PARK

173

Bridgeport

BRIDGEPORT HILL RD NE

WENATCHEE
NATIONAL
FOREST

47°59'03"

DOUGLAS

47°58'45"

LAKE
CHELAN

LAKE
ENTIAT

17

7

RAND M°NALLY

CHELAN

Greens
Landing

Azwell

ROAD B NE

174

Shrine
Beach

97

17

ROAD R NE

Manson

Echo Valley
Ski Resort

Mill Bay
Casino

WAPATO WY

971

150

47°52'07"

A   **B**   **C**   **D**   **E**

47°51'48"

120°12'50"

120°02'30"

119°52'11"

119°41'51"

119°31'31"

119°21'12"

SEE **28** MAP

MAP
19

1:380,160
1 in. = 6 mi.

0   4   8
miles

N

MAP
19

SEE 9 MAP

48°40'25"

20

20

CLARK AV'S

Republic

48°39'43"

21

20

1

Hart Ranch
Airport

COLVILLE NATIONAL FOREST

48°33'29"

Aeneas

48°32'47"

OKANOGAN NATIONAL FOREST

2

A

A

A

48°26'32"

48°25'50"

21

3

155

Disautel

OKANOGAN

A

48°19'35"

48°18'53"

MAP 18 SEE

SEE 20 MAP

4

OMAK
LAKE

OWHI
LAKE

COLVILLE
INDIAN
RESERVATION

FERRY

BRIDGE   CREEK   RD

155

48°12'38"

48°11'57"

CACHE

CREEK   RD

5

TWIST

Nespelem

Colville
Indian
Agency

21

RUFUS
WOODS
LAKE

48°05'42"

155

BUFFALO
LAKE

48°05'00"

Keller

6

Belvidere

McGinnis
Lake

DOUGLAS

Seatons
Grove

Elmer City

Lone
Pine

47°58'45"

174

Coulee Dam

Colville Confederated Tribes

47°58'03"

FRANKLIN D ROOSEVELT
LAKE

Grand Coulee

Lakeview
Terrace

COULEE
DAM NATIONAL
RECREATION
AREA

7

174

Electric
City

East
Heights

Grand
Coulee Dam
Airport

BANKS
LAKE

GRANT

LINCOLN

47°51'48"

155

STEAMBOAT
ROCK
STATE PARK

N
ALMIRA
RD

BAGDAD   RD

174

21

47°51'06"

A   B   C   D   E

119°21'11"   119°10'51"   119°00'32"   118°50'12"   118°39'53"   118°29'34"

SEE 29 MAP

MAP
20

1:380,160
1 in. = 6 mi.

0   4   8

miles

N

MAP
20

SEE 10 MAP

48°39'43"   48°38'39"

LAKE ROOSEVELT
NATIONAL
RECREATION AREA

25

395

Kettle Falls

20

20

25

COLVILLE
NATIONAL
FOREST

1

WILLIAMS LAKE RD

395

COLVILLE
NATIONAL
FOREST

1

48°32'47"   48°31'42"

Colville
Colville
Municipal
Airport

20

ARTMAN GIBSON RD

CRYSTAL
FALLS
STATE
PARK

2

RICE RD

Orin

Arden

ORIN RD

395

2

48°25'50"   48°24'46"

Rice

3

Daisy

Addy

COLVILLE
NATIONAL
FOREST

3

COLVILLE INDIAN RESERVATION

Inchelium

Maud

Bluecreek

Sand Canyon
Airport

2902

3

FERRY

48°18'53"   48°17'49"

NORTH
TWIN LAKE

Gifford

Chewelah
Musuem

Chewelah

SEE
MAP
19

2

BRIDGE CREEK RD

TWIN LAKES RD

SOUTH
TWIN LAKE

25

CEDONIA ADDY RD

Chewelah
Casino

395

SEE
MAP
21

4

48°11'57"   48°10'53"

Kewa

Waitts
Lake

Valley

WAITTS
LAKE

BULLDOG CREEK RD

5

Cedonia

SPRINGDALE-HUNTERS RD

STEVENS

231

395

5

48°05'00"   48°03'56"

Hunters

Loon
Lake

Fruitland

292

Springdale

LOON
LAKE

6

LAKE ROOSEVELT
NATIONAL
RECREATION AREA

25

231

6

47°58'03"   47°56'59"

RAND MCNALLY

SPOKANE INDIAN RESERVATION

Ford

Tumtum

LONG
LAKE

7

Fort
Spokane

Miles

FRANKLIN D
ROOSEVELT
LAKE

LAKE ROOSEVELT
NATIONAL
RECREATION AREA

FRANKLIN
D ROOSEVELT
LAKE

Seven
Bays

MILES CRESTON RD

LINCOLN

25

LAKE ROOSEVELT
NATIONAL
RECREATION AREA

Wellpinit

291

Sunset
Bay

291

7

47°51'06"   47°50'03"

118°29'33"   118°19'13"   118°08'54"   117°58'35"   117°48'16"   117°37'57"

A   B   C   D   E

SEE 30 MAP

MAP
21

MAP
21

SEE 11 MAP

1:380,160
1 in. = 6 mi.

0   4   8
miles

N

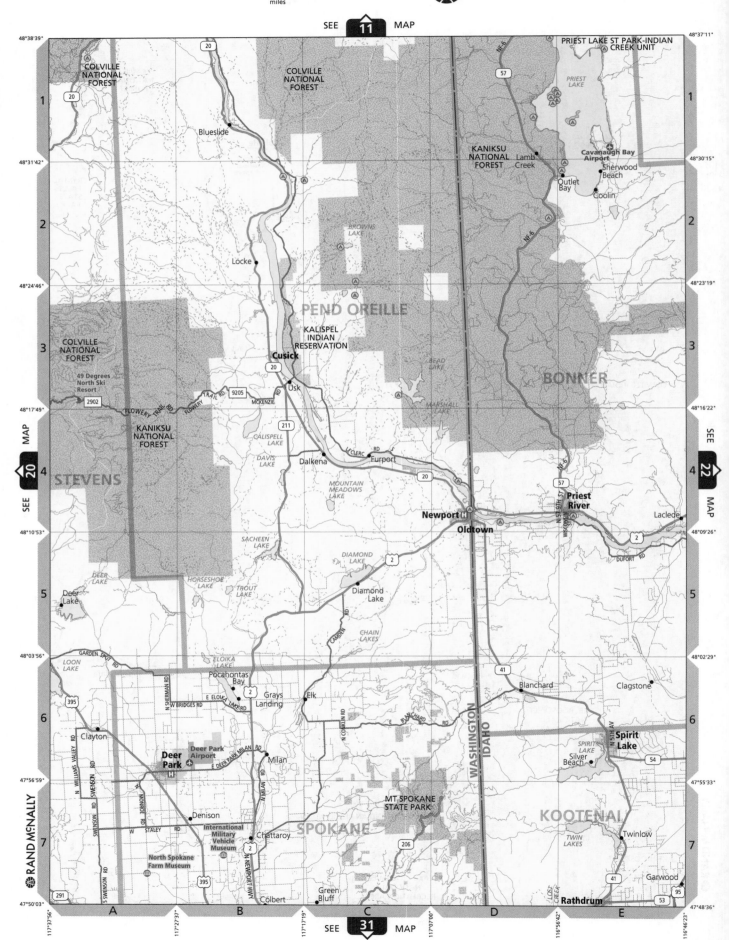

MAP
22

1:380,160
1 in. = 6 mi.

0   4   8
miles

MAP
22

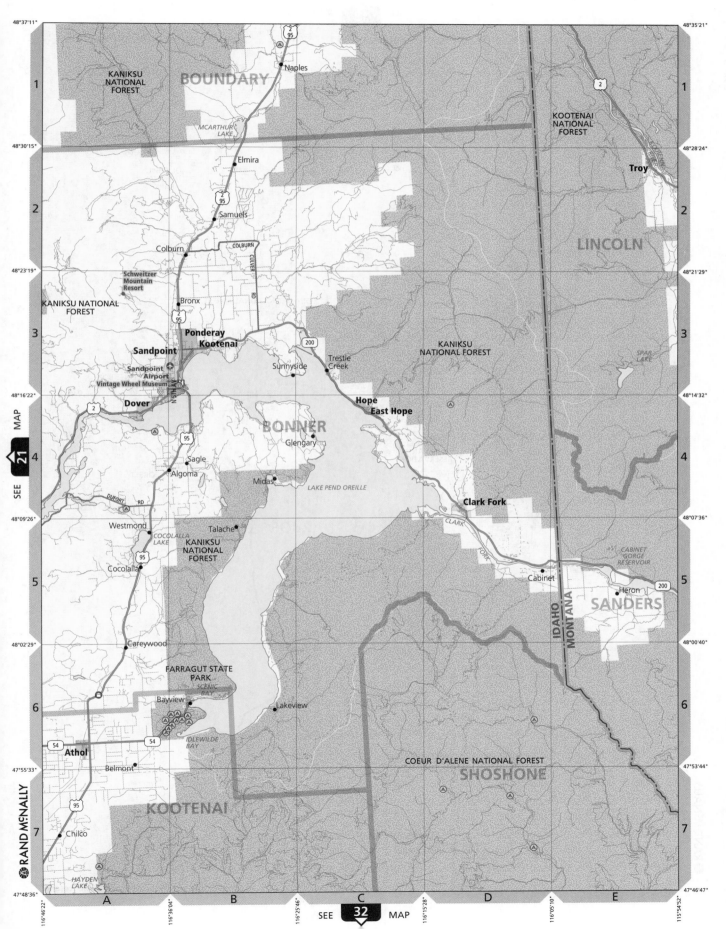

KANIKSU NATIONAL FOREST

BOUNDARY

Naples

KOOTENAI NATIONAL FOREST

Troy

MCARTHUR LAKE

Elmira

LINCOLN

Samuels

Colburn

COLBURN

CULVER RD

Schweitzer Mountain Resort

Bronx

Ponderay
Kootenai

Sandpoint

Sandpoint Airport
Vintage Wheel Museum

Sunnyside

Trestle Creek

KANIKSU NATIONAL FOREST

SPAR LAKE

Hope
East Hope

Dover

BONNER

Glengary

SEE MAP **21**

Sagle

Algoma

Midas

LAKE PEND OREILLE

Clark Fork

DUFORT RD

Westmond

Talache

KANIKSU NATIONAL FOREST

CLARK FORK

CABINET GORGE RESERVOIR

Cocolalla

COCOLALLA LAKE

Cabinet

Heron

SANDERS

IDAHO MONTANA

Careywood

FARRAGUT STATE PARK

SCENIC BAY

Bayview

Lakeview

IDLEWILDE BAY

COEUR D'ALENE NATIONAL FOREST

Athol

SHOSHONE

Belmont

KOOTENAI

Chilco

HAYDEN LAKE

48°37'11"
48°30'15"
48°23'19"
48°16'22"
48°09'26"
48°02'29"
47°55'33"
47°48'36"

48°35'21"
48°28'24"
48°21'29"
48°14'32"
48°07'36"
48°00'40"
47°53'44"
47°46'47"

116°46'22"   116°36'04"   116°25'46"   116°15'28"   116°05'10"   115°54'52"

A   B   C   D   E

1 2 3 4 5 6 7

MAP
23

MAP
23

1:380,160
1 in. = 6 mi.

0   4   8
miles

N

SEE 13 MAP

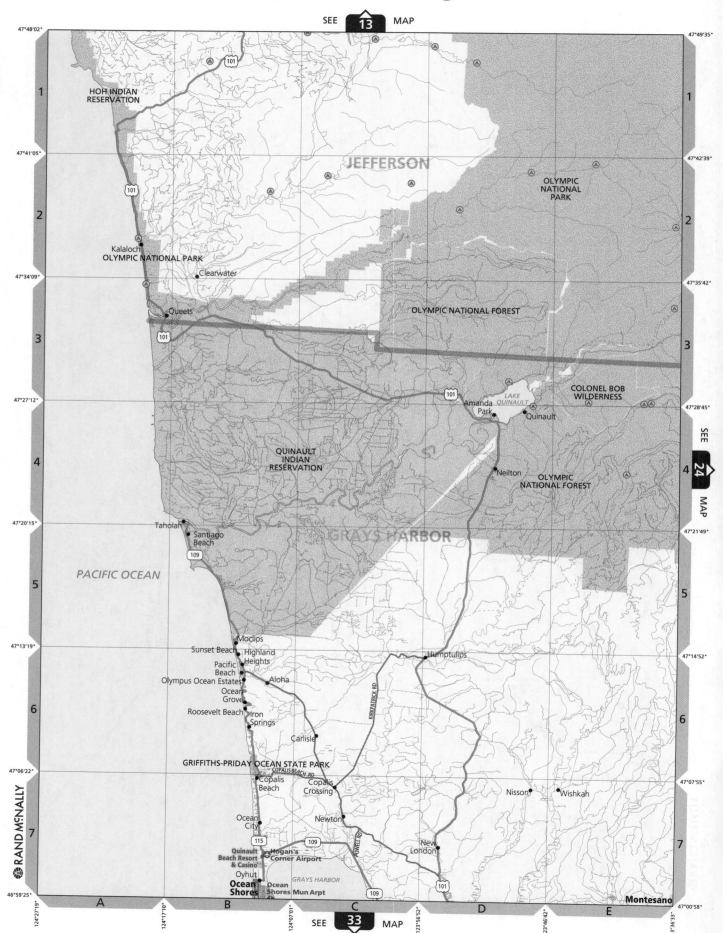

47°48'02"

47°49'35"

HOH INDIAN
RESERVATION

101

1

1

47°41'05"

JEFFERSON

OLYMPIC
NATIONAL
PARK

47°42'39"

101

2

2

Kalaloch
OLYMPIC NATIONAL PARK

Clearwater

OLYMPIC NATIONAL FOREST

47°34'09"

47°35'42"

Queets

101

3

3

LAKE
QUINAULT

COLONEL BOB
WILDERNESS

47°27'12"

101

Amanda
Park

Quinault

47°28'45"

QUINAULT
INDIAN
RESERVATION

Neilton

OLYMPIC
NATIONAL
FOREST

4

4

SEE 24 MAP

47°20'15"

Taholah

Santiago
Beach

109

GRAYS HARBOR

47°21'49"

PACIFIC OCEAN

5

5

47°13'19"

Moclips

Sunset Beach

Highland
Heights

Humptulips

47°14'52"

Pacific
Beach

Olympus Ocean Estates

Aloha

Ocean
Grove

Roosevelt Beach

Iron
Springs

KIRKPATRICK RD

6

6

Carlisle

GRIFFITHS-PRIDAY OCEAN STATE PARK

COPALIS BEACH RD

47°06'22"

Copalis
Beach

Copalis
Crossing

Nisson

Wishkah

47°07'55"

Ocean
City

Newton

POWELL RD

7

7

115

109

New
London

Quinault
Beach Resort
& Casino

Hogan's
Corner Airport

Oyhut

Ocean
Shores

Ocean
Shores Mun Arpt

GRAYS HARBOR

101

Montesano

46°59'25"

109

47°00'58"

124°27'19"   124°17'10"   B   124°07'01"   C   123°56'52"   D   123°46'42"   E   123°36'33"

A   B   C   D   E

SEE 33 MAP

MAP
24

MAP
24

1:380,160
1 in. = 6 mi.

0   4   8
miles

SEE 14 MAP

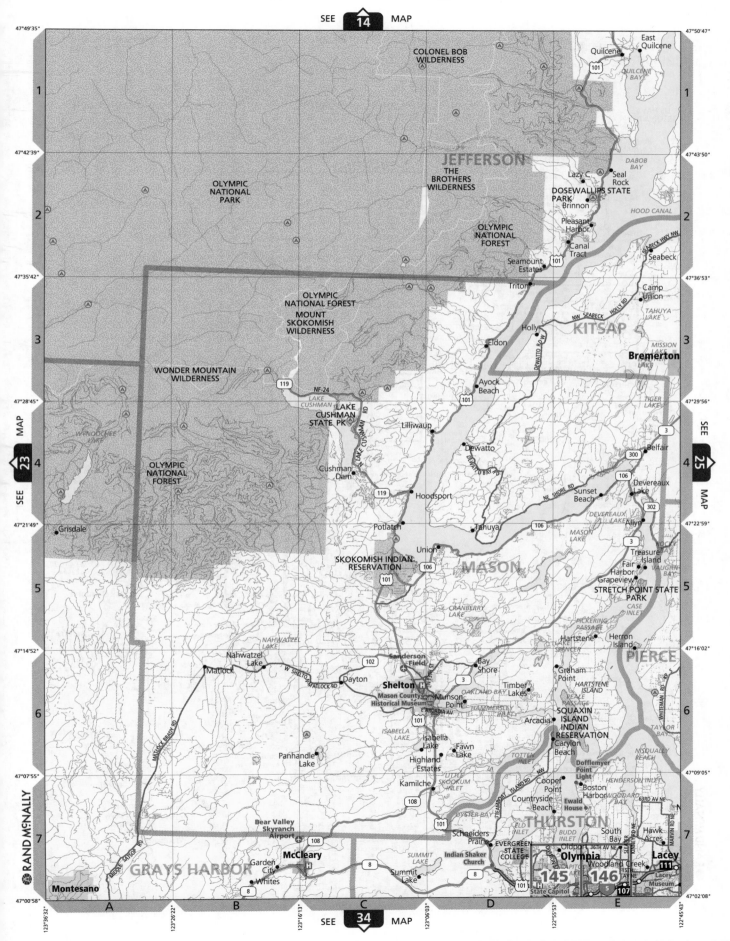

SEE 23 MAP

SEE 25 MAP

SEE 34 MAP

RAND McNALLY

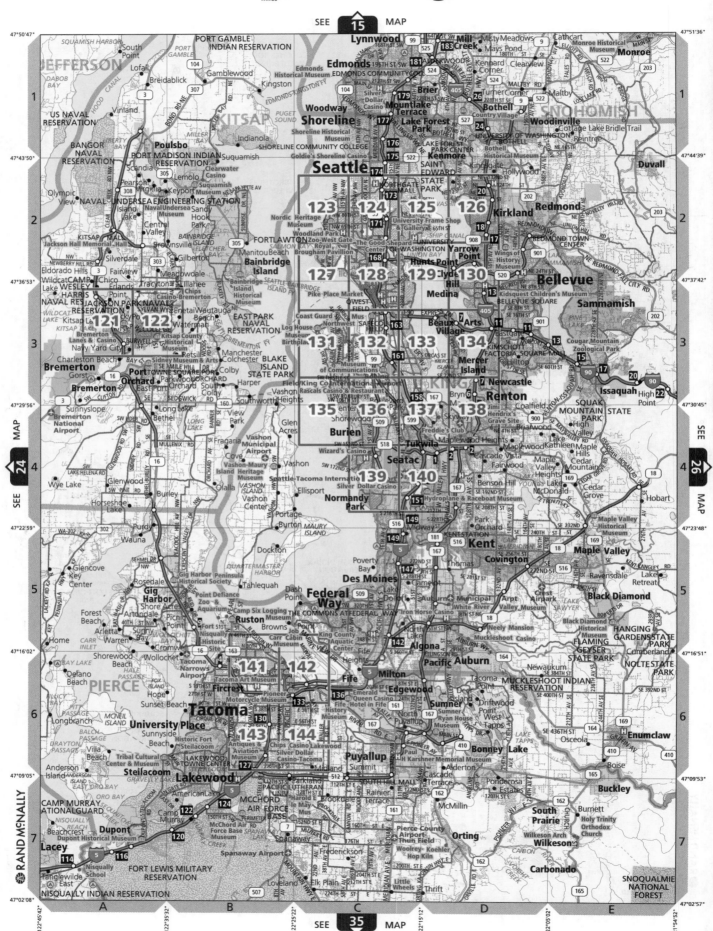

MAP
25

1:380,160
1 in. = 6 mi.

0   4   8
miles

N

MAP
25

SEE **15** MAP

47°50'47"

47°51'36"

JEFFERSON

SQUAMISH HARBOR

South Point

Lofall

DABOB BAY

PORT GAMBLE INDIAN RESERVATION

104

Breidablick

Gamblewood

Kingston

Edmonds Historical Museum

EDMONDS COMMUNITY COLLEGE

Lynnwood

99   525   183

Mill Creek

Misty Meadows

9   Cathcart

Monroe Historical Museum

Monroe

522   203

Edmonds

181

524

Clearview

Kennard Corner

US NAVAL RESERVATION

Vinland

3

307

Indianola

Suquamish

Woodway

Shoreline

Brier

179   405   26

Bothell

SNOHOMISH

Maltby

522

Poulsbo

KITSAP

PORT MADISON INDIAN RESERVATION

Clearwater Casino

177

Mountlake Terrace

527

Country Village

Woodinville

47°43'50"

47°44'39"

BANGOR NAVAL RESERVATION

Scandia

305

Lemolo

Suquamish Museum

Shoreline Historical Museum

176

Lake Forest Park

UNIVERSITY OF WASHINGTON Bothell

Cottage Lake Bridle Trail

Duvall

Olympic View

NAVAL UNDERSEA ENGINEERING STATION

308

Keyport

Seattle

175   522

Kenmore

SAINT EDWARD STATE PARK

Kingsgate

Hollywood

Pearson

Virginia

Naval Undersea Museum

Sandy Hook

174

Goldie's Shoreline Casino

123   124   125   126

Kirkland

Redmond

2

KITSAP MALL

Central Valley

BAINBRIDGE FLETCHER BAY

305

Nordic Heritage Museum

NW 80TH ST

Woodland Park Zoo

171

University Frame Shop & Gallery

18   17

REDMOND TOWN CENTER

202

203

Jackson Hall Memorial Hall

Silverdale

303

Gilberton

Manitou Beach

FORT LAWTON

The Good Shepard Center

UNIVERSITY OF WASHINGTON

908

Wings of History Museum

Eldorado Hills

Fairview

3

Meadowdale

Bainbridge Island

168   Royal Brougham Pavilion

Yarrow Point

Hunts Point

901

47°36'53"

47°37'42"

Wildcat Lake

CAMP WESLEY HARRIS

Chico

Erlands Point

Tracyton

Illahee

Chips Casino-Bremerton

127   128   129   130

Clyde Hill

Kidsquest Children's Museum

Bellevue

13

BELLEVUE SQUARE

Sammamish

202

NAVAL RES JACKSON PARK NAVAL RESERVATION

Enetai

Wautauga Beach

Bainbridge Island Historical Museum

SEATTLE-BAINBRIDGE ISLAND FY

Pike Place Market

WEST FIELD

Medina

405

Beaux Arts Village

11

Eastgate

901

Cougar Mountain Zoological Park

WILDCAT LAKE

Kitsap Lk

CREEK

121   122

RockyPt

Kitsap County Historical Museum

EAST PARK NAVAL RESERVATION

Coast Guard Mus

163

131   132   133   134

KIMSCHOTT FACTORIA

SQUARE MALL

15

17

3

Bremerton Lanes & Casino

Manchester

Colchester

BLAKE ISLAND STATE PARK

Log House Museum

Museum of Communications

161   Mercer Island

Hilltop

90

20

Navy Yard City

Sidney Museum & Arts

Northwest SEAFIELD FIELD

99

Newcastle

Issaquah

Bremerton

Charleston Beach

Gorst

PORT TOWNE SQUARE ORCHARD

Harper

Field

King Co International Airport

158   167

7

Renton

Jimi Hendrix's Grave Site

SQUAK MOUNTAIN STATE PARK

High Point

22

47°29'56"

47°30'45"

16

East Port Orchard

South Colby

Vashon Heights

Rascals Casino & Restaurant

135   136   137   138

Skyway

900

Briarwood

High Valley

Bremerton National Airport

SEDGWICK

160

Glen Acres

enter Shorewood

509   599   518

Freddie's Club

Maplewood Heights

Maplewood

Lake Kathleen

Maple Hills

Maple Valley

3

Sunnyslope

Long Lake

Burien

Tukwila

Cedar Mountain

SEE 24 MAP

Bethel

View Park

Wizard's Casino

SW 160TH ST

Cascade Vista

Fairwood

Maple Valley Heights

Cedar Grove

SEE 26 MAP

Wye Lake

MULLENIX RD

Fragaria

Seatac

Benson Hill

Young's Lake

McDonald

Hobart

47°22'59"

47°23'48"

Horseshoe Lake

Burley

Vashon-Maury Island Heritage Museum

Seattle-Tacoma International Airport

151   Hydroplane & Raceboat Museum

139   140

Silver Dollar Casino

516   149   181   516   Kent

LAKE HELENA RD

Glenwood

Vashon

Ellisport

Normandy Park

Midway

KENT STATION

169

Maple Valley Historical Museum

18

302

Purdy

WA-302

Portage

MAURY ISLAND

Burton

147   167

Thomas

Covington

516

Ravensdale

Lake Retreat

Wauna

SEHMEL DR

Dockton

QUARTERMASTER HARBOR

Poverty Bay

Des Moines

509   Dash Point

Federal Way

Cameron

18

Maple Valley

47°16'02"

47°16'51"

Glencove

Key Center

Rosedale

Gig Harbor Peninsula Historical Society

Tahlequah

Point Defiance Zoo & Aquarium

Camp Six Logging Museum

THE COMMONS AT FEDERAL WAY

Iron Horse Casino

White River Valley Museum

Arpt

Airpark

Black Diamond

Forest Beach

Artondale

Gig Harbor

Shore Acres

Picnic Point

Fort 5151

Browns Point

Neely Mansion

Black Diamond Historical Museum

HANGING GARDENS STATE PARK

Arletta

Sunny Bay

Ruston

Nisqually Historic Site

King County Aquatic Center

Job Corps

Fife Heights

142   Algona

Muckleshoot Casino

Cumberland

FLAMING GEYSER STATE PARK

NOLTE STATE PARK

Home

CARR INLET

Warren

Cromwell

16   163

Tacoma Narrows Airport

Carr Cabin Museum

Pacific

Auburn

164

Newaukum

Shorewood Beach

HALE PASSAGE

Tacoma Art Museum

141   142

Milton

Edgewood

Sumner

Deer Island

MUCKLESHOOT INDIAN RESERVATION

Enumclaw

Delano Beach

Wollochet

FOX ISLAND

Fircrest

Motorcycle Museum

Pioneer

136   Emerald Queen Casino

Fife

161

167   North Puyallup

Ryan House Museum

Sumner

Driftwood Point

West Tapps

410

DRAYTON PASSAGE

Hope

27TH

133   Fife History Museum

167

Paul H Karshner Memorial Museum

164   169

Villa Beach

PIERCE

Sunset Beach

Tacoma

130   University Place

Sunnyside Beach

143   144

Antiques & Aviation Museum

Chips Casino Lakewood Silver Dollar Casino-Tacoma

Puyallup

SOUTH HILL MALL

Bonney Lake

Boise

Anderson Island

Steilacoom

Tribal Cultural Center & Museum

LAKEWOOD TOWNE CENTER

127   196TH ST E

Midland

Summit

410

410

47°09'05"

47°09'53"

CAMP MURRAY NATIONAL GUARD

Lakewood

American Lake

5

McCHORD AIR FORCE BASE

122   124   McChord Air Force Base Museum

Parkland

PACIFIC LUTHERAN UNIV

Harold le May Mus

Cascade

162   Ponderosa Estates

165

Buckley

South Prairie

Burnett

Holy Trinity Orthodox Church

RAND McNALLY

Beachcrest

Dupont Historical Museum

Dupont

120

7

Spanaway

Rainier Terrace

Brookdale

161

McMillin

Orting

Wilkeson Arch

Wilkeson

47°02'08"

Lacey

114

5

116

Tanglewilde East

Nisqually School

FORT LEWIS MILITARY RESERVATION

Spanaway Airport

507

Loveland RD

Elk Plain

212TH ST E

Frederickson

Little Wheels

Thrift

Pierce County Airport Thun Field

Woolrey-Koehler Hop Kiln

162

Carbonado

165

SNOQUALMIE NATIONAL FOREST

47°02'57"

NISQUALLY INDIAN RESERVATION

A   B   SEE 35 MAP   C   D   E

MAP
26

MAP
26

1:380,160
1 in. = 6 mi.
0   4   8
miles

N

SEE 16 MAP

47°51'36"   47°52'02"

STEVENS PASS HWY   2   **Sultan**   **Gold Bar**   MAY CREEK

2

FOGARTY CREEK

Index

SNOHOMISH

BEAR CREEK   JOAN CREEK   BOULDER CREEK

SNOQUALMIE NATIONAL FOREST

HENRY M. JACKSON WILDERNESS

1

LEWIS CREEK   NORTH FORK   TROUT CREEK   JULY CREEK

PROCTOR CREEK   DUPES CREEK

STEVENS PASS HWY

BARCLAY CREEK   FOURTH CREEK   EAGLE CREEK

WENATCHEE NATIONAL FOREST

Baring
2

47°44'39"   47°45'05"

Grotto
2   Stevens Pass Ski Resort

LAKE JOY   Lake Joy

Skykomish   SNOQUALMIE NATIONAL FOREST

ALPINE LAKES WILDERNESS

2

TOLT RESERVOIR

TOLT RIVER

203   Stillwater

Carnation

47°37'42"   47°38'08"

PHILIPPA LAKE   CALLIGAN LAKE

COPPER LAKE

MARMOT LAKE

203

202   Spring Glen

Fall City

LAKE HANCOCK

ALPINE LAKES WILDERNESS

LAKE DOROTHY   OTTER LAKE   BIG HEART LAKE

3

Snoqualmie

Lake Alice   Preston   Northwest Railway Museum

KING

SNOQUALMIE LAKE   LAKE ANGELINE   CHETWOOT LAKE

3

SNOQUALMIE NATIONAL FOREST

47°30'45"   25   90   27   202   **North Bend**

31   32   Tanner   Snoqualmie Valley Historical Museum

34

WENATCHEE NATIONAL FOREST

47°31'11"

18   Harmon Heights

RATTLESNAKE LAKE

SNOW LAKE

WAPTUS LAKE

4

Cedar Falls   38   38   42

Summit at Snoqualmie-Alpental   Alpental

52   Snoqualmie   The Summit at Snoqualmie

903

MASONRY POOL

47°23'48"   47   45   53   Pass   Ski Acres Ski Resort

CHESTER MORSE LAKE

90   54   Hyak

LITTLE KACHESS LAKE

47°24'14"

Kangley   Selleck

GOLD CREEK RD   Hyak Ski Resort

KEECHELUS LAKE

KITTITAS

KACHESS LAKE   CLE ELUM LAKE

5

Kanaskat   KANASKET-PALMER STATE PARK   Palmer

HOWARD HANSON RESERVOIR

Kachees Ridge

Lake Kachees

903

SNOQUALMIE NATIONAL FOREST

62   63

47°16'51"   47°17'17"

SALMON LA SAC RD

Driftwood Acres

6

SNOQUALMIE NATIONAL FOREST

LAKE EASTON STATE PARK   70

Cabin Creek   LAKE EASTON   71   Pine Glen

Easton   Sun Island   74   90

6

47°09'53"   410   ENUMCLAW CHINOOK PASS HWY   47°10'19"

PIERCE

Greenwater

WHITE RIVER

WENATCHEE NATIONAL FOREST

7

CLEARWATER WILDERNESS

SNOQUALMIE NATIONAL FOREST

Crystal Village   410

NORSE PEAK WILDERNESS

YAKIMA   SNOQUALMIE NATIONAL FOREST

7

47°02'56"   A   B   C   D   E   47°03'22"

RAND McNALLY

SEE MAP 25   SEE MAP 27

MAP
27

MAP
27

1:380,160
1 in. = 6 mi.

0   4   8
miles

N

SEE **17** MAP

47°52'02"   47°52'06"

HENRY M. JACKSON
WILDERNESS

WENATCHEE NATIONAL
FOREST

Telma

LAKE
WENATCHEE

1

LAKE WENATCHEE HWY 207

Lake Wenatchee
State Airport

LAKE WENATCHEE
STATE PARK

CHIWAWA RIVER RD

FISH
LAKE

1

2

Merritt

47°45'05"   47°45'09"

Mason
Creek
State
Airport

Coles
Corner

Plain

Ardenvoir

Earthquake
Point

WENATCHEE NATIONAL FOREST

2

ALPINE LAKES WILDERNESS

2

CHUMSTICK HWY

Entiat

LAKE
ENTIAT

2

47°38'08"   47°38'12"

Leavenworth
Winter
Sports Club

Upper
Valley
Museum

CHELAN

Orondo

97

97

Nutcracker
Museum

3

Leavenworth

2

Peshastin

Dryden

Cashmere
Museum &
Pioneer
Village

ALT
97

3

97

2

WENATCHEE
NATIONAL
FOREST

97

Riverbend

SEE
MAP
26

4

ALPINE
LAKES
WILDERNESS

Cashmere
Dryden
Airport

Cashmere

Monitor

SUNSET HWY

97

2

N WESTERN AV

ALT
97

Sunnyslope

SEE
MAP
28

4

28

47°31'11"   47°31'15"

47°24'14"

WENATCHEE CONFLUENCE STATE PARK

WENATCHEE VALLEY COLLEGE
North Central Washington Museum

285

**East
Wenatchee**

STH ST

Kenroy

Wenatchee

CHERRY ST

GRANT RD

Peardot

47°24'18"

8TH ST SE

28

South
Wenatchee

5

Wenatchee
Heights

5

47°17'17"

Spring
Creek

CLE ELUM LAKE

Mission
Ridge Ski
Resort

47°17'20"

Lakedale

903

Ronald

Roslyn

Liberty

KITTITAS

6

Roslyn
Museum

Cle Elum
Historical
Telephone
Museum

Cle Elum
Municipal
Airport

97

WENATCHEE NATIONAL FOREST

6

78

80

90

84

**Cle
Elum**

84

85

970

970

47°10'19"

Teanaway

10

47°10'23"

7

WENATCHEE
NATIONAL
FOREST

93

YAKIMA RIVER

10

97

7

90

Thorp

47°03'22"   47°03'26"

A   B   C   D   E

120°03'58"   120°53'48"   120°43'38"   120°33'27"   120°23'17"   120°13'06"

SEE **37** MAP

MAP
28

1:380,160
1 in. = 6 mi.
0   4   8
miles

N

MAP
28

SEE 18 MAP

SEE MAP 27

SEE MAP 29

47°52'06"
47°51'47"

150 Chelan
LAKE CHELAN
CHELAN-STEHEKIN-LUCERNE FY
S LAKESHORE RD
NAVARRE COULEE RD
WENATCHEE NATIONAL FOREST
ALT 97
97
Lake Chelan Museum
Chelan Falls
CHELAN
971
ROAD 15 NW
LAKE ENTIAT
ROAD 14 NW
ROAD 14 NE
MAIN ST
ROAD B NE
172
Mansfield
Mansfield Airport
172
17
ROAD R NE
1

47°45'09"
47°44'50"

ALT 97
97
LAKE ENTIAT
97
Lamoine
Withrow
ROAD C NW
GRIMES LAKE
JAMESON LAKE
St. Andrews
DO
2

47°38'12"
47°37'53"

Entiat Museum
Entiat
Waterville   Waterville Airport
2
Douglas County Historical Museum
Douglas
DOUGLAS
172
ROAD C NW
2
2
17
SUN LAKES STATE PARK
17
3

47°31'15"
47°30'56"

MEADOWS RD
COULEE RD
PARK LAKE
BLUE LAKE
Blue Lake
LENORE LAKE
17
LAKE LENORE CAVES STATE PARK
Stratford
4

47°24'18"
47°23'59"

GRANT RD
Pangborn Memorial Airport
4TH ST SE
BATTERMAN RD
Palisades
SOAP LAKE
A
Soap Lake
28
Westmont Acres
Lakeview Park
28
17
5

Rock Island
28
Malaga
CHELAN
Grant County Historical Museum
Ephrata
Ephrata Municipal Airport
S BASIN ST SW
282
5

47°17'20"
47°17'02"

28
GRANT
28
Winchester
MOSES LAKE
17
6

Quincy
28
28
ROAD C NW
Crescent Bar
281
6

47°10'23"
47°10'05"

KITTITAS
WANAPUM LAKE
283
WINCHESTER WASTEWAY
POTHOLES RESERVOIR
7

281
151   154
90
164   169
90
A
SW
ROAD C SW
POTHOLES RESERVOIR
7

BASELINE RD W
Sunland Estates
SILICA RD SW
149
George
90

47°03'26"
47°03'08"

A   B   C   D   E

120°13'05"
120°02'55"
119°52'45"
119°42'34"
119°32'24"
119°22'13"

MAP
29

MAP
29

1:380,160
1 in. = 6 mi.

0   4   8
miles

N

SEE 19 MAP

47°51'47"
47°51'06"

STEAMBOAT ROCK STATE PARK
BANKS LAKE
ROAD 52 NE W NE
ROAD 50 NE
155
ROAD V NE
21
174

DOUGLAS

BANKS LAKE

1

Creston
2

Wilbur Airport
Wilbur

47°44'50"
47°44'09"

Govan

ROAD 36 NE

Almira

Hartline
2
155

ROAD 50 NE
ALMIRA RD
N
ALMIRA ST N
2

Fordair

47°37'53"
47°37'12"

2
Coulee City
SUN LAKES STATE PARK

ROAD 36 NE
MONSON RD E

LINCOLN

3

21

COFFEEPOT LAKE

47°30'56"
47°30'15"

SUMMER FALLS STATE PARK
BILLY CLAPP LAKE

MAP 28 SEE

SEE 30 MAP

STAFFORD LAKE

GRANT

KINER RD

4

Wilson Creek
4TH ST N
SPRAUGE ST
28
Krupp
URQUHART

47°23'59"
47°23'18"

28

Irby

28
Odessa
H
SYLVAN LAKE
5

5

BATUM RD
HIGHWAY 21

47°17'02"
47°16'21"

21

6

Grant County International Airport
TYNDELL RD NE
BIG BEND COMMUNITY COLLEGE

BATUM RD

ADAMS

6

Ruff

47°10'05"
47°09'24"

17
Moses Lake Municipal Airport

Wheeler ROAD 3 NE
ROSENOFF RD
E ROSENOFF RD

W

Moses Lake
H
Moses Lake Museum & Art Center
BUS 90
90

175
BROADWAY
90

174   176   179   182   184   188   I 90   196   206   90   7

ROAD O SE
ROAD U SE
DEAL RD
N

47°10'05"

7

MOSES LAKE

McDonald
17
W SCHRAG RD
21

POTHOLES RESERVOIR

47°03'08"
47°02'27"

119°22'12"   119°12'02"   119°01'52"   118°51'42"   118°41'32"   118°31'21"

A   B   C   D   E

SEE 39 MAP

RAND McNALLY

MAP
30

1:380,160
1 in. = 6 mi.
0   4   8
miles

N

MAP
30

SEE 20 MAP

47°51'06"

COLVILLE INDIAN
RESERVATION
Lincoln
FRANKLIN D.
ROOSEVELT LAKE
Seven Bays Airport

STEVENS

FRANKLIN D.
ROOSEVELT
LAKE

SPOKANE
INDIAN
RESERVATION

Little
Falls

Long
Lake

LONG
LAKE

47°50'02"

FARWELL RD

MILES-CRESTON RD

DR

BACHLELOR

25

LAKE ROOSEVELT
NATIONAL
RECREATION AREA

231

MISSILE SITE RD

W   COULEE-HITE

1

47°44'09"

2

Mondovi

231

Reardan

COULEE-HITE

RD

W

47°43'05"

Lincoln County
Historical
Museum

12TH ST

2

Davenport

2

Espanola

Espanola RD

231

Deep
Creek

FAIRCHILD
AIR FORCE
BASE

2

47°37'12"

28

231

WEST
MEDICAL
LAKE

Espanola

902

47°36'08"

LINCOLN

MEDICAL LAKE

Medical Lake

SILVER
LAKE

S BROOKS RD

S LEFEVRE ST

3

Waukon

SPOKANE

CLEAR
LAKE

Silver
Lake

3

Edwall

SALNAVE RD

Clear
Lake

BLUESTEM RD

BLUESTEM RD

264

47°30'15"

ROCKLYN RD

231

90

47°29'11"

SEE
29
MAP

Harrington

395

SEE
31
MAP

4

28

23

904

TOKYO

257   Tyler

4

47°23'18"

HARRINGTON

254

47°22'15"

Mohler

FISHTRAP
LAKE

AMBER
LAKE

Amber

MULLINIX

28   Lamona

WILLIAMS
LAKE

5

SPRAGUE HIGHWAY RD

DOWNS
LAKE

5

395

245

W MARTIN RD

47°16'21"

Sprague

WILLIAMS LAKE RD

47°15'18"

SPRAGUE
LAKE

23

N HILLS RD

ALKALI
LAKE

ROCK
LAKE

6

90

PALM
LAKE

Lamont

6

395

231

MUD LAKE

WHITMAN

E DANEKAS RD

47°09'24"

226

47°08'21"

Ritzville
Municipal
Airport

ADAMS

90

E   ROSENOFF   RD

Ritzville

E   WELLSANDT   RD

COW LAKE

23

Ewan

RAND McNALLY

BUS
90
H   221

220

N HILLS RD

215   90   220

7

261

E URQUHART RD

E HARDER RD

7

47°02'27"

PAHA PACKARD RD

395

118°31'21"

A

118°21'10"

B

118°11'01"

C

118°00'51"

D

117°50'41"

E

117°40'31"

47°01'24"

SEE 40 MAP

MAP
31

MAP
31

1:380,160
1 in. = 6 mi.

0   4   8
miles

SEE [21] MAP

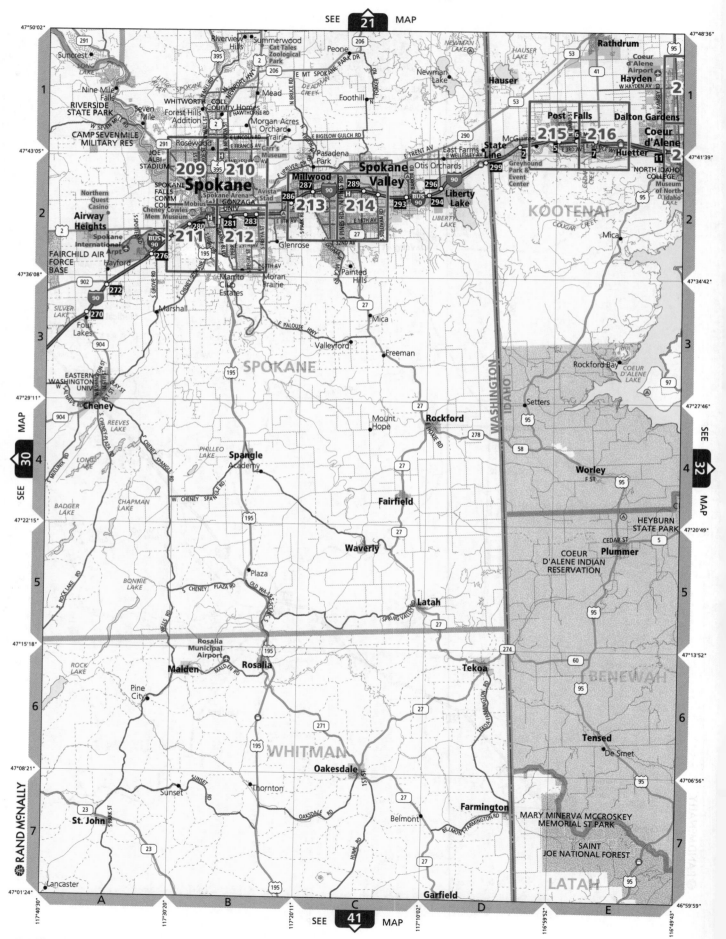

SEE [30] MAP

SEE [32] MAP

SEE [41] MAP

MAP
32

MAP
32

1:380,160
1 in. = 6 mi.

0   4   8
miles

N

SEE 22 MAP

47°48'36"

47°46'47"

HAYDEN
LAKE

RAHORN RD

Hayden
Lake

O'ROURKE
BAY

Clarksville

1   17   Hayden

Honeysuckle
Hills

COEUR D'ALENE NATIONAL FOREST

Prichard

NF-505

OLD RIVER RD

NF-9

1

Dalton Gardens

Coeur
d'Alene

47°41'39"   18   14

FERNAN
LAKE

47°39'50"

BEAVER CREEK RD

Delta

15 Fernan
Lake Village

COEUR
D'ALENE
LAKE

90

Wolf
Lodge

2

22

2

Eddyville

97

KOOTENAI

34

Shoshone
County
Airport

Staff
House
Museum

47°34'42"

ROSE
LAKE

Kingston

48

47°32'54"

3

39

43

45

90

54

Cataldo   40   Pinehurst

Smelterville

51

97

KILLARNEY
LAKE

Rose
Lake

Page

Kellogg

57

Silverton

Osburn

BUS
90

60

3

COEUR D'ALENE LAKE

3

THOMPSON
LAKE   BLUE
LAKE

Medimont

COEUR
D'ALENE
NATIONAL
FOREST

ANDERSON
LAKE

BLACK
LAKE

SWAN
LAKE

47°27'46"

COEUR D'ALENE LAKE

CAVE
LAKE

47°25'58"

97

Harrison

CRYSTAL
LAKE WILDERNESS
STUDY AREA

SHOSHONE

4

3

SAINT JOE
NATIONAL
FOREST

4

MAP
31
SEE

COEUR
D'ALENE
LAKE

97

ROUND
LAKE

HEYBURN
STATE PARK

Chatcolet

BENEWAH
LAKE

Ramsdell

3

St. Maries
Municipal
Airport

NF-50

47°20'49"

Pedee

Rocky
Point

Parkline

5

Milltown

47°19'01"

CHATCOLET
LAKE

COEUR
D'ALENE INDIAN
RESERVATION

4TH ST

St.
Joe

St. Maries

5

Calder

NF-50

Marble
Creek

5

47°13'52"

3

47°12'05"

BENEWAH

6

Santa

SAINT JOE
NATIONAL
FOREST

6

6

Fernwood

Emida

47°06'56"

3

47°05'08"

Sanders

GRANDMOTHER MOUNTAIN WILDERNESS STUDY AREA

7

SAINT JOE NATIONAL FOREST

43

Clarkia

SAINT
JOE NATIONAL FOREST

7

6

NF-15

LATAH

46°59'59"

46°58'12"

116°49'42"   116°39'33"   A   B   116°29'24"   C   116°19'15"   D   116°09'07"   E   115°58'58"

MAP
33

1:380,160
1 in. = 6 mi.

0   4   8
miles

N

MAP
33

SEE **23** MAP

46°59'25"

47°00'57"

Ocean
Shores
149

109 Grays
Harbor
City **Hoquiam**

Arnold
Polson Park &
Museum **Aberdeen**

Montesano

101

Bowerman
Airport

Aberdeen
Museum
of History

Grays Harbor Historical Seaport

GRAYS HARBOR

101 Junction
City

12 Central
Park

1

Westport
Historical
Maritime
Museum

105

Markham

Cosmopolis

GRAYS HARBOR COLLEGE

Melbourne

1

WESTPORT
LIGHT
STATE
PARK

Westport
Airport
150

105

Ocosta

107

101

46°52'28"

Westport

Bay
City

Artic

46°54'00"

105

2

Grayland

2

GRAYLAND BEACH STATE PARK
SOUTH BEACH STATE PARK

46°45'31"

46°47'03"

SHOALWATER INDIAN RESERVATION

Dexter by
the Sea

105

WILLAPA BAY

Willapa
Harbor
Airport

101

3

Tokeland

PARK AV

Old
Willapa

3

101

105

Raymond

Willapa

46°38'34"

LEADBETTER
POINT
STATE
PARK

Bay
Center

101

Pacific County
Historical Society
Museum

**South
Bend**

East
Raymond

6

46°40'06"

SEE

Rhodesia
Beach

Menlo

34

103

MAP

4

PACIFIC OCEAN

Holcomb

4

STACKPOLE RD

Oysterville

PACIFIC

6

46°31'38"

46°33'10"

Nahcotta
Ocean Park
BAY AV

Nemah

5

VERNON AV

Klipsan
Beach

*LONG
ISLAND*

101

5

PACIFIC WY

46°24'41"

46°26'13"

103

4

*NASELLE
RIVER*

6

Pacific
Coast
Cranberry
Museum

SANDRIDGE RD

101

WAHKIAKUM

6

World Kite
Museum &
Hall of Fame

Naselle

4

Deep
River

4 Grays
River

Long Beach
Seaview

Holman

101

401

Rosburg

46°17'44"

Ilwaco

Port of Ilwaco Airport

Stringtown

403

46°19'15"

CAPE
DISAPPOINTMENT
STATE
PARK

Ilwaco
Heritage
Museum

100

Chinook

ALTOONA-PILLAR ROCK RD

Altoona

Pillar
Rock

7

**FORT
COLUMBIA STATE PARK**

401

**WASHINGTON
OREGON**

7

FORT
STEVENS STATE PARK

101

ASTORIA BR

CLATSOP

*JETTY
LAGOON*

Fort Steven
State Park
& Museum

Fort
Stevens **Warrenton**

Astoria

46°10'47"

46°12'19"

A   124°13'50"   B   124°03'50"   C   123°53'49"   D   123°43'49"   E

124°23'50"

123°33'49"

SEE **43** MAP

RAND MºNALLY

MAP
34

MAP
34

1:380,160
1 in. = 6 mi.
0   4   8
miles

N

SEE [24] MAP

47°00'57"

Montesano
Brady
Satsop
Elma
MONTE-ELMA RD
Elma Municipal Airport
Greenwood
South Elma
Malone
Porter
GRAYS HARBOR COUNTY FAIRGROUNDS
[8]
[12]

GRAYS HARBOR

Cedarville

[12]

46°54'00"

THURSTON

Washington State Capital Museum
FW Schmidt House
Lacey
Tumwater
Olympia
Long Lake Rec Hall
Delphi Country Club
Delphi School
Henderson House Museum
Black Lake School
Evergreen Shores
Wilderness Woodsmuir
45TH AVE SE
Glen Eden Park
Lake Pattison
[147]
[148]
Kellys Korner
Olympia Mun
Olympia Flight Museum
Sunwood Lakes
Olympia Mun Arpt
William Owen Bush Monument
East Olympia
[99]
South Union
FORT LEWIS MILITARY RESERVATION
Scott Lake
OFFUT
Mima Mounds Natural Area Preserve
Littlerock
[121]
MILLERSYLVANIA STATE PARK
113TH AVE SW
Offutt Lake
MCINTOSH LAKE
[5]
George Washington Rutledge House
MAYTOWN RD SW
[95]
Maytown
Tenino
Quarry House
[507]
[507]

Gate School
Gate
Rochester Elementary School
Miller-Brewer House
OLD HIGHWAY 99 SW
Colvin House
SOUTH SOUND SPEEDWAY
[507]

46°47'03"

Oakville
CHEHALIS INDIAN RESERVATION
[12]
Rochester
Fort Henness Site
Grand Mound
Bucoda
BUCODA HWY SE
Seatco Prison Site
Ticknor School
Lucky Eagle Casino
Jaaska House & Warehouse
Jonas Erickson Farmstead
[88]

Fords Prairie
[507]
Galvin
W REYNOLDS AV
[151]
Centralia
[81]

Chehalis-Central Airport
[79]
Chehalis
Whitney Esttes
Sunset West
Bunker
Bazinet Eddition
[152]
Veterans Memorial Museum
[76]
Adna
[6]
[603]
[5]

Dryad
Doty
Forest
[72]
[71]
Fircrest Eddition
[508]

PACIFIC
Curtis
LEWIS
Napavine
[6]
Klaber
BOISTFORT RD
Pe Ell
[68]
[12]
John R Jackson House Historic Site
LEWIS & CLARK STATE PARK

Lebam
[6]
Frances

46°33'10"

WILDWOOD RD
[603]
Winlock
[63]
[5]
TUCKER RD

46°26'13"

Toledo
[60]
6TH ST SW
[505]

Vader
WILLOCK-VADER RD
7TH ST
[59]
[506]
[57]
[506]

Ryderwood
MORSE ST
[411]

46°19'15"

WASHINGTON
OREGON
WAHKIAKUM
[4]
[5]
[407]
[52]
Mt St Helens National Volcanic Monument
[411]
[504]
Toutle
[504]
Streeters
Skamokawa
ELOCHOMAN VALLEY RD
SILVER LAKE
Silver Lake
Castle Rock Exhibit Hall
[49]
CLATSOP
[4]
BUS 5
[48]
CLATSOP STATE FOREST
Castle Rock
Brownsmead
COWLITZ
[46]
Pleasant Hill
[411]

46°12'19"

SEE [44] MAP

SEE [33] MAP

SEE [35] MAP

A   B   C   D   E

RAND McNALLY

MAP
35

1:380,160
1 in. = 6 mi.

0   4   8

miles

N

MAP
35

SEE **25** MAP

47°02'08"

Evergreen
Estates

510

MULLEN RD SE

**NISQUALLY
INDIAN
RESERVATION**

Red Wind
Casino

CHAMBERS
LAKE

7

260TH ST E

Rocky Woods

70TH AVE

264TH ST E

MERIDIAN AV

Fairfax

**CLEARWATER
WILDERNESS**

165

Roy

YELM HWY SE

LAKE ST
CLAIR

510

SPANAWAY MCKENNA HWY

507

MUCK CREEK

Salsich
Lumber

8TH AV E

161

Kapowsin

LAKE
KAPOWSIN

1

46°55'10"

**FORT LEWIS
MILITARY
RESERVATION**

RAINIER RD SE

Company Superintendent's
House

Yelm

Mckenna

BALD HILL RD SE

702

TANWAX
LAKE

Clear
Lake

ORVILLE RD E

Clay
City

CLEAR LAKE

OHOP
LAKE

PIERCE

165

46°55'59"

2

MILITARY RD SE

507

Rainier

148TH AV SE

VAIL RD SE

L.N. Rice
House

HARTS
LAKE

EATONVILLE CUT OFF RD

SILVER
LAKE

Pioneer
Farm
Museum

Swanson
Airport

Eatonville

LITTLE MASHEL RIVER

**MT RAINIER
NATIONAL
PARK**

2

VAIL

153RD AV SE

Lackamas
School

Lackamas
School

CLEAR
LAKE

46°48'14"

THURSTON

J Gary
Fenton
Historical
Marker

SKOOKUMCHUCK
RESERVOIR

LAKE
LAWRENCE

Johnson
House

La Grande

7

Alder

ALDER
LAKE

SKOOKUMCHUCK RIVER

**GLACIER
VIEW
WILDERNESS**

46°49'01"

3

Elbe Church National
Historic Site

706

Elbe

National

NISQUALLY RIVER

Summit
House

Ashford

Hidden
Valley

706

46°41'16"

MINERAL
LAKE

Mineral

Paradise
Estates

**SNOQUALMIE
NATIONAL
FOREST**

46°42'04"

SEE **34** MAP

SEE **36** MAP

4

**GIFFORD
PINCHOT
NATIONAL
FOREST**

**GIFFORD
PINCHOT
NATIONAL
FOREST**

4

Alpha

Cinebar

508

46°34'19"

Onalaska

LEONARD RD

CINEBAR RD

**IKE
KINSWA
STATE PARK**

122

HARMONY RD

MAYFIELD
LAKE

LEWIS

508

7

Morton

2ND ST

HWY ST

Randle

12

46°35'07"

5

12

Salkum

SILVERCREEK RD

12

Mossyrock

COWLITZ RIVER

12

Glenoma

**Randle-
Kiona
Airpark**

131

5

Ethel

Silver Creek

COWLITZ RIVER

SWOFFORD
POND

RIFFE
LAKE

CISPUS RIVER

46°27'22"

46°28'10"

6

505

504

SPIRIT LAKE HWY

GIFFORD
PINCHOT NATIONAL
FOREST

SKAMANIA

6

46°20'25"

COWLITZ

COLDWATER
LAKE

**MT ST
HELENS
NATIONAL
MONUMENT**

46°21'12"

7

504

SPIRIT
LAKE

CASTLE
LAKE

7

46°13'28"

A   B   C   D   E

46°14'15"

SEE **45** MAP

122°43'43" 122°33'42" 122°23'41" 122°13'39" 122°03'38" 121°53'37"

MAP
36

MAP
36

1:380,160
1 in. = 6 mi.

0   4   8
miles

N

SEE 26 MAP

47°02'56"

CLEARWATER
WILDERNESS

SNOQUALMIE
NATIONAL FOREST

PIERCE

KITTITAS

47°03'22"

WENATCHEE
NATIONAL
FOREST

NORSE
PEAK
WILDERNESS

SAND CREEK

ALDER CREEK

CROW CREEK

WEST QUARTZ CREEK

410

1

WHITE RIVER

410

MATHER MEMORIAL PKWY

Crystal
Mountain
Ski Resort

Crystal
Mountain

Cliffdell

46°55'58"

Sunrise

MORSE CREEK

AMERICAN RIVER

410

Goose
Prairie

46°56'24"

BUMPING
LAKE

BOULDER CREEK

BUMPING RIVER

THUNDER CREEK

SCAB CREEK

2

MT RAINIER NATIONAL PARK

SNOQUALMIE NATIONAL FOREST

NORTH FORK CREEK

46°49'01"

123

BUMPING RIVER

DEEP CREEK

TWIN
SISTERS
LAKES

LITTLE HINDOO CREEK

LOOKOUT CREEK

THREE CREEKS

46°49'27"

3

Longmire

PARADISE RD

Longmire
Museum

STEVENS CANYON RD

Ohanapecosh

WILLIAM
O. DOUGLAS WILDERNESS

RATTLESNAKE CREEK

SHELL CREEK

3

NISQUALLY RIVER

46°42'04"

SNOQUALMIE
NATIONAL
FOREST

TATOOSH
WILDERNESS

INDIAN CREEK

46°42'30"

SEE 35 MAP

SEE 37 MAP

4

12

CREEK

RIMROCK
LAKE

12

Rimrock

White Pass

White Pass
Ski Resort

CLEAR
LAKE

YAKIMA

NORTH FORK TIETON CREEK

SOUTH FORK TIETON CREEK

4

COWLITZ RIVER

12

Packwood

PACKWOOD
LAKE

46°35'07"

SNOQUALMIE NATIONAL FOREST

46°35'33"

5

12

LEWIS

GOAT ROCKS WILDERNESS

BEAR CREEK

CONRAD CREEK

MIDDLE FORK ANTANUM CREEK

5

46°28'10"

GIFFORD
PINCHOT NATIONAL
FOREST

WALUPT
LAKE

KLICKITAT MEADOW

COYOTE CREEK

BUTTE MEADOWS

46°28'36"

6

ELKHORN
CREEK

PETROSS
CREEK

DIAMOND FORK

PISCOE CREEK

KINGFISH CREEK

6

46°21'12"

TWO
LAKES

YAKIMA INDIAN
RESERVATION

KLICKITAT RIVER

46°21'38"

7

SKAMANIA

MUDDY FORK CREEK

CLEARWATER CREEK

FISH LAKE STREAM

CORAL CREEK

WEST FORK KLICKITAT RIVER

SWAMP CREEK

7

MOUNT
ADAMS
WILDERNESS

46°14'15"

46°14'41"

121°53'36"   A   121°43'35"   B   121°33'34"   C   121°23'32"   D   121°13'31"   E   121°03'29"

SEE 46 MAP

RAND M?NALLY

MOWICH
LAKE

CARBON RIVER

MAP
37

MAP
37

1:380,160
1 in. = 6 mi.

0   4   8
miles

N

SEE 27 MAP

47°03'22"
47°03'25"

101 10 97
90 Bowers Field
Ellensburg
E HELENA AV
Wild Goose Casino
W 14TH AV CENTRAL WASHINGTON UNIVERSITY
106 Kittitas County Historical Museum
E CAPITOL AV
H
KITTITAS
BUS 90
HWY Kittitas
110 115
CLEMAN RD
90

46°56'24"
46°56'28"

410
KITTITAS

Pinecliff
821
SNOQUALMIE
NATIONAL
FOREST
NORTH FORK CREEK
ROCK CREEK
WEMAS CREEK
82
11

46°49'27"
46°49'31"

RATTLESNAKE CREEK
LITTLE RATTLESNAKE CREEK
INDIAN CREEK
NORTH FORK OAK CREEK
PINE CANYON
WENAS DAM
DRY CREEK
LONGMIRE RD

46°42'30"
46°42'34"

410
SELAH VALLEY CANAL
NACHES-WENAS RD
821
12
OLD NACHES HWY
Naches
12
HWY
YAKIMA FIRING CENTER
82
OAK CREEK
SOUTH FORK OAK CREEK
NORTH FORK CREEK
COWICHE CANYON
FRENCH CANYON
CLEMAN'S VIEW PARK &
SPORTS COMPLEX
Tieton
NACHES
TIETON RD
Naches
Basket
Fort
Eschbach
26
SELAH
SELAH LOOP RD
East Selah
HARRISON RD
SPEYER RD
WENAS CREEK
SELAH CREEK
SNOQUALMIE
NATIONAL
FOREST
12
REYNOLDS CREEK
SUMMITVIEW RD
Cowiche
Gleed
MAPLEWAY RD
823
Rambler
Park
30 29
Pomona
Heights
Selah
31

46°42'30"
SEE 36 MAP
SEE 38 MAP

46°35'33"
46°35'37"

Gromore
TIETON DR
Harwood
SUMMITVIEW DR
STONE RD
96TH AV
80TH AV
72ND AV
NORTH AV
Yakima
Yakima Valley Museum &
Hist Association
Nob Hill
Casino
H
STATE
FAIR PARK
33
Terrace
Heights
Yakima Valley Trolleys
34
AV
36
Casino
Caribbean
Moxee
FAUCHER RD
BROADWAY RD

46°35'33"

NORTH FORK AHTANUM CREEK
SWANN RD
GILBERT RD
COTTONWOOD CANYON
STEIN RD
OCCIDENTAL
Yakima Air
Terminal/McAllister
McAllister
Museum or
Aviation
Union Gap
37
38
Central Washington
Agricultural Museum
24

Tampico
AHTANUM RD
Ahtanum
Wiley
City
SPRING CREEK
HATTON CREEK
AHTANUM CANAL
40
HIGHLINE CANAL

46°28'36"
46°28'39"

Saint at
Joseph's
Mission
Ahtanum
YAKIMA
Parker
LATERAL
WILBUR CANAL
97
82
Donald
44
Sawyer
SUNNYSIDE CANAL
ROZA CANAL

46°28'36"

NORTH FORK SIMCOE CREEK
LATUM CREEK
NORTH MEDICINE CREEK
HIGHLINE CANAL
MAIN CANAL
BROWNSTOWN RD
BROWN LATERAL
VOGLER LATERAL
OW WAPATO RD
WAPATO RD
HARRAH RD
DRAIN 2
Wapato
W 1ST ST
W 9TH ST
82
BUENA RD
Buena
Zillah
CHERRY RD

46°21'38"
46°21'42"

YAKIMA
INDIAN RESERVATION
WAHTUM CREEK
SIMCOE CREEK
AGENCY CREEK
BARNEY CREEK
WEST CREEK
OTNEY FLAT DRAIN
Brownstown
MUD LAKE DRAIN
Harrah
BRANCH RD
DRAIN 3
Adamsview
Park
220
Toppenish
FORT RD
50
52 54
Toppenish Museum
American
Hop Museum
Legend's
Casino
H
DRAIN 4
White Swan
FORT RD
FORT SIMCOE RD
SIPHON CANAL
SIPHON UNIT 2 CANAL
MARION DRAIN
TOPPENISH CREEK
SNAKE CREEK
MEYERS RD
BUENA HWY
22
TOPPENISH DRAIN

46°14'41"
46°14'45"

TOPPENISH CREEK
STATUS CREEK
97
MULE DRY CREEK

A   B   C   D   E

RAND MCNALLY

121°03'28" 120°53'27" 120°43'26" 120°33'24" 120°23'23" 120°13'21"

MAP
38

MAP
38

1:380,160
1 in. = 6 mi.

0　　　4　　　8
miles

N

SEE 28 MAP

47°03'25"　　　47°03'07"

SALSA RD SW

90

143

ROAD SW

FRENCHMAN HILLS RD

139

Vantage

46°56'28"　　46°56'10"

136

26

243

KITTITAS

WANAPUM LAKE

WATERMASTER HEADQUARTERS

Royal City

26

262

Royal Camp

A-SE RD

OSULLIVAN DAM RD

POTHOLES RESERVOIR

POTHOLES STATE PARK

2　　　2

Wanapum Village

BEVERLY BURKE RD

GRANT

46°49'31"　　46°49'13"

Beverly

Smyrna

26

Schawana

PRIEST RAPIDS LAKE

3　　　3

Mattawa

24-SW RD

24

243

46°42'34"　　46°42'15"

SADDLE MOUNTAIN LAKE

SEE 37 MAP

MAP 37

YAKIMA FIRING CENTER

Desert Airport

Desert Aire

ROAD SW

24

4　　　4

243

SEE 39 MAP

MAP 39

SQUAW CREEK

CREEK

46°35'37"　　46°35'18"

24

240

HANFORD NUCLEAR RESERVATION

5　　　5

24

241

YAKIMA

46°28'39"　　46°28'21"

BENTON

HANFORD RD

6　　　6

241

240

YAKIMA VALLEY HWY

46°21'42"　　46°21'23"

82

58

VANBELLE RD

Granger

12

Outlook

SNIPES LATERAL

RACCOON RD

SUNNYSIDE CANAL

Sunnyside Museum

MID VALLEY MALL

Sunnyside Municipal Airport

Richland

West Richland

225

HORN RD

COYOTE CREEK

223

63

E LINCOLN AV

YAKIMA VALLEY HWY

7　　　7

67

69

Sunnyside

82

Grandview

WASHINGTON STATE UNIVERSITY PROSSER

SUNNYSIDE CANAL

CHANDLER CANAL

W OLD INLAND EMPIRE HWY

82

93

HORN RD

Benton City

224

22

Satus

GRIFFIN LAKE

SULPUR CREEK WASTEWAY

241

73

75

12

YAKIMA VALLEY CEM CO GRANDVIEW

W 5TH ST

GRANDVIEW PAVEMENT RD

88

12

Kiona

12

196

82

YAKIMA INDIAN RESERVATION

RAND McNALLY

46°14'45"　　46°14'26"

A　　B　　C　　D　　E

120°13'20"　120°03'19"　119°53'17"　119°43'16"　119°33'15"　119°23'13"

SEE 48 MAP

MAP
39

MAP
39

1:380,160
1 in. = 6 mi.
0   4   8
miles

SEE 29 MAP

N

47°03'07"
47°02'26"

GRANT

21

POTHOLES
RESERVOIR
POTHOLES
STATE
PARK
262

17

Lind
Airport
Lind

OSULLIVAN DAM RD
W LIND-WARDEN RD E
LIND-WARDEN RD
N ST
395

SODA
LAKE

170
Warden

LIND-KAHLOTUS RD

46°56'10"
46°55'29"

1

ADAMS

McMANAMON RD

17

BOOKER RD

21

S RD

2

Othello
E MAIN ST
E SCOOTNEY ST

26

Cunningham

26

46°49'13"
46°48'32"

24

S JOHNSON RD

Hatton

S RADAR

395

21

17

3

24

W MUSE RD
MAIL RD
POTHOLES
CANAL

EAGLE
LAKES

MOON RD

HENDRICKS RD

SCOOTENEY
RESERVOIR

Connell

46°42'15"
46°41'35"

SEE 38 MAP

260

Connell
City
Airport

21

263

260
Kahlotus

SEE 40 MAP

4

SAGEHILL RD

HAVLINA RD

DEVILS CANYON RD

Basin
City

17

395

LAKE
HERBERT
G WEST

ROAD 170

263

46°35'18"
46°34'38"

Mesa

BLANTON RD

5

FORTY A
WADE WAY

395

OVERTURF RD

LAKE
SACAJAWEA

HANFORD
NUCLEAR
RESERVATION

RINGOLD RD

46°28'21"
46°27'41"

FRANKLIN

ELTOPIA WEST RD
Eltopia

6

BENTON

FLATS RD

NORTH RD

GLADE RD

TAYLOR RD

395

JUNIPER
DUNES
WILDERNESS

46°21'24"
46°20'43"

240
Richland

WASHINGTON
STATE UNIVERSITY
TRI-CITIES

WALLA WALLA

Eureka

7

COLUMBIA RD

STEVENS DR

GEORGE WASHINGTON WY

HORN RAPIDS
COMPLEX
ATHLETIC
Richland
Airport

224

395

124

West
Richland

203

Three Rivers
Children's
Museum
DUST
DEVILS
STAD
Columbia River
Exhibition

Joker's Casino
& Sports Bar

182

Tri-Cities
Airport

204

Pasco

EDGAR BROWN
MEMORIAL
STADIUM

HARBOR RD

LAKE
WALLULA

124

82

KEENE RD

COLUMBIA BASIN COLLEGE
Kennewick
W COURT ST
395

12

LAKE
WALLULA

46°14'26"
46°13'46"

A   B   C   D   E
119°23'12"   119°13'11"   119°03'10"   118°53'08"   118°43'07"   118°33'06"

SEE 49 MAP

MAP
40

MAP
40

1:380,160
1 in. = 6 mi.
0   4   8
miles

N

SEE 30 MAP

47°02'26"
47°01'23"

395

261

Ralston

LIND-RALSTON RD

1

BENGE-RITZVILLE RD

TWELVE MILE LAKE

Winona

ENDICOTT WEST RD

Endicott

Honn Farm
Airport

46°55'29"
46°54'26"

ADAMS

N

E. BENGE-WINONA RD

Benge

LIFT RD

2

46°48'32"
46°47'29"

26

261

Lacrosse

26

Lacrosse
Airport

WHITMAN

127

Washtucna

26

Hooper

3

46°41'35"
46°40'32"

260
261

Hay

LAKE BRYAN

261

SEE 39 MAP

FRANKLIN

260

LOWER DEADMAN RD

SEE 41 MAP

KAHLOTUS LAKE

LAKE HERBERT G WEST

LYONS
FERRY STATE
PARK

4

Ayer

46°34'38"
46°33'35"

LAKE SACAJAWEA

127

Lower Monumental
State Airport

LYONS FERRY RD

LYONS FERRY RD

12

Dodge

Scott
Seed Farm
Airport

Starbuck

261

GARFIELD

12

5

46°27'41"
46°26'38"

12

Turner

126

COLUMBIA

WALLA WALLA

6

46°20'43"
46°19'41"

Dayton

Baileysburg

WILLIAM T
WOOTEN
STATE
PARK

124

Prescott

124

Touchet Valley
Airport

12

7

UMATILLA
NATIONAL
FOREST

125

Waitsburg

12

46°13'46"
46°12'44"

A   B   C   D   E

118°33'05"   118°23'04"   118°13'03"   118°03'02"   117°53'01"   117°43'00"

SEE 50 MAP

MAP
41

1:380,160
1 in. = 6 mi.

0   4   8
miles

N

MAP
41

SEE 31 MAP

47°01'23"
46°59'58"

SAINT JOE NATIONAL FOREST

23
Steptoe

14TH ST
Garfield

Elberton

27

95

Potlatch Junction

6

Potlatch

6TH ST
6

Hampton

1

195

272

195

DIVISION ST

Palouse

95

LATAH

6

66

46°54'26"
46°53'01"

Endicott

ENDICOTT ST
JOHN RD

ENDICOTT

EAST RD

Diamond

272

272

WHITMAN

Viola

2

26

ALMOTA RD

Colfax

PALOUSE ALBION RD

27

95

46°47'29"
46°46'05"

127

Dusty

SOMMERS RD

194

GOOSE CREEK RD

ALBION RD

Albion

PULLMAN-ALBION RD

195

Palouse Discovery Science Center

Pullman-Moscow Regional Airport

Appaloosa Museum & Heritage Center

LINE ST

McConnell Mansion

WEST

8

Moscow

Joel

3

194

ALMOTA RD

WILBUR GULCH RD

EWARTSVILLE RD

270

194

Bohler Gymnasium

270

WASHINGTON STATE UNIVERSITY-PULLMAN

S GRAND AV

Pullman

Clarence D Martin Stadium

WASHINGTON

IDAHO

46°40'32"
46°39'08"

LAKE BRYAN

ALMOTA RD

FERRY RD

GRANITE RD

CASEY CREEK RD

WAWAWAI GRADE RD

195

Johnson

WAWAWAI RD

95

4

LOWER DEADMAN RD

KIRBY-MAYVIEW RD

N

DEADMAN RD

WAWAWAI RIVER

WAWAWAI RD

RIMROCK RD

Colton

Genesee

LOWER GRANITE LAKE

46°33'35"
46°32'11"

GARFIELD

E BLAIR ST

LEON RD

Uniontown

COW CREEK RD

195

US HIGHWAY 95

NEZ PERCE INDIAN RESERVATION

5

IDAHO

NEZ PERCE NATIONAL HISTORICAL PARK

12

Pataha City

MAIN ST

Pomeroy

KIRBY-MAYVIEW RD

193

95

Lewis-Clark Center for Arts & History

US HIGHWAY 12

12

95 N

46°26'38"
46°25'14"

15TH ST

12

WAWAWAI RIVER RD

12

Clarkston

D ST

ELM ST

Valley View Heights

LEWIS-CLARK STATE COLLEGE

11TH AV

128

Silcott

BRIDGE ST

SCENIC

Clarkston Heights

6TH AV

RIVERSIDE DR

16TH AV

PRESTON AV

Lewiston

6

128

HELLS GATE STATE PARK

Asotin Museum

Lewiston-Nez Perce County Airport

RIPON AV

TAMMANY CREEK RD

1ST ST
Asotin

NEZ PERCE

46°19'41"
46°18'17"

ASOTIN

7

RAND McNALLY

UMATILLA NATIONAL FOREST

129

SNAKE RIVER

46°12'44"
46°11'20"

A   B   C   D   E

117°43'00"   117°32'59"   117°22'58"   117°12'58"   117°02'57"   116°52'57"

SEE 51 MAP

MAP
42

1:380,160
1 in. = 6 mi.

0   4   8
miles

N

MAP
42

SEE 32 MAP

46°59'58"   46°58'11"

6

SAINT JOE NATIONAL FOREST   SHOSHONE   SAINT JOE
NATIONAL FOREST

NF-71

1   1

NF-15

6   Harvard   3

Princeton

NF-58

46°53'01"   46°51'14"

9   Bovill

NF-68

Avon   LATAH

2   NF-50   2

Deary   Helmer   8   Elk River

8   TAFT ST
1ST ST

46°46'05"   46°44'18"

DWORSHAK
RESERVOIR

Park

3   3   3
Troy

8

99

DWORSHAK
RESERVOIR

46°39'08"   46°37'21"

Dent

Kendrick   DWORSHAK
STATE PARK

Cameron   Southwick   CLEARWATER

MAIN ST
WAUNCHER   GULCH   RD

41   4   Juliaetta   P1   4
MAP

Leland   Cavendish

3   NEZ PERCE

SEE

46°32'11"   46°30'25"

STATE HIGHWAY 3   12   Lenore   CLEARWATER   RIVER

Myrtle   US   HIGHWAY   17   12   Ahsahka

5   Peck   Orofino   Orofino   5
Municipal   MICHIGAN AV
Spalding   Airport

12   GIFFORD REUBENS RD
SUMMIT GRADE RD

Spalding   HEWETT RD   Gifford   12
Site

46°25'14"   Greer   11   46°23'28"

NEZ PERCE
Lapwai   NATIONAL
HISTORICAL PARK

Sweetwater   Culdesac   7

6   US   HIGHWAY   95   REUBENS-GIFFORD RD   IDAHO   6

95   LEWIS

WEBB RD   95   NEZ PERCE   Woodland
Reubens   INDIAN RESERVATION

Mohler

46°18'17"   62   46°16'31"
64   12

62
64

Craigmont
Municipal
Airport   7

7   Winchester   Craigmont   Nezperce   64   7

Waha   7
162
WINCHESTER   95   162
LAKE STATE PARK   IDAHO   IDAHO

46°11'20"   46°09'35"

A   B   C   D   E

116°52'56"   116°42'56"   116°32'56"   116°22'56"   116°12'56"   116°02'56"

SEE 52 MAP

RAND M\!NALLY

MAP
43

MAP
43

1:380,160
1 in. = 6 mi.

0   4   8

miles

SEE   33   MAP

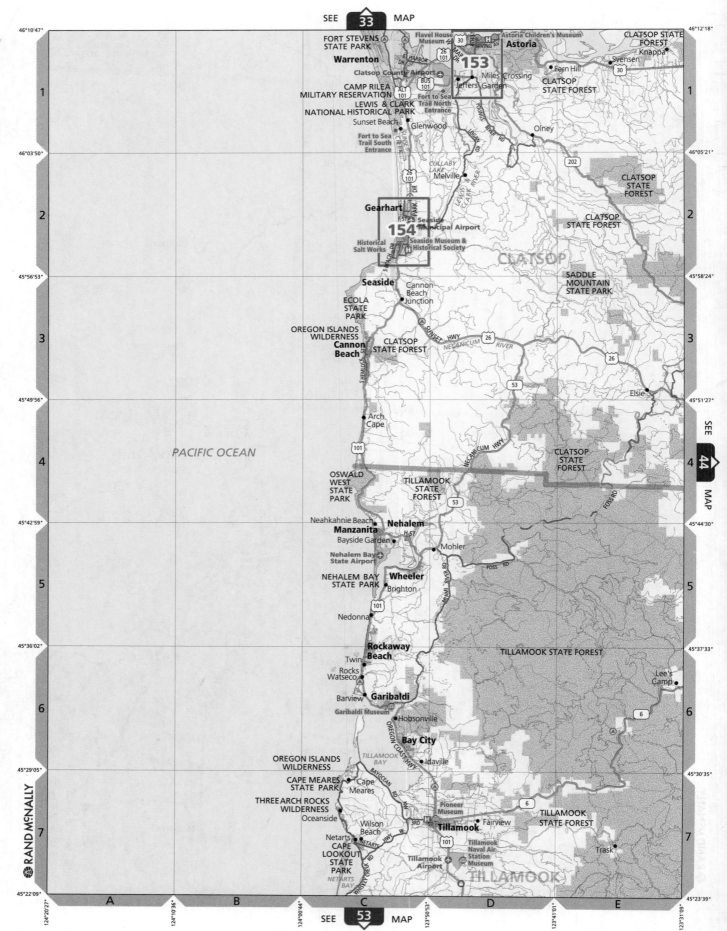

FORT STEVENS
STATE PARK

Flavel House
Museum

Astoria Children's Museum

CLATSOP STATE
FOREST

Warrenton

Astoria

Knappa

Clatsop County Airport

153

Fern Hill

Svensen

CAMP RILEA
MILITARY RESERVATION

BUS
101

Jeffers
Garden

Miles Crossing

CLATSOP
STATE FOREST

Fort to Sea
Trail North
Entrance

Olney

LEWIS & CLARK
NATIONAL HISTORICAL PARK

Sunset Beach

Glenwood

202

Fort to Sea
Trail South
Entrance

CLATSOP
STATE
FOREST

CULLABY
LAKE

26
101

Melville

CLATSOP
STATE FOREST

Gearhart

154

Seaside
Municipal Airport

CLATSOP

SADDLE
MOUNTAIN
STATE PARK

Historical
Salt Works

Seaside Museum &
Historical Society

Seaside

Cannon
Beach
Junction

ECOLA
STATE
PARK

SUNSET HWY

26

OREGON ISLANDS
WILDERNESS

NECANICUM RIVER

**Cannon
Beach**

CLATSOP
STATE FOREST

53

Elsie

SHEMLOCK

Arch
Cape

101

PACIFIC OCEAN

NECANICUM HWY

CLATSOP
STATE
FOREST

OSWALD
WEST
STATE
PARK

TILLAMOOK
STATE
FOREST

FOSS RD

53

Neahkahnie Beach

Nehalem

H ST

Manzanita

Bayside Garden

Mohler

FOSS RD

Nehalem Bay
State Airport

NEHALEM BAY
STATE PARK

Wheeler

Brighton

MIAMI RIVER RD

101

Nedonna

**Rockaway
Beach**

TILLAMOOK STATE FOREST

Twin
Rocks
Watseco

Lee's
Camp

Barview

Garibaldi

6

Garibaldi Museum

Hobsonville

OREGON COAST HWY

Bay City

OREGON ISLANDS
WILDERNESS

TILLAMOOK
BAY

Idaville

6

CAPE MEARES
STATE PARK

Cape
Meares

TILLAMOOK
STATE FOREST

THREE ARCH ROCKS
WILDERNESS

BAYOCEAN RD

Pioneer
Museum

Oceanside

Fairview

Wilson
Beach

3RD ST

Tillamook

Netarts

NETARTS HWY

101

Tillamook
Naval Air
Station
Museum

Trask

CAPE
LOOKOUT
STATE
PARK

WHISKEY CREEK RD

Tillamook
Airport

NETARTS BAY

TILLAMOOK

SEE
44
MAP

SEE   53   MAP

A   B   C   D   E

46°10'47"   46°12'18"
46°03'50"   46°05'21"
45°56'53"   45°58'24"
45°49'56"   45°51'27"
45°42'59"   45°44'30"
45°36'02"   45°37'33"
45°29'05"   45°30'35"
45°22'09"   45°23'39"

124°20'27"   124°10'36"   124°00'44"   123°50'53"   123°41'01"   123°31'09"

MAP
44

MAP
44

1:380,160
1 in. = 6 mi.
0   4   8
miles

N

SEE MAP 34

SEE MAP 43

SEE MAP 45

SEE MAP 54

RAND McNALLY

WAHKIAKUM

CLATSOP STATE FOREST
Bradwood
Wahkiakum County Historical Museum
Cathlamet
Puget Island
30
409
PUGET ISLAND
Taylorville
Westport
Woodson
Marshland
Quincy
Inglis
47
Clatskanie
Historical Flippin Castle
30
202
Mayger
Willow Grove
432
Longview
4
LOWER COLUMBIA INDUSTRIAL WY
155
156
Kelso
Eufaula Heights
Coal Creek
OCEAN BEACH HWY
Lexington
Beacon Hill
Butler Acres
5
411
42
40
COWLITZ
Ostrander
WASHINGTON
OREGON
E OCEAN BEACH HWY
BEAVER FALLS RD
QUICK-MAYGER RD
ALSTON-MAYGER RD
Alston
36
Kelso Longview Airport
Rose Valley
Vision Acres
Carrolls

CLATSOP STATE FOREST
2
CLATSOP
Jewell
202
Birkenfeld
Mist
47
Natal
47 202
APIARY RD
Rainier
Lindberg
Prescott
Goble
32
30
27
Kalama
FERN HILL RD
MESSNER RD
CANAAN RD

COLUMBIA
3
Pittsburg
CLATSOP STATE FOREST
Keasey
Columbia County Historical Society Museum
Vernonia Airfield
Treharne
Vernonia
Vernonia Museum
ROSE AV
NEHALEM HWY
Chapman
Yankton
Deer Island
Columbia City
Woodland
22
21
503
5
St. Helens
McNulty
Warren
CLARK
Ridgefield
PIONEER ST

26
SUNSET HWY
4
TILLAMOOK
47 202
NEHALEM HWY
Tophill
Timber
Scofield
HARES CANYON STATE PARK
47
Buxton
26
Manning
Glenwood
WASHINGTON
Scappoose
Watts Pioneer Museum
DUTCH CANYON RD
SCAPPOOSE VERNONIA HWY
COLUMBIA AV
MCNARY LAKE
STURGEON LAKE
MUD LAKE
501
Sara
STEELMAN LAKE
GREEN LAKE
LAKE RIVER
CAMPBELL LAKE

5
TILLAMOOK STATE FOREST
6
WILSON RIVER HWY
WILSON RIVER HWY
NEHALEM HWY
Gales Creek
6
Banks
55
North Plains
57
59
26
61
62
West Union
Helvetia
Bethany
James F Bybee House
Burlington
30
MULTNOMAH
Vancouver
VANCOUVER LAKE
Portland
15
16
N MARINE DR
N COLUMBIA BLVD
LOMBARD
SMITH LAKE

NW GALES CREEK RD
8
Forest Grove
Verboort
Pacific University Museum
PACIFIC AV
PACIFIC UNIVERSITY
Dilley
Cornelius
NEHALEM HWY
Hillsboro
Portland Hillsboro Airport
Hillsboro Stadium
SE MAIN ST
8
219
NW EVERGREEN RD
64
65
Cedar Mill
PORTLAND COMMUNITY COLLEGE-ROCK CREEK
Washington County Museum
UNIVERSITY OF PORTLAND
Bonny Slope
Aloha
CEDAR HILLS CROSSING
BEAVERTON TOWN SQUARE
STREETS OF TANASBOURNE
OREGON GRADUATE INSTITUTE
67
68
69
71
West Slope
Green Hills
Sylvan
Pittock Mansion
73
16
Raleigh Hills
10

7
Cherry Grove
47
Seghers
Gaston
Laurelwood
BARNEY RESERVOIR
YAMHILL
Wapato
10
SW HILLSBORO HWY
SW FARMINGTON RD
SW RIVER RD
219
Laurel
Midway
Scholls
210
Kinton
99W
6
293
292
Lake Oswego
Tigard
King City
PORTLAND COMMUNITY COLLEGE
WASHINGTON SQUARE
Metzger
SYLVANIA
217
Beaverton
296
16
Green Hills

46°12'18"
46°05'21"
45°58'24"
45°51'27"
45°44'30"
45°37'33"
45°30'35"
45°23'39"

46°13'27"
46°06'30"
45°59'33"
45°52'36"
45°45'39"
45°38'41"
45°31'44"
45°24'47"

123°31'08"
123°21'16"
123°11'24"
123°01'32"
122°51'40"
122°41'48"

MAP
45

1:380,160
1 in. = 6 mi.

0   4   8
miles

N

1

MT ST HELENS
NATIONAL
MONUMENT

GIFFORD
PINCHOT
NATIONAL
FOREST

COWLITZ

MERRILL
LAKE

NF-25

2

Cougar
SWIFT
RESERVOIR
Northwoods
CURLY CREEK RD

SPUR
503
YALE
LAKE

GIFFORD PINCHOT NATIONAL FOREST

Woodland
Park
Kings
Lakeside
LAKE MERWIN
503
Yale

3

503
Chelatchie
NE 419TH S
Amboy

SKAMANIA

503

NE 399TH STNE SORENSON RD
NE 394TH ST
NE 389TH ST
NELSON RD
NE 379TH ST
Fargher
Lake

La Center
View-Air
Airport
TRAPPER
CREEK
WILDERNESS

MAP
44
SEE

La Center
New Phoenix Casino
Chips &
Palace
Casino
Yacolt

4

PIONEER ST
14
Pioneer
Goheen
Airport
Cherry
Grove
Heisson
MOULTON
FALLS
STATE
PARK
Stabler

Ridgefield
BATTLE
GROUND
LAKE
STATE
PARK
Venersborg

NE 219TH ST
Dollar's
Corner
NE 199TH ST
Battle
Ground

5
Cedars North
Airport
NW 179TH ST
NE 178TH ST
Meadow
Glade
503
NE 159TH ST
Hockinson
CLARK

5

WASHINGTON
STATE
UNIVERSITY
VANCOUVER
36
Barberton
Brush
Prairie
NE 152ND AV
NE 119TH ST
Orchards
COLUMBIA RIVER
GORGE NATIONAL
SCENIC AREA

Salmon
Creek
7
Felida
5
205
32
Sifton
500
Proebstel
NE 88TH ST
NE 53RD ST
CAMP
BONNEVILLE
Stevenson

Hazel
Dell
St
Walnut
Grove
Minnehaha
30
Fern
Prairie
Cascade Locks
BEACON
ROCK
STATE
PARK

6

Covington
Hse
500
NE 112TH AV
NE 39TH ST
500
14
Bonneville
North
Bonneville
41

45°38'41"
501
1
158
3
159
H
160
28
SE BLAIR RD
Skamania
84
40
Bonneville
37

CLARK
COLL
308
5
Vancouver
NW 38TH AV
14
Dodson
35
Henry J
Kaiser
Wendel
Shipyard Animal Cons
Mus of
LACAMAS
LAKE
CLARK HWY
84
30

307
306
PORTLAND INTERNATIONAL
Int'l Arpt
205
10
Camas
Parkersville
Site
Prindle
14
MARK O.
HATFIELD
WILDERNESS

7

1
162
163
24
164
Washougal
Two Rivers Heritage Museum
29
30
31
COLUMBIA
RIVER GORGE
NATIONAL
SCENIC
AREA

99E
Overlook Hse
Portland
Maywood Park
NE SANDY BLVD
FAIRVIEW
Portland
Troutdale
Arpt
Historic Columbia
River Highway
25
28
Bridal
Veil
Latourell
Falls

Portland Alien Mus
13
Fairview
30
18
30
Corbett
22
84
GUY
W TALBOT
STATE PARK

166
167
168
Wood Village
Troutdale
Springdale
Orient
MULTNOMAH
MOUNT HOOD
NATIONAL FOREST

296
298
REED COLL
26
MT HOOD COMM COLL
Gresham Pioneer Museum
BULL RUN
RESERVOIR
NO 1

7

Portland
170
Milwaukie
16
213
Battin
Happy
Valley
Gresham
Orient
Cottrell
BULL RUN
RESERVOIR
NO 2
ROSLYN
LAKE

Lake
Oswego
Oak Grove
224
Sunnyside
Damascus
Boring
Sandy
CLACKAMAS

A   B   C   D   E

MAP
45

MAP
46

MAP
46

1:380,160
1 in. = 6 mi.

0   4   8
miles

N

SEE 36 MAP

46°14'15"
46°14'40"

1

MOUNT
ADAMS
WILDERNESS

YAKIMA
INDIAN
RESERVATION

ICE CREEK
TROUT CREEK
WEST FORK
WHITE CREEK
LYON SPRING

1

GIFFORD
PINCHOT
NATIONAL FOREST

46°07'17"
46°07'43"

2

INDIAN
HEAVEN
WILDERNESS

SKAMANIA

YAKIMA

BRUSH CREEK

2

Draper
Springs
Camp

Glenwood

GLENWOOD-GOLDENDALE RD

46°00'20"
46°00'46"

Trout Lake
Airport

Trout
Lake

RIVER RD

TROUT LAKE HWY

3

141

SKAMANIA

KLICKITAT

BZ-GLENWOOD HWY

3

141

GIFFORD PINCHOT
NATIONAL FOREST

Gilmer

BZ Corner

45°53'23"
45°53'48"

SEE 45 MAP

4

Husum

Appleton

Wahkiacus

Klickitat

142

4

SEE 47 MAP

WIND RIVER RD

Willard

Mill A

COLUMBIA RIVER
GORGE NATIONAL
SCENIC AREA

45°46'26"
45°46'51"

Carson

Home
Valley

Hood

Cook

W JEWETT BLVD

White Salmon

COLUMBIA RIVER
GORGE NATIONAL
SCENIC AREA

5

14

Stevenson

Underwood

Bingen

E STEUBEN ST

14

Lyle

5

WASHINGTON
OREGON

30

84

Hood River

69

Mosier

84

44

47

51

84

55

56

58

62

63

WYGANT
STATE PARK

Hood
River
County
Historical
Museum

76

Rowena

LAKE
CELILO

45°39'28"
45°39'54"

Cascade
Locks

Cascade
Locks
State
Airport

Hood River
Airport

Columbia Gorge
Discovery Center

Murdock

30

197

14

84

88

MARK O.
HATFIELD
WILDERNESS

HOOD RIVER HWY

SUMMIT DR

POWELL HWY

Odell

MT HOOD HWY

The
Dalles

Chenoweth

82

W 6TH ST

83

The Dalles Municipal
Airport

85

2ND ST

87

Wonder
Works
Children's Museum

Petersburg

6

St. Peter's
Landmark

Fort
Dalles Museum

H

OLNEY RD

THREEMILE RD

6

HOOD RIVER

Dee

LOST LAKE RD

Trout
Creek

E MT HOOD HWY

WASCO

45°32'31"
45°32'56"

Hutson
Museum

Mount
Hood

35

THREEMILE RD

197

LOST
LAKE

Parkdale

MT HOOD HWY

NE-18

Boyd

BULL
RUN
LAKE

NE-1810

MOUNT HOOD
NATIONAL
FOREST

Cooper Spur
Ski Area

NF-1720

Dufur

DUFUR VALLEY RD

7

7

45°25'34"
45°25'59"

MOUNT HOOD WILDERNESS

A   B   C   D   E

SEE 56 MAP

121°15'24"   121°42'31"   121°32'38"   121°22'46"   121°12'53"   121°03'00"

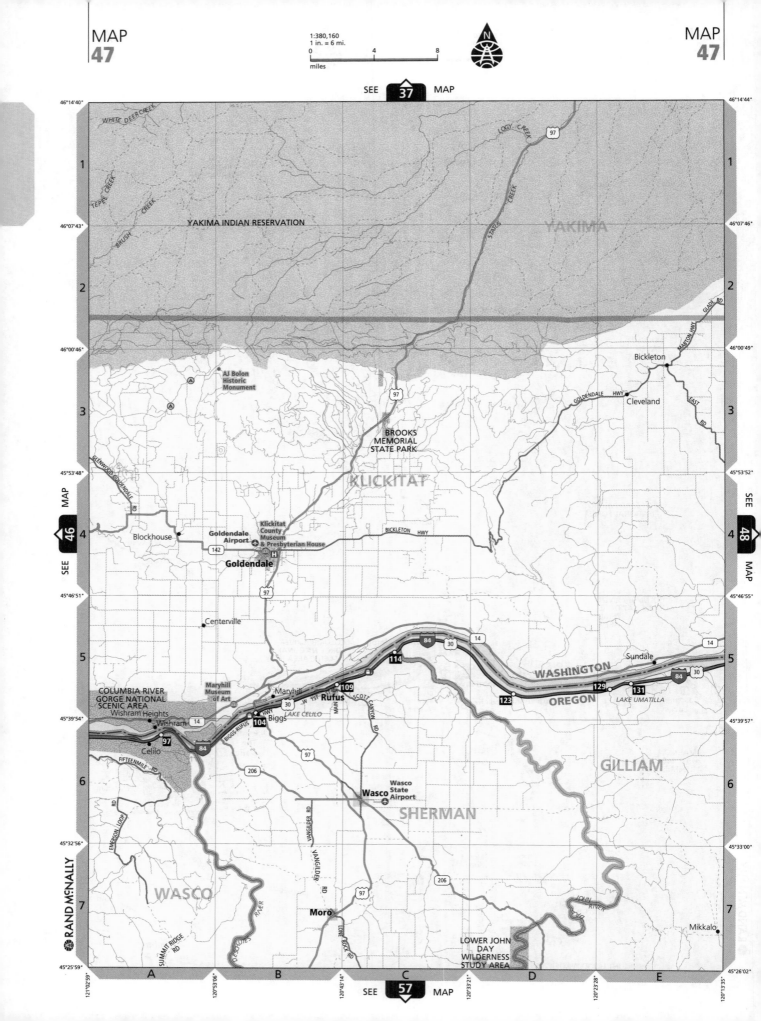

MAP
47

MAP
47

1:380,160
1 in. = 6 mi.

0   4   8

miles

SEE 37 MAP

WHITE DEER CREEK

97

LOGY CREEK

46°14'40"
46°14'44"

1

YAKIMA INDIAN RESERVATION

YAKIMA

STATUS CREEK

TEPEE CREEK

CREEK

BRUSH CREEK

46°07'43"
46°07'46"

2

GLADE RD

MARLTON HWY

46°00'46"
46°00'49"

Bickleton

AJ Bolon
Historic
Monument

97

GOLDENDALE HWY

Cleveland

EAST RD

3

BROOKS
MEMORIAL
STATE PARK

KLICKITAT

45°53'48"
45°53'52"

SEE

48

MAP

SEE MAP

46

GLENWOOD-GOLDENDALE RD

Blockhouse

Goldendale
Airport

142

Klickitat
County
Museum
& Presbyterian House

Goldendale

BICKLETON HWY

4

45°46'51"
45°46'55"

97

Centerville

Maryhill
Museum
of Art

84

30

14

Sundale

5

114

WASHINGTON

84

30

14

COLUMBIA RIVER
GORGE NATIONAL
SCENIC AREA

Maryhill

109

Rufus

W 1ST

SCOTT CANYON RD

OREGON

129

131

45°39'54"

Wishram Heights

Wishram

14

30

LAKE CELILO

Biggs

MAIN

123

Lake Umatilla

45°39'57"

97

84

Celilo

BIGGS-RUFUS HWY

104

FIFTEENMILE RD

GILLIAM

206

97

45°32'56"

EMERSON LOOP RD

VANGILDER RD

Wasco
State
Airport

Wasco

45°33'00"

6

SHERMAN

SUMMIT RIDGE RD

DESCHUTES RIVER

VANGILDER RD

206

JOHN DAY RIVER

WASCO

97

Mikkalo

7

Moro

LONE ROCK RD

LOWER JOHN
DAY
WILDERNESS
STUDY AREA

45°25'59"
45°26'02"

RAND MCNALLY

A   B   C   D   E

121°02'59"   120°53'06"   120°43'14"   120°33'21"   120°23'28"   120°13'35"

SEE 57 MAP

MAP
48

1:380,160
1 in. = 6 mi.

0   4   8
miles

N

MAP
48

SEE 38 MAP

46°14'44"
46°14'26"

Grandview

North Prosser

GRIFFIN LAKE

241

22

Mabton

80

CHANDLER CANAL

Whitstran

KENNEWICK MANN CANAL

E BADGER RD

82

12

Prosser Airport

82

221

H

22

Prosser

Benton County Historical Museum

COUNTY WELL RD

TRAVIS RD

1

1

YAKIMA INDIAN RESERVATION

46°07'46"
46°07'28"

SELLARDS RD

SELLARDS RD

YAKIMA

GLADE CREEK

BENTON

221

2

2

MCKINLEY SPRINGS RD

46°00'49"
46°00'31"

3

3

Paterson

14

KLICKITAT

Patterson Junction

Irrigon

45°53'52"
45°53'34"

MAP
47

14

LAKE UMATILLA

MCCORMACK SLOUGH

730

SEE 49 MAP

CROW BUTTE STATE PARK

WASHINGTON

UMATILLA ORDNANCE DEPOT

SEE 47

OREGON

165

COLUMBIA RIVER HWY

14

151

159

30

164

168

OLD OREGON TRAIL HWY

171

84

30

177

4

184

Boardman

Boardman Airport

COLUMBIA RIVER HWY

179

45°46'55"
45°46'37"

EAST RD

14

147

WILLOW LAKE

HEPPNER HWY

30

84

Roosevelt

LAKE UMATILLA

ROOSEVELT GRADE RD

BOARDMAN BOMBING RANGE

5

5

Arlington

Arlington Municipal Airport

45°39'57"
45°39'39"

74

GILLIAM

Cecil

MORROW

BIG BUTTER CREEK RD

6

6

LEXINGTON-ECHO HWY

45°33'00"
45°32'42"

19

207

MCNAB LN

Ione

74

7

7

Olex

IONE RD

GOOSEBERRY RD

GOOSEBERRY RD

IONE RD

RHEA CREEK RD

E ST

Lexington Airport

Lexington

JOHN DAY HWY

45°26'02"
120°13'35"

A
120°03'42"

B
119°53'49"

SEE 58 MAP

C
119°43'56"

D
119°34'04"

E
119°47'61"

45°25'45"

MAP
49

1:380,160
1 in. = 6 mi.
0   4   8
miles

N

MAP
49

SEE **39** MAP

Richland
104
GAGE BLVD
COLUMBIA CENTER
MALL
W SYLVESTER
240
Crazy Moose Casino
LAKE
WALLULA
Celebrities
Casino
397
Pasco
12
124
Island
Casino
Vista Field
82
109
205 **206**
Cable Bridge Casino
Burbank
Heights
Burbank
Kennewick
E 27TH AV
113
W 45TH AV
BOWLES RD
CHEMICAL DR
E
12
N DALLAS RD
NESTLE RD
W 10TH AV
395
OLYMPIA
S OAK ST
COLUMBIA CANAL
E BADGER RD
RD
114
Finley
397
397
KENNEWICK MAIN CANAL
CLODFELTER RD
S
SELLARDS RD
395
WALLA WALLA

BENTON
82
Wallula
Fort Walla Walla
Heritage Marker
LAKE
WALLULA
Lowden
S PLYMOUTH RD
Touchet
12
122
Wallula
Junction
12
Gardena
WASHINGTON
395
OREGON
82
131
14
Plymouth
LAKE
UMATILLA
COLUMBIA RIVER HWY
730
Umatilla
HAT ROCK
STATE PARK
730
730
**Power
City**
395
37
PENDLETON-COLD
COLD
SPRINGS
RESERVOIR
SPRINGS
Helix
UMATILLA
DEPOT
5
207
PENDLETON-COLD HWY
HOLDMAN HELIX HWY
W ELM AV
H
N 1ST ST
NE 10TH ST
334
ATHENA-HOLDMAN HWY
HAVANA-HELIX
Hermiston Municipal
Airport
395
DR
Hermiston
10
MAIN ST
NORTHGATE
Adams
207
82
180
182
30
Stanfield
Echo
84
188
193
37
11
MADISON RD
320 RD
PENDLETON CTO
UMATILLA
OREGON-WASHINGTON HWY
11
Cayuse
198
199
207
331
1300
202
84
Eastern
Oregon
Regional
Airport
Pendleton
207
209
H
Mission
Rieth
210
213
RIETH RD
Round-
Up Hall of
Fame Museum
Umatilla
County
Historical
Museum
216
Wildhorse
Resort
Casino
S MARKET RD
84
BIG BUTTER CREEK RD
MCKAY
RESERVOIR
30
395
224
**UMATILLA INDIAN
RESERVATION**
BUTTER CREEK RD
MORROW
Pilot Rock
74 HWY
HEPPNER
74
395

SEE **48** MAP

SEE **50** MAP

RAND McNALLY

A   B   C   D   E

MAP
50

1:380,160
1 in. = 6 mi.
0   4   8
miles

MAP
50

SEE **40** MAP

46°13'46"

46°12'44"

1

COLUMBIA

125

Dixie

WENAHA-
TUCANNON WILDERNESS

46°06'48"

46°05'46"

Walla Walla
Regional
Airport

WALLA WALLA

Ski Bluewood
Ski Resort

BORLESKE
STADIUM
207
WHITMAN
COLLEGE
ISAACS
208
Walla Walla

2

12

Martin Field
WALLA
WALLA
WALLA COLLEGE
College Place
Fort
Walla Walla
Museum Complex

125

Kooskooskie

WASHINGTON
OREGON

45°59'51"

45°58'49"

332

Umapine

Sunnyside

WENAHA-
TUCANNON
WILDERNESS

SUNNYSIDE RD

11

3

E BROADWAY AV

Milton-Freewater

Frazier
Farmstead
Museum

WALLOWA

11

45°52'54"

45°51'52"

SEE **49** MAP

SEE **51** MAP

4

332

Athena

UMATILLA

334

Weston

BANISTER RD

OREGON-WASHINGTON HWY

11

204

Tollgate

45°45'57"

45°44'55"

Adams

Spout
Springs
Ski Area

5

UMATILLA
INDIAN
RESERVATION

Bingham
Springs

NORTH FORK
UMATILLA
WILDERNESS

Palmer
Junction

Gibbon

Thornhollow

204

45°38'59"

45°37'58"

6

UMATILLA
NATIONAL FOREST

UNION

228

WALLOWA LAKE HWY

82

EMIGRANT SPRINGS
STATE PARK

Elgin

84

S 8TH AV

45°32'02"

45°31'01"

Meacham

238

Summerville

SUMMERVILLE RD

82

7

Imbler

RAND McNALLY

UMATILLA NATIONAL
FOREST
WHITMAN
NATIONAL
FOREST

Kamela

243

WHITMAN
NATIONAL
FOREST

WHITMAN
NATIONAL
FOREST

45°25'05"

45°24'04"

118°34'47"   A   118°24'54"   B   118°15'02"   C   118°05'10"   D   117°55'18"   E   117°45'25"

SEE **60** MAP

MAP
51

MAP
51

1:380,160
1 in. = 6 mi.

0   4   8

miles

N

SEE 41 MAP

46°12'44"   46°11'20"

UMATILLA NATIONAL FOREST
GARFIELD

ASOTIN

Anatone

WASHINGTON
IDAHO

NEZ
PERCE

COLUMBIA

46°05'46"   46°04'23"

129

FIELDS
SPRINGS
STATE PARK

WENAHA-
TUCANNON
WILDERNESS

WALLOWA
NATIONAL
FOREST

WASHINGTON
OREGON

SNAKE RIVER

45°58'49"   45°57'26"

Troy

UMATILLA NATIONAL FOREST

Flora

HELLS CANYON
NATIONAL
RECREATION
AREA

45°51'52"   45°50'29"

MAP 50 SEE

3

WALLOWA
NATIONAL
FOREST

SEE 52 MAP

45°44'55"   45°43'32"

WALLOWA

Minam

45°37'58"   45°36'35"

82

WALLOWA

LAKE

HWY

3

Wallowa

82

45°31'01"   45°29'38"

WHITMAN
NATIONAL
FOREST

Lostine

STATE ST

RAND MCNALLY

WALLOWA NATIONAL FOREST

WALLOWA LAKE

HWY

Enterprise
Enterprise Municipal
Airport

82

WALLOWA
NATIONAL
FOREST

UNION

EAGLE CAP WILDERNESS

45°24'04"   45°22'41"

A   B   C   D   E

117°45'25"   117°35'32"   117°25'41"   117°15'49"   117°05'57"   116°56'05"

SEE 61 MAP

MAP
52

MAP
52

1:380,160
1 in. = 6 mi.

0   4   8

miles

N

SEE 42 MAP

46°11'20"

46°09'34"

Ferdinand

NEZ PERCE
NATIONAL
HISTORICAL PARK

162

NEZ PERCE
INDIAN
RESERVATION

1

1

LEWIS

Greencreek

95

46°04'23"

46°02'37"

NEZ PERCE

Cottonwood
Municipal
Airport

Cottonwood

Keuterville

OLD HIGHWAY 7

2

2

SNOWHOLE RAPIDS
WILDERNESS STUDY AREA

95   Fenn

7

Idaho
County
Airport

45°57'26"

45°55'41"

13

Grangeville

Mount
Idaho

IDAHO
OREGON

IDAHO

95

Snowhaven
Ski Area

3

3

SNAKE RIVER

45°50'29"

45°48'44"

MAP
51
SEE

White Bird

4

4

WALLOWA
NATIONAL
FOREST

45°43'32"

45°41'47"

HELLS
CANYON
WILDERNESS

Slate
Creek

NEZ PERCE
NATIONAL
FOREST

5

95

5

HELLS
CANYON
NATIONAL
RECREATION AREA

45°36'35"

45°34'50"

Imnaha

Lucile

6

6

NEZ PERCE
NATIONAL
FOREST

45°29'38"

45°27'54"

WALLOWA
NATIONAL
FOREST

MARK ST

WALLOWA

HELLS
CANYON
WILDERNESS

Riggins

7

7

95

45°22'41"

PAYETTE NATIONAL FOREST

45°20'57"

RAND McNALLY

A   B   C   D   E

116°56'05"   116°46'13"   116°36'22"   116°26'30"   116°16'39"   116°06'48"

SEE 62 MAP

MAP 53

MAP 53

1:380,160
1 in. = 6 mi.

0   4   8
miles

N

SEE **43** MAP

45°22'08"
45°23'38"

NETARTS BAY

Pleasant Valley

TILLAMOOK STATE FOREST

101

CAPE LOOKOUT STATE PARK

SIUSLAW NATIONAL FOREST

Hemlock

SAND LAKE

Sand Lake

TILLAMOOK

Beaver

BLAINE RD

Blaine

UPPER NESTUCCA RD

NESTUCCA RIVER RD

45°15'11"
45°16'41"

Tierra Del Mar

SANDLAKE RD

Woods

BROOTEN RD

FERRY RD

Hebo

SIUSLAW NATIONAL FOREST

THREE RIVERS HWY

GILBERT CREEK RD

Pacific City

Cloverdale

NESTUCCA BAY

45°08'14"
45°09'44"

Winema Beach

Oretown

22

YAMHILL

Neskowin

OREGON ISLANDS WILDERNESS

SIUSLAW NATIONAL FOREST

Grand Ronde Agency

45°01'17"

CASCADE HEAD NATIONAL SCENIC RESEARCH AREA

101

18

HEBO RD

Valley Junction

Grand Ronde

Spirit Mountain Casino

18
22

45°02'41"

Otis

PACIFIC OCEAN

Roads End

Rose Lodge

Chinook Winds Casino Resort

Neotsu

SEE **54** MAP

NW JETTY AV

DEVILS LAKE

NE 14TH ST

101

EAST DEVILS LAKE STATE PARK

4

Lincoln City

SIUSLAW NATIONAL FOREST

44°54'20"
44°55'50"

SILETZ BAY

Salishan

Kernville

Gleneden Beach

Coronado Shores

Siletz Bay State Airport

POLK

Lincoln Beach

VALSETZ LAKE

5

BOILER BAY STATE PARK

229

Valsetz

Depoe Bay

44°47'24"
44°48'53"

ROCKY CREEK STATE SCENIC VIEWPOINT

101

OTTER CREST STATE PARK

Otter Rock

SILETZ INDIAN RESERVATION

BEVERLY BEACH STATE PARK

Logsden

Beverly Beach

Camp Twelve

Siletz

411

6

LINCOLN

44°40'27"
44°41'55"

OLALLA RESERVOIR

YAQUINA RIVER

BENTON

Newport

SILETZ HWY

20

Nortons

Nye Books House

229

180

EDDYVILLE-BLODGETT

411

Nashville

NE EADS ST

Eddyville

Summit

20

H

S COAST HWY

Toledo

Elk City

ELLMAKER STATE PARK WAYSIDE

Burnt Woods

SOUTH BEACH STATE PARK

YAQUINA BAY

Toledo

20

7

Toledo State Airport

Blodgett

Newport Municipal Airport

44°33'30"
44°34'58"

RAND McNALLY

A   B   C   D   E

124°17'10"   124°07'27"   123°57'44"   123°48'01"   123°38'18"   123°28'34"

SEE **63** MAP

MAP 54

MAP 54

1:380,160
1 in. = 6 mi.

0   4   8
miles

N

SEE 44 MAP

SEE 53 MAP

SEE 55 MAP

SEE 64 MAP

RAND MCNALLY

WASHINGTON
CLACKAMAS
YAMHILL
POLK
MARION
LINN
BENTON

TILLAMOOK STATE FOREST
MCGUIRE RESERVOIR

King City · Tigard · Lake Oswego
Durham · Rivergrove
Tualatin · Norwood · Stafford
Sherwood
Wilsonville
MOLALLA RIVER ST PK
Canby
Barlow · Aurora
Donald
Hubbard
Lenhardt Airport
Woodburn
Gervais
Mt Angel
Monitor · Marquam
Silverton
Rockie · Four Corners

Cove Orchard
Yamhill
Carlton
Newberg
GEORGE FOX UNIV
Hoover-Minthorn Museum House
Sportsman Airpark
Dundee
CHAMPOEG STATE PARK
Pioneer Mothers Memorial Cabin Museum
Robert Newell House Museum
St Paul
Lafayette
McMINNVILLE
CHEMEKETA COMMUNITY COLL
LINFIELD COLLEGE MCMINNVILLE
Evergreen Aviation Museum
McMinnville Municipal Airport
Dayton
Eola Village
Whiteson
Unionvale
Bellevue
Sheridan
Willamina
Ballston
Amity
McCoy
Perrydale
SIUSLAW NATIONAL FOREST
WILLAMETTE MISSION STATE PARK
Brooks Society & Mus
Quinaby · Brooks
Labish Village
Queen of Angels Monastery
SILVER FALLS STATE PARK
Keizer
VOLCANOES STADIUM
Hayesville
CHEMEKETA COMMUNITY COLLEGE
Gilbert House Children's Museum
Oregon State Capitol
Jason Lee Manor
Four Corners
McNary Field
Salem
Pratum
Dallas
POLK COUNTY MUSEUM
Eola
Fir Villa
Rickreall
Falls City
Bridgeport
Independence State Airport
Paul Jensen Arctic Museum
WESTERN OREGON UNIV
Independence
Monmouth
Heritage Museum
Prewitt-Allen Archaeology Museum
CORBAN COLL
Aumsville
Turner
Sublimity
Shaw
Stayton
West Stayton
Pedee
Airlie
Buena Vista
Suver
Marion
North Santiam
West Scio
Scio
Kings Valley
Hoskins
Jefferson
Shelburn
Crabtree
Larwood
Adair Village
Lewisburg
MCDONALD STATE PARK
Millersburg
Draperville
Albany
Albany Regional Mus
Albany Municipal Airport
Corvallis
Wren
Riverside

MAP
55

MAP
55

1:380,160
1 in. = 6 mi.

0   4   8
miles

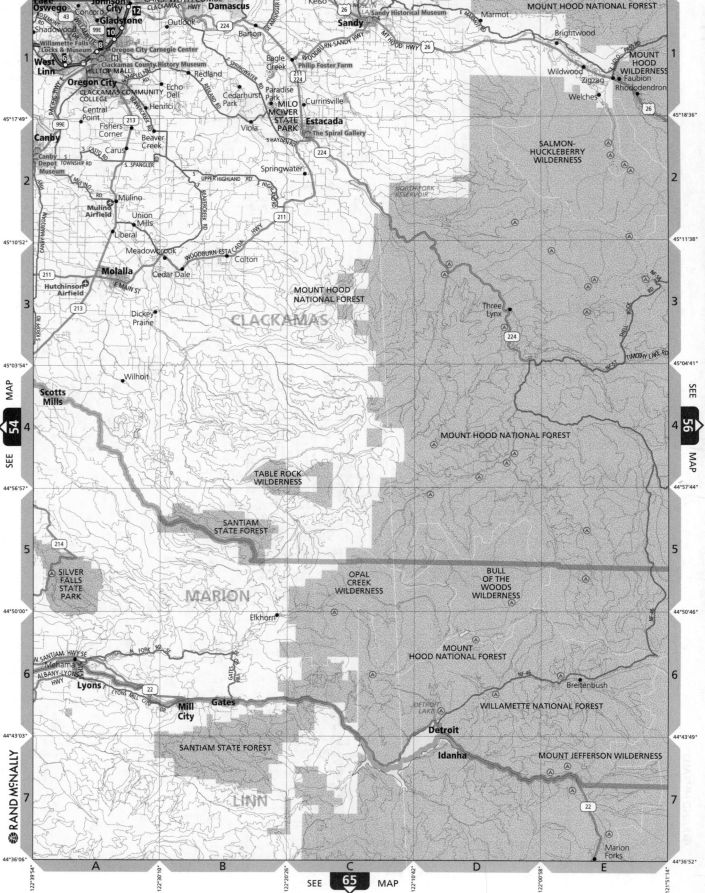

SEE 45 MAP

45°24'46"
45°25'33"

Lake Oswego
Johnson City
CAMP WITHYCOMBE
Damascus
Kelso
Sandy Historical Museum
MOUNT HOOD NATIONAL FOREST

Rosemont Rd
Concord
Shadowood
CLACKAMAS HWY
Barton
SCHIEFFELIN RD
Marmot
E MARMOT RD
Brightwood

Willamette Falls Locks & Museum
Gladstone
Outlook
224
Eagle Creek
WOODBURN-SANDY HWY
26
MT HOOD HWY
Wildwood
MOUNT HOOD WILDERNESS

West Linn
Oregon City Carnegie Center
Redland
S SPRINGWATER RD
Philip Foster Farm
211 224
26
Zigzag
Faubion
Rhododendron

Oregon City
Clackamas County History Museum
HILLTOP MALL
Echo Dell
Cedarhurst Park
Paradise Park
Currinsville
Welches

CLACKAMAS COMMUNITY COLLEGE
Henrici
MILO MCIVER STATE PARK
Estacada

Central Point
BEAVERCREEK RD
213
Viola
The Spiral Gallery
SALMON-HUCKLEBERRY WILDERNESS

Canby
Fishers Corner
Beaver Creek
S HAYDEN RD
224

Canby Depot Museum
TOWNSHIP RD
S CASTO RD
Carus
S SPANGLER RD
UPPER HIGHLAND RD
Springwater

S MILL INO RD
Mulino
BEAVERCREEK RD
S HIGHLAND RD
NORTH FORK RESERVOIR

Mulino Airfield
Union Mills
211
45°10'52"
45°11'38"

CANBY-MARQUAM HWY
Liberal
WOODBURN-ESTACADA HWY
Three Lynx

Meadowbrook
Colton
MOUNT HOOD NATIONAL FOREST
224

211
Hutchinson Airfield
Molalla
E MAIN ST
Cedar Dale
NF 57

213
S KROFF RD
Dickey Prairie
CLACKAMAS
TIMOTHY LAKE RD

45°03'54"
45°04'41"

Wilhoit

Scotts Mills
MOUNT HOOD NATIONAL FOREST

SEE 54 MAP
SEE 56 MAP

44°56'57"
44°57'44"

TABLE ROCK WILDERNESS

214
SANTIAM STATE FOREST

SILVER FALLS STATE PARK
MARION
OPAL CREEK WILDERNESS
BULL OF THE WOODS WILDERNESS

44°50'00"
44°50'46"

Elkhorn
NF 46

MOUNT HOOD NATIONAL FOREST

N SANTIAM HWY SE
N FORK RD SE
GATES HILL RD SE

Mehama
ALBANY-LYONS HWY
Breitenbush

Lyons
22
LYONS MILL CITY DR
Mill City
Gates
NF 46
DETROIT LAKE
WILLAMETTE NATIONAL FOREST

44°43'03"
44°43'49"

SANTIAM STATE FOREST
Detroit

Idanha
MOUNT JEFFERSON WILDERNESS

LINN
22

44°36'06"
44°36'52"

Marion Forks

A   B   C   D   E

122°39'54"   122°30'10"   122°20'26"   122°10'42"   122°00'58"   121°51'14"

SEE 65 MAP

RAND MCNALLY

MAP
56

MAP
56

1:380,160
1 in. = 6 mi.

0   4   8
miles

N

SEE **46** MAP

45°25'33"
45°25'58"

NF-18
NF-1810

1

MOUNT
HOOD
WILDERNESS

Mt Hood
Meadows
Ski Resort

HOOD HWY

BADGER
CREEK
WILDERNESS

DUFUR VALLEY RD

NF-44

197

TYGH RIDGE RD
OLD TYGH RD

Mount Hood
Skibowl- West

Government
Camp

35

MT HOOD HWY

HOOD RIVER

45°18'36"
45°19'01"

26

Mt Hood
Skibowl- East

2

CLACKAMAS

SALMON-
HUCKLEBERRY
WILDERNESS

MOUNT
HOOD
NATIONAL
FOREST

NF-43

NF-8

Tygh Valley

216

WAMIC MKT RD

ROCK CREEK DAM RD

Wamic

197

DESCHUTES RIVER RD

45°11'38"
45°12'03"

NF-58

TIMOTHY
LAKE

CLEAR
LAKE

26

S-507

NF-2651

Maupin

197

3

NF-57

NF-42

SKYLINE RD

Pine
Grove

216

Wapinitia

RESERVATION RD

WHITE
RIVER
FALLS
STATE PARK

45°04'41"
45°05'06"

MAP **55** SEE

MOUNT
HOOD NATIONAL FOREST

WASCO

3

SEE **57** MAP

4

26

WAPINITIA RD

44°57'44"
44°58'09"

SIMNASHO RD

9

Simnasho

3

5

WARM
SPRINGS
INDIAN
RESERVATION

Indian
Head
Casino

South
Junction

44°50'46"
44°51'11"

MARION

OLALLIE
LAKE

26

6

MOUNT
JEFFERSON
WILDERNESS

Gateway

WARM
Warm
Springs

WARM SPRINGS HWY

CROOKED RIVER
NATIONAL
GRASSLAND

NE FERNLN

44°43'49"
44°44'14"

26

FIR LN

NE FIR LN

NE CLARK DR

97

JEFFERSON

LAKE
SIMTUSTUS

NW ELK DR

7

LINN

Seekseequa

Madras City-
County
Airport

Madras

SW BELMONT LN

44°36'52"
44°37'17"

RAND MCNALLY

A   B   C   D   E

121°51'13"   121°41'29"   121°31'45"   121°22'00"   121°12'16"   121°02'32"

SEE **66** MAP

DESCHUTES
NATIONAL FOREST

MAP
57

MAP
57

1:380,160
1 in. = 6 mi.

0   4   8
miles

SEE 47 MAP

45°25'58"   45°26'02"

206

CENTER RIDGE RD

1   1

97

Grass Valley
RUTLEDGE   LN

WHITE
RIVER
FALLS
STATE PARK

RUTLEDGE LN

WASCO-HEPPNER HWY

45°19'01"   45°19'04"

216

HWY

BEND RD

DESCHUTES RIVER

SHERMAN   **GILLIAM**

2   2

SHERARS BRIDGE

BALL   LN

216   206

HORSESHOE

97

LIBERTY LN

45°12'03"   45°12'07"

Kent
DECKER RD

LOWER
JOHN DAY
WILDERNESS
STUDY AREA

3   3

NORTH POLE
RIDGE
WILDERNESS
STUDY AREA

45°05'06"   45°05'10"

97

MAP
56
SEE

4   4

SEE
MAP
58

197

WASCO

Shaniko
4TH ST

44°58'09"   44°58'12"

97

JOHN DAY
FOSSIL BEDS
NATIONAL
MONUMENT

218   218

SHANIKO-FOSSIL HWY

5   5

MAIN ST

Antelope

218

293

SPRING BASIN
WILDERNESS
STUDY
AREA

44°51'11"   44°51'15"

97

ANTELOPE HWY

Willowdale

6   6

JEFFERSON   **WHEELER**

97

44°44'14"   44°44'18"

Ashwood

CROOKED
RIVER
NATIONAL
GRASSLAND

7   7

JOHN DAY FOSSIL
BEDS NATIONAL
MONUMENT

44°37'17"   44°37'20"

A   B   C   D   E

121°02'31"   120°52'47"   120°43'03"   120°33'18"   120°23'34"   120°13'50"

SEE 67 MAP

MAP
58

1:380,160
1 in. = 6 mi.
0   4   8
miles

MAP
58

N

SEE **48** MAP

45°26'02"
45°25'44"

1

SOCIAL RIDGE LN

74
207

HEPPNER HWY   74

Heppner H

RHEA CREEK RD

45°19'04"
45°18'46"

JOHN DAY HWY

19

206

2

WILLOW CREEK RD

206
207

Condon
206

Condon State Airport

Ruggs

MORROW

207

45°12'07"
45°11'49"

GILLIAM

Hardman

3

SEE **57** MAP

45°05'10"
45°04'52"

Mayville

Lonerock

19

SEE **59** MAP

4

SEE

Fossil

SHANIKO-FOSSIL HWY

44°58'12"
44°57'55"

UMATILLA NATIONAL FOREST

207

5

19

Top

44°51'15"
44°50'57"

WILLOW ST

WHEELER

Spray

GRANT

Monument

19
207

19

KIMBERLY-LONG CREEK HWY

6

Service Creek

19

Kimberly

44°44'18"
44°44'00"

19

SERVICE CREEK-MITCHELL HWY

7

JOHN DAY FOSSIL BEDS NATIONAL MONUMENT

RAND McNALLY

207

44°37'20"
44°37'03"

120°13'49"   A   120°04'04"   B   119°54'20"   C   119°44'36"   D   119°34'52"   E   119°25'07"

SEE **68** MAP

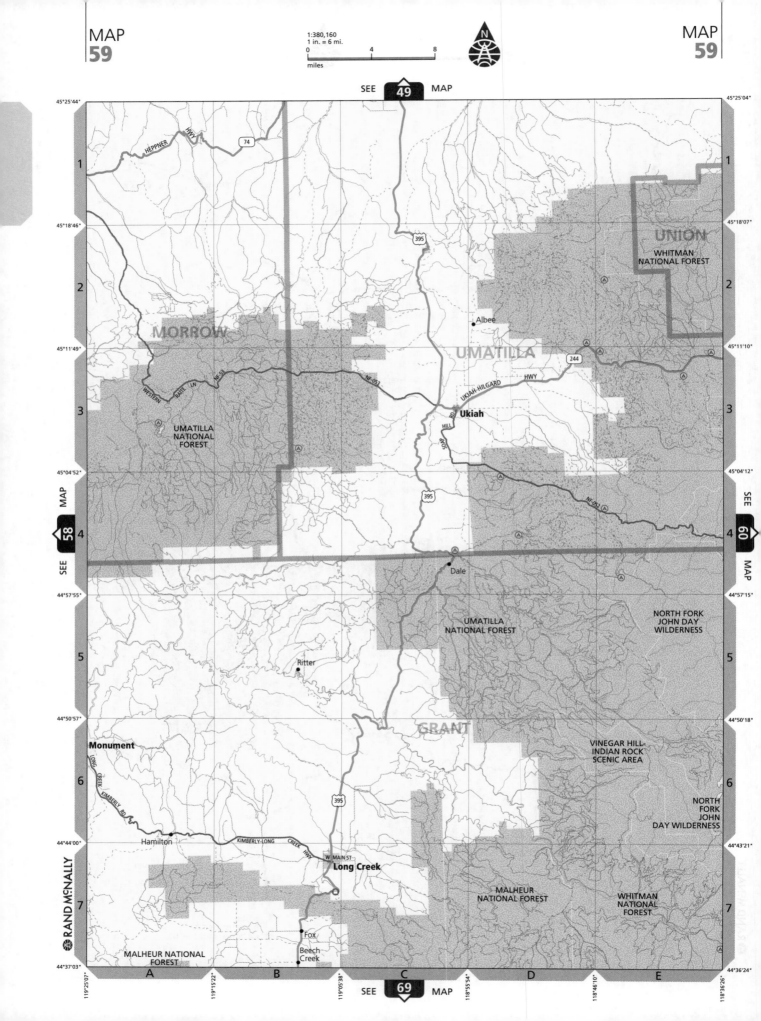

MAP
59

MAP
59

1:380,160
1 in. = 6 mi.
0   4   8
miles

N

SEE **49** MAP

45°25'44"   45°25'04"

HEPPNER HWY

74

395

45°18'46"   45°18'07"

UNION

WHITMAN
NATIONAL FOREST

MORROW

Albee

UMATILLA

244

NF-053   UKIAH-HILGARD   HWY

45°11'49"   45°11'10"

WESTERN ROUTE LN   NF-53

Ukiah

HILL

SOAP RD

UMATILLA
NATIONAL
FOREST

45°04'52"   45°04'12"

395   NF-052

SEE **58** MAP

SEE **60** MAP

44°57'55"   44°57'15"

Dale

NORTH FORK
JOHN DAY
WILDERNESS

UMATILLA
NATIONAL FOREST

Ritter

44°50'57"   44°50'18"

GRANT

VINEGAR HILL-
INDIAN ROCK
SCENIC AREA

Monument

LONG CREEK

KIMBERLY RD

395

NORTH
FORK
JOHN
DAY WILDERNESS

44°44'00"   44°43'21"

Hamilton   KIMBERLY-LONG   CREEK HWY

W MAIN ST

Long Creek

MALHEUR
NATIONAL FOREST

WHITMAN
NATIONAL
FOREST

Fox

Beech
Creek

MALHEUR NATIONAL
FOREST

44°37'03"   44°36'24"

A   B   C   D   E

119°25'07"   119°15'22"   119°05'38"   118°55'54"   118°46'10"   118°36'26"

SEE **69** MAP

MAP
60

MAP
60

1:380,160
1 in. = 6 mi.

0   4   8
miles

N

SEE **50** MAP

45°25'04"

UMATILLA

UMATILLA
NATIONAL
FOREST

WHITMAN
NATIONAL
FOREST

Alicel

WHITMAN
NATIONAL
FOREST

45°24'03"

84

248

1

Hilgard

256

84

Perry

257 259 30

261 Island City

237

Cove

MAIN ST

1

Think Link Discovery
Museum for Children

1ST ST

COVE HWY

244

EASTERN OREGON UNIVERSITY

ISLAND AVE

ADAMS AV

La Grande

La Grande-
Union County
Airport

265

45°18'07"

45°17'06"

268

203

2

Starkey

UNION

270

UNION-COVE HWY

Union County
Museum

2

244

84 273

Union

MEDICAL SPRINGS HWY

45°11'10"

NF-51

45°10'09"

278

237

WHITMAN
NATIONAL
FOREST

Telocaset

3

3

45°04'12"

THIEF VALLEY
RESERVOIR

45°03'12"

MAP
59
SEE

NF-052

283

285 **North Powder**

SEE
61
MAP

4

ANTHONY LAKES HWY

ELLIS RD

N. POWDER RIVER LN

84

4

NF-52

ANTHONY LAKE RD

Anthony
Lakes
Ski Area

30

UMATILLA
NATIONAL
FOREST

NF-73

44°57'15"

44°56'15"

Eastern
Oregon
Museum

NORTH FORK
JOHN DAY
WILDERNESS

NORTH FORK
JOHN DAY
WILDERNESS

Rock
Creek

Haines

5

GRANT

BAKER

LA GRANDE-BAKER HWY

CHANDLER LN

203

5

NF-73

POCAHONTAS RD

298

Baker City
Airport

44°50'18"

Wingville

Granite

Pocahontas

302

UMATILLA
NATIONAL
FOREST

Oregon Trail Regional Museum

10TH ST

304

6

24

WHITMAN
NATIONAL
FOREST

Baker City

6

GRANITE HILL HWY

Sumpter

7 84

VINEGAR HILL-INDIAN
ROCK SCENIC AREA

220

SUMPTER STAGE HWY

44°43'21"

44°42'20"

Greenhorn

PHILLIPS LAKE

7

7

7

NF 7

Whitney

WHITMAN
NATIONAL
FOREST

DOOLEY MOUNTAIN HWY

7

AUSTIN SPUR

44°36'24"

A   B   C   D   E

SEE **70** MAP

118°36'25"   118°26'41"   118°16'58"   118°07'14"   117°57'30"   117°47'46"

44°35'23"

MAP
61

MAP
61

1:380,160
1 in. = 6 mi.

0   4   8

miles

N

SEE **51** MAP

45°24'03"   45°22'40"

82

David & Lee Manuel Museum

Joseph

Joseph State Airport

Wallowa County Museum

Ferguson Ridge Ski Area

IMNAHA HWY

82

WALLOWA

WALLOWA LAKE

1

WALLOWA NATIONAL FOREST

Wallowa Lake Resort

WALLOWA NATIONAL FOREST

45°17'06"   45°15'43"

WALLOWA

2

EAGLE CAP WILDERNESS

WALLOWA NATIONAL FOREST

NF-39

45°10'09"   45°08'47"

203

UNION

HELLS CANYON NATIONAL RECREATION AREA

3

WHITMAN NATIONAL FOREST

EAGLE CAP WILDERNESS

45°03'12"   45°01'50"

MAP **60** SEE

Pondosa

Medical Springs

WHITMAN NATIONAL FOREST

HELLS CANYON NATIONAL RECREATION AREA

SEE **62** MAP

4

NF-39

44°56'15"   44°54'53"

HOUGHTON CREEK RD

Carson

Jimtown

203

Halfway

BAKER-COPPERFIELD   HWY

5

KEATING RD

RD

Pine

44°49'18"   44°47'56"

86

BAKER

New Bridge

86

SUNNYSLOPE LN

86

MAIN ST

Richland

6

BROWNLEE RESERVOIR

44°42'20"   44°40'59"

OLD OREGON TRAIL

313

Pleasant Valley

HWY

317

84

OREGON IDAHO

7

PAYETTE NATIONAL FOREST

44°35'23"   44°34'02"

WHITMAN NATIONAL FOREST

Durkee

327

117°44'45"   117°38'02"   117°28'18"   117°18'35"   117°08'52"   116°59'08"

A   B   C   D   E

SEE **71** MAP

MAP
62

MAP
62

1:380,160
1 in. = 6 mi.
0   4   8
miles

N

SEE [52] MAP

45°22'40"
45°20'56"

1

WALLOWA
NATIONAL
FOREST

WALLOWA

HELLS CANYON
WILDERNESS

OREGON
IDAHO

NEZ PERCE
NATIONAL
FOREST

Pollock

[95]

IDAHO

Pinehurst

45°15'43"
45°13'59"

2

HELLS CANYON
NATIONAL
RECREATION AREA

NF-39

HELLS
CANYON
RESERVOIR

HELLS
CANYON
WILDERNESS

PAYETTE
NATIONAL
FOREST

45°08'47"
45°07'03"

HELLS
CANYON
WILDERNESS

GOOSE
LAKE

3

Cuprum

PAYETTE
NATIONAL FOREST

Brundage
Mountain

HOMESTEAD
WILDERNESS
STUDY AREA

NF-39

Bear

[95]

45°01'50"
45°00'06"

Homestead

ADAMS

LOST VALLEY
RESERVOIR

MAP
[61]

NF-454

Tamarack

New
Meadows

Meadows

4

WHITMAN
NATIONAL
FOREST

[86]

OXBOW
RESERVOIR

Pine
Ridge

[95]

[55]

McCall

SEE

BAKER

[71]

44°54'53"
44°53'09"

SHEEP
MOUNTAIN
WILDERNESS
STUDY AREA

Starkey

5

BROWNLEE
RESERVOIR

Fruitvale

Brownlee

44°47'56"
44°46'13"

Council Municipal
Airport

Council

6

WASHINGTON

[95]

44°40'59"
44°39'16"

Goodrich

[71]

BOISE
NATIONAL
FOREST

7

Mesa

RAND MCNALLY

Cambridge
Cambridge Museum

[95]

INDIAN VALLEY RD

Indian
Valley

44°34'02"
44°32'19"

A   B   C   D   E

116°59'08"   116°49'24"   116°39'41"   116°29'58"   116°20'16"   116°10'33"

SEE [72] MAP

MAP
63

MAP
63

1:380,160
1 in. = 6 mi.

0   4   8

miles

N

SEE 53 MAP

44°33'29"   44°34'58"

Newport
Forfar
101
ONA BEACH
STATE PARK

Seal
Rock

Harlan

OREGON COAST HWY

44°26'32"   44°28'01"

Bayshore
ALSEA BAY
179
Eckman
Lake

DRIFT CREEK
WILDERNESS

LINCOLN

SIUSLAW
NATIONAL FOREST

34

SIUSLAW
NATIONAL FOREST

ALSEA HWY

Waldport
34

Tidewater

Wakonda
Beach

SIUSLAW
NATIONAL
FOREST

Little
Albany

34

Alsea

ISLIS ST

San
Marine

BENTON

44°19'36"   44°21'04"

SOUTH FORK RD

Yachats
Little Log
Church Museum

NEPTUNE STATE
PARK

44°12'39"   44°14'07"

CUMMINS CREEK
WILDERNESS

101

SIUSLAW
NATIONAL FOREST

PACIFIC OCEAN

ROCK CREEK
WILDERNESS

Horton

Blachly

SEE 64 MAP

CARL G WASHBURNE
MEMORIAL STATE PARK

Triangle
Lake

TRIANGLE
LAKE

OREGON ISLANDS
WILDERNESS

44°05'42"   44°07'10"

LANE

Deadwood

36

Greenleaf

MERCER
LAKE

Brickerville

Tide

Swisshome

Walton

VAUGHAN RD

Heceta
Beach

Mapleton

Heceta Junction

126

Tiernan

Florence
Dolly Wares
Doll Museum

Florence
Municipal
Airport

SPRUCE ST

126

43°58'45"   44°00'13"

Siuslaw
Pioneer
Museum

Three Rivers
Casino

Glenada

101

WOAHINK
LAKE

JESSIE M HONEYMAN
MEMORIAL STATE PARK

**Dunes
City**

OREGON DUNES
NATIONAL
RECREATION AREA

Westlake

Siltcoos

Alma

SILTCOOS
LAKE

Ada
Station

43°51'48"   43°53'16"

DOUGLAS

TAHKENITCH
LAKE

SIUSLAW
NATIONAL FOREST

SMITH RIVER

101

SMITH RIVER

43°44'52"   43°46'19"

A   B   C   D   E

SEE 74 MAP

124°13'59"   124°04'24"   123°54'49"   123°45'14"   123°35'39"   123°26'03"

MAP
64

MAP
64

1:380,160
1 in. = 6 mi.

0   4   8
miles

N

SEE MAP 54

44°34'58"
44°36'05"

177 178

Albany

Benton County Historical Museum

Philomath

RESER STADIUM

OSU STATE UNIVERSITY
BYP 34
CORVALLIS-LEBANON

SE PHILOMATH

CHAPEL DR

Corvallis

SW 53RD ST

S 53RD ST

ALSEA HWY

20

34

99W

20

Tangent

228

99E

HWY

Lebanon

W OAK ST

Lebanon Museum

Lebanon State Airport

S MAIN ST

S SANTIAM HWY

SPICER

SANTIAM HWY

LACOMB DR

Lacomb

KIWITZ RD

BREWSTER RD

Crowfoot

Waterloo

1

BELLINGER SCALE RD

BERLIN RD

N 1ST ST

Corvallis Municipal Airport

99W

HWY

BELLFOUNTAIN

DECKER RD

GREENBERRY RD

Greenberry

PACIFIC HWY

FAYETTEVILLE DR

Shedd

BOSTON

PLAINVIEW DR

SAND

ROCK HILL DR

Sodaville

20

44°28'01"
44°29'08"

BENTON

Peoria

ALBANY-JUNCTION

99E

LINN

Brownsville

Linn County Historical Museum

228

HALSEY-SWEET HOME HWY

Crawfordsville

East Linn Museum

N SIDE DR

MAIN ST

20

KOSTER LAKE

Sweet Home

2

Bellfountain

AMERICAN DR

Halsey

216

44°21'04"
44°22'11"

Alpine

KYE RD

99E

GAP RD

Holley

BROWN CREEK RD

Monroe

99W

DIAMOND HILL DR

Harrisburg

209

MARCOLA RD

3

ALPINE RD

PACIFIC HWY W

5

44°14'07"
44°15'14"

SEE MAP 63

Junction City

6TH AV

BIRCH

COBURG RD

RIVER RD

Cheshire

HWY

Franklin

Marcola

99

MAPLETON-JUNCTION

4

Alvadore

Eugene Airport-Mahlon Sweet Field

Oregon Air & Space Museum

BEACON DR W

CLEAR LAKE RD

COBURG

PEARL ST

199

Mohawk

Leaburg

MCKENZIE HWY

36

44°07'10"
44°08'17"

Noti

Elmira

Applegate Pioneer Museum

FERN RIDGE LAKE

99

IRVING DR

IRVING RD

7

BARGER

BELTLINE RD

180 181 182 183

MCKENZIE

HILL RD

YOLANDA AV

Walterville

126

MCKENZIE RIVER

5

FLORENCE-EUGENE HWY

126

Veneta

GREEN HILL RD

ROYAL AV

ROOSEVELT BLVD

195

194

Jordan Schnitzer Museum of Art

The Science Factory Children's Museum and Planetarium

MCKENZIE

BUS 126

126

Autzen Stadium

Springfield

MAIN ST

5TH ST

44°00'13"
44°01'19"

VAUGHN RD

Vaughn

W 11TH AV

BAILEY HILL RD

Eugene

184

185

186

187

188

Lane County Historical Museum

HAWKINS LN

18TH AV

Museum

40TH AV

AGATE

S A ST

Glenw

189

HYWY 126

MAIN ST

S 57TH ST

Crow

LANE

Lane Community College

DILLARD RD

188

Goshen

Jasper

FALL CREEK LAKE

6

5

Pleasant Hill

Fall Creek

DEXTER LAKE

Elijah Bristow State Park

Lowell

58

186

99

Creswell

182

Dexter

58

LOOKOUT POINT LAKE

43°53'16"
43°54'22"

Walker

GOSHEN-DIVIDE HWY

WILLAMETTE HWY

7

Lorane

COTTAGE GROVE-LORANE RD

Saginaw

176

WILLAMETTE NATIONAL FOREST

SIUSLAW RIVER

Cottage Grove Museum

9TH ST

Cottage Grove State Airport

DORENA LAKE

RAND McNALLY

SMITH RIVER

Cottage Grove

UMPQUA NATIONAL FOREST

43°46'19"
43°47'25"

SEE MAP 75

A   B   C   D   E

123°26'03"   123°16'27"   123°06'52"   122°57'16"   122°47'41"   122°38'05"

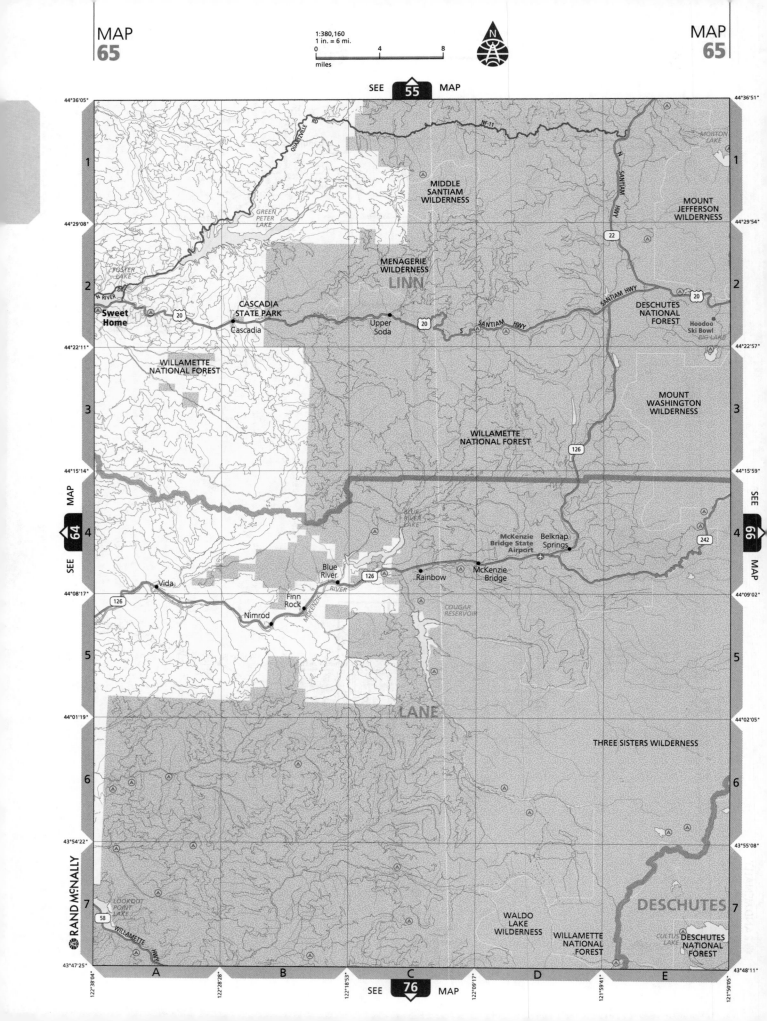

MAP
65

MAP
65

1:380,160
1 in. = 6 mi.

0   4   8

miles

N

SEE 55 MAP

44°36'05"
44°36'51"

1

MORTON
LAKE

MIDDLE
SANTIAM
WILDERNESS

NF-11

N SANTIAM HWY

MOUNT
JEFFERSON
WILDERNESS

44°29'08"
44°29'54"

22

MENAGERIE
WILDERNESS

LINN

2

QUARTZVILLE RD

GREEN
PETER
LAKE

FOSTER
LAKE

N RIVER DR

Sweet
Home

20

CASCADIA
STATE PARK

Cascadia

Upper
Soda

20

S SANTIAM HWY

SANTIAM HWY

DESCHUTES
NATIONAL
FOREST

20

Hoodoo
Ski Bowl
BIG LAKE

44°22'11"
44°22'57"

WILLAMETTE
NATIONAL FOREST

3

MOUNT
WASHINGTON
WILDERNESS

WILLAMETTE
NATIONAL FOREST

126

44°15'14"
44°15'59"

MAP
64
SEE

BLUE
RIVER
LAKE

McKenzie
Bridge State
Airport

Belknap
Springs

4

SEE
66
MAP

242

Vida

Blue
River

126

Rainbow

McKenzie
Bridge

44°08'17"
44°09'02"

126

Finn
Rock

Nimrod

MCKENZIE RIVER

COUGAR
RESERVOIR

5

LANE

44°01'19"
44°02'05"

THREE SISTERS WILDERNESS

6

7

LOOKOUT
POINT
LAKE

58

WILLAMETTE HWY

DESCHUTES

WALDO
LAKE
WILDERNESS

WILLAMETTE
NATIONAL
FOREST

CULTUS
LAKE

DESCHUTES
NATIONAL
FOREST

43°54'22"
43°55'08"

43°47'25"
43°48'11"

RAND M?NALLY

122°38'04"
A
122°28'28"
B
122°18'53"
C
122°09'17"
D
121°59'41"
E
121°50'05"

SEE 76 MAP

MAP
66

MAP
66

1:380,160
1 in. = 6 mi.
0   4   8
miles

N

SEE 56 MAP

44°36'51"

LINN
MORTON LAKE
MOUNT JEFFERSON WILDERNESS
WARM SPRINGS INDIAN RESERVATION
WARM SPRINGS INDIAN RESERVATION
CROOKED RIVER NATIONAL GRASSLAND
LAKE SIMTUSTUS
Madras

LAKE BILLY CHINOOK
THE COVE PALISADES STATE PARK
Metolius
DOVER LN
SW GEM LN
97
SW HWY

1   1

44°29'54"   44°30'19"

64
SW GRAHAM RD
SW FEATHER LN
Culver
SW IRIS LN
HAYSTACK RESERVOIR
26

JEFFERSON
SW HAYSTACK DR
SE LAUREL LN

Camp Sherman

2   2

SANTIAM HWY
20
SUTTLE LAKE
Crooked River Ranch
CROOKED RIVER NATIONAL GRASSLAND

44°22'57"   44°23'22"

WILLAMETTE NATIONAL FOREST
Black Butte Ranch
GREEN RIDGE RD
INDIAN FORD RD
Camp Polk
Tetherow Crossing
Terrebonne
NE SMITH ROCK WY
NW ODEM AV
NW COYNER AV
NE O'NEIL
NE O'NEIL HWY
NORTH CANAL

MOUNT WASHINGTON WILDERNESS
MCKENZIE HWY
242
CAMP POLK RD
2610
126
MCKENZIE HWY
126
HOLMES RD
BUCKHORN RD
97
NW 19TH ST

3   3

Sisters
20
Redmond Airport-Roberts Field
126
OCHOCO HWY

44°15'59"   44°16'24"

242
WILLAMETTE NATIONAL FOREST
FALLS RD
CLINE
SW HELMHOLTZ
NW 61ST
SW 27TH ST
Redmond
SE O'NEIL HWY

SEE 65 MAP   SEE 67 MAP

4   4

INNES MARKET RD
SW 61ST ST
REDMOND HWY
SW POWELL

44°09'02"   44°09'27"

LANE
TUMALO RESERVOIR
Tumalo
TUMALO RD
20
97
Deschutes Junction
NORTH CANAL
POWELL BUTTE HWY

5   5

COOLEY RD
CASCADE VILLAGE SHOPPING CENTER
Bend Municipal Airport
ALFALFA MARKET RD
DESCHUTES
189 **190**
CENTRAL OREGON COMMUNITY COLLEGE
MALL WAGNER MALL
HAMBY RD
NEFF RD
BYRAM RD
STENKAMP RD

THREE SISTERS WILDERNESS
The Sage House
SHOPS AT THE OLD MILL DISTRICT
Vince Genna Stadium
BEAR CREEK
BEN BARR RD
GOSNEY RD
DOODS RD

Bend
191 **192**
WARD RD
CENTRAL OREGON

44°02'05"   44°02'30"

46
DESCHUTES NATIONAL FOREST
46
SW BROOKSWOOD
BAKER RD
97
KNOTT RD
BILLADEAU RD
RICKARD RD
OLD MARKET RD
20
BADLANDS WILDERNESS STUDY AREA

Elk Lake
Mt Bachelor Ski Area
SPARKS LAKE
ELK LAKE
HOSMER LAKE
High Desert Museum
NF-18
NF-1815
CENTRAL OREGON

6   6

LAVA LAKE

43°55'08"   43°55'32"

NF-41
COTTONWOOD
AIRPORT RD
DESCHUTES NATIONAL FOREST

NF-45
Sunriver
SUNRIVER VILLAGE MALL

CULTUS LAKE
46
Sunriver Airport
40
CENTURY DR
97
NEWBERRY NATIONAL VOLCANIC MONUMENT

7   7

CRANE PRAIRIE RESERVOIR
42
LAVA CAST FOREST

43°48'11"   43°48'35"

RAND McNALLY

A   B   C   D   E

SEE 77 MAP

121°50'05"   121°40'28"   121°30'53"   121°21'16"   121°11'41"   121°02'04"

MAP
66

MAP
67

MAP
67

1:380,160
1 in. = 6 mi.

0　　　　　4　　　　　8
miles

N

SEE **57** MAP

44°37'16"　　　　　　　　　　　　　　　　　　　　　　　　　44°37'20"

JEFFERSON

WHEELER

CROOKED
RIVER
NATIONAL
GRASSLAND

26

OCHOCO
HWY

44°30'19"　　　　　　　　　　　　　　　　　　　　　　　　44°30'22"

OCHOCO
NATIONAL FOREST

MILL
CREEK
WILDERNESS

BRIDGE CREEK
WILDERNESS

1

2

26

44°23'22"　　　　　　　　　　　　　　　　　　　　　　　　44°23'25"

NW
MADRAS-PRINEVILLE
HWY

N LAMONTA RD

MCKAY RD

OCHOCO
NATIONAL
FOREST

370　NW　O'NEIL　HWY

Prineville
H Bowman Museum

OCHOCO
SATE PARK

26

3

E 3RD ST

Prineville
Airport

SE PAUINA HWY

OCHOCO
RESERVOIR

CROOK

44°16'24"　　　　　　　　　　　　　　　　　　　　　　　　44°16'28"

Powell
Butte

126

380

SEE **66** MAP

4

27

44°09'27"　　　　　　　　　　　　　　　　　　　　　　　　44°09'31"

JOHNSON-RANCH-RD

PRINEVILLE
RESERVOIR

PRINEVILLE
RESERVOIR
STATE
PARK

Post

380

SEE **68** MAP

Alfalfa

SW RESERVOIR RD　SE RESERVOIR RD

5

44°02'30"　　　　　　　　　　　　　　　　　　　　　　　　44°02'33"

OCHOCO
NATIONAL
FOREST

ANTELOPE
FLAT
RESERVOIR

BADLANDS
WILDERNESS STUDY
AREA

6

HWY

27

43°55'32"　　　　　　　　　　　　　　　　　　　　　　　　43°55'36"

CROOKED RIVER HWY

7

20

DESCHUTES

CENTRAL OREGON HWY 20

Brothers

DESCHUTES
NATIONAL FOREST

43°48'35"　　　　　　　　　　　　　　　　　　　　　　　　43°48'39"

A　　　　　B　　　　　C　　　　　D　　　　　E

121°02'04"　120°52'27"　　120°42'52"　　120°33'15"　120°23'39"　120°14'03"

SEE **78** MAP

MAP
68

MAP
68

1:380,160
1 in. = 6 mi.

0   4   8
miles

N

SEE **58** MAP

44°37'20"
44°37'02"

207

26

Mitchell

OCHOCO HWY

1

19

JOHN DAY
FOSSIL BEDS
NATIONAL
MONUMENT

OCHOCO
NATIONAL
FOREST

44°30'22"
44°30'05"

BRIDGE CREEK
WILDERNESS

26

26

WHEELER

JOHN DAY HWY

Dayville

26

2

ALDRICH
MOUNTAIN
WILDERNESS
STUDY AREA

44°23'25"
44°23'07"

OCHOCO
NATIONAL
FOREST

MALHEUR
NATIONAL
FOREST

3

BLACK
CANYON
WILDERNESS

GRANT

44°16'28"
44°16'10"

MAP **67** SEE

SEE **69** MAP

4

NORTH FORK
WILDERNESS
STUDY
AREA

MERWIN
RESERVOIR
NUMBER 3

MALHEUR
NATIONAL FOREST

44°09'31"
44°09'13"

380

Paulina

380

SE PAULINA HWY

SE PAULINA-SUPLEE RD

63

63

5

CROOK

44°02'33"
44°02'16"

OCHOCO
NATIONAL
FOREST

6

SOUTH FORK
WILDERNESS
STUDY
AREA

SAND
HOLLOW
WILDERNESS
STUDY AREA

MALHEUR
NATIONAL
FOREST

43°55'36"
43°55'18"

GERRY
MOUNTAIN
WILDERNESS
STUDY AREA

OCHOCO
NATIONAL FOREST

HARNEY

7

RAND McNALLY

43°48'39"
43°48'21"

A   B   C   D   E

120°14'02"   120°04'26"   119°54'50"   119°45'14"   119°35'38"   119°26'02"

SEE **79** MAP

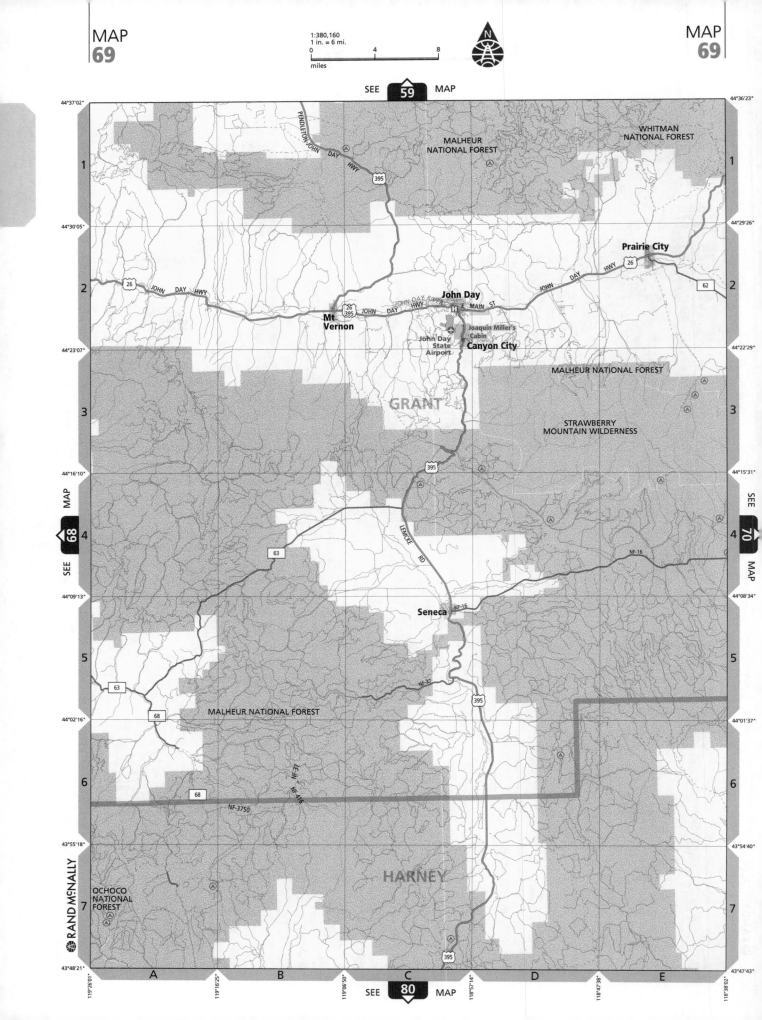

MAP
70

MAP
70

1:380,160
1 in. = 6 mi.

0   4   8

miles

N

SEE **60** MAP

44°36'23"

Austin
Bates

AUSTIN SPUR

WHITMAN
NATIONAL
FOREST

WHITMAN
NATIONAL
FOREST

26

26

245

WHITMAN
NATIONAL
FOREST

UNITY
RESERVOIR

44°29'26"

245 Hereford

44°28'26"

BAKER

Unity

N 1ST AV

26

44°22'29"

62

NF-11

NF-16

Ironside

26

44°21'29"

MONUMENT
ROCK
WILDERNESS

3

STRAWBERRY
MOUNTAIN
WILDERNESS

44°15'31"

SEE **69** MAP

MALHEUR
NATIONAL
FOREST

NF-16

62

44°14'31"

SEE **71** MAP

NF-16

MALHEUR

4

NF-16

GRANT

44°08'34"

BEAVER DAM
CREEK WILDERNESS
STUDY
AREA

44°07'35"

5

44°01'37"

CASTLE
ROCK
WILDERNESS
STUDY AREA

44°00'37"

MALHEUR
RIVER-BLUEBUCKET
CREEK WILDERNESS
STUDY AREA

BEULAH
RESERVOIR

6

HARNEY

43°54'40"

43°53'40"

7

Drewsey

CENTRAL OREGON HWY
GOLD CREEK
WILDERNESS STUDY
AREA

20

43°47'43"

A   118°28'25"   B   118°18'50"   C   118°09'14"   D   117°59'39"   E   117°50'03"

118°38'01"

43°46'44"

SEE **81** MAP

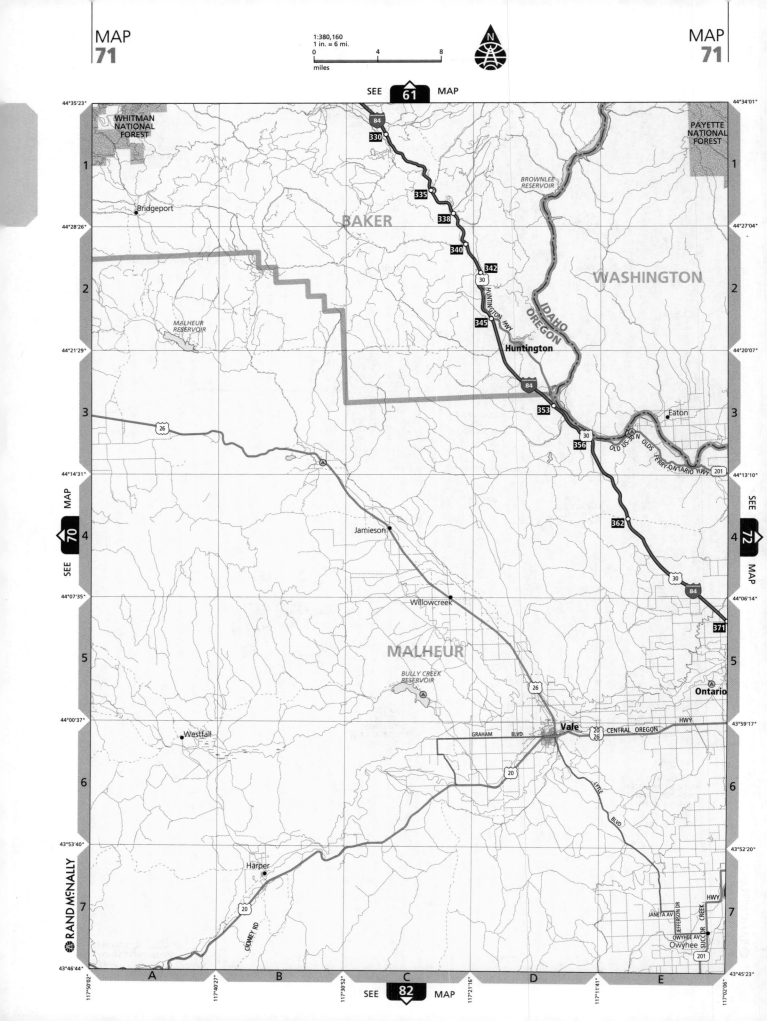

MAP
71

MAP
71

1:380,160
1 in. = 6 mi.

0   4   8
miles

N

SEE 61 MAP

WHITMAN
NATIONAL
FOREST

PAYETTE
NATIONAL
FOREST

84
330

335

338

340

342

30

345

Huntington

84

353

30
356

30
201

362

30
84

371

BAKER

WASHINGTON

BROWNLEE
RESERVOIR

IDAHO
OREGON

HUNTINGTON HWY

OLD US-30 N   OLDS FERRY-ONTARIO HWY

Eaton

Bridgeport

MALHEUR
RESERVOIR

26

Jamieson

Willowcreek

MALHEUR

BULLY CREEK
RESERVOIR

26

Ontario

Westfall

Vale

GRAHAM   BLVD

20
26   CENTRAL OREGON

HWY

20

LYTLE

BLVD

Harper

20

CROWLEY RD

JANETA AV

SUCCOR CREEK

HWY

JEFFERSON DR

OWYHEE AV

Owyhee

201

SEE 70 MAP

SEE 72 MAP

SEE 82 MAP

44°35'23"   44°34'01"
44°28'26"   44°27'04"
44°21'29"   44°20'07"
44°14'31"   44°13'10"
44°07'35"   44°06'14"
44°00'37"   43°59'17"
43°53'40"   43°52'20"
43°46'44"   43°45'23"

117°50'02"   117°40'27"   117°30'52"   117°21'16"   117°11'41"   117°02'06"

A   B   C   D   E

1   2   3   4   5   6   7

MAP
72

MAP
72

1:380,160
1 in. = 6 mi.

0   4   8
miles

N

SEE 62 MAP

44°34'01"

PAYETTE
NATIONAL
FOREST

95

BEN ROSS
RESERVOIR

PAYETTE
NATIONAL
FOREST

ADAMS

1

44°32'18"

1

Lee Williams
Memorial
Airport
Midvale

44°27'04"

MANN CREEK
RESERVOIR

CRANE CREEK
RESERVOIR

BOISE
NATIONAL
FOREST

2

44°25'22"

2

WASHINGTON

RILEY BUTTE RD

INDIAN VALLEY RD

SAGE HEN
RESERVOIR

44°20'07"

95

44°18'25"

3

3

Weiser
H

PADDOCK
VALLEY
RESERVOIR

Ola

44°13'10"

Annex

SPUR
95

Weiser Municipal
Airport

44°11'28"

201

95

MAP
71

SEE

MALHEUR

4

BOISE

44°06'14"

PAYETTE

44°04'32"

4

371

52

Payette Municipal
Airport

2ND AV S

84

Payette

OLDS

FERRY-ONTARIO HWY

Washoe

374

BUS
30

95

5

GEM

43°57'35"

5

201

Ontario

B76

Fruitland

Four Rivers Cultural Center
Museum

Sweet

Ontario
Municipal
Airport

TREASURE
VALLEY

COMMUNITY COLLEGE

Ramsey

52

Cairo

30
95

43°59'17"

OREGON

IDAHO

30

New
Plymouth

52

BLACK
CANYON
RESERVOIR

3

6

CENTRAL

20
26

95

30

52

Letha

Northside

52

52

6

43°57'35"

9

84

W HIGHWAY 52

Emmett

H

Nyssa

BOWMAN RD

43°52'20"

20
26

13

Emmett
Municipal
Airport

55

Apple
Valley

16

Fort Boise
Original Site

LITTLE FREEZEOUT RD

17

ADA

HORSESHOE BEND RD

7

RAND McNALLY

ROSSORN RD

EAST IDL DR

SCOTT DR

PARMA RD

Parma

Parma
Airport

Fort Boise
Replica

CANYON

CANAL C-LINE RD

95

MARKET RD

CONWAY RD

CREEK HOLLOW

CONWAY

HIGHWAY GULCH

30

C-LINE CANAL

WILLOW CREEK

EDNA LN

16

EMMETT HWY

7

43°45'23"

117°02'05"

A

116°52'30"

B

116°42'56"

C

SEE 83 MAP

116°33'21"

D

116°23'46"

E

116°14'12"

43°43'42"

MAP
73

1:380,160
1 in. = 6 mi.

0   4   8
miles

N

MAP
73

43°43'03"

43°44'51"

1

43°36'06"

43°37'54"

2

43°29'10"

43°30'58"

PACIFIC OCEAN

OREGON DUNES
NATIONAL
RECREATION
AREA

Hauser

3

Shorewood

43°22'13"

Southwest
Oregon
Regional
Airport

**North
Bend**

101

VIRGINIA

Artist Loft Gallery

SOUTHWESTERN OREGON COMMUNITY
COL

193 1

43°24'01"

COOS
BAY

ELROD AV

Coos Art
Museum

**Coos
Bay**

Barview

LIBBY

SEE
74
MAP

4

Charleston

Libby

43°15'17"

SHORE
ACRES
STATE
PARK

SOUTH
SLOUGH

101

43°17'04"

HWY

42

Green
Acres

5

43°08'20"

BULLARDS BEACH
STATE PARK

101

COOS

Coquille

42S

43°10'08"

Bullards

Prosper

Riverton

OREGON ISLANDS
WILDERNESS

Bandon

42S

Winterville

COQUILLE-BANDON

6

Coquille River
Museum
**Bandon State
Airport**

BEACH LOOP RD

ELK RD

FAT

43°01'24"

BANDON
STATE
PARK

43°03'11"

7

Fourmile

101

42°54'28"

42°56'15"

A   B   C   D   E

124°58'06"   124°48'40"   124°39'14"   124°29'47"   124°20'20"   124°10'53"

SEE 85 MAP

CURRY

MAP
74

1:380,160
1 in. = 6 mi.

0   4   8
miles

N

MAP
74

SEE 63 MAP

43°44'51"

43°46'18"

1

OREGON DUNES
NATIONAL
RECREATION
AREA

Gardiner

East
Gardiner

SIUSLAW
NATIONAL FOREST

101

FIR AV

Winchester
Bay

Reedsport

Green
Acres

UMPQUA
LIGHTHOUSE
STATE
PARK

CLEAR
LAKE

Scottsburg

38

A ST

UMPQUA HWY

Elkton

38

1

43°37'54"

43°39'21"

OREGON DUNES
NATIONAL RECREATION
AREA

WILLIAM M TUGMAN
STATE PARK

EEL
LAKE

ELLIOTT
STATE FOREST

LOON
LAKE

DOUGLAS

Lakeside

TEN MILE
LAKE

NORTH TEN
MILE LAKE

OREGON COAST HWY

101

UMPQUA RIVER

ELKTON-SUTHERLIN HWY

2

2

43°30'58"

Saunders Lake

43°32'25"

138

3

HAYNES
INLET

Glasgow

Allegany

33

43°24'01"

94
MAP

Cooston

43°25'28"

Coos Bay

D ST

COOS RIVER

Dellwood

Millwood

TYEE RD

3

SEE
73
MAP

101

Millington

Umpqua

6

4

4

43°17'04"

COOS-SUMNER RD

Sumner

43°18'31"

SEE
75
MAP

COOS

Melrose

13

5

Fairview

McKinley

13B

5

FAIRVIEW-MCKINLEY RD

LONE PINE LN

51

COUNTY ROAD

COQUILLE-FAIRVIEW RD

43°10'08"

Coquille

42

MARIA C JACKSON
STATE PARK

COUNTY ROAD 5B

Lookingglass

43°11'34"

COOS BAY-ROSEBURG HWY

Sitkum

COUNTY ROAD 5D

Norway

Gravelford

RESTON RD

Winston

107

6

Arago

FORK LN

42

99

6

Arago HWY

SPRUCE ST

8TH ST

Coos County
Logging Museum

Tenmile

Dillard

DILLARD HWY

43°03'11"

Myrtle Point

43°04'37"

Broadbent

Bridge

Camas
Valley

BEN IRVING
RESERVOIR

7

7

ALBERT H POWERS
STATE PARK

Remote

42

Gaylord

42°56'14"

42°57'41"

A   B   C   D   E

124°10'53"   124°01'26"   123°51'59"   123°42'31"   123°33'04"   123°23'37"

SEE 86 MAP

RAND MᶜNALLY

MAP 75

MAP 75

1:380,160
1 in. = 6 mi.

0   4   8
miles

N

SEE 64 MAP

WILLAMETTE NATIONAL FOREST

43°46'18"
43°47'25"

SMITH RIVER

COUNTY ROAD 116

Cottage Grove
Latham   172
170
LATHAM RD

Walden

DORENA LAKE

PACIFIC HWY

Curtin   163
Anlauf   162
161
160
159

LANE

COTTAGE GROVE LAKE

LONDON RD

Dorena

Culp Creek

Disston

1

43°39'21"
43°40'27"

38 99
38   UMPQUA HWY
Drain

EAGLE VALLEY RD

154   8
8A

SHOESTRING RD

ELKHEAD RD

7

Yoncalla
99

150

2

43°32'25"
43°33'31"

148

146
5

50   DRIVER VALLEY RD

142

140   Old Town   22

Oakland
Oakland Museum

138   N 1ST ST
STEARNS LN

Fair Oaks

19

Nonpareil

3

43°25'28"
43°26'34"

SEE 74 MAP

SUTHERLIN-UMPQUA RD

Sutherlin Municipal Airport
136
135   Sutherlin

OAKLAND-SHADY HWY

Wilbur

ELKTON-SUTHERLIN HWY

4

43°18'31"
43°19'37"

SEE 76 MAP

Steamboat
138

DEL RIO RD

UMPQUA COMMUNITY COLLEGE
129
Winchester

NORTH BANK RD

NORTH UMPQUA RIVER

Glide

Idleyld Park

North Umpqua Village

DOUGLAS

167
99
127
Roseburg Municipal Airport
Newton Creek
H
195   196

138

17

Peel

5

43°11'34"
43°12'40"

123   42 99   Roseburg

Dixonville

BUCKHORN RD

121

Green
120
119
42 99

Glengary

Winston

UMPQUA NATIONAL FOREST

6

43°04'37"
43°05'43"

DILLARD
113

SOUTH UMPQUA HWY

112
PACIFIC HWY

Myrtle Creek

108
Myrtle Creek Municipal Airport
106   99

5

Tri-City

Days Creek

TILLER TRAIL HWY

7

RAND MCNALLY

103
Riddle   RIDDLE BYP

42°57'41"
42°58'46"

123°23'36"   123°14'09"   123°04'41"   122°55'14"   122°45'46"   122°36'18"

A   B   C   D   E

SEE 87 MAP

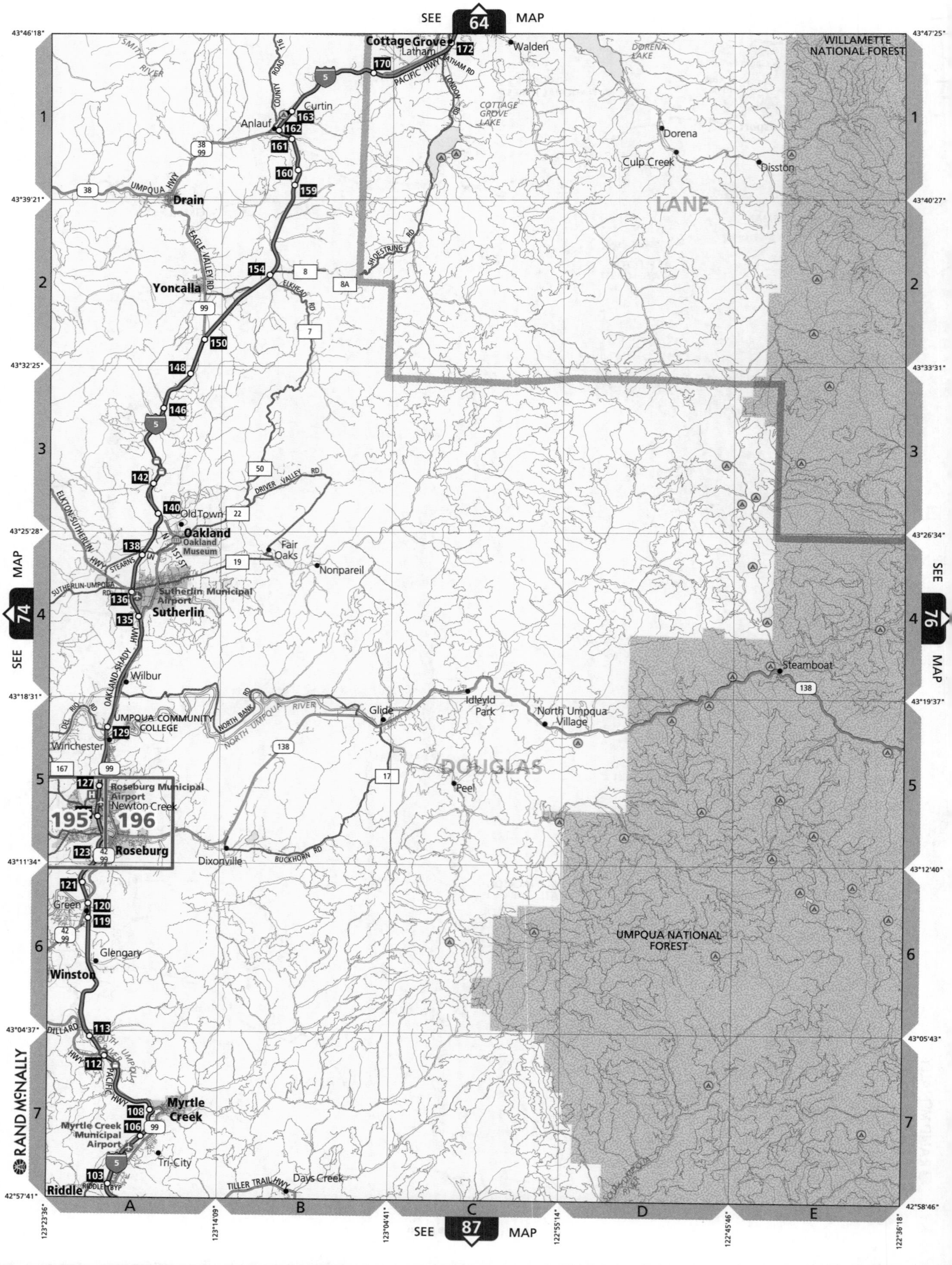

MAP
76

1:380,160
1 in. = 6 mi.

0   4   8

miles

N

MAP
76

SEE 65 MAP

43°47'25"

THREE SISTERS
WILDERNESS

WALDO
LAKE
WILDERNESS

CRANE
PRAIRIE
RESERVOIR

43°48'10"

Oakridge
State
Airport

Westfir

58

Oakridge

MIDDLE FORK
WILLAMETTE RIVER

WALDO
LAKE

DESCHUTES

1

HILLS
CREEK LAKE

LANE

43°40'27"

43°41'13"

WILLAMETTE
NATIONAL
FOREST

2

58

Willamette
Pass Ski
Area

DESCHUTES
NATIONAL FOREST

DAVIS
LAKE

2

Cascade
Summit

O'DELL
LAKE

43°33'31"

43°34'16"

DIAMOND PEAK
WILDERNESS

Crescent
Lake

MIDDLE FORK
WILLAMETTE RIV

3

CRESCENT
LAKE

3

SUMMIT
LAKE

43°26'34"

58

OREGON
CASCADES
RECREATION
AREA

KLAMATH

MAP

75

BOULDER
CREEK
WILDERNESS

4

SEE

4

43°19'37"

43°20'22"

LEMOLO
LAKE

MOUNT
THIELSEN
WILDERNESS

138

NORTH UMPQUA RIVER

Toketee
Falls

UMPQUA RIVER

5

UMPQUA NATIONAL FOREST

N UMPQUA HWY

MILLER
LAKE

5

138

DOUGLAS

43°12'40"

43°13'25"

Diamond
Lake

6

DIAMOND
LAKE

MOUNT
THIELSEN
WILDERNESS

WINEMA
NATIONAL
FOREST

6

ROGUE-
UMPQUA
DIVIDE
WILDERNESS

230

138

43°05'43"

43°06'28"

DIAMOND LAKE HWY

138

ROGUE RIVER

232

Diamond Lake
Junction

THE DALLES-CALIFORNIA HWY

7

ROGUE
RIVER
NATIONAL
FOREST

CRATER LAKE
NATIONAL PARK

NORTH ENTRANCE RD

7

230

97

JACKSON

42°58'46"

42°59'31"

A   B   C   D   E

122°36'18"   122°26'50"   122°17'22"   122°07'54"   121°58'27"   121°48'59"

MAP
77
SEE

MAP
77

MAP
77

1:380,160
1 in. = 6 mi.

0   4   8

miles

N

SEE **66** MAP

43°48'10"
43°48'35"

LAVE CAST FOREST

CRANE PRAIRIE RESERVOIR

1

42

S CENTURY DR

BURGESS RD

42

97

HUNTINGTON RD

43

DESCHUTES

PAULINA LAKE

EAST LAKE

43°41'13"
43°41'37"

WICKIUP RESERVOIR

La Pine

DESCHUTES RIVER

NEWBERRY NATIONAL VOLCANIC MONUMENT

2

DAVIS LAKE

THE DALLES-CALIFORNIA HWY

43°34'16"
43°34'40"

97

31

DESCHUTES NATIONAL FOREST

DESCHUTES NATIONAL FOREST

3

Gilchrist

CRESCENT CUT OFF RD

Crescent Airport

Crescent

43°27'19"
43°27'43"

SEE **76** MAP

SEE **78** MAP

FREMONT HWY

4

58

97

31

FORT ROCK STATE PARK

WILLAMETTE HWY

COUNTY ROAD 5-10

43°20'22"
43°20'46"

KLAMATH

LAKE

Fort Rock

5

43°13'25"
43°13'49"

Chemult

97

WINEMA NATIONAL FOREST

FREMONT NATIONAL FOREST

FREMONT HWY

6

Beaver Marsh

COUNTY ROAD 5-10

31

43°06'28"
43°06'52"

Silver Lake

EAST BAY RD

7

SILVER

LAKE RD

NF-28

42°59'31"
42°59'55"

A   B   C   D   E

121°48'58"
121°39'30"
121°30'02"
121°20'34"
121°11'06"
121°01'38"

SEE **89** MAP

MAP
78

MAP
78

1:380,160
1 in. = 6 mi.

0   4   8

miles

N

SEE **67** MAP

43°48'35"

20

CENTRAL   OREGON   HWY

CROOK

1

HAMPTON BUTTE
WILDERNESS
STUDY AREA

43°41'37"

43°41'41"

20

DESCHUTES

DESCHUTES
NATIONAL
FOREST

2

2

43°34'40"

43°34'44"

3

3

DEVIL'S GARDEN
LAVA BED WILDERNESS
STUDY AREA

SQUAW RIDGE
LAVA BED
WILDERNESS
STUDY AREA

43°27'43"

43°27'47"

SEE
MAP
77

4

FOUR CRATERS
LAVA BED
WILDERNESS
STUDY AREA

SAND
DUNES
WILDERNESS
STUDY AREA

4

SEE
79
MAP

43°20'46"

43°20'50"

LAKE

5

5

COUNTY
ROAD   5-10

Christmas
Valley

43°13'49"

Christmas
Valley Airport

COUNTY   ROAD   5-14

43°13'52"

COUNTY   ROAD   5-14

5-14E

6

6

31

FREMONT
HWY

43°06'52"

43°06'55"

SILVER
LAKE

7

FREMONT
NATIONAL
FOREST

DIABLO
MOUNTAIN
WILDERNESS
STUDY AREA

7

31

42°59'55"

42°59'58"

121°01'37"

A   120°52'09"   B   120°42'41"   C   120°33'13"   D   120°23'45"   E   120°14'16"

SEE **90** MAP

MAP
79

1:380,160
1 in. = 6 mi.

0   4   8
miles

N

MAP
79

SEE 68 MAP

43°48'38"

43°48'21"

1

CROOK

HAMPTON
BUTTE
WILDERNESS
STUDY AREA

OCHOCO
NATIONAL
FOREST

1

COUGAR
WELL WILDERNESS
STUDY AREA

43°41'41"

43°41'23"

Hampton

DESCHUTES

2

20

2

43°34'44"

*CHICKAHOMINY
RESERVOIR*

43°34'26"

20   CENTRAL   OREGON   HWY   20
395
Riley

3

49

395

3

HARNEY

43°27'47"

43°27'29"

LAKEVIEW-BURNS HWY

MAP
78
SEE

4

SEE
80
MAP

4

43°20'50"

43°20'32"

LAKE

395

5

49   395

5

Wagontire

43°13'52"

43°13'35"

COUNTY   ROAD   5-14

6

6

43°06'55"

43°06'38"

7

395

7

42°59'58"

42°59'41"

A   120°04'48"   B   119°55'20"   C   119°45'51"   D   119°36'24"   E

120°14'16"

119°26'55"

MAP
80

1:380,160
1 in. = 6 mi.

0   4   8
miles

N

SEE **69** MAP

MAP
80

43°48'21"

MALHEUR NATIONAL
FOREST

127

MALHEUR NATIONAL FOREST

43°47'42"

1

395

1

43°41'23"

OCHOCO
NATIONAL
FOREST

43°40'45"

2

127

127

BURNS
PAIUTE INDIAN
RESERVATION

Harney County Historical Museum

Old Camp
Casino

Burns

Hines

395

20

CENTRAL   OREGON   HWY

Burns
Municipal
Airport

STEENS

78

20

2

43°34'26"

78

205

43°33'48"

20
395

CENTRAL OREGON HWY

20
395

128

3

78

3

43°27'29"

MOON
RESERVOIR

Lawen

43°26'51"

78

SEE **79** MAP

4

HARNEY

MALHEUR LAKE

SEE **81** MAP

4

43°20'32"

STINKING
LAKE

DERRICK
LAKE

MALHEUR LAKE

43°19'54"

5

MUD LAKE

205

5

HARNEY
LAKE

43°13'35"

43°12'57"

404

6

WEED
LAKE

DRY LAKE
RESERVOIR

6

43°06'38"

COUNTY ROAD 404

43°06'00"

7

DIAMOND GRAIN CAMP RD

205

Diamond

7

RAND McNALLY

42°59'41"

A   119°17'27"   B   119°07'59"   C   118°58'31"   D   118°49'03"   E   118°39'35"

42°59'03"

MAP
81

MAP
81

1:380,160
1 in. = 6 mi.

0   4   8
miles

N

SEE [70] MAP

43°47'42"

20

CENTRAL OREGON HWY

CENTRAL OREGON HWY

20

Juntura

SPERRY CREEK
WILDERNESS
STUDY
AREA

GOLD CREEK
WILDERNESS
STUDY
AREA

1

43°40'45"

20

Oard's
Museum

Buchanan

312

WARM SPRINGS
RESERVOIR

CAMP CREEK
WILDERNESS
STUDY AREA

43°39'46"

2

43°33'48"

312

Riverside

43°32'49"

3

43°26'51"

312

78

Crane

HARNEY

MALHEUR

43°25'52"

MAP
[80]
SEE

SEE
[82]
MAP

4

43°19'54"

MALHEUR
LAKE

New
Princeton

CROWLEY RD

43°18'55"

5

78

404

STEENS HWY

43°12'57"

78

43°11'58"

6

DRY LAKE
RESERVOIR

43°06'00"

43°05'01"

7

STONEHOUSE
WILDERNESS
STUDY
AREA

TEN CENT
LAKE

HEATH LAKE
WILDERNESS
STUDY AREA

SHEEPSHEAD
MOUNTAINS
WILDERNESS STUDY
AREA

78

SADDLE BUTTE
WILDERNESS
STUDY AREA

PALOMINO HILLS
WILDERNESS
STUDY AREA

42°59'03"

118°39'34"

A

118°30'06"

B

118°20'39"

C

SEE [93] MAP

118°11'11"

D

118°01'44"

E

42°58'05"

117°52'16"

MAP
82

1:380,160
1 in. = 6 mi.

0   4   8
miles

N

MAP
82

SEE 71 MAP

43°46'43"

20

43°45'23"

201

Adrian

GOLD CREEK
WILDERNESS
STUDY
AREA

1

1

SUCCOR CREEK HWY

43°39'46"

CAMP CREEK
WILDERNESS
STUDY
AREA

43°38'26"

201

COTTONWOOD
CREEK
WILDERNESS
STUDY AREA

LAKE
OWYHEE
STATE
PARK

2

WILD
HORSE BASIN
WILDERNESS
STUDY
AREA

2

DRY CREEK
WILDERNESS
STUDY AREA

43°32'49"

43°31'29"

3

*LAKE
OWYHEE*

3

HONEYCOMBS
WILDERNESS
STUDY
AREA

43°25'52"

43°24'32"

MAP 81 SEE

DRY
CREEK BUTTES
WILDERNESS
STUDY AREA

SEE 83 MAP

4

MALHEUR

4

43°18'55"

SLOCUM
CREEK
WILDERNESS
STUDY AREA

43°17'36"

Rockville

CEDAR
MOUNTAIN
WILDERNESS
STUDY AREA

UPPER LESLIE
GULCH
WILDERNESS
STUDY AREA

5

BLUE CANYON
WILDERNESS
STUDY AREA

5

43°11'58"

43°10'39"

LOWER OWYHEE
CANYON WILDERNESS
STUDY AREA

OWYHEE
BREAKS
WILDERNESS
STUDY AREA

6

JORDAN
CRATERS
WILDERNESS
STUDY AREA

*UPPER
COW LAKE*

6

43°05'01"

43°03'42"

*LOWER
COW LAKE*

SADDLE
BUTTE
WILDERNESS
STUDY AREA

CLARKS
BUTTE
WILDERNESS
STUDY AREA

7

ION HWY

7

95

RAND MᶜNALLY

42°58'05"

A   B   C   D   E

42°56'46"

117°52'15"

117°42'48"

117°32'21"

117°23'53"

117°14'26"

117°04'59"

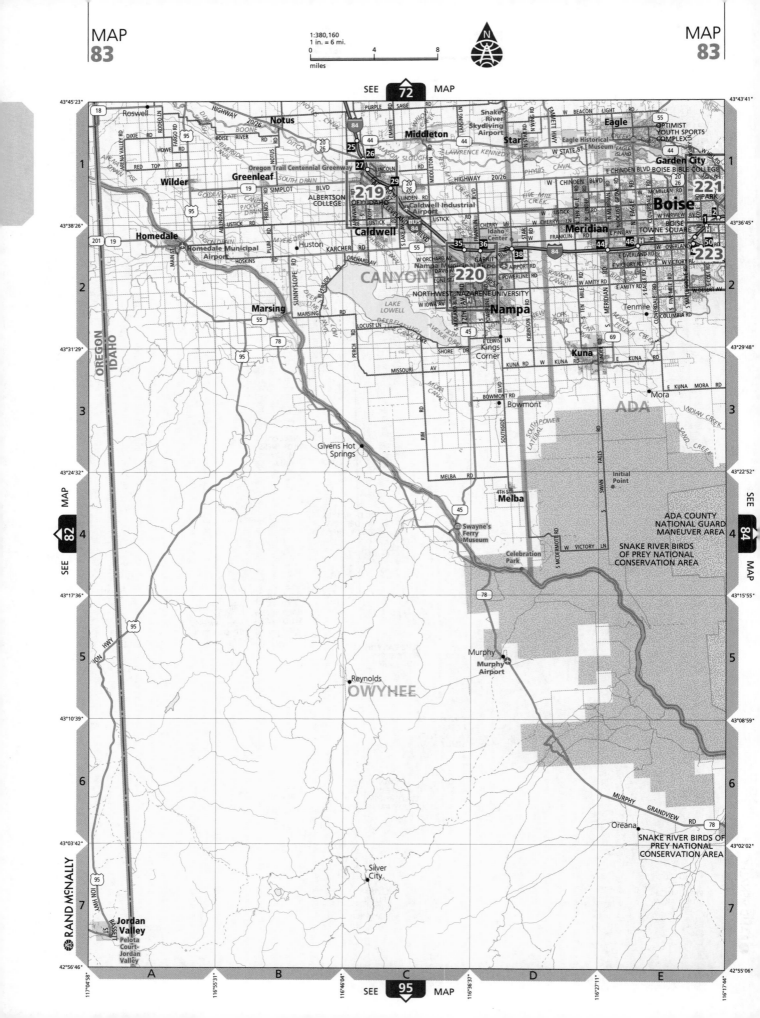

MAP
84

1:380,160
1 in. = 6 mi.

0   4   8

miles

N

MAP
84

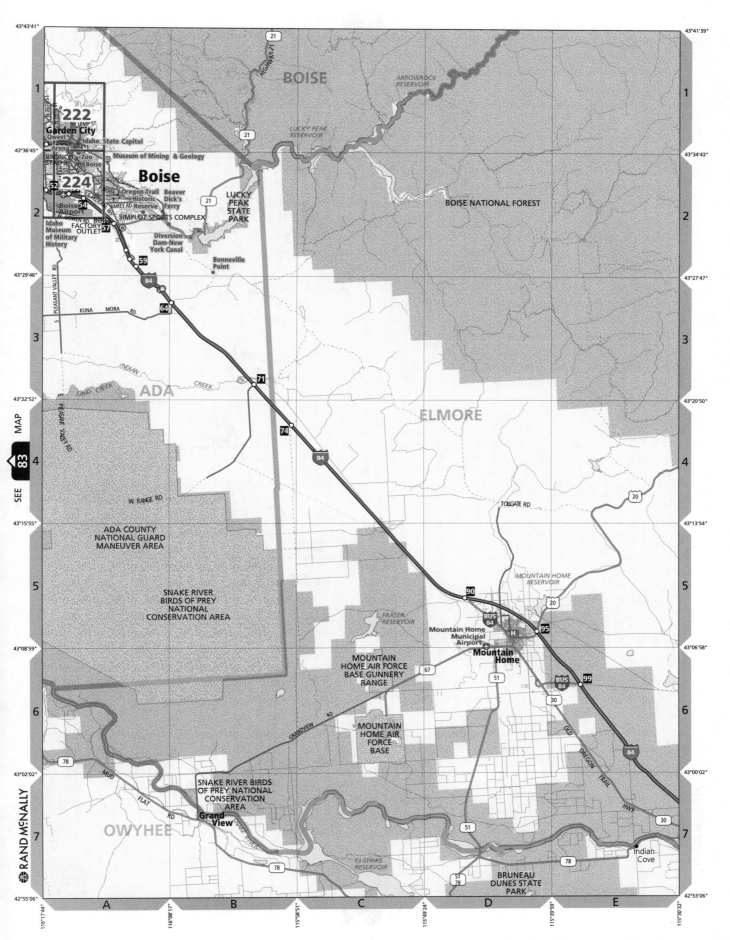

43°43'41"

43°36'45"

43°29'48"

43°22'52"

MAP
83
SEE

43°15'55"

43°08'59"

43°02'02"

42°55'06"

43°41'39"

43°34'43"

43°27'47"

43°20'50"

43°13'54"

43°06'58"

43°00'02"

42°53'06"

BOISE

ARROWROCK
RESERVOIR

LUCKY PEAK
RESERVOIR

BOISE NATIONAL FOREST

222
Garden City
Qwest
Arena
BRONCO
STAD
Zoo
Boise
Idaho State Capitol
Museum of Mining & Geology
Boise
224
52
54
Boise
Airport
57
Idaho
Museum
of Military
History
GOWEN RD
Oregon Trail
Historic
FAMILY RD Reserve
SIMPLOT SPORTS COMPLEX
Beaver
Dick's
Ferry
LUCKY
PEAK
STATE
PARK
Diversion
Dam-New
York Canal
Bonneville
Point

59
84
64
KUNA MORA RD
S PLEASANT VALLEY RD
INDIAN
CREEK
SAND CREEK
ADA

71
74
84

ELMORE

S PLEASANT VALLEY RD

W RANGE RD

ADA COUNTY
NATIONAL GUARD
MANEUVER AREA

SNAKE RIVER
BIRDS OF PREY
NATIONAL
CONSERVATION AREA

TOLLGATE RD

20

MOUNTAIN HOME
RESERVOIR

90
BUS
84
Mountain Home
Municipal
Airport
Mountain Home
20
95
H

FRASER
RESERVOIR

MOUNTAIN
HOME AIR FORCE
BASE GUNNERY
RANGE
67
51
BUS
84
99

MOUNTAIN
HOME AIR
FORCE
BASE
GRANDVIEW RD
30

84
OLD OREGON TRAIL

78
MUD
FLAT RD
SNAKE RIVER BIRDS
OF PREY NATIONAL
CONSERVATION
AREA
Grand
View
51

HWY

30

OWYHEE

78
CJ STRIKE
RESERVOIR
51
78
BRUNEAU
DUNES STATE
PARK
78
Indian
Cove

RAND MCNALLY

A   B   C   D   E

116°17'44"   116°08'17"   115°58'51"   115°49'24"   115°39'59"   115°30'32"

MAP
85

1:380,160
1 in. = 6 mi.

0   4   8
miles

N

MAP
85

SEE 73 MAP

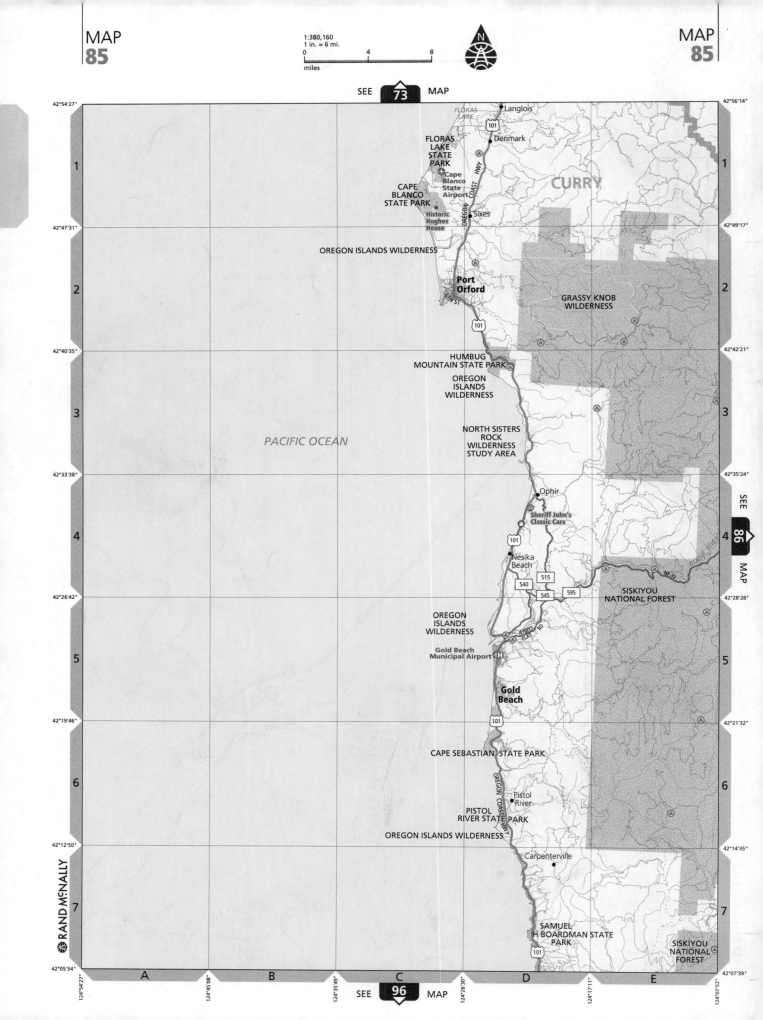

42°54'27"   42°56'14"

FLORAS
LAKE   Langlois

101

Denmark

FLORAS
LAKE
STATE
PARK

CURRY

1   1

Cape
Blanco
State
Airport

CAPE
BLANCO
STATE PARK

OREGON COAST HWY

Sixes

Historic
Hughes
House

42°47'31"   42°49'17"

OREGON ISLANDS WILDERNESS

GRASSY KNOB
WILDERNESS

2   2

Port
Orford

6TH ST

101

42°40'35"   42°42'21"

HUMBUG
MOUNTAIN STATE PARK

OREGON
ISLANDS
WILDERNESS

3   3

PACIFIC OCEAN

NORTH SISTERS
ROCK
WILDERNESS
STUDY AREA

42°33'38"   42°35'24"

Ophir

SEE

Sheriff John's
Classic Cars

86

4   4

MAP

101

Nesika
Beach

515
540
545   595

ROGUE RIVER

NF-33

SISKIYOU
NATIONAL FOREST

42°26'42"   42°28'28"

OREGON
ISLANDS
WILDERNESS

JERRYS FLAT RD

Gold Beach
Municipal Airport   H

5   5

Gold
Beach

101

42°19'46"   42°21'32"

CAPE SEBASTIAN STATE PARK

6   6

OREGON COAST HWY

Pistol
River

PISTOL
RIVER STATE PARK

OREGON ISLANDS WILDERNESS

42°12'50"   42°14'35"

Carpenterville

7   7

SAMUEL
H BOARDMAN STATE
PARK

SISKIYOU
NATIONAL
FOREST

101

42°05'54"   42°07'39"

A   B   C   D   E

124°54'27"   124°45'08"   124°35'49"   124°26'30"   124°17'11"   124°07'52"

SEE 96 MAP

MAP
86
MAP
86

1:380,160
1 in. = 6 mi.
0   4   8
miles

SEE 74 MAP

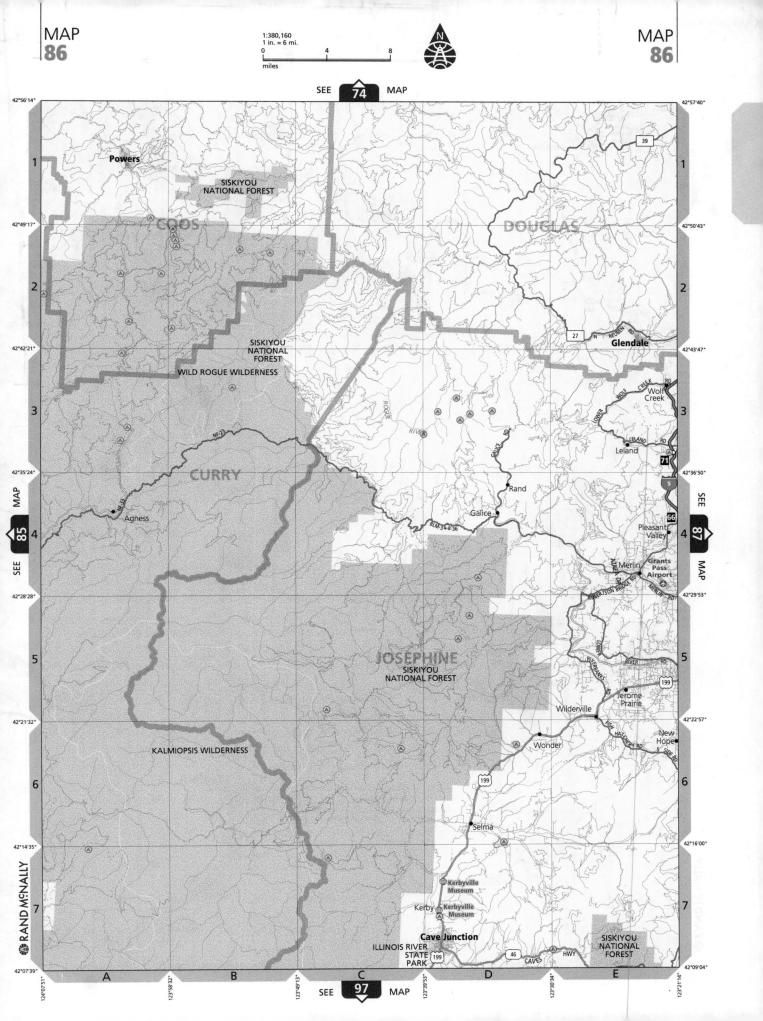

42°56'14"
42°57'40"

1   1

Powers

SISKIYOU
NATIONAL FOREST

COOS

DOUGLAS

42°49'17"
42°50'43"

2   2

39

27

SISKIYOU
NATIONAL
FOREST

Glendale

42°42'21"
42°43'47"

WILD ROGUE WILDERNESS

3   3

NF-33

ROGUE

RIVER

GALICE RD.

Wolf
Creek

LELAND RD.

Leland

71

CURRY

42°35'24"
42°36'50"

SEE 85 MAP

NF-33

Agness

Rand

Galice

BLM-34-8-36

5

66

Pleasant
Valley

SEE 87 MAP

4   4

Merlin

Grants
Pass
Airport

ROBERTSON BRIDGE RD.

MERLIN RD.

42°28'28"
42°29'53"

RIVERBANKS RD.

RIVER RD.

5   5

JOSEPHINE
SISKIYOU
NATIONAL FOREST

Jerome
Prairie

199

Wilderville

42°21'32"
42°22'57"

New
Hope

Wonder

FISH HATCHERY RD.

S. SIDE RD.

KALMIOPSIS WILDERNESS

6   6

199

Selma

42°14'35"
42°16'00"

7   7

Kerbyville
Museum

Kerby

Kerbyville
Museum

Cave Junction

ILLINOIS RIVER
STATE
PARK

199

46

CAVES HWY

SISKIYOU
NATIONAL
FOREST

42°07'39"
42°09'04"

A   B   C   D   E

124°07'51"   123°58'32"   123°49'13"   123°39'53"   123°30'34"   123°21'14"

SEE 97 MAP

RAND McNALLY

MAP
87

1:380,160
1 in. = 6 mi.

0   4   8
miles

N

MAP
87

SEE 75 MAP

42°57'40"
42°58'45"

Riddle
102
101
39
Seven
Feathers
Casino
99   99
21   98   Canyonville
5

227

Tiller

UMPQUA NATIONAL FOREST

DOUGLAS

42°50'43"
42°51'48"

GALESVILLE
RESERVOIR

Drew

227

ROGUE RIVER
NATIONAL
FOREST

Azalea
88
Fortune
Branch
86
Quines Creek
83
PACIFIC HWY
80
5
78

42°43'47"
42°44'52"

227

TILLER TRAIL HWY

ROGUE RIVER
NATIONAL FOREST

LOST
CREEK LAKE

JOSEPH STEWART
STATE PARK
62

CRATER LAKE HWY

Sunny
Valley

GRAVE CREEK

PLEASANT CREEK

227
62
Trail

42°36'50"
42°37'55"

SEE
MAP
86

66

5
61

JOSEPHINE

Shady
Cove

62

MEADOWS RD

BUTTE FALLS HWY

BIG BUTTE CREEK

SEE
MAP
88

42°29'53"
42°30'58"

Grants
Pass
197
58

Wimer

JACKSON

234

VALLEY HWY

62

AGATE RD

Eagle
Point
234

Rogue
River
48

Sams
Valley

RAMSEY RD
SAMS

CRATER LAKE HWY

NICK
YOUNG
RD

White City

LITTLE BUTTE CREEK

LICK CREEK

140

SARDINE CREEK

Gold Hill
2ND AV
1ST AV

Table
Rock

ANTELOPE HWY
140

SPRING CREEK DR
YANKEE CREEK

Lakecreek
140

199
Grants
Pass
Museum
of Art

99

43
45

40

OLD STAGE RD

TABLE ROCK RD

35

99

Crater
Rock
Museum

VILAS RD E

Rogue Valley
International-Medford
Airport

62

AGATE
RESERVOIR

ANTELOPE CREEK

42°22'57"
42°24'02"

238

Murphy

CARIS CREEK

Central Point

BEALL LN

ROSS LN

BEAR CREEK

FREEMAN RD

DELTA WATERS RD

27

198

Medford
CENTER

42°16'00"
42°17'05"

JACKSONVILLE HWY

Applegate
238

HAMBUG CREEK

Rogue
Valley
33
MALL

Kids Imagination Discovery Space
Beekman House
Jacksonville Children's Museum
Museum of Southern
Oregon History
Jacksonville
238

COLUMBUS AV

CENTRAL AV

STAGE RD

PHOENIX RD

S FOOTHILL RD

PACIFIC HWY
24

Phoenix
99

APPLEGATE RIVER

Ruch

SPENCER GULCH

POORMANS CREEK

21

Talent
19

42°09'04"
42°10'08"

KINCAID RD
Williams

THOMPSON CREEK

FERRIS GULCH RD

UPPER APPLEGATE RD

FOREST CREEK

Ashland
199

200

OREGON
UNIVERSITY

Ashland
Municipal Airport

5

66

SOUTHERN
ROGUE RIVER NATIONAL FOREST

RAND M℃NALLY

A   B   C   D   E

123°21'14"   123°11'54"   123°02'34"   122°53'14"   122°43'55"   122°34'35"

MAP
88

MAP
88

SEE 76 MAP

1:380,160
1 in. = 6 mi.

0   4   8

miles

N

42°58'45"   42°59'30"

UMPQUA   ROGUE-UMPQUA
NATIONAL DIVIDE WILDERNESS
FOREST

DOUGLAS

CRATER LAKE

232

CRATER
LAKE
NATIONAL
PARK

97

230

62

Union
Creek

ROGUE
RIVER
NATIONAL
FOREST

62

WINEMA
NATIONAL FOREST

1

42°51'48"   42°52'33"

SOUTH ENTRANCE

62

2

42°44'52"   42°45'36"

RED BLANKET CREEK

MIDDLE ROGUE RIVER

Prospect

Cascade
Gorge

62

HIGHWAY

Prospect
State
Airport

Fort
Klamath

4TH ST

WEED RD

Fort Klamath
Historical
Frontier Post

3

62

LOST
CREEK
LAKE

ROGUE RIVER

SEVENMILE   RD

LOOSLEY RD

KLAMATH

CRATER LAKE HWY

97

COLLIER
MEMORIAL
STATE PARK

ROGUE RIVER
NATIONAL
FOREST

JACKSON

SOUTH FORK ROGUE RIVER

SKY LAKES
WILDERNESS

Klamath
Agency

CHILOQUIN HWY

Pine
Ridge

42°37'55"   42°38'39"

SEE
MAP
87

SEE
MAP
89

Chiloquin

WINEMA
NATIONAL
FOREST

4

Depot
Library &
Museum

Butte
Falls

821

62

427

Kla-Mo-
Ya Casino

AGENCY
LAKE

42°30'58"   42°31'43"

821

SOUTH FORK FOURBIT CREEK

WILLOW
LAKE

FOURMILE
LAKE

WINEMA NATIONAL
FOREST   Rocky
Point

SOS RD

97

CHILOQUIN RD

MODOC POINT RD

5

RYE
SPRING

UPPER KLAMATH LAKE

Modoc
Point

140

BUTTE FALLS FISH LAKE RD

Fish Lake
Resort

140

140

SHOALWATER
BAY

42°24'02"   42°24'46"

Lost Creek
Covered
Bridge

FISH
LAKE

LAKE OF
THE WOODS

MOUNTAIN
LAKES
WILDERNESS

WOCUS
BAY

97

6

SOUTH FORK BUTTE CREEK

LITTLE
CREEK

DEAD INDIAN RD

ASPEN
LAKE

42°17'05"   42°17'49"

FROG CREEK

PRAIRIE RD

HOWARD
PRAIRIE
LAKE

CLOVER

CREEK

RD

WINEMA NATIONAL FOREST

LONG
LAKE

Wocus

LAKESHORE DR

140

7

RAND McNALLY

COVE   CREEK

HYATT

HYATT
RESERVOIR

Klamath Falls

140

66

A   B   C   D   E

122°34'34"   122°25'14"   122°15'54"   122°06'34"   121°57'14"   121°47'54"

42°10'08"   42°10'53"

MAP
89

1:380,160
1 in. = 6 mi.

0   4   8
miles

N

MAP
89

SEE 77 MAP

42°59'30"

42°59'54"

THOMPSON
RESERVOIR

NF-28

1

WINEMA
NATIONAL
FOREST

FREMONT NATIONAL FOREST

LAKE

1

42°52'33"

42°52'57"

2

WINEMA NATIONAL FOREST

SYCAN
MARSH

2

KLAMATH
MARSH

42°45'36"

42°46'00"

FREMONT NATIONAL FOREST

3

A

3

42°38'39"

42°39'03"

HAWKS
LAKE

SEE 88 MAP

SEE 90 MAP

NF-3312

4

A

4

42°31'43"

42°32'07"

WILD
BILLY
LAKE

KLAMATH

COUNTY ROAD 1257

5

Sprague
River

140

Beatty

Odessa

5

140

42°24'46"

42°25'10"

Bly

6

WHITELINE
RESERVOIR

SWAN
LAKE

140

42°17'49"

42°18'13"

FREMONT NATIONAL FOREST

6

OREGON
INSTITUTE
OF TECHNOLOGY

140

BLY MOUNTAIN CTO

GERBER
RESERVOIR

7

201 202th
Falls

H

39

Favell
Museum
of Western
Art

97

140

KLAMATH FALLS-LAKEVIEW HWY

DAIRY-BONANZA HWY

Dairy

70

ALKALI
LAKE

MARKET ST

Bonanza

NORTH ST

LOST RIVER

7

42°10'53"

42°11'16"

A   B   C   D   E

121°47'53"   121°38'33"   121°29'13"   121°19'52"   121°10'32"   121°01'12"

RAND M?NALLY

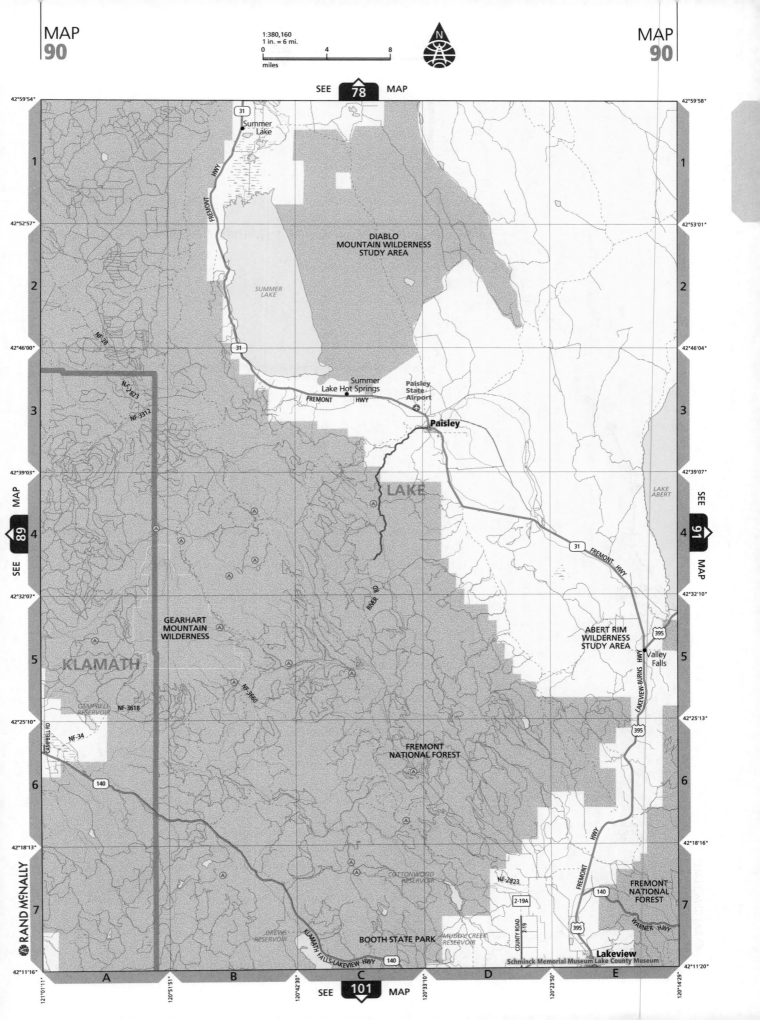

MAP
91

1:380,160
1 in. = 6 mi.

0   4   8

miles

N

MAP
91

SEE 79 MAP

Alkali Lake
Station

395

LAKEVIEW-BURNS HWY

HARNEY

 OREJANA
CANYON
WILDERNESS
STUDY AREA

FRENCHGLEN RD

395

LAKE
ABERT

LAKEVIEW-BURNS HWY

BLUEJOINT
LAKE

TURPIN
LAKE

STONE
CORRAL
LAKE

CAMPBELL
LAKE

MAP
90
SEE

395

FLAGSTAFF
LAKE

MUGWUMP
LAKE

UPPER
CAMPBELL
LAKE

HART MOUNTAIN RD

SEE
92
MAP

ANDERSON
LAKE

SWAMP
LAKE

COUNTY ROAD 3-12

ABERT RIM
WILDERNESS
STUDY
AREA

LAKE

SPANISH
LAKE

COUNTY ROAD 3-12

COUNTY ROAD 3-10

Plush

HART
LAKE

DESERT
LAKE

MOUND
LAKE

ALGER
LAKE

LONG
LAKE

COUNTY ROAD 3-13

FREMONT
NATIONAL
FOREST

WOOL
LAKE

CRUMP
LAKE

FISHER
LAKE

GUANO CREEK
WILDERNESS
STUDY AREA

JACK
LAKE

FISH
CREEK RIM
WILDERNESS
STUDY AREA

SHIRK
LAKE

140

PELICAN
LAKE

140

A   B   C   D   E

MAP
92

1:380,160
1 in. = 6 mi.

0   4   8
miles

N

MAP
92

SEE 80 MAP

42°59'40"

42°59'03"

1

OREJANA CANYON WILDERNESS STUDY AREA

205

BACA LAKE

KNOX POND

1

42°52'43"

42°52'06"

FRENCHGLEN HWY

2

BRIDGE CREEK WILDERNESS STUDY AREA

Frenchglen

BLITZEN RIVER WILDERNESS STUDY AREA

2

42°45'47"

412

LONG HOLLOW RD

STEENS MOUNTAIN WILDERNESS

42°45'09"

3

ROCK CREEK RESERVOIR

FRENCHGLEN RD 412

205

3

42°38'50"

42°38'12"

SEE
91
MAP

202

HARNEY

SOUTH FORK OF THE DONNER AND BLITZEN RIVER WILDERNESS STUDY AREA

SEE
93
MAP

4

STEENS MOUNTAIN WILDERNESS

4

42°31'53"

42°31'15"

5

LAKE

202

5

42°24'56"

42°24'19"

202

6

BASQUE HILLS WILDERNESS STUDY AREA

STEENS MOUNTAIN WILDERNESS

202

6

42°17'59"

RINCON WILDERNESS STUDY AREA

42°17'22"

RAND McNALLY

7

SPAULDING WILDERNESS STUDY AREA

PUEBLO MOUNTAINS WILDERNESS STUDY AREA

7

42°11'03"

42°10'25"

119°27'46"   A   119°18'26"   B   119°09'06"   C   118°59'46"   D   118°50'26"   E   118°41'06"

SEE 103 MAP

MAP
93

MAP
93

1:380,160
1 in. = 6 mi.

0   4   8
miles

N

SEE 81 MAP

42°59'03"

STONEHOUSE
WILDERNESS
STUDY
AREA

JUNIPER
LAKE

HEATH
LAKE
WILDERNESS
STUDY AREA

SHEEPSHEAD
MOUNTAINS
WILDERNESS
STUDY AREA

SADDLE BUTTE
WILDERNESS
STUDY
AREA

42°58'04"

78

1

1

LOWER
STONEHOUSE
WILDERNESS
STUDY AREA

PALOMINO
HILLS
WILDERNESS
STUDY AREA

42°52'06"

42°51'07"

2

TABLE
MOUNTAIN
WILDERNESS
STUDY AREA

WILDCAT CANYON
WILDERNESS
STUDY AREA

2

MANN
LAKE

WEST PEAK
WILDERNESS
STUDY
AREA

42°45'09"

42°44'11"

3

WINTER
RANGE
WILDERNESS
STUDY AREA

3

EAST ALVORD
WILDERNESS
STUDY AREA

42°38'12"

42°37'14"

SEE 92 MAP

ALVORD DESERT
WILDERNESS
STUDY AREA

MALHEUR

SEE 94 MAP

4

HARNEY

STEENS
MOUNTAIN
WILDERNESS

4

42°31'15"

42°30'17"

5

5

42°24'19"

42°23'21"

ALVORD
LAKE

6

TWELVEMILE
CREEK
WILDERNESS
STUDY AREA

6

42°17'22"

202

42°16'24"

Fields

201

7

FIFTEENMILE
CREEK
WILDERNESS
STUDY AREA

7

PUEBLO MOUNTAINS
WILDERNESS
STUDY
AREA

201

WILLOW CREEK WILDERNESS STUDY AREA
MAHOGANY RIDGE WILDERNESS STUDY AREA

OREGON
CANYON
WILDERNESS
STUDY AREA

42°10'25"

42°09'28"

A   B   C   D   E

118°41'05"   118°31'45"   118°22'25"   118°13'05"   118°03'45"   117°54'26"

SEE 104 MAP

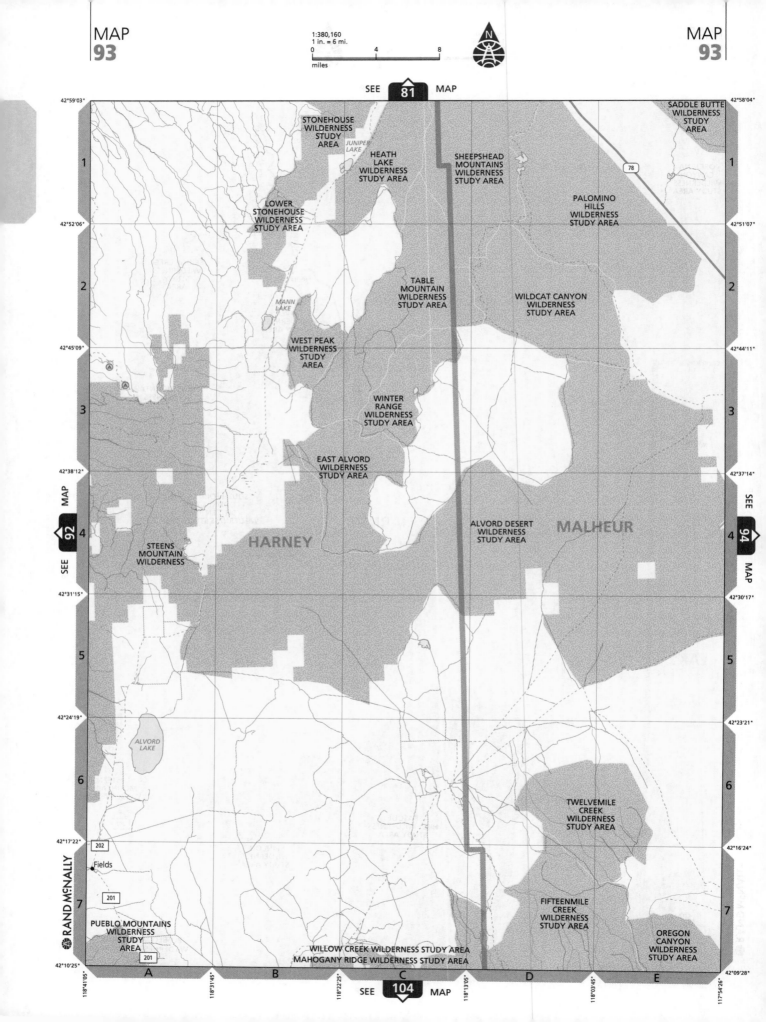

MAP
94

MAP
94

1:380,160
1 in. = 6 mi.
0   4   8
miles

N

SEE 82 MAP

CLARKS BUTTE
WILDERNESS
STUDY
AREA

Charbonneau
Grave Site

● Danner

Jean Baptiste
Charbonneau

95

SADDLE BUTTE
WILDERNESS
STUDY AREA

LOWER OWYHEE
CANYON
WILDERNESS
STUDY AREA

● Arock

ANTELOPE
RESERVOIR

1

95

LITTLE
GRASSY
RESERVOIR

● Rome

78

● Burns
Junction

95

2

3

95

MALHEUR

SEE 93 MAP

✈ Rome State Airport

95

ALVORD
DESERT
WILDERNESS
STUDY AREA

BOWDEN
HILLS
WILDERNESS
STUDY AREA

SEE 95 MAP

4

95

● Basque

OWYHEE
CANYON
WILDERNESS
STUDY AREA

5

6

95

RAND MC NALLY

OREGON CANYON
WILDERNESS
STUDY
AREA

UPPER WEST
LITTLE OWYHEE
WILDERNESS
STUDY AREA

LOOKOUT
BUTTE
WILDERNESS
STUDY AREA

7

SEE 105 MAP

A   B   C   D   E

42°58'04"
42°51'07"
42°44'11"
42°37'14"
42°30'17"
42°23'21"
42°16'24"
42°09'28"

42°56'45"
42°49'48"
42°42'52"
42°35'55"
42°28'59"
42°22'02"
42°15'06"
42°08'10"

117°54'25"
117°45'05"
117°35'46"
117°26'26"
117°17'07"
117°07'47"

MAP
95

1:380,160
1 in. = 6 mi.

0   4   8
miles

N

MAP
95

SEE [83] MAP

1

2

LITTLE
JACKS CREEK
WILDERNESS
STUDY AREA

42°56'45"
42°49'48"
42°42'52"
42°35'55"

42°55'05"
42°48'09"
42°41'12"
42°34'16"

NORTH FORK
OWYHEE RIVER
WILDERNESS
STUDY AREA

3

OWYHEE

POLE CREEK
WILDERNESS
STUDY AREA

4

OREGON
IDAHO

MAP
[94]
SEE

SQUAW
CREEK CANYON
WILDERNESS
STUDY AREA

UPPER
DEEP CREEK
WILDERNESS
STUDY AREA

HORSEHEAD
SPRING
WILDERNESS
STUDY AREA

MIDDLE FORK
OWYHEE RIVER
WILDERNESS
STUDY AREA

5

WEST FORK
RED CANYON
WILDERNESS
STUDY AREA

42°28'59"
42°22'02"

42°27'20"
42°20'24"

6

OWYHEE
CANYON
WILDERNESS
STUDY AREA

42°15'06"
42°13'27"

RAND McNALLY

7

LOOKOUT
BUTTE
WILDERNESS
STUDY AREA

LITTLE
OWYHEE RIVER
WILDERNESS
STUDY AREA

DUCK
VALLEY
INDIAN
RESERVATION

MALHEUR

42°08'10"

A   B   C   D   E

42°06'31"

117°07'46"   116°58'27"   116°49'08"   116°39'49"   116°30'30"   116°21'11"

SEE [106] MAP

MAP
96

MAP
96

1:380,160
1 in. = 6 mi.

0   4   8

miles

N

SEE 85 MAP

SAMUEL H BOARDMAN STATE PARK

101

OREGON ISLANDS WILDERNESS

Brookings
State
Airport

CURRY

SISKIYOU
NATIONAL
FOREST

Brookings

Chetco Valley
Historical
Society
Museum

OREGON COAST HWY

101

OREGON
CALIFORNIA

Lucky 7 Casino

Smith
River

SMITH RIVER

MOSELEY RD DR

LOWER LAKE RD

Fort
Dick

LAKE
TALAWA

D3

Lake
Earl

101

LAKE
EARL

Felterwood

199

Jack
McNamara
Field

DEL NORTE

Crescent City

FRONT ST

D2

Bertsch
Terrace

1

2

3

4

SEE 97 MAP

199

DEL NORTE COAST REDWOODS PARK

REDWOOD
NATIONAL PARK

REDWOOD HWY

101

PACIFIC OCEAN

5

6

7

REDWOOD
NATIONAL
PARK

42°05'53"
41°58'57"
41°52'01"
41°45'05"
41°38'09"
41°31'14"
41°24'18"
41°17'22"

42°07'38"
42°00'42"
41°53'46"
41°46'50"
41°39'54"
41°32'58"
41°26'02"
41°19'06"

A   B   C   D   E

124°50'53"
124°41'42"
124°32'30"
124°23'19"
124°14'08"
124°04'56"

MAP
97

1:380,160
1 in. = 6 mi.

0   4   8

miles

N

MAP
97

SEE 86 MAP

42°07'38"

KALMIOPSIS
WILDERNESS

CURRY

Illinois
Valley
Illinois
Valley
Airport

Bridgeview

199

O'Brien

JOSEPHINE

Takilma

CAVES HWY

46

OREGON
CAVES NATIONAL
MONUMENT

1

ROGUE RIVER
NATIONAL
FOREST

42°09'03"

42°00'42"

OREGON
CALIFORNIA

GATEWAY STATE WAYSIDE

SISKIYOU NATIONAL FOREST

RED BUTTES
WILDERNESS

42°02'07"

MORTH FORK SMITH RIVER

2

SISKIYOU
WILDERNESS

2

41°53'46"

41°55'10"

Gasquet

199

Patrick
Creek

3

SMITH RIVER
NATIONAL
RECREATION AREA

SISKIYOU WILDERNESS

Happy Camp
Airport

96

Happy
Camp

41°48'14"

3

199

Hiouchi
Valley

Douglas
Park

41°46'50"

JEDEDIAH
SMITH
REDWOODS
STATE PARK
REDWOOD NATIONAL
PARK

MAP

96

SEE

4

DEL
NORTE COAST
REDWOODS
PARK

Clear
Creek

SEE

98

MAP

4

41°39'54"

SIX RIVERS
NATIONAL
FOREST

SMITH RIVER

SOUTH FORK

SISKIYOU

KLAMATH
NATIONAL FOREST

96

41°41'18"

5

101

5

41°32'58"

Requa

Klamath

REDWOOD
NATIONAL
PARK

KLAMATH GLEN RD

Klamath
Glen

HOOPA VALLEY
INDIAN RESERVATION

SISKIYOU WILDERNESS

DEL NORTE

MARBLE
MOUNTAIN
WILDERNESS

41°34'22"

6

REDWOOD HWY

41°26'02"

SIX RIVERS NATIONAL FOREST

6

41°27'25"

RAND M°NALLY

PRAIRIE
CREEK
REDWOODS
STATE PARK

HWY

HUMBOLDT

KLAMATH RIVER

Somes
Bar

7

MARBLE MOUNTAIN
WILDERNESS

7

101

REDWOOD
NATIONAL
PARK

Pecwan

169

96

SALMON RIVER

41°19'06"

A   B   C   D   E

124°04'55"   123°55'43"   123°46'32"   123°37'20"   123°28'08"   123°18'56"

41°20'29"

MAP
98

SEE 87 MAP

MAP
98

1:380,160
1 in. = 6 mi.
0   4   8
miles

N

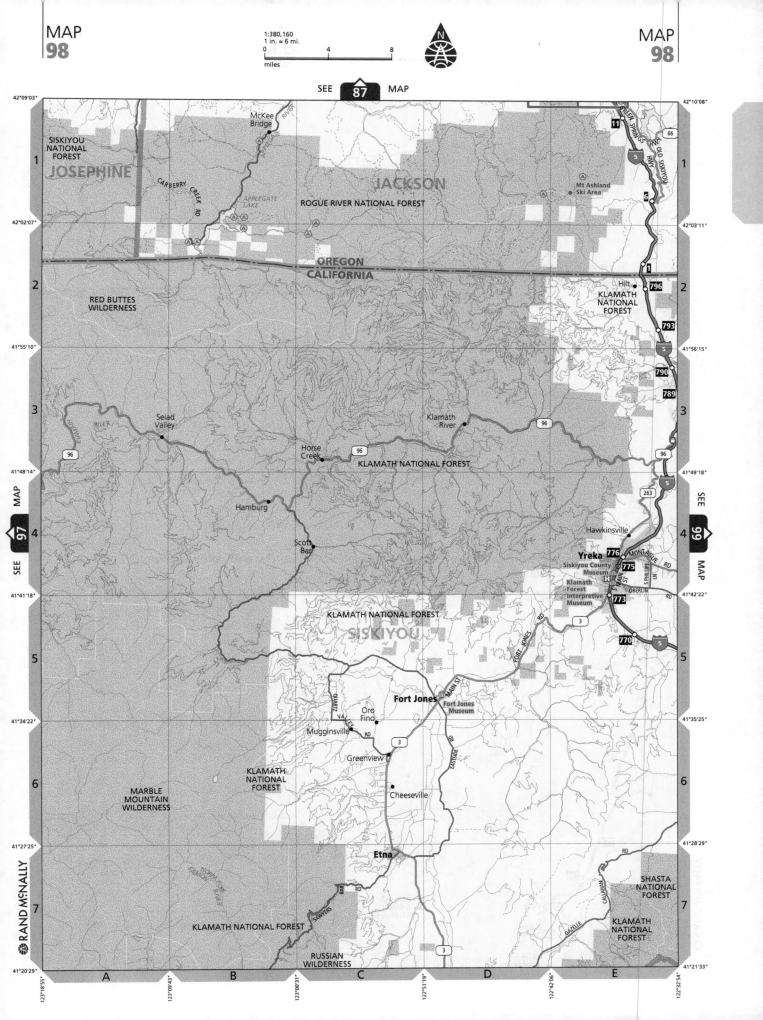

SISKIYOU NATIONAL FOREST

JOSEPHINE

McKee Bridge

CARBERRY CREEK RD

APPLEGATE LAKE

JACKSON

ROGUE RIVER NATIONAL FOREST

Mt Ashland Ski Area

66

11

6

OREGON
CALIFORNIA

1

RED BUTTES WILDERNESS

Hilt

KLAMATH NATIONAL FOREST

796

793

790

789

Seiad Valley

Klamath River

96

96

KLAMATH NATIONAL FOREST

96

Horse Creek

96

263

Hamburg

96

Scott Bar

Hawkinsville

Yreka
Siskiyou County Museum
Klamath Forest Interpretive Museum

776

775

MONTAGUE RD

S PHILLIPS LN

OBERLIN RD

773

3

KLAMATH NATIONAL FOREST

SISKIYOU

FORT JONES RD

EASTSIDE RD

770

5

Fort Jones
Fort Jones Museum
MAIN ST

QUARTZ VALLEY RD

Oro Fino

Mugginsville

3

Greenview

MARBLE MOUNTAIN WILDERNESS

KLAMATH NATIONAL FOREST

Cheeseville

Etna

SHASTA NATIONAL FOREST

KLAMATH NATIONAL FOREST

NORTH FORK SALMON RIVER

SAWYERS BAR RD

GAZELLE

CALLAHAN RD

3

KLAMATH NATIONAL FOREST

RUSSIAN WILDERNESS

RAND MCNALLY

SEE 97 MAP

SEE 99 MAP

A   B   C   D   E

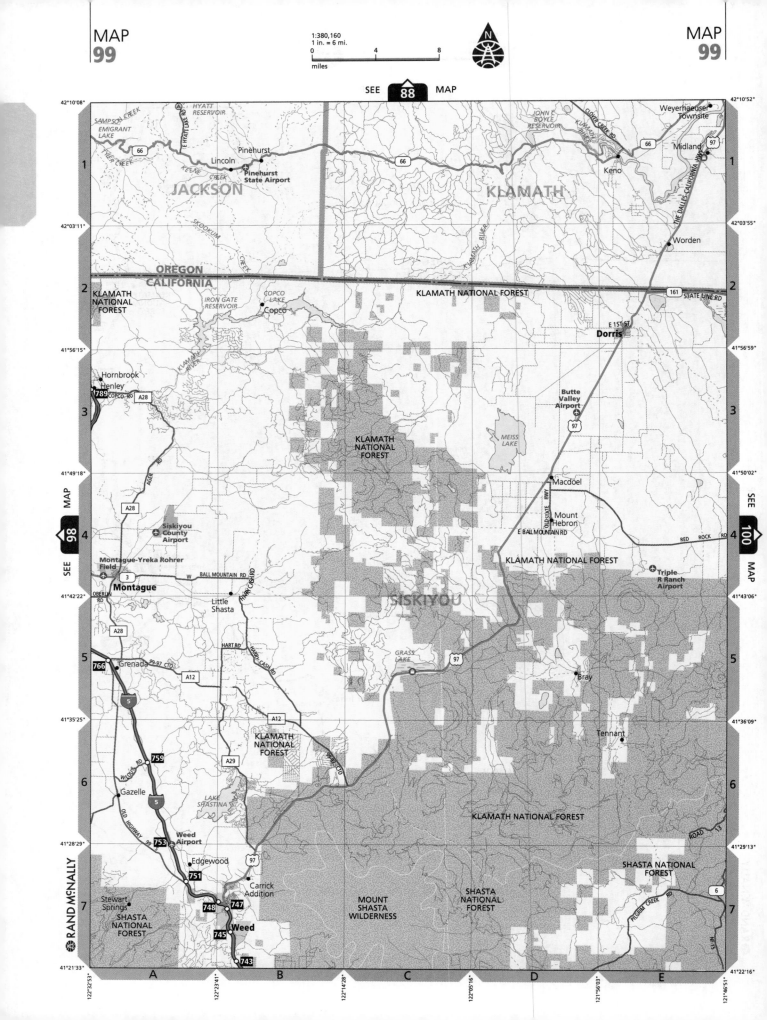

MAP
99

MAP
99

1:380,160
1 in. = 6 mi.
0   4   8
miles

N

SEE 88 MAP

42°10'08"

SAMPSON CREEK
EMIGRANT LAKE
HYATT RESERVOIR
E HYATT LAKE RD
TYLER CREEK
KEENE CREEK
SKOOKUM CREEK

66
Lincoln
Pinehurst
Pinehurst State Airport

JACKSON

66

KLAMATH

JOHN C BOYLE RESERVOIR
CLOVER CREEK RD
KLAMATH RIVER

Weyerhaeuser Townsite

66
Keno
Midland
97
THE DALLES CALIFORNIA HWY

42°10'52"

42°03'11"
42°03'55"

OREGON
CALIFORNIA

Worden

2

KLAMATH NATIONAL FOREST
IRON GATE RESERVOIR
COPCO LAKE
Copco

KLAMATH NATIONAL FOREST

161 STATE LINE RD

E 1ST ST
Dorris

2

41°56'15"
41°56'59"

Hornbrook
Henley
789
COPCO RD
A28
KLAMATH RIVER

KLAMATH NATIONAL FOREST

KLAMATH NATIONAL FOREST

MEISS LAKE

Butte Valley Airport

97

3

41°49'18"
41°50'02"

AGER RD
A28

Siskiyou County Airport

Montague-Yreka Rohrer Field
3
Montague
OBERLIN RD
A28
W BALL MOUNTAIN RD
HART CASH RD

Little Shasta

Macdoel
OLD STATE HWY
Mount Hebron
E BALL MOUNTAIN RD

KLAMATH NATIONAL FOREST

RED ROCK RD

Triple R Ranch Airport

MAP
98
SEE

4

41°42'22"
41°43'06"

SISKIYOU

5

766
Grenada
99-97 CTO
A12
HART RD
HART CASH RD

GRASS LAKE

97

Bray

41°35'25"
41°36'09"

5

A12
A29

KLAMATH NATIONAL FOREST

99-97 CTO

Tennant

6

759
Gazelle
OLD HIGHWAY 99
WAGON RD
LAKE SHASTINA

KLAMATH NATIONAL FOREST

ROAD 13

6

41°28'29"
41°29'13"

753
Weed Airport
Edgewood
751
97
Carrick Addition

SHASTA NATIONAL FOREST

SHASTA NATIONAL FOREST

MOUNT SHASTA WILDERNESS

SHASTA NATIONAL FOREST

PILGRIM CREEK RD

6

7

Stewart Springs
SHASTA NATIONAL FOREST
748
747
745
Weed
743

7

41°21'33"
41°22'16"

A   122°32'53"   B   122°23'41"   C   122°14'28"   122°05'16"   D   121°56'03"   E   121°46'51"

MAP
100

1:380,160
1 in. = 6 mi.

0   4   8

miles

N

MAP
100

SEE **89** MAP

42°10'52"

Klamath Falls International Airport
SOUTHSIDE EXPWY
Klamath Falls
Falcon Heights
Henley

140
Olene

FREMONT NATIONAL FOREST

GERBER RESERVOIR

ROUND VALLEY RESERVOIR

42°11'16"

SPRING LAKE

KLAMATH

Lorella

Hot Springs

1

42°03'55"

39

42°04'19"

WILLOW VALLEY RESERVOIR

Merrill

KLAMATH FALLS-MALIN HWY
S MERRILL RD
MALONE RD
HATFIELD HWY

50
Malin

OREGON
CALIFORNIA

Langell Valley

2

161
STATE LINE RD
161
Ainsworth Corner

139

LOWER KLAMATH LAKE

LOST RIVER

Malin Airport
OLD MALIN HWY

41°56'59"

EAST   WEST   RD
HILL RD
MAIN ST

Tulelake

E CR-104

N COUNTY ROAD 112

114

41°57'22"

KLAMATH LAKE

TULE LAKE SUMP

Newell

Tulelake Municipal Airport
141

CLEAR LAKE RESERVOIR

3

114

41°50'02"

MODOC NATIONAL FOREST

NF-10

41°50'26"

SEE **99** MAP

RED ROCK RD

LAVA BEDS NATIONAL MONUMENT

MODOC

4

SEE **101** MAP

41°43'06"

NF-15

41°43'29"

SISKIYOU

NF-10

5

KLAMATH NATIONAL FOREST

97
Tionesta

41°36'09"

NF-44N50
MEDICINE LAKE RD
MEDICINE LAKE

41°36'33"

DAVIS RD

15

MEDICINE LAKE RD

6

ROAD 13

6
NF-15
NF-49

MODOC NATIONAL FOREST

139

HACKAMORE RD

41°29'13"

41°29'36"

SHASTA NATIONAL FOREST

LOOKOUT

PIT RIVER

7

NF-49

41°22'16"

A   B   C   D   E

41°22'40"

121°46'50"   121°37'37"   121°28'25"   121°19'12"   121°09'59"   121°00'46"

MAP
101

MAP
101

1:380,160
1 in. = 6 mi.

0   4   8

miles

N

SEE **90** MAP

42°11'16"   42°11'19"

DREWS
RESERVOIR

140

KLAMATH FALLS-LAKEVIEW HWY

Five
Corners

Lakeview   Lake County Museum

Lake County
Airport

H

FREMONT
NATIONAL
FOREST

STRAWBERRY
RESERVOIR

KLAMATH

BEAR
VALLEY
LAKE

FREMONT NATIONAL FOREST

DOG LAKE

LAKE

West
Side

395

FREMONT

1

42°04'19"   42°04'22"

TULE
LAKE

RENNER
LAKE

GOOSE
LAKE

HWY

2

OREGON
CALIFORNIA

New Pine
Creek

2

41°57'22"   41°57'26"

395

GOOSE LAKE

Willow
Ranch

9

3

41°50'26"   41°50'29"

MAP
100
SEE

MODOC NATIONAL FOREST

XL RANCH INDIAN
RESERVATION

9

SEE
MAP
102

4

395

Davis
Creek

41°43'29"   41°43'33"

XL RANCH
INDIAN
RESERVATION

MODOC

MODOC
NATIONAL
FOREST

5

41°36'33"   41°36'36"

BIG SAGE
RESERVOIR

6

299

271

XL RANCH
INDIAN RESERVATION

299

Daphnedale
Park

395

41°29'36"   41°29'39"

139

299

PIT RIVER

Alturas
Alturas
Municipal Airport

60

7

139
299

54

CENTERVILLE RD

60

California
Pines

California
Pines
Airport

395

SOUTH
WARNER
WILDERNESS

Canby

41°22'40"   41°22'43"

A   B   C   D   E

121°00'46"   120°15'33"   120°42'20"   120°33'07"   120°23'55"   120°14'42"

MAP
102

1:380,160
1 in. = 6 mi.

0   4   8

miles

N

MAP
102

SEE **91** MAP

42°11'19"   **42°11'02"**

1   **1**

FISH
CREEK
RIM WILDERNESS
STUDY AREA

Adel

GREASER
RESERVOIR

MCRESERVOIR   LITTLE
RESERVOIR

140

140

LAKE

SPAULDING
WILDERNESS
STUDY
AREA

42°04'22"   **42°04'05"**

COLEMAN
LAKE

140

FREMONT
NATIONAL
FOREST

2   **2**

OREGON
CALIFORNIA

OREGON
NEVADA

34

MODOC
NATIONAL
FOREST

SHELDON
CONTIGUOUS
WILDERNESS
STUDY AREA

41°57'26"   **41°57'09"**

3   **3**

34A

FORT
BIDWELL
INDIAN
RESERVATION

Fort
Bidwell

MOSQUITO
LAKE

CALCUTTA
LAKE

SWAN LAKE
RESERVOIR

41°50'29"   **41°50'12"**

34A

COW LAKE

MAP
SEE
101

9

MIDDLE
LAKE

34

4   **4**

SEE
103
MAP

1

CROOKS
LAKE

UPPER
LAKE

41°43'33"   **41°43'16"**

MUD LAKE

MASSACRE RIM
WILDERNESS
STUDY
AREA

MODOC

CALIFORNIA
NEVADA

MASSACRE
LAKE

5   **5**

ALKALI
LAKE

WASHOE

MIDDLE
LAKE

Lake
City

34

WEST
LAKE

41°36'36"   **41°36'19"**

1

8A

8A

Vya

8A

FORTYNINE
LAKE

8A

6   **6**

Cedarville
Airport

299

34

299

Cedarville

CENTRAL
LAKE

41°29'40"   **41°29'23"**

SOUTH WARNER
CONTIGUOUS
WILDERNESS
STUDY AREA

MIDDLE
ALKALI
LAKE

7   **7**

HIGH
ROCK
CANYON
WILDERNESS

SOUTH
WARNER
WILDERNESS

1

34

41°22'43"   **41°22'27"**

A   **B**   **C**   **D**   **E**

120°14'41"   120°05'28"   119°56'16"   119°47'03"   119°37'50"   119°28'38"

MAP
103

MAP
103

1:380,160
1 in. = 6 mi.

0   4   8

miles

N

SEE **92** MAP

42°11'02"

42°10'25"

SPAULDING
WILDERNESS
STUDY AREA

BASQUE HILLS
WILDERNESS
STUDY
AREA

RINCON
WILDERNESS
STUDY AREA

PUEBLO
MOUNTAINS
WILDERNESS
STUDY AREA

HARNEY

LAKE

42°04'05"

42°03'28"

HAWK MOUNTAIN WILDERNESS STUDY AREA

140

SAGE
HEN HILLS
WILDERNESS
STUDY
AREA

OREGON
NEVADA

41°57'09"

41°56'32"

BIG SPRING
RESERVOIR

CONTINENTAL
LAKE

34A

140

140

8A

41°50'12"

41°49'35"

SEE MAP **102**

SEE **104** MAP

MAP

MASSACRE
RIM WILDERNESS
STUDY
AREA

41°43'16"

41°42'39"

ADLER
CREEK
WILDERNESS
STUDY AREA

8A

HUMBOLDT

BLUE LAKES
WILDERNESS
STUDY
AREA

WASHOE

41°36'19"

41°35'42"

SUMMIT
LAKE INDIAN
RESERVATION

SUMMIT
LAKE

41°29'23"

41°28'46"

RAND M°NALLY

EAST FORK
HIGH ROCK
CANYON
WILDERNESS

NORTH BLACK
ROCK RANGE
WILDERNESS

BLACK
ROCK
DESERT
WILDERNESS

HIGH
ROCK
CANYON
WILDERNESS

41°22'27"

41°21'50"

A   B   C   D   E

119°28'37"   119°19'24"   119°10'12"   119°00'59"   118°51'47"   118°42'34"

1 2 3 4 5 6 7

MAP
104

MAP
104

1:380,160
1 in. = 6 mi.

0   4   8

miles

N

SEE 93 MAP

42°10'25"   42°09'27"

201

1

MAHOGANY
RIDGE
WILDERNESS
STUDY AREA

WILLOW
CREEK
WILDERNESS
STUDY AREA

FIFTEENMILE
CREEK
WILDERNESS
STUDY AREA

OREGON
CANYON
WILDERNESS
STUDY AREA

MALHEUR

PUEBLO
MOUNTAINS
WILDERNESS
STUDY AREA

RED MOUNTAIN
WILDERNESS
STUDY
AREA

42°03'28"   **HARNEY**   42°02'30"

201

DISASTER PEAK
WILDERNESS
STUDY AREA

**OREGON
NEVADA**

2

Denio

292

140

41°56'32"   41°55'34"

3   140

41°49'35"   41°48'38"

MAP 103 SEE

4

SEE 105 MAP

41°42'39"   **HUMBOLDT**   KINGS VALLEY RD   293   KINGS RIVER RD   41°41'42"

BLUE LAKES
WILDERNESS
STUDY
AREA

5

41°35'42"   140   41°34'45"

6   *QUINN
RIVER
LAKES*

140

FORT MCDERMITT
INDIAN
RESERVATION

41°28'46"   41°27'49"

7   140

BLACK ROCK
DESERT
WILDERNESS

NORTH
JACKSON
MOUNTAINS
WILDERNESS

41°21'50"   41°20'53"

A   **B**   **C**   **D**   **E**

118°42'33"   118°33'21"   118°24'08"   118°14'56"   118°05'44"   117°56'31"

MAP
105

MAP
105

1:380,160
1 in. = 6 mi.

0   4   8
miles

SEE 94 MAP

N

42°09'27"

OREGON
CANYON
WILDERNESS
STUDY AREA

MALHEUR

UPPER WEST LITTLE
OWYHEE WILDERNESS
STUDY AREA

OWYHEE CANYON
WILDERNESS
STUDY
AREA

LOOKOUT BUTTE
WILDERNESS
STUDY AREA

1

42°08'09"

ION HWY

95

42°02'30"

FORT McDERMITT INDIAN RESERVATION

42°01'13"

OREGON
NEVADA

793

Mc Dermitt

41°55'34"

COUNTY LINE RD

793

2

41°54'16"

95

HUMBOLDT NATIONAL FOREST

41°48'38"

3

41°47'20"

SEE 104 MAP

SEE 106 MAP

41°41'42"

95

4

41°40'24"

HUMBOLDT

NORTH FORK OF
THE LITTLE
HUMBOLDT RIVER
WILDERNESS STUDY AREA

5

290

41°34'45"

293 KINGS RIVER RD

Orovada

41°33'28"

SANTA ROSA-
PARADISE
PEAK
WILDERNESS

HINKEY RD

95

6

Paradise
Valley

290

41°27'49"

CHIMNEY DAM
RESERVOIR

41°26'32"

140

7

95

PARADISE HWY

41°20'53"

A   B   C   D   E

117°56'31"   117°47'19"   117°38'07"   117°28'54"   117°19'43"   117°10'31"

41°19'36"

MAP
106

MAP
106

1:380,160
1 in. = 6 mi.

0   4   8

miles

N

SEE 95 MAP

42°08'09"

LOOKOUT
BUTTE
WILDERNESS
STUDY AREA

OREGON
IDAHO

LITTLE
OWYHEE RIVER
WILDERNESS
STUDY AREA

OWYHEE

DUCK
VALLEY
INDIAN
RESERVATION

42°06'31"

1

JUNIPER
BASIN
RESERVOIR

1

MALHEUR

42°01'13"

OREGON
NEVADA

IDAHO
NEVADA

41°59'34"

SOUTH FORK
OWYHEE RIVER
WILDERNESS
STUDY AREA

2

DUCK
VALLEY
INDIAN
RESERVATION

2

OWYHEE
CANYON
WILDERNESS
STUDY AREA

41°54'17"

41°52'39"

3

3

41°47'20"

41°45'42"

MAP
105

SEE

4

ELKO

4

41°40'24"

41°38'47"

HUMBOLDT

5

5

41°33'28"

41°31'51"

NORTH FORK OF THE
LITTLE HUMBOLDT
RIVER WILDERNESS
STUDY AREA

6

6

41°26'32"

41°24'55"

CHIMNEY DAM
RESERVOIR

LITTLE
HUMBOLDT RIVER
WILDERNESS STUDY
AREA

7

7

RAND MCNALLY

41°19'36"

41°17'59"

A   B   C   D   E

117°10'30"   117°01'18"   116°52'07"   116°42'55"   116°33'44"   116°24'32"

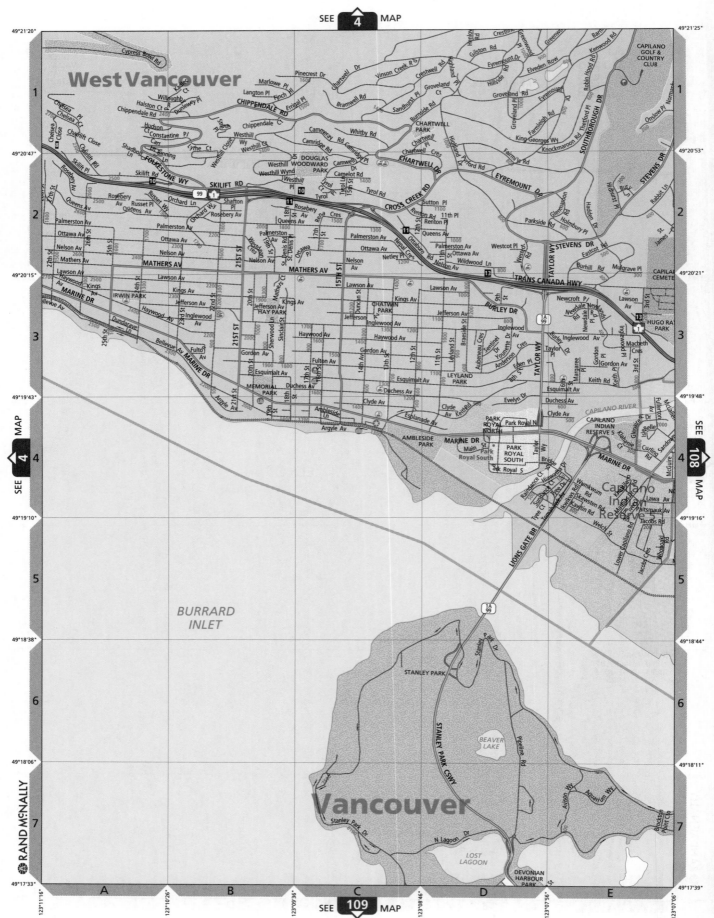

MAP
108

MAP
108

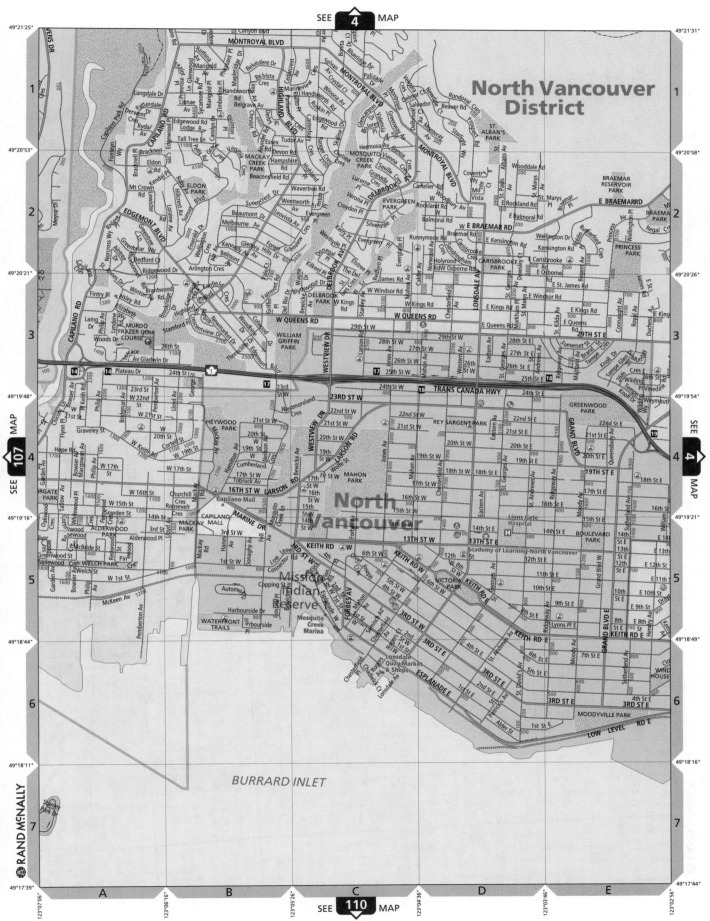

SEE 4 MAP

SEE 107 MAP

SEE 4 MAP

SEE 110 MAP

1:30,000
1 in. = 2500 ft.
0   0.25   0.5
miles

N

North Vancouver
District

North
Vancouver

Mission
Indian
Reserve

BURRARD INLET

RAND MᶜNALLY

MAP 109

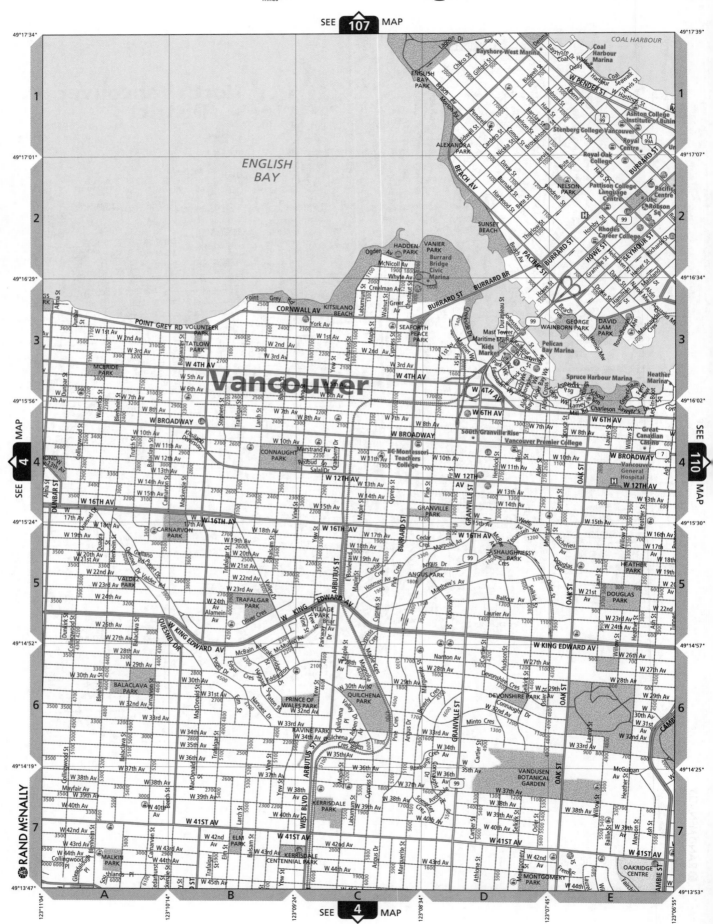

MAP 109

1:30,000
1 in. = 2500 ft.

SEE 107 MAP

SEE 4 MAP

SEE 110 MAP

SEE 4 MAP

ENGLISH BAY

Vancouver

RAND M?NALLY

MAP
110

1:30,000
1 in. = 2500 ft.
0   0.25   0.5
miles

N

MAP
110

BURRARD INLET

Vancouver

MAP
111

1:30,000
1 in. = 2500 ft.
0   0.25   0.5
miles

MAP
111

SEE 14 MAP

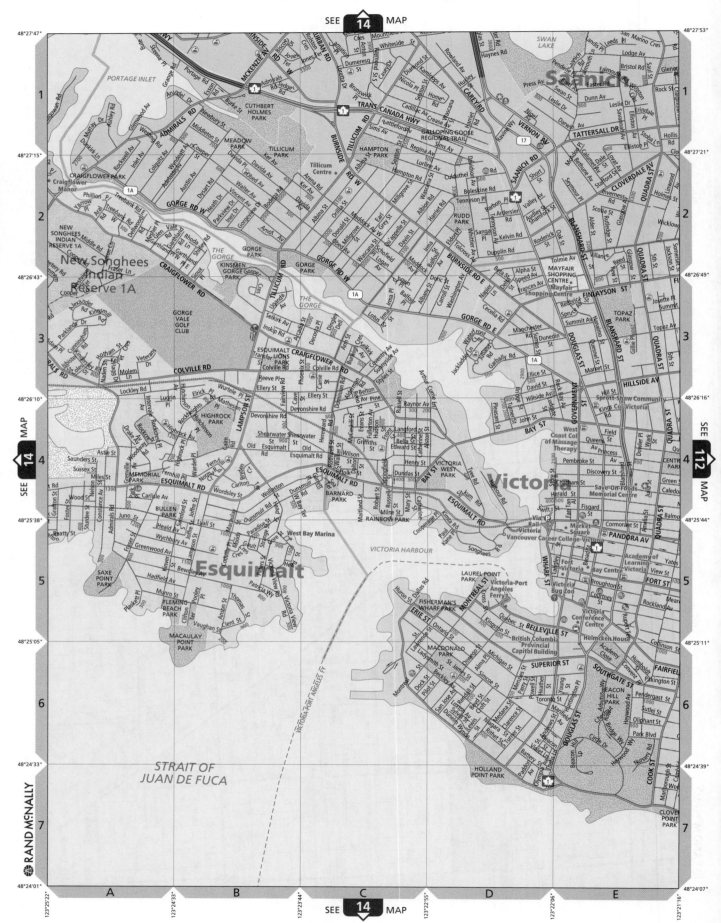

SEE 14 MAP

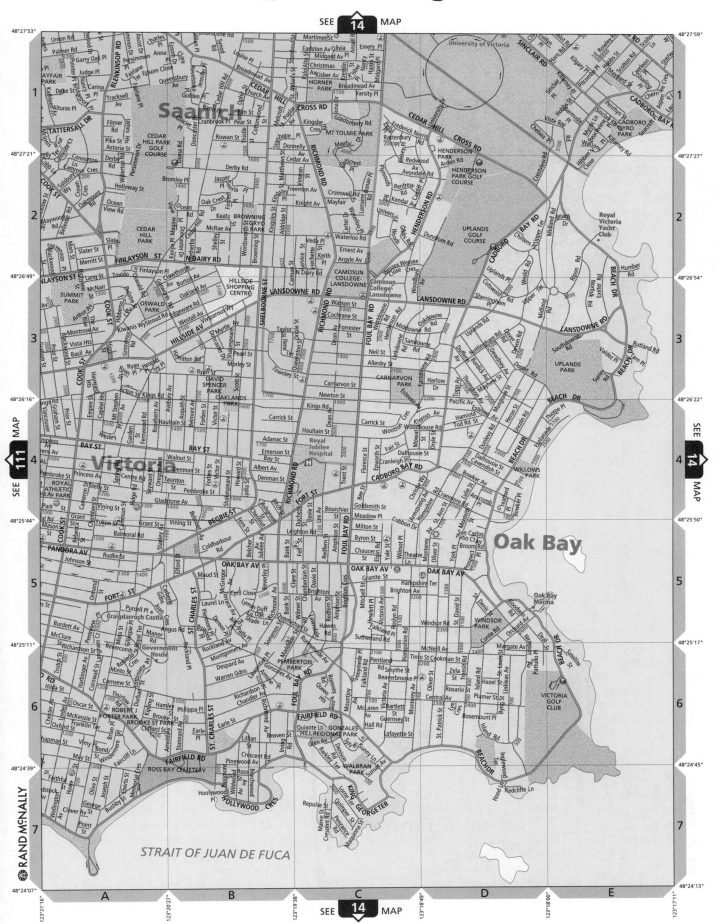

MAP
113

MAP
113

MAP
114

MAP
114

1:30,000
1 in. = 2500 ft.
0   0.25   0.5
miles

SEE 15 MAP

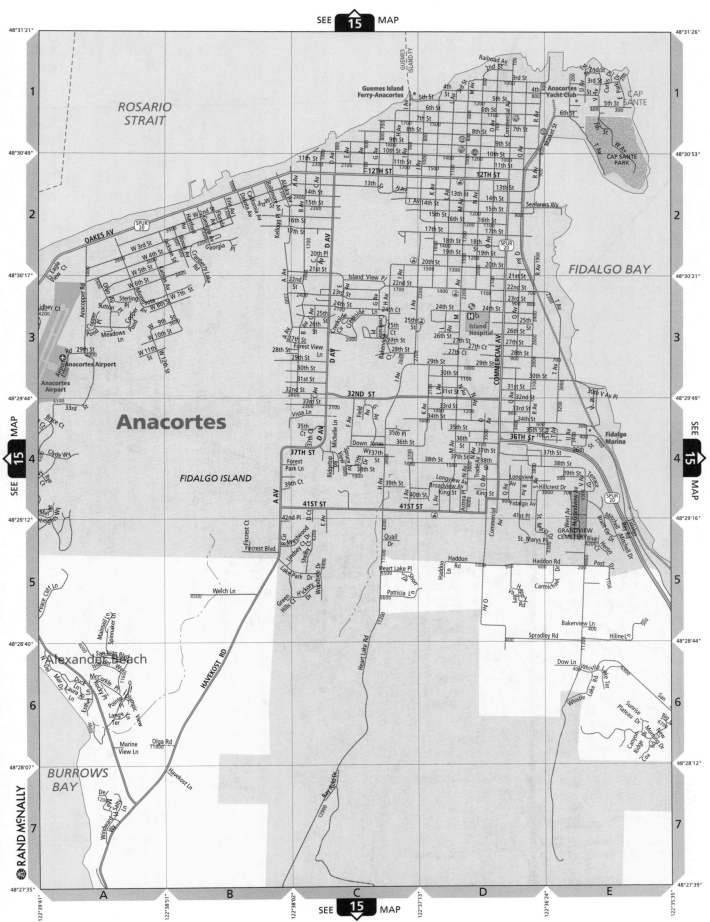

ROSARIO
STRAIT

FIDALGO BAY

CAP SANTE

CAP SANTE PARK

Anacortes

FIDALGO ISLAND

Anacortes Airport

Alexander Beach

BURROWS BAY

SEE 15 MAP

SEE 15 MAP

SEE 15 MAP

MAP
115

MAP
115

1:30,000
1 in. = 2500 ft.
0   0.25   0.5
miles

SEE 15 MAP

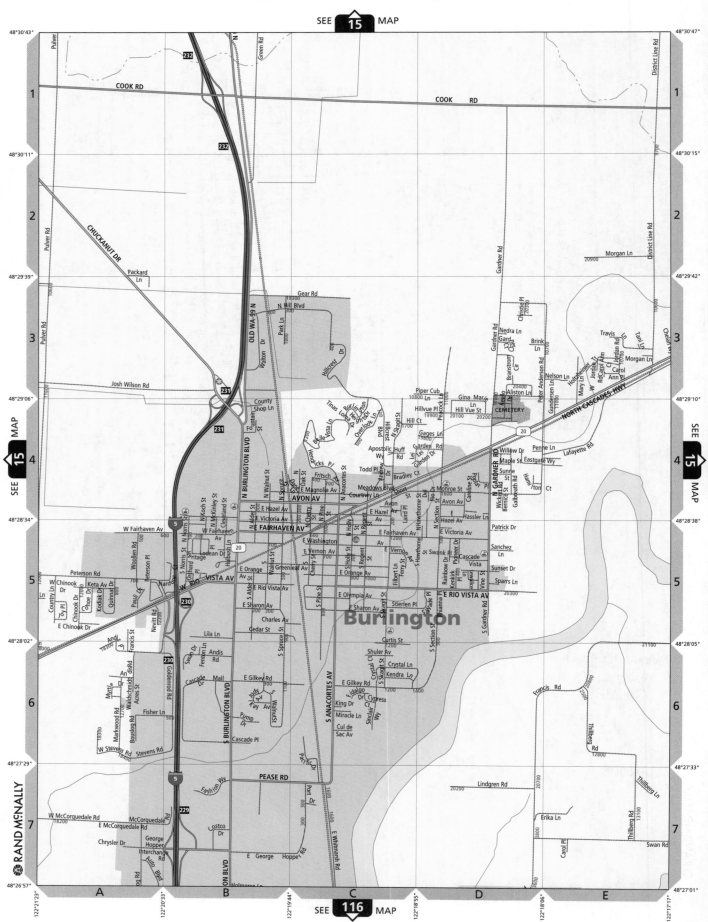

SEE 15 MAP

SEE 15 MAP

SEE 116 MAP

MAP
116

MAP
116

1:30,000
1 in. = 2500 ft.
0   0.25   0.5
miles

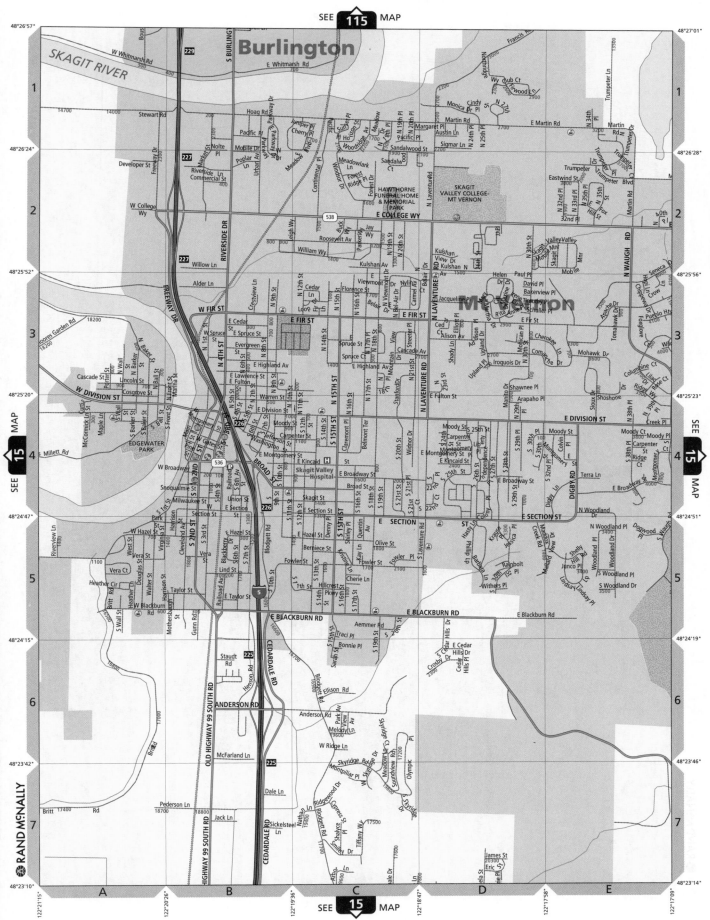

SEE **115** MAP

Burlington

SKAGIT RIVER

Mt Vernon

SKAGIT VALLEY COLLEGE-MT VERNON

HAWTHORNE FUNERAL HOME & MEMORIAL PARK

EDGEWATER PARK

Skagit Valley Hospital

SEE **15** MAP

SEE **15** MAP

SEE **15** MAP

MAP
117

MAP
117

1:30,000
1 in. = 2500 ft.
0   0.25   0.5
miles

SEE ⌂ **14** MAP

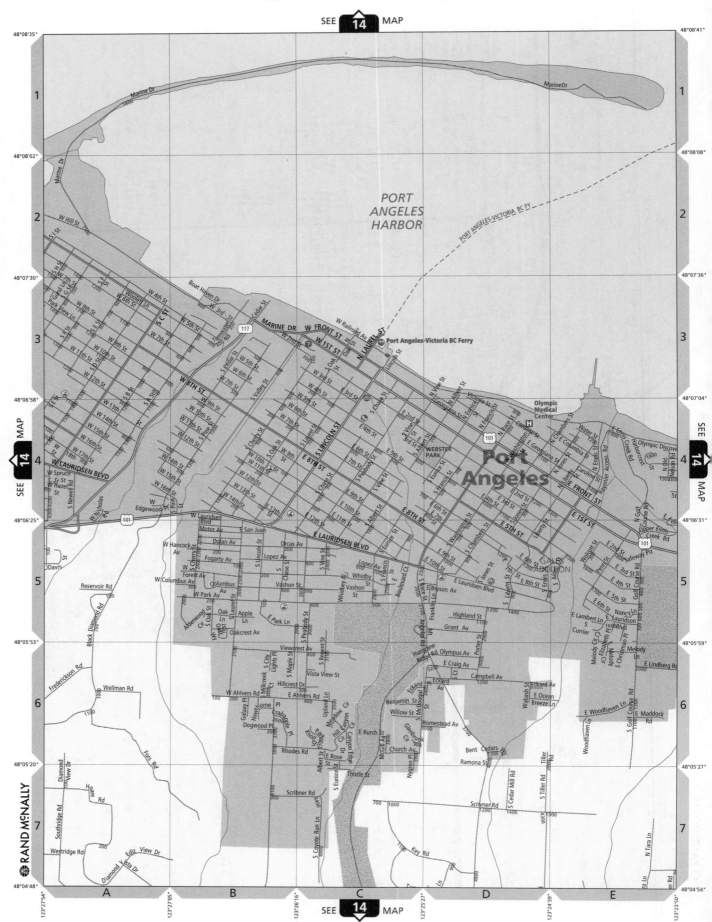

48°08'35"
48°08'41"

48°08'02"
48°08'08"

48°07'30"
48°07'36"

48°06'58"
48°07'04"

48°06'25"
48°06'31"

48°05'53"
48°05'59"

48°05'20"
48°05'27"

48°04'48"
48°04'54"

1

2

3

4

5

6

7

MAP
⊲ **14**
SEE MAP

SEE
⊲ **14**
MAP

*PORT
ANGELES
HARBOR*

PORT ANGELES-VICTORIA BC FY

Port Angeles-Victoria BC Ferry

Marine Dr

MarineDr

MARINE DR   W FRONT ST

W 1ST ST

N LAUREL ST

W 8TH ST

W LAURIDSEN BLVD

E LAURIDSEN BLVD

E 8TH ST

E 5TH ST

E 1ST ST

E FRONT ST

Olympic
Medical
Center

WEBSTER
PARK

**Port
Angeles**

GALES
ADDITION

RAND M^cNALLY

A   B   C   D   E

123°27'54"
123°27'05"
123°26'16"
123°25'27"
123°24'39"
123°23'50"

SEE ⌄ **14** MAP

MAP
118

MAP
118

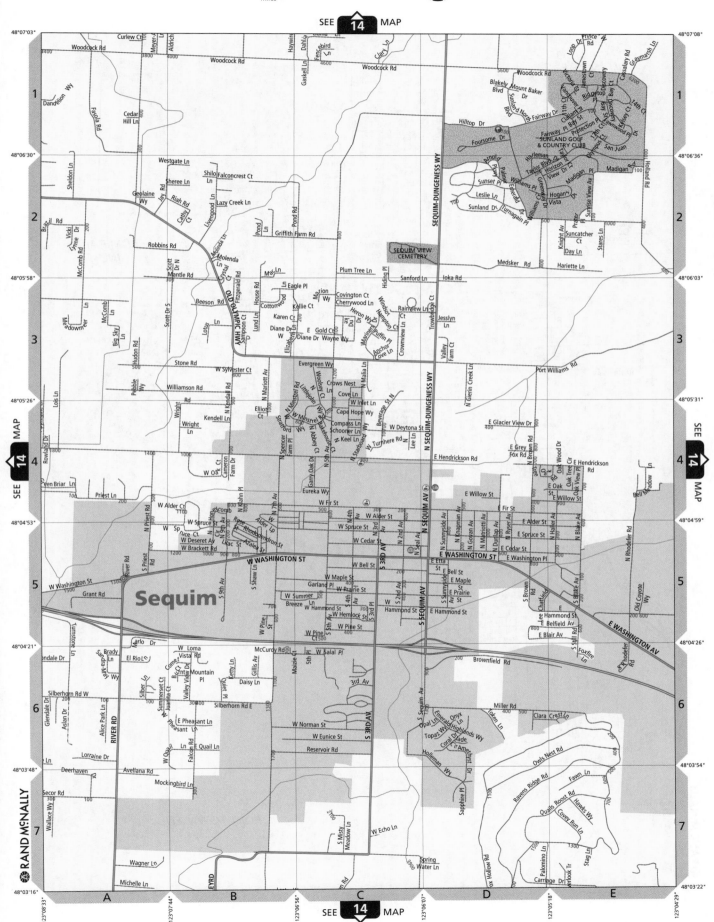

1:30,000
1 in. = 2500 ft.
0   0.25   0.5
miles

Sequim

RAND McNALLY

MAP
119

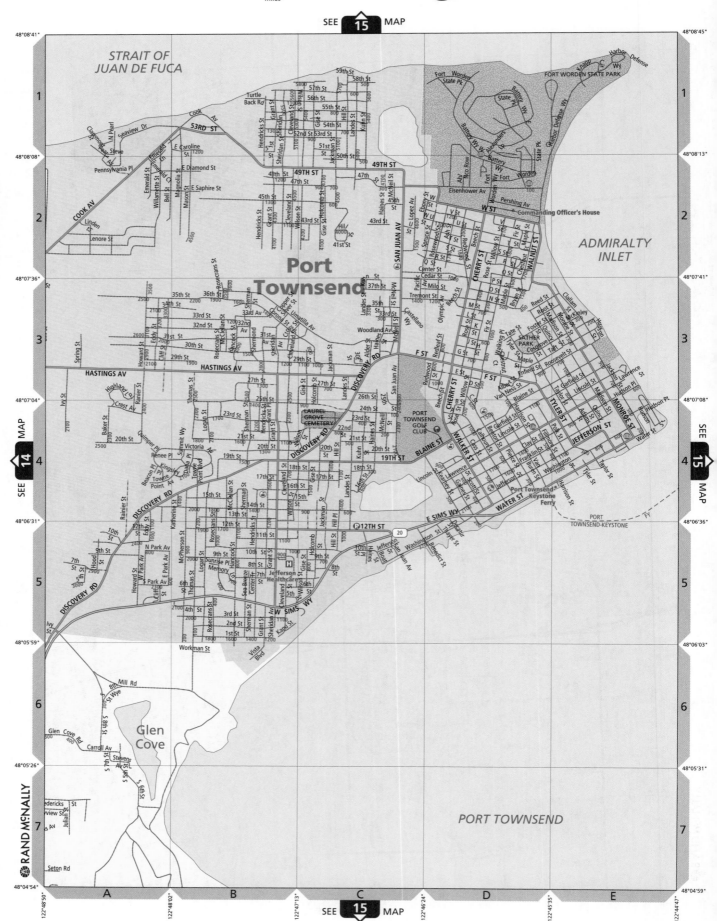

MAP
119

1:30,000
1 in. = 2500 ft.
0   0.25   0.5
miles

SEE 15 MAP

STRAIT OF
JUAN DE FUCA

Port
Townsend

ADMIRALTY
INLET

FORT WORDEN STATE PARK

HASTINGS AV

DISCOVERY RD

Glen
Cove

PORT TOWNSEND

SEE 15 MAP

MAP
120

MAP
120

1:30,000
1 in. = 2500 ft.
0   0.25   0.5
miles

SEE 15 MAP

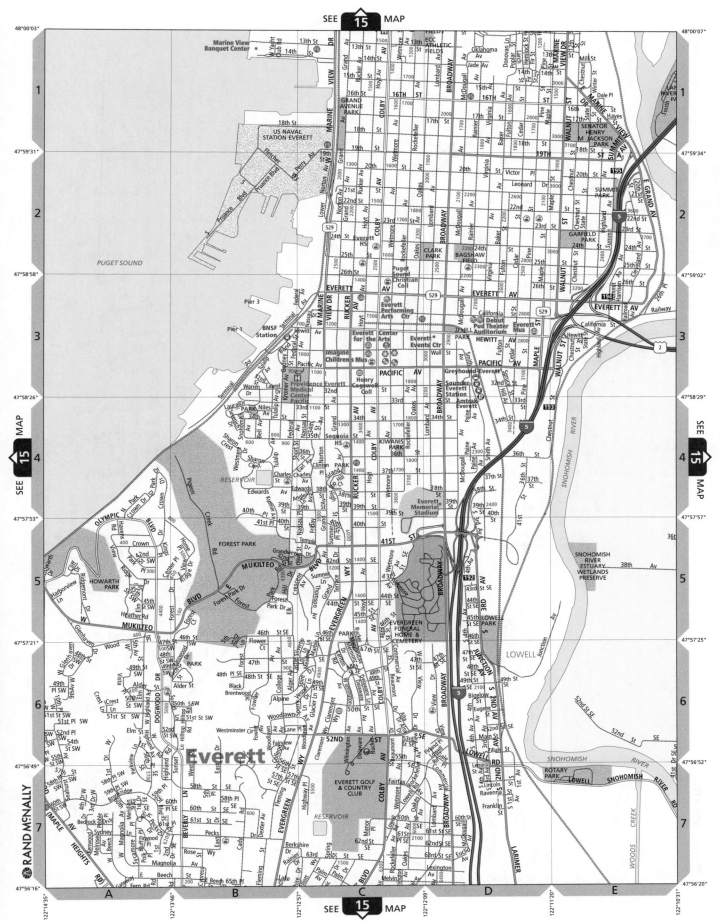

48°00'03"   48°00'07"

47°59'31"   47°59'34"

47°58'58"   47°59'02"

47°58'26"   47°58'29"

47°57'53"   47°57'57"

47°57'21"   47°57'25"

47°56'49"   47°56'52"

47°56'16"   47°56'20"

122°14'35"   122°13'46"   122°12'57"   122°12'09"   122°11'20"   122°10'31"

SEE 15 MAP

PUGET SOUND

Everett

RAND McNALLY

MAP
121

1:30,000
1 in. = 2500 ft.
0   0.25   0.5
miles

MAP
121

SEE 25 MAP

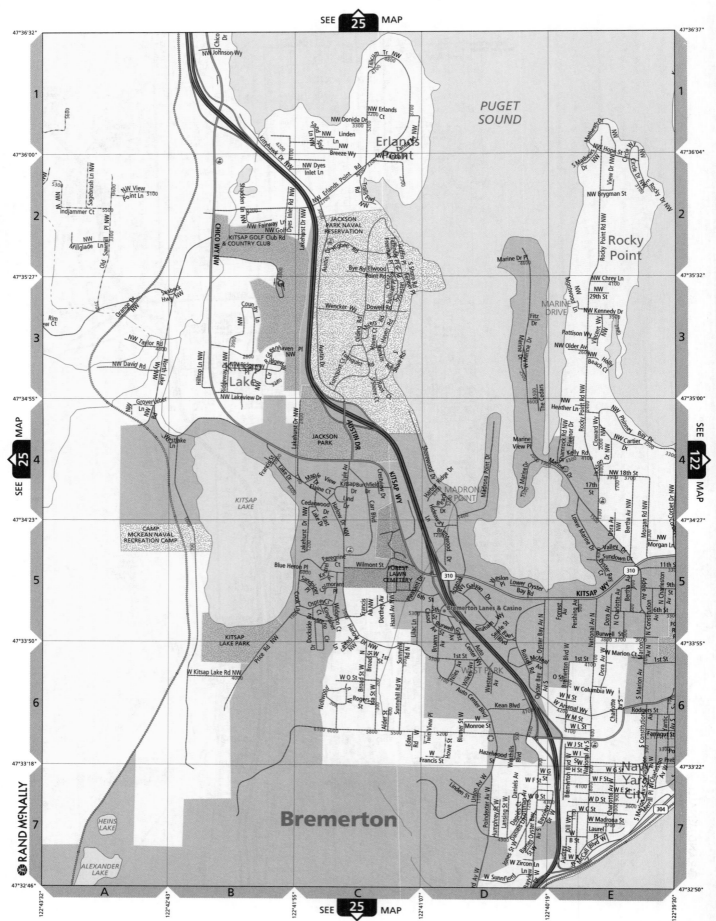

PUGET SOUND

Erlands Point

Rocky Point

MARINE DRIVE

Jackson Park Naval Reservation

KITSAP GOLF CLUB & COUNTRY CLUB

Chico Lake

Kitsap Lake

CAMP MCKEAN NAVAL RECREATION CAMP

JACKSON PARK

FOREST LAWN CEMETERY

KITSAP LAKE PARK

WEST PARK

Bremerton

Navy Yard City

HEINS LAKE

ALEXANDER LAKE

MADRONA POINT

SEE 25 MAP

SEE 122 MAP

SEE 25 MAP

RAND MᶜNALLY

47°36'32"
47°36'37"
47°36'00"
47°36'04"
47°35'27"
47°35'32"
47°34'55"
47°35'00"
47°34'23"
47°34'27"
47°33'50"
47°33'55"
47°33'18"
47°33'22"
47°32'46"
47°32'50"

122°43'32"
122°42'43"
122°41'55"
122°41'07"
122°40'19"
122°39'30"

A   B   C   D   E

1   2   3   4   5   6   7

MAP
122

1:30,000
1 in. = 2500 ft.
0   0.25   0.5
miles

MAP
122

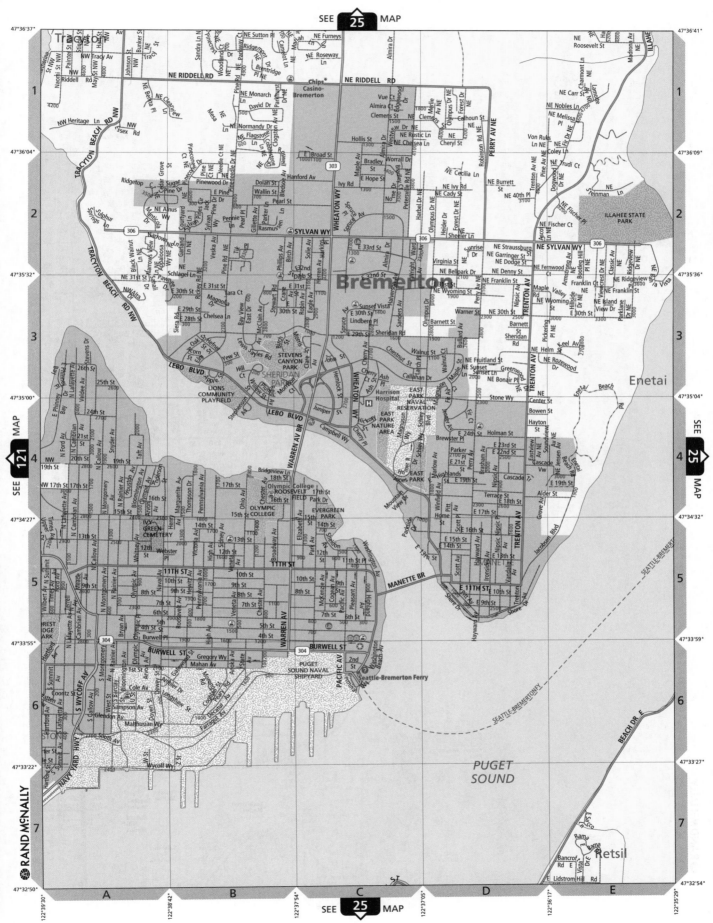

SEE **25** MAP

SEE **121** MAP

SEE **25** MAP

SEE **25** MAP

Bremerton

Enetai

PUGET SOUND

Keyport / Ketsil

RAND McNALLY

MAP
123

MAP
123

SEE 25 MAP

1:30,000
1 in. = 2500 ft.
0   0.25   0.5
miles

SEE 25 MAP

SEE 124 MAP

SEE 127 MAP

RAND McNALLY

MAP 124

MAP 124

1:30,000
1 in. = 2500 ft.

SEE 25 MAP

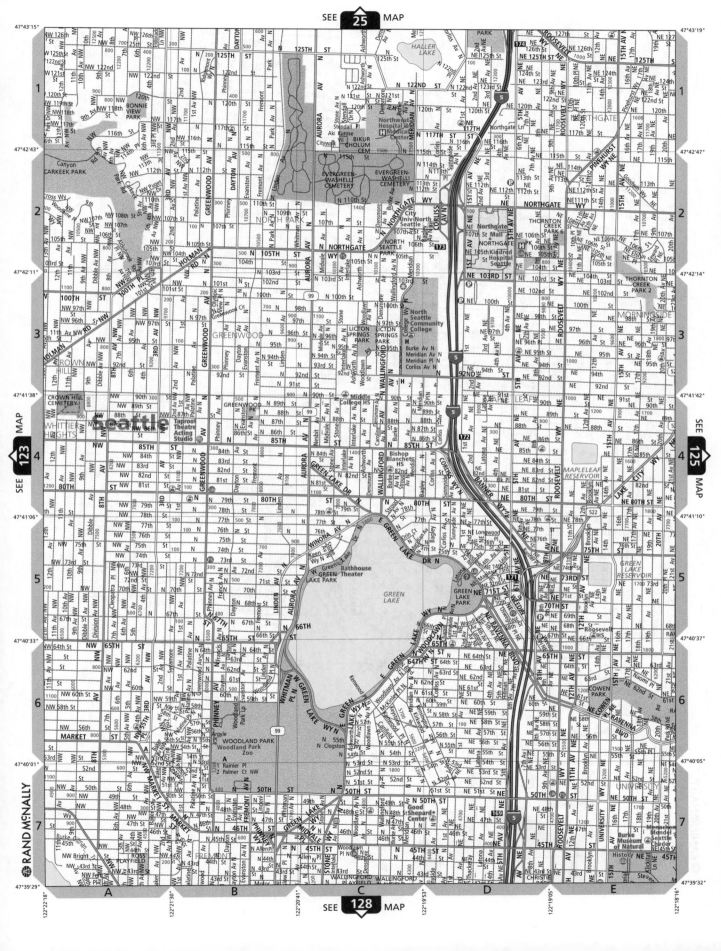

SEE 128 MAP

MAP
125

MAP
125

1:30,000
1 in. = 2500 ft.

0   0.25   0.5
miles

SEE 25 MAP

SEE 124 MAP

SEE 126 MAP

SEE 129 MAP

RAND McNALLY

MAP
126

1:30,000
1 in. = 2500 ft.
0   0.25   0.5
miles

MAP
126

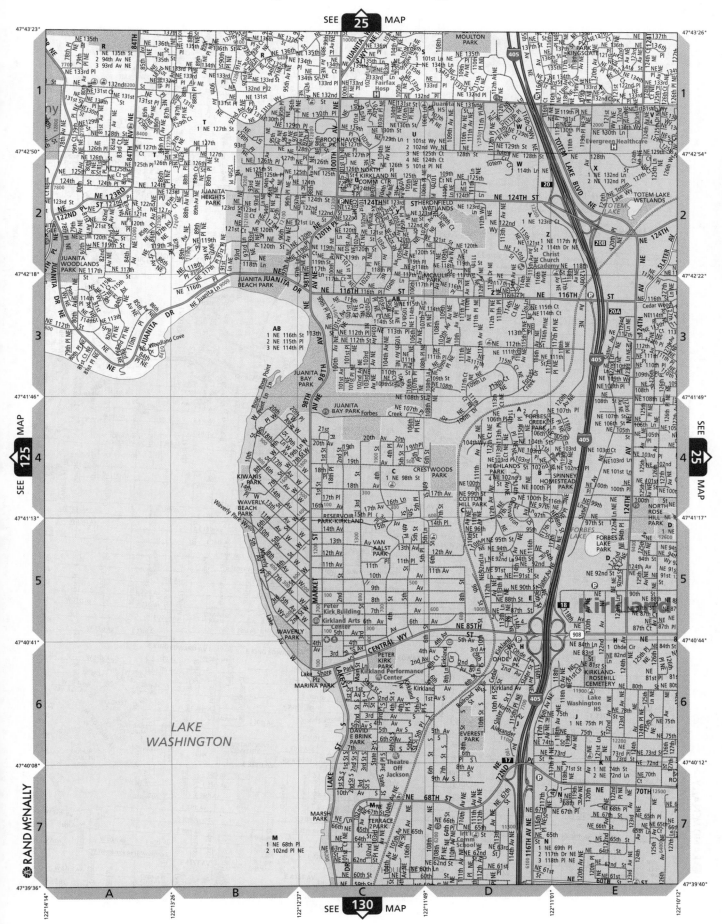

RAND MᶜNALLY

MAP
127

1:30,000
1 in. = 2500 ft.
0   0.25   0.5
miles

SEE 123 MAP

SEE 25 MAP

SEE 128 MAP

Seattle

PUGET
SOUND

A
1 40th Av W
2 Altavista Pl W
3 Mountain Dr W

B
1 Montvale Ct W
2 Constance Dr W
3 W Clise Ct

C
1 22nd Av W
2 Thorndyke Pl W

F
1 SW California Pl
2 Elm Pl SW
3 California Ln SW
4 Sunset Av SW
5 Palm Av SW
6 SW Maryland Pl

D
1 Constance Dr W

SEE 131 MAP

MAP
128

1:30,000
1 in. = 2500 ft.
0   0.25   0.5
miles

MAP
128

SEE 124 MAP

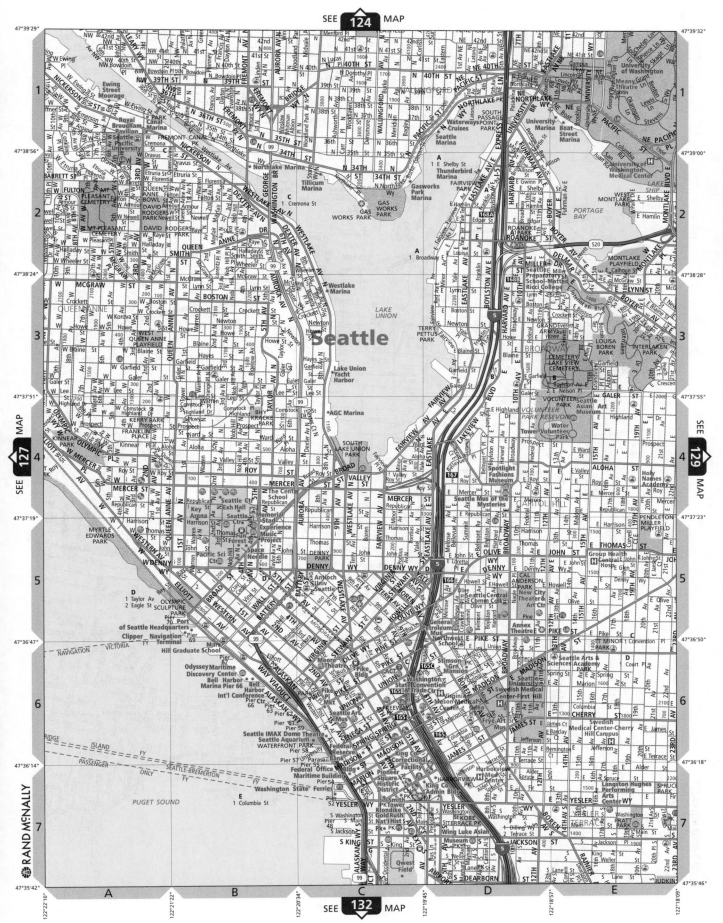

SEE 127 MAP

SEE 129 MAP

SEE 132 MAP

RAND MCNALLY

MAP
129

MAP
129

1:30,000
1 in. = 2500 ft.
0   0.25   0.5
miles

SEE 125 MAP

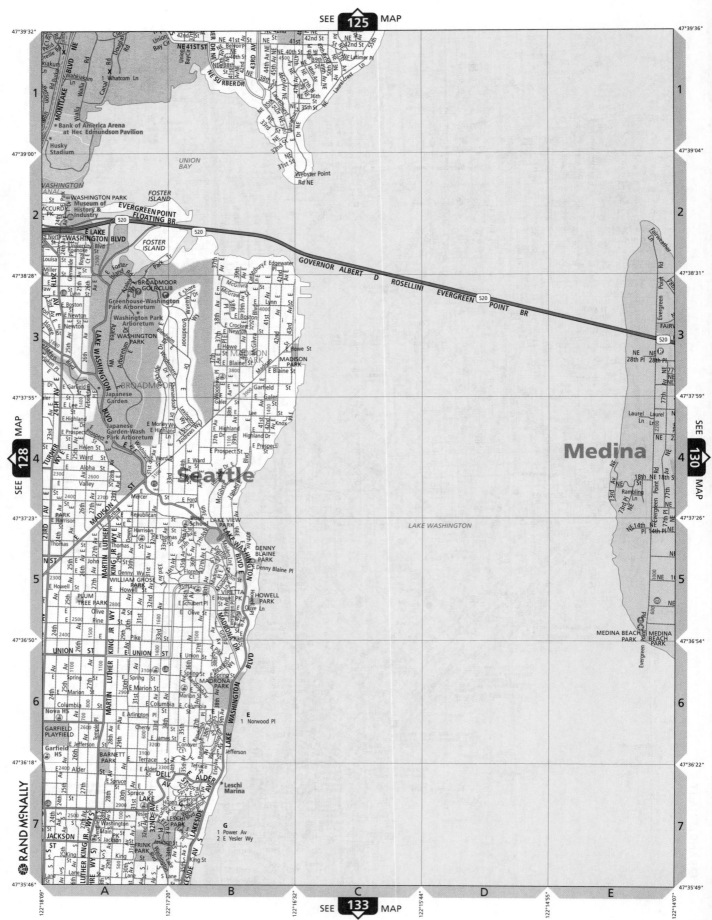

SEE 128 MAP

SEE 130 MAP

Medina

Seattle

LAKE WASHINGTON

UNION BAY

SEE 133 MAP

RAND MCNALLY

MAP
130

MAP
130

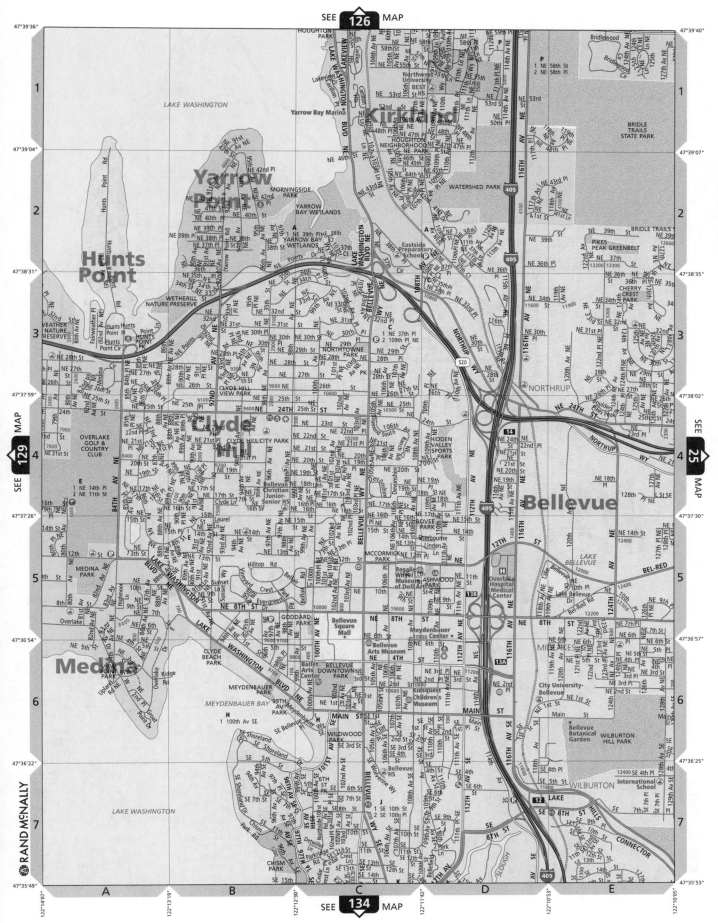

MAP
131

1:30,000
1 in. = 2500 ft.

0   0.25   0.5

miles

MAP
131

SEE 127 MAP

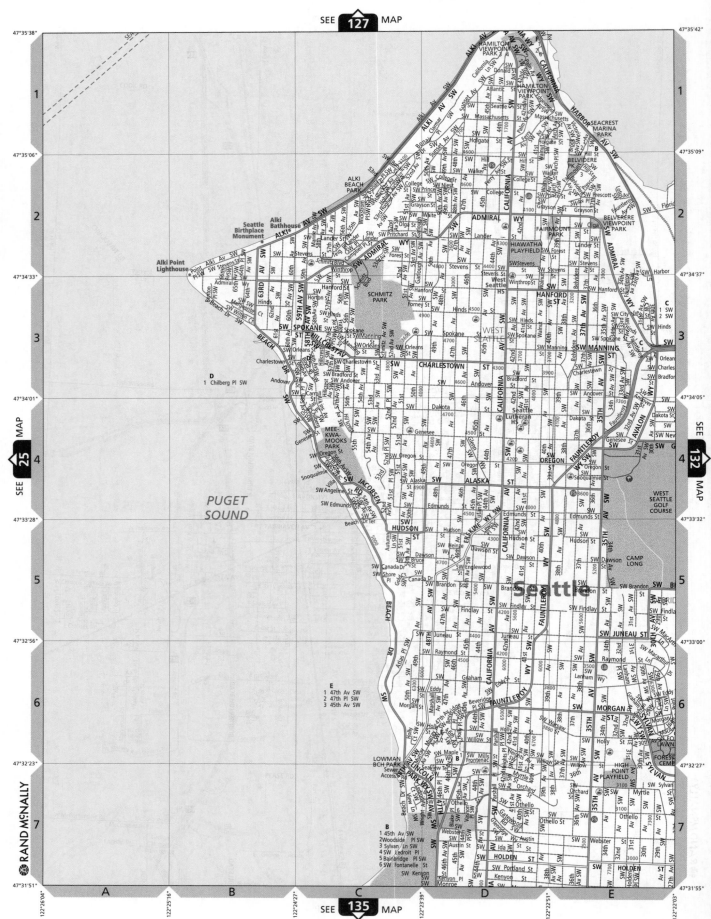

SEE 25 MAP

SEE 132 MAP

SEE 135 MAP

PUGET
SOUND

Seattle

RAND McNALLY

MAP
132

1:30,000
1 in. = 2500 ft.

0   0.25   0.5

miles

MAP
132

SEE [128] MAP

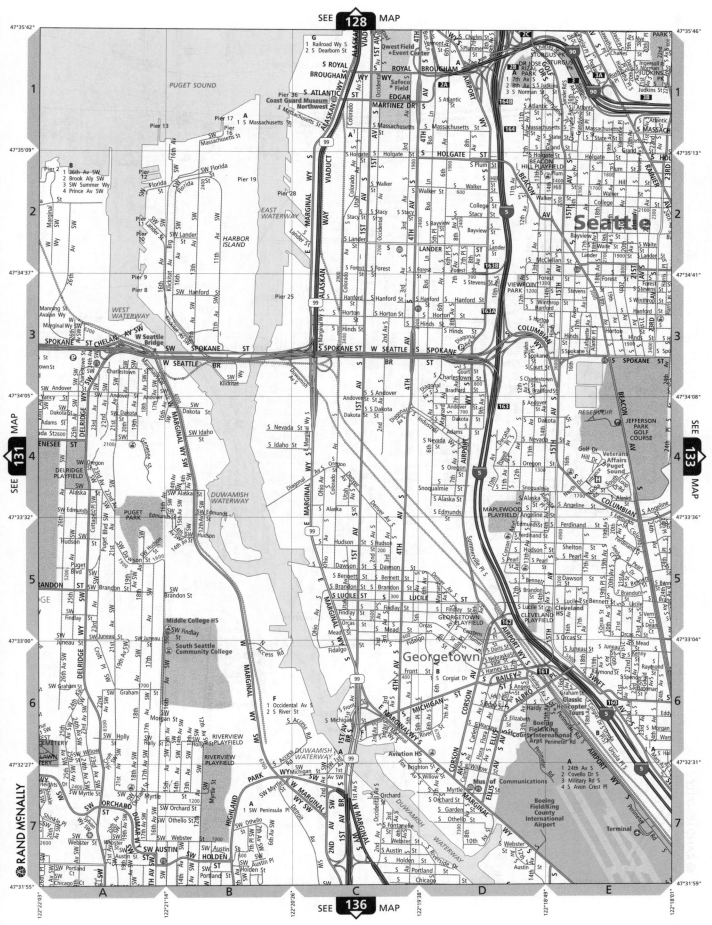

SEE [131] MAP

SEE [133] MAP

SEE [136] MAP

RAND MCNALLY

MAP
133

MAP
133

1:30,000
1 in. = 2500 ft.

0   0.25   0.5

miles

SEE 129 MAP

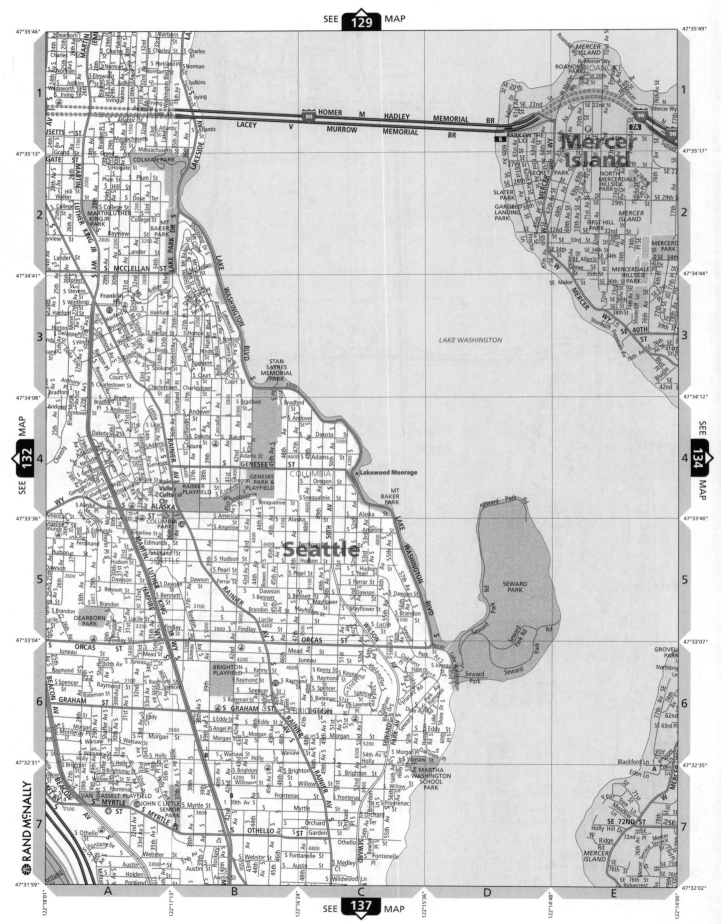

SEE 132 MAP

SEE 134 MAP

SEE 137 MAP

RAND M°NALLY

MAP
134

MAP
134

1:30,000
1 in. = 2500 ft.
0   0.25   0.5
miles

SEE 130 MAP

SEE 133 MAP

SEE 25 MAP

SEE 138 MAP

RAND McNALLY

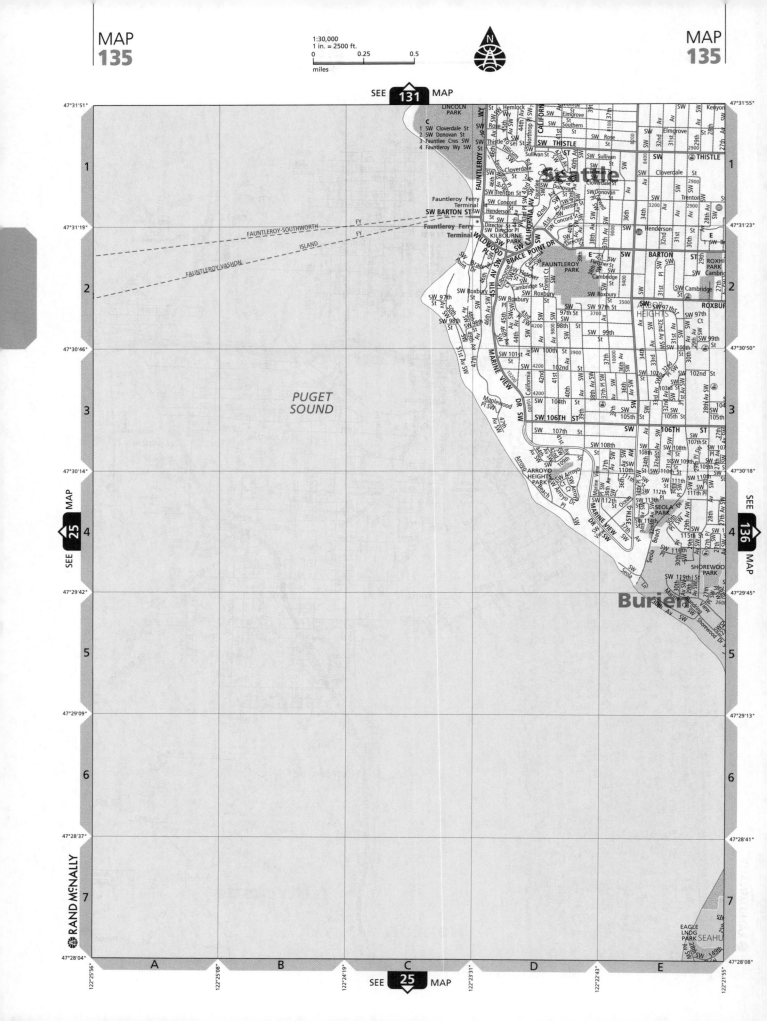

MAP
136

MAP
136

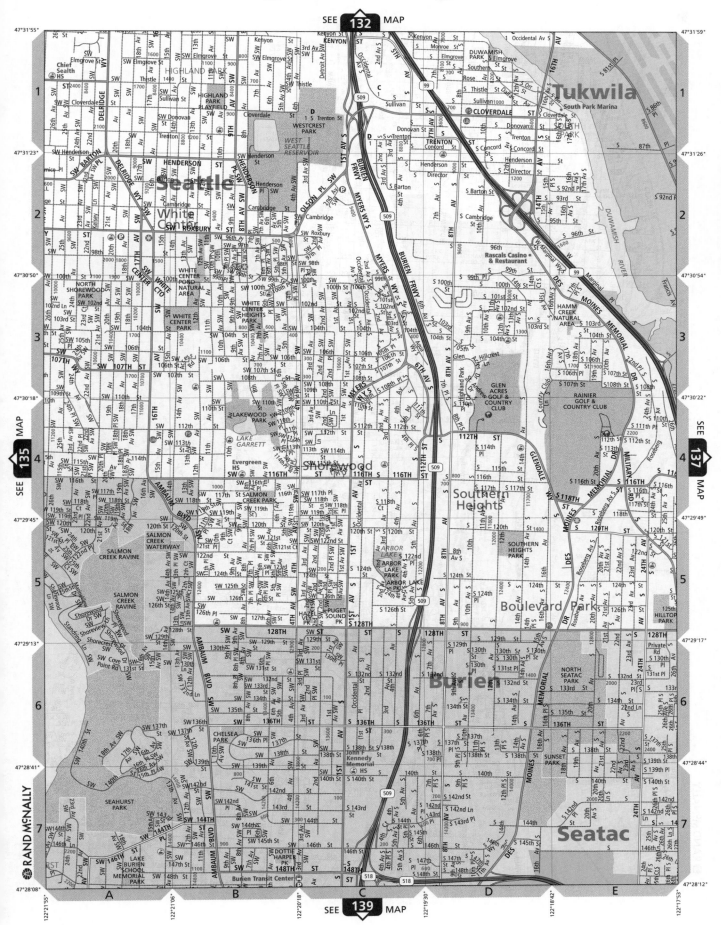

1:30,000
1 in. = 2500 ft.
0   0.25   0.5
miles

SEE 135 MAP

SEE 137 MAP

SEE 139 MAP

RAND MCNALLY

MAP
137

MAP
137

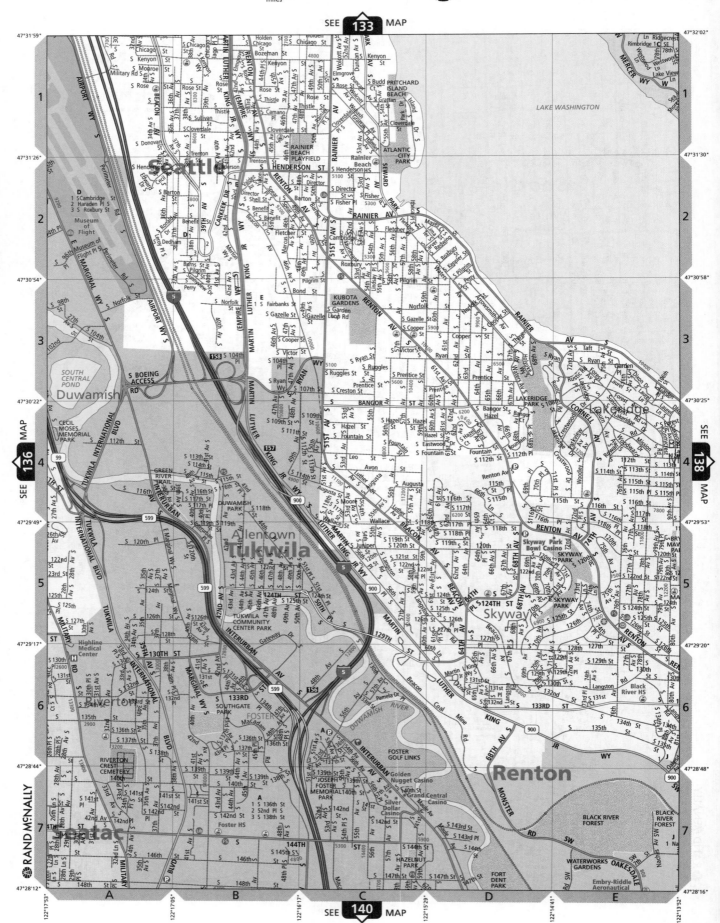

1:30,000
1 in. = 2500 ft.

0   0.25   0.5
miles

SEE 133 MAP

SEE 136 MAP

SEE 138 MAP

SEE 140 MAP

RAND McNALLY

MAP
138

MAP
138

1:30,000
1 in. = 2500 ft.

0   0.25   0.5
miles

SEE **134** MAP

SEE **25** MAP

MAP
139

MAP
139

MAP
140

MAP
140

1:30,000
1 in. = 2500 ft.
0   0.25   0.5
miles

SEE 137 MAP

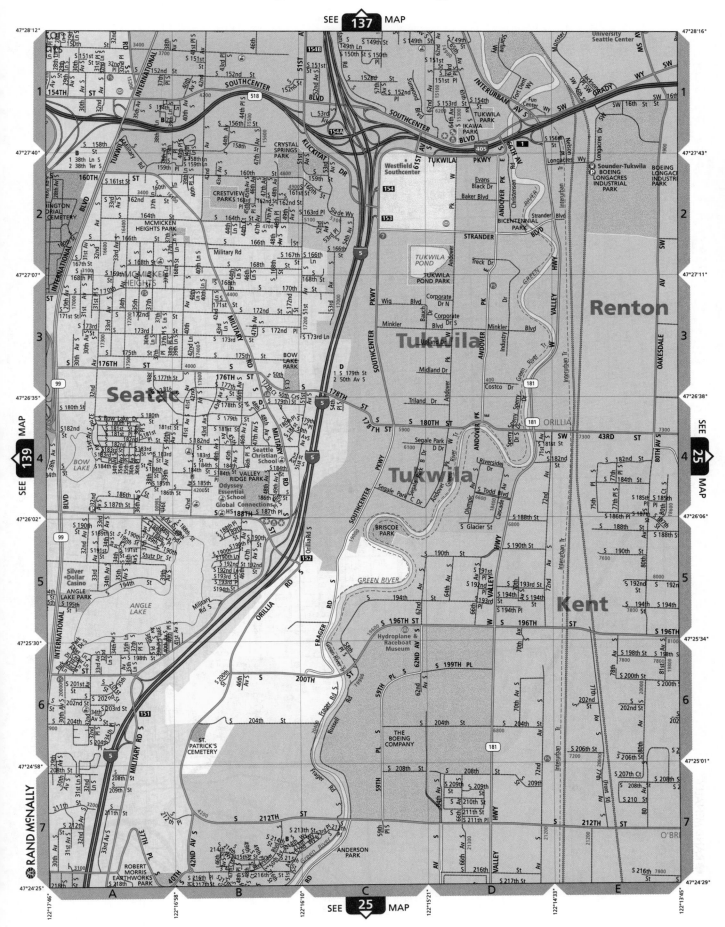

SEE 139 MAP

SEE 25 MAP

SEE 25 MAP

RAND McNALLY

MAP
141

MAP
141

1:30,000
1 in. = 2500 ft.

0   0.25   0.5

miles

SEE 25 MAP

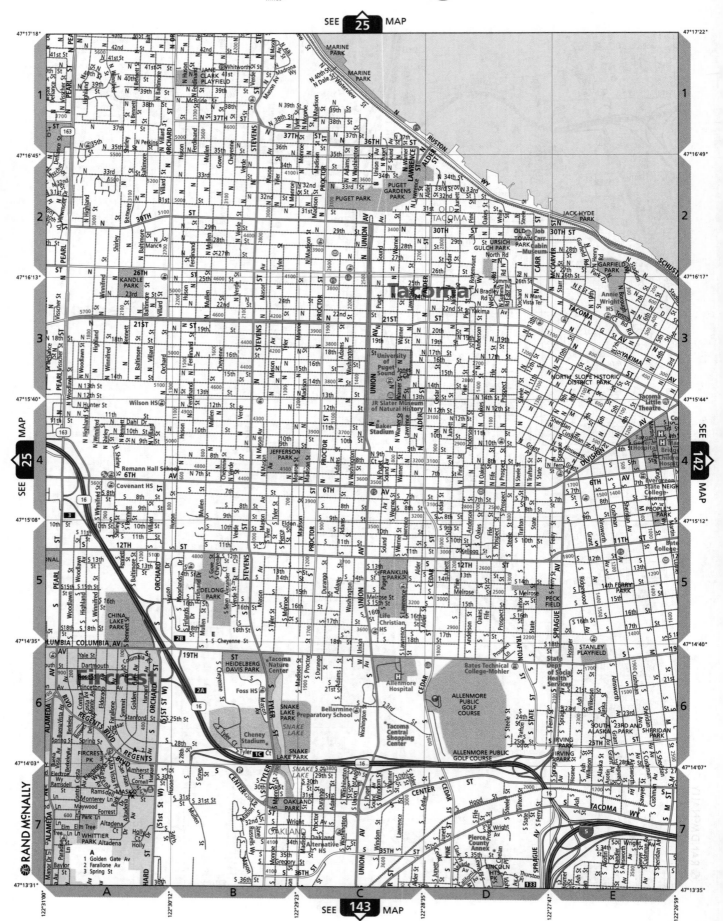

SEE 25 MAP

SEE 142 MAP

SEE 143 MAP

Tacoma

Fircrest

RAND MCNALLY

A
1 Golden Gate Av
2 Farallone Av
3 Spring St

MAP
142

MAP
142

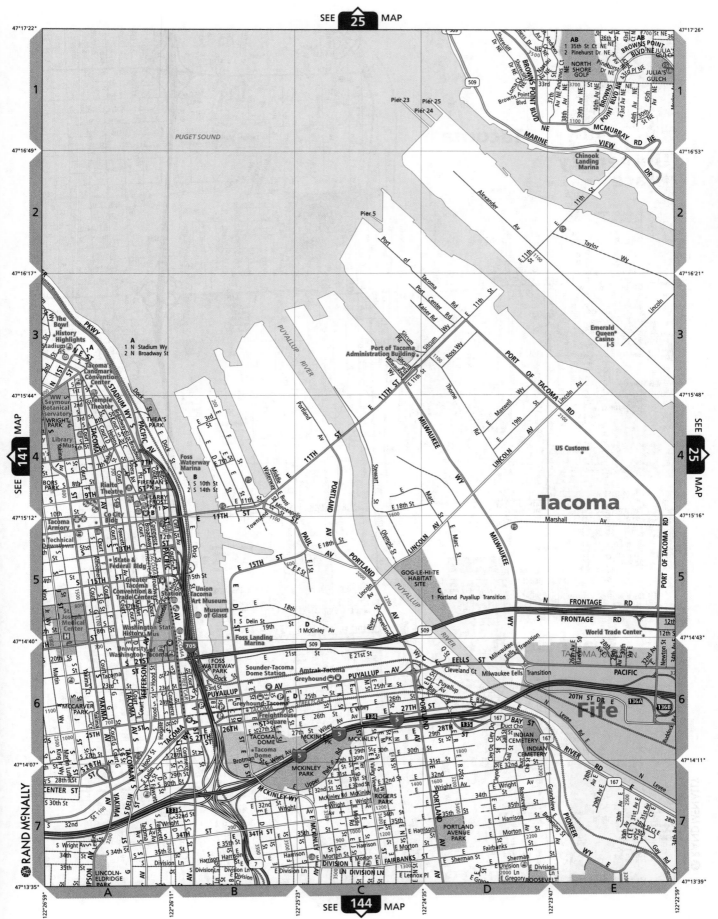

1:30,000
1 in. = 2500 ft.
0   0.25   0.5
miles

PUGET SOUND

Tacoma

Fife

RAND MCNALLY

MAP
143

MAP
143

1:30,000
1 in. = 2500 ft.
0   0.25   0.5
miles

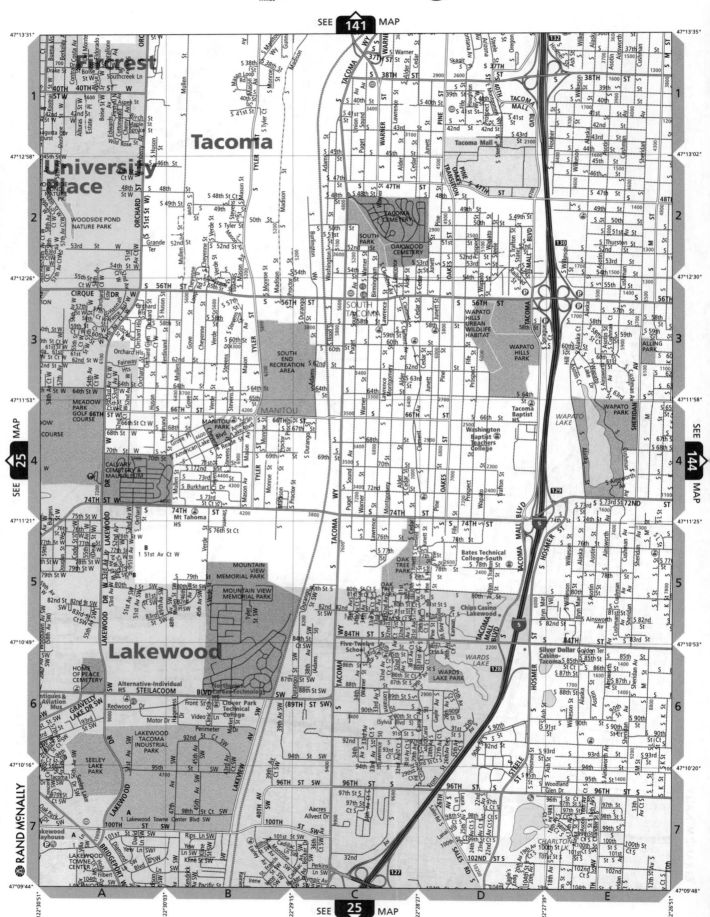

SEE 25 MAP

MAP
144

MAP
144

1:30,000
1 in. = 2500 ft.
0   0.25   0.5
miles

N

SEE 142 MAP

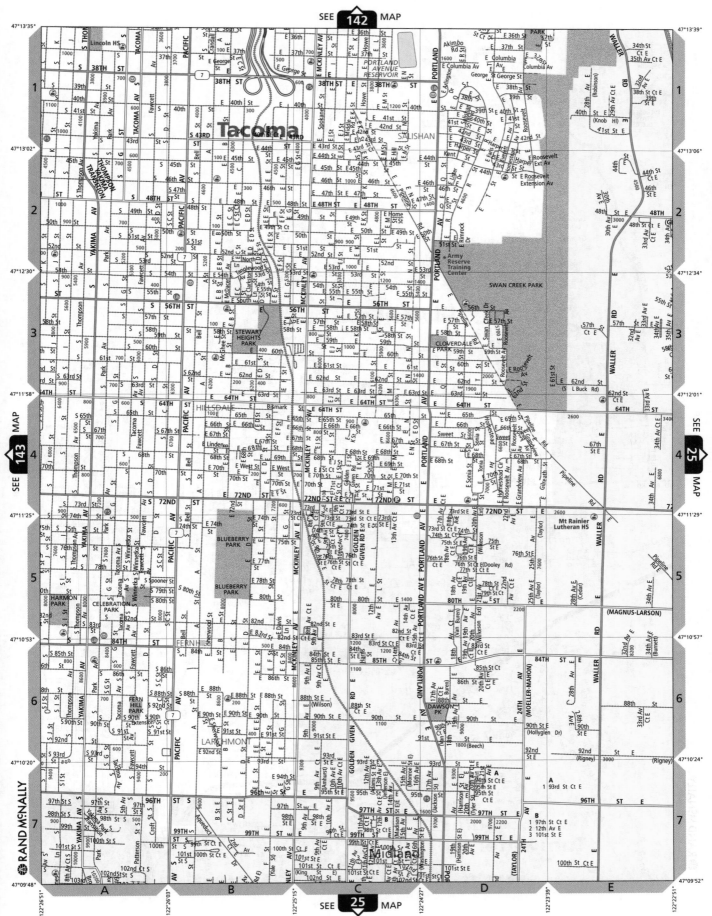

SEE 143 MAP

SEE 25 MAP

SEE 25 MAP

Tacoma

Midland

RAND M\=NALLY

MAP
145

MAP
145

1:30,000
1 in. = 2500 ft.
0   0.25   0.5
miles

SEE 24 MAP

Oldport

BUDD INLET

Evergreen State College

Olympia

Louise Lake

Grass Lake Park

Yauger Park

Capital Medical Center

Westfield Capital

Ken Lake

Tumwater

Marathon Park

South Puget Sound Community College

Capitol Lake Park

Capitol Lake

Washington State Capitol

Capitol Lake

SEE 24 MAP

SEE 146 MAP

SEE 147 MAP

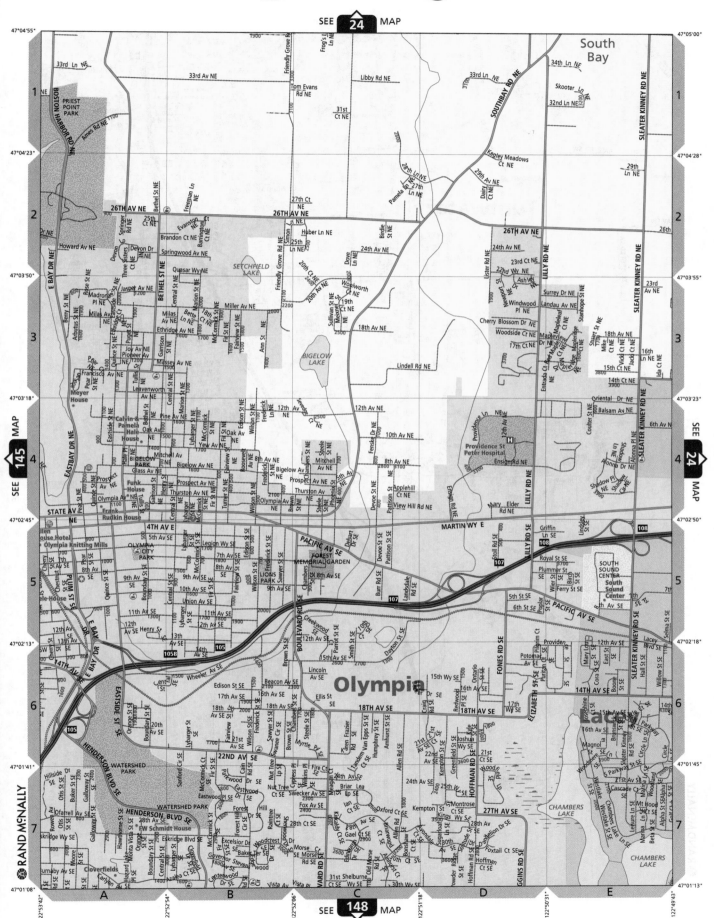

MAP
147

1:30,000
1 in. = 2500 ft.
0   0.25   0.5
miles

N

MAP
147

SEE **145** MAP

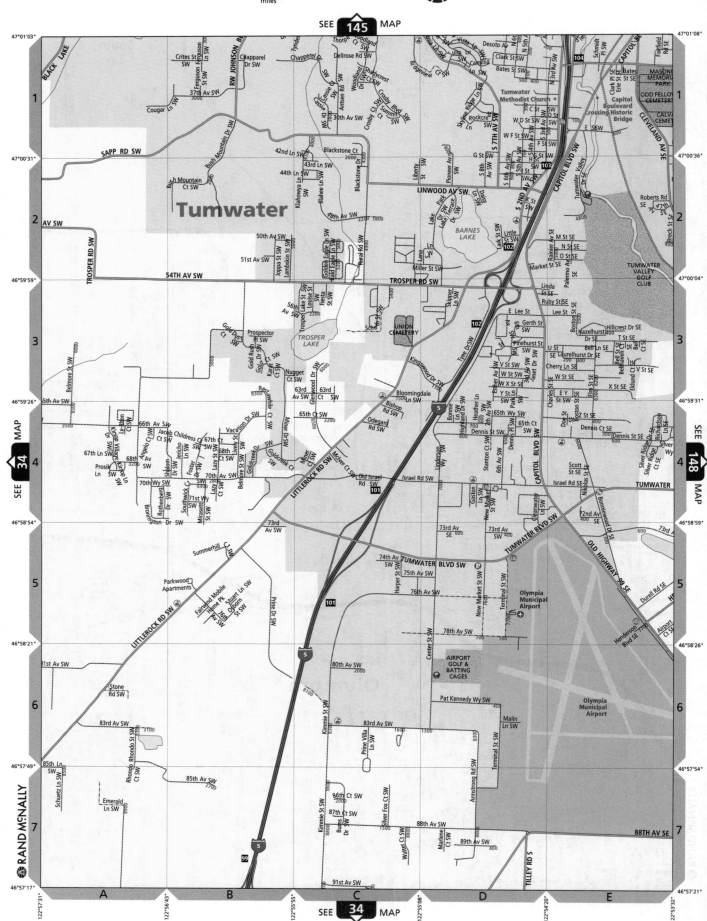

SEE **34** MAP

SEE **34** MAP

SEE **148** MAP

RAND M?NALLY

MAP 148

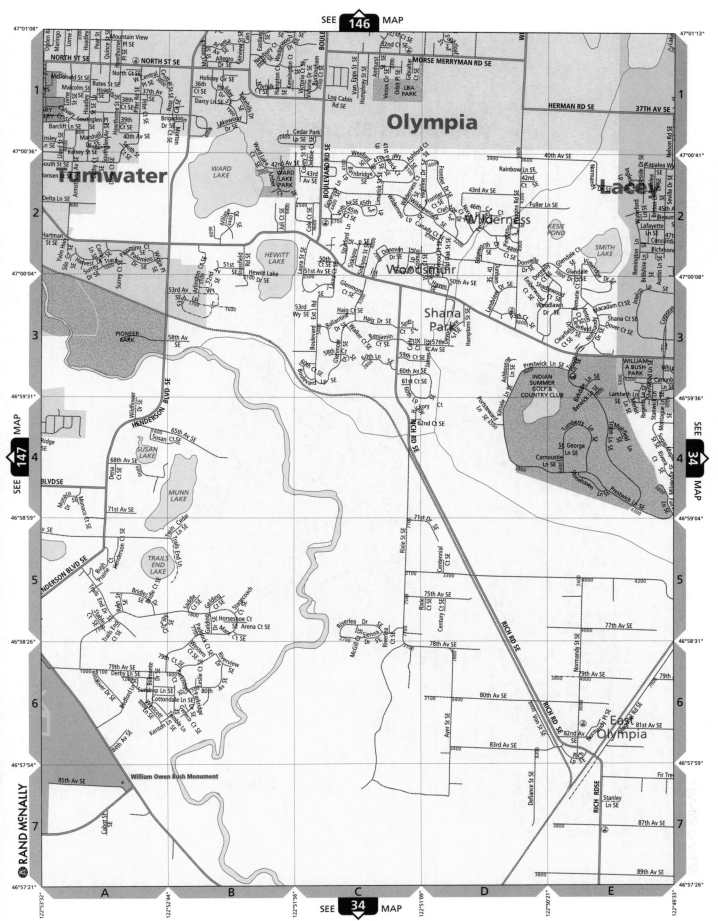

MAP 148

MAP
149

MAP
149

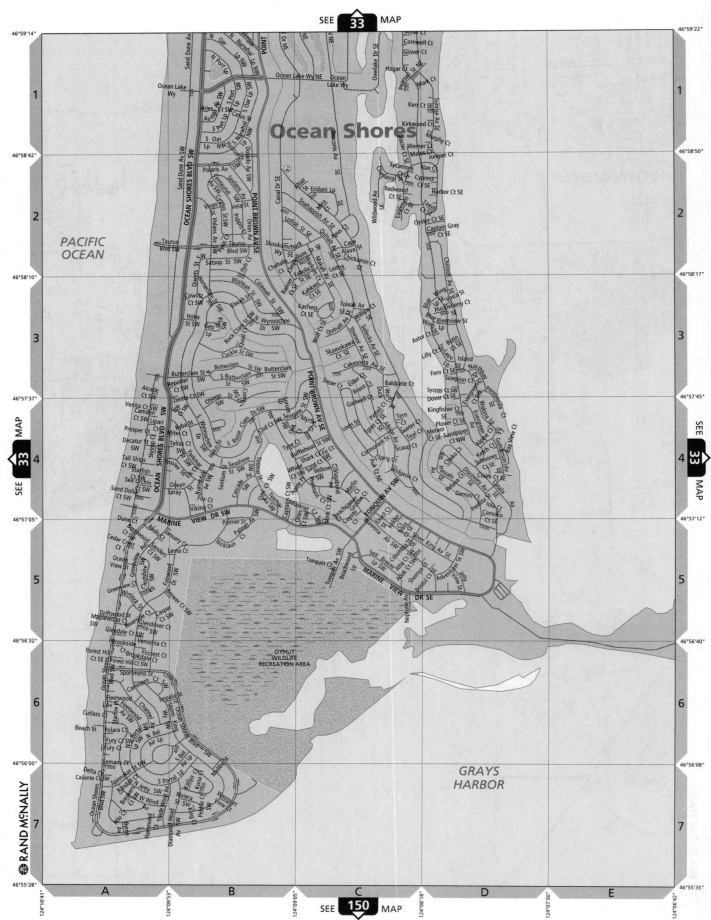

Ocean Shores

PACIFIC
OCEAN

SEE 33 MAP

SEE 33 MAP

OYHUT
WILDLIFE
RECREATION AREA

GRAYS
HARBOR

RAND M^cNALLY

MAP
150

MAP
150

1:30,000
1 in. = 2500 ft.
0   0.25   0.5
miles

N

SEE 149 MAP

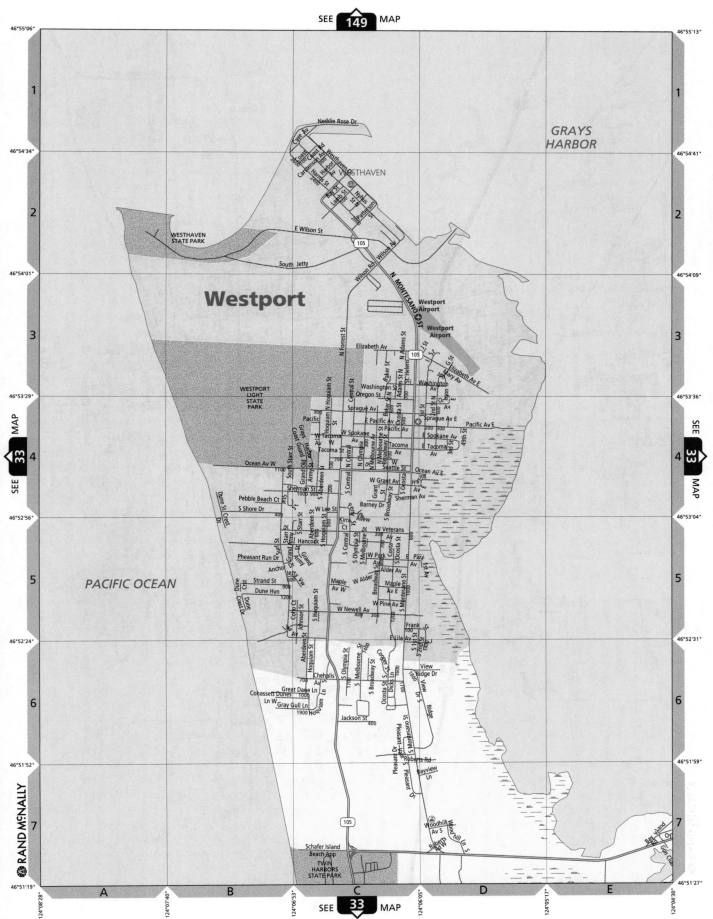

Westport

GRAYS HARBOR

WESTHAVEN STATE PARK

WESTHAVEN

Neddie Rose Dr
Cove Av
Coral
Silver Coast Rd
Carstenson Av
Westhaven Dr
Harms St
Harbor Av
Bay St
Lamb St
St N
Patterson
Nyhus St

E Wilson St

105

Wilson Rd
Wilson Av
N MONTESANO ST

South Jetty

Westport Airport

Westport Airport

N Forrest St

Elizabeth Av

N Adams St
St Helens
105
G St
Mary Av
Elizabeth Av E

Baker St
Washington St
Oregon St
Washington
Av

WESTPORT LIGHT STATE PARK

Central St
N Hoquiam St

Sprague Av
Pacific
N Adams St N
N Ocosta St

Sprague Av E
Pacific Av E

E Pacific Av
Pacific Av
W Spokane
W Tacoma
W
Tacoma St
N Melbourne St
S Melbourne St
N Central
N Olympia
Tacoma
Av
E Spokane Av
E Tacoma
Av
49th St
3rd St

Ocean Av W
South Starr St
Coast Guard
Grand Old Army St
N Central
N Aberdeen St
Seattle St
Ocean Av E

Sherman St
S Aberdeen St
W Grant Av
Grant
S Ocosta St
Broadway St
Sherman Av
Hst

Pebble Beach Ct
S Shore Dr
Dune St Crest Dr
Barney Dr
Nyra
Avew
Kirra Ct

Starr St
Aberdeen St
W Lee St
S Central
W Veterans
S Melbourne St
S Ocosta St
Park

Hancock
S Hoquiam St
Grand
Grand Army Way
W Park
S 3rd St

Pheasant Run Dr
Anchor
Jetty Vw
W Alder St
Alder Av
Maple
Av E

Strand St
Surf St
S Grand Army
Maple Av W
Broadway Av
W Pine Av

PACIFIC OCEAN

Dune Hvn
Dune Crest Dr
S Hoquiam St
Colic Ct
Johnson St
W Newell Av
Frank
E Lila St
S 1st St

Av
Aberdeen St
Hoquiam St
S Olympia St
Melbourne St
Cooper
S Montesano St
View Ridge Dr
View Ridge Dr S

Chehalis Av
Great Dane Ln
Gray Gull Ln
S Broadway St
Dicks St
S Ocosta St
Cohassett Dunes Ln W
Hoquiam St
Jackson St
Pleasant Ln S

Roberts Rd
Pleasant Dr
Bayview Ln

105

Woodhill Av S
Woodhill Ln S
Bay Island Rd
Gun Club

Schafer Island Beach App
TWIN HARBORS STATE PARK

46°55'06"   46°55'13"
46°54'34"   46°54'41"
46°54'01"   46°54'09"
46°53'29"   46°53'36"
46°52'56"   46°53'04"
46°52'24"   46°52'31"
46°51'52"   46°51'59"
46°51'19"   46°51'27"

124°08'28"   124°07'40"   124°06'53"   124°06'05"   124°05'17"   124°04'30"

SEE 33 MAP
SEE 33 MAP
SEE 33 MAP

A   B   C   D   E

1   2   3   4   5   6   7

MAP
151

1:30,000
1 in. = 2500 ft.

0   0.25   0.5
miles

MAP
151

SEE 34 MAP

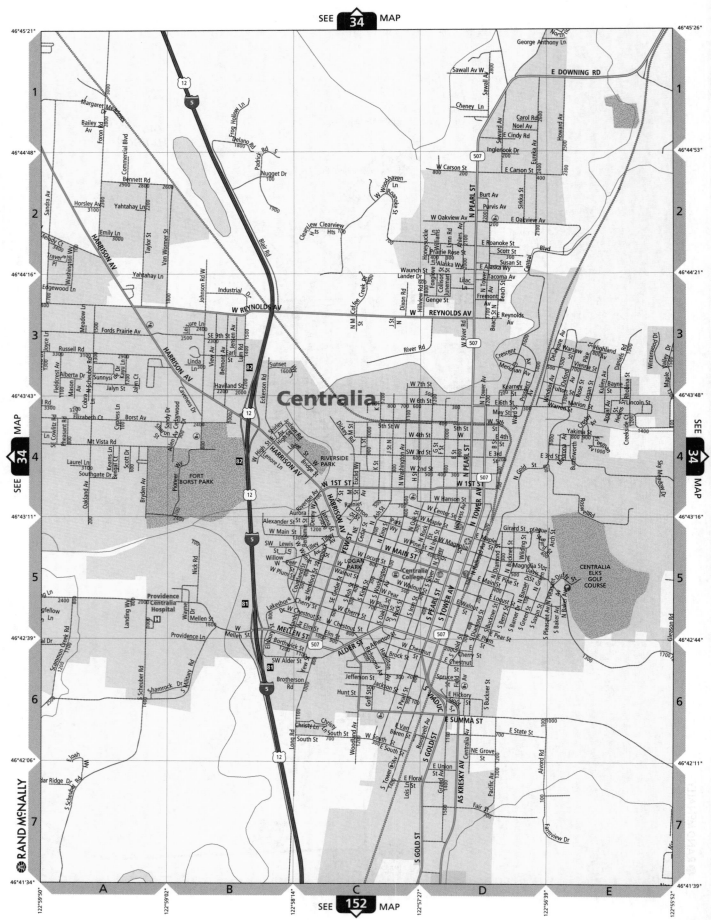

SEE 34 MAP

SEE 34 MAP

Centralia

FORT BORST PARK

RIVERSIDE PARK

Providence Centralia Hospital H

CENTRALIA ELKS GOLF COURSE

SEE 152 MAP

A   B   C   D   E

MAP 152

MAP 152

1:30,000
1 in. = 2500 ft.

SEE 151 MAP

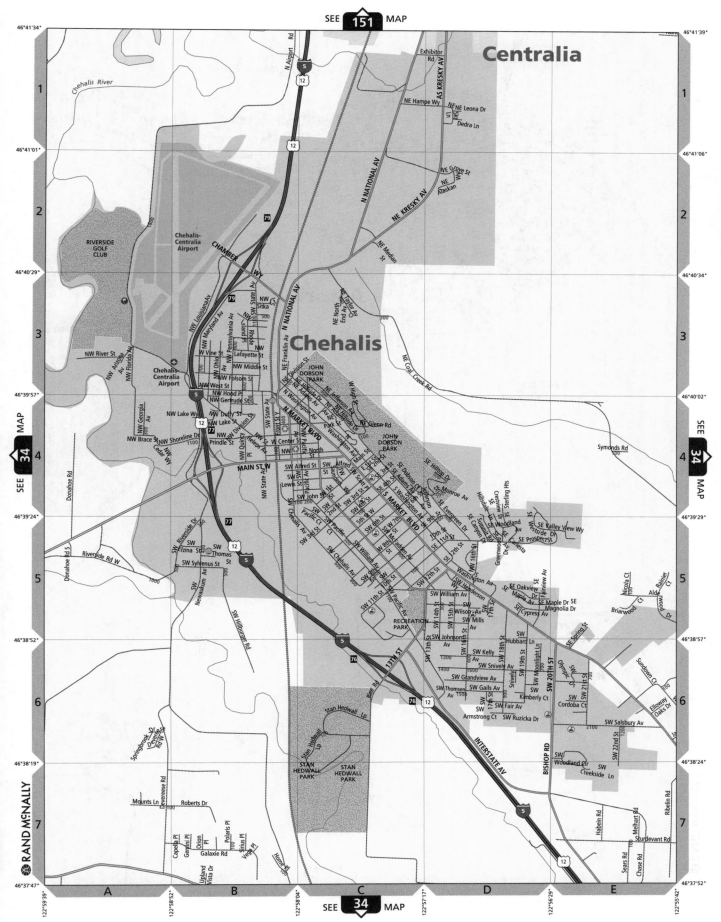

MAP
153

1:30,000
1 in. = 2500 ft.
0   0.25   0.5
miles

SEE **43** MAP

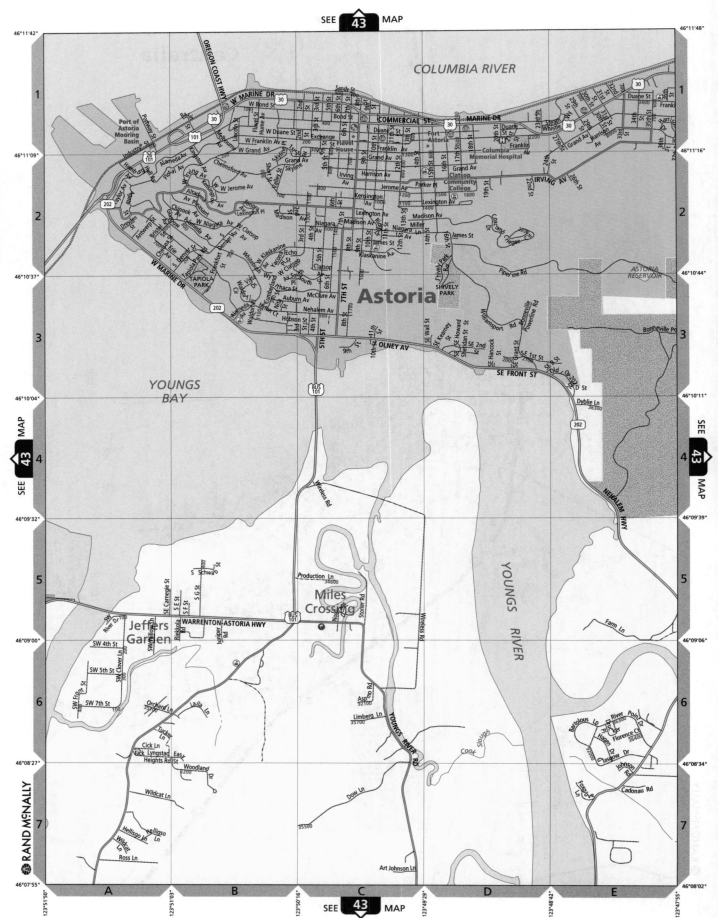

COLUMBIA RIVER

Astoria

YOUNGS BAY

YOUNGS RIVER

Port of Astoria Mooring Basin

Miles Crossing

Jeffers Garden

SEE **43** MAP

SEE **43** MAP

MAP
153

MAP
154

MAP
154

1:30,000
1 in. = 2500 ft.
0   0.25   0.5
miles

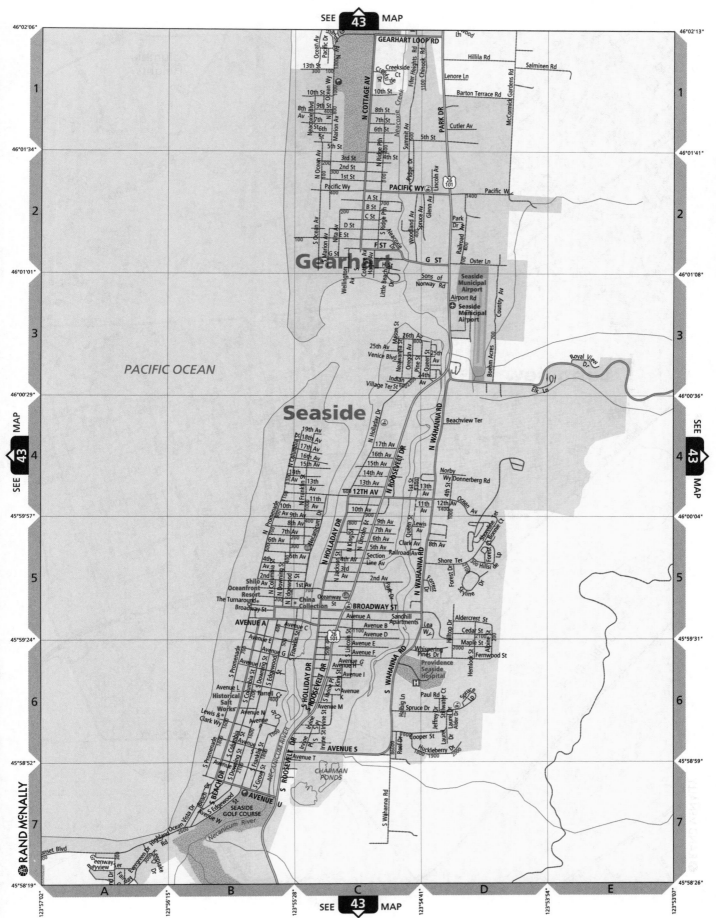

SEE ▲ 43 MAP

SEE 43 MAP

SEE 43 MAP

SEE ▼ 43 MAP

PACIFIC OCEAN

Gearhart

Seaside

RAND McNALLY

MAP
155

1:30,000
1 in. = 2500 ft.

0   0.25   0.5
miles

MAP
155

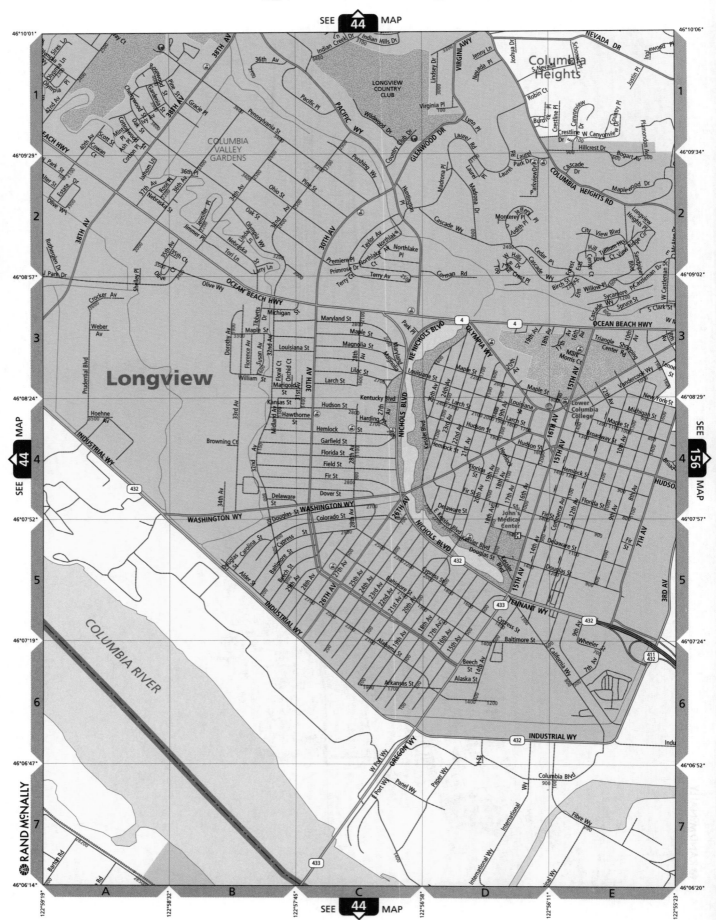

Columbia
Heights

COLUMBIA
VALLEY
GARDENS

LONGVIEW
COUNTRY
CLUB

Longview

COLUMBIA RIVER

A   B   C   D   E

MAP
156

MAP
156

1:30,000
1 in. = 2500 ft.

0.25   0.5

miles

N

SEE 44 MAP

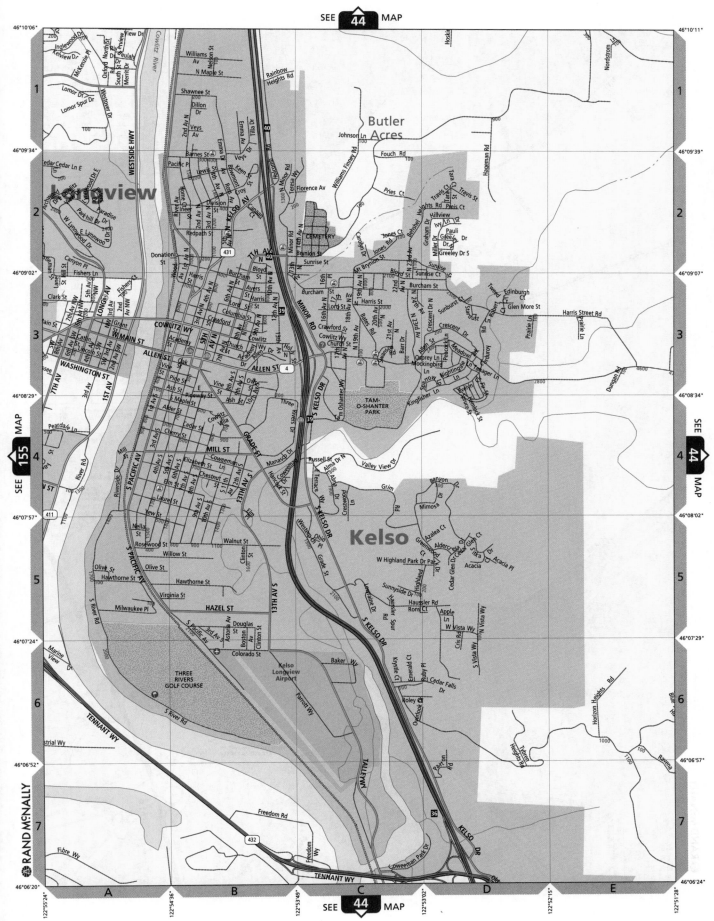

Longview

Butler
Acres

Kelso

SEE 155 MAP

SEE 44 MAP

THREE
RIVERS
GOLF COURSE

Kelso
Longview
Airport

TAM-
O-SHANTER
PARK

SEE 44 MAP

A   B   C   D   E

MAP
157

MAP
157

1:30,000
1 in. = 2500 ft.
0   0.25   0.5
miles

N

SEE 44 MAP

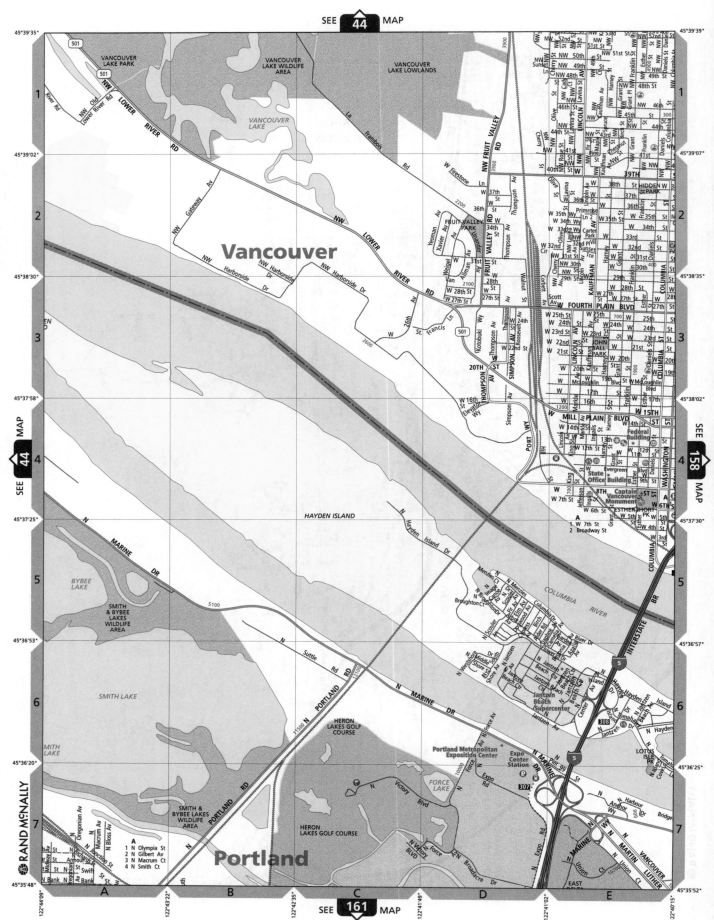

45°39'35"
45°39'39"

45°39'02"
45°39'07"

45°38'30"
45°38'35"

45°37'58"
45°38'02"

45°37'25"
45°37'30"

45°36'53"
45°36'57"

45°36'20"
45°36'25"

45°35'48"
45°35'52"

122°44'09"
122°43'22"
122°42'35"
122°41'49"
122°41'02"
122°40'15"

1
2
3
4
5
6
7

A   B   C   D   E

SEE 44 MAP

SEE 158 MAP

SEE 161 MAP

501

VANCOUVER LAKE PARK

VANCOUVER LAKE WILDLIFE AREA

VANCOUVER LAKE LOWLANDS

VANCOUVER LAKE

Vancouver

HAYDEN ISLAND

BYBEE LAKE

SMITH & BYBEE LAKES WILDLIFE AREA

SMITH LAKE

SMITH LAKE

SMITH & BYBEE LAKES WILDLIFE AREA

HERON LAKES GOLF COURSE

HERON LAKES GOLF COURSE

FORCE LAKE

COLUMBIA RIVER

LOTUS ISLE PK

Portland Metropolitan Exposition Center

Expo Center Station

Jantzen Beach Supercenter

Portland

RAND McNALLY

1 N Olympia St
2 N Gilbert Av
3 N Macrum Ct
4 N Smith Ct

MAP
158

MAP
158

1:30,000
1 in. = 2500 ft.
0   0.25   0.5
miles

N

SEE 45 MAP

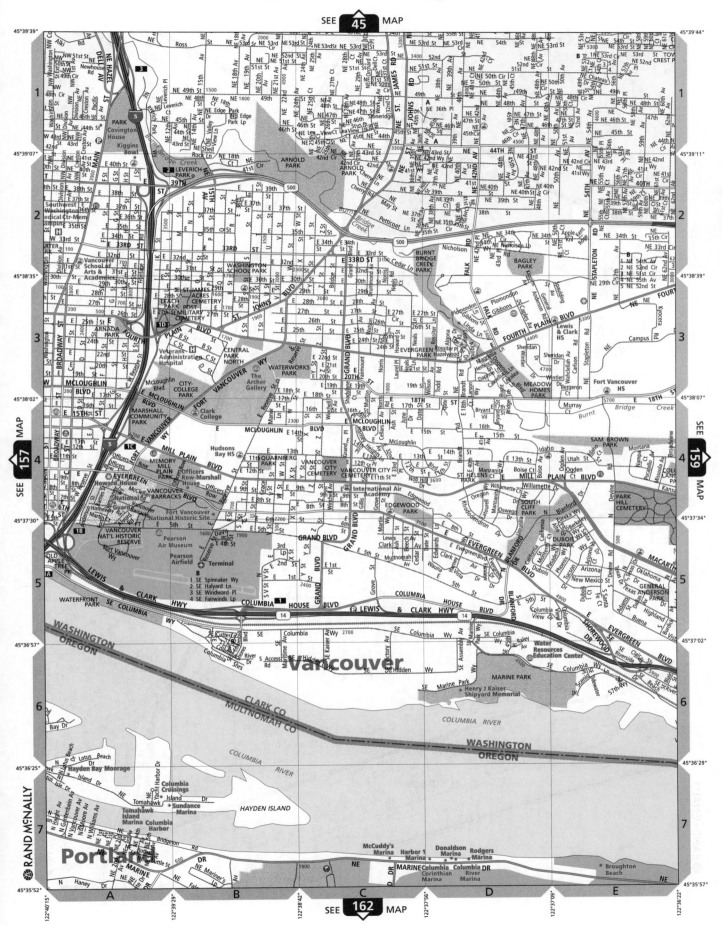

SEE 157 MAP
SEE 159 MAP
SEE 162 MAP

RAND McNALLY

MAP
159

1:30,000
1 in. = 2500 ft.
0   0.25   0.5
miles

MAP
159

SEE 45 MAP

SEE 158 MAP

SEE 160 MAP

SEE 163 MAP

RAND MCNALLY

MAP
160

MAP
160

1:30,000
1 in. = 2500 ft.
0   0.25   0.5
miles

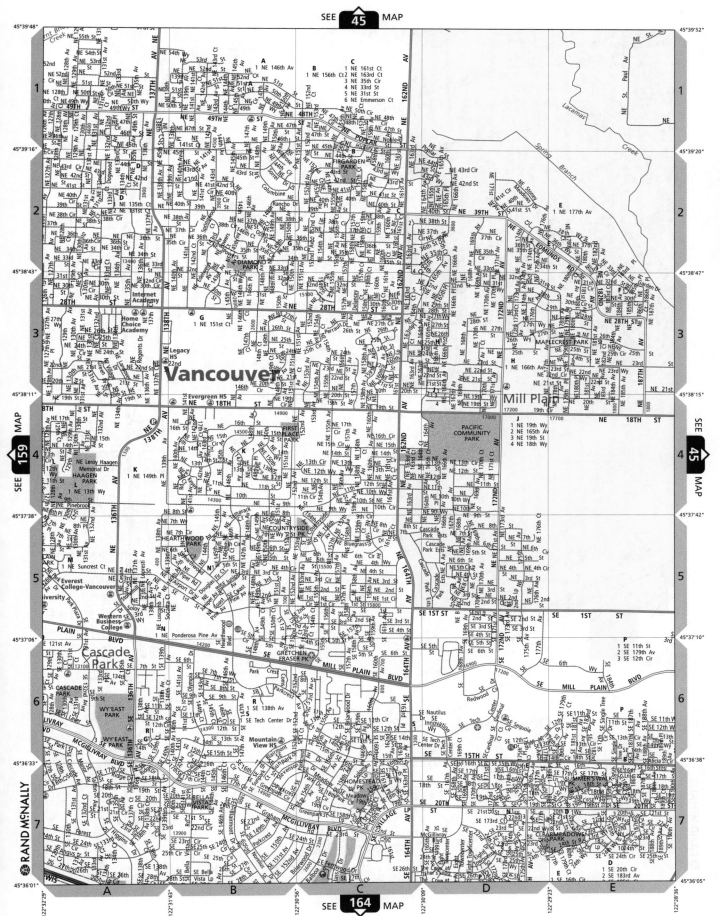

SEE 45 MAP

SEE 159 MAP

SEE 45 MAP

SEE 164 MAP

Vancouver

Mill Plain

Cascade Park

RAND MCNALLY

MAP
161

MAP
161

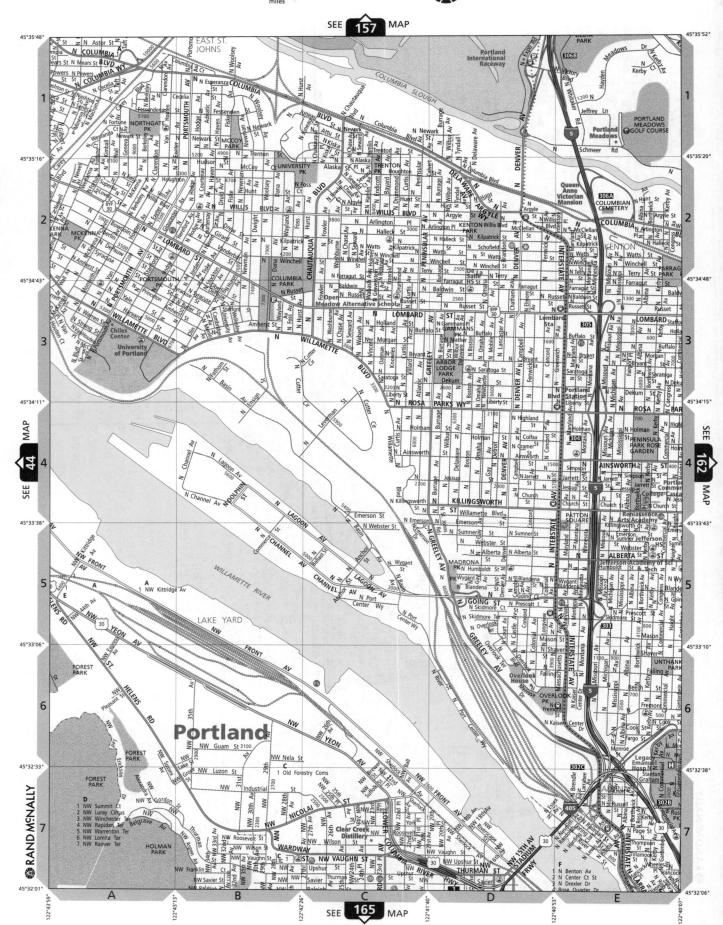

SEE 157 MAP

SEE 44 MAP

SEE 162 MAP

Portland

FOREST PARK

WILLAMETTE RIVER

LAKE YARD

D
1 NW Summit Ct
2 NW Luray Cirtus
3 NW Winchester Ter
4 NW Rapidan Ter
5 NW Warrenton Ter
6 NW Lomita Ter
7 NW Rainier Ter

SEE 165 MAP

MAP
162

1:30,000
1 in. = 2500 ft.
0   0.25   0.5
miles

MAP
162

SEE 158 MAP

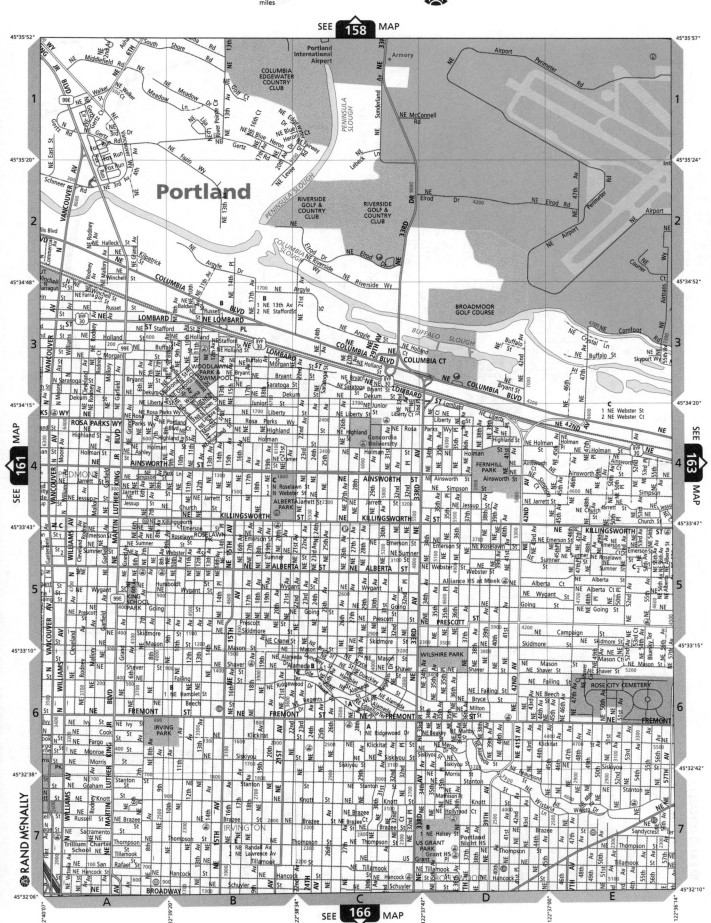

Portland

SEE 161 MAP

SEE 163 MAP

RAND MCNALLY

SEE 166 MAP

MAP
163

1:30,000
1 in. = 2500 ft.

0   0.25   0.5
miles

SEE 159 MAP

MAP
163

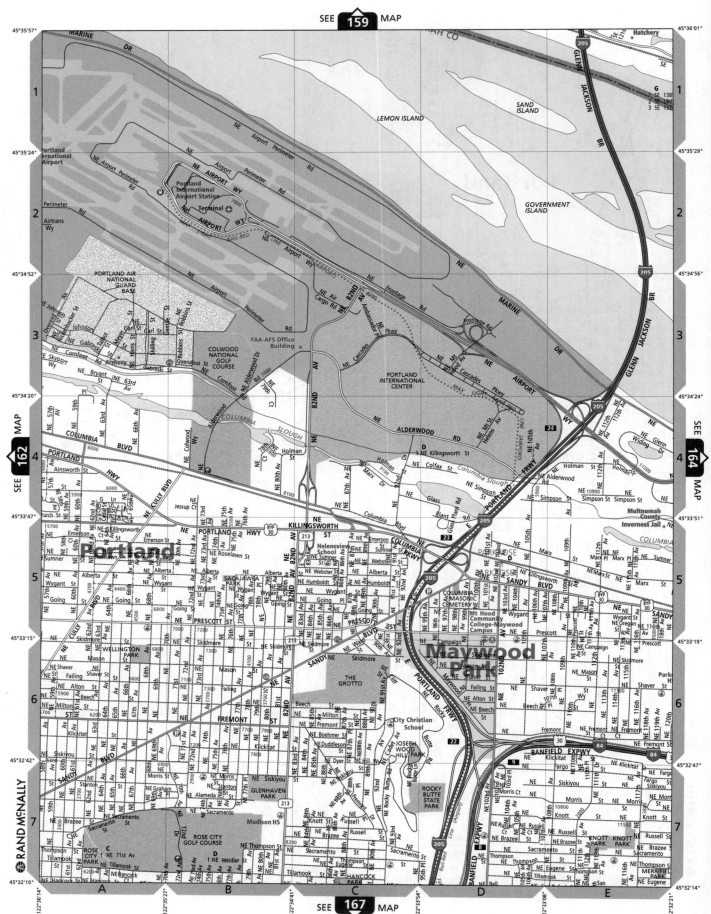

SEE 162 MAP

SEE 164 MAP

SEE 167 MAP

RAND M°NALLY

MAP
164

1:30,000
1 in. = 2500 ft.
0   0.25   0.5
miles

MAP
164

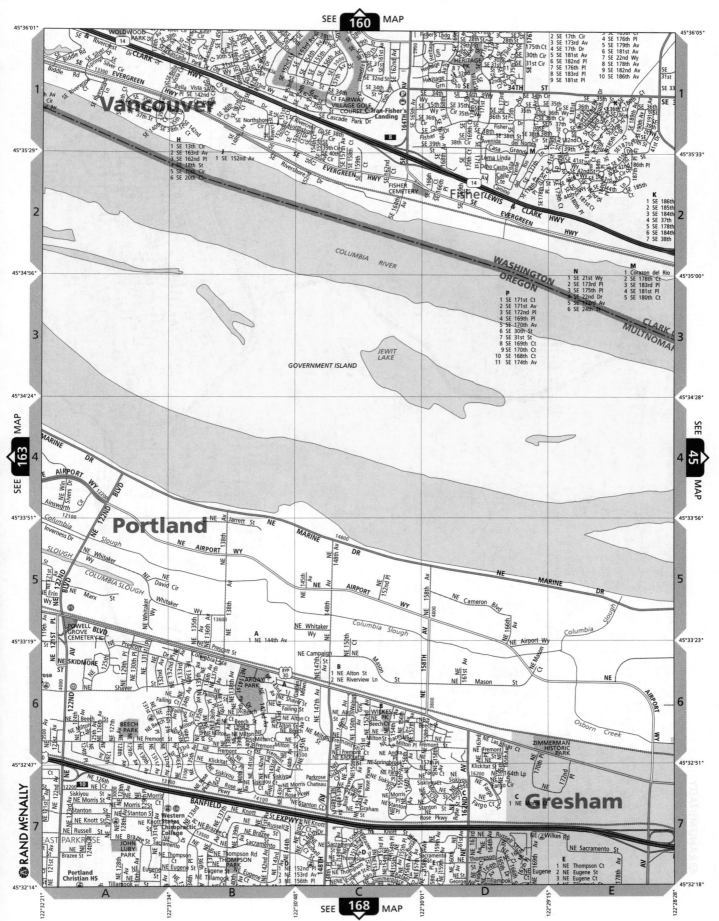

SEE 160 MAP

45°36'01"
45°35'29"
45°34'56"
45°34'24"
45°33'51"
45°33'19"
45°32'47"
45°32'14"

45°36'05"
45°35'33"
45°35'00"
45°34'28"
45°33'56"
45°33'23"
45°32'51"
45°32'18"

Vancouver

Fisher

COLUMBIA RIVER

WASHINGTON
OREGON

CLARK CO
MULTNOMAH

GOVERNMENT ISLAND

JEWIT
LAKE

Portland

Gresham

SEE 163 MAP
SEE 45 MAP

SEE 168 MAP

RAND M°NALLY

H
1 SE 13th Cir
2 SE 163rd Av
3 SE 162nd Pl
4 SE 18th St
5 SE 19th Cir
6 SE 20th Cir

J
1 SE 152nd Av

K
1 SE 186th
2 SE 185th
3 SE 184th
4 SE 37th
5 SE 178th
6 SE 184th
7 SE 38th

N
1 SE 21st Wy
2 SE 173rd Pl
3 SE 175th Pl
4 SE 22nd Dr
5 SE 173rd Av
6 SE 24th Pl

M
1 Corazon del Rio
2 SE 178th Ct
3 SE 183rd Pl
4 SE 181st Pl
5 SE 180th Ct

P
1 SE 171st Ct
2 SE 171st Av
3 SE 172nd Pl
4 SE 169th Pl
5 SE 170th Av
6 SE 30th St
7 SE 31st St
8 SE 169th Ct
9 SE 170th Ct
10 SE 168th Ct
11 SE 174th Av

A
1 NE 144th Av

B
1 NE Alton St
2 NE Riverview Ln

122°32'21"
122°31'34"
122°30'48"
122°30'01"
122°29'15"
122°28'28"

MAP
165

1:30,000
1 in. = 2500 ft.
0   0.25   0.5
miles

MAP
165

SEE 161 MAP

Portland

SEE 169 MAP

SEE 44 MAP

SEE 166 MAP

RAND M?NALLY

MAP
166

1:30,000
1 in. = 2500 ft.

0   0.25   0.5
miles

N

MAP
166

SEE **162** MAP

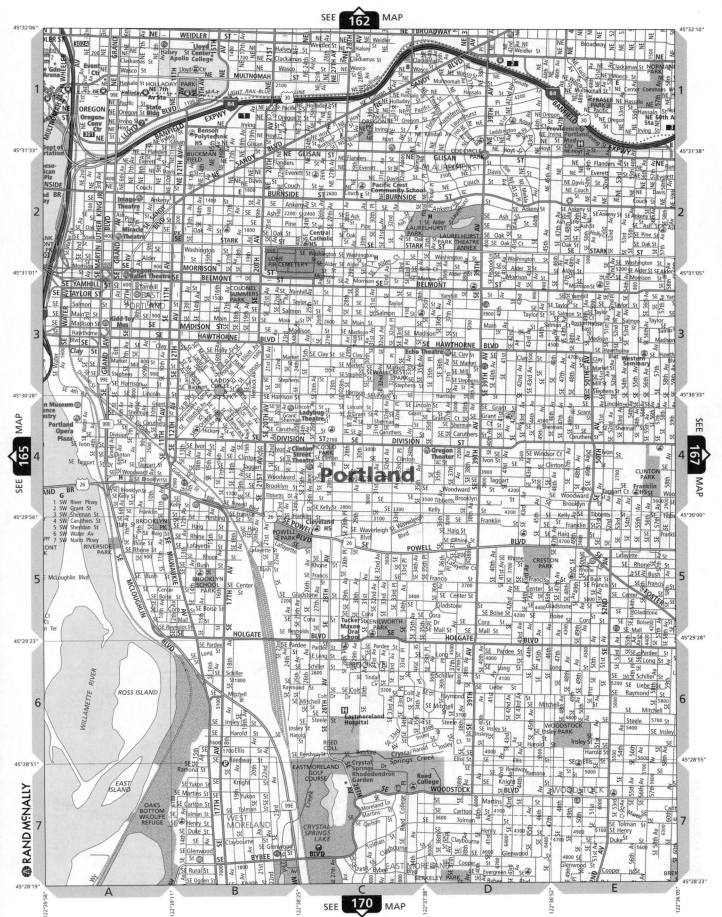

Portland

RAND McNALLY

SEE **165** MAP

SEE **167** MAP

1 SW River Pkwy
2 SW Grant St
3 SW Sherman St
4 SW Caruthers St
5 SW Sheridan St
6 SW Water Av
7 SW Naito Pkwy

SEE **170** MAP

MAP
167

MAP
167

1:30,000
1 in. = 2500 ft.

0   0.25   0.5
miles

SEE 163 MAP

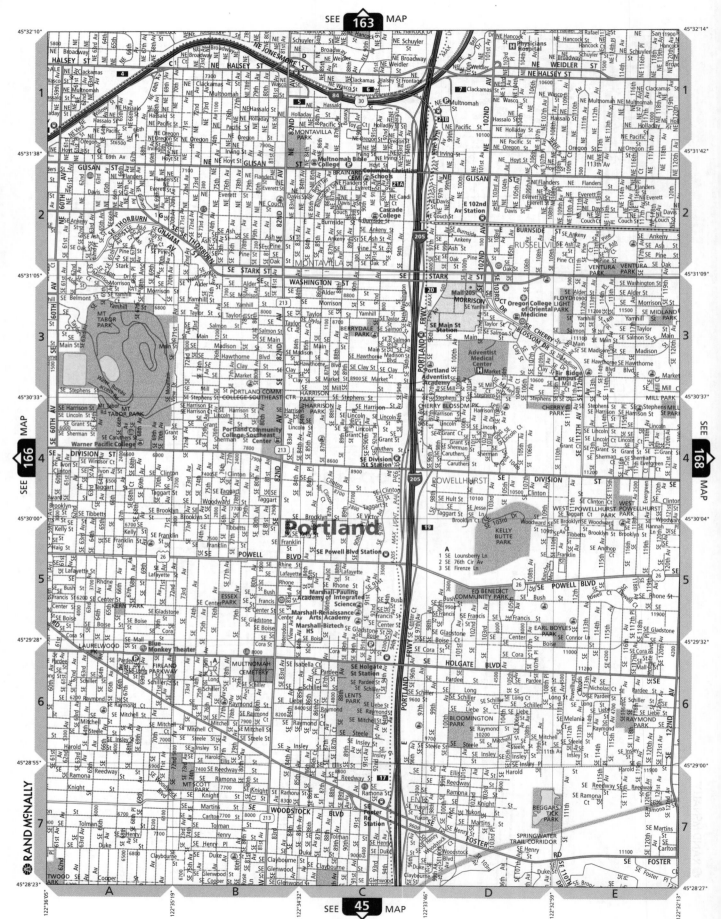

Portland

SEE 166 MAP

SEE 168 MAP

SEE 45 MAP

MAP
168

MAP
168

1:30,000
1 in. = 2500 ft.
0   0.25   0.5
miles

SEE 164 MAP

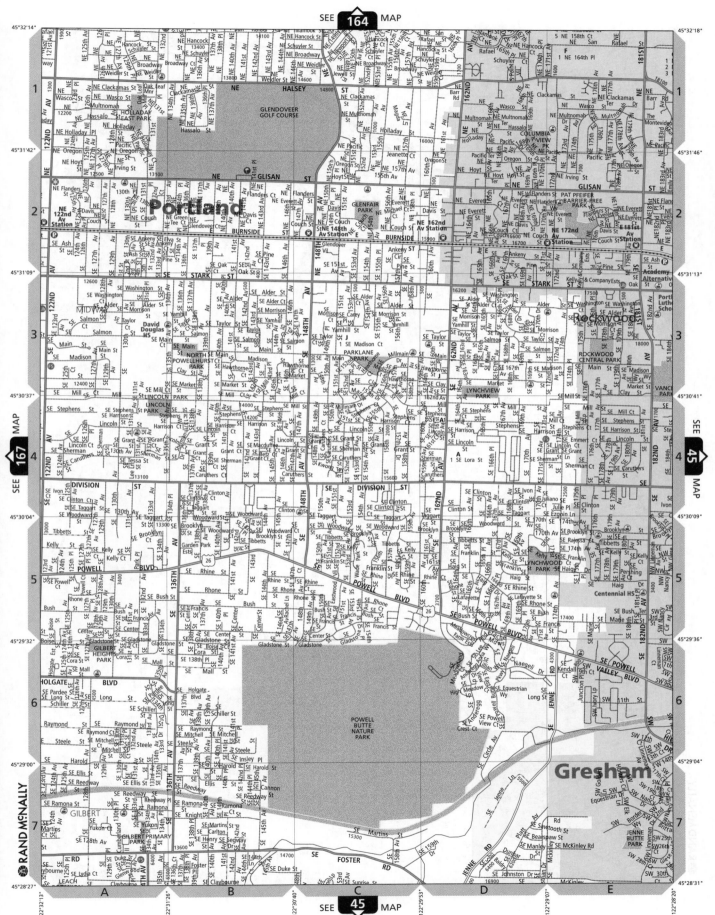

Portland

Gresham

SEE 167 MAP

SEE 45 MAP

SEE 45 MAP

RAND McNALLY

MAP
169

MAP
169

1:30,000
1 in. = 2500 ft.
0   0.25   0.5
miles

SEE 165 MAP

Portland

**Lake
Oswego**

Englewood

BURLINGAME

TRYON CREEK STATE PARK

RIVERVIEW CEMETERY

GRAND ARMY OF THE CEMETERY

OSWEGO LAKE COUNTRY CLUB

ROSSMAN PARK

MILLENNIUM PLAZA PARK

Oswego Lake

JANTZEN ISLAND

SPRINGBROOK PARK

WALUGA PARK

SEE 44 MAP

SEE 170 MAP

SEE 54 MAP

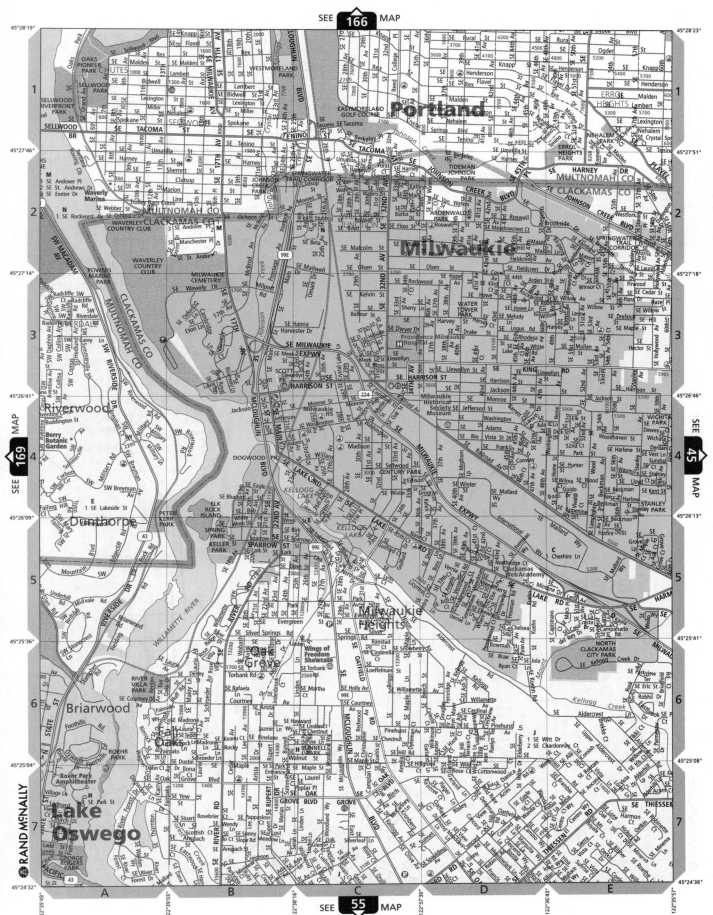

MAP
170

MAP
170

1:30,000
1 in. = 2500 ft.

0   0.25   0.5

miles

SEE **166** MAP

SEE **55** MAP

SEE **169** MAP

SEE **45** MAP

RAND MCNALLY

MAP
171

MAP
171

1:30,000
1 in. = 2500 ft.

0   0.25   0.5
miles

SEE 54 MAP

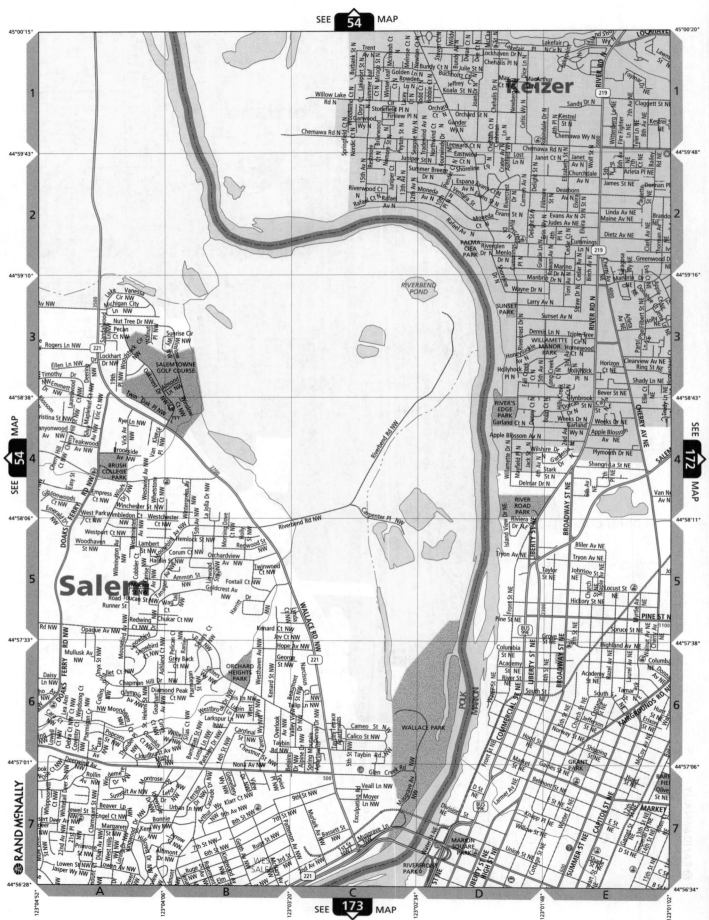

Keizer

Salem

SEE 54 MAP

SEE 172 MAP

RAND McNALLY

SEE 173 MAP

MAP
172

MAP
172

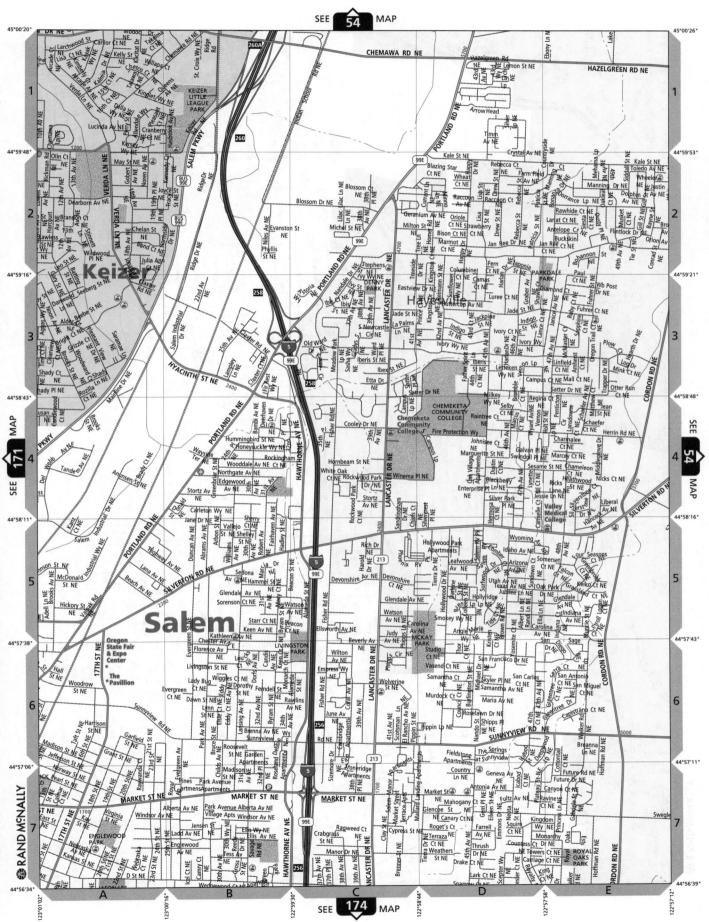

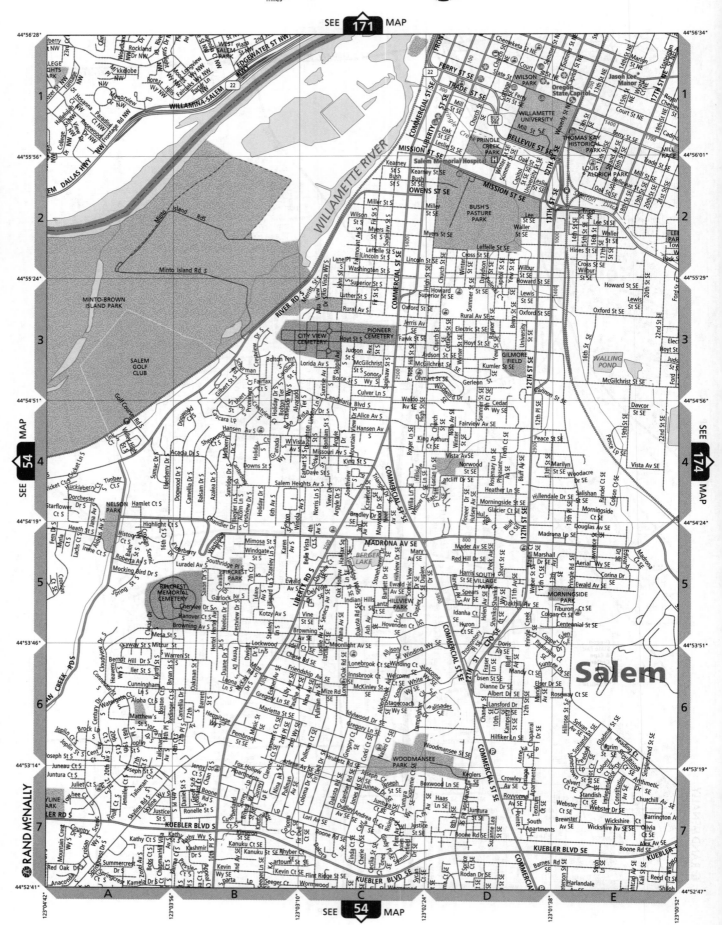

MAP
173

MAP
173

1:30,000
1 in. = 2500 ft.
0   0.25   0.5
miles

SEE 171 MAP

SEE 54 MAP

SEE 174 MAP

SEE 54 MAP

Salem

RAND MCNALLY

WILLAMETTE RIVER

MINTO-BROWN
ISLAND PARK

SALEM GOLF
CLUB

BUSH'S PASTURE PARK

KUEBLER BLVD S

KUEBLER BLVD SE

MAP
174

MAP
174

1:30,000
1 in. = 2500 ft.
0   0.25   0.5
miles

N

SEE 172 MAP

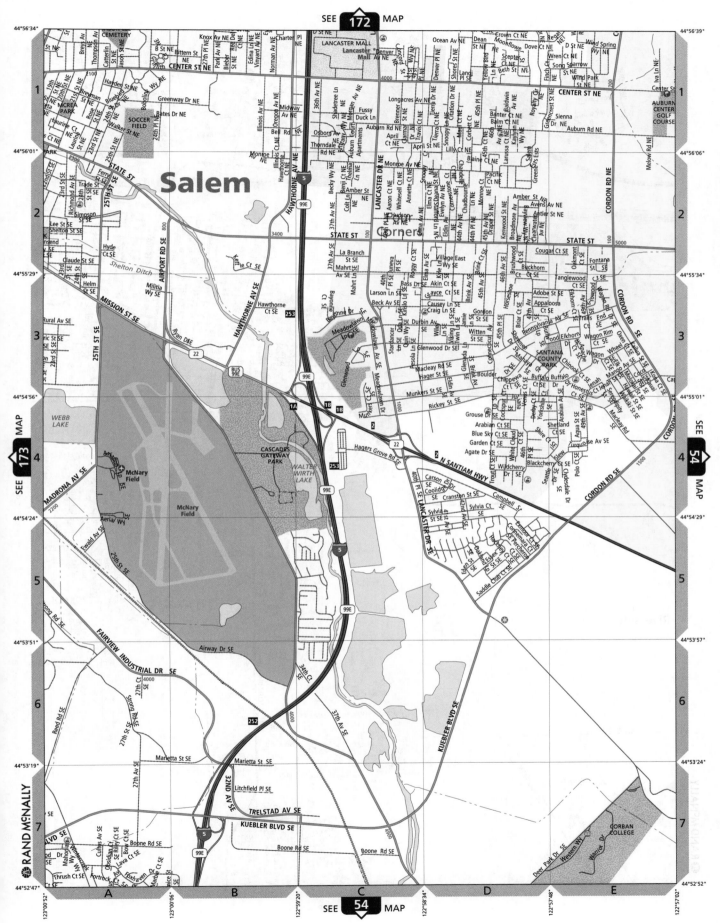

Salem

SEE 173 MAP

SEE 54 MAP

SEE 54 MAP

RAND MCNALLY

MAP
175

MAP
175

1:30,000
1 in. = 2500 ft.

0   0.25   0.5

miles

SEE 54 MAP

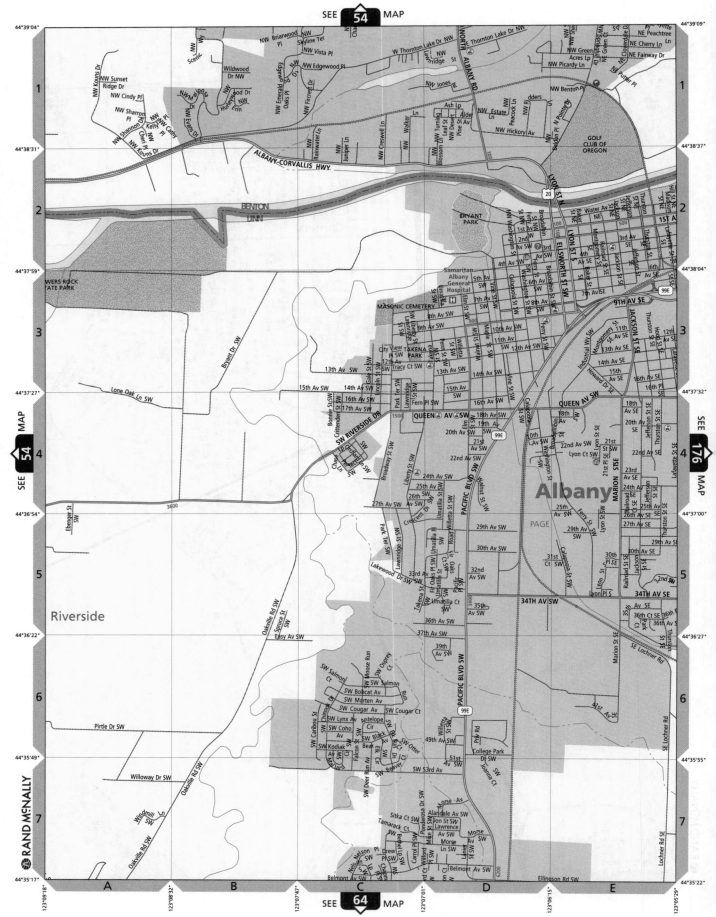

SEE 54 MAP

SEE 176 MAP

SEE 64 MAP

Albany

Riverside

MAP
176

MAP
176

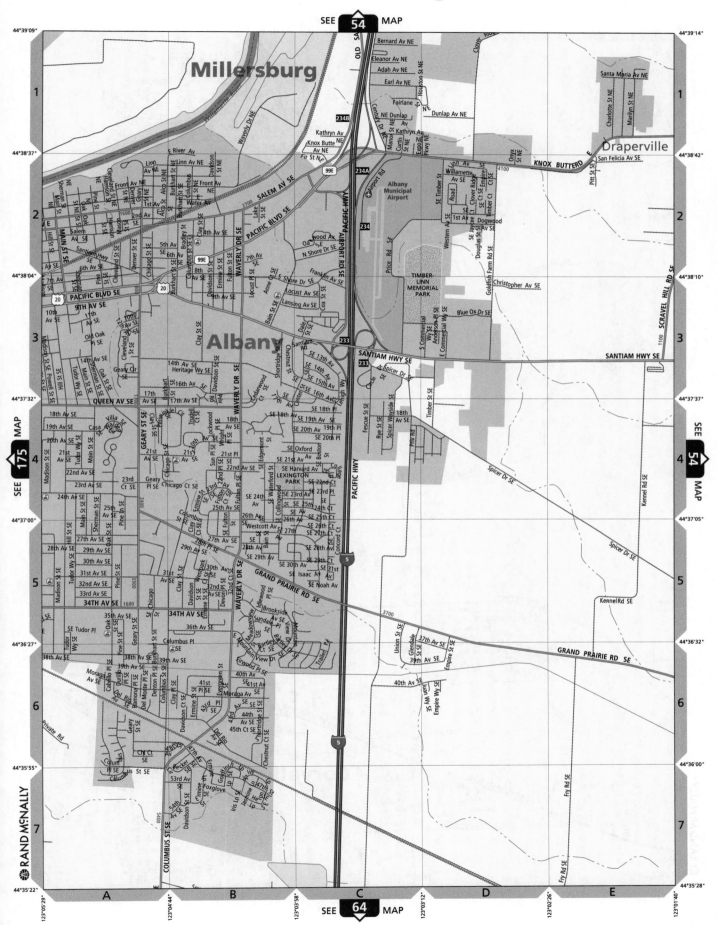

1:30,000
1 in. = 2500 ft.
0   0.25   0.5
miles

N

Millersburg

Albany

Draperville

SEE 175 MAP

SEE 54 MAP

SEE 64 MAP

RAND MCNALLY

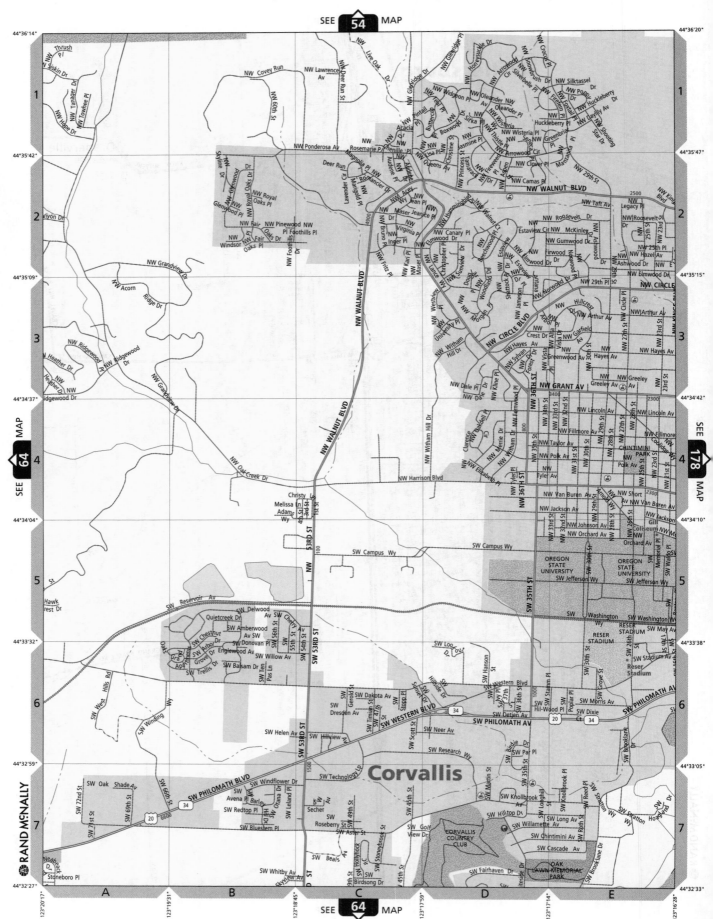

MAP
178

MAP
178

1:30,000
1 in. = 2500 ft.
0   0.25   0.5
miles

N

SEE 54 MAP

Corvallis

SEE 177 MAP

SEE 64 MAP

SEE 64 MAP

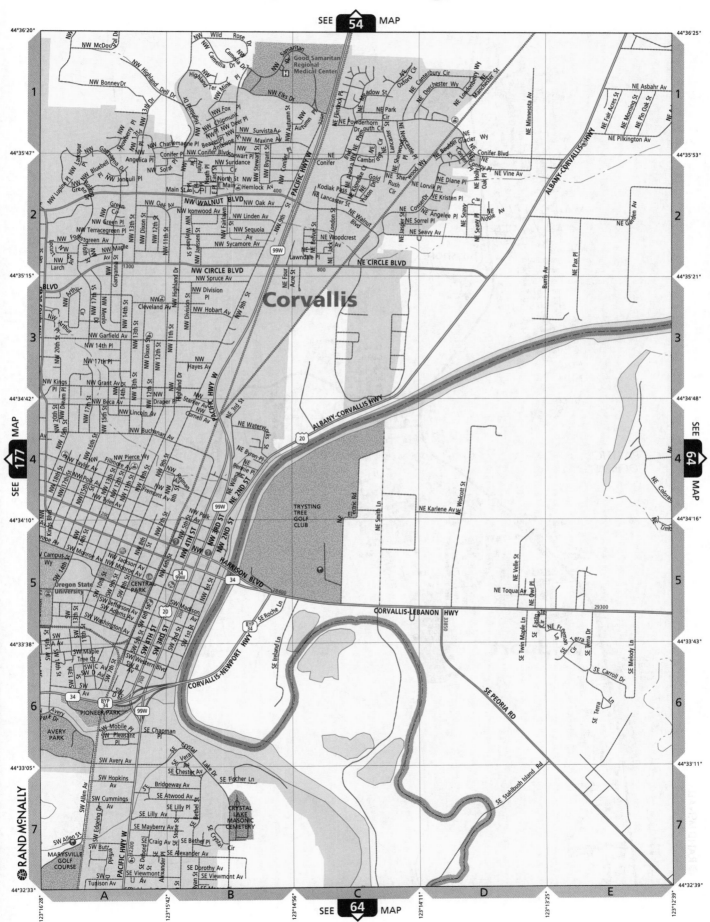

RAND M?NALLY

44°36'20"
44°35'47"
44°35'15"
44°34'42"
44°34'10"
44°33'38"
44°33'05"
44°32'33"

44°36'25"
44°35'53"
44°35'21"
44°34'48"
44°34'16"
44°33'43"
44°33'11"
44°32'39"

123°16'28"
123°15'42"
123°14'56"
123°14'11"
123°13'25"
123°12'39"

A   B   C   D   E

1   2   3   4   5   6   7

MAP
179

MAP
179

1:30,000
1 in. = 2500 ft.
0   0.25   0.5
miles

SEE 63 MAP

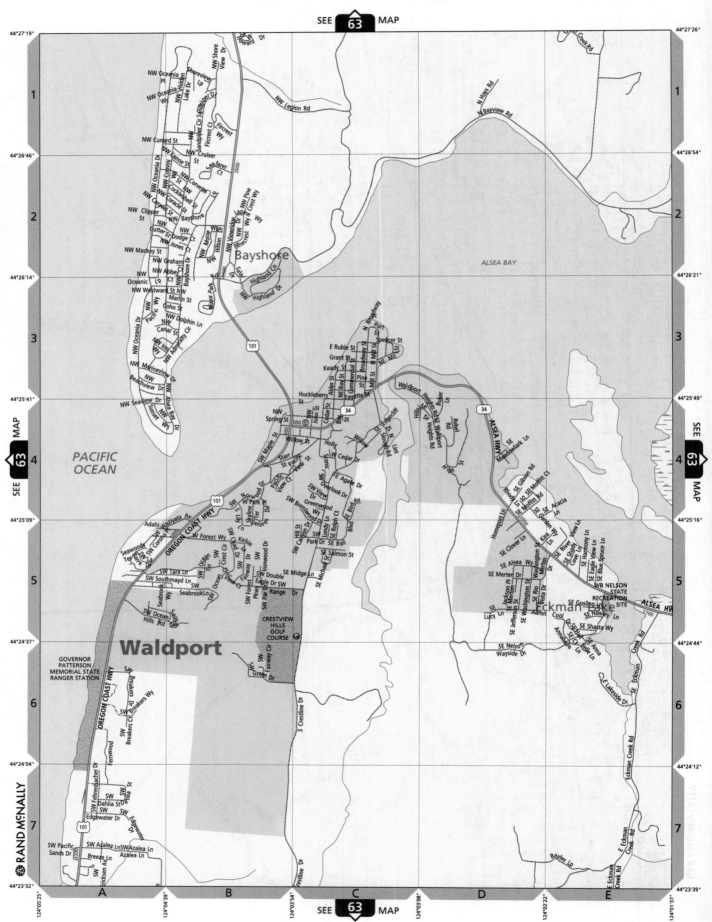

PACIFIC
OCEAN

ALSEA BAY

Bayshore

Waldport

GOVERNOR
PATTERSON
MEMORIAL STATE
RANGER STATION

CRESTVIEW
HILLS
GOLF
COURSE

Eckman Lake

WB NELSON
STATE
RECREATION
SITE

SEE 63 MAP

SEE 63 MAP

MAP
180

MAP
180

1:30,000
1 in. = 2500 ft.
0   0.25   0.5
miles

SEE 64 MAP

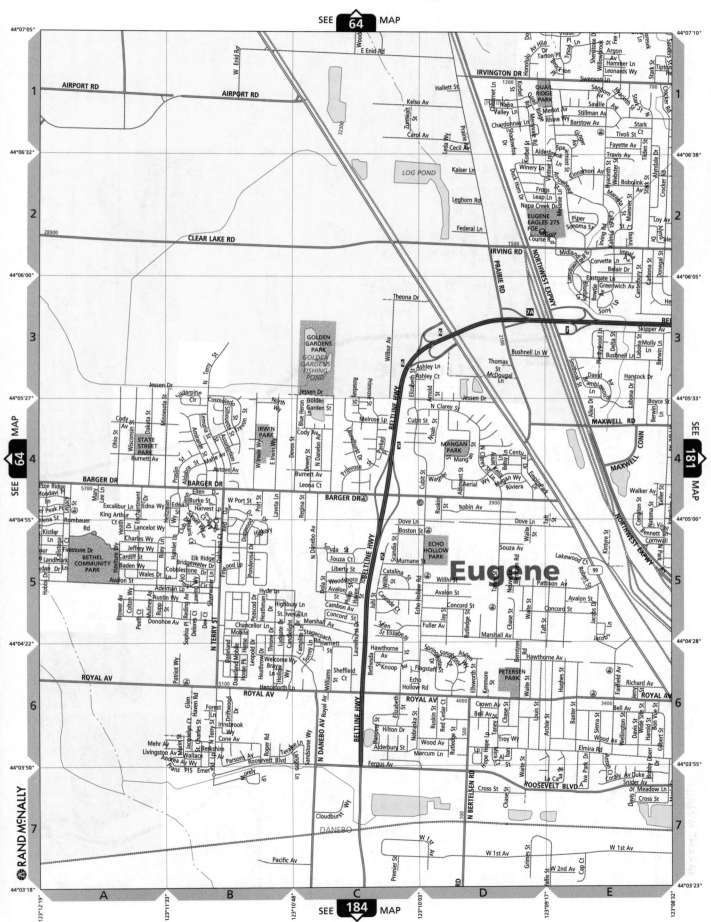

SEE 184 MAP

RAND MCNALLY

SEE 64 MAP

SEE 181 MAP

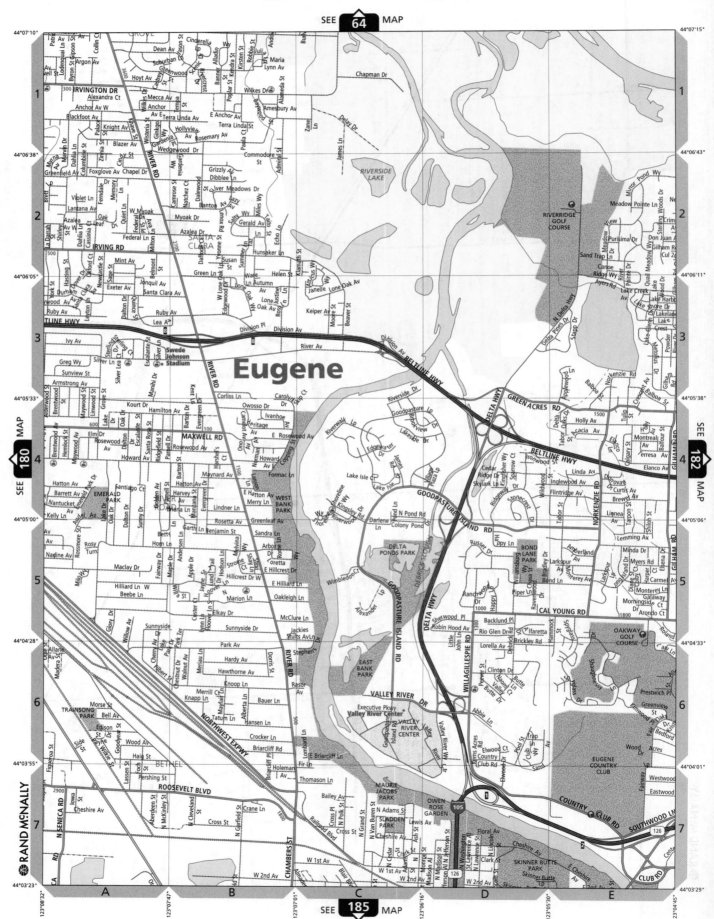

MAP
182

MAP
182

1:30,000
1 in. = 2500 ft.
0   0.25   0.5
miles

N

SEE 64 MAP

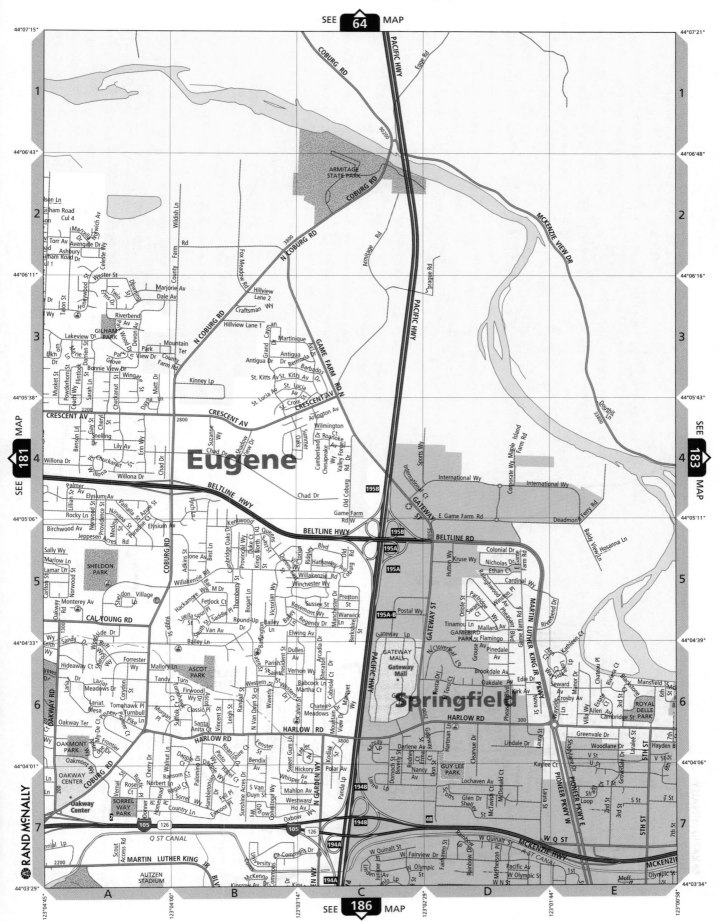

SEE 181 MAP

SEE 183 MAP

SEE 186 MAP

Eugene

Springfield

RAND McNALLY

MAP
183

MAP
183

1:30,000
1 in. = 2500 ft.

0   0.25   0.5
miles

N

SEE MAP

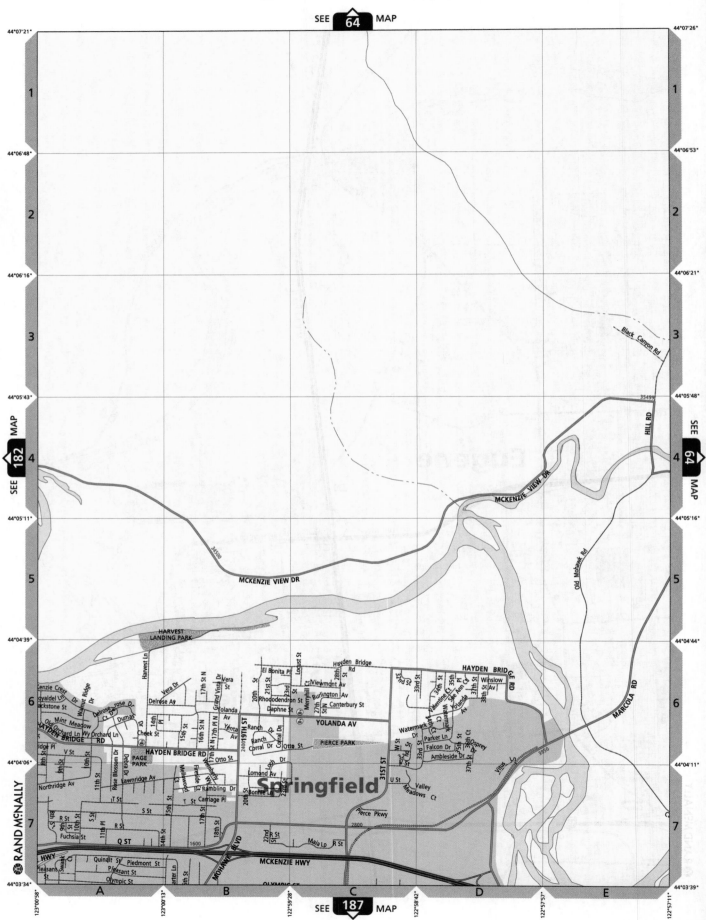

MAP
184

1:30,000
1 in. = 2500 ft.
0   0.25   0.5
miles

MAP
184

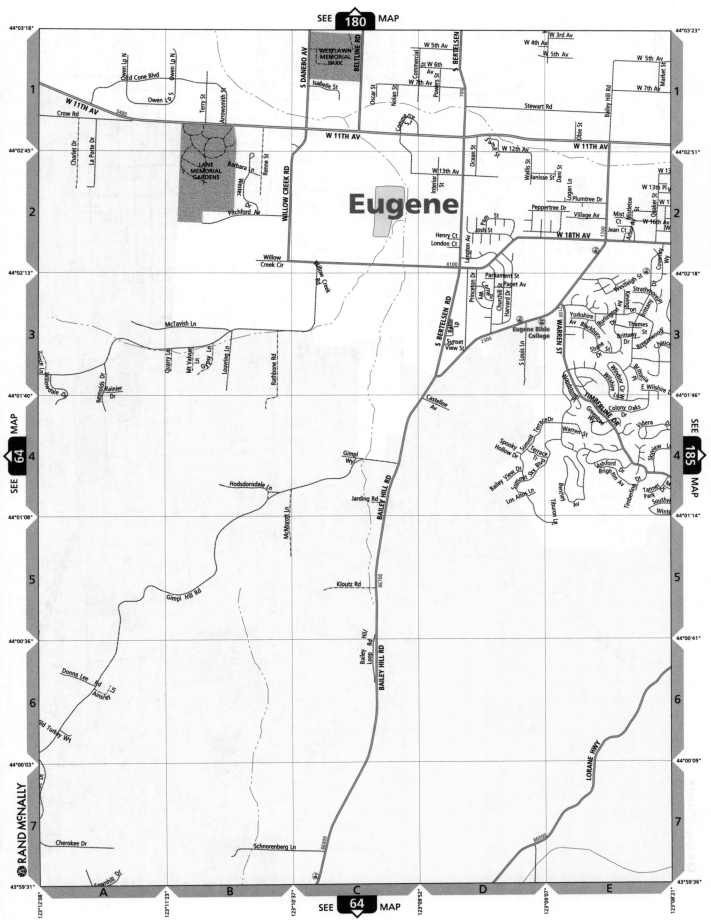

SEE 180 MAP

SEE 64 MAP
SEE 185 MAP

Eugene

WESTLAWN MEMORIAL PARK
LANE MEMORIAL GARDENS
Eugene Bible College

SEE 64 MAP

RAND McNALLY

MAP
185

MAP
185

1:30,000
1 in. = 2500 ft.
0   0.25   0.5
miles

SEE 181 MAP

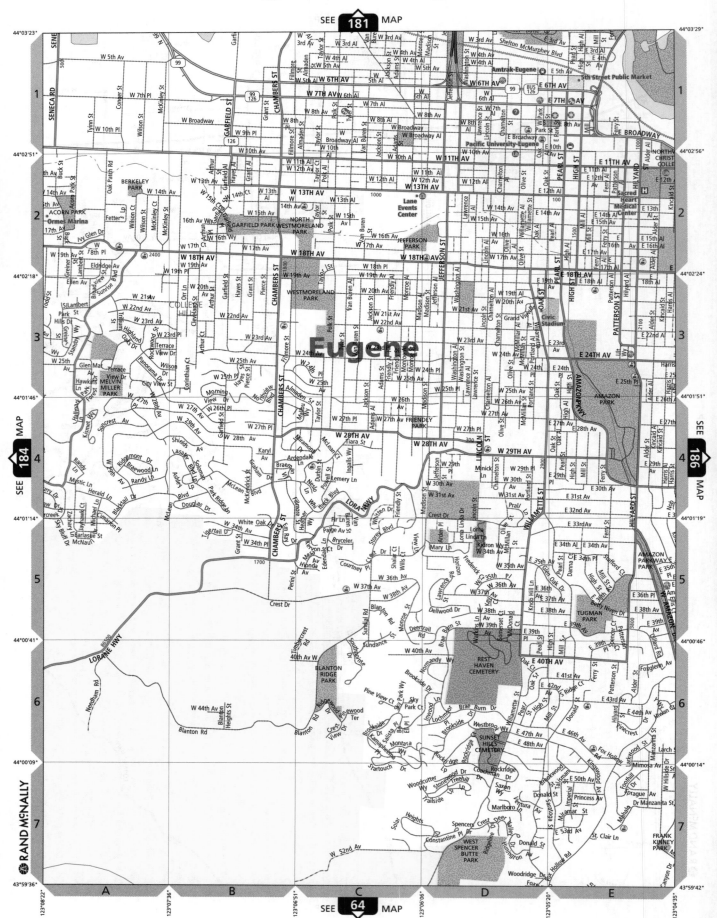

Eugene

SEE 184 MAP

SEE 186 MAP

SEE 64 MAP

MAP
186

MAP
186

1:30,000
1 in. = 2500 ft.
0   0.25   0.5
miles

N

SEE 182 MAP

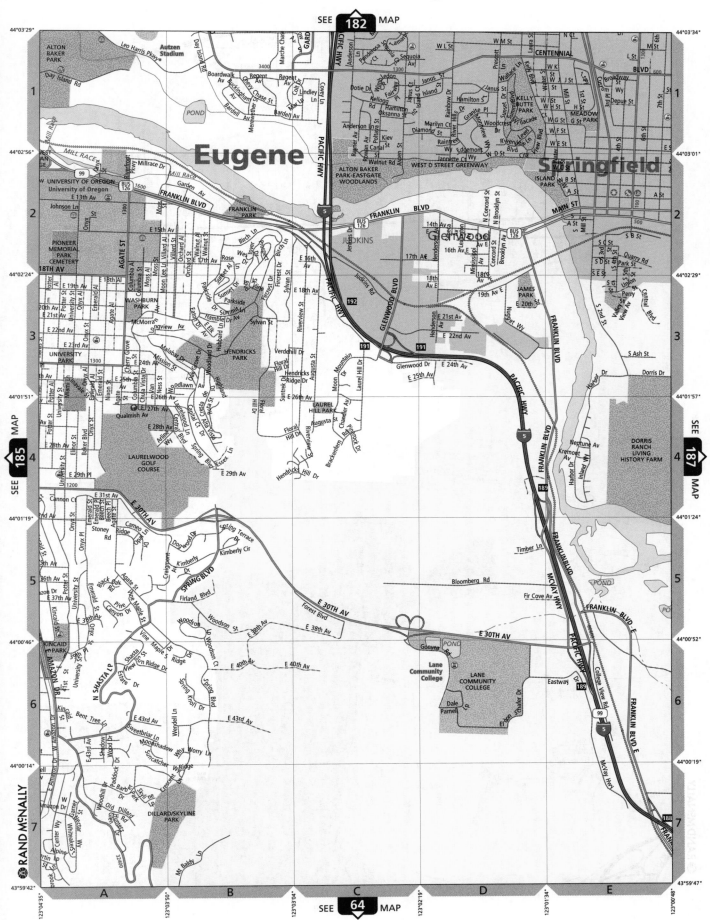

44°03'29"
44°02'56"
44°02'24"
44°01'51"
44°01'19"
44°00'46"
44°00'14"
43°59'42"

44°03'34"
44°03'01"
44°02'29"
44°01'57"
44°01'24"
44°00'52"
44°00'19"
43°59'47"

Eugene

Springfield

Glenwood

ALTON BAKER PARK

Autzen Stadium

UNIVERSITY OF OREGON
University of Oregon

PIONEER MEMORIAL PARK CEMETERY

WASHBURN PARK

HENDRICKS PARK

UNIVERSITY PARK

LAUREL HILL PARK

LAURELWOOD GOLF COURSE

KINCAID PARK

DILLARD/SKYLINE PARK

Lane Community College

LANE COMMUNITY COLLEGE

DORRIS RANCH LIVING HISTORY FARM

ALTON BAKER PARK-EASTGATE WOODLANDS

WEST D STREET GREENWAY

MEADOW PARK

KELLY BUTTE PARK

JAMES PARK

ISLAND PARK

MILL RACE

FRANKLIN BLVD

MAIN ST

PACIFIC HWY

GLENWOOD BLVD

FRANKLIN BLVD

McVAY HWY

E 30TH AV

Bloomberg Rd

FRANKLIN BLVD E

College View Rd

McVay Hwy

SPRING BLVD

E 30TH AV

SHASTA LP

AMAZON DR

SEE 185 MAP

SEE 187 MAP

SEE 64 MAP

A   B   C   D   E

1   2   3   4   5   6   7

MAP
187

MAP
187

1:30,000
1 in. = 2500 ft.

0   0.25   0.5
miles

SEE **183** MAP

Springfield

SEE **186** MAP

SEE **188** MAP

SEE **64** MAP

RAND MNALLY

MAP
188

MAP
188

1:30,000
1 in. = 2500 ft.
0   0.25   0.5
miles

N

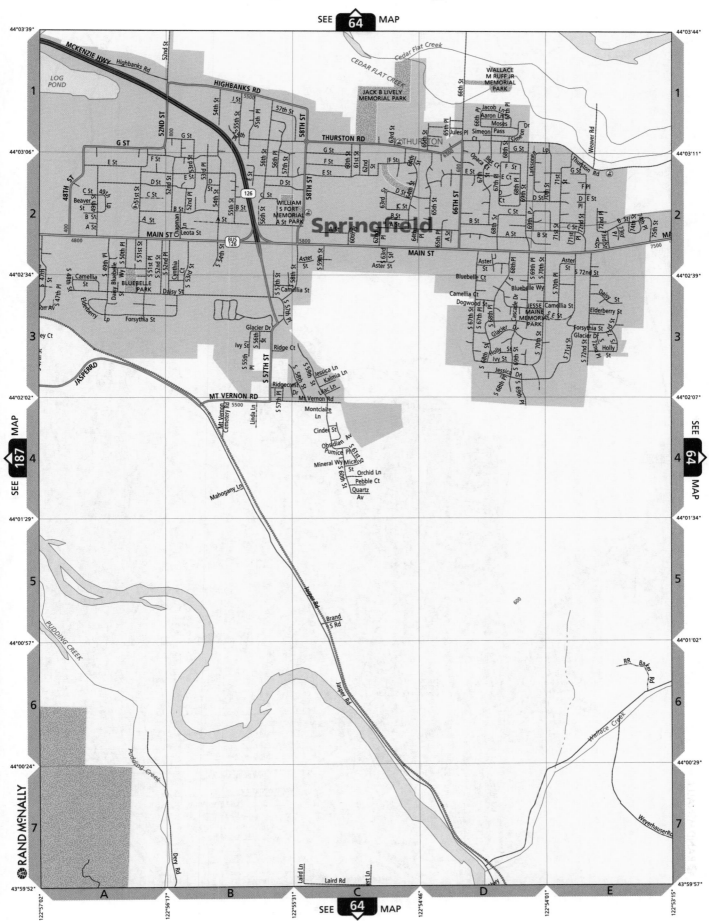

SEE [64] MAP

44°03'39"
44°03'44"

MCKENZIE HWY   Highbanks Rd

LOG
POND

52nd St

Highbanks Rd

HIGHBANKS RD

Cedar Flat Creek

CEDAR FLAT CREEK

JACK B LIVELY
MEMORIAL PARK

WALLACE
M RUFF JR
MEMORIAL
PARK

66th St

1

1

52ND ST
54th St
J St
55th St
55th Pl
57th St
58TH ST
THURSTON RD
62nd St
THURSTON

66th Pl
66th Pl
Jacob Ln
Aaron Ln
Moses
Simeon Dr
Pass

Weaver Rd

44°03'06"
44°03'11"

G ST
E St
G St
F St
56th St
56th Pl
57th Pl
58TH ST
G St
F St
E St
60th St
61st St
62nd St
F St
64th St
65th St
65th Pl
Jules Pl
Simeon
Iliet Ct
Opaca Ln
66th St
G St
Larksome
Lp
Thurston Rd
71st St
G St
F Pl

48TH ST
D St
52nd St
E St
53rd Pl
D St
54th St
E St
56th St
D St
63rd St
C St
64th St
66TH ST
67th St
68th St
C Et
C Ct
69th St
D St
70th St
71st St
P Pl
D St
E St

2
C St
Beaver
49th
S 51st St
52nd St
54th St
55th St
B St
56th St
B St
C St
A St
B St
68th St
C St
A St
B St
71st St
71st Pl
Spiel
72nd Pl
73rd Pl
74th Ln
75th St
2

B St
49th Pl
A St
52nd St
Leota St
A St
A St
Chapman
A St
WILLIAM
S FORT
MEMORIAL
A St PARK

Springfield

A St
MAP

MAIN ST
BUS 126
5800
MAIN ST
7500

44°02'34"
44°02'39"

S 47th St
S 48th St
S 49th St
S 50th Pl
S 51st St
S 51st Pl
S 52nd St
Cynthia
Ct
S 54th St
Aster
St
S 59th Pl
Aster St
63rd St
Aster St
Aster
Bluebelle Ct
S 68th St
S 69th Pl
S 70th Pl
Aster
S 72nd St

Camellia
St
Daisy
Bluebelle
Wy
S 52nd Pl
BLUEBELLE
PARK
Daisy St
S 55th St
S 58th St
Camellia St
Bluebelle Ct
Camellia Ct
Bluebelle Wy
Daisy
St

Elderberry
Lp
Forsythia St
S 57th St
Dogwood
S 67th St
S 67th Pl
S 68th St
JESSE
MAINE
MEMORIAL
PARK
Camellia St
Cascade
St
Elderberry St

3
on Av
ey Ct
Glacier Dr
Ivy St
S 56th St
Ridge Ct
S 57TH ST
Jessica Ln
Kalmia Ln
Holly
S 68th St
Ivy St
Glacier
S 70th Pl
Forsythia St
Glacier Dr
S 71st St
S 72nd Pl
Holly
St
3

JASPER RD
Ridgecrest
Dr
S 58th St
S 59th St
lac Ln
Jessica
S 68th St
S 69th Pl
St Dr

44°02'02"
44°02'07"

MT VERNON RD
Mt Vernon Rd
SEE
187
MAP
Mt Vernon
Cemetery Rd
Linda Ln
5500
S 57th Pl
Montclaire
Ln

SEE
64
MAP

4
Cindel St
Obsidian
Pumice Pl
Mineral Wy
S 61st St
Av
Mica
St
Orchid Ln
S 60th St
Pebble Ct
Quartz
Av
4

44°01'29"
44°01'34"

Mahogany Ln

5
Jasper Rd
5

Brand
S Rd
600

44°00'57"
44°01'02"

PUDDING CREEK
RR Bader
Rd

6
Jasper Rd
Wallace Creek
6

Pudding Creek

44°00'24"
44°00'29"

RAND McNALLY

Dery Rd

Laird Ln
Laird Rd

Weyerhauser Rd

ert Ln

7
7

43°59'52"
43°59'57"

122°57'02"
122°56'17"
122°55'31"
122°55'46"
122°54'01"
122°53'15"

A   B   C   D   E

SEE [64] MAP

MAP
189

MAP
189

1:30,000
1 in. = 2500 ft.
0   0.25   0.5
miles

N

SEE 66 MAP

44°07'06"   44°07'07"
1   1

Tyler Rd
63800

RILEY RD
Mountain
Mead

Tumalo Creek Rd

44°06'33"   44°06'35"
2   2

Goldspur Wy
Klippel Rd
BuckDr
Saddleback Pl
Fawn Ln
Palla Ln
NW Skyline Ranch Rd

Deschutes River

Cox Ln Rd
Mathers Rd

Glen Vista Rd

44°06'01"   44°06'03"
3   3

Saddleback Ln
Doe Ln
Lookout Dr
Stag Dr
Rocher Wy

Chaney Rd
NE OB RILEY
Chaney Rd South

NW Sawyer
NW Sower Ct
NW Brogan Rd
Slagstad Ct
NW Sower

NW Archie Briggs Rd
NW Northcliff
NW Lower Village Wy
NW Mesa Verde
Firerock Rd
Soft Breeze
Caddisfly Ln

44°05'28"   44°05'30"
4   4

SHEVLIN REGIONAL PARK

AWBREY GLEN GOLF CLUB
NW Rawlins Ct
NW Kirkaldy Ct
NW Morris Ct
NW Fishwick Ct
NW Hilton Ct
NW Messen St
NW Sargent Wy
Cir
NW Kidd
NW Champion
NW Conrad Dr
NW Braid Dr
NW Vardon Ct
NW Fernie Ct
NW Wethered

NW Foxwood Pl
NW Greenleaf Wy
NW Greenbrier
NW Chelsea Dr
Chelsea Dr
NW Yosemite
NW Olympic Ct
NW Bryce
Canyon Ln
NW Haleakala Wy
Moonstone
Carnelian

RIVER'S EDGE GOLF COURSE

SEE 66 MAP
SEE 190 MAP

44°04'56"   44°04'58"

NW Squirrel Tail Ln
Mt Hood Av
Mt Shasta Dr
Mt Jefferson
NW Commons
Sage
NW Park
NW Shevlin Park Rd
NW Skyline Ranch Rd
NW Whitworth Wy
NW Strath Wy
NW Melville
NW McDermott
Anderson
NW Arrowlead
NW Mekte Pl
NW Perspective Dr
NW Windwood
NW Panorama Dr
NW Constellation Dr
NW Remarkable Dr
NW Balitch
Rye Cir
NW Greta
NW Prairie
NW Bungalow Dr
NW Heights
NW Fairway
SYLVAN PARK
NW Winslow Dr
NW Overlook Dr
NW Colver
NW Healy
NW Colonial Dr
NW Redfield
NW Farewell
NW Kenwood
NW Austin
NW Elliot
NW Hale
NW Meissner
NW Divot Dr
NW 11th Green Pl
Second
The Dr
NW 11th

5   5

44°04'24"   44°04'25"

McClain Dr
NW Kreth
NW Kelly
NW Skyline
Ranch Rd
NW Brickyard
NW Darnel Wy
NW Marken St
NW Scandia Lp
NW Jeffer St
NW Rainbow Ln
NW Nordic Av
NW Cousins Pl
NW Locke Ct
NW Dabkin
NW Regency St
NW O'Brien Ct
NW Twilight
NW Dwight Dr
Keenan
NW Nightfall
NW Starview Dr
NW Okane Ct
NW Lawrence Dr
NW Three Sisters Dr
NW Moore
NW Clark Ct
NW Welcome
NW Gill
NW Promontory
NW Peoples
NW Foley
NW Coe Ct
NW Glassow
NW Gunway Dr
NW Gleneville Dr
NW City View Dr
NW Summit Dr
SUMMIT PARK
NW Wyeth
NW Milton
NW Lucas
NW Fickett Ct
Promontory
NW Pilot View Pl
Compass Ln
NW Scenic Heights

6   6

44°03'51"   44°03'53"

NW Anderson Ranch Rd
NW Chianti Ln
NW Shiraz Ln
NW Pinot Ct
NW Celilo Ln
NW Wild Meadow Dr
NW Reserve
Camp Ct
NW Lepage Pl
NW Shields
NW Pompy Pl
NW Lemhi
NW Pryor
NW McNeal
NW Monterey
NW Sugar
NW Vicksburg Av
NW Trenton Av
NW Saginaw Av
NW Quincy Av
HILLSDALE PARK
NW Vicksburg Av
NW Utica Av
NW Roanoke Av
NW Saginaw Av
NW Quincy Av
HILLSIDE PARK
NW Hillside Park Dr
NW Hillpine
NW Stone Hill Dr
Stonepine
NW Evergreen
NW West Hills Av
NW Iowa Av
NW Easties
NW Morelock Ct
NW Greyhawk
NW Todd
Hawk Dr
NW 5th
NW 7th
NW 8th
NW Yellowtail
Crest Dr
NW Wilming
NW Vicksburg

Bend
CENTRAL OREGON COMMUNITY COLLEGE
Oregon State University-Cascades
NW College Loop Rd
NW College Wy
NW Shevlin Park Rd
NW Mt Washington Dr

NW Rimrock Dr
NW Palisades Dr
NW City Heights Dr
NW Rock Rd

44°03'19"   44°03'21"
7   7

RAND McNALLY

NW Crossing Dr
NW Clearwater Dr
NW Charbonneau St
NW Fort Clatsop St
NW John Fremont St
NW Lewis
NW Meriwether
NW Colter Av
NW High Lakes Ln
NW Ordway
NW Crossing Dr
NW Drouillard Av
NW Dorion
NW Frazer
NW Flagline Dr
NW Cabot
NW Jack
NW Lake St
NW Skyliners Rd

SUNSET VIEW PARK

NW Portland Av
NW Newport Av
NW 18th Pl
NW Newport Dr
NW 18th St
NW Knobhill
Blvd
NW Kingston Av
NW Jacksonville
NW Milwaukee Av
NW Lexington Av
NW Nashville Av
NW Drake Rd
NW Glen Rd
BROOKS PARK
HARMON PARK
DRAKE PARK
The Sage House
NW Milne
NW Franklin Av
NW Hartford Av
NW Ithaca Av
NW Columbia
NW Federal
NW Harmon
NW Hixon Av
NW Fresno Av
NW Kansas Av
NW State St
NW Congress St

SEE 66 MAP
SEE 191 MAP

A   B   C   D   E

121°22'30"   121°21'45"   121°21'00"   121°20'14"   121°19'29"   121°18'43"

MAP
190

MAP
190

1:30,000
1 in. = 2500 ft.
0   0.25   0.5
miles

SEE 66 MAP

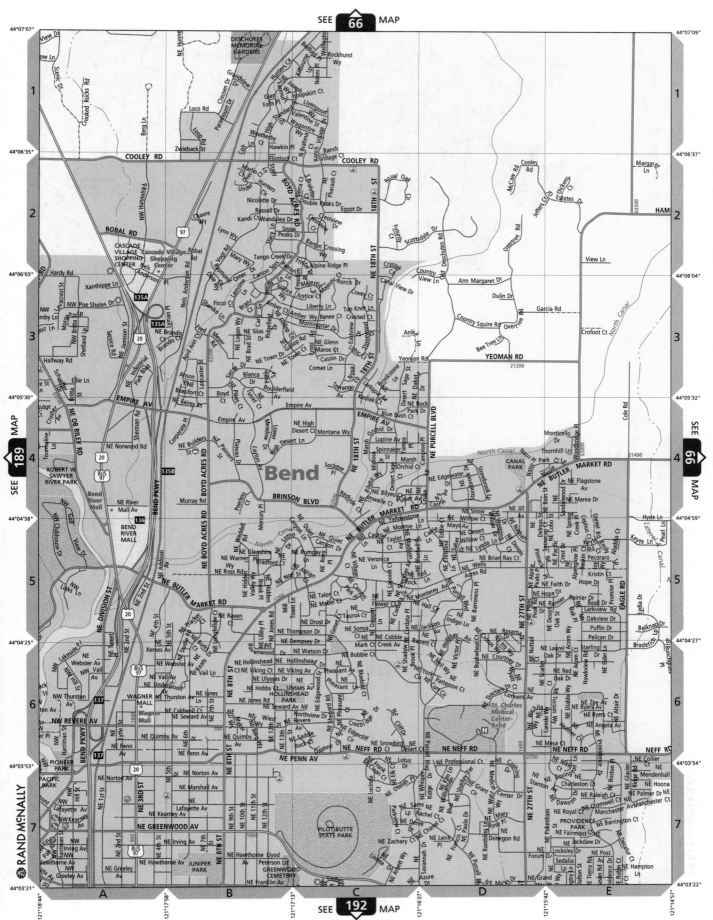

Bend

SEE 189 MAP

SEE 66 MAP

SEE 192 MAP

RAND McNALLY

MAP
191

1:30,000
1 in. = 2500 ft.
0   0.25   0.5
miles

MAP
191

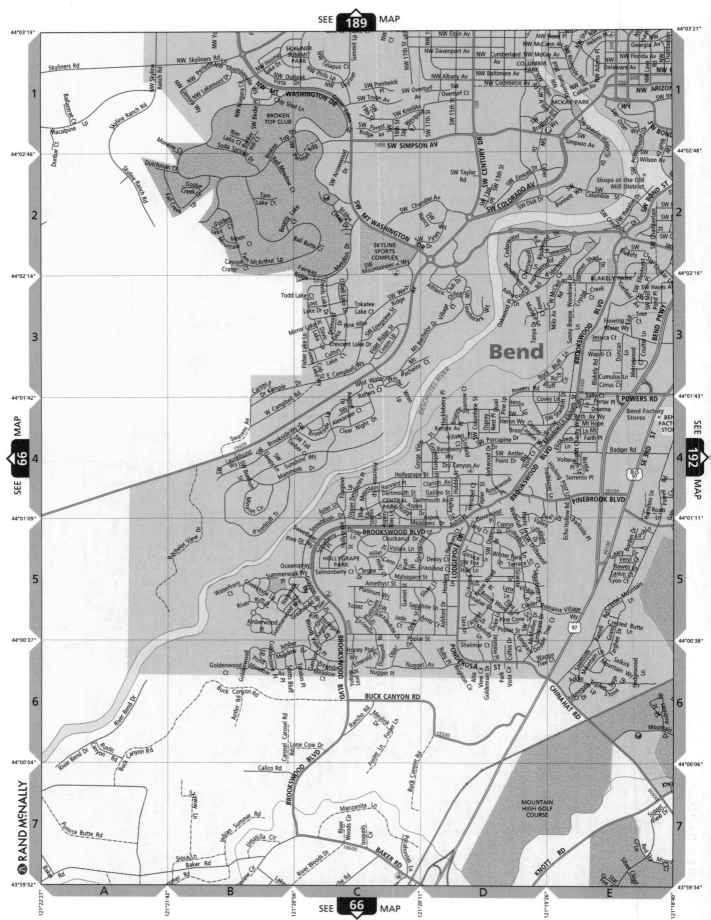

SEE **189** MAP

SEE **66** MAP

SEE **192** MAP

SEE **66** MAP

Bend

RAND McNALLY

44°03'19"
44°02'46"
44°02'14"
44°01'42"
44°01'09"
44°00'37"
44°00'04"
43°59'32"

44°03'21"
44°02'48"
44°02'16"
44°01'43"
44°01'11"
44°00'38"
44°00'06"
43°59'34"

MAP
192

MAP
192

1:30,000
1 in. = 2500 ft.

0   0.25   0.5

miles

SEE 190 MAP

SEE 191 MAP

SEE 66 MAP

SEE 66 MAP

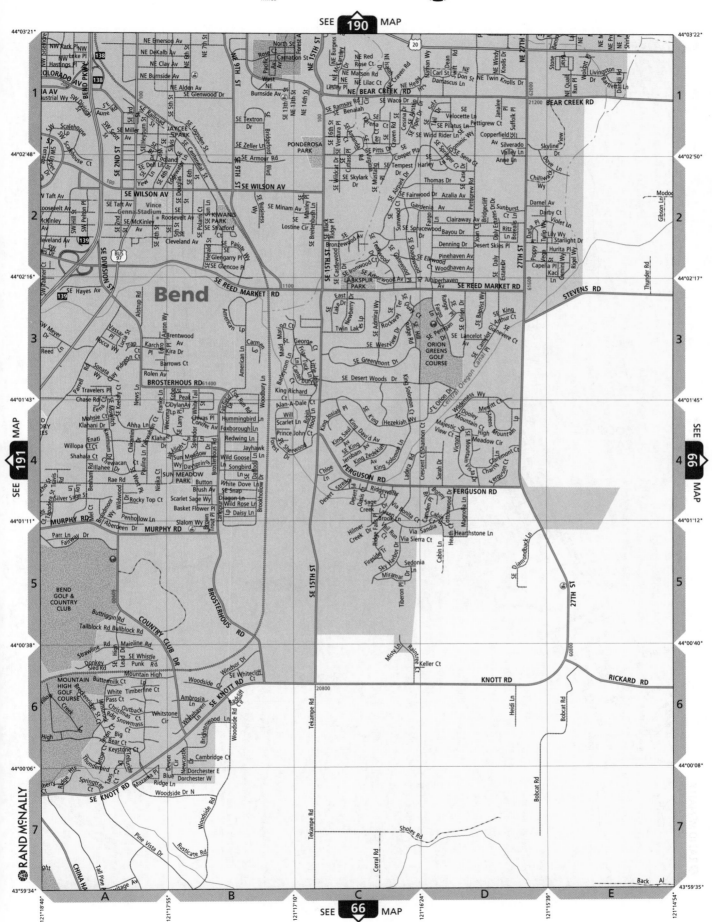

Bend

RAND McNALLY

MAP
193

MAP
193

1:30,000
1 in. = 2500 ft.
0   0.25   0.5
miles

N

SEE 73 MAP

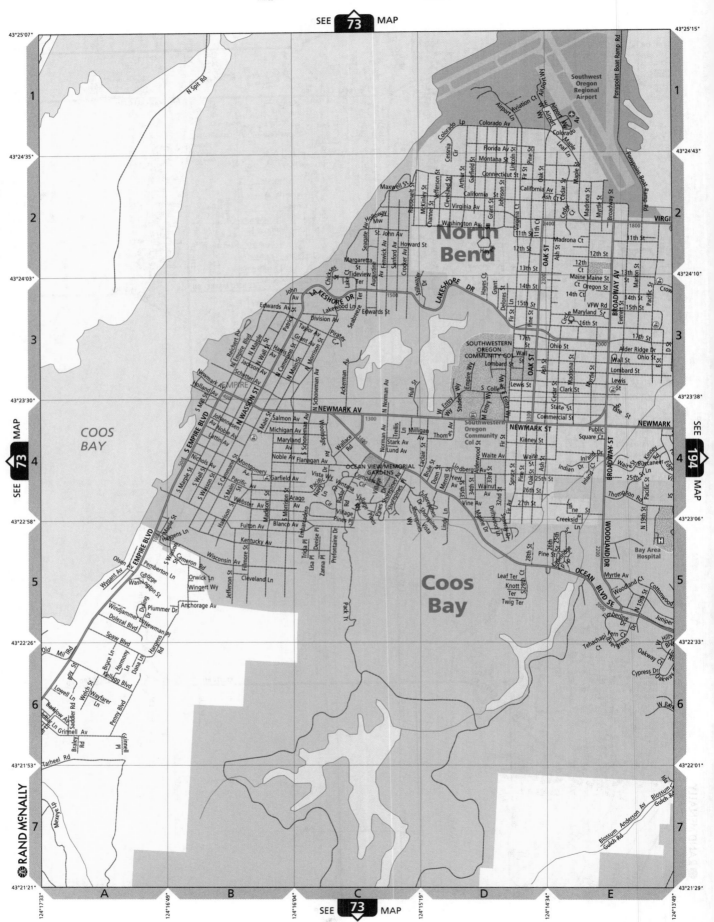

SEE 73 MAP
SEE 73 MAP
SEE 194 MAP

North Bend

COOS BAY

Coos Bay

Southwest Oregon Regional Airport

SOUTHWESTERN OREGON COMMUNITY GOL

Southwestern Oregon Community Col

OCEAN VIEW MEMORIAL GARDENS

Bay Area Hospital

MAP
194

MAP
194

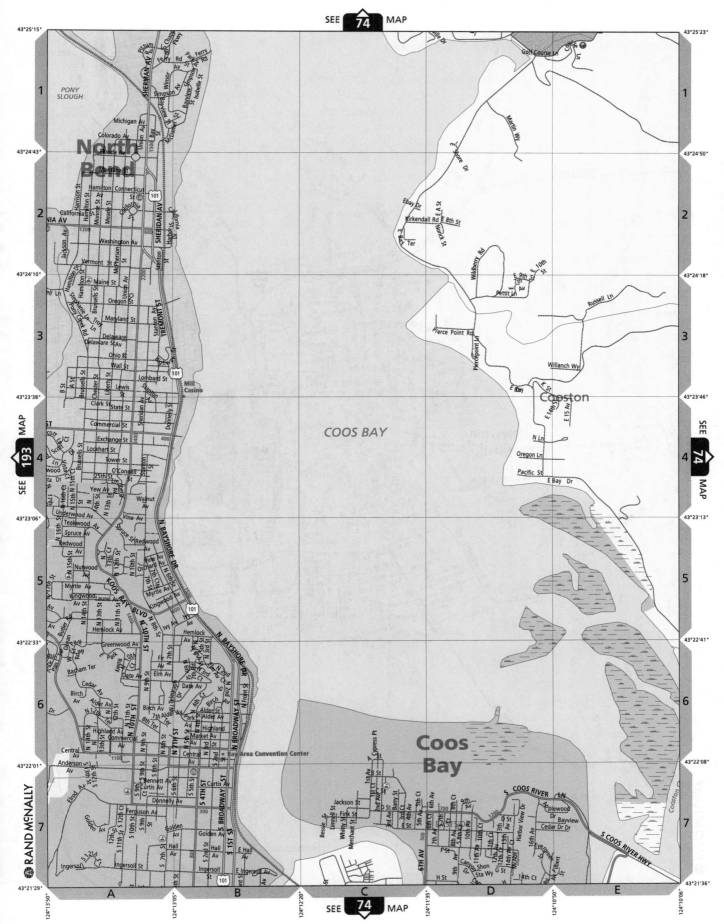

MAP
195

MAP
195

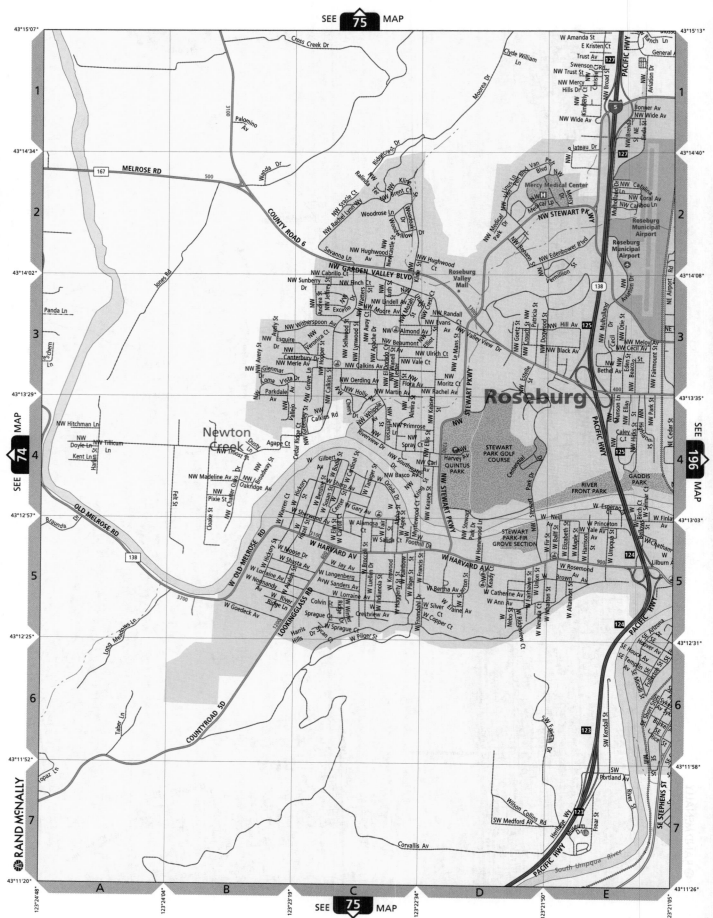

1:30,000
1 in. = 2500 ft.

0   0.25   0.5
miles

MAP
196

MAP
196

1:30,000
1 in. = 2500 ft.
0   0.25   0.5
miles

N

SEE 75 MAP

Roseburg

SEE 195 MAP

SEE 75 MAP

NORTH ROSEBURG

NE Diamond Lake Blvd
SE Oak Av
SE Pine St

RAND McNALLY

SEE 75 MAP

43°15'13"   43°15'18"
43°14'40"   43°14'46"
43°14'08"   43°14'14"
43°13'35"   43°13'41"
43°13'03"   43°13'09"
43°12'31"   43°12'36"
43°11'58"   43°12'04"
43°11'26"   43°11'32"

123°21'05"   123°20'20"   123°19'36"   123°18'51"   123°18'06"   123°17'22"

A   B   C   D   E
1   2   3   4   5   6   7

MAP
197

MAP
197

1:30,000
1 in. = 2500 ft.
0   0.25   0.5
miles

N

SEE 87 MAP

42°28'26"
42°27'54"
42°27'21"
42°26'49"
42°26'17"
42°25'44"
42°25'12"
42°24'40"

42°28'32"
42°28'00"
42°27'27"
42°26'55"
42°26'22"
42°25'50"
42°25'18"
42°24'45"

SEE 87 MAP

SEE 87 MAP

Grants Pass

Fruitdale

Three Rivers Community Hospital

MITCHELL PARK

GEORGE H ECKSTEIN PARK

GRANTS PASS PKWY

PACIFIC HWY
REDWOOD HWY
WILLIAMS HWY
ROGUE RIVER HWY
FOOTHILL BLVD
LINCOLN RD
Rogue River

RAND M?NALLY

123°21'26" 123°20'42" 123°19'58" 123°19'14" 123°18'30" 123°17'46"

A   B   C   D   E

SEE 87 MAP

MAP
198

MAP
198

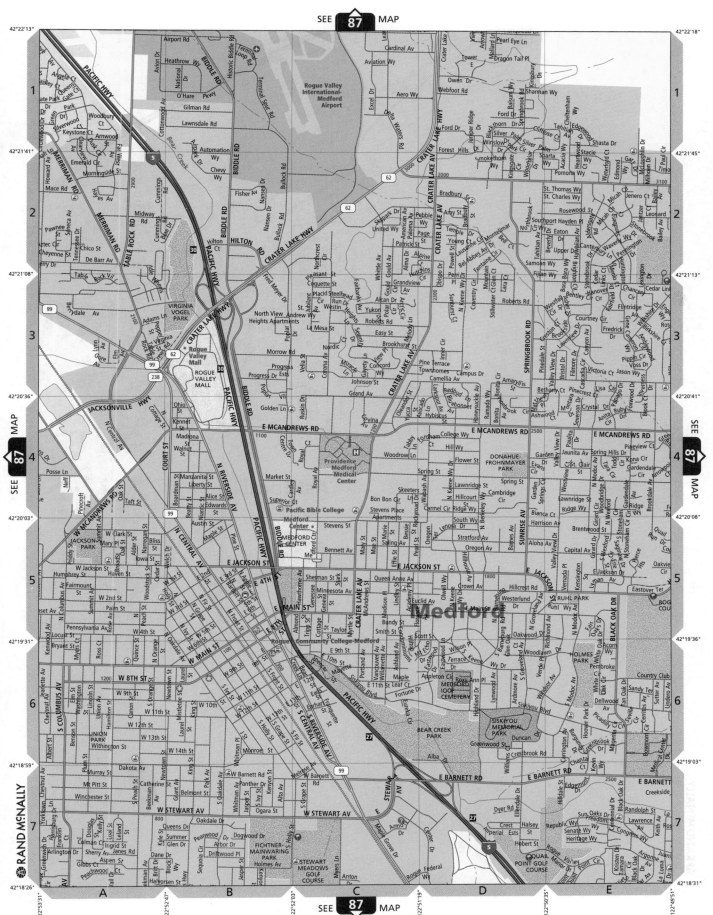

1:30,000
1 in. = 2500 ft.
0   0.25   0.5
miles

MAP
199

MAP
199

1:30,000
1 in. = 2500 ft.
0   0.25   0.5
miles

N

SEE 87 MAP

SEE 87 MAP

SEE 200 MAP

SEE 98 MAP

42°13'21"   42°13'26"
42°12'49"   42°12'53"
42°12'16"   42°12'21"
42°11'44"   42°11'49"
42°11'12"   42°11'16"
42°10'39"   42°10'44"
42°10'07"   42°10'11"
42°09'35"   42°09'39"

122°45'34"   122°44'50"   122°44'06"   122°43'23"   122°42'39"   122°41'55"

A   B   C   D   E

1   2   3   4   5   6   7

Ashland

S VALLEY
W Jackson Rd
Nauvoo Mobile Nauvoo
Ests   Mobile Ests
Jackson Rd
Bear Creek
PACIFIC HWY
Mill Rd
Eagle
N Mountain Av

Frank Hill Rd
McKenzie Canyon Rd
Patrick Ln

Ashland Creek
Quiet Ln   Oxford   Coyentry Pl
Tudor St   Sunflower
York St   Glenflower Av   DOG PARK
Kent   Glenbrook   Almeda Dr
Cedar Wy   W Nevada St   Alder Ln   E Nevada St   E Nevada St
Norton St   Eastgeling   Clovis Av   E Nevada St
Fox St   Lindsay   Cambridge St   Cypress Cir   Fair
Schofields   Michele Av   Oaks Av   Pavilion
Lakota Wy   Vista Dr   Randy   Oak Meadows Pl   Nandina   Meadows
Sheridan St   Elizabeth   Otis St   N Laurel St   Mountain View Dr   Dr S
Tucker St   Grant St   Willow St   Draper St   Sleepy Hollow Dr
Greenbriar Pl   SCENIC PARK   Draper Av   Oaklawn   Sylvia
Wiley St   Maple   Ashland Community   Helman St   Tolliver Ln   Briscoe
Chestnut   St   Hospital   Orange Av   Park St   Oaklawn Av   Clinton St
Dogwood Wy   Coolidge St   Ohio St   Jessica Ln   Carol   N Mountain Av
Prather St   Luna   Vista St   Soott Glenn   Patterson   Lynn St
Paige St   Wimer St   Rock St   W Hersey St   Walter   Poplar Pl   Ripga
Grandview Dr   Nursery St   Skidmore   VOGEL PARK   Crispin   Clear Creek   Russell St
Benjamin Ct   Susan Ln   Van Ness Av   Central Av   Rogue St
Alta Av   West St   Manzanita St   Hersey St   RAILROAD DISTRICT PARK   Villa Gree
Orchard St   Sunshine Cir   Historic Ashland   A St   Phelps   9th
Nyla Ln   Skycrest Dr   Grandview Dr   Logan Dr   Armory   N Pioneer St   N 1st St   N 2nd   8th St
Sunnyview   Scenic Dr   Nob Hill St   LITHIA WY   Golden Spike   B St   7th St   St Al
Westwood   Piedmont Dr   Church   N Main St   N 3rd St   6th St   Emerick St
Creekside Rd   HALD STRAWBERRY PARK   Pine St   Baum   Linden Av   Will Dodge   C St   5th St   Eureka St
Wood Rd   Birdsong   Strawberry   Alnut St   Nutley St   N Beach   500   1000
Myrt Rd   Wrights Creek   Vista   SISKIYOU BLVD   Eureka St
Montview Av   Wightman St   W Fork St   Allison St   Beswick Wy   Blaine St
Gresham St   Pearl St   Fairview St   99
Summit St   Iowa St   Morton St   Alida   Morse Av   TRIANGLE PARK
Hillcrest St   Auburn St   Kearney St   Sherman St   Harrison St   Alaska St   Larkin Ln
LITHIA PARK   Gresham St   Holly St   Idaho St
Merrill St   Liberty St   Pennsylvania St
Merrill Cir   Taylor St   Altamont St   Henry St
Heather St   Pracht St   Ashland St
Hill   Lantern Dr   Guthrie St   Pioneer St   GLENWOOD PARK
Winter Dr   Jennifer   Henry   Friendship St   Clarence   Beach St
Forest St   Glenwood Dr   Pleas
Granite St Ashland   Waterline   Logan Rd   Cascade Ln   Pros
Ashland Creek Dr   Glenview Dr   Morton St   Wildwood Wy
S Mountain Av
Ivy St
Ashland Loop Rd
Elk

Wrights Creek
Ashland Mine Rd

MAP 200

MAP 200

1:30,000
1 in. = 2500 ft.
0   0.25   0.5
miles

N

SEE 87 MAP

SEE 199 MAP

SEE 87 MAP

42°13'26"
42°13'30"
42°12'53"
42°12'58"
42°12'21"
42°12'25"
42°11'49"
42°11'53"
42°11'16"
42°11'21"
42°10'44"
42°10'48"
42°10'11"
42°10'16"
42°09'39"
42°09'44"

122°41'55"
122°41'11"
122°40'27"
122°39'43"
122°38'59"
122°38'15"

Ashland

PACIFIC HWY

Gaerky Creek

Maddox Ln

Pompadour Dr

E Nevada St
E Nevada
PlotView Rd
Gaerky Creek Rd

Spark Pl
Tony Pt
Bulder Creek
Creek
Stone Wy
Nepenthe Rd
Ashland Acres Rd
Jensen Ln

NORTH MOUNTAIN PARK

E Hills Dr

SCENIC HILL MEMORIAL PARK

Square Dr
Seena Ln
Rome
Village
Old Willow Ln
Kirk Ln
Orchid St
Rose Ln
N Wightman
Blue Heron Wy
Mill Pond Rd
Mallard

GARFIELD PARK
California Ct
California St
Lincoln St
Garfield St
Iowa St
Quincy St
SOUTHERN OREGON UNIVERSITY
Campus Wy
Webster
Homes Av
Creek Dr
Dollarhide Wy
Meadow
Brooks Ln
Crocker
Abbott
Tolman Creek
Pk
Clay St
Engle St
E MAIN ST

Southern Oregon University
Palm Av
Avery St
Bridge St
Wightman St
Walker Av
Stadium St
Hunter Ct
Lit Wy
N College Wy
College Wy
Parker St
Normal Av
Ray Ln
MOUNTAIN VIEW CEMETERY
Birchwood Ln
YMCA PARK
YMCA

2200

Madrone St
Roca
Fern St
Monroe St
Oregon St
Frances St
SHERWOOD PARK
Sherwood St
Fremont
Faith Av
CLAY STREET PARK
Garden Apartments
Stratford
Mickelson St
ASHLAND ST
Jefferson Av
Washington St
Sutton Pl
Spring Creek
Oak Knoll Dr
Oak Hill Cir
Fairway Cir
Applegate Wy

Elkader St
Leonard St
Indiana St
Windsor St
Fielder St
Elms St
Woodland Dr
Garden Way Park
Clark Av
Harmony Ln
SISKIYOU BLVD
Joy Av
Park St
Mae St
Ventura Cir
Wine St
Gresham St
Iowa St
Kelma Wy
Grizzly Dr
Cub Ct
Jefferson Av
E St
Acorn Cir
Pines Ct
Twin Pines Ct
OAK KNOLL GOLF COURSE

Emma St
Penny Palmer Rd
Pinecrest Ter
Sunset Av
Walker Av
Garden Wy
Ross Ln
Weissenback
Hillview Wy
Plaza Av
Linda Av
Terra Av
Diane St
Black Dr
Barbara St
Apella
Old Mill Wy
Hill Dr
Eagle Creek
Spring St
Mistletoe Rd
Jefferson St
Benson Wy
W Pebble Beach Dr
W Oak Knoll Dr
Augusta Ct
St Andrew
Barrington Cir
CROWSON RD
Maywood Wy
Hillendale Dr
Hidden Ln

Ponderosa Dr
Oneida Cir
Hiawatha
Deer Vista Ln
Paradise Ln
Bristol St
Dover Av
Peachey Rd
Hope St
Nezla St
Mary Jane Av
Verda Av
Chitwood Ln
Mohawk St
Crestview Dr
Tamarack Pl
Dragonfly Ln
Canyon Park Dr
Oak Wy
BELLVIEW
Morada Ln
Black Wy
Apple
Greenmeadow
Sam Evans Pl
Lupine Dr
Oredson Todd Woods

Highwood
Statite Rd
Powerline Ter

SISKIYOU MOUNTAIN PARK

Tolman Creek Rd
Moonlight Dr

BYERS LAKE

GREEN SPRINGS HWY
Bear Creek
Clayton Creek
Skeeten Dr

Dead Indian Memorial Rd
Ashland Municipal Airport

I-5
99
66
14
200

SEE 98 MAP

RAND McNALLY

MAP
201

MAP
201

1:30,000
1 in. = 2500 ft.

0   0.25   0.5
miles

N

SEE 89 MAP

42°16'05"   42°16'07"

1   1

42°15'32"   42°15'35"

2   2

42°15'00"   42°15'03"

3   3

42°14'28"   42°14'30"

SEE 88 MAP   SEE 202 MAP

4   4

42°13'55"   42°13'58"

5   5

42°13'23"   42°13'25"

6   6

42°12'50"   42°12'53"

7   7

42°12'18"   42°12'21"

A   B   C   D   E

121°49'08"   121°48'24"   121°47'40"   121°46'56"   121°46'12"   121°45'28"

SEE 89 MAP

RAND McNALLY

UPPER
KLAMATH
LAKE

Klamath
Falls

LAKE EWAUNA

PELICAN CITY

OREGON INSTITUTE
OF TECHNOLOGY

Oregon Institute
of Technology

Merle
West
Medical
Center

HARBOR
LINKS
GOLF
COURSE

MOORE
PARK

MOORE
PARK

VETERANS
PARK

CEMETERY

THE DALLES-CALIFORNIA HWY

KIT CARSON HWY

LAKEPORT BLVD

NEVADA ST

OREGON AV

MAIN ST

E MAIN ST

ESPLANADE ST

KLAMATH AV

S 6TH ST

N 11TH ST

SHASTA W

Sykes Av

MAP
202

1:30,000
1 in. = 2500 ft.
0   0.25   0.5
miles

MAP
202

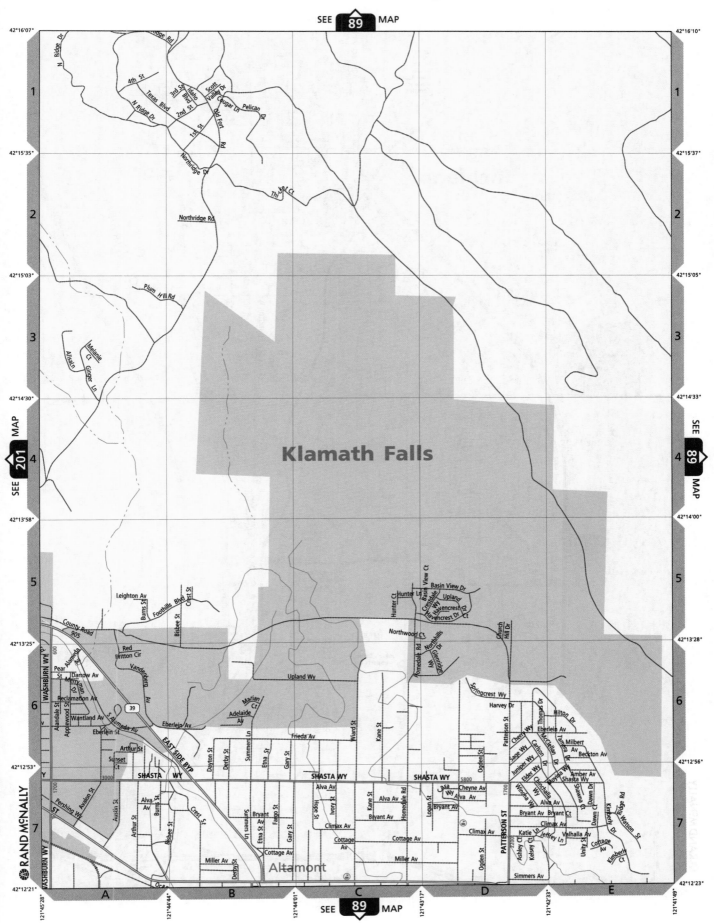

42°16'07"
42°16'10"

42°15'35"
42°15'37"

42°15'03"
42°15'05"

42°14'30"
42°14'33"

42°13'58"
42°14'00"

42°13'25"
42°13'28"

42°12'53"
42°12'56"

42°12'21"
42°12'23"

Klamath Falls

SEE 201 MAP

SEE 89 MAP

1   2   3   4   5   6   7

A   B   C   D   E

N Ridge Dr
4th St
3rd St
Idaho Blvd
Scott Valley Dr
Cougar Ln
Pelican Dr
Texas Blvd
N Ridge Dr
2nd St
1st St
Old Fort Rd
Northridge Dr
Thl et Ct
Northridge Rd
Plum Hill Rd
Melanie Ct
Ginger Ln
Alisan
Leighton Av
Burns St
Foothills Blvd
Bisbee St
Crest St
Basin View Ct
Basin View Dr
Hunter Ln
Upland
Crestdale Wy
Havencrest Dr
Hunter Ct
Havencrest Dr
Church Hill Dr
County Road 905
Northwood Ct
Northwood Ct
Northhills Dr
Glenridge Dr
Homedale Rd
Red Britton Cir
Vandenberg Av
Upland Wy
Springcrest Wy
Harvey Dr
Milton Dr
Patterson St
Cherry Wy
Eberlein Av
Tamra Ct
Milbert Av
Beckton Av
Pear St
Alameda St
Darrow Av
Merry man Dr
Marian Ct
Adelaide Av
Wiard St
Kane St
Sage Wy
Thomas Dr
McClellan Dr
Carlton Dr
Reclamation Av
39
EAST SIDE BYP
Eberlein Av
Frieda Av
Juniper Wy
Clinchalla
Rovita Ct
Alandale St
Applewood St
Wantland Av
S Alameda Av
Dayton St
Derby St
Summers Ln
Etna St
Gary St
Ogden St
Elder Wy
Alva Av
Amber Ct
Shasta Wy
Eberlein St
Arthur St
Sunset Ct
3000
SHASTA WY
SHASTA WY
SHASTA WY
5800
Winona Wy
Bryant Av
Bryant Ct
Dawn Dr
Shawna Wy
Dawn Dr
Kimberly
Watson St
Pershing Wy
1700
Avalon St
Alva Av
Burns St
Crest St
Kane St
Alva Av
Homedale Rd
sa Wy
Cheyne Av
1700
Bryant Av
Bryant Av
Climax Ct
Valhalla Av
Austin St
Arthur St
Bisbee St
Summers Ln
Bryant
Fargo St
Etna St
Gary St
Hope St
Ivory St
Climax Av
Logan St
Bryant Av
Climax Av
Katie Ln
Jeffrey Ln
Kimberly Dr
WASHBURN WY
RAND MC NALLY
Cottage Av
Miller Av
Derby St
Altamont
Cottage Av
Cottage Av
Miller Av
Ogden St
Unity St
Kelsey Ct
Ashley Ct
Kimberly Ct
Simmers Av
Ocean

121°45'28"
121°44'44"
121°44'01"
121°43'17"
121°42'33"
121°41'49"

MAP
203

1:30,000
1 in. = 2500 ft.
0   0.25   0.5
miles

SEE 39 MAP

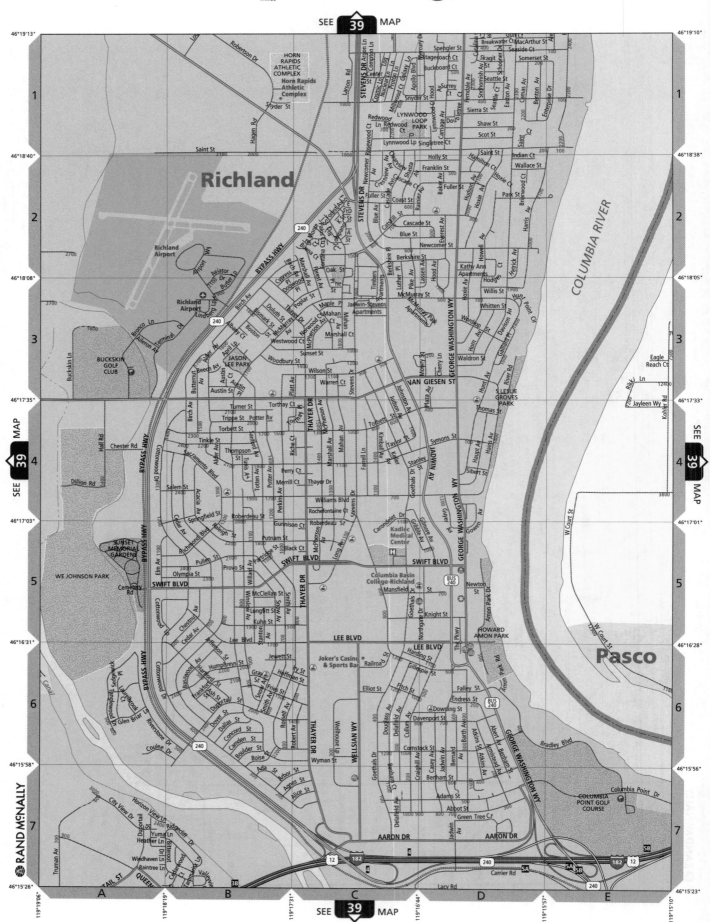

SEE 39 MAP

SEE 39 MAP

SEE 39 MAP

MAP
203

RAND MCNALLY

MAP 204 MAP 204

1:30,000
1 in. = 2500 ft.
miles 0 0.25 0.5

N

SEE 39 MAP

Pasco

Tri-Cities Airport

Tri-Cities Airport

SUN WILLOWS GOLF COURSE

PASCO GOLFLAND

COLUMBIA BASIN COLLEGE

Columbia Basin College

CITY VIEW CEMETERY

HIGHLAND PARK

Edgar Brown Memorial Stadium

EDGAR BROWN MEMORIAL STADIUM

Lourdes Medical Center

Amtrak-Pasco

VOLUNTEER PARK

SYLVESTER PARK

MEMORIAL PARK

COLUMBIA MEMORIAL GARDENS

Crazy Moose Casino

PASCO YOUTH BASEBALL COMPLEX

MERCIER PARK

LAKE WALLULA

RAND MCNALLY

SEE 39 MAP
SEE 39 MAP

A B C D E

MAP
205

1:30,000
1 in. = 2500 ft.
0   0.25   0.5
miles

N

MAP
205

SEE MAP

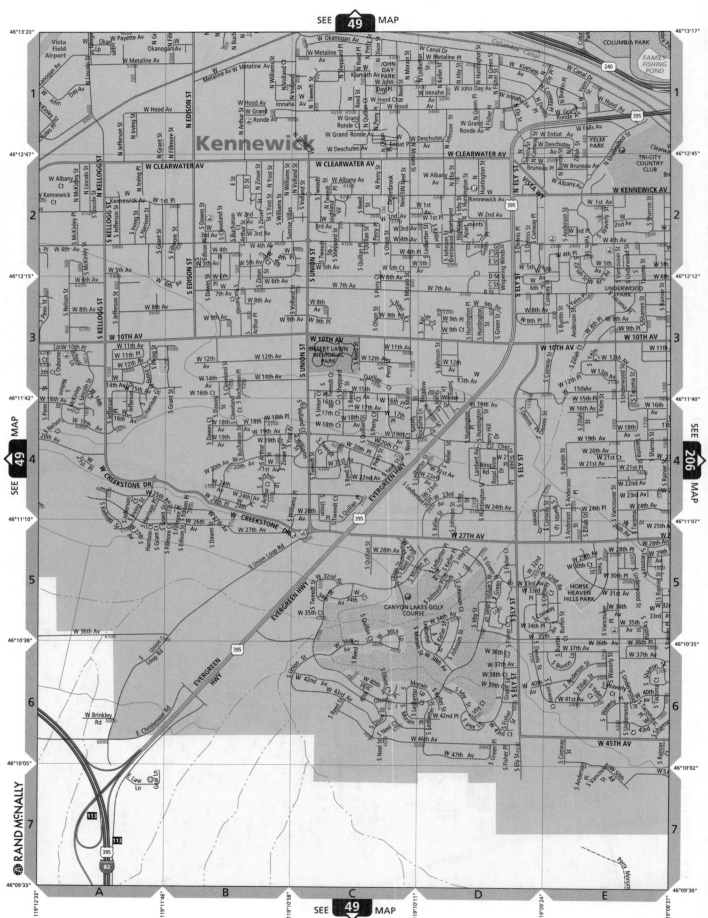

SEE 49 MAP

SEE 49 MAP

SEE 206 MAP

RAND McNALLY

MAP
206

1:30,000
1 in. = 2500 ft.
0   0.25   0.5
miles

N

MAP
206

SEE 204 MAP

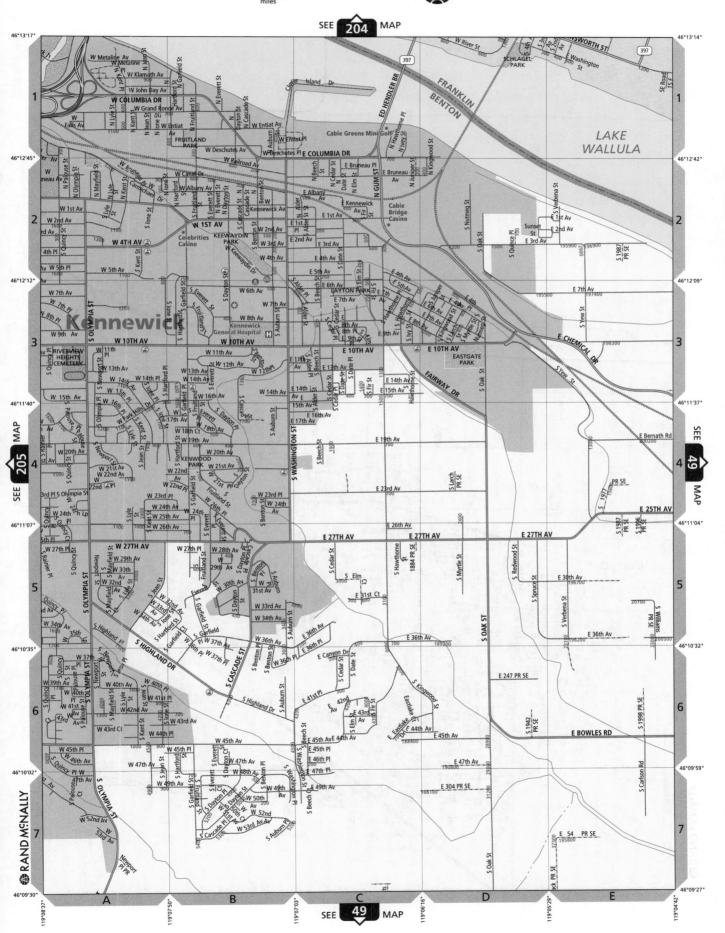

SEE 205 MAP

SEE 49 MAP

SEE 49 MAP

RAND McNALLY

MAP
207

MAP
207

1:30,000
1 in. = 2500 ft.
0   0.25   0.5
miles

N

SEE **50** MAP

46°05'31"
46°05'27"

46°04'59"
46°04'54"

46°04'26"
46°04'22"

46°03'54"
46°03'50"

46°03'21"
46°03'17"

46°02'49"
46°02'45"

46°02'17"
46°02'12"

46°01'44"
46°01'40"

SEE **50** MAP
SEE **208** MAP

1   2   3   4   5   6   7

A   B   C   D   E

118°24'20"   118°23'33"   118°22'46"   118°21'59"   118°21'12"   118°20'25"

Place names

Walla Walla

College Place

Garrett

Streets and features

N 4th Av
Carrie Av
Edith Av
May Av
W George
Par 72 Dr
W Rees Av
W Moore St
Dell Av
W Elm St
W Pine St
W Cherry St
Washington Park
Newtown Rd
Campbell Rd
Baldwin Rd
N Hussey Rd
Gose St
Duncan Ln
Rome St
Electric Av
Bearsville Ln
Lois
E Finch St
Fleetwood
NE Empire
Artesia Av
NE Dawson St
Chelan St
NE Villa
NE Troutdale Av
Westar
Hatch St
Drumheller
Davis Av
Finch Ln
Electric St
Locati Ln
Damson St
NE Belroy St
Belroy St
NE Alden St
Karo
W Rose St
Blue Mountain Mall
Wallula Rd
Finch
NE Redwood
Pine Deccio Ln
NE Spitzenburg
NE Lambert Rd
NE Della Rd
Cargill Cir
S Maple St
NE Tamarack St
NE Andy Ln
NE Deccio Rd
Pearl St
Garnet St
Topaz St
Jasper St
Emerald St
W Poplar St
Blalock Dr
Campbell Rd
Hussey St
NW B St
Pont-Marr
NE Pinewood
NE Ln
Birch St
NE Cedar St
NE Elder Pl
NE C St
SE Andrew Ln
NE Larch Av
SE Larch Av
NM Evans Av
NW Evans Ct
Destiho Av
NE Adams St
NE Bade Av
NE Ash Av
Birch Av
E Whitman Dr
Kiwanis Park
Davin Dr
Crestlane
JM Wainwright Memorial VA Medical Ctr
Rancho Villa
S 15th St
Callanan Dr
Walla Walla Park
Hulsey St
SW 1st St
SW 2nd St
SW Dailey
SW 3rd St
SW Clay St
SE Ash Av
SE Ash St
SE 2nd
Walla Walla College
SW 4th St
SE 3rd St
SE 4th St
Village Wy
Fairway
Walla Walla Country Club
Evans Av
W 6th St
SW 5th St
SW 6th St
City Shop Al
S College Av
SE 6th St
SE Hillcrest Dr
SE Barkspur
Garrison Village Wy
Garrison
SE Creekside Dr
Covey Ct
SE Admiral
SE Emerson
Crosshaven
Dana Dr
Suncrest Ter
Davis Av
SW 7th St
SW 8th St
SE 8th St
Granite
Granite Dr
Agate
Mica St
Stone
Creek Pl
Shale
Gemstone
Smith Dr
SW Grandview St
SW 9th St
SE Birch St
SE 9th St
SE Brentwood
SE Waine Av
SE 11th
S College Av
Anvil Ln
Wayne Ln
Whitney Rd
Brickner Rd
SW 10th St
SW 11th St
SW Puff
SE 10th St
SE Stanford Dr
SE Mountain View Dr
SE Robin Dr
SE Dove Ln
Walla Walla Country Club
Ironwood
Mercita Dr
SW 12th St
SE 12th St
13th St
SE Linda Dr
SE Scenic View Dr
SE Sky
SE Larch
SE Raven
SE Osprey Ln
Highland Rd
Country Club Rd
Leroux
Lancer Ln
Highland Rd
SW McKinney Av
SW Valley St
Summit Pl
SE Broadway Ln
Central
SE Valley Dr
Mallard
SE Freedom
Independence
Justice Av
SE Constitution Dr
Chisholm Ct
Fairfield Dr
Lancer Rd
Williams Rd
Moionnier Rd
Lampert St
SE Cedar Bend Dr
Winona
SE Harsh
Jessica Av
Taumarson Rd
Prospect Av
Christenson Rd
SE Rory Ct
SE Grassland Ct
SE Clover Ct
Gray Lynn Dr
Tay Lyn
Plaza Wy

13TH AV N
N 2nd Av
S 4th Av
S 9th Av
S 11th Av
W Rees Av
W Rose St
W Poplar St
Dalles Military Rd
Taumarson Rd

US 12
BUS 12
125

MAP
208

MAP
208

1:30,000
1 in. = 2500 ft.

0   0.25   0.5
miles

N

SEE 50 MAP

SEE 207 MAP

SEE 50 MAP

SEE 50 MAP

Walla Walla

Walla Walla Regional Airport

VETERANS MEMORIAL GOLF COURSE

BORLESKE STADIUM

WHITMAN COLLEGE

PIONEER PARK

WALLA WALLA GENERAL HOSPITAL

TIETAN PARK

MOUNTAIN VIEW CEMETERY

GABRIEL PARK

E ISAACS AV

MELROSE ST

E ALDER ST

WHITMAN ST

E CHESTNUT ST

BRYANT AV

E TIETAN ST

W TIETAN ST

RESER RD

E PROSPECT RD

AIRPORT RD

TAUSICK WY

SCHOOL AV

FERN ST

CLINTON ST

RAND McNALLY

46°05'27"
46°04'54"
46°04'22"
46°03'50"
46°03'17"
46°02'45"
46°02'12"
46°01'40"

46°05'22"
46°04'50"
46°04'17"
46°03'45"
46°03'13"
46°02'40"
46°02'08"
46°01'35"

118°20'25"   118°19'38"   118°18'51"   118°18'04"   118°17'17"   118°16'30"

A   B   C   D   E
1   2   3   4   5   6   7

MAP
209

MAP
209

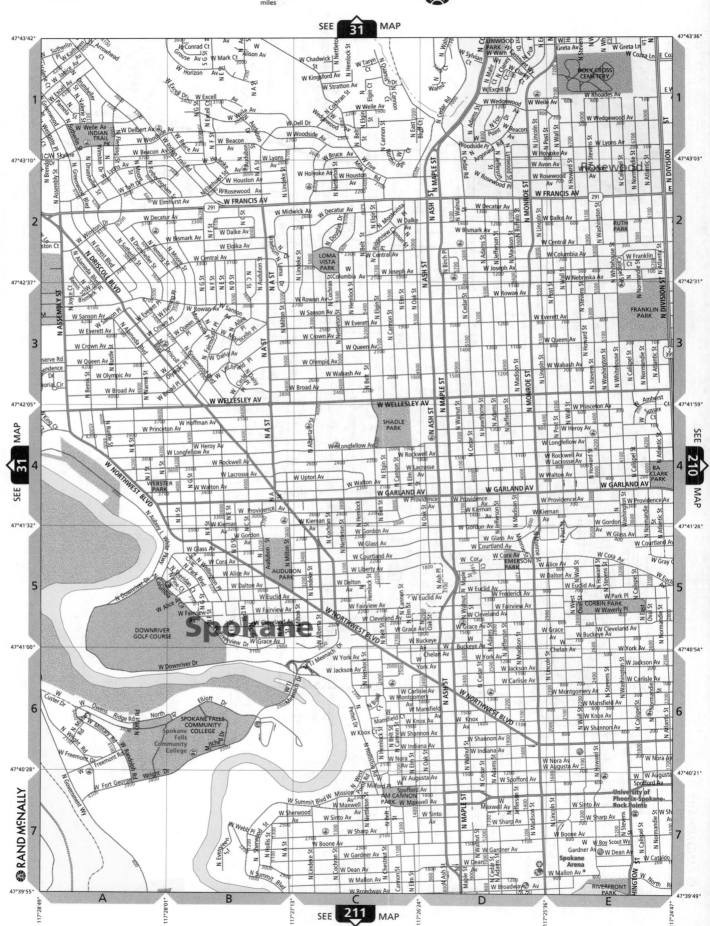

MAP
210

MAP
210

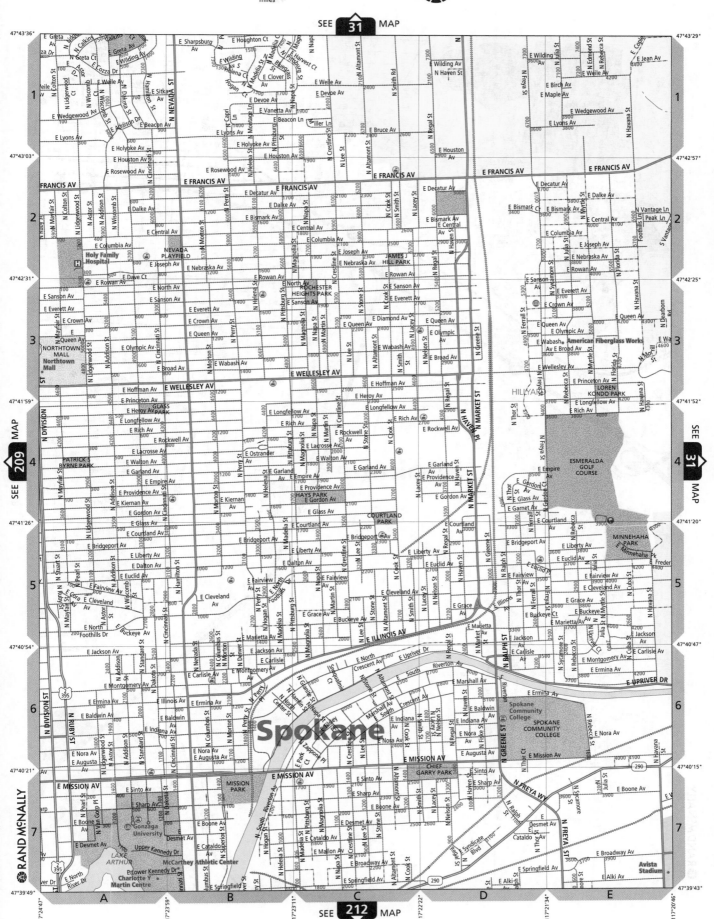

MAP
211

1:30,000
1 in. = 2500 ft.
0   0.25   0.5
miles

MAP
211

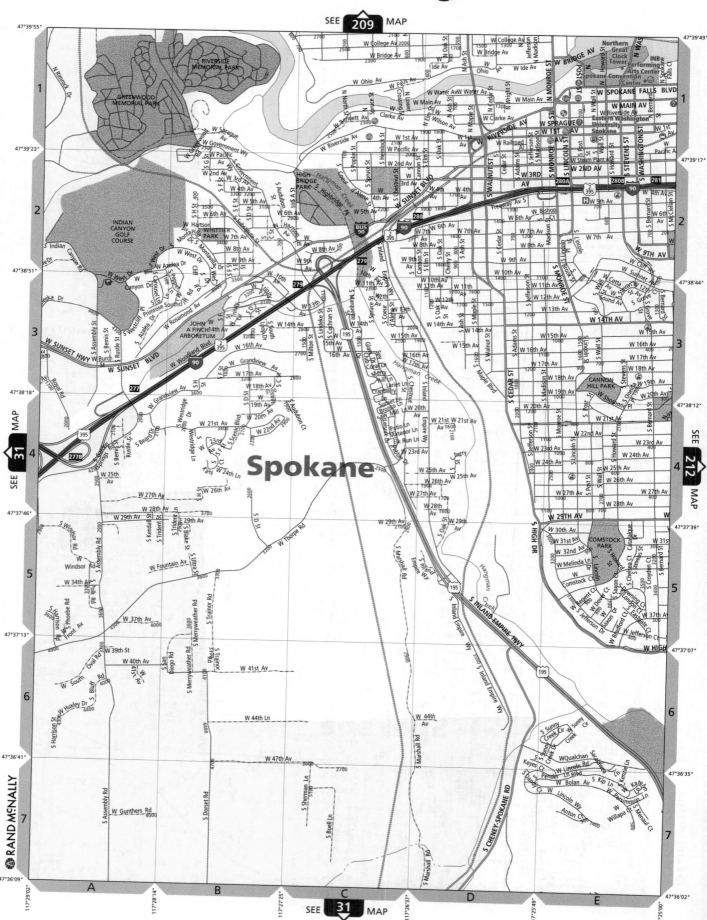

Spokane

SEE **31** MAP

SEE **212** MAP

RAND MᶜNALLY

MAP
212

MAP
212

1:30,000
1 in. = 2500 ft.
0   0.25   0.5
miles

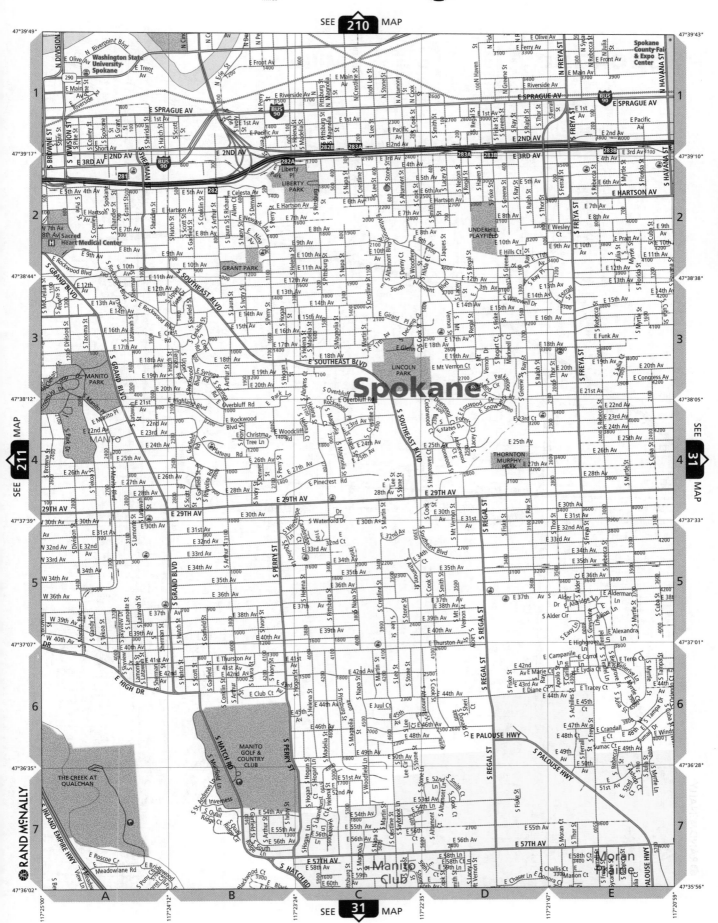

SEE 210 MAP

SEE 211 MAP

SEE 31 MAP

SEE 31 MAP

Spokane

RAND McNALLY

MAP
213

MAP
213

1:30,000
1 in. = 2500 ft.
0   0.25   0.5
miles

SEE **31** MAP

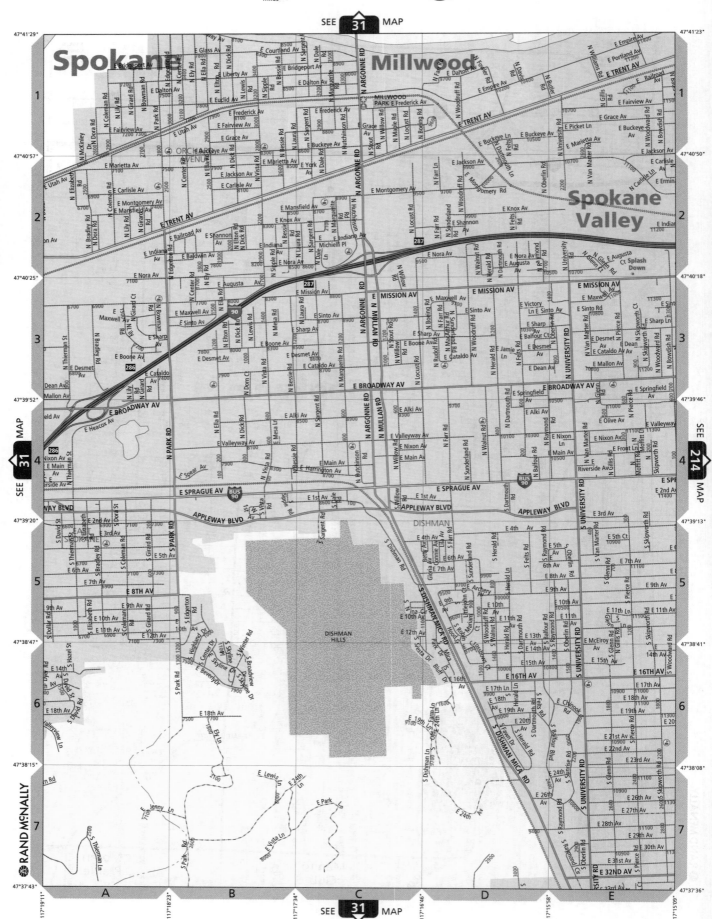

Spokane

Millwood

Spokane
Valley

SEE **31** MAP

SEE **31** MAP

MAP **31** SEE

SEE **214** MAP

RAND M°NALLY

DISHMAN
HILLS

MAP
214

1:30,000
1 in. = 2500 ft.
0   0.25   0.5
miles

MAP
214

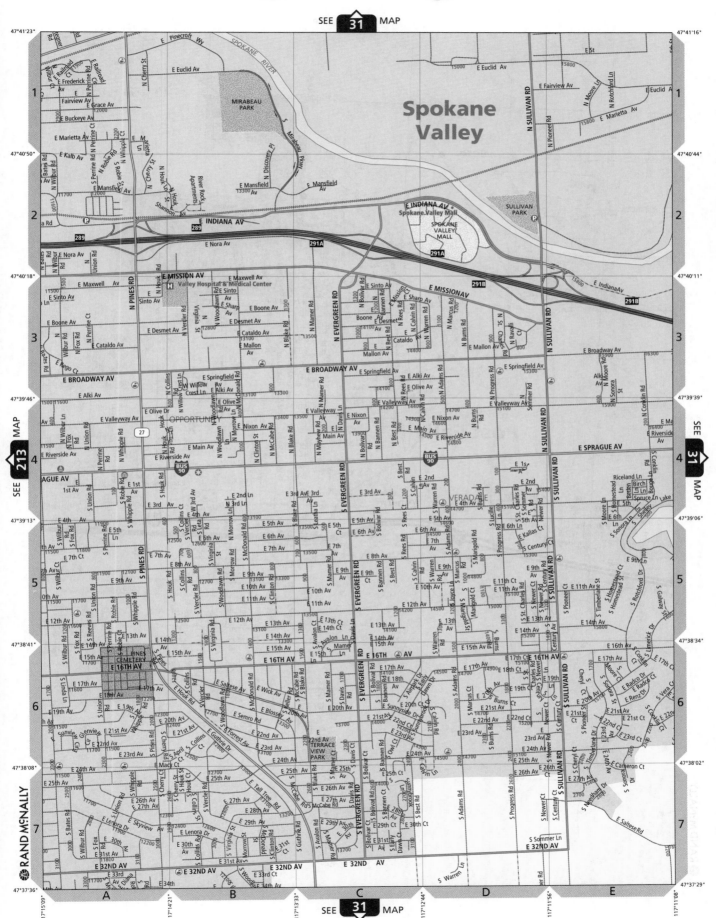

Spokane
Valley

MIRABEAU
PARK

SULLIVAN
PARK

SPOKANE
VALLEY
MALL

Valley Hospital & Medical Center

OPPORTUNITY

VERADALE

PINES
CEMETERY

TERRACE
VIEW
PARK

MAP
215

MAP
215

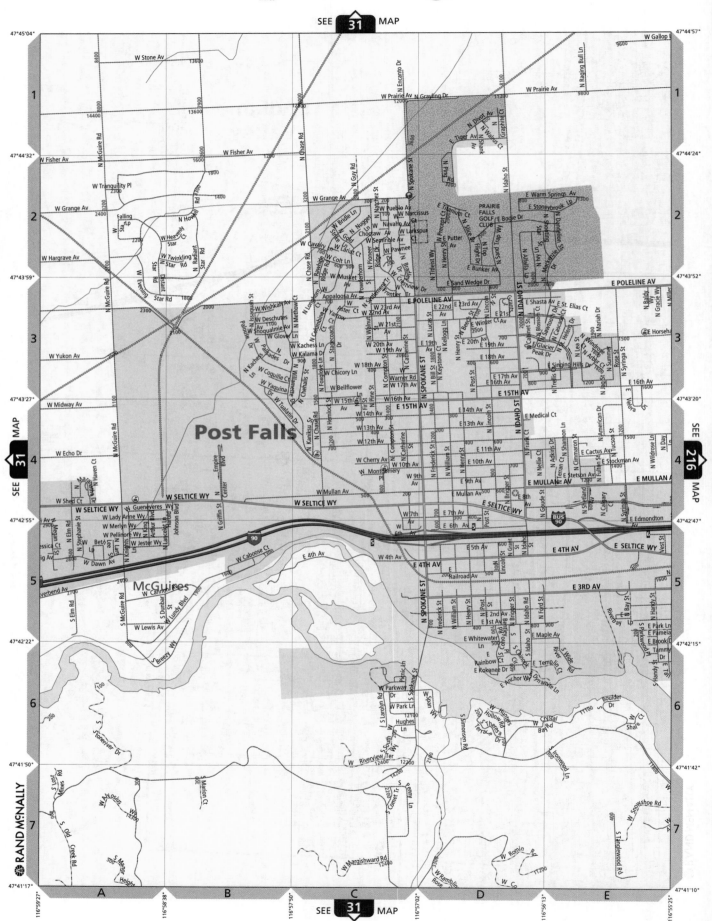

SEE **31** MAP

MAP
216

MAP
216

1:30,000
1 in. = 2500 ft.

0   0.25   0.5

miles

N

SEE **31** MAP

47°44'57"

47°44'49"

1

W Prairie Av

W Prairie Av   W Prairie Av   W Prairie Av

9600

N Carolwood Ct

E Killdeer Ln

47°44'24"

47°44'17"

N Greenferry Rd

E Bluegrass Ln

W Nighthawk Dr

W Century Dr

N Meyer Rd

W Big Sky Dr

2

E Wheelbarrow Rd

E Early
Dawn Av

N Trapper Ln

N Cranston Ct

E Poleline Av

47°43'52"

E POLELINE AV   E POLELINE AV   E Poleline Av   N Meyer Rd   E Poleline Av

47°43'45"

E Ridgeview Dr

E 22nd Av

N Reiswig Rd

E Greta Av

ROSS POINT-RATHDRUM HWY

3

E Horsehaven Av

E Horsehaven Av

E Lacewood Ln

E Roger Dr

E Octavia
Ct

E 16th Av

E 16th Av   E 16th Av

N Spice Ct   N Heidi Ct

47°43'20"

E Bantam Ct

47°43'12"

E Lapis Ct

SEE **215** MAP

SEE **31** MAP

4

E Bremington St

E Azalea Av

N Glasgow Dr

E Quail Acres Rd

E Royal Dr   E Heather Ln

E Inverness Dr

E Mullan Av

E MULLAN AV   E MULLAN AV   N Inverness Dr   HIGHLANDS GOLF & COUNTRY CLUB

E Polston Av

E Jenalan St   E Covington Av

N McDonald   N Dundee Dr

47°42'47"

E Central Av

E Primrose   E Frazier   5200

47°42'40"

Schneidmiller Av

7

7

90

E SELTICE WY

5

Coeur D Alene Av

E 3RD AV

N Greenferry Rd

E 3rd Av

E Osler St

E 3rd Av

E SELTICE WY

E 2nd Av

E Diana Ct

Commerce Lp

E 1st Av

E Maplewood Dr

CommerceLp

E Newome Ct

E Maplewood Av

47°42'15"

E Bark St

E Mountain
View Dr

47°42'07"

E Plaza Dr

E Woodcrest Dr

E Ponderosa Blvd

E Weatherby

**Post
Falls**

E Maplewood Av

E Shore
Pines Ct

E Rivercrest Dr

W Harbor Dr

6

E Meadow
Ln

E Canvasback Av

HARBOR ISLAND
Ebbtide Dr

W Island
View Dr

W Driftwood Dr

W Dixon Ct

47°41'42"

W Michael Wy

W Patrick Dr

47°41'35"

W Heavenly
View Ln

S Cassius Ct

W Highland Dr

7

George Ln

W
Turtle Wy

Cedar Creek

47°41'10"

47°41'03"

A   B   C   D   E

SEE **31** MAP

MAP
217

MAP
217

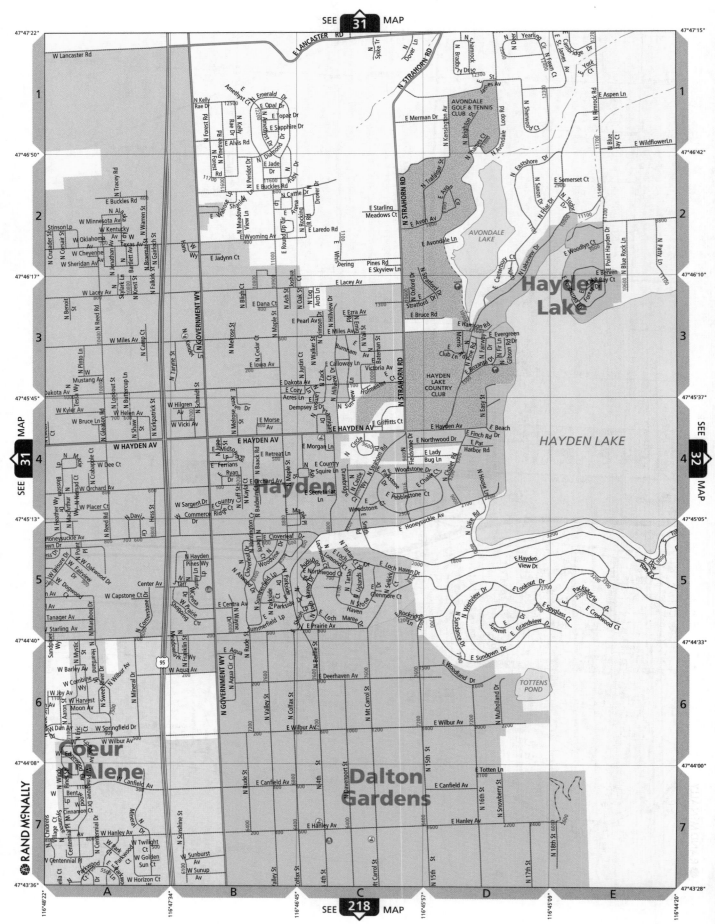

SEE 31 MAP

1:30,000
1 in. = 2500 ft.
0   0.25   0.5
miles

N

SEE 31 MAP

SEE 32 MAP

SEE 218 MAP

RAND McNALLY

MAP
218

MAP
218

1:30,000
1 in. = 2500 ft.

0   0.25   0.5
miles

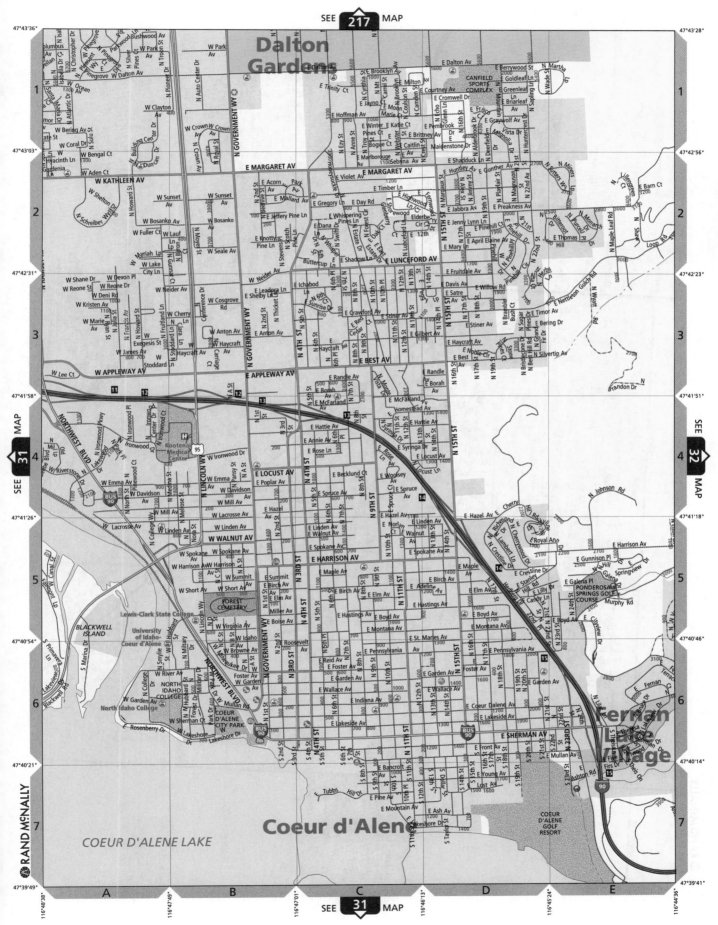

Coeur d'Alene
COEUR D'ALENE LAKE
Dalton Gardens
Fernan Lake Village

MAP
219

MAP
219

1:30,000
1 in. = 2500 ft.
0   0.25   0.5
miles

N

SEE **83** MAP

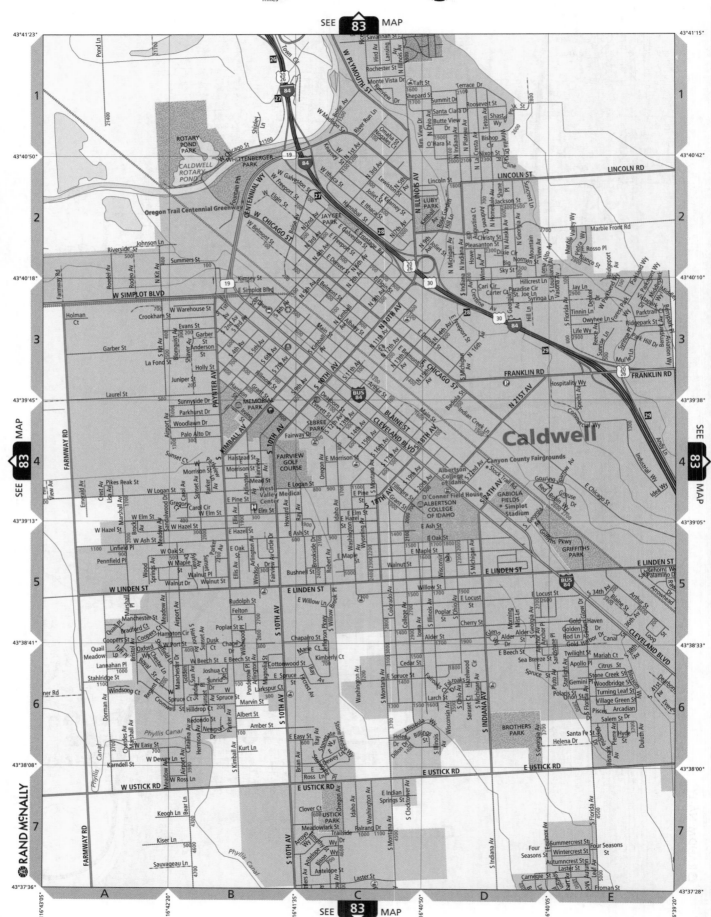

SEE **83** MAP

SEE **83** MAP

SEE **83** MAP

Caldwell

MAP
220

MAP
220

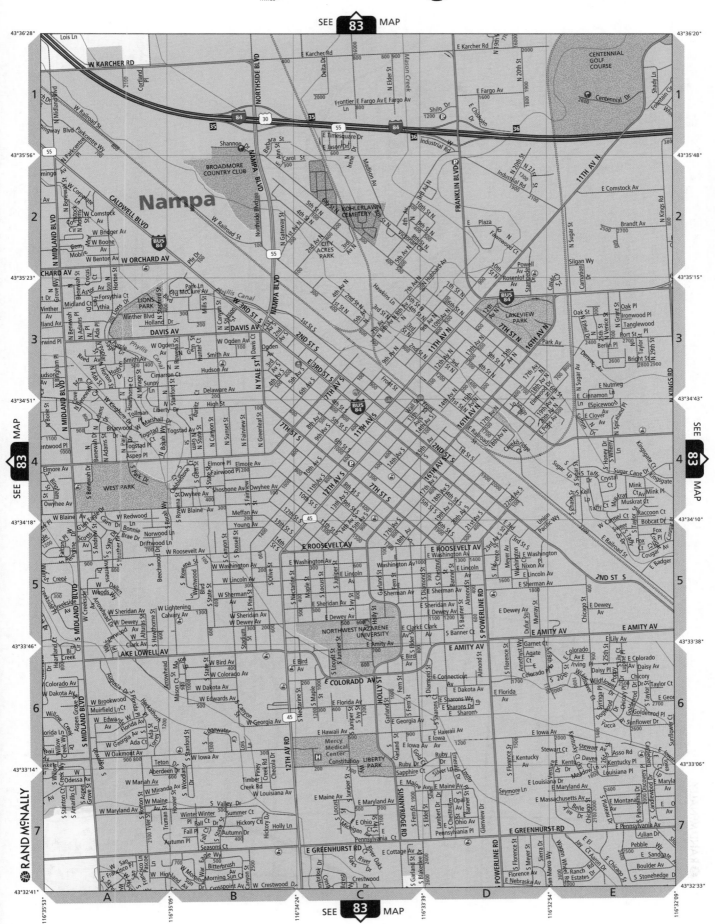

MAP
221

1:30,000
1 in. = 2500 ft.

0.25   0.5
miles

N

SEE 83 MAP

MAP
221

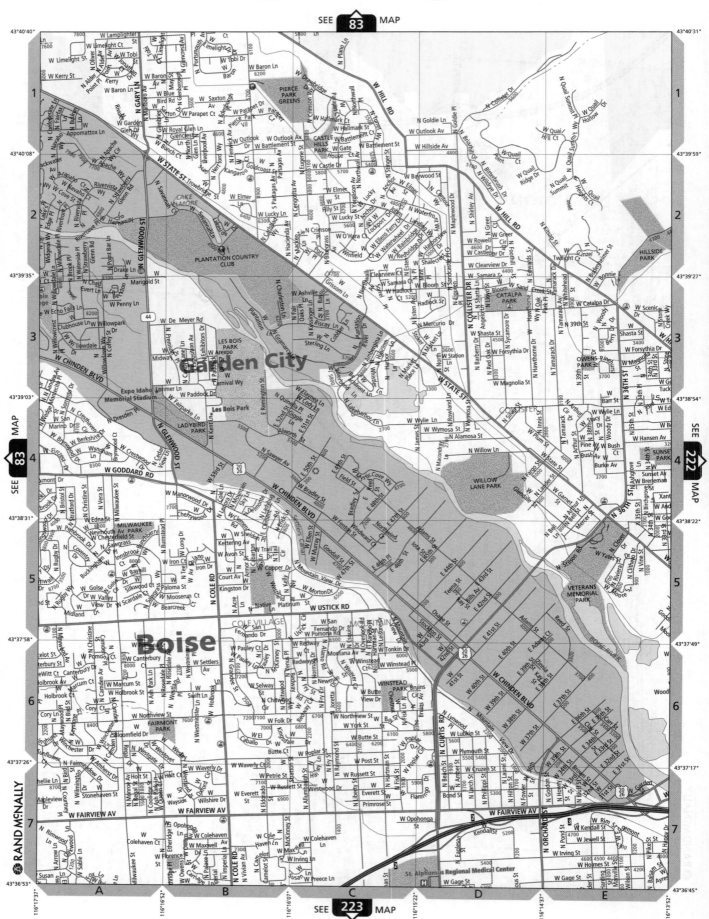

SEE 83 MAP

SEE 222 MAP

SEE 223 MAP

RAND McNALLY

MAP
222

MAP
222

1:30,000
1 in. = 2500 ft.
0   0.25   0.5
miles

N

SEE 84 MAP

Boise

SEE 221 MAP

SEE 84 MAP

SEE 224 MAP

QUAIL HOLLOW GOLF CLUB

CRANE CREEK COUNTRY CLUB

HIGHLANDS

CAMEL'S BACK PARK

HULLS GULCH PARK

BOISE HILLS

NORTHSIDE

ELM GROVE PARK

FAIRVIEW PARK

KATHRYN ALBERTSON PARK

RIVERSIDE PARK

SHORELINE PARK

MILITARY RESERVE

FORT BOISE PARK & SKATE PARK

FOOTHILL EAST RESERVE

MEMORIAL PARK

O'Farrell Cabin

Alexander House

Idaho State Capitol

Steunenberg Memorial

Boise Centre on the Grove

Qwest Arena

St. Luke's Regional Medical Center

Stevens Henager College

FAIRVIEW AV
184
20 26

43°40'31"
43°39'59"
43°39'27"
43°38'54"
43°38'22"
43°37'49"
43°37'17"
43°36'45"

43°40'23"
43°39'50"
43°39'18"
43°38'45"
43°38'13"
43°37'41"
43°37'08"
43°36'36"

116°13'52"
116°13'07"
116°12'22"
116°11'37"
116°10'52"
116°10'07"

A   B   C   D   E

1 2 3 4 5 6 7

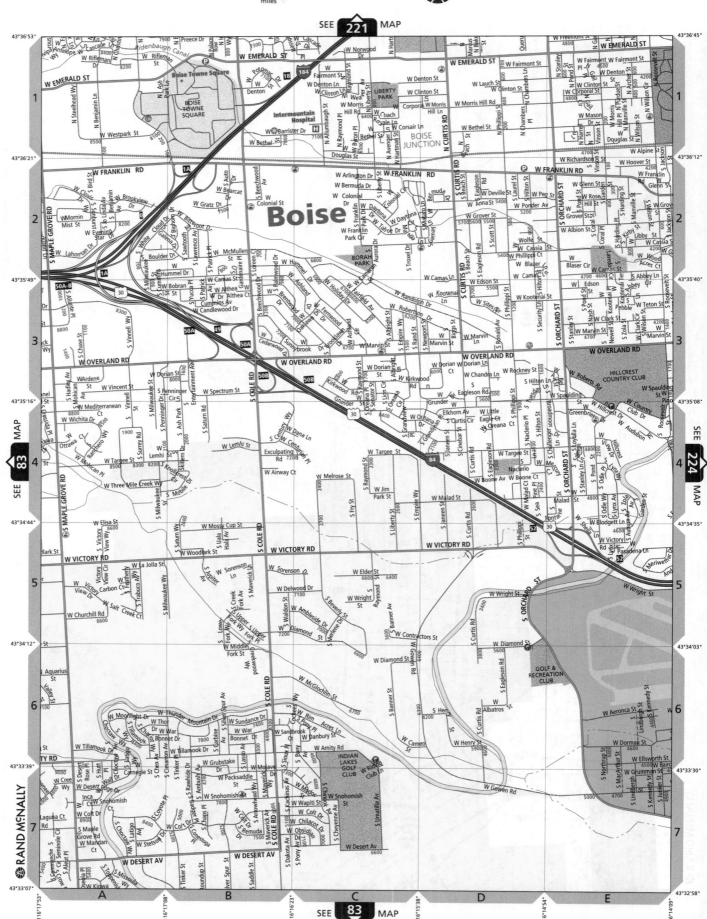

MAP
223

MAP
223

1:30,000
1 in. = 2500 ft.
0   0.25   0.5
miles

SEE 221 MAP

Boise

SEE 83 MAP

SEE 224 MAP

SEE 83 MAP

RAND M?NALLY

MAP
224

MAP
224

1:30,000
1 in. = 2500 ft.
0   0.25   0.5
miles

N

SEE 222 MAP

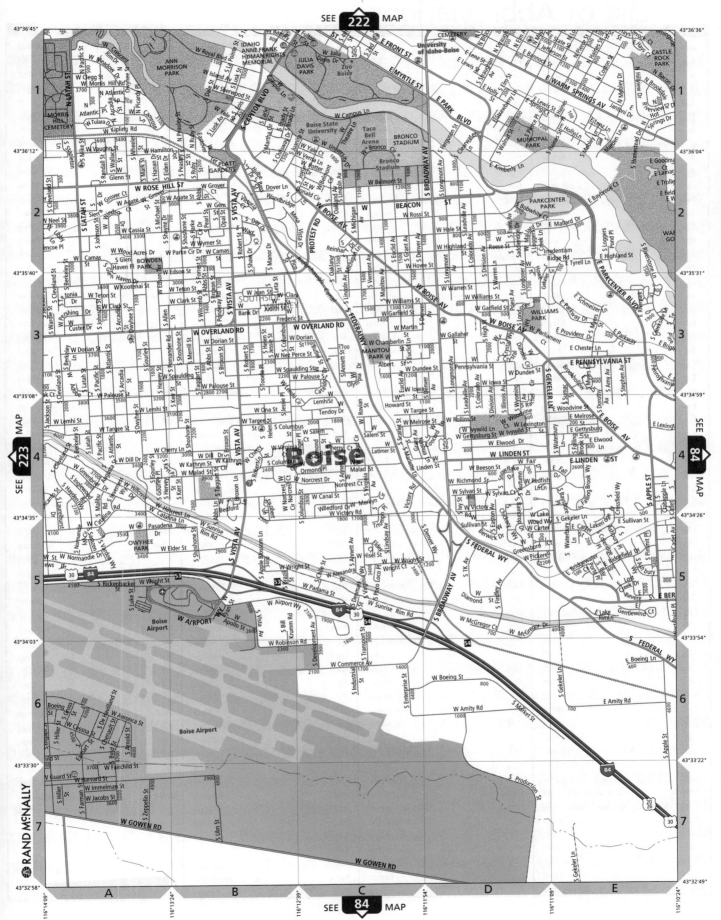

SEE 223 MAP

SEE 84 MAP

SEE 84 MAP

RAND MCNALLY

List of Abbreviations

Admin	Administration	Co	County	Jct	Junction	Reg	Regional
Agri	Agricultural	Ct	Court	Knl	Knoll	Res	Reservoir
Ag	Agriculture	Ct Hse	Court House	Lk	Lake	Rst	Rest
AFB	Air Force Base	Cv	Cove	Lndg	Landing	Rdg	Ridge
Arpt	Airport	Cr	Creek	Ln	Lane	Riv	River
Al	Alley	Cres	Crescent	Lib	Library	Rd	Road
Amer	American	Cross	Crossing	Ldg	Lodge	St.	Saint
Anx	Annex	Curv	Curve	Lp	Loop	Ste.	Sainte
Arc	Arcade	Cto	Cut Off	Mnr	Manor	Sci	Science/Scientific
Arch	Archaeological	Dept	Department	Mkt	Market	Shop Ctr	Shopping Center
Aud	Auditorium	Dev	Development	Mdw	Meadow	Shr	Shore
Avd	Avenida	Diag	Diagonal	Med	Medical	Skwy	Skyway
Av	Avenue	Div	Division	Mem	Memorial	S	South
Bfld	Battlefield	Dr	Drive	Metro	Metropolitan	Spr	Spring
Bch	Beach	Drwy	Driveway	Mw	Mews	Sq	Square
Bltwy	Beltway	E	East	Mil	Military	Stad	Stadium
Bnd	Bend	El	Elevation	Ml	Mill	St For, SF	State Forest
Bio	Biological	Env	Environmental	Mon	Monument	St Hist Site, SHS	State Historic Site
Blf	Bluff	Est	Estate	Mtwy	Motorway	St Nat Area, SNA	State Natural Area
Blvd	Boulevard	Exh	Exhibition	Mnd	Mound	St Pk, SP	State Park
Brch	Branch	Expm	Experimental	Mt	Mount	St Rec Area, SRA	State Recreation Area
Br	Bridge	Expo	Exposition	Mtn	Mountain	Sta	Station
Brk	Brook	Expwy	Expressway	Mun	Municipal	St	Street
Bldg	Building	Ext	Extension	Mus	Museum	Smt	Summit
Bur	Bureau	Fclt	Facility	Nat'l	National	Symph	Symphony
Bus	Business	Frgds	Fairgrounds	Nat'l For, NF	National Forest	Sys	Systems
Bswy	Busway	ft	Feet	Nat'l Hist Pk, NHP	National Historic Park	Tech	Technical/Technology
Byp	Bypass	Fy	Ferry	Nat'l Hist Site, NHS	National Historic Site	Ter	Terrace
Bywy	Byway	Fld	Field	Nat'l Mon, NM	National Monument	Terr	Territory
Cl	Calle	Flt	Flat	Nat'l Pk, NP	National Park	Thtr	Theater
Cljn	Callejon	For	Forest	Nat'l Rec Area, NRA	National Recreation Area	Theol	Theological
Cmto	Caminito	Fk	Fork	Nat'l Wld Ref, NWR	National Wildlife Refuge	Thwy	Throughway
Cm	Camino	Ft	Fort	Nat	Natural	Toll Fy	Toll Ferry
Cyn	Canyon	Found	Foundation	NAS	Naval Air Station	TIC	Tourist Information Center
Cap	Capitol	Frwy	Freeway	Nk	Nook	Twp	Township
Cath	Cathedral/Catholic	Gdn	Garden	N	North	Trc	Trace
Cswy	Causeway	Gen Hosp	General Hospital	Orch	Orchard	Trfwy	Trafficway
Cem	Cemetery	Gln	Glen	Ohwy	Outer Highway	Tr	Trail
Ctr	Center/Centre	GC	Golf Course	Ovl	Oval	Tran	Transit
Cent	Central	Gov't	Government	Ovlk	Overlook	Transp	Transportation
Cir	Circle	Grn	Green	Ovps	Overpass	Tun	Tunnel
Crlo	Circulo	Grds	Grounds	Pk	Park	Tpk	Turnpike
CH	City Hall	Grv	Grove	Pkwy	Parkway	Unps	Underpass
Civ	Civic	Hbr	Harbor/Harbour	Pas	Paseo	Univ	University
Clf	Cliff	Hvn	Haven	Psg	Passage	Vly	Valley
Clb	Club	HQs	Headquarters	Pass	Passenger	Vet	Veterans
Cltr	Cluster	Ht	Height	Pth	Path	Vw	View
Col	Coliseum	Hts	Heights	Pn	Pine	Vil	Village
Coll	College	HS	High School	Pl	Place	Vis Bur	Visitors Bureau
Com	Common	Hwy	Highway	Pln	Plain	Vis	Vista
Coms	Commons	Hl	Hill	Plgnd	Playground	Wk	Walk
Comm	Community	Hist	Historic/Historical	Plz	Plaza	Wy	Way
Co.	Company	Hllw	Hollow	Pt	Point	W	West
Cons	Conservation	Hosp	Hospital	Pnd	Pond	Wld	Wildlife
Cont HS	Continuation High School	Hse	House	Pres	Preserve	WMA	Wildlife Management Area
Conv & Vis Bur	Convention and Visitors Bureau	Ind Res	Indian Reservation	Prov	Provincial		
Conv Ctr	Convention Center	Info	Information	RR	Railroad		
Cor	Corner	Inst	Institute	Rwy	Railway		
Corp	Corporation	Int'l	International	Rch	Ranch		
Corr	Corridor	I	Island	Rcho	Rancho		
Cte	Corte	Is	Islands	Rec	Recreation		
CC	Country Club	Isl	Isle	Ref	Refuge		

2 INDEX

INDEX 2

PROV-7 Lougheed Hwy

Street Index

STREET
City State Map# Grid

HIGHWAYS

ALT - Alternate Route
BIA - Bureau of Indian Affairs
BUS - Business Route
CO - County Highway/Road
FM - Farm to Market Road
HIST - Historic Highway
I - Interstate Highway
LP - State Loop
PK - Park & Recreation Road
PROV - Provincial Highway
RTE - Other Route
SPR - State Spur
SR - State Route/Highway
TCH - Trans-Canada Highway
US - United States Highway

B-3
Wasco Co OR 56 D4
B-3 Simnasho Hot-Springs Rd
Wasco Co OR 56 D5
B-3 Wapinitia Rd
Wasco Co OR 56 D4
B-9
Wasco Co OR 56 C5
B-9 Simnasho Rd
Wasco Co OR 56 C5
CO-1
Modoc Co CA 102 A6
CO-1 Surprise Valley Rd
Modoc Co CA 102 A7
CO-2
Ferry Co WA 20 A4
CO-2 Bridge Creek Rd
Ferry Co WA 20 A4
CO-2-19A
Lake Co OR 90 D7
CO-2-19A Thomas Creek Lp
Lake Co OR 90 D7
CO-3
Ferry Co WA 20 B3
CO-3 Inchelium-Kettle Falls Rd
Ferry Co WA 20 B3
CO-6
Douglas Co OR 74 E4
CO-6 Garden Valley Rd
Douglas Co OR 74 E4
CO-7
Douglas Co OR 75 B2
CO-7 Elkhead Rd
Douglas Co OR 75 B2
CO-8
Douglas Co OR 75 B2
CO-8 Scotts Valley Rd
Douglas Co OR 75 B2
CO-8A
Douglas Co OR 75 B2
CO-8A Scotts Valley Rd
Douglas Co OR 75 B2
CO-9
Modoc Co CA 101 E4
Modoc Co CA 102 A4
CO-9 Fandango Pass Rd
Modoc Co CA 101 E3
Modoc Co CA 102 A4
CO-13
Douglas Co OR 74 E5
CO-13 Melrose Rd
Douglas Co OR 74 E5
CO-13B
Douglas Co OR 74 E5
Douglas Co OR 195 A2
Roseburg OR 195 B5
CO-13B Old Melrose Rd
Douglas Co OR 74 E5
Douglas Co OR 195 A4
Roseburg OR 195 B5
CO-17
Douglas Co OR 75 B5
CO-17 Buckhorn Rd
Douglas Co OR 75 B5
CO-19
Douglas Co OR 75 B4
CO-19 Nonpareil Rd
Douglas Co OR 75 B4
CO-21
Douglas Co OR 87 A1
CO-21 Canyonville-Riddle Rd
Douglas Co OR 87 A1
CO-22
Douglas Co OR 75 B3
CO-22 Driver Valley Rd
Douglas Co OR 75 B3
CO-24
Grant Co OR 60 B6
CO-27
Douglas Co OR 86 E2
CO-27 Cow Creek Rd
Douglas Co OR 86 E2
CO-33
Douglas Co OR 74 E4
CO-33 Tyee Rd
Douglas Co OR 74 E4
CO-39
Douglas Co OR 86 E1
Douglas Co OR 87 A1
CO-39 Cow Creek Rd
Douglas Co OR 86 E1
CO-39 Riddle Bypass Rd
Douglas Co OR 87 A1
CO-40
Deschutes Co OR 66 C7
CO-40 Spring River Rd
Deschutes Co OR 66 C7
CO-42
Deschutes Co OR 66 B7
Deschutes Co OR 77 A1
CO-42 S Century Dr
Deschutes Co OR 66 B7
Deschutes Co OR 77 A1
CO-43
Deschutes Co OR 77 B1
CO-43 Burgess Rd
Deschutes Co OR 77 B1
CO-46
Bend OR 66 C6
Bend OR 191 A4
Deschutes Co OR 66 C6
Deschutes Co OR 191 A4
CO-46 Cascade Lakes Hwy
Deschutes Co OR 66 A6
CO-46 SW Century Dr
Bend OR 66 C6
Bend OR 191 A4
Deschutes Co OR 66 C6
Deschutes Co OR 191 A4
CO-50
Douglas Co OR 75 B3
CO-50 Medley-Elkhead Rd
Douglas Co OR 75 B3
CO-54
Modoc Co CA 101 B7
CO-54 Centerville Rd
Modoc Co CA 101 B7
CO-60
Modoc Co CA 101 B7
CO-60 Centerville Rd
Modoc Co CA 101 B7
CO-62
Grant Co OR 69 E2
Grant Co OR 70 A2
CO-62 Logan Valley Rd
Grant Co OR 69 E2
CO-62 NF-14
Grant Co OR 70 A2
CO-63
Grant Co OR 68 D5
Grant Co OR 69 B4
CO-63 Izee Hwy
Grant Co OR 68 D5
Grant Co OR 69 A5
CO-64
Jefferson Co OR 66 C1
CO-64 SW Montgomery Rd
Jefferson Co OR 66 C1
CO-68
Grant Co OR 69 A5
Harney Co OR 69 A6
CO-68 Izee-Officer Ranch Rd
Grant Co OR 69 A5
Harney Co OR 69 A6
CO-97
Modoc Co CA 100 C5
CO-97 Tionesta Rd
Modoc Co CA 100 C5
CO-107
Winston OR 74 E6
CO-107 Lookingglass Rd
Winston OR 74 E6
CO-114
Modoc Co CA 100 C3
CO-127
Harney Co OR 80 A1
CO-127 Hines Logging Rd
Harney Co OR 80 B2
CO-128
Harney Co OR 80 C3
CO-128 Greenhouse Ln
Harney Co OR 80 C3
CO-141
Modoc Co CA 100 C3
CO-167
Douglas Co OR 75 A5
Douglas Co OR 195 A2
CO-167 Melrose Rd
Douglas Co OR 75 A5
Douglas Co OR 195 A2
CO-201
Harney Co OR 93 A7
Harney Co OR 104 A1
CO-201 Fields Denio Rd
Harney Co OR 93 A7
Harney Co OR 104 A1
CO-202
Harney Co OR 92 D6
Harney Co OR 93 A7
CO-202 Catlow Valley Rd
Harney Co OR 92 D5
Harney Co OR 93 A7
CO-271
Modoc Co CA 101 D6
CO-312
Harney Co OR 81 A3
CO-312 Crane-Buchanan Rd
Harney Co OR 81 A2
CO-397
Benton Co WA 49 B1
CO-404
Harney Co OR 80 E6
Harney Co OR 81 A5
CO-404 Lava Beds Rd
Harney Co OR 80 E6
Harney Co OR 81 A5
CO-412
Harney Co OR 92 C3
Lake Co OR 92 A3
CO-412 Rock Creek Rd
Harney Co OR 92 A3
Lake Co OR 92 A3
CO-515
Curry Co OR 85 D4
CO-515 Cedar Valley Rd
Curry Co OR 85 D4
CO-540
Curry Co OR 85 D4
CO-540 Edson Creek Rd
Curry Co OR 85 D4
CO-545
Curry Co OR 85 D4
CO-545 N Bank Rogue River Rd
Curry Co OR 85 D4
CO-595
Curry Co OR 85 D4
CO-595 Jerrys Flat Rd
Curry Co OR 85 D4
CO-821
Jackson Co OR 88 A4
CO-821 Butte Flls Fish Lake Rd
Jackson Co OR 88 B5
CO-1300
Umatilla Co OR 49 B5
CO-1300 Rieth Rd
Umatilla Co OR 49 B5
CO-2610
Deschutes Co OR 66 C3
CO-2610 Camp Polk Rd
Deschutes Co OR 66 C3
CO-2902
Stevens Co WA 20 E4
Stevens Co WA 21 A3
CO-2902 Flowery Trail Rd
Stevens Co WA 20 E4
Stevens Co WA 21 A3
CO-9205
Pend Oreille Co WA 21 B3
CO-9205 Westside Calispell Rd
Pend Oreille Co WA 21 B3
CO-9425
Stevens Co WA 10 D6
CO-9425 Clugston-Onion Cr Rd
Stevens Co WA 10 D6
CO-A12
Siskiyou Co CA 99 B6
CO-A12 99-97 Cto
Siskiyou Co CA 99 A5
CO-A28
Siskiyou Co CA 99 A3
CO-A28 Ager Rd
Siskiyou Co CA 99 A3
CO-A28 Montague Grenada Rd
Siskiyou Co CA 99 A5
CO-A29
Siskiyou Co CA 99 B6
CO-A29 Big Springs Rd
Siskiyou Co CA 99 B6
CO-D2
Del Norte Co CA 96 E4
CO-D2 Elk Valley Rd
Del Norte Co CA 96 E4
CO-D3
Del Norte Co CA 96 E3
CO-D3 Lake Earl Dr
Del Norte Co CA 96 E3
CO-P1
Clearwater Co ID 42 C4
I-5
Albany OR 54 C7
Albany OR 176 C6
Ashland OR 87 E7
Ashland OR 200 A2
Bellingham WA 113 D1
Burlington WA 115 B5
Burlington WA 116 B1
Central Point OR 198 A1
Centralia WA 151 B6
Chehalis WA 34 D4
Chehalis WA 152 D7
Clark Co WA 45 A4
Cowlitz Co WA 34 D6
Cowlitz Co WA 44 E3
Cowlitz Co WA 156 B1
Creswell OR 64 C6
Des Moines WA 140 A7
Douglas Co OR 75 B1
Douglas Co OR 87 A3
Douglas Co OR 195 E1
Eugene OR 182 C5
Eugene OR 186 E6
Everett WA 120 D4
Federal Way WA 25 C6
Fife WA 142 D6
Grants Pass OR 197 D3
Jackson Co OR 87 C5
Jackson Co OR 98 E1
Jackson Co OR 198 A1
Jackson Co OR 199 D1
Jackson Co OR 200 C5
Josephine Co OR 86 E4
Josephine Co OR 87 A5
Josephine Co OR 197 E3
Kelso WA 156 D7
Kent WA 25 C5
King Co WA 137 C5
King Co WA 140 B5
Lacey WA 146 E5
Lakewood WA 25 B7
Lakewood WA 143 D5
Lane Co OR 64 C6
Lane Co OR 75 B1
Lane Co OR 182 C7
Lane Co OR 186 D4
Lane Co OR 187 A7
Lewis Co WA 34 E5
Lewis Co WA 151 B1
Lewis Co WA 152 D7
Linn Co OR 54 C7
Linn Co OR 64 C3
Linn Co OR 176 C5
Marion Co OR 54 D3
Marion Co OR 172 C5
Marion Co OR 174 C1
Marysville WA 15 D5
Medford OR 198 D7
Mt Vernon WA 116 B5
Olympia WA 24 E7
Olympia WA 145 E7
Olympia WA 146 B6
Pierce Co WA 25 A7
Pierce Co WA 143 D6
Portland OR 157 E6
Portland OR 161 E4
Portland OR 162 A7
Portland OR 165 E3
Portland OR 166 A2
Portland OR 169 B2
Roseburg OR 195 E5
Salem OR 54 D5
Salem OR 172 C3
Salem OR 174 C2
Seatac WA 140 B5
Seattle WA 124 D1
Seattle WA 128 D7
Seattle WA 132 D4
Seattle WA 133 A7
Seattle WA 137 B3
Siskiyou Co CA 98 E4
Siskiyou Co CA 99 A5
Skagit Co WA 15 C3
Skagit Co WA 115 B1
Skagit Co WA 116 B5
Snohomish Co WA 15 D7
Springfield OR 182 C4
Springfield OR 186 D4
Tacoma WA 141 E7
Tacoma WA 142 C6
Tacoma WA 143 D5
Thurston Co WA 25 A7
Thurston Co WA 34 D2
Thurston Co WA 147 B7
Tukwila WA 137 C7
Tukwila WA 140 C4
Tumwater WA 145 E7
Tumwater WA 147 C5
Vancouver WA 157 E5
Vancouver WA 158 A1
Whatcom Co WA 5 A5
Wilsonville OR 54 E1
Woodburn OR 54 D3
Yreka CA 98 E4
I-5 BUS
Castle Rock WA 34 D7
I-5 BUS Huntington Av S
Castle Rock WA 34 D7
I-5 Interstate Br
Portland OR 157 E5
Vancouver WA 157 E5
I-5 Marquam Br
Portland OR 165 E3
Portland OR 166 A3
I-5 Pacific Hwy
Albany OR 54 C7
Albany OR 176 C5
Ashland OR 87 E7
Ashland OR 200 A2
Central Point OR 198 A1
Creswell OR 64 C6
Douglas Co OR 75 A3
Douglas Co OR 87 A1
Douglas Co OR 195 E7
Eugene OR 182 C4
Eugene OR 186 E6
Grants Pass OR 197 D3
Jackson Co OR 87 E7
Jackson Co OR 98 E1
Jackson Co OR 198 A1
Jackson Co OR 199 D1
Jackson Co OR 200 B3
Josephine Co OR 86 E4
Josephine Co OR 87 A5
Josephine Co OR 197 D3
Lane Co OR 64 C6
Lane Co OR 182 C4
Lane Co OR 186 E6
Lane Co OR 187 A7
Linn Co OR 54 C7
Linn Co OR 64 C3
Linn Co OR 176 C6
Marion Co OR 54 C6
Medford OR 198 D7
Roseburg OR 195 E5
Springfield OR 182 C7
Springfield OR 186 D4
I-5 Umpqua Hwy
Douglas Co OR 75 B1
Lane Co OR 75 B1
I-82
Benton Co WA 38 B7
Benton Co WA 39 A7
Benton Co WA 48 C1
Benton Co WA 49 A1
Benton Co WA 205 A7
Kittitas Co WA 37 D2
Umatilla Co OR 49 A4
Yakima Co WA 37 D5
Yakima Co WA 38 A7
I-84
Ada Co ID 83 E2
Ada Co ID 84 A3
Ada Co ID 223 D4
Baker Co OR 60 E6
Baker Co OR 61 B7
Baker Co OR 71 D3
Boise ID 83 E2
Boise ID 223 D4
Boise ID 224 A5
Caldwell ID 219 C2
Canyon Co ID 83 C1
Canyon Co ID 219 B1
Canyon Co ID 220 A1
Elmore Co ID 84 C4
Gilliam Co OR 47 E5
Gilliam Co OR 48 A5
Gresham OR 164 E7
Hood River Co OR 46 A5
Malheur Co OR 71 E4
Malheur Co OR 72 A5
Meridian ID 83 D2
Morrow Co OR 48 C4
Mosier OR 46 D5
Multnomah Co OR 45 C6
Nampa ID 220 B1
Payette Co ID 72 B6
Portland OR 163 E6
Portland OR 164 A6
Portland OR 166 E1
Portland OR 167 C1
Sherman Co OR 47 A6
Umatilla Co OR 48 E4
Umatilla Co OR 49 E6
Umatilla Co OR 50 A6
Union Co OR 60 D2
Wasco Co OR 46 E6
Wasco Co OR 47 A6
I-84 BUS
Caldwell ID 83 C2
Caldwell ID 219 C3
Elmore Co ID 84 E6
Nampa ID 220 C4
I-84 BUS 2nd St S
Nampa ID 220 B3
I-84 BUS E 3rd St S
Nampa ID 220 B3
I-84 BUS W 3rd St S
Nampa ID 220 C4
I-84 BUS 11th Av N
Nampa ID 220 D3
I-84 BUS 11th Av S
Nampa ID 220 C3
I-84 Banfield Expwy
Gresham OR 164 E7
Portland OR 163 E6
Portland OR 164 B7
Portland OR 166 E1
Portland OR 167 C1
I-84 Blaine St
Caldwell ID 219 B3
I-84 BUS Caldwell Blvd
Nampa ID 220 A2
I-84 BUS Centennial Wy
Caldwell ID 219 C3
I-84 BUS Cleveland Blvd
Caldwell ID 83 C2
Caldwell ID 219 E5
I-84 Columbia River Hwy
Morrow Co OR 48 C4
Multnomah Co OR 45 C6
I-84 BUS Garrity Blvd
Nampa ID 220 D3
I-84 Old Oregon Trail Hwy
Baker Co OR 60 E4
Baker Co OR 61 B7
Baker Co OR 71 D3
Malheur Co OR 71 E4
Malheur Co OR 72 A5
Morrow Co OR 48 E4
Umatilla Co OR 48 E4
Union Co OR 60 D2
I-90
Adams Co WA 29 E7
Adams Co WA 30 B7
Bellevue WA 134 E2
Coeur d'Alene ID 218 E7
Fernan Lake Village ID 218 E6
Grant Co WA 28 E7
Grant Co WA 29 A7
Grant Co WA 38 B1
Issaquah WA 25 E3
King Co WA 25 E3
King Co WA 26 C5
King Co WA 133 C1
King Co WA 134 C3
Kittitas Co WA 26 E6
Kittitas Co WA 27 C7
Kittitas Co WA 37 C1
Kittitas Co WA 38 A1
Kootenai Co ID 32 A2
Kootenai Co ID 216 D5
Kootenai Co ID 218 E7
Liberty Lake WA 31 D2
Lincoln Co WA 30 D5
Mercer Island WA 133 E1
Mercer Island WA 134 D3
Post Falls ID 215 D5
Post Falls ID 216 A5
Seattle WA 132 E1
Seattle WA 133 C1
Shoshone Co ID 32 E3
Spokane WA 211 E2
Spokane WA 212 C1
Spokane Co WA 30 E4
Spokane Co WA 31 A3
Spokane Co WA 211 A4
Spokane Valley WA 31 C2
Spokane Valley WA 212 E1
Spokane Valley WA 213 D2
Spokane Valley WA 214 D2
I-90 BUS
Adams Co WA 30 A7
Coeur d'Alene ID 218 A4
Ellensburg WA 37 D1
Grant Co WA 29 A7
Moses Lake WA 29 A7
Osburn ID 32 E3
Post Falls ID 215 E5
Ritzville WA 30 A7
Shoshone Co ID 32 E3
Spokane WA 211 A3
Spokane WA 212 B1
Spokane Co WA 31 A2
Spokane Co WA 211 C2
Spokane Valley WA 31 C2
Spokane Valley WA 212 E1
Spokane Valley WA 213 B4
Spokane Valley WA 214 B4
I-90 BUS W 1st Av
Adams Co WA 30 A7
Ritzville WA 30 A7
I-90 BUS E 2nd Av
Spokane WA 212 A1
I-90 BUS W 2nd Av
Spokane WA 211 E2
Spokane WA 212 A1
I-90 BUS E 3rd Av
Spokane WA 212 A2
I-90 BUS W 3rd Av
Spokane WA 211 E2
Spokane WA 212 A2
I-90 BUS E Appleway Av
Spokane Co WA 31 C2
Spokane Valley WA 31 C2
I-90 BUS S Canyon Rd
Ellensburg WA 37 D1
I-90 BUS S Geiger Blvd
Spokane Co WA 31 A2
Spokane Co WA 211 C2
I-90 Homer M Hadley Mem Br
King Co WA 133 C1
Mercer Island WA 133 D1
Seattle WA 133 C1
I-90 Lacey V Murrow Mem Br
King Co WA 133 D1
Mercer Island WA 133 D1
Seattle WA 133 B1
I-90 BUS Northwest Blvd
Coeur d'Alene ID 218 B6
I-90 BUS N Ramsey Rd
Coeur d'Alene ID 218 A4
I-90 BUS E Seltice Wy
Post Falls ID 215 D4
I-90 BUS E Sherman Av
Coeur d'Alene ID 218 D6
I-90 BUS N Spokane St
Post Falls ID 215 E5
I-90 BUS E Sprague Av
Spokane WA 212 E1
Spokane Valley WA 212 E1
Spokane Valley WA 213 D4
Spokane Valley WA 214 D4
I-90 BUS E Sprague Av Acc 1
Spokane WA 212 B2
I-90 BUS E Sprague Av Acc 3
Spokane WA 212 B1
I-90 BUS W Sunset Blvd
Spokane WA 211 C2
Spokane Co WA 211 A3
I-90 BUS W Sunset Hwy
Spokane WA 211 A3
Spokane Co WA 211 A3
I-105
Eugene OR 181 D7
Eugene OR 182 B7
Eugene OR 185 D1
Lane Co OR 182 C7
Springfield OR 182 C7
I-182
Franklin Co WA 39 A7
Franklin Co WA 204 A4
Pasco WA 39 A7
Pasco WA 204 A4
Richland WA 39 A7
Richland WA 203 E7
I-184
Boise ID 221 D7
Boise ID 222 A7
Boise ID 223 C1
I-205
Clackamas Co OR 54 E1
Clark Co WA 45 A5
Clark Co WA 159 C1
Maywood Park OR 163 D7
Multnomah Co OR 45 A6
Multnomah Co OR 163 E1
Portland OR 45 A7
Portland OR 163 E4
Portland OR 167 C1
Tualatin OR 54 E1
Vancouver WA 45 A6
Vancouver WA 159 D2
Vancouver WA 163 E1
I-205 Glenn Jackson Br
Multnomah Co OR 45 A6
Multnomah Co OR 163 E1
Portland OR 163 E3
Vancouver WA 45 A6
Vancouver WA 163 E1
I-205 E Portland Frwy
Maywood Park OR 163 D7
Portland OR 163 E3
Portland OR 167 C2
I-205 Veterans Memorial Hwy
Clackamas Co OR 54 E1
Portland OR 45 A7
Tualatin OR 54 E1
I-405
Bellevue WA 25 D3
Bellevue WA 130 D2
Bellevue WA 134 D1
Bothell WA 25 D1
King Co WA 126 D1
King Co WA 134 C6
Kirkland WA 126 D1
Kirkland WA 130 D2
Newcastle WA 134 C6
Portland OR 161 E7
Portland OR 165 D3
Renton WA 134 C6
Renton WA 138 C5
Renton WA 140 E1
Tukwila WA 140 D1
I-405 Stadium Frwy
Portland OR 161 E7
Portland OR 165 D3
I-705
Tacoma WA 142 B6
PROV-1A
Abbotsford BC 5 C4
Colwood BC 14 B2
Cowichan Valley BC 3 E5
Cowichan Valley BC 4 A6
Esquimalt BC 111 A2
Langley BC 5 B4
Saanich BC 111 C3
Surrey BC 4 E3
Surrey BC 5 A3
Vancouver BC 4 D2
Vancouver BC 107 D5
Vancouver BC 109 E1
Vancouver BC 110 B4
Victoria BC 111 D3
View Royal BC 111 A2
West Vancouver BC 107 D3
PROV-1A Admirals Rd
Esquimalt BC 111 A2
Saanich BC 111 A2
View Royal BC 111 A2
PROV-1A Dunsmuir St
Vancouver BC 109 E2
Vancouver BC 110 A2
PROV-1A Dunsmuir Viaduct
Vancouver BC 110 A2
PROV-1A Fraser Hwy
Abbotsford BC 5 C4
Langley BC 5 B4
Surrey BC 5 A3
PROV-1A W Georgia St
Vancouver BC 107 D7
Vancouver BC 109 E1
Vancouver BC 110 A2
PROV-1A Georgia Viaduct
Vancouver BC 110 A2
PROV-1A Goldstream Av
Colwood BC 14 B2
PROV-1A Gorge Rd E
Saanich BC 111 C3
Victoria BC 111 D3
PROV-1A Gorge Rd W
Saanich BC 111 C3
Victoria BC 111 C3
PROV-1A Island Hwy
Esquimalt BC 111 A2
View Royal BC 111 A2
PROV-1A King George Hwy
Surrey BC 4 E3
PROV-1A Kingsway
Vancouver BC 4 D2
Vancouver BC 110 E7
PROV-1A Lions Gate Br
Vancouver BC 107 D5
West Vancouver BC 107 E4
PROV-1A Main St
Vancouver BC 110 B4
PROV-1A Marine Dr
West Vancouver BC 107 E4
PROV-1A Melville St
Vancouver BC 109 E1
PROV-1A Osborne Bay Rd
Cowichan Valley BC 4 A6
PROV-1A W Pender St
Vancouver BC 109 E1
PROV-1A Stanley Park Cswy
Vancouver BC 4 D2
Vancouver BC 107 D5
PROV-1A Taylor Wy
West Vancouver BC 107 D3
PROV-3
Central Kootenay BC 10 D2
Central Kootenay BC 11 E3
Fraser Valley BC 6 D2
Fraser Valley BC 7 A3
Hope BC 6 D2
Kootenay Boundary BC 9 C4
Kootenay Boundary BC 10 A4
Okanagan-Similkam BC 7 E1
Okanagan-Similkam BC 8 D4
PROV-3 Crowsnest Hwy
Central Kootenay BC 10 E2
Central Kootenay BC 11 B4
Fraser Valley BC 6 D2
Hope BC 6 D2
Kootenay Boundary BC 9 E3
Kootenay Boundary BC 10 A4
Okanagan-Similkam BC 7 D1
Okanagan-Similkam BC 8 D4
PROV-3 Hope-Princeton Hwy
Fraser Valley BC 6 E2
Fraser Valley BC 7 A3
Okanagan-Similkam BC 7 C4
PROV-3A
Central Kootenay BC 10 E1
Central Kootenay BC 11 E1
Okanagan-Similkam BC 8 C3
PROV-3B
Kootenay Boundary BC 10 E4
Kootenay Boundary BC 11 A3
Trail BC 10 E4
PROV-4
Nanaimo District BC 3 A2
PROV-4 Alberni Hwy
Nanaimo District BC 3 A2
PROV-4A
Nanaimo District BC 3 B2
PROV-4A Alberni Hwy
Nanaimo District BC 3 B2
PROV-5
Fraser Valley BC 6 D1
PROV-5 Coquihalla Hwy
Fraser Valley BC 6 D1
PROV-5A
Okanagan-Similkam BC 7 D1
PROV-6
Central Kootenay BC 10 E1
Central Kootenay BC 11 B2
Pend Oreille Co WA 11 B4
PROV-6 Crowsnest Hwy
Central Kootenay BC 11 B3
PROV-7
Fraser Valley BC 5 E3
Fraser Valley BC 6 C1
Hope BC 6 C1
Kent BC 6 A3
Maple Ridge BC 5 C3
Pitt Meadows BC 5 A2
Port Coquitlam BC 5 A2
Vancouver BC 109 E4
Vancouver BC 110 D4
PROV-7 E Broadway
Vancouver BC 110 D4
PROV-7 W Broadway
Vancouver BC 109 E4
Vancouver BC 110 A4
PROV-7 Lougheed Hwy
Fraser Valley BC 5 E3
Fraser Valley BC 6 C1
Hope BC 6 C1

Street Index

4 INDEX
INDEX 4
SR-39
SR-126 Garfield St

Street Index

STREET
City State Map# Grid

SR-39
Klamath Co OR 202 A7
Klamath Falls OR 89 A7
Klamath Falls OR 201 C3
Klamath Falls OR 202 A7
SR-39 S 5th St
Klamath Falls OR 201 C5
SR-39 6th St
Klamath Falls OR 201 E7
SR-39 S 6th St
Klamath Co OR 202 A7
Klamath Falls OR 201 D6
Klamath Falls OR 202 A7
SR-39 S 12th St
Klamath Falls OR 201 D5
SR-39 East Side Byp
Klamath Co OR 202 A6
Klamath Falls OR 202 A6
SR-39 Esplanade St
Klamath Falls OR 201 D5
SR-39 Kit Carson Wy
Klamath Falls OR 201 C3
SR-39 Klamath Av
Klamath Falls OR 201 C6
SR-39 Klamath Falls-Malin Hwy
Klamath Co OR 100 A1
SR-39 Main St
Klamath Falls OR 201 C6
SR-39 The Dalles-California Hy
Klamath Falls OR 201 B2
SR-41
Bonner Co ID 21 D6
Kootenai Co ID 21 E7
Kootenai Co ID 31 E1
Kootenai Co ID 216 C4
Post Falls ID 216 B4
Rathdrum ID 31 E1
SR-41 Ross Point-Rathdrum Hwy
Kootenai Co ID 216 B4
Post Falls ID 216 B4
SR-42
Coos Co OR 73 E5
Coquille OR 74 A6
Douglas Co OR 74 C7
Douglas Co OR 75 A6
Douglas Co OR 195 E7
Roseburg OR 75 A5
Roseburg OR 195 E7
SR-42 Coos Bay-Roseburg Hwy
Coos Co OR 73 E5
Coquille OR 74 A6
Douglas Co OR 74 E6
Douglas Co OR 75 A6
Douglas Co OR 195 E7
Roseburg OR 75 A5
Roseburg OR 195 E7
SR-42 SE Stephens St
Douglas Co OR 195 E7
Roseburg OR 195 E7
SR-42S
Coos Co OR 73 E5
SR-42S Coquille-Bandon Hwy
Coos Co OR 73 D6
SR-43
Clackamas Co OR 170 A6
Lake Oswego OR 55 A1
Lake Oswego OR 169 E7
Lake Oswego OR 170 A7
Multnomah Co OR 170 A5
Portland OR 165 E5
Portland OR 169 E2
Portland OR 170 A5
SR-43 SW Hood Av
Portland OR 165 E5
SR-43 SW Kelly Av
Portland OR 165 E4
SR-43 SW Macadam Av
Multnomah Co OR 170 A2
Portland OR 165 E5
Portland OR 169 E2
Portland OR 170 A2
SR-43 Pacific Hwy
Lake Oswego OR 55 A1
Lake Oswego OR 169 E7
Lake Oswego OR 170 A1
SR-43 Riverside Dr
Clackamas Co OR 170 A5
Lake Oswego OR 170 A5
SR-43 SW Riverside Dr
Clackamas Co OR 170 A5
Multnomah Co OR 170 A5
Portland OR 170 A5
SR-43 N State St
Clackamas Co OR 170 A6
Lake Oswego OR 170 A7
SR-43 S State St
Lake Oswego OR 169 E7
Lake Oswego OR 170 A7
SR-44
Ada Co ID 83 E1
Ada Co ID 221 A3
Boise ID 221 A1
Canyon Co ID 83 C1
Garden City ID 83 E1
Garden City ID 221 A3
SR-44 N Glenwood St
Ada Co ID 221 A3
Boise ID 221 A2
Garden City ID 221 A3
SR-44 W State St
Ada Co ID 83 E1
Ada Co ID 221 A1
Boise ID 221 A1
Garden City ID 83 E1
Garden City ID 221 A1
SR-45
Canyon Co ID 83 C2
Nampa ID 220 C4
Owyhee Co ID 83 C4
SR-45 2nd St S
Nampa ID 220 C4
SR-45 E 3rd St S
Nampa ID 220 C4
SR-45 12th Av S
Nampa ID 220 C4
SR-45 12th Av Rd
Nampa ID 220 B6
SR-46
Josephine Co OR 86 D7
Josephine Co OR 97 E1
SR-46 Caves Hwy
Josephine Co OR 86 D7
Josephine Co OR 97 E1
SR-47
Columbia Co OR 44 B4
Washington Co OR 44 C5
Yamhill Co OR 54 C2
SR-47 Mist-Clatskanie Hwy
Columbia Co OR 44 B1
SR-47 Nehalem Hwy
Washington Co OR 44 C5
SR-47 Nehalem Hwy N
Columbia Co OR 44 C3
SR-47 Nehalem Hwy S
Columbia Co OR 44 B4
SR-47 Tualatin Valley Hwy
Washington Co OR 44 C7
Yamhill Co OR 54 C2
SR-49
Harney Co OR 79 D5
SR-49 Lakeview-Burns Hwy
Harney Co OR 79 E3
SR-50
Klamath Co OR 100 C2
SR-50 Klamath Falls-Malin Hwy
Klamath Co OR 100 C2
SR-51
Elmore Co ID 84 D7
Owyhee Co ID 84 D7
Polk Co OR 54 B5
SR-51 Independence Hwy
Polk Co OR 54 B5
SR-52
Boise Co ID 72 E6
Gem Co ID 72 C6
Malheur Co OR 72 A5
Payette Co ID 72 B5
SR-52 W Highway 52
Gem Co ID 72 D7
SR-52 Payette Spur
Malheur Co OR 72 A5
SR-53
Clatsop Co OR 43 D3
Hauser ID 31 D1
Kootenai Co ID 21 E7
Kootenai Co ID 31 D1
Tillamook Co OR 43 D4
SR-53 Necanicum Hwy
Clatsop Co OR 43 D3
Tillamook Co OR 43 D4
SR-54
Kootenai Co ID 21 E6
Kootenai Co ID 22 A6
SR-55
Ada Co ID 72 E7
Adams Co ID 62 E4
Boise Co ID 72 E7
Canyon Co ID 83 C2
Eagle ID 83 E1
Marsing ID 83 B2
Nampa ID 83 C2
Nampa ID 220 B2
SR-55 2nd St S
Nampa ID 220 B3
SR-55 W 3rd St S
Nampa ID 220 B3
SR-55 Caldwell Blvd
Nampa ID 220 A1
SR-55 Karcher Rd
Canyon Co ID 83 C2
Nampa ID 83 C2
SR-55 Nampa Blvd
Nampa ID 220 B2
SR-57
Bonner Co ID 11 D7
Bonner Co ID 21 D1
Priest River ID 21 E4
SR-57 N 57
Priest River ID 21 E4
SR-57 NF-6
Bonner Co ID 21 E4
SR-57 NF-302
Bonner Co ID 11 D7
SR-58
Klamath Co OR 76 E4
Klamath Co OR 77 A4
Kootenai Co ID 31 D4
Lane Co OR 64 E6
Lane Co OR 65 A7
Lane Co OR 76 A1
Lane Co OR 187 A7
SR-58 Willamette Hwy
Klamath Co OR 76 E4
Klamath Co OR 77 A4
Lane Co OR 64 D6
Lane Co OR 65 A7
Lane Co OR 76 D2
Lane Co OR 187 A7
SR-60
Benewah Co ID 31 E6
SR-62
Eagle Point OR 87 D5
Jackson Co OR 87 E3
Jackson Co OR 88 A3
Klamath Co OR 88 E4
Lewis Co ID 42 D7
Medford OR 87 D6
Medford OR 198 C2
Shady Cove OR 87 D4
SR-62 Crater Lake Hwy
Jackson Co OR 87 E3
Jackson Co OR 88 C1
Klamath Co OR 88 D3
SR-62 Crater Lake Hwy
Medford OR 87 D6
Medford OR 198 C2
SR-62 Highway 62
Eagle Point OR 87 D5
Jackson Co OR 87 D4
Jackson Co OR 88 A3
Shady Cove OR 87 D4
SR-64
Lewis Co ID 42 E7
SR-66
Ashland OR 200 E6
Jackson Co OR 87 E7
Jackson Co OR 98 E1
Jackson Co OR 99 A1
Jackson Co OR 200 C5
Klamath Co OR 88 E7
Klamath Co OR 99 E1
Whitman Co WA 41 D2
SR-66 Ashland St
Ashland OR 200 E6
Jackson Co OR 200 C5
SR-66 Green Springs Hwy
Ashland OR 200 D6
Jackson Co OR 87 E7
Jackson Co OR 98 E1
Jackson Co OR 99 A1
Jackson Co OR 200 E7
Klamath Co OR 88 E7
Klamath Co OR 99 C1
SR-66 Palouse Cove Rd
Whitman Co WA 41 D2
SR-67
Elmore Co ID 84 D6
SR-69
Ada Co ID 83 E2
SR-70
Klamath Co OR 89 B7
SR-70 Dairy-Bonanza Hwy
Klamath Co OR 89 B7
SR-71
Baker Co OR 62 A5
Washington Co ID 62 B7
SR-74
Morrow Co OR 48 C7
Morrow Co OR 49 B7
Morrow Co OR 58 D1
Morrow Co OR 59 B1
Umatilla Co OR 49 B7
SR-74 Heppner Hwy
Morrow Co OR 48 B6
Morrow Co OR 49 B7
Morrow Co OR 58 D1
Morrow Co OR 59 B1
Umatilla Co OR 49 C7
SR-78
Burns OR 80 C2
Harney Co OR 80 D3
Harney Co OR 81 A5
Malheur Co OR 81 D7
Malheur Co OR 93 E1
Malheur Co OR 94 A2
Owyhee Co ID 83 B2
Owyhee Co ID 84 D7
SR-78 Crane Blvd
Burns OR 80 C2
SR-78 Murphy Grandview Rd
Owyhee Co ID 83 E6
Owyhee Co ID 84 A6
SR-78 Steens Hwy
Harney Co OR 80 E4
Harney Co OR 81 A4
SR-82
Union Co OR 50 E6
Union Co OR 51 A6
Wallowa Co OR 51 B6
Wallowa Co OR 61 D1
SR-82 Joseph-Wallowa Lake Hwy
Wallowa Co OR 61 D1
SR-82 Wallowa Lake Hwy
Union Co OR 50 E6
Union Co OR 51 A6
Wallowa Co OR 51 B6
Wallowa Co OR 61 D1
SR-86
Baker Co OR 61 E6
Baker Co OR 62 A4
SR-86 Baker-Copperfield Hwy
Baker Co OR 61 A6
Baker Co OR 62 A4
SR-92
Granite Falls WA 15 E6
Snohomish Co WA 15 E6
SR-92 Granite Falls Hwy
Granite Falls WA 15 E6
SR-96
Humboldt Co CA 97 D7
Siskiyou Co CA 97 E3
Siskiyou Co CA 98 D3
Snohomish Co WA 15 D7
SR-96 Bigfoot Scenic Hwy
Humboldt Co CA 97 D7
SR-96 E Lowell Larimer Rd
Snohomish Co WA 15 D7
SR-97
Kootenai Co ID 31 E3
Kootenai Co ID 32 A2
SR-99
Ashland OR 199 D2
Ashland OR 200 C6
Canyonville OR 87 A1
Central Point OR 87 C6
Des Moines WA 139 E7
Douglas Co OR 74 E6
Douglas Co OR 75 A6
Douglas Co OR 195 E7
Douglas Co OR 196 A1
Eugene OR 180 E6
Eugene OR 181 A7
Eugene OR 185 B1
Eugene OR 186 A2
Everett WA 15 D7
SR-99
Grants Pass OR 197 D6
Jackson Co OR 87 C6
Jackson Co OR 199 C2
Jackson Co OR 200 C6
Josephine Co OR 197 C1
King Co WA 136 E3
King Co WA 137 A5
Lane Co OR 64 B5
Lane Co OR 180 B1
Lane Co OR 186 E6
Lane Co OR 187 A7
Latah Co ID 42 A3
Lynnwood WA 25 C1
Medford OR 198 B4
Roseburg OR 75 A5
Roseburg OR 195 E6
Roseburg OR 196 A4
Seatac WA 139 E6
Seatac WA 140 A3
Seattle WA 25 C3
Seattle WA 124 C3
Seattle WA 128 B5
Seattle WA 132 C1
Seattle WA 136 C1
Springfield OR 186 E6
Talent OR 87 D7
Tukwila WA 136 E3
Tukwila WA 137 A4
Tukwila WA 140 A1
Winston OR 74 E6
Yoncalla OR 75 A2
SR-99 1st St
Lane Co OR 187 A7
SR-99 1st Av Br S
Seattle WA 132 C6
SR-99 E 6th Av
Eugene OR 185 D1
SR-99 W 6th Av
Eugene OR 185 D1
SR-99 NW 6th St
Grants Pass OR 197 C4
SR-99 SW 6th St
Grants Pass OR 197 C4
SR-99 E 7th Av
Eugene OR 185 D1
SR-99 W 7th Av
Eugene OR 185 B1
SR-99 NE 7th St
Grants Pass OR 197 C4
SR-99 SE 7th St
Grants Pass OR 197 D3
SR-99 Alaskan Way Viaduct
Seattle WA 128 C7
Seattle WA 132 C1
SR-99 Aurora Av N
Seattle WA 25 C2
Seattle WA 124 C3
Seattle WA 128 B2
SR-99 E Broadway
Eugene OR 185 E1
Eugene OR 186 A2
SR-99 N Central Av
Medford OR 198 B5
SR-99 S Central Av
Medford OR 198 B5
SR-99 Coos Bay-Roseburg Hwy
Douglas Co OR 75 A6
Douglas Co OR 195 E7
Roseburg OR 75 A5
Roseburg OR 195 E7
SR-99 Court St
Medford OR 198 B4
SR-99 Dillard Hwy
Douglas Co OR 74 E6
Winston OR 74 E6
SR-99 Evergreen Wy
Everett WA 15 D7
SR-99 Franklin Blvd
Eugene OR 186 A2
SR-99 Franklin Blvd E
Lane Co OR 186 E7
Lane Co OR 187 A7
SR-99 Front St
Yoncalla OR 75 A2
SR-99 George Washington Br
Seattle WA 128 B1
SR-99 Goshen-Divide Hwy
Lane Co OR 64 C6
SR-99 International Blvd
Des Moines WA 139 E7
Seatac WA 139 E6
Seatac WA 140 A3
Tukwila WA 140 A2
SR-99 Lithia Wy
Ashland OR 199 D3
SR-99 E Main St
Ashland OR 199 D3
SR-99 N Main St
Ashland OR 199 D2
Canyonville OR 87 A1
Jackson Co OR 199 C2
SR-99 E Marginal Wy S
Seattle WA 25 C3
Seattle WA 132 C5
SR-99 Mill St
Eugene OR 185 E1
SR-99 North Old Pacific Hwy
Douglas Co OR 75 A7
SR-99 Old Willamette Hwy S
Lane Co OR 187 A7
SR-99 Pacific Hwy
Eugene OR 186 D3
Grants Pass OR 197 C1
Josephine Co OR 197 B1
Lane Co OR 186 E3
Lane Co OR 187 A7
Springfield OR 186 E6
SR-99 Pacific Hwy S
Des Moines WA 139 E7
Seatac WA 139 E7
SR-99 Pacific Hwy W
Lane Co OR 64 B4
SR-99 S Pacific Hwy
Talent OR 87 D7
SR-99 SE Pine St
Roseburg OR 195 E6
Roseburg OR 196 A6
SR-99 N Riverside Av
Medford OR 198 B5
SR-99 S Riverside Av
Medford OR 198 C7
SR-99 Rogue River Hwy
Grants Pass OR 197 D6
Jackson Co OR 87 B5
Josephine Co OR 197 D6
SR-99 Rogue Valley Hwy
Central Point OR 87 C6
Jackson Co OR 87 C6
SR-99 Siskiyou Blvd
Ashland OR 199 E4
Ashland OR 200 C6
Jackson Co OR 200 C6
SR-99 NE Stephens St
Douglas Co OR 75 A5
Douglas Co OR 196 A1
Roseburg OR 75 A5
Roseburg OR 196 A4
SR-99 SE Stephens St
Douglas Co OR 195 E7
Roseburg OR 195 E7
Roseburg OR 196 A5
SR-99 Tukwila Int'l Blvd
King Co WA 137 A5
Seatac WA 140 A1
Tukwila WA 137 A5
Tukwila WA 140 A1
SR-99 Umpqua Hwy
Douglas Co OR 75 A1
SR-99 Willamette Hwy
Lane Co OR 187 A7
SR-99E
Albany OR 54 C7
Albany OR 64 C1
Albany OR 175 E3
Albany OR 176 C2
Clackamas Co OR 54 E3
Clackamas Co OR 55 A2
Clackamas Co OR 170 C6
Gervais OR 54 D3
Linn Co OR 64 C1
Linn Co OR 176 C1
Marion Co OR 54 D3
Marion Co OR 172 C5
Marion Co OR 174 C1
Milwaukie OR 170 B2
Portland OR 45 A6
Portland OR 157 E7
Portland OR 161 E1
Portland OR 162 A5
Portland OR 166 A4
Portland OR 170 C1
Salem OR 172 C2
Salem OR 174 C5
SR-99E BUS
Jefferson OR 54 C6
Keizer OR 172 B2
Marion Co OR 54 C6
Salem OR 54 C4
Salem OR 171 D5
Salem OR 172 B2
Salem OR 173 D1
Salem OR 174 A2
SR-99E BUS N 2nd St
Jefferson OR 54 C6
Marion Co OR 54 C6
SR-99E 9th Av SE
Albany OR 175 E3
Albany OR 176 A3
SR-99E Albany-Junction Cty Hwy
Albany OR 64 C1
Linn Co OR 64 C3
SR-99E BUS Bellevue St SE
Salem OR 173 D1
SR-99E BUS Commercial St NE
Salem OR 171 D5
SR-99E BUS Ferry St SE
Salem OR 173 D1
SR-99E BUS Front St NE
Salem OR 171 D7
Salem OR 173 D1
SR-99E BUS Front St SE
Salem OR 173 D1
SR-99E NE Grand Av
Portland OR 162 A7
Portland OR 166 A2
SR-99E SE Grand Av
Portland OR 166 A4
SR-99E BUS Liberty St NE
Salem OR 54 C4
Salem OR 171 D7
SR-99E N Martin L King Jr Blvd
Portland OR 157 E7
Portland OR 161 E1
Portland OR 162 A1
SR-99E NE ML King Jr Blvd
Portland OR 45 A6
Portland OR 162 A5
Portland OR 166 A2
SR-99E SE ML King Jr Blvd
Portland OR 166 A2
SR-99E SE McLoughlin Blvd
Clackamas Co OR 55 A1
Clackamas Co OR 170 C6
Milwaukie OR 170 C5
Portland OR 166 A4
Portland OR 170 C1
SR-99E BUS Mission St SE
Salem OR 173 E2
Salem OR 174 A2
SR-99E Pacific Blvd SE
Albany OR 175 E3
Albany OR 176 B2
SR-99E Pacific Blvd SE
Linn Co OR 176 C2
SR-99E Pacific Blvd SW
Albany OR 54 C7
Albany OR 175 D4
SR-99E Pacific Hwy
Linn Co OR 176 C1
SR-99E Pacific Hwy E
Clackamas Co OR 54 E3
Clackamas Co OR 55 A2
SR-99E Portland Rd NE
Gervais OR 54 D3
Marion Co OR 54 D3
Marion Co OR 172 C2
Salem OR 172 C2
SR-99E BUS Pringle Pkwy SE
Salem OR 173 D1
SR-99E BUS Salem Hwy
Salem OR 171 D7
SR-99E BUS Salem Pkwy
Keizer OR 172 B2
Salem OR 171 D5
Salem OR 172 B2
SR-99E BUS N Santiam Hwy
Salem OR 174 B4
SR-99E BUS Trade St SE
Salem OR 173 D1
SR-99W
Benton Co OR 54 B7
Benton Co OR 64 B1
Benton Co OR 178 C1
Corvallis OR 54 B7
Corvallis OR 178 B4
Polk Co OR 54 B4
Portland OR 165 D7
Portland OR 169 B2
Tigard OR 44 E7
Yamhill Co OR 54 D1
SR-99W NW 3rd St
Corvallis OR 178 B4
SR-99W SW 3rd St
Corvallis OR 178 B5
SR-99W NW 4th St
Corvallis OR 178 B5
SR-99W SW 4th St
Corvallis OR 178 B5
SR-99W SW Barbur Blvd
Portland OR 165 D6
Portland OR 169 A2
SR-99W SW Naito Pkwy
Portland OR 165 E4
SR-99W Pacific Hwy W
Benton Co OR 54 B7
Benton Co OR 64 B1
Benton Co OR 178 C1
Corvallis OR 54 B7
Corvallis OR 178 B2
Yamhill Co OR 54 B3
SR-99W N Pacific Hwy W
Polk Co OR 54 B4
SR-99W S Pacific Hwy W
Polk Co OR 54 B5
SR-99W SW Pacific Hwy
Tigard OR 44 E7
SR-99W SW Pacific Hwy W
Yamhill Co OR 54 D1
SR-100
Pacific Co WA 33 C7
SR-100 Fort Canby Rd
Pacific Co WA 33 C7
SR-102
Mason Co WA 24 C6
SR-102 W Dayton Airport Rd
Mason Co WA 24 C6
SR-103
Pacific Co WA 33 C6
SR-103 Pacific Wy
Pacific Co WA 33 C6
SR-103 Stackpole Rd
Pacific Co WA 33 C4
SR-104
Edmonds WA 25 C1
Jefferson Co WA 14 E7
Jefferson Co WA 15 A7
Kitsap Co WA 15 A7
Kitsap Co WA 25 B1
SR-104 Hood Canal Floating Br
Jefferson Co WA 15 A7
Kitsap Co WA 15 A7
SR-104 Main St
Edmonds WA 25 C1
SR-105
Grays Harbor Co WA 33 C1
Grays Harbor Co WA 150 C7
Pacific Co WA 33 C3
Pacific Co WA 150 C7
Westport WA 150 C3
SR-105 N Montesano St
Westport WA 150 C3
SR-105 State Route 105
Grays Harbor Co WA 150 C7
SR-106
Mason Co WA 24 D5
SR-107
Grays Harbor Co WA 33 E1
SR-108
Grays Harbor Co WA 24 C7
Mason Co WA 24 C7
SR-108 W State Route 108
Mason Co WA 24 C7
SR-109
Grays Harbor Co WA 23 C7
Grays Harbor Co WA 33 C1
SR-110
Clallam Co WA 12 E7
Clallam Co WA 13 A6
Forks WA 13 A6
SR-110 La Push Rd
Clallam Co WA 12 E7
Clallam Co WA 13 A6
Forks WA 13 A6
SR-112
Clallam Co WA 13 A3
Clallam Co WA 14 A5
SR-113
Clallam Co WA 13 B5
SR-113 Burnt Mountain Rd
Clallam Co WA 13 B5
SR-115
Grays Harbor Co WA 23 B7
SR-116
Jefferson Co WA 15 A6
SR-117
Clallam Co WA 117 B3
Port Angeles WA 117 B3
SR-117 S Tumwater Access Rd
Clallam Co WA 117 B3
Port Angeles WA 117 B3
SR-119
Mason Co WA 24 B3
SR-119 N Lake Cushman Rd
Mason Co WA 24 C4
SR-119 NF-24
Mason Co WA 24 B3
SR-121
Thurston Co WA 34 E1
SR-121 Tilley Rd S
Thurston Co WA 34 E1
SR-122
Lewis Co WA 35 B5
SR-122 Silvercreek Rd
Lewis Co WA 35 B5
SR-123
Pierce Co WA 36 C3
SR-124
Walla Walla Co WA 39 E7
Walla Walla Co WA 40 A7
Walla Walla Co WA 49 C1
SR-125
College Place WA 207 C7
Walla Walla WA 207 E3
Walla Walla Co WA 40 B7
Walla Walla Co WA 50 B1
Walla Walla Co WA 207 D3
SR-125 SPUR
Walla Walla WA 207 D3
SR-125 N 9th Av
Walla Walla WA 207 E4
SR-125 S 9th Av
Walla Walla WA 207 E4
SR-125 13th Av N
Walla Walla WA 207 D2
Walla Walla Co WA 207 D2
SR-125 W Pine St
Walla Walla WA 207 E3
Walla Walla Co WA 207 D3
SR-125 SPUR W Pine St
Walla Walla WA 207 D3
SR-126
Columbia Co WA 40 E6
Crook Co OR 66 E4
Crook Co OR 67 A4
Deschutes Co OR 66 C3
Eugene OR 181 D7
Eugene OR 182 A7
Eugene OR 184 E1
Eugene OR 185 B1
Lane Co OR 63 B5
Lane Co OR 64 E5
Lane Co OR 65 C4
Lane Co OR 182 C7
Lane Co OR 184 B1
Lane Co OR 188 E2
Linn Co OR 65 D3
Springfield OR 64 D5
Springfield OR 182 C7
Springfield OR 183 A7
Springfield OR 187 E1
Springfield OR 188 B2
SR-126 BUS
Eugene OR 185 D1
Eugene OR 186 C2
Lane Co OR 186 D2
Springfield OR 64 C5
Springfield OR 186 C2
Springfield OR 187 E2
Springfield OR 188 B2
SR-126 BUS E 6th Av
Eugene OR 185 D1
SR-126 W 6th Av
Eugene OR 185 D1
SR-126 BUS W 6th Av
Eugene OR 185 D1
SR-126 BUS E 7th Av
Eugene OR 185 D1
SR-126 W 7th Av
Eugene OR 185 B1
SR-126 BUS W 7th Av
Eugene OR 185 D1
SR-126 W 11th Av
Eugene OR 184 E1
Eugene OR 185 B2
Lane Co OR 184 B1
SR-126 BUS S A St
Lane Co OR 186 E2
Springfield OR 186 E2
Springfield OR 187 A2
SR-126 BUS E Broadway
Eugene OR 185 E1
Eugene OR 186 A2
SR-126 Clear Lk-Belknap Sprs H
Linn Co OR 65 D3
SR-126 Florence-Eugene Hwy
Lane Co OR 63 B5
Lane Co OR 64 B5
SR-126 BUS Franklin Blvd
Eugene OR 186 C2
Lane Co OR 186 D2
Springfield OR 186 C2
SR-126 Garfield St
Eugene OR 185 B1

Street Index

STREET
City State Map# Grid

SR-310 6th St
Bremerton WA 122 A5
SR-310 N Callow Av
Bremerton WA 122 A5
SR-310 Kitsap Wy
Bremerton WA 121 E5
Bremerton WA 122 A5
Kitsap Co WA 121 E5
Kitsap Co WA 122 A5
SR-320
Umatilla Co OR 49 A5
SR-320 Madison Rd
Umatilla Co OR 49 A5
SR-331
Umatilla Co OR 49 E5
SR-332
Umatilla Co OR 50 A3
SR-334
Umatilla Co OR 49 D4
Umatilla Co OR 50 A4
SR-334 Athena-Holdman Hwy
Umatilla Co OR 49 D4
SR-334 Holdman Helix Hwy
Umatilla Co OR 50 A4
SR-370
Crook Co OR 67 A3
SR-370 NW O'Neil Hwy
Crook Co OR 67 A3
SR-380
Crook Co OR 67 C4
Crook Co OR 68 A5
SR-380 SE Paulina Hwy
Crook Co OR 67 C4
Crook Co OR 68 A5
SR-397
Benton Co WA 49 C1
Benton Co WA 206 E3
Kennewick WA 206 C1
Pasco WA 49 B1
Pasco WA 204 E5
Pasco WA 206 C1
SR-397 S 10th Av
Pasco WA 204 D7
SR-397 E Ainsworth St
Pasco WA 204 D7
Pasco WA 206 E1
SR-397 W Ainsworth St
Pasco WA 204 D7
SR-397 E Chemical Dr
Benton Co WA 49 C1
Benton Co WA 206 E3
Kennewick WA 206 C2
SR-397 Ed Hendler Br
Kennewick WA 206 C1
Pasco WA 206 C1
SR-397 N Gum St
Kennewick WA 206 C1
SR-397 S Gum St
Kennewick WA 206 C2
SR-397 N Oregon Av
Pasco WA 204 E5
SR-397 S Oregon Av
Pasco WA 49 B1
Pasco WA 204 E7
Pasco WA 206 E1
SR-401
Pacific Co WA 33 D6
SR-403
Wahkiakum Co WA 33 E7
SR-403 Altoona-Pillar Rock Rd
Wahkiakum Co WA 33 E7
SR-407
Wahkiakum Co WA 34 B7
SR-407 Elochoman Valley Rd
Wahkiakum Co WA 34 B7
SR-409
Wahkiakum Co WA 44 B1
SR-410
Bonney Lake WA 25 D6
King Co WA 25 E6
King Co WA 26 A7
Pierce Co WA 25 E6
Pierce Co WA 26 B7
Pierce Co WA 36 C1
Yakima Co WA 36 E1
Yakima Co WA 37 B3
SR-410 SE Enmclw-Chnk Pass Rd
King Co WA 25 E6
King Co WA 26 A7
SR-411
Cowlitz Co WA 34 D7
Cowlitz Co WA 44 D1
Cowlitz Co WA 155 E6
Cowlitz Co WA 156 A4
Kelso WA 156 A3
Lewis Co WA 34 D6
Lincoln Co OR 53 C6
Longview WA 155 E6
Longview WA 156 A4
SR-411 1st Av
Cowlitz Co WA 156 A3
Kelso WA 156 A3
Longview WA 156 A4
SR-411 1st Av NW
Cowlitz Co WA 156 A3
Kelso WA 156 A3
SR-411 3rd Av
Cowlitz Co WA 155 E6
Cowlitz Co WA 156 A4
Longview WA 155 E6
Longview WA 156 A4
SR-411 Logsden Rd
Lincoln Co OR 53 C6
SR-411 West Side Hwy
Cowlitz Co WA 156 A3
Kelso WA 156 A3
Longview WA 156 A3
SR-411 Westside Hwy
Cowlitz Co WA 34 D7
Cowlitz Co WA 44 D1
Cowlitz Co WA 156 A1
Kelso WA 156 A3
Lewis Co WA 34 D6
Longview WA 156 A2
SR-427
Klamath Co OR 88 E4
SR-427 Modoc Point Rd
Klamath Co OR 88 E4
SR-431
Kelso WA 156 B2
SR-431 N Kelso Av
Kelso WA 156 B2
SR-431 N Pacific Av
Kelso WA 156 B3
SR-432
Cowlitz Co WA 44 D1
Cowlitz Co WA 155 E6
Cowlitz Co WA 156 B7
Kelso WA 156 C7
Longview WA 44 D1
Longview WA 155 E6
SR-432 3rd Av
Cowlitz Co WA 155 E6
Longview WA 155 E6
SR-432 Industrial Wy
Cowlitz Co WA 155 D6
Longview WA 155 D6
SR-432 Nichols Blvd
Longview WA 155 D5
SR-432 NW Nichols Blvd
Longview WA 155 C3
SR-432 Tennant Wy
Cowlitz Co WA 155 E6
Cowlitz Co WA 156 B7
Kelso WA 156 D7
Longview WA 155 E5
SR-432 Willow Grv Conn Rd
Cowlitz Co WA 44 D1
Longview WA 44 D1
SR-433
Cowlitz Co WA 155 C7
Longview WA 155 D5
Rainier OR 155 C7
SR-433 Oregon Wy
Cowlitz Co WA 155 C7
Longview WA 155 D5
Rainier OR 155 C7
SR-500
Clark Co WA 45 A6
Clark Co WA 158 D2
Clark Co WA 159 D1
Vancouver WA 45 A6
Vancouver WA 158 B2
Vancouver WA 159 D1
SR-500 NE 267th Av
Clark Co WA 45 B6
SR-500 NE Fourth Plain Rd
Clark Co WA 45 B5
SR-501
Clark Co WA 44 E5
Clark Co WA 157 A1
Vancouver WA 45 A6
Vancouver WA 157 A1
Vancouver WA 158 A4
SR-501 E 15th St
Vancouver WA 158 A4
SR-501 W 15th St
Vancouver WA 157 E4
Vancouver WA 158 A4
SR-501 NW Lower River Rd
Clark Co WA 44 E5
Clark Co WA 157 A1
Vancouver WA 157 A1
SR-501 E Mill Plain Blvd
Vancouver WA 158 A4
SR-501 W Mill Plain Blvd
Vancouver WA 45 A6
Vancouver WA 157 E4
Vancouver WA 158 A4
SR-503
Clark Co WA 45 C3
Cowlitz Co WA 44 E3
Cowlitz Co WA 45 A3
SR-503 SPUR
Cowlitz Co WA 45 C2
SR-503 Lewis River Rd
Cowlitz Co WA 44 E3
Cowlitz Co WA 45 A3
SR-503 SPUR Lewis River Rd
Cowlitz Co WA 45 C2
SR-503 NE Lewisville Hwy
Clark Co WA 45 B4
SR-503 NE Yale Bridge Rd
Clark Co WA 45 C3
SR-504
Castle Rock WA 34 E7
Cowlitz Co WA 34 E7
Cowlitz Co WA 35 A6
Skamania Co WA 35 C7
SR-504 Spirit Lake Hwy
Castle Rock WA 34 D7
Cowlitz Co WA 34 D7
SR-504 Spirit Lake Mem Hwy
Cowlitz Co WA 35 C7
Skamania Co WA 35 C7
SR-505
Lewis Co WA 34 E6
Lewis Co WA 35 A6
SR-506
Cowlitz Co WA 34 D6
Lewis Co WA 34 D6
SR-507
Centralia WA 151 D3
Lewis Co WA 34 D3
Lewis Co WA 151 D2
Pierce Co WA 25 B7
Pierce Co WA 35 B1
Roy WA 35 B1
Tenino WA 34 E2
Thurston Co WA 34 E2
Thurston Co WA 35 A2
SR-507 W 6th St
Centralia WA 151 D4
SR-507 Alder St
Centralia WA 151 D5
SR-507 Bucoda Hwy SE
Tenino WA 34 E2
Thurston Co WA 34 E2
SR-507 W Cherry St
Centralia WA 151 D6
SR-507 E Downing Rd
Centralia WA 151 D1
Lewis Co WA 151 D1
SR-507 Mellen St
Centralia WA 151 C6
SR-507 N Pearl St
Centralia WA 151 D2
Lewis Co WA 151 D2
SR-507 S Pearl St
Centralia WA 151 D5
SR-507 Spanaway McKenna Hwy
Pierce Co WA 25 B7
Pierce Co WA 35 B1
Roy WA 35 B1
SR-507 N Tower Av
Centralia WA 151 D4
SR-507 S Tower Av
Centralia WA 151 D5
SR-508
Lewis Co WA 34 E4
Lewis Co WA 35 A4
SR-509
Burien WA 25 C4
Burien WA 136 C5
Burien WA 139 C4
Des Moines WA 139 C7
Federal Way WA 25 C5
Fife WA 142 E5
King Co WA 136 C2
Normandy Park WA 139 C3
Seatac WA 139 D3
Seattle WA 132 C7
Seattle WA 136 C1
Tacoma WA 142 C6
SR-509 1st Av S
Burien WA 139 C3
Des Moines WA 139 C7
Normandy Park WA 139 C3
SR-509 1st Pl S
Des Moines WA 139 C7
Normandy Park WA 139 C7
SR-509 1st Av Br S
Seattle WA 132 C7
SR-509 S 21st St
Tacoma WA 142 B6
SR-509 S 174th St
Burien WA 139 C3
Normandy Park WA 139 C3
SR-509 S 216th Pl
Des Moines WA 139 C7
Normandy Park WA 139 C7
SR-509 S 216th St
Des Moines WA 139 C7
Normandy Park WA 139 C7
SR-509 Ambaum Blvd S
Burien WA 139 C4
SR-509 Burien Frwy
King Co WA 136 C2
Seattle WA 136 C2
SR-509 SW Dash Point Rd
Federal Way WA 25 C5
SR-509 Des Moines Memorial Dr
Burien WA 139 C4
Seatac WA 139 C4
SR-509 Marine View Dr
Tacoma WA 142 D1
SR-509 Marine View Dr S
Des Moines WA 139 C7
SR-509 Pacific Av
Tacoma WA 142 B6
SR-510
Thurston Co WA 35 A1
SR-510 St. Clair Cut Off Rd SE
Thurston Co WA 35 A1
SR-510 Yelm Hwy SE
Thurston Co WA 35 A1
SR-512
Lakewood WA 143 C7
Pierce Co WA 25 C7
Puyallup WA 25 C7
SR-513
Seattle WA 125 C6
Seattle WA 128 E2
Seattle WA 129 A1
SR-513 NE 45th St
Seattle WA 125 A7
SR-513 Montlake Blvd E
Seattle WA 128 E2
SR-513 Montlake Blvd NE
Seattle WA 125 A7
Seattle WA 128 E2
Seattle WA 129 A1
SR-513 Sand Point Wy NE
Seattle WA 125 C6
SR-515
Renton WA 138 C6
SR-515 S Grady Wy
Renton WA 138 B7
SR-515 Main Av S
Renton WA 138 C6
SR-515 Talbot Rd S
Renton WA 138 B7
SR-516
Covington WA 25 E5
Des Moines WA 25 C4
Kent WA 25 C4
SR-516 SE 272nd St
Covington WA 25 E5
SR-516 Canyon Dr
Kent WA 25 D5
SR-516 S Kent des Moines Rd
Des Moines WA 25 C4
Kent WA 25 C4
SR-518
Burien WA 25 C4
Burien WA 136 C7
Seatac WA 25 C4
Seatac WA 136 D7
Seatac WA 139 E1
Seatac WA 140 A1
Tukwila WA 140 B1
SR-520
Bellevue WA 25 D2
Bellevue WA 130 C2
Clyde Hill WA 130 B3
Hunts Point WA 130 D3
King Co WA 129 B2
Kirkland WA 130 C2
Medina WA 129 B2
Medina WA 130 D3
Seattle WA 128 E2
Seattle WA 129 A2
Yarrow Point WA 130 B3
SR-520 Evergrn Pt Floating Br
Seattle WA 129 A2
SR-520 Gov Rsllni Evrgrn Pt Br
King Co WA 129 B2
Medina WA 129 B2
Seattle WA 129 B2
SR-522
Lake Forest Park WA 25 C2
Monroe WA 25 E1
Seattle WA 124 E4
Seattle WA 125 A1
Snohomish Co WA 25 E1
Woodinville WA 25 D1
SR-522 Bothell Wy NE
Lake Forest Park WA 25 C2
SR-522 Lake City Wy NE
Seattle WA 124 E4
Seattle WA 125 A3
SR-524
Lynnwood WA 25 D1
Snohomish Co WA 25 D1
SR-524 196th St SW
Lynnwood WA 25 D1
Snohomish Co WA 25 D1
SR-524 Maltby Rd
Snohomish Co WA 25 D1
SR-525
Island Co WA 15 B6
Mukilteo WA 15 C7
Snohomish Co WA 15 C7
Snohomish Co WA 25 D1
SR-525 Mukilteo Speedway
Mukilteo WA 15 C7
Snohomish Co WA 15 C7
SR-526
Everett WA 15 D7
SR-526 Boeing Frwy
Everett WA 15 D7
SR-527
Bothell WA 25 D1
Mill Creek WA 15 D7
SR-527 Bothell Everett Hwy
Bothell WA 25 D1
Mill Creek WA 15 D7
SR-528
Marysville WA 15 D6
SR-528 64th St NE
Marysville WA 15 D6
SR-529
Everett WA 15 D6
Everett WA 120 D3
SR-529 Everett Av
Everett WA 120 C3
SR-529 Maple St
Everett WA 120 D3
SR-529 W Marine View Dr
Everett WA 15 D6
Everett WA 120 D3
SR-529 Pacific Av
Everett WA 120 D3
SR-530
Arlington WA 15 D5
Snohomish Co WA 15 D5
Snohomish Co WA 16 A4
SR-530 Arlington-Darrington Rd
Snohomish Co WA 15 E4
Snohomish Co WA 16 A4
SR-531
Marysville WA 15 D5
Snohomish Co WA 15 D5
SR-531 172nd St NE
Marysville WA 15 D5
Snohomish Co WA 15 D5
SR-532
Island Co WA 15 C4
Snohomish Co WA 15 C4
SR-534
Skagit Co WA 15 C3
SR-536
Mt Vernon WA 116 B4
Skagit Co WA 15 C2
Skagit Co WA 116 A3
SR-536 S 1st St
Mt Vernon WA 116 B4
SR-536 W Division St
Mt Vernon WA 116 B4
Skagit Co WA 116 A3
SR-536 Kincaid St
Mt Vernon WA 116 B4
SR-536 E Kincaid St
Mt Vernon WA 116 B4
SR-536 Memorial Hwy
Mt Vernon WA 116 A3
Skagit Co WA 15 C2
Skagit Co WA 116 A3
SR-538
Mt Vernon WA 116 C2
SR-538 E College Wy
Mt Vernon WA 116 B2
SR-538 W College Wy
Mt Vernon WA 116 C2
SR-539
Bellingham WA 5 B6
Whatcom Co WA 5 B6
SR-539 Guide Meridian Rd
Bellingham WA 5 B6
Whatcom Co WA 5 C5
SR-542
Bellingham WA 5 C6
Bellingham WA 113 D1
Whatcom Co WA 5 D6
Whatcom Co WA 6 A5
SR-542 Mt Baker Hwy
Bellingham WA 5 C6
Whatcom Co WA 5 D6
Whatcom Co WA 6 B6
SR-542 E Sunset Dr
Bellingham WA 113 D1
SR-544
Whatcom Co WA 5 C6
SR-544 Everson-Goshen Rd
Whatcom Co WA 5 C6
SR-544 E Pole Rd
Whatcom Co WA 5 C6
SR-546
Whatcom Co WA 5 C5
SR-546 E Badger Rd
Whatcom Co WA 5 C5
SR-547
Whatcom Co WA 5 D5
SR-547 Kendall Rd
Whatcom Co WA 5 D5
SR-547 Reese Hill Rd
Whatcom Co WA 5 D5
SR-548
Whatcom Co WA 5 A5
SR-548 Blaine Rd
Whatcom Co WA 5 A5
SR-548 Grandview Rd
Whatcom Co WA 5 B6
SR-599
King Co WA 137 A4
Tukwila WA 25 C4
Tukwila WA 137 B6
SR-603
Lewis Co WA 34 D4
Lewis Co WA 152 A7
SR-702
Pierce Co WA 35 B1
SR-706
Pierce Co WA 35 E3
SR-793
Humboldt Co NV 105 B2
Malheur Co OR 105 B2
SR-793 Cordero Mine Rd
Humboldt Co NV 105 B2
Malheur Co OR 105 B2
SR-821
Kittitas Co WA 37 D2
Yakima Co WA 37 D3
SR-821 Canyon Rd
Kittitas Co WA 37 D2
SR-823
Selah WA 37 D4
SR-823 N Wenas Rd
Selah WA 37 D4
SR-900
King Co WA 25 D4
King Co WA 137 D6
Renton WA 137 E7
Renton WA 138 C4
Seattle WA 137 B3
Tukwila WA 137 C5
SR-900 S 2nd St
Renton WA 138 B6
SR-900 S 3rd St
Renton WA 138 B7
SR-900 Bronson Wy N
Renton WA 138 C6
SR-900 Bronson Wy S
Renton WA 138 C6
SR-900 Houser Wy S
Renton WA 138 B6
SR-900 Main Av S
Renton WA 138 C6
SR-900 Martin L King Jr Wy
King Co WA 137 C5
Renton WA 137 E7
Seattle WA 137 C5
Tukwila WA 137 B4
SR-900 Martin L King Jr Wy S
Seattle WA 137 B3
Tukwila WA 137 C4
SR-900 Mill Av S
Renton WA 138 C6
SR-900 NE Park Dr
Renton WA 138 C4
SR-900 Rainier Av S
Renton WA 138 B6
SR-900 SE Renton-Issaquah Rd
King Co WA 25 D4
SR-900 Sunset Blvd N
Renton WA 138 C6
SR-900 Sunset Blvd NE
Renton WA 138 C6
SR-900 NE Sunset Blvd
Renton WA 138 D4
SR-900 SW Sunset Blvd
Renton WA 137 E7
Renton WA 138 A7
SR-901
Bellevue WA 25 D3
Redmond WA 25 D2
SR-901 W Lk Sammamish Pkwy NE
Redmond WA 25 D2
SR-901 W Lk Sammamish Pkwy SE
Bellevue WA 25 D3
SR-902
Medical Lake WA 30 E3
Spokane Co WA 30 E3
Spokane Co WA 31 A3
SR-902 W Medical Lake Rd
Spokane Co WA 31 A3
SR-903
Kittitas Co WA 26 E5
Kittitas Co WA 27 A6
SR-903 Salmon la Sac Rd
Kittitas Co WA 26 E5
SR-904
Spokane Co WA 30 E4
Spokane Co WA 31 A3
SR-904 Lt Col M Andersn Mem Hy
Spokane Co WA 30 E4
Spokane Co WA 31 A3
SR-908
Kirkland WA 25 D2
Kirkland WA 126 E5
SR-908 NE 85th St
Kirkland WA 126 E5
SR-908 Lake Washington Blvd NE
Kirkland WA 25 D2
SR-970
Kittitas Co WA 27 B6
SR-971
Chelan Co WA 18 A7
Chelan Co WA 28 A1
SR-971 S Lakeshore Rd
Chelan Co WA 18 A7
SR-971 Navarre Coulee Rd
Chelan Co WA 28 A1
TCH-1
Abbotsford BC 5 C4
Burnaby BC 4 E2
Capital BC 14 A2
Chilliwack BC 6 A3
Cowichan Valley BC 3 E4
Cowichan Valley BC 4 A5
Cowichan Valley BC 14 A1
Fraser Valley BC 6 B2
Hope BC 6 C2
Langford BC 14 A2
Langley Township BC 5 B3
Nanaimo District BC 3 E4
North Vancouver BC 4 D2
North Vancouver BC 108 E3
North Vancouver Dist BC 108 A3
Saanich BC 14 B2
Saanich BC 111 C1
Surrey BC 5 A3
Vancouver BC 4 E2
Victoria BC 14 B2
Victoria BC 111 E5
West Vancouver BC 4 C1
West Vancouver BC 107 B2
West Vancouver BC 108 A3
TCH-1 Douglas St
Saanich BC 14 B2
Saanich BC 111 D2
Victoria BC 14 B2
Victoria BC 111 D7
TCH-1 Trans Canada Hwy
Abbotsford BC 5 C4
Burnaby BC 4 E2
Capital BC 14 A2
Chilliwack BC 6 A3
Cowichan Valley BC 3 E5
Cowichan Valley BC 4 A7
Cowichan Valley BC 14 A1
Fraser Valley BC 6 B2
Hope BC 6 C2
Langford BC 14 A2
Langley Township BC 5 B3
Nanaimo District BC 3 E4
North Vancouver BC 4 D2
North Vancouver BC 108 D3
N Vancouver Dist BC 108 B3
Saanich BC 111 C1
Surrey BC 5 A3
Vancouver BC 4 E2
Victoria BC 111 D7
West Vancouver BC 4 C1
West Vancouver BC 107 B2
West Vancouver BC 108 A3
US-2
Bonner Co ID 21 E5
Bonner Co ID 22 B3
Boundary Co ID 22 B1
Chelan Co WA 27 B2
Douglas Co WA 27 E4
Douglas Co WA 28 E3
Dover ID 22 A4
Everett WA 120 E3
Gold Bar WA 26 B1
Grant Co WA 29 B2
King Co WA 26 C1
Lincoln Co MT 22 E1
Lincoln Co WA 29 E1
Lincoln Co WA 30 C2
Pend Oreille Co WA 21 C5
Snohomish Co WA 15 E7
Snohomish Co WA 16 B7
Snohomish Co WA 26 B1
Snohomish Co WA 120 E3
Spokane WA 31 B2
Spokane WA 209 E3
Spokane WA 210 A7
Spokane WA 211 C2
Spokane WA 212 A1
Spokane Co WA 21 B7
Spokane Co WA 30 E2
Spokane Co WA 31 B1
Spokane Co WA 209 E2
Spokane Co WA 211 A4
Sultan WA 16 A7
Sultan WA 26 A1
US-2 N Browne St
Spokane WA 212 A1
US-2 S Browne St
Spokane WA 212 A1
US-2 N Division St
Spokane WA 31 B2
US-2 N Division St
Spokane WA 209 E3
Spokane WA 210 A7
Spokane WA 212 A1
Spokane Co WA 209 E2
US-2 S Division St
Spokane WA 212 A1
US-2 Hewitt Av
Everett WA 120 C3
US-2 N Newport Hwy
Spokane WA 31 B1
Spokane Co WA 21 B7
Spokane Co WA 31 B1
US-2 N Ruby St
Spokane WA 210 A7
US-2 W Stevens Av
Snohomish Co WA 26 A1
Sultan WA 26 A1
US-2 Stevens Pass Hwy
Gold Bar WA 26 B1
Snohomish Co WA 15 E7
Snohomish Co WA 16 A7
Snohomish Co WA 26 B1
Sultan WA 16 A7
US-2 NE Stevens Pass Hwy
King Co WA 26 C1
US-2 Sunset Hwy
Chelan Co WA 27 E4
US-12
Asotin Co WA 41 D6
Benton Co WA 38 D7
Benton Co WA 48 D1
Centralia WA 151 B4
Chehalis WA 152 B1
Clarkston WA 41 E5
Clearwater Co ID 42 D5
Columbia Co WA 40 C7
Franklin Co WA 49 C1
Franklin Co WA 204 A4
Garfield Co WA 40 E5
Garfield Co WA 41 A5
Grandview WA 38 B7
Grays Harbor Co WA 33 E1
Grays Harbor Co WA 34 B2
Lewis Co ID 42 D5
Lewis Co WA 34 E5
Lewis Co WA 35 A5
Lewis Co WA 36 C4
Lewis Co WA 151 B6
Lewis Co WA 152 C1
Nez Perce Co ID 42 B5
Pasco WA 39 B7
Pasco WA 49 C1
Pasco WA 204 B4
Richland WA 203 C7
Thurston Co WA 34 C2
Walla Walla WA 207 C3
Walla Walla WA 208 A2
Walla Walla Co WA 40 C7
Walla Walla Co WA 49 D2
Walla Walla Co WA 50 A2
Walla Walla Co WA 207 C3
Walla Walla Co WA 208 E1
Yakima WA 37 C4
Yakima Co WA 36 E4
Yakima Co WA 37 A4
Yakima Co WA 38 A7
US-12 BUS
Walla Walla WA 207 E3
Walla Walla WA 208 D2
Walla Walla Co WA 208 E2
US-12 BUS N 2nd Av
Walla Walla WA 207 E3
US-12 Bridge St
Clarkston WA 41 E5
US-12 BUS E Isaacs Av
Walla Walla WA 208 D2
Walla Walla Co WA 208 E2
US-12 US Highway 12
Nez Perce Co ID 42 C5
US-20
Ada Co ID 83 E1
Albany OR 54 C7
Albany OR 175 D2
Albany OR 176 A3
Bend OR 190 A5
Bend OR 192 E1
Benton Co OR 53 E7
Benton Co OR 54 A7
Benton Co OR 64 A1
Benton Co OR 175 C2
Benton Co OR 177 A7
Benton Co OR 178 B4
Boise ID 83 E1
Boise ID 84 A2
Boise ID 221 E7
Boise ID 222 A7
Boise ID 224 D4
Caldwell ID 219 E3
Canyon Co ID 72 A7
Canyon Co ID 83 B1
Canyon Co ID 219 B1
Corvallis OR 64 B1
Corvallis OR 177 E6
Corvallis OR 178 C4
Deschutes Co OR 66 C4
Deschutes Co OR 67 A7
Deschutes Co OR 78 C1
Deschutes Co OR 79 A2
Deschutes Co OR 189 E1
Deschutes Co OR 190 A1
Deschutes Co OR 192 E1
Elmore Co ID 84 E5
Garden City ID 221 B4
Harney Co OR 79 D3
Harney Co OR 80 C2
Harney Co OR 81 A2
Jefferson Co OR 66 A2
Lake Co OR 79 A2
Lincoln Co OR 53 D7
Linn Co OR 54 D7
Linn Co OR 64 E2
Linn Co OR 65 C2
Linn Co OR 176 C3
Malheur Co OR 70 D7
Malheur Co OR 71 D6
Malheur Co OR 72 A6

9 INDEX
INDEX 9
Black Oak Dr
W Chinden Blvd US-20

Street Index

STREET City State Map# Grid

Black Oak Dr
Medford OR 198 E5
Blaine Rd
Blaine WA 5 A5
Tillamook Co OR 53 D1
Blaine Rd SR-548
Blaine WA 5 A5
Blaine St
Caldwell ID 83 C1
Caldwell ID 219 C4
Port Townsend WA 119 C4
Blaine St I-84 BUS
Caldwell ID 83 C1
Caldwell ID 219 C4
SE Blair Rd
Clark Co WA 45 C6
E Blair St
Uniontown WA 41 D5
NE Blakeley St
Seattle WA 125 A7
Blakely Av NE
Bainbridge Island WA 25 B3
E Blanchard Rd
Spokane Co WA 21 C6
N Blanford Dr
Vancouver WA 158 D5
S Blanford Dr
Vancouver WA 158 D5
Blanshard St
Saanich BC 111 E3
Victoria BC 111 E2
Blanshard St PROV-17
Saanich BC 111 E3
Victoria BC 111 E2
Blanton Rd
Connell WA 39 C5
Franklin Co WA 39 C5
Blenkinsop Rd
Saanich BC 112 A1
BLM-34-8-36
Josephine Co OR 86 D4
Bluestem Rd
Lincoln Co WA 30 C3
N Bluff Rd
Surrey BC 5 A4
White Rock BC 5 A4
SE Bluff Rd
Clackamas Co OR 45 C7
Blundell Rd
Richmond BC 4 D3
Bly Mountain Cto
Klamath Co OR 89 C7
Bob Straub Pkwy
Springfield OR 188 B3
S Boeing Access Rd
Seattle WA 137 B3
Tukwila WA 137 A3
E Boise Av
Boise ID 84 A2
Boise ID 224 E4
W Boise Av
Boise ID 84 A2
Boise ID 224 D3
Boise River Rd
Canyon Co ID 83 B1
Boistfort Rd
Lewis Co WA 34 C5
NW Boistfort St
Chehalis WA 152 B4
Bond Rd NE
Kitsap Co WA 25 B1
Poulsbo WA 25 B1
Bond Rd NE SR-307
Kitsap Co WA 25 B1
Poulsbo WA 25 B1
NW Bond St
Bend OR 189 E7
Bend OR 190 A7
Bend OR 191 E1
SW Bond St
Bend OR 191 E1
Bend OR 192 A2
S Booker Rd
Adams Co WA 39 B2
S Boone St
Aberdeen WA 33 D1
S Boone St SR-105
Aberdeen WA 33 D1
Boones Ferry Rd
Clackamas Co OR 169 B6
Lake Oswego OR 169 A7
Multnomah Co OR 169 C4
Portland OR 169 C4
SW Boones Ferry Rd
Multnomah Co OR 169 D3
Portland OR 169 C4
NW Booth St
Grants Pass OR 197 C4
SW Booth St
Grants Pass OR 197 B4
Boren Av
Seattle WA 128 C5
Boren Av S
Seattle WA 128 D7
Boston St
Seattle WA 128 B3
Boston Harbor Rd NE
Olympia WA 146 A1
Thurston Co WA 146 A1
Boston Mill Dr
Linn Co OR 64 C2
NE Bothell Wy
Kenmore WA 25 D1
NE Bothell Wy SR-522
Kenmore WA 25 D1
Bothell Everett Hwy
Bothell WA 25 D1
Bothell Everett Hwy SR-527
Bothell WA 25 D1
Boulder Av
Vancouver WA 159 C5
Boulevard Cres
North Vancouver BC 108 E4
Boulevard Rd SE
Olympia WA 146 C6
Olympia WA 148 C1
Thurston Co WA 148 C2
Boulevard St
Bellingham WA 113 B5
Boundary Rd
Abbotsford BC 5 E4
Chilliwack BC 5 E4
Bowen Rd
Nanaimo BC 3 D3
W Bow Hill Rd
Skagit Co WA 15 C1
W Bow Hill Rd SR-237
Skagit Co WA 15 C1
E Bowles Rd
Benton Co WA 49 B1
Benton Co WA 206 E6
Bowman Rd
Gem Co ID 72 C7
Bowmont Rd
Canyon Co ID 83 D3
Boyd Acres Rd
Bend OR 190 B4
NE Boyd Acres Rd
Bend OR 190 B5
Boyer Av E
Seattle WA 128 E2
Seattle WA 129 A3
Boylston Av E
Seattle WA 128 D3
SW Brace Point Dr
Seattle WA 135 D2
Bradner Rd
Abbotsford BC 5 C4
E Braemar Rd
N Vancouver Dist BC 108 E2
Brainers Rd
Island Co WA 15 B6
Branch Rd
Yakima Co WA 37 D6
SW Brandon St
Seattle WA 131 E5
Seattle WA 132 A5
Brewster Rd
Lebanon OR 64 D1
Linn Co OR 64 D1
W Bridge Av
Spokane WA 211 E1
Bridge St
Clarkston WA 41 D6
Bridge St US-12
Clarkston WA 41 D6
SW Bridge St
Grants Pass OR 197 A5
Bridge Wy N
Seattle WA 128 B1
Bridge Creek Rd
Ferry Co WA 19 E4
Ferry Co WA 20 A4
Bridgeport Rd
Polk Co OR 54 A5
Bridgeport Wy SW
Lakewood WA 143 A7
Bridgeport Hill Rd NE
Douglas Co WA 18 D7
W Bridges Rd
Spokane Co WA 21 B6
Brinson Blvd
Bend OR 190 B4
Britton Rd
Bellingham WA 5 C6
Whatcom Co WA 5 C6
Broad St
Mt Vernon WA 116 B4
Seattle WA 128 C4
Broadmead Rd
Yamhill Co OR 54 B3
Broadmoor Rd
Island Co WA 15 C5
Broadway
Bellingham WA 113 C2
Everett WA 15 D7
Everett WA 120 D5
Seattle WA 128 D6
Broadway E
Seattle WA 128 D5
E Broadway
Eugene OR 185 E1
Eugene OR 186 A2
Vancouver BC 4 D2
Vancouver BC 110 C4
E Broadway PROV-7
Vancouver BC 4 D2
Vancouver BC 110 C4
E Broadway SR-99
Eugene OR 185 E1
Eugene OR 186 A2
E Broadway SR-126 BUS
Eugene OR 185 E1
Eugene OR 186 A2
N Broadway
Portland OR 161 E7
Portland OR 162 A7
Portland OR 165 E1
NE Broadway
Portland OR 162 A7
Portland OR 166 C1
NW Broadway
Portland OR 165 E1
SW Broadway
Portland OR 165 D3
W Broadway
Vancouver BC 4 D2
Vancouver BC 109 E4
Vancouver BC 110 A4
W Broadway PROV-7
Vancouver BC 109 E4
Vancouver BC 110 A4
Broadway Av
North Bend OR 193 E3
Snohomish Co WA 25 E1
E Broadway Av
Milton-Freewater OR 50 B3
E Broadway Av
Spokane WA 210 E7
Spokane Valley WA 210 E7
Spokane Valley WA 213 E3
Spokane Valley WA 214 A3
S Broadway Av
Boise ID 222 D7
Boise ID 224 D5
S Broadway Av US-20
Boise ID 224 D5
S Broadway Av US-26
Boise ID 224 D5
W Broadway Av
Moses Lake WA 29 A7
W Broadway Av I-90 BUS
Moses Lake WA 29 A7
W Broadway Av SR-171
Moses Lake WA 29 A7
Broadway Br
Portland OR 165 E1
SW Broadway Dr
Portland OR 165 D4
Broadway St
Coos Bay OR 193 E4
North Bend OR 193 E4
Seaside OR 154 C5
Vancouver WA 158 A3
Broadway St NE
Salem OR 171 E6
N Broadway St
Coos Bay OR 194 B6
N Broadway St US-101
Coos Bay OR 194 B6
S Broadway St
Coos Bay OR 194 B7
S Broadway St US-101
Coos Bay OR 194 B7
Bronson Wy N
Renton WA 138 C6
Bronson Wy N SR-900
Renton WA 138 C6
Bronson Wy NE
Renton WA 138 C6
Bronson Wy S
Renton WA 138 C6
Bronson Wy S SR-900
Renton WA 138 C6
Brookdale Rd E
Pierce Co WA 25 C7
S Brooks Rd
Spokane Co WA 30 E3
Brookswood Blvd
Bend OR 191 C5
Deschutes Co OR 191 B7
SW Brookswood Blvd
Bend OR 191 E2
Brooten Rd
Tillamook Co OR 53 C2
Brosterhous Rd
Bend OR 192 A3
Deschutes Co OR 192 B6
N Browne St
Spokane WA 212 A1
N Browne St US-2
Spokane WA 212 A1
N Browne St US-395
Spokane WA 212 A1
S Browne St
Spokane WA 212 A2
S Browne St US-2
Spokane WA 212 A2
S Browne St US-395
Spokane WA 212 A2
Browns Point Blvd NE
Tacoma WA 142 E1
Brownstown Rd
Yakima Co WA 37 C6
N Bruce Rd
Spokane Co WA 31 B1
Brush Creek Rd
Linn Co OR 64 D3
Bryant Av
Walla Walla WA 208 B4
Walla Walla Co WA 50 B2
Walla Walla Co WA 208 C4
Bryant Rd
Lake Oswego OR 169 A7
Buck Canyon Rd
Deschutes Co OR 191 C6
Buckhorn Rd
Deschutes Co OR 66 D3
Douglas Co OR 75 B5
Buckhorn Rd CO-17
Douglas Co OR 75 B5
Bucoda Hwy SE
Thurston Co WA 34 D3
Bucoda Hwy SE SR-507
Thurston Co WA 34 D3
Buena Rd
Yakima Co WA 37 E6
Buena Rd SR-22
Yakima Co WA 37 E6
Buena Wy
Toppenish WA 37 E6
Buena Wy SR-22
Toppenish WA 37 E6
Buena Vista Rd
Polk Co OR 54 B6
Bulldog Creek Rd
Stevens Co WA 20 E5
Bulldog Creek Rd SR-232
Stevens Co WA 20 E5
Burdett Av
Victoria BC 111 E5
Burgess Rd
Deschutes Co OR 77 B1
Burgess Rd CO-43
Deschutes Co OR 77 B1
Burien Frwy
King Co WA 136 D3
Seattle WA 136 C2
Burien Frwy SR-509
King Co WA 136 D3
Burien Frwy SR-509
Seattle WA 136 C2
Burley Dr
West Vancouver BC 107 D3
N Burlington Blvd
Burlington WA 115 B4
Skagit Co WA 115 B4
N Burlington Blvd SR-20
Burlington WA 115 B5
S Burlington Blvd
Burlington WA 115 B5
Burlington WA 116 B1
S Burlington Blvd SR-20
Burlington WA 115 B5
Burn Rd
Snohomish Co WA 15 E5
Burnside Br
Portland OR 165 E2
Portland OR 166 A2
Burnside Rd E
Saanich BC 111 D2
Victoria BC 111 D2
Burnside Rd W
Saanich BC 111 C2
Victoria BC 111 C2
View Royal BC 14 B2
W Burnside Rd
Portland OR 165 A2
E Burnside St
Gresham OR 168 B2
Multnomah Co OR 168 B2
Portland OR 166 B2
Portland OR 167 D2
Portland OR 168 B2
W Burnside St
Portland OR 165 C2
Burnt Mountain Rd
Clallam Co WA 13 B5
Burnt Mountain Rd SR-113
Clallam Co WA 13 B5
Burrard Br
Vancouver BC 109 D3
Burrard St
Vancouver BC 109 C5
Vancouver BC 110 A1
Burrard St PROV-7A
Vancouver BC 110 A1
N Burton Rd
Vancouver WA 159 A3
Burwell St
Bremerton WA 25 A3
Bremerton WA 122 A6
Kitsap Co WA 122 C6
Burwell St SR-304
Bremerton WA 25 A3
Bremerton WA 122 C6
Kitsap Co WA 122 C6
NE Butler Market Rd
Bend OR 190 C5
Deschutes Co OR 190 E4
Butte Falls Hwy
Jackson Co OR 87 E4
Butte Falls Fish Lake Rd
Jackson Co OR 88 B5
Butte Flls Fish Lake Rd CO-821
Jackson Co OR 88 B5
Butter Creek Rd
Umatilla Co OR 49 B7
Butteville Rd NE
Marion Co OR 54 D3
SE Bybee Blvd
Portland OR 166 B7
Bypass Hwy
Richland WA 203 A4
Bypass Hwy SR-240
Richland WA 203 A5
Byram Rd
Deschutes Co OR 66 E5
Byron Av
Bellingham WA 113 D5
Bz-Glenwood Hwy
Klickitat Co WA 46 D3

C

C Av
La Grande OR 60 C1
C St
Vancouver WA 158 A4
NE C St
College Place WA 50 B2
College Place WA 207 B5
Walla Walla WA 207 C5
S C St
Port Angeles WA 117 A3
W C St
Moscow ID 41 E3
W C St US-95
Moscow ID 41 E3
Cache Creek Rd
Ferry Co WA 19 D5
Cadboro Bay Rd
Oak Bay BC 112 C4
Saanich BC 112 E2
Victoria BC 112 C4
Cain Rd SE
Olympia WA 148 B1
Caldwell Blvd
Nampa ID 220 A2
Caldwell Blvd I-84 BUS
Nampa ID 220 A2
Caldwell Blvd SR-55
Nampa ID 220 A2
California Av SW
Seattle WA 25 C3
Seattle WA 131 D6
Seattle WA 135 D1
California Wy SW
Seattle WA 131 D1
Callahan Dr
Bremerton WA 122 C3
N Callow Av
Bremerton WA 122 A6
N Callow Av SR-304
Bremerton WA 122 A6
N Callow Av SR-310
Bremerton WA 122 A5
Cal Young Rd
Eugene OR 181 D5
Eugene OR 182 A5
Cambie Br
Vancouver BC 110 A3
Cambie St
Vancouver BC 109 E6
Vancouver BC 110 A4
Camden Rd
Pend Oreille Co WA 21 C5
SW Cameron Rd
Portland OR 165 A6
Cameron Wy
Mt Vernon WA 116 B3
Camp Adair Rd
Benton Co OR 54 B7
Campbell Rd
Klamath Co OR 90 A6
Camp Polk Rd
Deschutes Co OR 66 B3
Camp Polk Rd CO-2610
Deschutes Co OR 66 B3
W Campus Wy
Bellingham WA 113 B5
Canaan Rd
Columbia Co OR 44 D3
S Canal Blvd
Redmond OR 66 D4
Canby-Marquam Hwy
Clackamas Co OR 55 A3
SW Canyon Ct
Multnomah Co OR 165 A3
Portland OR 165 A3
Canyon Rd
Kittitas Co WA 37 D1
Canyon Rd E
Pierce Co WA 25 C7
SW Canyon Rd
Portland OR 165 C2
Canyon Creek Rd
Skamania Co WA 45 C6
Cape Arago Hwy
Coos Co OR 73 E4
Coos Co OR 193 A6
Capilano Rd
N Vancouver Dist BC 107 E4
N Vancouver Dist BC 108 A1
E Capitol Av
Ellensburg WA 37 D1
Capitol Blvd S
Olympia WA 145 E7
Tumwater WA 145 E7
Capitol Blvd SW
Olympia WA 145 E7
Tumwater WA 145 E7
Tumwater WA 147 D4
N Capitol Blvd
Boise ID 222 C7
S Capitol Blvd
Boise ID 222 C7
Boise ID 224 B1
SW Capitol Hwy
Portland OR 165 C7
Portland OR 169 A3
SW Capitol Hwy SR-10
Portland OR 165 C7
Capitol St NE
Salem OR 171 E7
Salem OR 173 E1
Capitol Wy N
Olympia WA 145 E5
Capitol Wy S
Olympia WA 145 E6
Carberry Creek Rd
Jackson Co OR 98 A1
Carey Rd
Saanich BC 111 D1
Carkeek Dr S
Seattle WA 137 B2
E Carlisle Av
Spokane WA 210 D6
Carlsborg Rd
Clallam Co WA 14 C5
Carman Dr
Lake Oswego OR 169 A7
S Carmichael Dr
Kennewick WA 206 B2
N Carr St
Tacoma WA 141 D2
SW Caruthers St
Portland OR 165 D4
SW Caruthers St US-26
Portland OR 165 D4
SW Cascade Av
Chehalis WA 152 C4
Cascade Hwy NE
Marion Co OR 54 E4
Cascade Hwy NE SR-213
Marion Co OR 54 E4
Cascade Hwy SE
Marion Co OR 54 E5
S Cascade St
Benton Co WA 206 B6
Kennewick WA 206 B6
Case Rd SW
Thurston Co WA 147 D7
Tumwater WA 147 D7
Casey Creek Rd
Garfield Co WA 41 B4
S Casto Rd
Clackamas Co OR 55 A2
E Catching Slough Rd
Coos Co OR 194 E7
Catherine St
Victoria BC 111 C4
Caves Hwy
Josephine Co OR 86 D7
Josephine Co OR 97 E1
Caves Hwy SR-46
Josephine Co OR 86 D7
Josephine Co OR 97 E1
Cays Rd
Clallam Co WA 14 C5
Cedar Rd
Nanaimo District BC 3 E3
Cedar St
Mission BC 5 D3
Plummer ID 31 E5
Cedar St SR-5
Plummer ID 31 E5
S Cedar St
Spokane WA 211 D3
Tacoma WA 141 C6
Cedardale Rd
Mt Vernon WA 116 B6
Skagit Co WA 116 B6
Cedar Grove Rd SE
King Co WA 25 E4
Cedar Hill Cross Rd
Oak Bay BC 112 C1
Saanich BC 112 B1
Cedonia-Addy Rd
Stevens Co WA 20 C4
Centennial Blvd
Springfield OR 186 D1
Springfield OR 187 B1
W Centennial Blvd
Eugene OR 186 C1
Lane Co OR 186 C1
Springfield OR 186 E1
Centennial Wy
Caldwell ID 219 B2
Centennial Wy I-84 BUS
Caldwell ID 219 B2
Centennial Wy SR-19
Caldwell ID 219 B2
Center St NE
Marion Co OR 174 C1
Salem OR 171 D7
Salem OR 173 D1
Salem OR 174 B1
S Center St
Fircrest WA 141 A6
Tacoma WA 141 B7
Tacoma WA 142 A7
Center Ridge Rd
Wasco Co OR 57 A1
Center St Br
Salem OR 171 D7
Center St Br SR-22
Salem OR 171 C7
Centerville Rd
Modoc Co CA 101 B7
Centerville Rd CO-54
Modoc Co CA 101 B7
Central Av
Oroville WA 8 E5
N Central Av
Medford OR 198 B5
N Central Av SR-99
Medford OR 198 B5
S Central Av
Medford OR 198 C6
S Central Av SR-99
Medford OR 198 C6
W Central Av
Coos Bay OR 194 A6
Central Wy
Kirkland WA 126 C6
Central Oregon Hwy
Deschutes Co OR 66 E6
Deschutes Co OR 67 B7
Deschutes Co OR 78 D1
Harney Co OR 79 D3
Harney Co OR 80 B3
Harney Co OR 81 A1
Malheur Co OR 70 E7
Malheur Co OR 71 E6
Malheur Co OR 72 A6
Malheur Co OR 81 C1
Nyssa OR 72 A6
Central Oregon Hwy SR-201
Malheur Co OR 72 A6
Nyssa OR 72 A6
Central Oregon Hwy US-20
Deschutes Co OR 66 E6
Deschutes Co OR 67 B7
Deschutes Co OR 78 C1
Harney Co OR 79 D3
Harney Co OR 80 D2
Harney Co OR 81 A1
Malheur Co OR 70 E7
Malheur Co OR 71 E6
Malheur Co OR 72 A6
Malheur Co OR 81 C1
Nyssa OR 72 A6
Central Oregon Hwy US-26
Malheur Co OR 71 E6
Malheur Co OR 72 A6
Nyssa OR 72 A6
Central Oregon Hwy US-395
Harney Co OR 79 D3
Harney Co OR 80 B3
S Century Dr
Deschutes Co OR 66 C7
Deschutes Co OR 77 A1
S Century Dr CO-42
Deschutes Co OR 66 C7
Deschutes Co OR 77 A1
SW Century Dr
Bend OR 191 D2
Deschutes Co OR 66 C6
Deschutes Co OR 191 A4
SW Century Dr CO-46
Bend OR 191 A4
Deschutes Co OR 66 C6
Deschutes Co OR 191 A4
Chalet Rd
North Saanich BC 4 B7
Chamber Wy
Chehalis WA 152 B2
Chambers St
Eugene OR 181 B7
Eugene OR 185 B3
Lane Co OR 185 B5
W Champion St
Bellingham WA 113 C3
Chandler Ln
Baker Co OR 60 E5
N Channel Av
Portland OR 161 C5
Chapel Dr
Benton Co OR 64 A1
S Charleston Blvd
Bremerton WA 122 A6
S Charleston Blvd SR-304
Bremerton WA 122 A6
SW Charlestown St
Seattle WA 131 D3
Chartwell Dr
West Vancouver BC 107 C2
N Chautauqua Blvd
Portland OR 161 C2
NW Chehalis Av
Chehalis WA 152 B4
Chelan Av SW
Seattle WA 132 A3
Chemawa Rd NE
Keizer OR 171 E1
Keizer OR 172 C1
Marion Co OR 172 C1
Salem OR 172 B1
E Chemical Dr
Benton Co WA 49 B1
Benton Co WA 206 E3
Kennewick WA 49 B1
Kennewick WA 206 E3
E Chemical Dr SR-397
Benton Co WA 49 B1
Benton Co WA 206 E3
Kennewick WA 49 B1
Kennewick WA 206 E3
S Cheney-Plaza Rd
Cheney WA 31 A4
S Cheney Plaza Rd
Spokane Co WA 31 B5
S Cheney Spangle Rd
Spokane Co WA 31 A4
W Cheney Spangle Rd
Spokane Co WA 31 B4
S Cheney-Spokane Rd
Spokane WA 31 B3
Spokane WA 211 D7
Spokane Co WA 31 B3
Spokane Co WA 211 D7
Cherry Av NE
Keizer OR 171 E4
Salem OR 171 E5
Cherry Ln
Ada Co ID 83 D2
Canyon Co ID 83 D2
W Cherry Ln
Meridian ID 83 D2
Cherry St
Port Townsend WA 119 D3
Wenatchee WA 27 E4
E Cherry St
Seattle WA 128 E6
Seattle WA 129 A6
W Cherry St
Centralia WA 151 D6
W Cherry St SR-507
Centralia WA 151 D6
SE Cherry Blossom Dr
Portland OR 167 D3
Chesaw Rd
Okanogan Co WA 8 E5
Okanogan Co WA 9 B6
E Chestnut St
Bellingham WA 113 C4
Walla Walla WA 208 A4
W Chestnut St
Bellingham WA 113 C4
Walla Walla WA 207 E4
Walla Walla WA 208 A4
Cheyne Rd
Zillah WA 37 E6
E Chicago St
Caldwell ID 83 C1
Caldwell ID 219 D3
W Chicago St
Caldwell ID 219 B2
Chico Wy NW
Bremerton WA 121 B4
Kitsap Co WA 121 B2
Chiloquin Hwy
Klamath Co OR 88 E4
Chiloquin Hwy SR-422
Klamath Co OR 88 E4
S Chiloquin Rd
Klamath Co OR 88 E5
China Hat Rd
Bend OR 191 E6
Deschutes Co OR 191 E6
Deschutes Co OR 192 A7
E Chinden Blvd
Boise ID 83 E1
Eagle ID 83 E1
E Chinden Blvd US-20
Boise ID 83 E1
Eagle ID 83 E1
E Chinden Blvd US-26
Boise ID 83 E1
Eagle ID 83 E1
W Chinden Blvd
Ada Co ID 83 D1
Boise ID 221 E7
Garden City ID 221 D6
W Chinden Blvd US-20
Ada Co ID 83 D1
Boise ID 221 E7
Garden City ID 221 D6

10 INDEX

INDEX 10

W Chinden Blvd US-26 — S Division St US-2

Street Index

STREET / City State	Map#	Grid
W Chinden Blvd US-26		
Ada Co ID	83	D1
Boise ID	221	E7
Garden City ID	221	D6
Chippendale Rd		
West Vancouver BC	107	B1
Chiwawa River Rd		
Chelan Co WA	27	C1
Chiwawa River Rd SR-3		
Chelan Co WA	27	C1
NE Chkalov Dr		
Vancouver WA	159	D5
SE Chkalov Dr		
Vancouver WA	159	D6
Chuckanut Dr		
Burlington WA	115	B4
Skagit Co WA	15	C2
Skagit Co WA	115	A2
Chuckanut Dr SR-11		
Burlington WA	115	B4
Skagit Co WA	15	C2
Skagit Co WA	115	A2
Chuckanut Dr N		
Bellingham WA	113	A7
Chuckanut Dr N SR-11		
Bellingham WA	113	A7
Church St		
Ashland OR	199	D3
Wilkeson WA	25	E7
Church St SR-165		
Wilkeson WA	25	E7
Cinebar Rd		
Lewis Co WA	35	B5
NE Circle Blvd		
Benton Co OR	178	C2
Corvallis OR	178	C2
NW Circle Blvd		
Corvallis OR	177	D3
Corvallis OR	178	B2
Cirque Dr W		
Tacoma WA	143	A3
University Place WA	25	B6
University Place WA	143	A3
Clackamas Hwy		
Clackamas Co OR	55	A1
Clackamas Hwy SR-212		
Clackamas Co OR	55	A1
Clackamas Hwy SR-224		
Clackamas Co OR	55	A1
Clare Av		
Bremerton WA	122	C4
Clarendon St		
Vancouver BC	110	E7
Clark Av S		
Republic WA	19	D1
Clark Av S SR-20		
Republic WA	19	D1
Clark Dr		
Vancouver BC	110	C4
NE Clark Dr		
Jefferson Co OR	56	E7
Clay St		
Cheney WA	31	A3
SE Clay St		
Portland OR	166	A3
SW Clay St		
Portland OR	165	E3
SW Clay St US-26		
Portland OR	165	E3
Clayburn Rd		
Abbotsford BC	5	D4
Clear Creek Rd NW		
Kitsap Co WA	25	A2
Clear Lake Rd		
Lane Co OR	64	B5
Lane Co OR	180	B2
W Clearwater Av		
Kennewick WA	205	C2
Cleman Rd		
Kittitas Co WA	37	D2
Cleveland Av SE		
Thurston Co WA	148	A2
Tumwater WA	145	E7
Tumwater WA	147	E1
Tumwater WA	148	A2
Cleveland Blvd		
Caldwell ID	83	C1
Caldwell ID	219	C4
Cleveland Blvd I-84 BUS		
Caldwell ID	83	C1
Caldwell ID	219	C4
SW Clifton Rd		
Kitsap Co WA	25	A3
Cline Falls Hwy		
Deschutes Co OR	66	D4
Clinton St		
Walla Walla WA	208	B2
Walla Walla Co WA	208	A1
S Clinton St		
Walla Walla WA	208	B3
Clise Pl W		
Seattle WA	127	C3
Cliveden Av		
Delta BC	4	E3
S Clodfelter Rd		
Benton Co WA	49	A2
Clover Creek Rd		
Klamath Co OR	88	C7
Klamath Co OR	99	D1
Cloverdale Av		
Saanich BC	111	E2
N Cloverdale Rd		
Boise ID	83	E1
S Cloverdale Rd		
Ada Co ID	83	E2
S Cloverdale St		
Seattle WA	136	D1
Cloverlawn Dr		
Grants Pass OR	197	D7
Josephine Co OR	87	A6
Josephine Co OR	197	D7
Clow Corner Rd		
Polk Co OR	54	B5
Club Rd		
Eugene OR	181	E7
Coal Creek Pkwy SE		
Bellevue WA	134	E4
S Coast Hwy		
Lincoln Co OR	53	B7
Newport OR	53	B7
S Coast Hwy US-101		
Lincoln Co OR	53	B7
Newport OR	53	B7
W Coast Rd		
Capital BC	13	E3
W Coast Rd PROV-14		
Capital BC	13	E3
Coast St		
Richland WA	203	C2
Coburg Rd		
Eugene OR	64	C5
Eugene OR	181	E7
Eugene OR	182	A5
Eugene OR	185	E1
Lane Co OR	64	C4
Lane Co OR	182	C2
N Coburg Rd		
Coburg OR	64	C4
Eugene OR	182	B3
Lane Co OR	64	C4
Lane Co OR	182	B2
N Cochran St		
Spokane WA	209	C5
Colburn Culver Rd		
Bonner Co ID	22	B2
Colby Av		
Everett WA	120	C1
N Cole Rd		
Boise ID	83	E1
Boise ID	221	B5
Boise ID	223	B1
S Cole Rd		
Ada Co ID	223	B5
Boise ID	83	E2
Boise ID	223	B5
N College Av		
College Place WA	207	B5
Walla Walla Co WA	207	B5
S College Av		
College Place WA	207	B6
Walla Walla Co WA	207	B6
S College Dr		
Bellingham WA	113	B6
E College Rd NE		
Marion Co OR	54	E4
N College St		
Newberg OR	54	D1
Yamhill Co OR	54	D1
N College St SR-219		
Newberg OR	54	D1
Yamhill Co OR	54	D1
E College Wy		
Mt Vernon WA	116	C2
E College Wy SR-538		
Mt Vernon WA	116	C2
NW College Wy		
Bend OR	189	C6
W College Wy		
Bellingham WA	113	B5
Mt Vernon WA	116	B2
W College Wy SR-538		
Mt Vernon WA	116	B2
N Collister Dr		
Boise ID	221	D3
E Colorado Av		
Nampa ID	220	C6
NW Colorado Av		
Bend OR	191	E1
Bend OR	192	A1
SW Colorado Av		
Bend OR	191	D2
Columbia Av		
Castlegar BC	10	E2
Fircrest WA	141	A6
Tacoma WA	141	A6
Columbia Av PROV-22		
Castlegar BC	10	E2
E Columbia Av		
Scappoose OR	44	E5
N Columbia Blvd		
Portland OR	44	E6
Portland OR	161	E2
Portland OR	162	A2
NE Columbia Blvd		
Portland OR	45	A6
Portland OR	162	A2
Portland OR	163	A4
NE Columbia Ct		
Portland OR	162	C3
E Columbia Dr		
Kennewick WA	206	C1
W Columbia Dr		
Kennewick WA	206	A1
NE Columbia Pkwy		
Portland OR	163	C5
NE Columbia Pkwy US-30 BYP		
Portland OR	163	C5
Columbia Rd		
Ada Co ID	83	E2
Columbia St		
Seattle WA	128	C7
Vancouver WA	157	E5
S Columbia St		
Seaside OR	154	B5
SW Columbia St		
Portland OR	165	D2
N Columbia Wy		
Portland OR	161	A1
SE Columbia Wy		
Vancouver WA	158	A5
Columbia Heights Rd		
Cowlitz Co WA	155	E2
Cowlitz Co WA	156	A3
Longview WA	155	E2
Longview WA	156	A3
Columbia House Blvd		
Vancouver WA	158	B5
S Columbian Wy		
Seattle WA	132	D3
Seattle WA	133	A4
Columbia River Hwy		
Irrigon OR	48	D4
Morrow Co OR	48	B4
Portland OR	161	C7
Umatilla Co OR	49	B3
Columbia River Hwy I-84		
Morrow Co OR	48	B4
Columbia River Hwy US-30		
Morrow Co OR	48	B4
Columbia River Hwy US-730		
Irrigon OR	48	D4
Morrow Co OR	48	D4
Umatilla Co OR	49	B3
S Columbus Av		
Medford OR	87	D6
Medford OR	198	A6
Columbus St SE		
Albany OR	176	A7
Linn Co OR	64	C1
Linn Co OR	176	A7
Colville Rd		
Esquimalt BC	111	B3
Commerce St		
Tacoma WA	142	A4
Commercial Av		
Anacortes WA	114	D3
Coos Bay OR	194	B6
Commercial Av SR-20 SPUR		
Anacortes WA	114	D3
E Commercial Av		
Coos Bay OR	194	B6
W Commercial Av		
Coos Bay OR	194	B6
Commercial Dr		
Vancouver BC	110	D3
Commercial St		
Astoria OR	153	C1
Commercial St US-30		
Astoria OR	153	C1
Commercial St NE		
Salem OR	171	D6
Salem OR	173	D1
Commercial St NE SR-99E BUS		
Salem OR	171	D6
Commercial St SE		
Salem OR	54	C5
Salem OR	173	D5
Commercial Diversion N		
Vancouver BC	110	D2
SE Concord Rd		
Clackamas Co OR	170	D7
N Conklin Rd		
Spokane Co WA	21	C6
Conway Rd		
Canyon Co ID	72	B7
Cook Av		
Jefferson Co WA	14	E5
Jefferson Co WA	119	A2
Port Townsend WA	14	E5
Port Townsend WA	15	A5
Port Townsend WA	119	A2
Cook Rd		
Skagit Co WA	15	C2
Skagit Co WA	115	A1
Cook St		
Saanich BC	111	E2
Saanich BC	112	A2
Victoria BC	111	E7
Victoria BC	112	A3
Cooley Rd		
Bend OR	66	D5
Bend OR	190	C2
Deschutes Co OR	189	E2
Deschutes Co OR	190	C2
Cooper Point Rd NW		
Thurston Co WA	145	B1
Cooper Point Rd SW		
Olympia WA	145	C7
Coos Bay-Roseburg Hwy		
Coos Co OR	73	E5
Coos Co OR	74	A6
Coquille OR	73	E5
Douglas Co OR	195	E7
Roseburg OR	195	E7
Coos Bay-Roseburg Hwy SR-42		
Coos Co OR	73	E5
Coos Co OR	74	A6
Coquille OR	73	E5
Douglas Co OR	195	E7
Roseburg OR	195	E7
Coos Bay-Roseburg Hwy SR-99		
Douglas Co OR	195	E7
Roseburg OR	195	E7
S Coos River Hwy		
Coos Bay OR	194	E7
Coos Co OR	194	E7
S Coos River Ln		
Coos Bay OR	194	D7
Coos Co OR	194	E7
Coos-Sumner Rd		
Coos Co OR	74	A4
Copalis Beach Rd		
Grays Harbor Co WA	23	B6
Copco Rd		
Siskiyou Co CA	99	A3
Copco Rd CO-A28		
Siskiyou Co CA	99	A3
Coquihalla Hwy		
Fraser Valley BC	6	D1
Coquihalla Hwy PROV-5		
Fraser Valley BC	6	D1
Coquille-Bandon Hwy		
Coos Co OR	73	E6
Coquille-Bandon Hwy SR-42S		
Coos Co OR	73	E6
Coquille-Fairview Rd		
Coos Co OR	74	A5
SW Corbett Av		
Portland OR	165	E4
SW Corbett Av US-26		
Portland OR	165	E4
Cordon Rd NE		
Marion Co OR	54	D5
Marion Co OR	172	E7
Marion Co OR	174	E1
Salem OR	172	E4
Cordon Rd SE		
Marion Co OR	174	E4
Salem OR	174	E4
Cordova Bay Rd		
Saanich BC	14	B2
Corliss Av N		
Seattle WA	124	D2
Corliss Wy N		
Seattle WA	124	D4
NW Cornelius Pass Rd		
Washington Co OR	44	E6
Cornell Av S		
King Co WA	137	E4
Seattle WA	137	E4
NW Cornell Rd		
Multnomah Co OR	165	A1
Portland OR	165	A1
Cornwall Av		
Bellingham WA	113	C3
Vancouver BC	109	B3
Corson Av S		
Seattle WA	132	D7
Corvallis Rd		
Polk Co OR	54	B6
Corvallis-Lebanon Hwy		
Linn Co OR	64	B1
Linn Co OR	178	C5
Corvallis-Lebanon Hwy SR-34		
Linn Co OR	64	B1
Linn Co OR	178	C5
Corvallis-Newport Hwy		
Corvallis OR	178	B6
Linn Co OR	178	B6
Corvallis-Newport Hwy SR-34		
Corvallis OR	178	B6
Corvallis-NewPrt Hwy SR-34 BYP		
Corvallis OR	178	B6
Linn Co OR	178	B6
Corvallis-Newport Hwy US-20		
Corvallis OR	178	B6
N Cottage Av		
Clatsop Co OR	154	C1
Gearhart OR	154	C1
S Cottage Av		
Gearhart OR	154	C2
Cottage Grove-Lorane Rd		
Lane Co OR	64	B7
Cottonwood Rd		
Deschutes Co OR	66	C7
Walla Walla WA	208	B6
Walla Walla Co WA	208	B6
Cottonwood Canyon Rd		
Yakima Co WA	37	B5
N Coulee-Hite Rd		
Spokane Co WA	30	E2
W Coulee-Hite Rd		
Spokane Co WA	30	E1
Coulee Meadows Rd		
Douglas Co WA	28	C4
Country Club Dr		
Bend OR	192	A5
Country Club Rd		
Clackamas Co OR	169	D6
Eugene OR	181	E7
Lake Oswego OR	169	C6
N Country Homes Blvd		
Spokane WA	209	D1
Spokane Co WA	209	D1
County Line Rd		
Humboldt Co NV	105	A2
Malheur Co OR	105	A2
County Line Rd SR-793		
Humboldt Co NV	105	A2
Malheur Co OR	105	A2
County Road 2-19		
Lake Co OR	90	D7
County Road 3-10		
Lake Co OR	91	C6
County Road 3-12		
Lake Co OR	91	C5
County Road 3-13		
Lake Co OR	91	B6
County Road 4-10		
Lake Co OR	77	D6
County Road 5-10		
Lake Co OR	77	E4
Lake Co OR	78	A5
County Road 5-14		
Lake Co OR	78	C5
Lake Co OR	79	A6
County Road 5-14F		
Lake Co OR	78	B6
County Road 5B		
Douglas Co OR	74	D6
County Road 5D		
Douglas Co OR	74	E6
Douglas Co OR	195	B6
Roseburg OR	195	B6
County Road 6		
Douglas Co OR	195	B2
Roseburg OR	195	C2
County Road 47		
Douglas Co OR	74	E6
County Road 51		
Douglas Co OR	74	E6
N County Road 112		
Modoc Co CA	100	C3
County Road 116		
Douglas Co OR	75	B1
County Road 404		
Harney Co OR	80	E7
County Road 1257		
Klamath Co OR	89	E5
County Well Rd		
Benton Co WA	48	D1
Court St		
Medford OR	198	B4
Court St SR-99		
Medford OR	198	B4
Court St NE		
Salem OR	173	E1
W Court St		
Pasco WA	39	B7
Pasco WA	204	B5
Cove Hwy		
Union Co OR	60	D1
Cove Hwy SR-237		
Union Co OR	60	D1
Cow Creek Rd		
Nez Perce Co ID	41	E5
Cowen Pl NE		
Seattle WA	124	E6
Cowlitz Wy		
Kelso WA	156	A3
Cowlitz Wy SR-4		
Kelso WA	156	A3
W Cowlitz Wy		
Cowlitz Co WA	156	A3
Kelso WA	156	A3
Longview WA	156	A3
W Cowlitz Wy SR-4		
Cowlitz Co WA	156	A3
Kelso WA	156	A3
Longview WA	156	A3
NW Coyner Av		
Deschutes Co OR	66	D3
E CR-104		
Modoc Co CA	100	C3
Craigflower Rd		
Esquimalt BC	111	B3
Victoria BC	111	B3
View Royal BC	111	A2
Crater Lake Av		
Medford OR	198	C3
Crater Lake Hwy		
Jackson Co OR	87	E3
Jackson Co OR	88	A2
Klamath Co OR	88	E3
Medford OR	198	D2
Crater Lake Hwy SR-62		
Jackson Co OR	87	E3
Jackson Co OR	88	A2
Klamath Co OR	88	E3
Medford OR	198	B2
W Creekstone Dr		
Kennewick WA	205	B5
Crescent Av		
Eugene OR	181	E4
Eugene OR	182	C4
Lane Co OR	182	C3
Crescent Rd		
Oak Bay BC	112	C6
Victoria BC	112	B6
Crescent Cut Off Rd		
Klamath Co OR	77	A3
Crescent Valley Dr NW		
Pierce Co WA	25	B5
Croisan Creek Rd S		
Salem OR	173	A4
Crooked River Hwy		
Crook Co OR	67	B7
Deschutes Co OR	67	B7
Crooked River Hwy SR-27		
Crook Co OR	67	B7
Deschutes Co OR	67	B7
Crosby Blvd SW		
Olympia WA	145	C7
Tumwater WA	145	C7
Crosscreek Dr		
West Vancouver BC	107	D2
Cross Creek Rd		
West Vancouver BC	107	C2
Crowfoot Rd		
Jackson Co OR	87	E4
Crowley Rd		
Malheur Co OR	71	B7
Malheur Co OR	81	E5
Crowsnest Hwy		
Okanagan-Similkam BC	7	E1
Okanagan-Similkam BC	8	D4
Crowsnest Hwy PROV-3		
Okanagan-Similkam BC	7	E1
Okanagan-Similkam BC	8	D4
Crowson Rd		
Ashland OR	200	D6
Jackson Co OR	200	D6
NE Cully Blvd		
Portland OR	163	A4
Cultus Bay Rd		
Island Co WA	15	C7
SW Culver Hwy		
Jefferson Co OR	66	E1
Metolius OR	66	E1
Curly Creek Rd		
Skamania Co WA	45	E2
N Curtis Rd		
Boise ID	221	D6
Boise ID	223	D1
Garden City ID	221	D6
S Curtis Rd		
Boise ID	223	D3
Custer Rd W		
Lakewood WA	143	A4
Custer Wy SE		
Tumwater WA	147	E1
Custer Wy SW		
Tumwater WA	147	E1
Cypress St		
Cowichan Valley BC	3	E6
Cypress St PROV-18		
Cowichan Valley BC	3	E6
D		
D Av		
Anacortes WA	15	B2
Anacortes WA	114	C3
D St		
Blaine WA	5	A5
Coos Bay OR	74	A4
Coos Bay OR	194	D7
Lewiston ID	41	E6
D St US-12		
Lewiston ID	41	E6
E D St		
Moscow ID	41	E3
Tacoma WA	142	B5
N Dairy Rd		
Saanich BC	112	B2
Victoria BC	112	B2
Dairy-Bonanza Hwy		
Klamath Co OR	89	C7
Dairy-Bonanza Hwy SR-70		
Klamath Co OR	89	B7
Dallas Rd		
Victoria BC	111	C5
Victoria BC	112	A7
N Dallas Rd		
Benton Co WA	49	A1
Dalles Military Rd		
College Place WA	207	C6
Walla Walla WA	207	D5
Walla Walla Co WA	207	D6
Damson Rd		
Snohomish Co WA	25	D1
N Danebo Av		
Eugene OR	180	C6
S Danebo Av		
Eugene OR	180	C7
Eugene OR	184	C1
E Danekas Rd		
Adams Co WA	30	B6
Darley Rd SE		
Marion Co OR	54	D6
Davis Av		
Nampa ID	83	C2
Nampa ID	220	B3
Davis Rd		
Siskiyou Co CA	100	A6
Dayton Av N		
Seattle WA	124	B1
S Dayton St		
Kennewick WA	206	B5
Dead Indian Rd		
Klamath Co OR	88	C6
Dead Indian Memorial Rd		
Ashland OR	200	D5
Jackson Co OR	200	D5
N Deadman Rd		
Garfield Co WA	41	B4
N Deal Rd		
Adams Co WA	29	C7
S Dearborn St		
Seattle WA	128	D7
Seattle WA	132	E1
S Dearborn St SR-167		
Seattle WA	128	D7
Decker Rd		
Benton Co OR	64	A2
Sherman Co OR	57	C3
Deer Creek-Boulder Creek Rd		
Ferry Co WA	9	E6
Ferry Co WA	10	A6
Deer Lake Rd		
Island Co WA	15	C6
E Deer Park Milan Rd		
Spokane Co WA	21	B6
Dejong Rd		
Polk Co OR	54	B4
Delaney Rd SE		
Marion Co OR	54	D5
N Delaware Av		
Portland OR	161	D2
Delbrook Av		
N Vancouver Dist BC	108	C2
S Delin St		
Tacoma WA	142	A7
Delmar Dr E		
Seattle WA	128	E2
Delridge Wy SW		
King Co WA	136	A2
Seattle WA	25	C3
Seattle WA	132	A6
Seattle WA	136	A2
Del Rio Rd		
Douglas Co OR	75	A5
Delta Hwy		
Eugene OR	181	D4
Lane Co OR	181	D3
Delta Line Rd		
Whatcom Co WA	5	B5
Deltaport Wy		
Delta BC	4	D4
Delta Waters Rd		
Medford OR	87	D6
Medford OR	198	C2
Dempsey Rd		
N Vancouver Dist BC	4	D1
Denman St		
Vancouver BC	109	D1
Denny Wy		
Seattle WA	128	C5
E Denny Wy		
Seattle WA	128	D5
Seattle WA	129	B5
W Denny Wy		
Seattle WA	128	A5
Densmore Av N		
Seattle WA	124	C1
N Denver Av		
Portland OR	161	D2
Depot Rd		
Lynden WA	5	C5
Derwent Wy		
Delta BC	4	E3
Deschutes Pkwy SW		
Olympia WA	145	D6
Tumwater WA	145	D7
Tumwater WA	147	E1
Deschutes Wy SW		
Tumwater WA	147	E1
Deschutes Market Rd		
Bend OR	190	E4
Deschutes Co OR	66	D5
Deschutes Co OR	190	E4
Deschutes River Rd		
Wasco Co OR	56	E3
W Desert Av		
Ada Co ID	83	E2
Ada Co ID	223	A7
Des Moines Memorial Dr		
Burien WA	136	E5
Burien WA	139	D4
Des Moines WA	139	D7
King Co WA	136	D7
Seatac WA	136	E5
Seatac WA	139	D7
Seattle WA	136	D2
Des Moines Memorial Dr SR-509		
Burien WA	139	D4
Seatac WA	139	C4
Devils Canyon Rd		
Franklin Co WA	39	E4
Devils Canyon Rd SR-263		
Franklin Co WA	39	E4
Dewatto Rd W		
Kitsap Co WA	24	D3
Dewatto Bay Rd		
Mason Co WA	24	D4
Dexter Av N		
Seattle WA	128	B2
S Diamond St		
Nampa ID	220	D6
Diamond Grain Camp Rd		
Harney Co OR	80	D7
Diamond Hill Dr		
Linn Co OR	64	B3
NE Diamond Lake Blvd		
Douglas Co OR	196	D5
Roseburg OR	196	B5
NE Diamond Lake Blvd SR-138		
Douglas Co OR	196	D5
Roseburg OR	196	B5
W Diamond Lake Hwy		
Douglas Co OR	76	B7
W Diamond Lake Hwy SR-230		
Douglas Co OR	76	B7
Digby Rd		
Mt Vernon WA	116	E4
Dike Rd		
Columbia Co OR	44	E5
Dillard Hwy		
Douglas Co OR	74	E6
Douglas Co OR	75	A7
Winston OR	74	E6
Dillard Hwy SR-99		
Douglas Co OR	74	E6
Douglas Co OR	75	A7
Winston OR	74	E6
Dillard Rd		
Eugene OR	64	C6
Eugene OR	186	A6
NW Dimmick St		
Grants Pass OR	197	B4
Discovery Av SE		
Ocean Shores WA	149	D5
Discovery Rd		
Jefferson Co WA	119	A5
Port Townsend WA	119	A4
S Discovery Rd		
Jefferson Co WA	119	A6
Port Townsend WA	119	A5
S Dishman Mica Rd		
Spokane Co WA	31	C2
Spokane Valley WA	213	C5
Division Av		
Tacoma WA	141	E4
Tacoma WA	142	A3
E Division Ln		
Tacoma WA	142	C7
Division St		
Palouse WA	41	D1
Division St SR-27		
Palouse WA	41	D1
Division St NW		
Olympia WA	24	D7
Olympia WA	145	C2
Thurston Co WA	145	C2
E Division St		
Mt Vernon WA	15	C3
Mt Vernon WA	116	E4
N Division St		
Spokane WA	209	E4
Spokane WA	210	A6
Spokane WA	212	A1
Spokane Co WA	209	E2
N Division St US-2		
Spokane WA	209	E4
Spokane WA	210	A6
Spokane WA	212	A1
Spokane Co WA	209	E2
N Division St US-395		
Spokane WA	209	E4
Spokane WA	210	A6
Spokane WA	212	A1
Spokane Co WA	209	E2
NE Division St		
Bend OR	190	A5
S Division St		
Spokane WA	212	A1
S Division St US-2		
Spokane WA	212	A2

12 INDEX

INDEX 12

NW Front Wy

High St NE

Street Index

STREET
City State Map# Grid

NW Front Wy
Chehalis WA 152 B4
N Frontage Rd
Tacoma WA 142 E5
S Frontage Rd
Tacoma WA 142 E5
Fruitdale Dr
Grants Pass OR 197 D7
Josephine Co OR 197 D7
Fruitdale Rd
Skagit Co WA 15 D2
Fruitvale Blvd
Yakima WA 37 C4
Fruit Valley Rd
Vancouver WA 157 D2
NW Fruit Valley Rd
Vancouver WA 157 D2
Fuhrman Av E
Seattle WA 128 D1
W Fulton St
Seattle WA 128 A2

G

G St
Gearhart OR 154 D2
Springfield OR 64 D5
Springfield OR 188 A1
E G St
Tacoma WA 142 B6
S G St
Tacoma WA 142 A7
Tacoma WA 144 A2
SE G St
Grants Pass OR 197 C5
SW G St
Grants Pass OR 87 A5
Grants Pass OR 197 B4
Josephine Co OR 197 B4
Gage Blvd
Richland WA 49 A1
E Galer St
Seattle WA 128 E4
W Galer St
Seattle WA 127 D3
NW Gales Creek Rd
Washington Co OR 44 B6
NW Gales Creek Rd SR-8
Washington Co OR 44 B6
Galice Rd
Josephine Co OR 86 D3
NW Galveston Av
Bend OR 189 D7
Game Farm Rd N
Eugene OR 182 C3
Lane Co OR 182 C3
Springfield OR 182 C3
Gap Rd
Linn Co OR 64 C3
N Garden St
Bellingham WA 113 C4
Boise ID 221 E7
N Garden Wy
Eugene OR 182 C7
S Garden Wy
Eugene OR 182 C7
Eugene OR 186 C1
Garden Spot Rd
Stevens Co WA 21 A5
NE Garden Valley Blvd
Roseburg OR 195 E3
Roseburg OR 196 A3
NW Garden Valley Blvd
Douglas Co OR 195 C2
Roseburg OR 195 C2
Garden Valley Rd
Douglas Co OR 195 B1
N Gardner Rd
Burlington WA 115 D4
Skagit Co WA 115 D4
S Gardner Rd
Burlington WA 115 D5
Skagit Co WA 115 D5
Garfield St
Eugene OR 185 B1
Garfield St SR-126
Eugene OR 185 B1
W Garfield St
Seattle WA 127 E3
W Garland Av
Spokane WA 209 D4
Spokane WA 210 A4
Garrity Blvd
Nampa ID 83 D2
Nampa ID 220 D3
Garrity Blvd I-84 BUS
Nampa ID 83 D2
Nampa ID 220 D3
N Gary Ln
Boise ID 83 E1
Boise ID 221 A1
Garden City ID 221 A2
N Gate Rd
Pierce Co WA 25 B7
Gates Hill Rd SE
Marion Co OR 55 B6
Gateway St
Lane Co OR 182 C4
Springfield OR 182 C4
Gazelle Callahan Rd
Siskiyou Co CA 98 E7
Gearhart Loop Rd
Clatsop Co OR 154 C1
Gearhart OR 154 C1
Geary St SE
Albany OR 176 A4
Gehring Rd
Pierce Co WA 144 E2
S Geiger Blvd
Spokane Co WA 211 A3
S Geiger Blvd I-90 BUS
Spokane Co WA 211 A3
S Gekeler Ln
Boise ID 224 D3

SW Gem Ln
Jefferson Co OR 66 D1
S Genesee St
Seattle WA 133 B4
SW Genesee St
Seattle WA 131 E4
Seattle WA 132 A4
S Genesee Wy
Seattle WA 133 C4
George Hopper Rd
Burlington WA 115 B7
George Hopper Interchange Rd
Burlington WA 115 B7
George Washington Br
Seattle WA 128 B2
George Washington Br SR-99
Seattle WA 128 B2
George Washington Wy
Richland WA 39 A7
Richland WA 203 D3
George Washington Wy SR-240
Richland WA 203 E7
G Washington Wy SR-240 BUS
Richland WA 203 D6
S Georgia Av
Caldwell ID 219 D5
W Georgia St
Vancouver BC 107 D7
Vancouver BC 109 E2
Vancouver BC 110 A2
W Georgia St PROV-1A
Vancouver BC 107 D7
Vancouver BC 109 E2
Vancouver BC 110 A2
W Georgia St PROV-99
Vancouver BC 107 D7
Vancouver BC 109 E2
Vancouver BC 110 A2
W Georgia St PROV-99A
Vancouver BC 110 A2
Georgia Viaduct
Vancouver BC 110 A2
Georgia Viaduct PROV-1A
Vancouver BC 110 A2
Georgia Viaduct PROV-99A
Vancouver BC 110 A2
NW Germantown Rd
Portland OR 44 E6
NE Gher Rd
Clark Co WA 159 D1
Vancouver WA 159 D1
SW Gibbs St
Portland OR 165 E4
NW Gibson Hill Rd
Albany OR 54 C7
Gifford Reubens Rd
Nez Perce Co ID 42 B5
Gilbert Rd
Richmond BC 4 D3
Yakima Co WA 37 C5
Gilbert Creek Rd
Yamhill Co OR 53 E2
SE Gilham Av
Portland OR 167 A2
Gilham Rd
Eugene OR 181 E5
Gilkey Rd
Linn Co OR 54 D7
Gillespie Rd
Capital BC 14 A3
Gilman Av W
Seattle WA 123 D7
Seattle WA 127 D1
Gilman Dr W
Seattle WA 127 E2
Glade Rd
Yakima Co WA 47 E2
Glade North Rd
Franklin Co WA 39 B7
Franklin Co WA 204 B1
Pasco WA 204 C1
Gladwin Rd
Abbotsford BC 5 D4
Glen Creek Rd NW
Salem OR 171 C7
Glendale Rd
Island Co WA 15 C7
Glendale Wy S
King Co WA 136 D4
Glenn Jackson Br
Multnomah Co OR 163 E1
Portland OR 163 E1
Vancouver WA 163 E1
Glenn Jackson Br I-205
Multnomah Co OR 163 E1
Portland OR 163 E1
Vancouver WA 163 E1
Glenwood Av
Everett WA 120 A7
Glenwood Blvd
Eugene OR 186 C3
Lane Co OR 186 C2
Springfield OR 186 C3
Glenwood Dr
Eugene OR 186 C3
Longview WA 155 C2
Glenwood Rd SW
Kitsap Co WA 25 A4
N Glenwood St
Ada Co ID 221 A3
Boise ID 221 A4
Garden City ID 221 A2
N Glenwood St SR-44
Ada Co ID 221 A3
Boise ID 221 A2
Garden City ID 221 A2
Glenwood-Goldendale Rd
Klickitat Co WA 46 D2
Klickitat Co WA 47 A3

NE Glisan St
Gresham OR 168 D2
Portland OR 45 A7
Portland OR 166 D2
Portland OR 167 D2
Portland OR 168 A2
NW Glisan St
Portland OR 165 E1
W Goddard Rd
Boise ID 221 A4
N Going St
Portland OR 161 D5
Gold Av
Greenwood BC 9 D4
Gold Av PROV-3
Greenwood BC 9 D4
S Gold St
Centralia WA 151 D6
Centralia WA 152 C1
Chehalis WA 152 C1
Lewis Co WA 151 D7
Lewis Co WA 152 C1
Gold Creek Rd
Kittitas Co WA 26 C4
Gold Creek Rd SR-906
Kittitas Co WA 26 C4
Goldendale Hwy
Klickitat Co WA 47 D3
Golden Gardens Dr NW
Seattle WA 123 C3
Golden Given Rd E
Pierce Co WA 144 C5
Tacoma WA 144 C4
Goldenrod Rd
Burlington WA 115 B5
Golf Dr S
Seattle WA 132 D1
Golf Course Rd
Island Co WA 15 A4
Goodpasture Island Rd
Eugene OR 181 C4
Gooseberry Rd
Ione OR 48 C7
Morrow Co OR 48 C7
Goose Creek Rd
Whitman Co WA 41 B3
Goose Creek Rd SR-194
Whitman Co WA 41 B3
Gordon Head Rd
Oak Bay BC 112 C1
Saanich BC 14 C2
Saanich BC 112 C1
Gorge Rd E
Saanich BC 111 C3
Victoria BC 111 D3
Gorge Rd E PROV-1A
Saanich BC 111 C3
Victoria BC 111 D3
Gorge Rd W
Saanich BC 14 B2
Saanich BC 111 C2
Victoria BC 14 B2
Victoria BC 111 C3
Gorge Rd W PROV-1A
Saanich BC 14 B2
Saanich BC 111 A2
Victoria BC 14 B2
Victoria BC 111 C3
Gose St
Walla Walla Co WA 50 B2
Walla Walla Co WA 207 B4
Goshen-Divide Hwy
Lane Co OR 64 C7
Goshen-Divide Hwy SR-99
Lane Co OR 64 C7
Gosney Ln
Deschutes Co OR 66 E6
Government St
Victoria BC 111 E4
N Government Wy
Coeur d'Alene ID 217 B7
Coeur d'Alene ID 218 B3
Dalton Gardens ID 217 B7
Dalton Gardens ID 218 B1
Hayden ID 217 B6
Kootenai Co ID 217 B6
Kootenai Co ID 218 B2
W Government Wy
Seattle WA 123 D7
Gov AD Rosellini Evergrn Pt Br
King Co WA 129 C2
Medina WA 129 E3
Seattle WA 129 C2
Gov Rsllni Evrgrn Pt Br SR-520
King Co WA 129 C2
Medina WA 129 E3
Seattle WA 129 C2
W Gowen Rd
Ada Co ID 84 A2
Ada Co ID 223 E7
Boise ID 84 A2
Boise ID 223 E7
Boise ID 224 A7
Gower Point Rd
Sunshine Coast BC 4 B1
Grade St
Kelso WA 44 D1
Kelso WA 156 B4
S Grady Wy
Renton WA 138 B7
S Grady Wy SR-515
Renton WA 138 B7
SW Grady Wy
Renton WA 140 E1
Tukwila WA 140 E1
Graham Blvd
Malheur Co OR 71 D6
SW Graham Rd
Jefferson Co OR 66 C1
S Graham St
Seattle WA 132 E6
Seattle WA 133 B6

E Grand Av
Everett WA 120 E2
NE Grand Av
Portland OR 162 A7
Portland OR 166 A1
NE Grand Av SR-99E
Portland OR 162 A7
Portland OR 166 A1
S Grand Av
Pullman WA 41 C3
S Grand Av SR-27
Pullman WA 41 C3
SE Grand Av
Portland OR 166 A3
SE Grand Av SR-99E
Portland OR 166 A2
Grand Blvd
North Vancouver BC 108 E4
Vancouver WA 158 C5
Grand Blvd E
North Vancouver BC 108 E6
S Grand Blvd
Spokane WA 31 B2
Spokane WA 212 A2
Grand St
Mission BC 5 D3
Grand Prairie Rd SE
Albany OR 54 C7
Albany OR 176 B5
Linn Co OR 176 E6
Grandview Hwy
Vancouver BC 110 E5
S Grandview Hwy
Vancouver BC 110 E5
Grandview Rd
Elmore Co ID 84 B6
Whatcom Co WA 5 A5
Grandview Rd SR-548
Whatcom Co WA 5 A5
Grandview Pavement Rd
Yakima Co WA 38 B7
Grandview Viaduct
Vancouver BC 110 C3
Grangemont Rd
Clearwater Co ID 42 E4
Granite Rd
Whitman Co WA 41 B3
Granite Falls Hwy
Snohomish Co WA 15 E6
Granite Falls Hwy SR-92
Snohomish Co WA 15 E6
Granite Hill Hwy
Sumpter OR 60 C6
Granite Hill Hwy SR-220
Sumpter OR 60 C6
NW Grant Av
Corvallis OR 177 E3
Corvallis OR 178 A3
Grant Rd
Douglas Co WA 27 E4
Douglas Co WA 28 A4
Grants Pass Pkwy
Grants Pass OR 197 D5
Grants Pass Pkwy US-199
Grants Pass OR 197 D5
Grants Pass Pkwy US-199 SPUR
Grants Pass OR 197 E5
Granville Br
Vancouver BC 109 D3
Granville Br PROV-99
Vancouver BC 109 D3
Granville St
Vancouver BC 4 D2
Vancouver BC 109 D4
Granville St PROV-99
Vancouver BC 4 D2
Vancouver BC 109 D5
Gravelly Lake Dr SW
Lakewood WA 143 A6
Gray Rd
Abbotsford BC 5 C3
Langley Township BC 5 C3
Grayback Rd
Josephine Co OR 97 E1
N Greeley Av
Portland OR 161 D5
Green Acres Rd
Eugene OR 181 D4
Lane Co OR 181 D3
Greenberry Rd
Benton Co OR 64 A2
Greencreek Rd
Idaho Co ID 52 D1
N Greene St
Spokane WA 210 D6
N Greenferry Rd
Post Falls ID 216 A5
S Greenferry Rd
Post Falls ID 216 A5
Green Hill Rd
Eugene OR 64 B5
Lane Co OR 64 B5
Lane Co OR 180 A1
E Greenhurst Rd
Nampa ID 220 D7
W Greenhurst Rd
Canyon Co ID 220 A7
Nampa ID 220 B7
Green Lake Dr N
Seattle WA 124 C4
E Green Lake Dr N
Seattle WA 124 C5
W Green Lake Dr N
Seattle WA 124 C5
Green Lake Wy N
Seattle WA 124 B7
E Green Lake Wy N
Seattle WA 124 C6
W Green Lake Wy N
Seattle WA 124 C6
Green Ridge Rd
Deschutes Co OR 66 B3

Green Springs Hwy
Ashland OR 200 D5
Jackson Co OR 98 E1
Jackson Co OR 200 E6
Green Springs Hwy SR-66
Ashland OR 200 D6
Jackson Co OR 98 E1
Jackson Co OR 200 E6
Greenwood Av N
Seattle WA 25 C2
Seattle WA 124 B3
NE Greenwood Av
Bend OR 190 A7
NE Greenwood Av US-20
Bend OR 190 A7
NW Greenwood Av
Bend OR 190 A7
Griffin Av
Enumclaw WA 25 E6
Griffin Av SR-164
Enumclaw WA 25 E6
Griffiths Wy
Vancouver BC 110 A2
S Grove Rd
Spokane Co WA 31 A3
Grove St
Marysville WA 15 D6
W Grove St
Boise ID 222 B7
Guard St
Friday Harbor WA 14 D1
Guide Meridian Rd
Whatcom Co WA 5 C6
Guide Meridian Rd SR-539
Whatcom Co WA 5 C6
Gull Harbor Rd NE
Olympia WA 146 A2
Thurston Co WA 146 A2
N Gum St
Kennewick WA 206 C2
N Gum St SR-397
Kennewick WA 206 C2
S Gum St
Kennewick WA 206 C2
S Gum St SR-397
Kennewick WA 206 C2

H

H Rd SE
Adams Co WA 39 A1
Grant Co WA 39 A2
H St
Blaine WA 5 A5
Nehalem OR 43 C5
H St US-101
Nehalem OR 43 C5
Haig Hwy
Kent BC 6 B3
Haig Hwy PROV-9
Kent BC 6 B3
Halladay St
Seattle WA 128 B2
NE Halsey St
Fairview OR 45 B7
Gresham OR 45 B7
Gresham OR 168 D1
Portland OR 166 D1
Portland OR 167 B1
Portland OR 168 B1
Halsey-Sweet Home Hwy
Linn Co OR 64 D2
Halsey-Sweet Home Hwy SR-228
Linn Co OR 64 D2
Hamby Rd
Deschutes Co OR 66 D5
Hamehook Rd
Deschutes Co OR 190 E2
Hamilton Av
North Vancouver BC 108 B4
N Hamilton St
Spokane WA 210 B7
Spokane WA 212 B1
E Hamlin St
Seattle WA 128 E2
Hammond Bay Rd
Nanaimo BC 3 D2
Hampton Rd
Whatcom Co WA 5 C5
Hanford Rd
Yakima Co WA 38 B6
Hanford Rd SR-241
Yakima Co WA 38 B6
SW Hanford St
Seattle WA 131 D3
Hannegan Rd
Whatcom Co WA 5 C6
Hansberry St NW
Kitsap Co WA 122 A1
Happy Valley Rd
Clallam Co WA 118 C7
Metchosin BC 14 A3
Sequim WA 118 B7
Harbor Av SW
Seattle WA 25 C3
Seattle WA 127 D7
Seattle WA 131 E1
E Harbor Dr
Warrenton OR 43 C1
SW Harbor Dr
Portland OR 165 E4
E Harder Rd
Adams Co WA 30 C7
Harding St
Richland WA 203 D6
Harding St SR-240 BUS
Richland WA 203 D6
Harkins St
Bremerton WA 122 D5
Harlan Dr
Klamath Co OR 89 A7
Harlow Rd
Eugene OR 182 B6

Harlow Rd
Lane Co OR 182 D6
Springfield OR 182 D6
Harmony Rd
Lewis Co WA 35 B5
Harmony Rd SR-122
Lewis Co WA 35 B5
SE Harmony Rd
Clackamas Co OR 170 E5
Milwaukie OR 170 E5
SE Harney Dr
Clackamas Co OR 170 E2
Portland OR 170 E2
Harrah Rd
Harrah WA 37 D6
Harrington Tokyo Rd
Harrington WA 30 B5
Lincoln Co WA 30 B5
Harris Av
Bellingham WA 113 A7
Harrison Av
Astoria OR 153 E1
Centralia WA 151 A3
Lewis Co WA 151 A2
Harrison Av NW
Olympia WA 145 C4
E Harrison Av
Coeur d'Alene ID 218 C5
N Harrison Blvd
Boise ID 222 B6
NW Harrison Blvd
Corvallis OR 177 E4
Corvallis OR 178 B5
Linn Co OR 178 B5
NW Harrison Blvd SR-34
Corvallis OR 178 B5
Linn Co OR 178 B5
NW Harrison Blvd US-20
Corvallis OR 178 B5
Harrison Rd
Yakima Co WA 37 D4
Harrison Rd SR-823
Yakima Co WA 37 D4
Harrison St
Seattle WA 128 B5
SE Harrison St
Milwaukie OR 170 C3
Harry Cash Rd
Siskiyou Co CA 99 B5
Hart Rd
Siskiyou Co CA 99 B5
S Hartford Av
Bremerton WA 122 A6
Hart Mountain Rd
Lake Co OR 91 D4
E Hartson Av
Spokane WA 212 E2
Spokane Valley WA 212 E2
Harvard Av E
Seattle WA 128 D2
W Harvard Av
Roseburg OR 195 D5
Roseburg OR 196 A5
W Harvard Av SR-138
Roseburg OR 195 E5
Roseburg OR 196 A5
Hastings Av
Port Townsend WA 119 B3
Hastings Av W
Jefferson Co WA 14 E5
E Hastings St
Vancouver BC 110 E2
E Hastings St PROV-7A
Vancouver BC 110 E2
W Hastings St
Vancouver BC 110 A2
W Hastings St PROV-7A
Vancouver BC 110 A2
S Hatch Rd
Spokane WA 212 B6
Spokane WA 212 B7
Hatfield Hwy
Klamath Co OR 100 B2
Hatfield Hwy SR-39
Klamath Co OR 100 B2
N Havana St
Spokane WA 210 E7
Spokane WA 212 E1
Spokane Valley WA 210 E7
Spokane Valley WA 212 E1
S Havana St
Spokane WA 212 E2
Spokane Valley WA 212 E2
Havana-Helix Hwy
Umatilla Co OR 49 E5
Havekost Rd
Anacortes WA 114 B6
Skagit Co WA 114 B6
N Haven Pl
Spokane WA 210 D4
N Haven St
Spokane WA 210 D3
Havillah Rd
Okanogan Co WA 9 A6
Havlina Rd
Franklin Co WA 39 D4
Hawkins Ln
Eugene OR 64 B6
Eugene OR 185 A2
Hawthorne Av NE
Salem OR 172 C4
Salem OR 174 B2
Hawthorne Av SE
Salem OR 174 B3
NW Hawthorne Av
Grants Pass OR 197 C3
SE Hawthorne Blvd
Portland OR 166 D3
Hawthorne Br
Portland OR 165 E3
E Hawthorne Rd
Spokane Co WA 31 B1
Haxton Wy
Whatcom Co WA 5 B7

E Hayden Av
Hayden ID 217 B4
Hayden Lake ID 217 C4
Kootenai Co ID 217 C4
W Hayden Av
Hayden ID 217 A4
Kootenai Co ID 31 E1
S Hayden Rd
Clackamas Co OR 55 B2
Hayden Bridge Rd
Lane Co OR 182 E6
Lane Co OR 183 A6
Springfield OR 182 E6
Springfield OR 183 A6
Hayden Bridge Wy
Lane Co OR 182 D6
Springfield OR 182 D6
NW Hayes Rd
Clark Co WA 45 A3
W Hayes St
Seattle WA 127 D3
Haynie Rd
Whatcom Co WA 5 B5
W Hays St
Boise ID 222 B6
SW Haystack Dr
Jefferson Co OR 66 E2
Hayward St
Mission BC 5 C3
E Hazel Av
Coeur d'Alene ID 218 D5
Kootenai Co ID 218 D5
Hazel St
Kelso WA 156 B5
NE Hazel Dell Av
Clark Co WA 45 A5
Clark Co WA 158 A1
Vancouver WA 158 A1
Hazelgreen Rd NE
Marion Co OR 54 D4
Marion Co OR 172 D1
Salem OR 54 D4
Salem OR 172 D1
Head St
Esquimalt BC 14 B2
Esquimalt BC 111 B4
Hebo Rd
Yamhill Co OR 53 E3
Hebo Rd SR-22
Yamhill Co OR 53 E3
E Helena Av
Ellensburg WA 37 D1
Heller Rd
Island Co WA 15 A4
Oak Harbor WA 15 A4
NW Helmholtz Wy
Deschutes Co OR 66 D3
SW Helmholtz Wy
Deschutes Co OR 66 D4
Hemlock St
Vancouver BC 109 D3
NW Hemlock St
Waldport OR 179 C4
NW Hemlock St SR-34
Waldport OR 179 C4
S Hemlock St
Cannon Beach OR 43 C3
Henderson Blvd SE
Olympia WA 146 A7
Olympia WA 148 B1
Thurston Co WA 147 E5
Thurston Co WA 148 A4
Tumwater WA 147 E5
Tumwater WA 148 B2
Henderson Pl SW
Seattle WA 136 B2
Henderson Rd
Oak Bay BC 112 C2
S Henderson St
Seattle WA 137 B2
SW Henderson St
Seattle WA 136 A2
Hendricks Rd
Franklin Co WA 39 A3
NE Hendricks Rd
Carlton OR 54 C1
Yamhill Co OR 54 C1
Heppner Hwy
Heppner OR 58 E1
Morrow Co OR 48 B5
Morrow Co OR 58 E1
Morrow Co OR 59 A1
Umatilla Co OR 49 B7
Heppner Hwy SR-74
Heppner OR 58 E1
Morrow Co OR 48 B5
Morrow Co OR 58 E1
Morrow Co OR 59 A1
Umatilla Co OR 49 B7
Herd Rd W
Cowichan Valley BC 4 A6
Herman Rd SE
Lacey WA 148 E1
Olympia WA 148 D1
Hewitt Rd
Nez Perce Co ID 42 A5
Hewitt Rd US-12
Nez Perce Co ID 42 A5
Hewitt Av
Everett WA 120 D3
Hewitt Av US-2
Everett WA 120 C3
E High Dr
Spokane WA 212 A6
S High Dr
Spokane WA 31 B2
Spokane WA 211 D5
W High Dr
Spokane WA 211 E6
Spokane WA 212 A6
High St
Eugene OR 185 E3
High St NE
Salem OR 171 D7

14 INDEX

INDEX 14

Street Index

Kuna Rd

E Main St

STREET City State Map# Grid

Kuna Rd
Canyon Co ID 83 D3
E Kuna Rd
Ada Co ID 83 E3
W Kuna Rd
Ada Co ID 83 D3
Kuna ID 83 D3
Kuna Mora Rd
Ada Co ID 84 A3
E Kuna Mora Rd
Ada Co ID 83 E3
Kyle Rd
Benton Co OR 64 A3

L

L St
Crescent City CA 96 E4
L St US-101
Crescent City CA 96 E4
E L St
Tacoma WA 142 C6
Labish Center Rd NE
Marion Co OR 54 D4
Lacey V Murrow Memorial Br
King Co WA 133 B1
Mercer Island WA 133 B1
Seattle WA 133 B1
Lacey V Murrow Mem Br I-90
King Co WA 133 B1
Mercer Island WA 133 B1
Seattle WA 133 B1
Lackey Rd KP N
Pierce Co WA 25 A5
Lacomb Dr
Linn Co OR 64 D1
Ladner Trunk Rd
Delta BC 4 E4
Ladner Trunk Rd PROV-10
Delta BC 4 D4
NE Lafayette Av
Bainbridge Island WA 25 B2
SE Lafayette Hwy
Yamhill Co OR 54 C3
N Lagoon Av
Portland OR 161 C5
Lagoon Rd
Colwood BC 14 B2
La Grande-Baker Hwy
Baker Co OR 60 E5
Haines OR 60 E5
Union Co OR 60 D2
La Grande-Baker Hwy SR-203
Union Co OR 60 D2
La Grande-Baker Hwy US-30
Baker Co OR 60 E5
Haines OR 60 E5
Union Co OR 60 D2
Lake Av
Harrison ID 32 A4
Lake Av SR-97
Harrison ID 32 A4
S Lake Av
Caldwell ID 83 C2
NW Lake Rd
Camas WA 45 B6
Clark Co WA 45 B6
Vancouver WA 45 B6
SE Lake Rd
Clackamas Co OR 170 E5
Milwaukie OR 170 C4
Lake St
Kirkland WA 126 C6
Lake St S
Kirkland WA 126 C7
Lake City Wy NE
Seattle WA 124 E4
Seattle WA 125 A2
Lake City Wy NE SR-522
Seattle WA 124 E4
Seattle WA 125 A3
N Lake Cushman Rd
Mason Co WA 24 C4
N Lake Cushman Rd SR-119
Mason Co WA 24 C4
Lake Dell Av
Seattle WA 129 A7
Lake Earl Dr
Del Norte Co CA 96 E3
Lake Earl Dr CO-D3
Del Norte Co CA 96 E3
SW Lake Helena Rd
Kitsap Co WA 25 A4
Lake Hills Connector
Bellevue WA 130 E7
Lake Louise Rd
Whatcom Co WA 5 C7
Lake Lowell Av
Nampa ID 220 A6
Lake of the Woods Hwy
Klamath Co OR 201 A7
Lake of the Woods Hwy SR-140
Klamath Co OR 201 A7
Lake Park Dr S
Seattle WA 133 B2
Lakes Rd
Cowichan Valley BC 4 A6
Lakes Rd PROV-1A
Cowichan Valley BC 4 A6
Lake Shore Dr
Canyon Co ID 83 C2
Lakeshore Dr
Coos Bay OR 193 D3
Klamath Co OR 88 E7
Klamath Co OR 201 A4
Klamath Falls OR 88 E7
Klamath Falls OR 201 B4
North Bend OR 193 D3
S Lakeshore Rd
Chelan Co WA 28 A1
S Lakeshore Rd SR-971
Chelan Co WA 28 A1
Lakeside Av
Seattle WA 129 B7
Lakeside Av S
Seattle WA 129 B7
Seattle WA 133 B1
Lakeview Av SW
Lakewood WA 143 B7
Lakeview Blvd
Lake Oswego OR 169 B7
Lakeview Blvd E
Seattle WA 128 D4
Lakeview Dr
Kirkland WA 126 C7
Kirkland WA 130 C1
Lakeview-Burns Hwy
Harney Co OR 79 E4
Lake Co OR 90 E5
Lake Co OR 91 B2
Lakeview-Burns Hwy SR-49
Harney Co OR 79 E4
Lakeview-Burns Hwy US-395
Harney Co OR 79 E4
Lake Co OR 90 E5
Lake Co OR 91 B2
Lake Washington Blvd
Bellevue WA 134 D1
Seattle WA 129 B6
Lake Washington Blvd E
Seattle WA 129 B5
Lake Washington Blvd N
Renton WA 138 C1
Lake Washington Blvd NE
Bellevue WA 130 A5
Clyde Hill WA 130 A5
Kirkland WA 126 C7
Kirkland WA 130 C2
Medina WA 130 A5
Newcastle WA 134 D7
Renton WA 134 C7
Renton WA 138 C1
Lake Washington Blvd S
Seattle WA 133 B2
Lake Washington Blvd SE
Bellevue WA 134 D3
Newcastle WA 134 C7
Renton WA 134 C7
E Lake Washington Blvd
Seattle WA 129 A2
Lakeway Dr
Bellingham WA 5 C7
Bellingham WA 113 D4
Lake Wenatchee Hwy
Chelan Co WA 27 B1
Lake Wenatchee Hwy SR-207
Chelan Co WA 27 B1
Lakewood Dr SW
Lakewood WA 143 A7
Lakewood Dr W
Lakewood WA 143 A5
Pierce Co WA 143 A5
Tacoma WA 143 A5
University Place WA 143 A5
Lakewood Rd
Snohomish Co WA 15 D5
Lakewood Rd SR-531
Snohomish Co WA 15 D5
Lamar Ln
Clallam Co WA 14 C5
N Lamonta Rd
Crook Co OR 67 A3
Lampson St
Esquimalt BC 111 B4
Lancaster Dr NE
Marion Co OR 172 C3
Marion Co OR 174 C2
Salem OR 172 C6
Salem OR 174 C1
Lancaster Dr NE SR-213
Marion Co OR 172 C6
Salem OR 172 C6
Lancaster Dr SE
Marion Co OR 174 C2
Salem OR 174 C4
E Lancaster Rd
Hayden ID 217 B1
Island Co WA 15 B6
Kootenai Co ID 217 C1
W Lancaster Rd
Hayden ID 217 B1
Kootenai Co ID 217 B1
S Lander St
Seattle WA 132 D2
Lands End Rd
North Saanich BC 4 B7
Lansdowne Rd
Oak Bay BC 112 E3
Saanich BC 112 B3
Victoria BC 112 B3
Lansing Ln
Canyon Co ID 83 C1
La Push Rd
Clallam Co WA 12 E7
Clallam Co WA 13 A6
La Push Rd SR-110
Clallam Co WA 12 E7
Clallam Co WA 13 A7
NE Larch Av
College Place WA 207 C5
SE Larch Av
College Place WA 207 C5
Larch St
Longview WA 155 D4
Larimer Rd
Everett WA 120 D7
N Larrabee Av
Portland OR 161 E7
Portland OR 165 E1
Larson Rd
North Vancouver BC 108 B4
Larson Rd Cres
North Vancouver BC 108 C4
Larwood Dr
Linn Co OR 54 E7
N Latah St
Boise ID 224 A1
S Latah St
Boise ID 84 A2
Boise ID 224 A2
Latham Rd
Lane Co OR 75 C1
Latona Av NE
Seattle WA 128 D1
Latoria Rd
Langford BC 14 A2
SE Laurel Ln
Jefferson Co OR 66 E2
N Laurel St
Port Angeles WA 117 C3
E Lauridsen Blvd
Port Angeles WA 117 C5
E Lauridsen Blvd US-101
Port Angeles WA 117 B5
W Lauridsen Blvd
Port Angeles WA 117 A4
N Laventure Rd
Mt Vernon WA 116 D4
Lawrence Rd
Whatcom Co WA 5 C6
Lawrence Rd SR-9
Whatcom Co WA 5 C6
Lawrence St
Port Townsend WA 119 E3
N Lawrence St
Tacoma WA 141 C2
Leary Av NW
Seattle WA 123 E6
NW Leary Wy
Seattle WA 123 E7
Seattle WA 124 A7
Seattle WA 128 A1
Lebo Blvd
Bremerton WA 122 B3
Le Clerc Rd N
Pend Oreille Co WA 11 B7
Leclerc Rd S
Pend Oreille Co WA 21 C4
Lee Blvd
Richland WA 203 C5
Lefeuvre Rd
Abbotsford BC 5 C4
S Lefevre St
Medical Lake WA 30 E3
Spokane Co WA 30 E3
S Lefevre St SR-902
Medical Lake WA 30 E3
Spokane Co WA 30 E3
Legoe Bay Rd
Whatcom Co WA 5 A7
Leif Erickson Dr
Astoria OR 153 E1
Leif Erickson Dr US-30
Astoria OR 153 E1
Leland Rd
Josephine Co OR 86 E3
Lemcke Rd
Grant Co OR 69 C4
Lemcke Rd US-395
Grant Co OR 69 C4
W Lemp St
Boise ID 84 A1
Boise ID 222 C5
Lenora St
Everett WA 120 D7
Leon Rd
Nanaimo District BC 3 A1
Nez Perce Co ID 41 D5
Whitman Co WA 41 D4
Leonard Rd
Lewis Co WA 35 A5
Leslie Rd
Richland WA 49 A1
W Leslie Rd
Benton Co WA 49 A1
E Lewis Ln
Canyon Co ID 83 D2
Lewis Rd
Clallam Co WA 14 C5
E Lewis St
Pasco WA 204 E6
W Lewis St
Pasco WA 204 D6
Lewis & Clark Br
Clatsop Co OR 153 A5
Cowlitz Co WA 155 C7
Rainier OR 155 C7
Warrenton OR 153 A5
Lewis & Clark Br US-101 BUS
Clatsop Co OR 153 A5
Warrenton OR 153 A5
Lewis & Clark Hwy
Camas WA 45 B6
Clark Co WA 164 E2
Vancouver WA 158 E5
Vancouver WA 159 B6
Vancouver WA 160 A7
Vancouver WA 164 D2
Lewis & Clark Hwy SR-14
Camas WA 45 B6
Clark Co WA 164 D2
Vancouver WA 158 A5
Vancouver WA 159 B6
Vancouver WA 160 A7
Vancouver WA 164 D2
Lewis & Clark Rd
Clatsop Co OR 153 A7
Clatsop Co OR 154 D3
Gearhart OR 154 D3
Seaside OR 154 D3
NE Lewisville Hwy
Clark Co WA 45 A4
NE Lewisville Hwy SR-503
Clark Co WA 45 A4
Lexington Av
Astoria OR 153 B2
W Lexington Av
Astoria OR 153 B2
Lexington-Echo Hwy
Morrow Co OR 48 D6
Umatilla Co OR 48 D6
Lexington-Echo Hwy SR-207
Morrow Co OR 48 D6
Umatilla Co OR 48 D6
Libby Dr
Coos Co OR 73 E4
Liberty Ln
Sherman Co OR 57 B2
Liberty Rd S
Salem OR 54 C5
Salem OR 173 B5
Liberty St NE
Salem OR 171 D6
Salem OR 173 D1
Liberty St NE SR-99E BUS
Salem OR 171 D6
Liberty St SE
Salem OR 173 D1
Lickman Rd
Chilliwack BC 5 E4
SW Lider Rd
Kitsap Co WA 25 A4
N Lieser Rd
Vancouver WA 159 B5
SE Lieser Rd
Vancouver WA 159 B6
Lilly Rd NE
Olympia WA 146 D4
Thurston Co WA 146 D3
Lilly Rd SE
Olympia WA 146 D5
Lincoln Av
Coquitlam BC 5 A2
Port Coquitlam BC 5 A2
Tacoma WA 142 D4
Vancouver WA 157 E3
Lincoln Av NE
Newcastle WA 138 C1
Renton WA 138 C1
E Lincoln Av
Sunnyside WA 38 B7
NW Lincoln Av
Vancouver WA 157 E1
Lincoln Rd
Caldwell ID 219 E2
Canyon Co ID 83 C1
Canyon Co ID 219 E2
Grants Pass OR 87 A5
Grants Pass OR 197 A5
Josephine Co OR 197 A5
E Lincoln Rd
Spokane WA 31 B1
Spokane Co WA 31 B1
Lincoln St
Bellingham WA 113 D5
Caldwell ID 219 D2
Canyon Co ID 219 D2
Eugene OR 64 C6
Eugene OR 185 D4
Hoquiam WA 33 D1
Lincoln St US-101
Hoquiam WA 33 D1
N Lincoln St
Port Angeles WA 117 C3
Spokane WA 211 E1
N Lincoln St US-101
Port Angeles WA 117 C3
S Lincoln St
Port Angeles WA 117 C4
Spokane WA 211 E2
S Lincoln St US-101
Port Angeles WA 117 C4
Lincoln Wy
Seattle WA 128 E1
N Lincoln Wy
Coeur d'Alene ID 218 B4
N Lincoln Wy US-95
Coeur d'Alene ID 218 B4
Lincoln Park Wy SW
Seattle WA 131 C7
Linden Av N
Seattle WA 124 B5
Linden Rd
Caldwell ID 83 C1
Canyon Co ID 83 C1
E Linden St
Boise ID 224 E4
Caldwell ID 219 D5
W Linden St
Boise ID 224 D4
Caldwell ID 219 A5
Canyon Co ID 219 A5
Linder Rd
Kuna ID 83 E3
N Linder Rd
Ada Co ID 83 D1
Meridian ID 83 D1
Lind-Kahlotus Rd
Adams Co WA 39 E2
Lind-Kahlotus Rd SR-21
Adams Co WA 39 E2
Lind-Ralston Rd
Adams Co WA 40 A1
E Lind-Warden Rd
Adams Co WA 39 D1
W Lind-Warden Rd
Adams Co WA 39 D1
Line St
Moscow ID 41 D3
Linton St
Coquitlam BC 5 B2
Linwood Av SW
Tumwater WA 147 D2
Lions Gate Br
Vancouver BC 107 D5
West Vancouver BC 107 D5
Lions Gate Br PROV-1A
Vancouver BC 107 D5
West Vancouver BC 107 D5
Lions Gate Br PROV-99
Vancouver BC 107 D5
West Vancouver BC 107 D5
Lithia Wy
Ashland OR 199 D3
Lithia Wy SR-99
Ashland OR 199 D3
Little Rd
San Juan Co WA 14 D2
Little Freezeout Rd
Canyon Co ID 72 C7
Gem Co ID 72 C7
Little Mountain Rd
Mt Vernon WA 15 C3
Mt Vernon WA 116 D5
Skagit Co WA 15 C3
Skagit Co WA 116 D5
Littlerock Rd SW
Thurston Co WA 147 C4
Tumwater WA 34 D1
Tumwater WA 147 D3
NE Lloyd Blvd
Portland OR 166 A1
Lockhaven Dr NE
Keizer OR 171 E1
Keizer OR 172 A1
Locust Av
Yakima Co WA 37 D4
E Locust Av
Coeur d'Alene ID 218 B4
Locust Ln
Canyon Co ID 83 C2
N Locust Grove Rd
Meridian ID 83 E1
Lodgepole Dr
Bend OR 191 D5
Logan Av N
Renton WA 138 B5
Logan Av S
Renton WA 138 B6
Logan Rd
Clatsop Co OR 43 D1
Log Cabin Rd SE
Olympia WA 148 B1
E Lolo Pass Rd
Clackamas Co OR 55 E1
NE Lombard Pl
Portland OR 162 B3
N Lombard St
Portland OR 44 E6
Portland OR 161 E3
Portland OR 162 A3
N Lombard St US-30 BYP
Portland OR 44 E6
Portland OR 161 E3
Portland OR 162 A3
NE Lombard St
Portland OR 162 C3
NE Lombard St US-30 BYP
Portland OR 162 A3
London Rd
Lane Co OR 75 C1
Lone Pine Ln
Coos Co OR 74 B5
Lone Rock Rd
Sherman Co OR 47 B7
Lone Star Rd
Nampa ID 83 C2
Nampa ID 220 B4
Long Av
Cowlitz Co WA 156 A3
Kelso WA 156 A3
Longview WA 156 A3
Long Creek Kimberly Rd
Grant Co OR 59 A6
Long Hollow Rd
Harney Co OR 92 C3
Long Hollow Rd SR-205
Harney Co OR 92 C3
Longmire Ln
Yakima Co WA 37 C3
Lonsdale Av
North Vancouver BC 108 D3
N Vancouver Dist BC 108 D3
Lookingglass Rd
Douglas Co OR 195 B5
Roseburg OR 195 B5
Lookout Hackmore Rd
Modoc Co CA 100 D7
Loosley Rd
Klamath Co OR 88 D3
Lorane Hwy
Eugene OR 185 C4
Lane Co OR 184 D7
Lane Co OR 185 B5
Lost Lake Rd
Hood River Co OR 46 B6
Snohomish Co WA 25 E1
Lotzgesell Rd
Clallam Co WA 14 D5
Lougheed Hwy
Coquitlam BC 5 A3
Mission BC 5 E3
Pitt Meadows BC 5 C3
Lougheed Hwy PROV-7
Coquitlam BC 5 A3
Mission BC 5 E3
Pitt Meadows BC 5 C3
W Louie Rd
Siskiyou Co CA 99 A6
Louisiana St
Longview WA 155 D4
NW Lovejoy St
Portland OR 165 C1
Lowell Rd
Everett WA 120 D6
Lowell Snohomish River Rd
Everett WA 120 E7
Lower Columbia River Hwy
Portland OR 161 C7
Lower Columbia River Hwy US-30
Portland OR 161 C7
Lower Deadman Rd
Garfield Co WA 40 E4
Garfield Co WA 41 A4
Lower Lake Rd
Del Norte Co CA 96 E3
Lower River Rd
Grants Pass OR 197 A5
Josephine Co OR 86 E5
Josephine Co OR 197 A5
NW Lower River Rd
Clark Co WA 44 E5
Clark Co WA 157 C2
Vancouver WA 44 E5
Vancouver WA 157 C2
NW Lower River Rd SR-501
Clark Co WA 44 E5
Clark Co WA 157 C2
Vancouver WA 44 E5
Vancouver WA 157 C2
Lower Waitsburg Rd
Walla Walla WA 208 A1
Walla Walla Co WA 208 A1
Lower Wolf Creek Rd
Josephine Co OR 86 E3
Low Level Rd E
North Vancouver BC 108 E6
W Loxie Eagans Blvd
Bremerton WA 121 E6
Kitsap Co WA 121 E6
Loyal Wy NW
Seattle WA 123 D4
S Lucile St
Seattle WA 132 C5
Luft Rd
Whitman Co WA 40 E2
E Lunceford Av
Coeur d'Alene ID 218 C2
SE Lusted Rd
Clackamas Co OR 45 C7
E Lynn St
Seattle WA 128 E3
W Lynn St
Seattle WA 127 C3
Lynn Valley Rd
North Vancouver BC 108 E4
N Vancouver Dist BC 108 E4
Lyon St N
Albany OR 175 D2
Lyon St N US-20
Albany OR 175 D2
Lyon St S
Albany OR 175 E2
Lyon St S US-20
Albany OR 175 E2
Lyons Ferry Rd
Columbia Co WA 40 B5
Walla Walla Co WA 40 B5
E Lyons Mill City Dr
Linn Co OR 55 A6
Mill City OR 55 A6
Lytle Blvd
Malheur Co OR 71 D6

M

M St
Hoquiam WA 33 D1
S M St
Port Angeles WA 14 B5
Tacoma WA 141 E7
Tacoma WA 143 E2
SE M St
Grants Pass OR 197 C5
SW M St
Grants Pass OR 197 C5
Mabton Hwy
Klickitat Co WA 47 E3
SW Macadam Av
Multnomah Co OR 170 A2
Portland OR 165 E6
Portland OR 169 E1
Portland OR 170 A2
SW Macadam Av SR-43
Multnomah Co OR 170 A2
Portland OR 165 E6
Portland OR 169 E1
Portland OR 170 A2
MacArthur Blvd
Vancouver WA 158 E4
Vancouver WA 159 A5
MacDonald St
Vancouver BC 109 B7
N Machias Rd
Snohomish Co WA 15 E6
S Machias Rd
Snohomish Co WA 15 E7
Mackenzie St
Vancouver BC 109 B6
Maclure Rd
Abbotsford BC 5 C4
Madison Rd
Umatilla Co OR 49 A5
Madison Rd SR-320
Umatilla Co OR 49 A5
Madison St
Everett WA 120 A7
Seattle WA 128 C6
E Madison St
Caldwell ID 219 C1
Seattle WA 25 C3
Seattle WA 128 D6
Seattle WA 129 A5
SE Madison St
Portland OR 166 B3
SW Madison St
Portland OR 165 E3
W Madison St
Caldwell ID 219 C1
NW Madras-Prineville Hwy
Crook Co OR 67 A3
Prineville OR 67 A3
NW Madras-Prineville Hwy US-26
Crook Co OR 67 A3
Prineville OR 67 A3
Madrona Av S
Salem OR 173 C5
Madrona Av SE
Salem OR 173 C5
Salem OR 174 A4
Madrona Dr
Seattle WA 129 B5
Magnolia Blvd W
Seattle WA 127 C3
E Magnolia St
Bellingham WA 113 C4
Magnus-Larson
Pierce Co WA 144 E5
Mail Rd
Adams Co WA 39 B3
Franklin Co WA 39 B3
Main Av S
Renton WA 138 C7
Main Av S SR-515
Renton WA 138 C7
Main Av S SR-900
Renton WA 138 C6
W Main Av
Spokane WA 211 E1
Spokane WA 212 A1
S Main Rd
Lebanon OR 64 D1
Linn Co OR 64 D1
Main St
Antelope OR 57 B5
Baker City OR 60 E6
Baker Co OR 61 D6
Bellevue WA 130 D6
Cove OR 60 E1
Edmonds WA 25 C1
Ferndale WA 5 B6
Fort Jones CA 98 D5
Homedale ID 83 A2
Kendrick ID 42 B4
Klamath Falls OR 89 A7
Klamath Falls OR 201 E5
Lane Co OR 186 D2
Lane Co OR 188 E2
Lynden WA 5 C5
Mansfield WA 28 D1
Okanagan-Similkam BC 8 D2
Owyhee Co ID 83 A2
Pomeroy WA 41 A5
Richland OR 61 D6
Rufus OR 47 B5
Siskiyou Co CA 98 D5
Springfield OR 64 D5
Springfield OR 186 E2
Springfield OR 187 B2
Springfield OR 188 A2
Steilacoom WA 25 B6
Sumner WA 25 D6
Sweet Home OR 64 E2
Tulelake CA 100 C2
Union Gap WA 37 D5
Vancouver WA 45 A6
Vancouver WA 158 A4
Vancouver BC 110 B6
Main St PROV-1A
Vancouver BC 110 B3
Main St PROV-3
Okanagan-Similkam BC 8 E4
Main St PROV-97
Okanagan-Similkam BC 8 D2
Main St PROV-99A
Vancouver BC 110 B3
Main St SR-3
Fort Jones CA 98 D5
Kendrick ID 42 B4
Siskiyou Co CA 98 D5
Main St SR-7
Baker City OR 60 E6
Main St SR-39
Klamath Falls OR 89 A7
Klamath Falls OR 201 C6
Main St SR-86
Baker Co OR 61 D6
Richland OR 61 D6
Main St SR-126
Lane Co OR 188 E2
Springfield OR 188 B2
Main St SR-126 BUS
Lane Co OR 186 D2
Springfield OR 64 D5
Springfield OR 186 E2
Springfield OR 187 B2
Springfield OR 188 A2
Main St SR-172
Mansfield WA 28 D1
Main St SR-218
Antelope OR 57 B5
Main St SR-237
Cove OR 60 E1
Main St US-12
Pomeroy WA 41 A5
Main St US-20
Sweet Home OR 64 E2
Main St US-97 BUS
Klamath Falls OR 89 A7
Klamath Falls OR 201 C6
Main St SE
Albany OR 176 A2
Main St W
Chehalis WA 34 D4
Chehalis WA 152 B4
Main St W SR-6
Chehalis WA 152 B4
E Main St
Ashland OR 87 E7
Ashland OR 199 D3
Ashland OR 200 A4
Hillsboro OR 44 D7
Jackson Co OR 200 A4

E Main St — **Street Index** — Mud Flat Rd SR-78

STREET / City State / Map# Grid

E Main St
John Day OR 69 D2
Klamath Falls OR 201 D5
Medford OR 198 B5
Molalla OR 55 A3
Othello WA 39 B2
E Main St SR-24
Othello WA 39 B2
E Main St SR-99
Ashland OR 199 D3
E Main St SR-211
Molalla OR 55 A3
E Main St US-26
John Day OR 69 C2
N Main St
Ashland OR 199 D3
Falls City OR 54 A5
Jackson Co OR 199 C2
Stanfield OR 49 B4
N Main St SR-99
Ashland OR 199 D3
Jackson Co OR 199 C2
N Main St US-395
Stanfield OR 49 B4
S Main St
Dallas OR 54 B5
Jefferson OR 54 C7
Marion Co OR 54 C7
Milton-Freewater OR 50 A3
Pendleton OR 49 D5
Willamina OR 54 A3
Yreka CA 98 E4
S Main St SR-3
Yreka CA 98 E4
S Main St SR-11
Milton-Freewater OR 50 A3
S Main St SR-18 BUS
Willamina OR 54 A3
S Main St SR-223
Dallas OR 54 B5
SE Main St
Milwaukie OR 170 B4
SW Main St
Portland OR 165 E3
W Main St
Boise ID 221 E7
Boise ID 222 B6
Centralia WA 151 C5
Cowlitz Co WA 156 A3
Kelso WA 156 A3
Long Creek OR 59 B7
Medford OR 198 B6
Monroe WA 25 E1
Malden Rd
Whitman Co WA 31 B6
Malone Rd
Klamath Co OR 100 B2
Siskiyou Co CA 100 B2
Maltby Rd
Snohomish Co WA 25 D1
Maltby Rd SR-524
Snohomish Co WA 25 D1
Manbrin Dr NE
Keizer OR 171 E3
Manette Br
Bremerton WA 122 C5
Kitsap Co WA 122 C5
SW Manning St
Seattle WA 131 E3
W Manor Pl
Seattle WA 127 D1
Manson Av
Powell River BC 1 A4
Maple St
Everett WA 120 D3
Nampa ID 220 C6
Maple St SR-529
Everett WA 120 D3
E Maple St
Bellingham WA 113 D5
N Maple St
Spokane WA 209 D2
S Maple St
Spokane WA 211 D1
Maple Bay Rd
Cowichan Valley BC 4 A6
Maple Grove Rd
Polk Co OR 54 A6
N Maple Grove Rd
Boise ID 223 A2
S Maple Grove Rd
Ada Co ID 83 E2
Ada Co ID 223 A4
Boise ID 223 A2
Maple Heights Rd
Everett WA 120 A7
S Maplelane Rd
Clackamas Co OR 55 A1
Maple Street Br
Spokane WA 209 D7
Spokane WA 211 D1
Mapleton-Junction City Hwy
Lane Co OR 64 A4
Mplton-Junction Cty Hwy SR-36
Lane Co OR 64 A4
Maple Valley Hwy
Renton WA 138 D7
Maple Valley Hwy SR-169
Renton WA 138 D7
SE Maple Valley Hwy
Renton WA 138 C6
SE Maple Valley Hwy SR-169
Renton WA 138 C6
Mapleway Rd
Yakima Co WA 37 C4
Maplewild Av SW
Burien WA 139 A1
W Maplewood Av
Bellingham WA 113 B1
Maplewood Rd
Saanich BC 112 A2
Maplewood Rd
Victoria BC 112 A2
Marble Front Rd
Caldwell ID 219 D2
Marcola Rd
Lane Co OR 64 E4
Lane Co OR 183 D7
Springfield OR 183 B7
E Margaret Av
Coeur d'Alene ID 218 B2
Kootenai Co ID 218 B2
E Marginal Wy S
Seattle WA 132 C2
Seattle WA 136 E1
Tukwila WA 136 E1
Tukwila WA 137 A2
E Marginal Wy S SR-99
Seattle WA 132 C5
W Marginal Wy S
Seattle WA 132 C7
W Marginal Wy SW
Seattle WA 132 C7
Marine Av
Powell River BC 1 A4
Marine Av PROV-101
Powell River BC 1 A4
Marine Dr
Astoria OR 153 D1
Burnaby BC 4 E3
North Vancouver BC 108 B4
N Vancouver Dist BC 107 E4
N Vancouver Dist BC 108 B4
Port Angeles WA 117 B3
Skagit Co WA 15 A2
Skagit Co WA 114 A5
Snohomish Co WA 15 C5
Surrey BC 4 E4
West Vancouver BC 4 C2
West Vancouver BC 107 D4
Whatcom Co WA 5 B7
Marine Dr PROV-1A
West Vancouver BC 107 E4
Marine Dr PROV-99
West Vancouver BC 107 E4
Marine Dr US-30
Astoria OR 153 D1
N Marine Dr
Portland OR 44 E6
Portland OR 157 A5
Portland OR 158 A7
NE Marine Dr
Gresham OR 164 E5
Portland OR 158 A7
Portland OR 163 B1
Portland OR 164 A4
NW Marine Dr
Vancouver BC 4 C2
SW Marine Dr
Vancouver BC 109 A7
W Marine Dr
Astoria OR 43 D1
Astoria OR 153 A2
W Marine Dr SR-202
Astoria OR 43 D1
Astoria OR 153 A2
W Marine Dr US-26
Astoria OR 153 B1
W Marine Dr US-30
Astoria OR 153 B1
W Marine Dr US-101
Astoria OR 153 A2
W Marine Dr US-101 BUS
Astoria OR 43 D1
Astoria OR 153 A2
N Marine Wy
Portland OR 157 E7
Mariner Wy
Coquitlam BC 5 A2
Marine View Dr
Tacoma WA 25 C5
Tacoma WA 142 D1
Marine View Dr SR-509
Tacoma WA 25 C5
Tacoma WA 142 D1
Marine View Dr S
Des Moines WA 139 C7
Marine View Dr S SR-509
Des Moines WA 139 C7
Marine View Dr SE
Ocean Shores WA 149 C5
Marine View Dr SW
Burien WA 139 A2
Normandy Park WA 139 B4
Ocean Shores WA 149 A5
Seattle WA 135 D3
E Marine View Dr
Everett WA 120 E1
W Marine View Dr
Everett WA 120 C1
W Marine View Dr SR-529
Everett WA 120 C1
Marion Rd SE
Marion Co OR 54 D6
Marion St
King Co WA 128 C7
Seattle WA 128 C7
Marion St NE
Salem OR 171 D7
Salem OR 173 E1
Marion St NE SR-22
Salem OR 171 D7
Marion St SE
Albany OR 54 C7
Albany OR 175 E4
Marion St Br
Salem OR 171 D7
Marion St Br SR-22
Salem OR 171 D7
N Market Blvd
Chehalis WA 152 B4
S Market Blvd
Chehalis WA 152 C4
Lewis Co WA 152 E6
N Market Pl
Spokane WA 210 D2
Market Rd
Canyon Co ID 72 B7
S Market Rd
Umatilla Co OR 49 E6
S Market Rd SR-331
Umatilla Co OR 49 E6
SE Market Rd
Clackamas Co OR 45 B7
SE Market Rd SR-212
Clackamas Co OR 45 B7
Market St
Bonanza OR 89 C7
Kirkland WA 126 C5
Tacoma WA 142 A4
Market St NE
Salem OR 171 E7
Salem OR 172 A7
Market St NE SR-213
Salem OR 172 C7
N Market St
Seattle WA 124 B7
Spokane WA 210 D4
Spokane Co WA 210 D2
NW Market St
Seattle WA 123 D6
Seattle WA 124 A6
SW Market St
Portland OR 165 D3
SW Market St US-26
Portland OR 165 D3
E Marmot Rd
Clackamas Co OR 55 D1
Marquam Br
Portland OR 165 E3
Portland OR 166 A3
Marquam Br I-5
Portland OR 165 E3
Portland OR 166 A3
E Marquam Rd NE
Marion Co OR 54 E3
Mt Angel OR 54 E3
Marshall Rd
Abbotsford BC 5 D4
Marsing Rd
Canyon Co ID 83 B2
NW Martin Rd
Washington Co OR 44 C6
W Martin Rd
Spokane Co WA 30 E5
Martin Wy E
Olympia WA 146 D5
Martin Luther King Jr Blvd
Eugene OR 181 E7
Eugene OR 182 A7
Eugene OR 186 B1
Lane Co OR 186 C1
N Martin Luther King Jr Blvd
Portland OR 157 E7
Portland OR 161 E1
Portland OR 162 A1
N Martin L King Jr Blvd SR-99E
Portland OR 157 E7
Portland OR 161 E1
Portland OR 162 A1
NE Martin Luther King Jr Blvd
Portland OR 162 A5
Portland OR 166 A2
NE ML King Jr Blvd SR-99E
Portland OR 162 A7
Portland OR 166 A2
SE Martin Luther King Jr Blvd
Portland OR 166 A2
SE ML King Jr Blvd SR-99E
Portland OR 166 A2
Martin Luther King Jr Pkwy
Lane Co OR 182 D5
Springfield OR 182 D5
Martin Luther King Jr Wy
King Co WA 137 C5
Renton WA 137 D6
Seattle WA 129 A6
Seattle WA 137 C5
Tukwila WA 137 C5
Martin L King Jr Wy SR-900
King Co WA 137 C5
Renton WA 137 D6
Seattle WA 137 C5
Tukwila WA 137 C5
Martin Luther King Jr Wy E
Seattle WA 129 A5
Martin Luther King Jr Wy S
Seattle WA 129 A7
Seattle WA 133 A5
Seattle WA 137 B3
Tukwila WA 137 B3
Martin L King Jr Wy S SR-900
Seattle WA 137 B3
Tukwila WA 137 B3
Marvin Rd NE
Lacey WA 24 E7
Thurston Co WA 24 E7
Marx St
Idaho Co ID 52 D7
Riggins ID 52 D7
Marx St US-95
Idaho Co ID 52 D7
Riggins ID 52 D7
Mary Gates Memorial Dr NE
Seattle WA 125 A7
Mary Hill Byp
Port Coquitlam BC 5 A3
Mary Hill Byp PROV-7B
Port Coquitlam BC 5 A3
S Massachusetts St
Seattle WA 132 E1
Seattle WA 133 A1
Mather Memorial Pkwy
Pierce Co WA 36 C2
Mather Memorial Pkwy SR-410
Pierce Co WA 36 C2
Mathers Av
West Vancouver BC 107 B2
Matlock Brady Rd
Mason Co WA 24 A6
W Maxwell Av
Spokane WA 209 D7
Maxwell Rd
Eugene OR 64 B5
Eugene OR 180 E4
Eugene OR 181 B4
Lane Co OR 180 E4
Maxwell Conn
Eugene OR 180 E4
Maytown Rd SW
Thurston Co WA 34 D2
SE May Valley Rd
King Co WA 25 E4
E McAndrews Rd
Jackson Co OR 198 A4
Medford OR 198 D4
W McAndrews Rd
Jackson Co OR 198 A4
Medford OR 198 A5
N McCarver St
Tacoma WA 141 E2
S McClellan St
Seattle WA 132 E2
Seattle WA 133 A2
Spokane WA 211 E2
S McDermott Rd
Ada Co ID 83 D4
McGill St
Vancouver BC 4 D2
Vancouver BC 110 E1
SE McGillivray Blvd
Vancouver WA 159 E6
Vancouver WA 160 A6
McGrath Rd
Deschutes Co OR 66 E5
W McGraw Pl
Seattle WA 128 A2
W McGraw St
Seattle WA 128 A3
McKay Rd
Crook Co OR 67 B3
McKenzie Av
Saanich BC 14 B2
Saanich BC 111 B1
McKenzie Hwy
Deschutes Co OR 66 C3
Lane Co OR 64 E5
Linn Co OR 66 A3
Springfield OR 64 C5
Springfield OR 182 D7
Springfield OR 183 B7
Springfield OR 187 E1
Springfield OR 188 A1
McKenzie Hwy SR-126
Deschutes Co OR 66 C3
Lane Co OR 64 E5
Springfield OR 64 C5
Springfield OR 182 E7
Springfield OR 183 B7
Springfield OR 187 E1
Springfield OR 188 A1
McKenzie Hwy SR-242
Linn Co OR 66 A3
McKenzie Rd
Pend Oreille Co WA 21 B3
McKenzie View Dr
Lane Co OR 64 C5
Lane Co OR 182 D2
Lane Co OR 183 A4
McKinley Av E
Pierce Co WA 144 C6
Tacoma WA 144 C5
E McKinley Av
Pierce Co WA 144 C4
Tacoma WA 142 C7
Tacoma WA 144 C3
McKinley Wy
Tacoma WA 142 B7
McKinley Springs Rd
Benton Co WA 48 C2
E McLoughlin Blvd
Vancouver WA 158 B4
SE McLoughlin Blvd
Clackamas Co OR 170 C6
Milwaukie OR 170 B4
Portland OR 166 A5
Portland OR 170 C1
SE McLoughlin Blvd SR-99E
Clackamas Co OR 170 C6
Milwaukie OR 170 B4
Portland OR 166 A5
Portland OR 170 C1
W McLoughlin Blvd
Vancouver WA 157 E3
Vancouver WA 158 A3
W McManamon Rd
Adams Co WA 39 A2
W McMillan Rd
Boise ID 83 E1
McMurray Rd NE
Tacoma WA 142 E1
McNab Ln
Morrow Co OR 48 B7
McTavish Rd
Abbotsford BC 5 C3
North Saanich BC 14 B1
McVay Hwy
Lane Co OR 186 E5
McVey Av
Lake Oswego OR 169 E7
NW Meadowlake Rd
Yamhill Co OR 54 B1
Meadows Rd
Jackson Co OR 87 C4
Medical Springs Hwy
Union Co OR 60 E2
Medical Springs Hwy SR-203
Union Co OR 60 E2
Medicine Lake Rd
Siskiyou Co CA 100 B5
Meissner Rd
Columbia Co OR 44 D3
Melba Rd
Canyon Co ID 83 C4
Mellen St
Centralia WA 151 B5
Mellen St SR-507
Centralia WA 151 B5
Melrose Rd
Douglas Co OR 195 A2
Melrose Rd CO-167
Douglas Co OR 195 A2
Melrose St
Lake Oswego OR 169 A5
Walla Walla WA 208 A2
Melville St
Vancouver BC 109 E1
Melville St PROV-1A
Vancouver BC 109 E1
Melville St PROV-99A
Vancouver BC 109 E1
Memorial Hwy
Mt Vernon WA 116 A3
Skagit Co WA 116 A3
Memorial Hwy SR-536
Mt Vernon WA 116 A3
Skagit Co WA 116 A3
W Mercer Pl
Seattle WA 128 A4
Mercer St
Seattle WA 128 C4
W Mercer St
Seattle WA 128 A4
E Mercer Wy
Mercer Island WA 134 B6
Mercer Island WA 138 A1
W Mercer Wy
Mercer Island WA 133 D2
Mercer Island WA 134 A6
Mercer Island WA 137 E1
Mercer Island WA 138 A1
Mercerwood Dr
Mercer Island WA 134 B3
Meridian E
Pierce Co WA 25 C7
Meridian E SR-161
Pierce Co WA 25 C7
S Meridian
Puyallup WA 25 C6
Meridian Av E
Pierce Co WA 25 C7
Pierce Co WA 35 C1
Meridian Av E SR-161
Pierce Co WA 25 C7
Pierce Co WA 35 C1
Meridian Av N
Seattle WA 124 C1
Shoreline WA 25 C1
N Meridian Rd
Meridian ID 83 E1
S Meridian Rd
Ada Co ID 83 E2
S Meridian Rd SR-69
Ada Co ID 83 E2
Meridian St
Bellingham WA 113 C1
Merlin Rd
Josephine Co OR 86 E4
S Merrill Rd
Klamath Co OR 100 B2
Siskiyou Co CA 100 B2
Merrill Creek Pkwy
Everett WA 120 A7
Merriman Rd
Central Point OR 198 A2
Jackson Co OR 198 A1
Medford OR 198 A2
Merrimount Dr
Mercer Island WA 134 A4
Metchosin Rd
Metchosin BC 14 B3
N Meyers Rd
Yakima Co WA 37 E7
Miami River Rd
Tillamook Co OR 43 D5
Michigan Av
Orofino ID 42 D5
S Michigan St
Seattle WA 132 C6
Middle Satsop Rd
Grays Harbor Co WA 24 A7
Middleton Rd
Canyon Co ID 83 C1
N Midland Blvd
Nampa ID 220 A2
S Midland Blvd
Canyon Co ID 220 A7
Nampa ID 83 C2
Nampa ID 220 A6
Midlothian Av
Vancouver BC 110 A6
N Midvale Pl
Seattle WA 124 C7
N Milan Rd
Spokane Co WA 21 B7
SE Mile Hill Dr
Kitsap Co WA 25 B3
SE Mile Hill Dr SR-160
Kitsap Co WA 25 B3
Miles-Creston Rd
Lincoln Co WA 20 B7
Lincoln Co WA 30 A1
Military Rd E
Pierce Co WA 25 C7
Military Rd S
King Co WA 25 C4
Military Rd S
King Co WA 136 E4
King Co WA 137 A5
Seatac WA 137 A5
Seatac WA 140 A7
Tukwila WA 137 A5
Tukwila WA 140 A1
Military Rd SE
Thurston Co WA 35 A2
Mill Av S
Renton WA 138 C7
Mill Av S SR-900
Renton WA 138 C7
Mill Rd
Jefferson Co WA 14 E5
Jefferson Co WA 119 A5
Port Townsend WA 14 E5
Port Townsend WA 119 A5
N Mill Rd
Spokane Co WA 31 B1
Mill St
Eugene OR 185 E1
Kelso WA 156 B4
Mill St SR-99
Eugene OR 185 E1
Mill St SR-126 BUS
Eugene OR 185 E1
Mill Bay Rd
Cowichan Valley BC 4 A7
Mill Creek Rd SE
Marion Co OR 54 D5
E Miller St
Seattle WA 128 D2
Miller Bay Rd NE
Kitsap Co WA 25 B1
E Mill Plain Blvd
Vancouver WA 158 A4
Vancouver WA 159 B5
E Mill Plain Blvd SR-501
Vancouver WA 158 A4
SE Mill Plain Blvd
Vancouver WA 159 E5
Vancouver WA 160 E6
W Mill Plain Blvd
Vancouver WA 157 E4
Vancouver WA 158 A4
W Mill Plain Blvd SR-501
Vancouver WA 157 E4
Vancouver WA 158 A4
Milwaukee Wy
Fife WA 142 D6
Tacoma WA 25 C5
Tacoma WA 142 D4
SE Milwaukie Av
Portland OR 166 A5
Portland OR 170 B1
SE Milwaukie Expwy
Clackamas Co OR 170 E6
Milwaukie OR 170 E6
SE Milwaukie Expwy SR-224
Clackamas Co OR 170 E6
Milwaukie OR 170 C4
Minor Rd
Kelso WA 156 C3
E Mission Av
Spokane WA 210 C6
Spokane Valley WA 213 E3
Spokane Valley WA 214 B3
W Mission Av
Spokane WA 209 E7
Spokane WA 210 A7
Mission St SE
Salem OR 173 C1
Salem OR 174 A2
Mission St SE SR-22
Salem OR 173 E2
Salem OR 174 A2
Mission St SE SR-99E BUS
Salem OR 173 E2
Salem OR 174 A2
Missle Site Rd
Lincoln Co WA 30 D1
Missouri Av
Canyon Co ID 83 C3
N Missouri Av
Portland OR 161 E4
SE Mitchell St
Portland OR 166 B6
Modoc Point Rd
Klamath Co OR 88 E5
Modoc Point Rd SR-427
Klamath Co OR 88 E5
Moeller-Mahon
Pierce Co WA 144 D6
Mohawk Blvd
Springfield OR 183 B7
Springfield OR 187 A1
Moncton St
Richmond BC 4 C3
Monmouth Hwy
Polk Co OR 54 B5
Monroe Av NE
Renton WA 138 E6
N Monroe Rd
Spokane Co WA 21 A7
Monroe St
Port Townsend WA 119 E4
N Monroe St
Spokane WA 31 B2
Spokane WA 209 D3
Spokane WA 211 E1
Spokane Co WA 209 D2
S Monroe St
Spokane WA 211 E2
Monson Rd E
Lincoln Co WA 29 C3
Monster Rd SW
Renton WA 137 D7
Montague Rd
Yreka CA 98 E4
Montague Rd SR-3
Yreka CA 98 E4
S Montana Av
Caldwell ID 219 C4
Monte Elma Rd
Elma WA 34 A1
Grays Harbor Co WA 34 A1
Monterey Pl NE
Newcastle WA 138 D2
Renton WA 138 D1
N Montesano St
Westport WA 150 C3
N Montesano St SR-105
Westport WA 150 C3
Montgomery Dr
Linn Co OR 54 D7
Montlake Blvd E
Seattle WA 128 E2
Seattle WA 129 A2
Montlake Blvd E SR-513
Seattle WA 128 E2
Montlake Blvd NE
Seattle WA 125 A7
Seattle WA 128 E1
Seattle WA 129 A1
Montlake Blvd NE SR-513
Seattle WA 125 A7
Seattle WA 128 E2
Seattle WA 129 A1
E Montlake Pl E
Seattle WA 129 A2
W Montlake Pl E
Seattle WA 128 E2
Montreal St
Victoria BC 111 D5
Montroyal Blvd
N Vancouver Dist BC 108 C1
Montvale Pl W
Seattle WA 127 C3
Moon Rd
Adams Co WA 39 C4
Franklin Co WA 39 C4
NE Morgan Ln
Grants Pass OR 197 D2
NW Morgan Ln
Grants Pass OR 197 C2
SW Morgan St
Seattle WA 131 E6
Morrison Br
Portland OR 165 E2
SE Morrison Ct
Portland OR 167 D3
SE Morrison St
Portland OR 166 B2
SW Morrison St
Portland OR 165 E2
E Morrison Knudson Plaza Dr
Boise ID 224 D1
Morse St
Cowlitz Co WA 34 D6
Morse St SR-506
Cowlitz Co WA 34 D6
Morse Merryman Rd SE
Olympia WA 148 C1
Moseley Rd
Del Norte Co CA 96 E3
Mottman Rd SW
Olympia WA 145 C7
Tumwater WA 145 B6
Mountain Hwy E
Pierce Co WA 25 B7
Mountain Hwy E SR-7
Pierce Co WA 25 B7
Mountain View Dr
Boise ID 221 B4
Mountain View Rd
Ferndale WA 5 A6
Whatcom Co WA 5 A6
Mt Angel Hwy NE
Marion Co OR 54 E4
Mt Angel OR 54 E4
Mt Hood Hwy
Clackamas Co OR 45 B7
Clackamas Co OR 55 C1
Clackamas Co OR 56 A2
Hood River Co OR 46 B7
Hood River Co OR 56 B1
Sandy OR 55 C1
Mt Hood Hwy SR-35
Hood River Co OR 46 B7
Hood River Co OR 56 B1
Mt Hood Hwy US-26
Clackamas Co OR 45 B7
Clackamas Co OR 55 C1
Clackamas Co OR 56 A2
Sandy OR 55 C1
E Mt Hood Hwy
Hood River Co OR 46 C6
E Mt Hood Hwy SR-35
Hood River Co OR 46 B6
Mt Lehman Rd
Abbotsford BC 5 C4
Mt Shasta Dr
Vancouver WA 159 C6
E Mt Spokane Park Dr
Spokane Co WA 31 C1
E Mt Spokane Park Dr SR-206
Spokane Co WA 31 B1
Mt Vernon Rd
Lane Co OR 188 B4
Springfield OR 188 B4
NW Mt Washington Dr
Bend OR 189 B7
Bend OR 190 A5
Bend OR 191 B1
SW Mt Washington Dr
Bend OR 191 C2
Mud Bay Rd W
Olympia WA 145 A4
Thurston Co WA 145 A4
Mud Flat Rd
Grand View ID 84 A7
Mud Flat Rd SR-78
Grand View ID 84 A6

16 INDEX
INDEX 16
E Mukilteo Blvd
Oregon Coast Hwy US-101

Street Index

STREET City State Map# Grid

E Mukilteo Blvd
Everett WA 120 B5
W Mukilteo Blvd
Everett WA 15 D7
Everett WA 120 A5
S Mulino Rd
Clackamas Co OR 55 A2
E Mullan Av
Kootenai Co ID 215 E4
Kootenai Co ID 216 A4
Post Falls ID 31 E1
Post Falls ID 215 D4
Post Falls ID 216 A4
N Mullan Rd
Spokane Valley WA 213 C4
Mullen Rd SE
Thurston Co WA 35 A1
SE Mullenix Rd
Kitsap Co WA 25 A4
S Mullinix Rd
Spokane Co WA 30 E5
Spokane Co WA 31 A4
SW Multnomah Blvd
Portland OR 169 A1
N Multnomah St
Portland OR 166 A1
NE Multnomah St
Portland OR 166 B1
Portland OR 167 B1
Munns Rd
Capital BC 14 B2
Murphy Rd
Bend OR 191 E5
Bend OR 192 A5
Murphy Grandview Rd
Owyhee Co ID 83 E6
Murphy Grandview Rd SR-78
Owyhee Co ID 83 E6
SW Murray Blvd
Beaverton OR 44 E7
W Muse Rd
Adams Co WA 39 B3
Franklin Co WA 39 B3
Myers Wy S
King Co WA 136 C2
Seattle WA 136 C2
NE Myra Rd
College Place WA 207 C5
Walla Walla WA 207 C5
Walla Walla Co WA 207 C5
S Myrtle Pl
Seattle WA 133 A7
E Myrtle St
Boise ID 224 C1
E Myrtle St US-20
Boise ID 224 C1
E Myrtle St US-26
Boise ID 224 C1
S Myrtle St
Seattle WA 133 A7
W Myrtle St
Boise ID 222 C7
Boise ID 224 C1
W Myrtle St US-20
Boise ID 222 C7
Boise ID 224 C1
W Myrtle St US-26
Boise ID 222 C7
Boise ID 224 C1

N

S N St
Port Angeles WA 14 B5
S Naches Rd
Yakima Co WA 37 C4
Naches Tieton Rd
Yakima Co WA 37 B4
Naches-Wenas Rd
Yakima Co WA 37 C3
NW Naito Pkwy
Portland OR 161 D7
Portland OR 165 E1
SW Naito Pkwy
Portland OR 165 E2
SW Naito Pkwy SR-10
Portland OR 165 E5
SW Naito Pkwy SR-99W
Portland OR 165 E5
Nampa Blvd
Nampa ID 220 B1
Nampa Blvd SR-55
Nampa ID 220 B1
Nanaimo Pkwy
Nanaimo BC 3 D2
Nanaimo Pkwy PROV-19
Nanaimo BC 3 D2
Nanaimo St
Vancouver BC 110 E6
N Nanaimo St
Vancouver BC 110 E2
Nanaimo Lakes Rd
Nanaimo BC 3 D3
National Av
Chehalis WA 152 B3
N National Av
Chehalis WA 152 B3
Lewis Co WA 152 C1
Navarre Coulee Rd
Chelan Co WA 28 A1
Navarre Coulee Rd SR-971
Chelan Co WA 28 A1
Navy Yard Hwy
Bremerton WA 122 A7
Kitsap Co WA 121 E7
Kitsap Co WA 122 A6
Navy Yard Hwy SR-304
Bremerton WA 122 A7
Kitsap Co WA 121 E7
Kitsap Co WA 122 A7
Neacoxie Dr
Gearhart OR 154 C2
Neah Bay Rd
Clallam Co WA 12 E3
Neah Bay Rd SR-112
Clallam Co WA 12 E3
Nealey Rd
Okanogan Co WA 9 B6
Necanicum Hwy
Tillamook Co OR 43 D4
Necanicum Hwy SR-53
Tillamook Co OR 43 D4
Neff Rd
Bend OR 190 E6
Deschutes Co OR 66 D5
Deschutes Co OR 190 E6
NE Neff Rd
Bend OR 190 D6
Deschutes Co OR 190 E6
Nehalem Hwy
Astoria OR 153 E3
Banks OR 44 C6
Clatsop Co OR 153 E4
Washington Co OR 44 B4
Nehalem Hwy SR-47
Banks OR 44 C6
Washington Co OR 44 B4
Nehalem Hwy SR-202
Astoria OR 153 E3
Clatsop Co OR 153 E4
Nehalem Hwy N
Columbia Co OR 44 B2
Nehalem Hwy N SR-47
Columbia Co OR 44 B2
Nehalem Hwy N SR-202
Columbia Co OR 44 B2
Nehalem Hwy S
Columbia Co OR 44 B4
Nehalem Hwy S SR-47
Columbia Co OR 44 B4
Nehalem Hwy S SR-202
Columbia Co OR 44 B4
Nelson St
Vancouver BC 109 E3
Vancouver BC 110 A3
NW Neptune Pl
Seattle WA 123 D3
Nestucca River Rd
Tillamook Co OR 53 E2
Netarts Hwy W
Tillamook Co OR 43 C7
Nevada Dr
Cowlitz Co WA 44 D1
Cowlitz Co WA 155 E1
Cowlitz Co WA 156 A1
Longview WA 155 D1
Nevada St
Klamath Falls OR 201 B4
N Nevada St
Spokane WA 31 B1
Spokane WA 210 B1
Newberg Hwy
Marion Co OR 54 D3
Woodburn OR 54 D3
Newberg Hwy SR-214
Marion Co OR 54 D3
Woodburn OR 54 D3
NW Newberry Hill Rd
Kitsap Co WA 25 A2
Newcastle Wy
Bellevue WA 134 E7
Newcastle WA 134 E7
NE New Columbia Pkwy
Portland OR 163 C5
NE New Columbia Pkwy US-30 BYP
Portland OR 163 C5
Newmark Av
Coos Bay OR 73 E4
Coos Bay OR 193 C4
North Bend OR 193 C4
Newmark St
Coos Bay OR 193 D4
North Bend OR 193 D4
North Bend OR 194 A4
Newport Av
Oak Bay BC 112 D5
NW Newport Av
Bend OR 189 E7
N Newport Hwy
Spokane Co WA 21 B7
Spokane Co WA 31 B1
N Newport Hwy US-2
Spokane Co WA 21 B7
Spokane Co WA 31 B1
SE Newport Wy
Bellevue WA 134 E4
King Co WA 25 D3
NF-6
Bonner Co ID 21 E4
NF-6 SR-57
Bonner Co ID 21 E4
NF-9
Shoshone Co ID 32 E2
NF-10
Modoc Co CA 100 C5
Siskiyou Co CA 100 C5
NF-11
Linn Co OR 65 D1
NF-14
Grant Co OR 70 A3
NF-14 CO-62
Grant Co OR 70 A3
NF-15
Latah Co ID 32 A7
Latah Co ID 42 A1
Siskiyou Co CA 99 E7
Siskiyou Co CA 100 A5
NF-15 SR-6
Latah Co ID 32 A7
Latah Co ID 42 A1
NF-16
Baker Co OR 70 C3
Grant Co OR 69 E4
Grant Co OR 70 A4
Malheur Co OR 70 B4
NF-18
Clackamas Co OR 56 A1
Deschutes Co OR 66 D6
Hood River Co OR 46 A7
NF-23
Curry Co OR 86 B3
NF-24
Mason Co WA 24 C3
NF-24 SR-119
Mason Co WA 24 C3
NF-25
Skamania Co WA 45 E2
NF-28
Lake Co OR 77 E7
Lake Co OR 89 E1
Lake Co OR 90 A2
NF-33
Curry Co OR 85 E4
Curry Co OR 86 A4
NF-34
Klamath Co OR 90 A6
NF-37
Grant Co OR 69 B6
NF-39
Baker Co OR 61 E4
Baker Co OR 62 A3
Wallowa Co OR 61 E2
Wallowa Co OR 62 A2
NF-41
Deschutes Co OR 66 C7
NF-42
Clackamas Co OR 56 A3
NF-43
Wasco Co OR 56 B3
NF-44
Wasco Co OR 56 C1
NF-44N50
Siskiyou Co CA 100 A6
NF-45
Deschutes Co OR 66 B7
NF-46
Clackamas Co OR 55 E6
NF-48
Wasco Co OR 56 C3
NF-49
Siskiyou Co CA 100 B6
NF-50
Benewah Co ID 32 C5
Latah Co ID 42 B2
NF-50 SR-9
Latah Co ID 42 B2
NF-51
Union Co OR 60 B3
NF-52
Grant Co OR 60 A4
NF-052
Umatilla Co OR 59 D4
Umatilla Co OR 60 A4
NF-53
Morrow Co OR 59 B3
NF-053
Umatilla Co OR 59 C3
NF-57
Clackamas Co OR 55 E4
Clackamas Co OR 56 A3
NF-58
Clackamas Co OR 55 E3
Clackamas Co OR 56 A3
Latah Co ID 42 A1
NF-58 SR-9
Latah Co ID 42 A1
NF-63
Jefferson Co OR 66 D1
NF-68
Clearwater Co ID 42 C2
Latah Co ID 42 C2
NF-68 SR-8
Clearwater Co ID 42 C2
Latah Co ID 42 C2
NF-71
Latah Co ID 42 C1
NF-71 SR-3
Latah Co ID 42 C1
NF-73
Grant Co OR 60 B5
NF-99
Skamania Co WA 35 D7
NF-416
Harney Co OR 69 B6
NF-454
Baker Co OR 62 A4
NF-454 SR-86
Baker Co OR 62 A4
NF-503
Shoshone Co ID 32 D2
NF-1720
Wasco Co OR 46 C7
NF-1810
Hood River Co OR 46 A7
Hood River Co OR 56 A1
NF-1815
Deschutes Co OR 66 D6
NF-2651
Wasco Co OR 56 B3
NF-2823
Klamath Co OR 90 A3
Lake Co OR 90 D7
NF-3312
Klamath Co OR 89 E4
Klamath Co OR 90 A3
NF-3618
Klamath Co OR 90 A5
NF-3660
Lake Co OR 90 B5
NF-3750
Harney Co OR 69 B6
Niagara Av
Astoria OR 153 C2
Nichols Blvd
Longview WA 155 C4
Nichols Blvd SR-432
Longview WA 155 C4
NE Nichols Blvd
Longview WA 155 C3
NW Nichols Blvd
Longview WA 155 C3
NW Nichols Blvd SR-432
Longview WA 155 C3
Nickerson St
Seattle WA 128 B1
W Nickerson St
Seattle WA 127 E1
Seattle WA 128 A1
Nick Young Rd
Jackson Co OR 87 D5
NW Nicolai St
Portland OR 161 B7
N Nine Mile Rd
Spokane WA 209 A2
No 1 Rd
Richmond BC 4 D3
No 2 Rd
Richmond BC 4 D3
No 3 Rd
Abbotsford BC 5 E4
No 4 Rd
Abbotsford BC 5 E4
Richmond BC 4 D3
No 6 Rd
Richmond BC 4 D3
Nooksack Rd
Nooksack WA 5 C6
Whatcom Co WA 5 C6
Nooksack Rd SR-9
Nooksack WA 5 C6
Whatcom Co WA 5 C6
Nordel Wy
Delta BC 4 E3
Norkenzie Rd
Eugene OR 181 E5
S Normandy Rd
Burien WA 139 C4
Normandy Park WA 139 C4
SW Normandy Rd
Burien WA 139 C4
Normandy Park WA 139 B4
SW Normandy Ter
Normandy Park WA 139 B4
North St
Bonanza OR 89 C7
North St SR-70
Bonanza OR 89 C7
North St SE
Olympia WA 148 A1
Tumwater WA 147 E1
Tumwater WA 148 A1
NW North Albany Rd
Albany OR 175 D1
North Bank Rd
Douglas Co OR 75 B5
North Cascades Hwy
Burlington WA 115 E4
Skagit Co WA 115 D4
North Cascades Hwy SR-20
Burlington WA 115 E4
Skagit Co WA 115 D4
North Entrance Rd
Klamath Co OR 76 D7
North Entrance Rd SR-232
Klamath Co OR 76 D7
Northgate Dr
Umatilla Co OR 49 D5
Northgate Dr SR-37
Umatilla Co OR 49 D5
N Northgate Wy
Seattle WA 124 C2
NE Northgate Wy
Seattle WA 124 D2
Seattle WA 125 A2
N Northlake Wy
Seattle WA 128 D1
NE Northlake Wy
Seattle WA 128 D1
Northport-Boundry Rd
Northport WA 10 E5
Northport-Boundry Rd SR-251
Northport WA 10 E5
Northport-Flat Creek Rd
Stevens Co WA 10 C7
Northside Blvd
Nampa ID 220 B1
Northup Wy
Bellevue WA 130 D3
Kirkland WA 130 D3
Northwest Av
Bellingham WA 113 B1
Northwest Blvd
Coeur d'Alene ID 218 A4
Northwest Blvd I-90 BUS
Coeur d'Alene ID 218 A4
W Northwest Blvd
Spokane WA 209 C5
Northwest Dr
Whatcom Co WA 5 B6
Northwest Expwy
Eugene OR 64 B5
Eugene OR 180 E3
Eugene OR 181 B6
Lane Co OR 64 B5
Lane Co OR 180 D1
Notus Rd
Notus ID 83 B1
NE Novelty Hill Rd
King Co WA 25 E2
N Nugent Rd
Whatcom Co WA 5 A7
Nusom Rd NE
Marion Co OR 54 D4

O

O Av
Anacortes WA 15 B2
Anacortes WA 114 D4
SE Oak Av
Roseburg OR 196 A5
SE Oak Av SR-138
Roseburg OR 196 A5
SW Oak Av
Roseburg OR 196 A5
SW Oak Av SR-138
Roseburg OR 196 A5
Oak St
Eugene OR 185 D3
Kelso WA 156 B3
North Bend OR 73 E4
North Bend OR 193 E2
Silverton OR 54 E4
Vancouver BC 4 D2
Vancouver BC 109 E5
Oak St PROV-99
Vancouver BC 109 E7
Oak St SR-213
Silverton OR 54 E4
S Oak St
Benton Co WA 49 B1
Benton Co WA 206 D5
Kennewick WA 206 D5
SW Oak St
Portland OR 165 E2
W Oak St
Lebanon OR 64 D1
Linn Co OR 64 D1
Oak Bay Av
Oak Bay BC 112 D5
Victoria BC 112 B5
Oakes Av
Anacortes WA 15 A2
Anacortes WA 114 B2
Oakes Av SR-20 SPUR
Anacortes WA 15 A2
Anacortes WA 114 B2
S Oakes St
Tacoma WA 143 D4
Oakesdale Av SW
Kent WA 140 E4
Renton WA 137 E7
Renton WA 140 E3
SE Oak Grove Blvd
Clackamas Co OR 170 C7
Oakland-Shady Hwy
Douglas Co OR 75 A5
Sutherlin OR 75 A5
Oakland-Shady Hwy SR-99
Douglas Co OR 75 A5
Sutherlin OR 75 A5
Oaks Av
Cle Elum WA 27 A6
Oaks Av SR-903
Cle Elum WA 27 A6
Oaksdale Rd
Whitman Co WA 31 C7
Oakway Rd
Eugene OR 182 A6
SE Oatfield Rd
Clackamas Co OR 170 C6
Milwaukie OR 170 C5
Oberlin Rd
Siskiyou Co CA 99 A4
Yreka CA 98 E4
Ob Riley Rd
Bend OR 190 A2
Deschutes Co OR 189 E2
Deschutes Co OR 190 A2
NE Ob Riley Rd
Bend OR 189 E3
Bend OR 190 A4
Deschutes Co OR 190 A2
Occidental Rd
Yakima Co WA 37 C5
Ocean Blvd NW
Coos Bay OR 193 C4
Ocean Blvd SE
Coos Bay OR 193 E5
Coos Bay OR 194 A6
Ocean Beach Hwy
Cowlitz Co WA 44 C1
Cowlitz Co WA 156 A3
Kelso WA 156 A3
Longview WA 44 C1
Longview WA 155 E3
Longview WA 156 A3
Ocean Beach Hwy SR-4
Cowlitz Co WA 44 C1
Cowlitz Co WA 156 A3
Kelso WA 156 A3
Longview WA 44 C1
Longview WA 155 E3
Longview WA 156 A3
E Ocean Beach Hwy
Wahkiakum Co WA 44 B1
E Ocean Beach Hwy SR-4
Wahkiakum Co WA 44 B1
Ocean Lake Wy NW
Ocean Shores WA 149 B1
Ocean Lake Wy SW
Ocean Shores WA 149 B1
Ocean Shores Blvd NW
Ocean Shores WA 149 B1
Ocean Shores Blvd SW
Ocean Shores WA 149 A4
Ochoco Hwy
Crook Co OR 66 E4
Crook Co OR 67 A4
Grant Co OR 68 A1
Wheeler Co OR 67 E1
Wheeler Co OR 68 A1
Ochoco Hwy SR-126
Crook Co OR 66 E4
Crook Co OR 67 A4
Ochoco Hwy US-26
Grant Co OR 68 A1
Wheeler Co OR 67 E1
Wheeler Co OR 68 A1
O'Dell Hwy
Hood River Co OR 46 C6
NW Odem Av
Deschutes Co OR 66 E3
Ohio St
Bellingham WA 113 C3
Old Bend-Redmond Hwy
Deschutes Co OR 66 D5
Deschutes Co OR 189 E1
Old Fairhaven Pkwy
Bellingham WA 113 B7
Old Fairhaven Pkwy SR-11
Bellingham WA 113 B7
Oldfield Rd
Saanich BC 14 B1
Old Highway 7
Idaho Co ID 52 E1
Old Highway 7 SR-7
Idaho Co ID 52 E1
Old Highway 30
Canyon Co ID 72 B7
Canyon Co ID 219 B1
Old Highway 99 S
Siskiyou Co CA 99 A6
Old Highway 99 SE
Thurston Co WA 147 E5
Thurston Co WA 148 A6
Tumwater WA 147 E5
Tumwater WA 148 A6
Old Highway 99 SW
Thurston Co WA 34 D2
Old Highway 99 South Rd
Mt Vernon WA 116 B5
Skagit Co WA 116 B6
W Old Inland Empire Hwy
Benton Co WA 38 D7
Old Malin Hwy
Klamath Co OR 100 C2
Modoc Co CA 100 C2
Old Melrose Rd
Douglas Co OR 195 A2
Roseburg OR 195 B5
Old Melrose Rd CO-13B
Douglas Co OR 195 B5
Roseburg OR 195 B5
W Old Melrose Rd
Roseburg OR 195 B5
Old Mohawk Rd
Lane Co OR 183 E4
Old Naches Hwy
Naches WA 37 B3
Old Olympic Hwy
Clallam Co WA 14 C5
Clallam Co WA 118 A2
Sequim WA 118 B3
Old Oregon Trail Hwy
Baker Co OR 61 A6
Elmore Co ID 84 E6
Morrow Co OR 48 D4
Umatilla Co OR 48 D4
Old Oregon Trail Hwy I-84
Baker Co OR 61 A6
Morrow Co OR 48 D4
Umatilla Co OR 48 D4
Old Oregon Trail Hwy SR-30
Elmore Co ID 84 E6
Old Oregon Trail Hwy US-30
Baker Co OR 61 A6
Morrow Co OR 48 D4
Umatilla Co OR 48 D4
Old River Rd
Shoshone Co ID 32 D2
Old Salem Rd NE
Linn Co OR 176 C1
Olds Ferry-Ontario Hwy
Malheur Co OR 71 E3
Malheur Co OR 72 A5
Olds Ferry-Ontario Hwy SR-201
Malheur Co OR 71 E3
Malheur Co OR 72 A5
Old Siskiyou Hwy
Jackson Co OR 98 E1
Old Siskiyou Hwy SR-273
Jackson Co OR 98 E1
Old Stage Rd
Jackson Co OR 87 C5
Old State Hwy
Siskiyou Co CA 99 D4
Old Tygh Rd
Wasco Co OR 56 E1
Old US-30 N
Malheur Co OR 71 E3
Old US-30 N SR-201
Malheur Co OR 71 E3
Old WA-99 N
Burlington WA 115 B3
Skagit Co WA 115 B3
Old WA-195-Scenic S
Spokane Co WA 31 B5
Old Willamette Hwy S
Lane Co OR 187 A7
Old Willamette Hwy S SR-99
Lane Co OR 187 A7
Old Youngs Bay Br
Astoria OR 153 C3
Clatsop Co OR 153 C4
Old Youngs Bay Br US-101 BUS
Astoria OR 153 C3
Clatsop Co OR 153 C4
SW Oleson Rd
Portland OR 44 E7
Washington Co OR 44 E7
Olive Wy
Seattle WA 128 C5
E Olive Wy
Seattle WA 128 D5
Olney Av
Astoria OR 153 C3
Olney Av SR-202
Astoria OR 153 C3
NE Olney Av
Bend OR 190 A6
NW Olney Av
Bend OR 190 A7
Olney Rd
Wasco Co OR 46 E6
Olson Pl SW
King Co WA 136 B2
Seattle WA 136 C2
S Olympia St
Benton Co WA 206 A7
Kennewick WA 49 B1
Kennewick WA 206 A3
Olympia Wy
Longview WA 155 D3
Olympic Blvd
Everett WA 120 A5
Olympic Hwy
Clallam Co WA 13 E5
Olympic Hwy US-101
Clallam Co WA 13 E5
W Olympic Pl
Seattle WA 128 A4
Olympic St
Springfield OR 187 D1
Olympic Wy NW
Olympia WA 145 D5
Olympic Wy W
Seattle WA 128 A4
Olympic View Dr
Edmonds WA 25 C1
Omak Av E
Omak WA 18 D3
Omak Av E SR-155
Omak WA 18 D3
NE O'Neil Hwy
Crook Co OR 66 E3
NE O'Neil Hwy SR-370
Crook Co OR 66 E3
NW O'Neil Hwy
Crook Co OR 67 A3
NW O'Neil Hwy SR-370
Crook Co OR 67 A3
NE O'Neil Wy
Deschutes Co OR 66 E3
S Orcas St
Seattle WA 25 D3
Seattle WA 132 E5
Seattle WA 133 C6
Orchard Av
Canyon Co ID 83 C2
Orchard Av SE
Kitsap Co WA 25 B4
W Orchard Av
Nampa ID 83 C2
Nampa ID 220 A2
Orchard St W
Fircrest WA 141 A6
Fircrest WA 143 A1
Tacoma WA 141 A6
Tacoma WA 143 A2
University Place WA 143 A2
N Orchard St
Boise ID 221 E7
Boise ID 223 E1
Garden City ID 221 E6
Tacoma WA 141 A1
S Orchard St
Ada Co ID 223 E7
Boise ID 223 E2
Fircrest WA 141 A6
Fircrest WA 143 A1
Tacoma WA 141 A6
Tacoma WA 143 A1
SW Orchard St
Seattle WA 132 A7
Oregon Av
Klamath Falls OR 201 C4
N Oregon Av
Pasco WA 204 E5
N Oregon Av SR-397
Pasco WA 204 E5
S Oregon Av
Pasco WA 204 E7
Pasco WA 206 E1
S Oregon Av SR-397
Pasco WA 204 E7
Pasco WA 206 E1
Oregon St
Astoria OR 153 A2
NE Oregon St
Portland OR 166 A1
SW Oregon St
Seattle WA 131 D4
Oregon Wy
Cowlitz Co WA 155 C6
Longview WA 155 C6
Rainier OR 155 C7
Oregon Wy SR-433
Cowlitz Co WA 155 C7
Longview WA 155 C6
Rainier OR 155 C7
Oregon Coast Hwy
Astoria OR 153 B1
Clatsop Co OR 153 B1
Clatsop Co OR 154 B7
Coos Co OR 73 D6
Coos Co OR 74 A2
Curry Co OR 85 D6
Curry Co OR 96 E1
Lincoln Co OR 63 B1
Lincoln Co OR 179 B5
North Bend OR 194 A2
Seaside OR 154 B7
Tillamook Co OR 43 C6
Tillamook Co OR 43 C6
Waldport OR 179 B5
Oregon Coast Hwy US-26
Astoria OR 153 A2
Clatsop Co OR 154 B7
Seaside OR 154 B7
Oregon Coast Hwy US-101
Astoria OR 153 B1
Clatsop Co OR 153 B1
Clatsop Co OR 154 B7
Coos Co OR 73 D6
Coos Co OR 74 A2
Curry Co OR 85 D1
Curry Co OR 96 E1

17 INDEX
INDEX 17
Oregon Coast Hwy US-101
N Ramsey Rd

Street Index

STREET
City State Map# Grid

Oregon Coast Hwy US-101
Lincoln Co OR 63 B1
Lincoln Co OR 179 B5
North Bend OR 194 A2
Seaside OR 154 B7
Tillamook OR 43 C6
Tillamook Co OR 43 C6
Waldport OR 179 B5
Oregon-Washington Hwy
Athena OR 50 A4
Pendleton OR 49 E5
Umatilla Co OR 49 E5
Umatilla Co OR 50 A4
Oregon-Washington Hwy SR-11
Athena OR 50 A4
Pendleton OR 49 E5
Umatilla Co OR 49 E5
Umatilla Co OR 50 A4
SE Orient Dr
Gresham OR 45 C7
Orillia Rd S
Kent WA 140 B7
King Co WA 140 B5
Seatac WA 140 B6
Orin Rice Rd
Stevens Co WA 20 C2
SW Orleans St
Seattle WA 131 C3
Orting Kapowsin Hwy E
Pierce Co WA 25 C7
Orville Rd E
Pierce Co WA 25 D7
Pierce Co WA 35 C2
Osullivan Dam Rd
Grant Co WA 38 E1
Grant Co WA 39 A1
Osullivan Dam Rd SR-262
Grant Co WA 38 E1
Grant Co WA 39 A1
S Othello St
Seattle WA 133 B7
Otter Point Rd
Capital BC 13 E3
E Overland Rd
Meridian ID 83 E2
W Overland Rd
Boise ID 83 E2
Boise ID 223 B3
Boise ID 224 C3
Overturf Rd
Franklin Co WA 39 D5
Owens St S
Salem OR 173 C2
Owens St SE
Salem OR 173 C2
Owyhee Av
Malheur Co OR 71 E7

P

Pacific Av
Bremerton WA 122 C6
Everett WA 120 C3
Forest Grove OR 44 C7
Kitsap Co WA 122 C6
Pierce Co WA 144 B7
Tacoma WA 25 B6
Tacoma WA 142 A5
Tacoma WA 144 B5
Pacific Av SR-7
Pierce Co WA 144 B7
Tacoma WA 25 B6
Tacoma WA 144 B6
Pacific Av SR-8
Forest Grove OR 44 C7
Pacific Av SR-304
Bremerton WA 122 C6
Kitsap Co WA 122 C6
Pacific Av SR-509
Tacoma WA 142 B6
Pacific Av SR-529
Everett WA 120 D3
Pacific Av S
Pierce Co WA 144 B7
Pacific Av S SR-7
Pierce Co WA 144 B7
Pacific Av SE
Lacey WA 146 E5
Olympia WA 146 E5
N Pacific Av
Cowlitz Co WA 44 D1
Kelso WA 156 B3
N Pacific Av SR-4
Kelso WA 156 B3
N Pacific Av SR-431
Kelso WA 156 B3
NW Pacific Av
Chehalis WA 152 B4
S Pacific Av
Kelso WA 156 A4
Pacific Blvd
Vancouver BC 109 E3
Vancouver BC 110 A3
Pacific Blvd SE
Albany OR 175 E3
Albany OR 176 B2
Linn Co OR 176 C2
Pacific Blvd SE SR-99E
Albany OR 175 E3
Albany OR 176 B2
Linn Co OR 176 C2
Pacific Blvd SE US-20
Albany OR 175 E3
Albany OR 176 A3
Pacific Blvd SW
Albany OR 175 D6
Pacific Blvd SW SR-99E
Albany OR 175 D6
Pacific Blvd SW US-20
Albany OR 175 D6
Pacific Hwy
Albany OR 176 C4
Ashland OR 200 A2
Central Point OR 198 A1
Douglas Co OR 75 A7
Douglas Co OR 87 A2
Douglas Co OR 195 E1
Eugene OR 182 C7
Eugene OR 186 C3
Grants Pass OR 197 E5
Jackson Co OR 87 B5
Jackson Co OR 198 B2
Jackson Co OR 199 D1
Jackson Co OR 200 B3
Josephine Co OR 197 E4
Lake Oswego OR 169 E7
Lake Oswego OR 170 A1
Lane Co OR 75 C1
Lane Co OR 182 C7
Lane Co OR 186 C3
Lane Co OR 187 A7
Linn Co OR 176 C1
Marion Co OR 54 C6
Medford OR 198 C6
Rogue River OR 87 B5
Roseburg OR 195 E1
Springfield OR 182 C5
Springfield OR 186 C1
Pacific Hwy I-5
Albany OR 176 C4
Ashland OR 200 C5
Central Point OR 198 A1
Douglas Co OR 75 A7
Douglas Co OR 87 A2
Douglas Co OR 195 E1
Eugene OR 182 C7
Eugene OR 186 C2
Grants Pass OR 197 E4
Jackson Co OR 87 B5
Jackson Co OR 198 B2
Jackson Co OR 199 D1
Jackson Co OR 200 D6
Josephine Co OR 197 E4
Lane Co OR 75 C1
Lane Co OR 182 C6
Lane Co OR 186 E6
Lane Co OR 187 A7
Linn Co OR 176 C1
Marion Co OR 54 C6
Medford OR 198 C6
Rogue River OR 87 B5
Roseburg OR 195 E1
Springfield OR 182 C7
Springfield OR 186 C3
Pacific Hwy SR-43
Lake Oswego OR 169 E7
Lake Oswego OR 170 A1
Pacific Hwy SR-99
Douglas Co OR 75 A7
Douglas Co OR 87 A2
Eugene OR 186 C3
Grants Pass OR 197 C1
Josephine Co OR 197 C1
Lane Co OR 186 E7
Lane Co OR 187 A7
Springfield OR 186 C3
Pacific Hwy SR-99E
Linn Co OR 176 C1
Marion Co OR 54 C6
Pacific Hwy SR-138
Douglas Co OR 195 E1
Roseburg OR 195 E1
Pacific Hwy E
Aurora OR 54 E2
Clackamas Co OR 55 A1
Fife WA 142 E6
Tacoma WA 142 D6
Pacific Hwy E SR-99E
Aurora OR 54 E2
Clackamas Co OR 55 A1
Pacific Hwy S
Des Moines WA 139 E7
Federal Way WA 25 C5
Seatac WA 139 E7
Pacific Hwy S SR-99
Des Moines WA 139 E7
Federal Way WA 25 C5
Seatac WA 139 E7
Pacific Hwy W
Benton Co OR 64 B3
Benton Co OR 178 C1
Corvallis OR 64 B2
Corvallis OR 178 B4
Newberg OR 54 C2
Pacific Hwy W SR-34
Corvallis OR 178 A6
Pacific Hwy W SR-99W
Benton Co OR 64 B3
Benton Co OR 178 C1
Corvallis OR 64 B2
Corvallis OR 178 B4
Newberg OR 54 C2
N Pacific Hwy W
Polk Co OR 54 B4
N Pacific Hwy W SR-99W
Polk Co OR 54 B4
S Pacific Hwy
Jackson Co OR 87 D6
Medford OR 87 D6
S Pacific Hwy SR-99
Jackson Co OR 87 D6
Medford OR 87 D6
S Pacific Hwy W
Polk Co OR 54 B6
S Pacific Hwy W SR-99W
Polk Co OR 54 B6
SW Pacific Hwy W
Tualatin OR 54 D1
Washington Co OR 54 D1
SW Pacific Hwy W SR-99W
Tualatin OR 54 D1
Washington Co OR 54 D1
NE Pacific Pl
Seattle WA 128 E1
Seattle WA 129 A1
Pacific St
Vancouver BC 109 D2
N Pacific St
Seattle WA 128 C1
NE Pacific St
Seattle WA 128 E1
Pacific Wy
Gearhart OR 154 C2
Longview WA 155 C1
Pacific Co WA 33 C5
Pacific Wy SR-103
Pacific Co WA 33 C5
N Paha-Packard Rd
Adams Co WA 30 A7
E Palouse Hwy
Spokane WA 212 D6
Spokane Co WA 31 B3
Spokane Co WA 212 D6
S Palouse Hwy
Spokane Co WA 212 D6
Palouse Albion Rd
Albion WA 41 C2
Whitman Co WA 41 C2
Pandora Av
Victoria BC 111 E5
Victoria BC 112 A5
Paradise Hwy
Humboldt Co NV 105 C7
Paradise Hwy SR-290
Humboldt Co NV 105 C7
Paradise Rd
Pierce Co WA 36 A3
Park Av
Raymond WA 33 D3
Park Av SR-105
Raymond WA 33 D3
Park Av N
Renton WA 138 C5
Park Av S
Pierce Co WA 144 A7
E Park Blvd
Boise ID 224 D1
Park Dr
Clatsop Co OR 154 D3
Gearhart OR 43 C2
Gearhart OR 154 D3
Seaside OR 154 D3
Park Dr US-26
Clatsop Co OR 154 D3
Gearhart OR 43 C2
Gearhart OR 154 D3
Seaside OR 154 D3
Park Dr US-101
Clatsop Co OR 154 D3
Gearhart OR 43 C2
Gearhart OR 154 D3
Seaside OR 154 D3
NE Park Dr
Renton WA 138 C4
NE Park Dr SR-900
Renton WA 138 C4
SW Park Pl
Portland OR 165 C2
Park Rd
Whatcom Co WA 5 D7
N Park Rd
Spokane Valley WA 213 B4
S Park Rd
Spokane Co WA 213 B5
Spokane Valley WA 31 C2
Spokane Valley WA 213 B5
S Park St
St. John WA 31 A7
E Parkcenter Blvd
Boise ID 224 E2
W Parkcenter Blvd
Boise ID 224 D2
SW Parkland Dr
Chehalis WA 152 C5
Parkway Blvd
Coquitlam BC 5 A2
S Pass Rd
Whatcom Co WA 5 D5
Patten Av
Bremerton WA 121 E6
Patterson St
Eugene OR 185 E3
Klamath Co OR 202 D7
SW Patton Rd
Multnomah Co OR 165 A4
Portland OR 165 A4
SE Paulina Hwy
Crook Co OR 67 B3
Crook Co OR 68 A5
SE Paulina Hwy SR-380
Crook Co OR 67 B3
Crook Co OR 68 A5
SE Paulina-Suplee Rd
Crook Co OR 68 C5
Paynter Av
Caldwell ID 219 B4
Peacock Hill Av NW
Pierce Co WA 25 B5
Pearl St
Eugene OR 185 E3
E Pearl St
Coburg OR 64 C4
N Pearl St
Centralia WA 34 D3
Centralia WA 151 D4
Lewis Co WA 151 D3
Tacoma WA 25 B5
Tacoma WA 141 A3
N Pearl St SR-163
Tacoma WA 25 B5
Tacoma WA 141 A2
N Pearl St SR-507
Centralia WA 34 D3
Centralia WA 151 D4
Lewis Co WA 151 D3
S Pearl St
Centralia WA 151 D5
Fircrest WA 141 A6
Tacoma WA 141 A5
S Pearl St SR-507
Centralia WA 151 D5
Pease Rd
Burlington WA 15 C2
Burlington WA 115 B7
Pencil Rd
Modoc Co CA 101 D6
W Pender St
Vancouver BC 109 E1
Vancouver BC 110 A1
W Pender St PROV-1A
Vancouver BC 109 E1
W Pender St PROV-7A
Vancouver BC 109 E1
Vancouver BC 110 A1
W Pender St PROV-99A
Vancouver BC 109 E1
Pendleton Cto
Umatilla Co OR 49 B5
Pendleton Cto SR-320
Umatilla Co OR 49 B5
Pendleton-Cold Springs Hwy
Umatilla Co OR 49 C4
Pendleton-Cold Sprs Hwy SR-37
Umatilla Co OR 49 C4
Pendleton-John Day Hwy
Grant Co OR 69 B1
Pendleton-John Day Hwy US-395
Grant Co OR 69 B1
Pendray St
Victoria BC 111 D5
N Peninsular Av
Portland OR 161 C2
NE Penn Av
Bend OR 190 C6
E Pennsylvania St
Boise ID 224 E3
Peoria Rd
Harrisburg OR 64 B1
Linn Co OR 64 B1
SE Peoria Rd
Linn Co OR 64 B1
Linn Co OR 178 D6
Perch Rd
Canyon Co ID 83 C3
Perimeter Rd
Pierce Co WA 25 B7
Perry Av NE
Kitsap Co WA 25 B3
Kitsap Co WA 122 D2
S Perry St
Spokane WA 31 B2
Spokane WA 212 B6
Spokane Co WA 212 C7
Perrydale Rd
Polk Co OR 54 B4
W Perrydale Rd
Polk Co OR 54 B4
SE Petrovitsky Rd
King Co WA 25 D4
S Phillipe Ln
Yreka CA 98 E4
SW Philomath Av
Corvallis OR 177 E6
Corvallis OR 178 A6
SW Philomath Av SR-34
Corvallis OR 177 D6
Corvallis OR 178 A6
SW Philomath Av US-20
Corvallis OR 177 E6
Corvallis OR 178 A6
Philomath Blvd
Benton Co OR 177 A7
Corvallis OR 177 A7
Philomath OR 177 A7
Philomath Blvd SR-34
Benton Co OR 177 A7
Corvallis OR 177 A7
Philomath OR 177 A7
Philomath Blvd US-20
Benton Co OR 177 A7
Corvallis OR 177 A7
Philomath OR 177 A7
SW Philomath Blvd
Benton Co OR 177 B7
Corvallis OR 177 B7
Corvallis OR 178 A6
Philomath OR 177 A7
SW Philomath Blvd SR-34
Benton Co OR 177 B7
Corvallis OR 177 B7
Corvallis OR 178 A6
Philomath OR 177 A7
SW Philomath Blvd US-20
Benton Co OR 177 B7
Corvallis OR 177 B7
Corvallis OR 178 A6
Philomath OR 177 A7
Phinney Av N
Seattle WA 124 B6
N Phinney Wy
Seattle WA 124 B7
N Phoenix Rd
Medford OR 87 D6
Piedmont Rd
Clallam Co WA 13 E5
Clallam Co WA 14 A5
Piedmont Rd SR-112
Clallam Co WA 13 E5
Clallam Co WA 14 A5
Pike St
Seattle WA 128 C6
E Pike St
Seattle WA 128 D5
Pilgrim Creek Rd
Siskiyou Co CA 99 E7
Pine Av
Harrison Hot Springs BC 6 B2
E Pine Av
Meridian ID 83 E2
SW Pine Rd
Kitsap Co WA 25 A4
Pine St
Nanaimo BC 3 D3
Seattle WA 128 C6
Silverton OR 54 E4
Pine St NE
Salem OR 171 D5
Salem OR 172 A5
S Pine St
Tacoma WA 141 D7
Tacoma WA 143 D1
SE Pine St
Roseburg OR 195 E6
Roseburg OR 196 A6
SE Pine St SR-99
Roseburg OR 195 E6
Roseburg OR 196 A6
SE Pine St SR-138
Roseburg OR 196 A5
SW Pine St
Grants Pass OR 197 B5
W Pine St
Walla Walla WA 207 D3
Walla Walla Co WA 207 D3
W Pine St SR-125
Walla Walla WA 207 D3
Walla Walla Co WA 207 C3
W Pine St SR-125 SPUR
Walla Walla WA 207 D3
Pinebrook Blvd
Bend OR 191 E4
Pinehurst Wy NE
Seattle WA 124 E2
Pine Oakes Transition
Tacoma WA 143 D2
N Pines Rd
Spokane Valley WA 31 C2
Spokane Valley WA 214 A4
N Pines Rd SR-27
Spokane Valley WA 31 C2
Spokane Valley WA 214 A4
S Pines Rd
Spokane Valley WA 31 C2
Spokane Valley WA 214 A5
S Pines Rd SR-27
Spokane Valley WA 31 C2
Spokane Valley WA 214 A5
Pinetree Wy
Coquitlam BC 5 A2
E Pioneer Av
Puyallup WA 25 C6
Pioneer Hwy
Snohomish Co WA 15 C4
Pioneer Pkwy E
Lane Co OR 182 E7
Springfield OR 182 E7
Springfield OR 186 E2
Pioneer Pkwy W
Lane Co OR 182 E6
Springfield OR 182 E7
Springfield OR 186 E2
Pioneer St
Ridgefield WA 44 E4
Ridgefield WA 45 A4
Pioneer St SR-501
Ridgefield WA 44 E4
Ridgefield WA 45 A4
Pioneer Wy
Gig Harbor WA 25 B5
Pioneer Wy E
Pierce Co WA 25 D7
Pierce Co WA 142 E7
Pierce Co WA 144 E1
Tacoma WA 142 D6
Pioneer Wy E SR-165
Pierce Co WA 25 D7
Pioneer Wy E SR-167
Tacoma WA 142 D6
Pitt Av
Bremerton WA 122 D5
Plainview Dr
Linn Co OR 64 C1
Plaza Wy
Walla Walla WA 50 B2
Walla Walla WA 207 E5
Walla Walla Co WA 50 B2
Walla Walla Co WA 207 E5
S Pleasant Valley Rd
Ada Co ID 84 A3
Ada Co ID 224 A7
Boise ID 84 A3
Boise ID 224 A7
Plum Rd
Canyon Co ID 83 B2
Plum St SE
Olympia WA 146 A5
S Plymouth Rd
Benton Co WA 49 A2
E Plymouth St
Caldwell ID 219 C1
W Plymouth St
Caldwell ID 219 C1
Pocahontas Rd
Baker Co OR 60 D6
Point Brown Av NE
Ocean Shores WA 149 B1
Point Brown Av SE
Ocean Shores WA 149 B2
Point Ellice Br
Victoria BC 111 D4
Point Grey Rd
Vancouver BC 109 A3
E Pole Rd
Whatcom Co WA 5 C6
E Pole Rd SR-544
Whatcom Co WA 5 C6
E Poleline Av
Kootenai Co ID 215 E3
Kootenai Co ID 216 A3
Post Falls ID 215 C3
E Ponderosa Blvd
Kootenai Co ID 216 B6
Post Falls ID 216 B6
Ponderosa St
Bend OR 191 D6
Deschutes Co OR 191 D6
E Poplar St
Walla Walla WA 208 A3
NE Poplar St
Clark Co WA 160 C1
Vancouver WA 160 C1
W Poplar St
College Place WA 207 C5
Walla Walla WA 207 C5
Walla Walla WA 208 A3
Port Wy
Vancouver WA 157 D4
Portal Wy
Whatcom Co WA 5 B5
Portland Av
Tacoma WA 142 C4
Portland Av E
Pierce Co WA 144 C6
E Portland Av
Pierce Co WA 144 D5
Tacoma WA 142 C6
Tacoma WA 144 D3
NW Portland Av
Bend OR 189 D7
Bend OR 190 A7
E Portland Frwy
Maywood Park OR 163 D6
Portland OR 163 C6
Portland OR 167 C6
E Portland Frwy I-205
Maywood Park OR 163 C6
Portland OR 163 C6
Portland OR 167 C6
NE Portland Hwy
Portland OR 162 E4
Portland OR 163 B5
NE Portland Hwy US-30 BYP
Portland OR 162 E4
Portland OR 163 B5
Portland Rd NE
Marion Co OR 54 D4
Marion Co OR 172 D1
Salem OR 172 A5
Portland Rd NE SR-99E
Marion Co OR 54 D4
Marion Co OR 172 D2
Salem OR 172 C3
N Portland Rd
Portland OR 157 C6
Portland OR 161 A1
Port of Tacoma Rd
Fife WA 142 E5
Tacoma WA 142 D3
N Portsmouth Av
Portland OR 161 B1
N Post St
Spokane WA 211 E1
Potter St
Bellingham WA 113 D4
N Powder River Ln
North Powder OR 60 D4
Union Co OR 60 D4
SE Powell Blvd
Gresham OR 168 E6
Portland OR 45 A7
Portland OR 166 C5
Portland OR 167 B5
Portland OR 168 C5
SE Powell Blvd US-26
Gresham OR 168 E6
Portland OR 45 A7
Portland OR 166 B5
Portland OR 167 B5
Portland OR 168 D5
W Powell Blvd
Gresham OR 168 E6
W Powell Blvd US-26
Gresham OR 168 E6
Powell Rd
Grays Harbor Co WA 23 C7
Powell Butte Hwy
Deschutes Co OR 66 E5
SW Powell Butte Hwy
Crook Co OR 66 E4
SE Powell Valley Blvd
Gresham OR 168 E6
Portland OR 168 E6
SE Powell Valley Blvd US-26
Gresham OR 168 E6
Portland OR 168 E6
Powerhouse Rd
Abbotsford BC 5 E5
E Powerline Rd
Nampa ID 83 D2
Nampa ID 220 E4
S Powerline Rd
Nampa ID 83 D2
Nampa ID 220 D5
Powers Rd
Bend OR 191 E4
Prairie Av
Port Coquitlam BC 5 A2
Prairie Rd
Eugene OR 64 B4
Eugene OR 180 D2
Lane Co OR 64 B4
Lane Co OR 180 D4
Skagit Co WA 15 C1
Prairie Central Rd
Chilliwack BC 6 A3
Pratt Rd
Sunshine Coast BC 4 B1
NE Prescott St
Maywood Park OR 163 C5
Portland OR 162 D5
Portland OR 163 B5
Prest Rd
Chilliwack BC 6 A4
Preston Av
Lewiston ID 41 E6
Princeton Av NE
Seattle WA 125 C7
NE Princeton Wy
Seattle WA 125 C6
Pringle Pkwy SE
Salem OR 173 D1
Pringle Pkwy SE SR-22
Salem OR 173 D1
Pringle Pkwy SE SR-99E BUS
Salem OR 173 D1
Prior St
Vancouver BC 110 B2
N Proctor St
Tacoma WA 141 C4
S Proctor St
Tacoma WA 141 C5
Prospect Av
Walla Walla Co WA 207 E6
Walla Walla Co WA 208 A6
E Prospect Rd
Walla Walla WA 208 A6
Walla Walla Co WA 208 A6
W Prospect Rd
Walla Walla Co WA 208 A6
Prospect St
Bellingham WA 113 C3
Klamath Falls OR 201 C5
Prospect Lake Rd
Saanich BC 14 B2
Protest Rd
Boise ID 224 C2
Puget St NE
Olympia WA 146 A4
Pullman-Albion Rd
Whitman Co WA 41 C3
NE Purcell Blvd
Bend OR 190 D4
Deschutes Co OR 190 D4
Purple Sage Rd
Canyon Co ID 83 C1
Puyallup Av
Tacoma WA 142 B6

Q

Q St
Port Townsend WA 119 D3
Springfield OR 64 C5
Springfield OR 182 E7
Springfield OR 183 A7
W Q St
Springfield OR 182 E7
Quadra St
Saanich BC 111 E2
Victoria BC 111 E5
Quartz Valley Rd
Siskiyou Co CA 98 C5
Quartzville Rd
Linn Co OR 65 B1
Quebec St
Vancouver BC 110 B3
Victoria BC 111 D5
Queen Av SE
Albany OR 175 E4
Albany OR 176 A4
Queen Av SW
Albany OR 175 E4
Linn Co OR 175 C4
Queen Anne Av N
Seattle WA 128 B3
Queen Anne Dr
Seattle WA 128 B2
W Queens Rd
N Vancouver Dist BC 108 C3
Queensbury Av
North Vancouver BC 108 E6
Queensgate Dr
Richland WA 203 A7
Quesnel Dr
Vancouver BC 109 A5
Quincy St
Port Townsend WA 119 E4
Quincy-Mayger Rd
Columbia Co OR 44 C1

R

N Race St
Port Angeles WA 117 D4
S Race St
Port Angeles WA 117 D4
S Radar Rd
Adams Co WA 39 B3
S Radar Rd SR-24
Adams Co WA 39 B3
Railroad Av
Mt Vernon WA 116 B5
Skagit Co WA 116 B5
Railway Av
Richmond BC 4 D3
Rainier Av N
King Co WA 138 A5
Renton WA 138 A5
Rainier Av S
King Co WA 137 E3
King Co WA 138 A4
Renton WA 138 B6
Seattle WA 25 C3
Seattle WA 128 E7
Seattle WA 132 E2
Seattle WA 133 C7
Seattle WA 137 C2
Rainier Av S SR-167
Renton WA 138 B7
Seattle WA 25 C3
Seattle WA 132 E1
Seattle WA 133 A4
Rainier Av S SR-900
Renton WA 138 B7
Rainier Rd SE
Thurston Co WA 35 A2
N Ralph St
Spokane WA 210 D6
Ramsey Rd
Jackson Co OR 87 C5
N Ramsey Rd
Coeur d'Alene ID 31 E1

18 INDEX

INDEX 18

N Ramsey Rd

Seymour St PROV-99A

Street Index

STREET / City State Map# Grid

N Ramsey Rd
Coeur d'Alene ID 218 A3
N Ramsey Rd I-90 BUS
Coeur d'Alene ID 218 A3
N Randolph Av
Portland OR 161 E7
W Range Rd
Ada Co ID 84 A4
Ravenna Av NE
Seattle WA 125 A4
NE Ravenna Blvd
Seattle WA 124 D5
Seattle WA 125 A6
W Raye St
Seattle WA 128 A2
Ray Nash Dr NW
Pierce Co WA 25 A5
S Redland Rd
Clackamas Co OR 55 B1
Redmond Wy
Redmond WA 25 D2
Redmond Wy SR-908
Redmond WA 25 D2
NE Redmond-Fall City Rd
King Co WA 25 E2
Sammamish WA 25 E2
NE Redmond-Fall City Rd SR-202
King Co WA 25 E2
Sammamish WA 25 E2
Red Rock Rd
Siskiyou Co CA 99 E4
Siskiyou Co CA 100 A4
Red Top Rd
Canyon Co ID 83 A1
Redwood Hwy
Crescent City CA 96 E4
Del Norte Co CA 96 E4
Grants Pass OR 197 B6
Humboldt Co CA 97 A6
Josephine Co OR 197 A6
Redwood Hwy US-101
Crescent City CA 96 E4
Del Norte Co CA 96 E4
Humboldt Co CA 97 A6
Redwood Hwy US-199
Grants Pass OR 197 B6
Josephine Co OR 197 A6
Reed St
Sedro-Woolley WA 15 D2
SE Reed Market Rd
Bend OR 192 B3
SW Reed Market Rd
Bend OR 191 E2
Bend OR 192 A2
W Rees Av
Walla Walla WA 207 D2
Reese Hill Rd
Whatcom Co WA 5 D5
Reese Hill Rd SR-547
Whatcom Co WA 5 D5
S Regal Rd
Spokane Co WA 212 D7
S Regal St
Spokane WA 31 B2
Spokane WA 212 D5
Spokane Co WA 212 D6
Regents Blvd
Fircrest WA 141 A6
Tacoma WA 141 A6
Reid Dr NW
Pierce Co WA 25 B5
Renton Av S
King Co WA 137 D5
King Co WA 138 A6
Renton WA 138 A6
Seattle WA 133 B7
Seattle WA 137 C3
Renton Av Ext
King Co WA 138 A6
Renton WA 138 A6
Renton-Issaquah Rd SE
Issaquah WA 25 D4
Renton-Issaquah Rd SE SR-900
Issaquah WA 25 D4
Reser Rd
Walla Walla WA 208 B6
Walla Walla Co WA 50 B2
Walla Walla Co WA 208 C6
Reservation Rd
Wasco Co OR 56 D4
SE Reservoir Rd
Crook Co OR 67 B5
SW Reservoir Rd
Crook Co OR 67 A5
Reston Rd
Douglas Co OR 74 D6
N Reuben Rd
Douglas Co OR 86 E2
N Reuben Rd CO-27
Douglas Co OR 86 E2
Reubens-Gifford Rd
Nez Perce Co ID 42 C6
NE Revere Av
Bend OR 190 A6
NW Revere Av
Bend OR 190 A6
W Reynolds Av
Centralia WA 34 D3
Centralia WA 151 B3
Lewis Co WA 34 D3
Lewis Co WA 151 B3
Rhea Creek Rd
Morrow Co OR 48 C7
Morrow Co OR 58 C1
Rhody Dr
Jefferson Co WA 15 A6
Rhody Dr SR-19
Jefferson Co WA 15 A6
Rich Rd SE
Thurston Co WA 34 E1
Thurston Co WA 148 C4
Richards Rd
Bellevue WA 134 E2
Richards Rd SE
Bellevue WA 134 E2
Richardsons Gap Rd
Linn Co OR 54 E7
Richmond Av
Victoria BC 112 B5
Richmond Frwy
Richmond BC 4 D3
Richmond Frwy PROV-91
Richmond BC 4 D3
Richmond Rd
Saanich BC 112 C3
Victoria BC 112 B4
Rickard Rd
Deschutes Co OR 66 D6
Deschutes Co OR 192 E6
NE Riddell Rd
Bremerton WA 122 C1
Kitsap Co WA 122 B1
NW Riddell Rd
Kitsap Co WA 122 A1
Riddle Byp
Douglas Co OR 75 A7
Rieth Rd
Umatilla Co OR 49 C5
Rieth Rd CO-1300
Umatilla Co OR 49 C5
Riley Butte Rd
Washington Co ID 72 D2
Rim Rd
Canyon Co ID 83 C3
Rimrock Rd
Colton WA 41 D4
Whitman Co WA 41 D4
Rimrock Rd SR-193
Colton WA 41 D4
Whitman Co WA 41 D4
Ringold Rd
Franklin Co WA 39 B5
E Rio Vista Av
Burlington WA 15 C2
Burlington WA 115 D5
Skagit Co WA 115 D5
W Rio Vista Av
Burlington WA 115 B5
W Rio Vista Av SR-20
Burlington WA 115 B5
Ripon Av
Lewiston ID 41 E6
River Dr
Richmond BC 4 D3
N River Dr
Linn Co OR 64 E2
Linn Co OR 65 A2
River Rd
Clallam Co WA 14 D6
Clallam Co WA 118 A6
Delta BC 4 E3
Eugene OR 64 B4
Eugene OR 181 A2
Klickitat Co WA 46 C3
Lake Co OR 90 C5
Lane Co OR 64 B4
Langley Township BC 5 B3
Sequim WA 118 A5
Wasco Co OR 46 E6
River Rd E
Pierce Co WA 25 C6
Pierce Co WA 142 E6
Tacoma WA 142 E6
River Rd E SR-167
Pierce Co WA 25 C6
Pierce Co WA 142 E6
Tacoma WA 142 E6
River Rd N
Keizer OR 54 C4
Keizer OR 171 E1
Salem OR 171 E3
River Rd N SR-219
Keizer OR 54 C4
Keizer OR 171 E1
Salem OR 171 E3
River Rd NE
Marion Co OR 54 D3
River Rd NE SR-219
Marion Co OR 54 D4
River Rd S
Salem OR 54 C5
Salem OR 173 B3
River Rd W
Delta BC 4 D4
SE River Rd
Clackamas Co OR 170 B7
Milwaukie OR 170 B5
SW River Rd
Washington Co OR 44 D7
W River St
Boise ID 222 B7
Riverbanks Rd
Josephine Co OR 86 E5
N Riverside Av
Medford OR 198 B4
N Riverside Av SR-99
Medford OR 198 B4
S Riverside Av
Medford OR 198 C6
S Riverside Av SR-99
Medford OR 198 C6
W Riverside Av
Spokane WA 211 D1
NW Riverside Blvd
Bend OR 189 E7
Riverside Dr
Albany OR 175 C4
Asotin Co WA 41 D6
Clackamas Co OR 170 A5
Lake Oswego OR 170 A5
Linn Co OR 175 C4
Mt Vernon WA 116 B2
Riverside Dr SR-43
Clackamas Co OR 170 A5
Lake Oswego OR 170 A5
Riverside Dr SR-129
Asotin Co WA 41 D6
Riverside Dr SW
Albany OR 54 B7
Albany OR 175 C4
Linn Co OR 54 B7
Linn Co OR 175 C4
SW Riverside Dr
Albany OR 175 C4
Clackamas Co OR 170 A5
Linn Co OR 175 C4
Multnomah Co OR 170 A3
Portland OR 170 A2
SW Riverside Dr SR-43
Clackamas Co OR 170 A5
Multnomah Co OR 170 A3
Portland OR 170 A2
Riverside Rd
Canyon Co ID 83 B2
Road 3 NE
Grant Co WA 29 B7
Road 13
Siskiyou Co CA 99 E6
Siskiyou Co CA 100 A6
Road 13 SR-6
Siskiyou Co CA 99 E6
Siskiyou Co CA 100 A6
Road 14 NE
Douglas Co WA 28 D1
Road 14 NE SR-172
Douglas Co WA 28 D1
Road 14 NW
Douglas Co WA 28 C1
Road 14 NW SR-172
Douglas Co WA 28 C1
Road 15 NW
Douglas Co WA 28 C1
Road 36 NE
Grant Co WA 29 A3
Road 50 NE
Grant Co WA 29 B1
Road 52 NE
Grant Co WA 29 B1
N Road 68
Pasco WA 39 B7
Road 170
Franklin Co WA 39 B4
Road B NE
Douglas Co WA 18 C7
Douglas Co WA 28 C1
Road C NW
Douglas Co WA 28 C2
Grant Co WA 28 D6
Road C NW SR-172
Douglas Co WA 28 C2
Road C SW
Grant Co WA 28 D7
Grant Co WA 38 D1
Road L SW
Grant Co WA 38 C4
Road O NE
Grant Co WA 29 B7
Road O SE
Grant Co WA 29 B7
Road O SW
Grant Co WA 38 B1
Road Q SW
Grant Co WA 38 C1
Road R NE
Douglas Co WA 18 E7
Douglas Co WA 28 E2
Grant Co WA 29 B1
Road R NE SR-17
Douglas Co WA 18 E7
Douglas Co WA 28 E2
Road U NE
Grant Co WA 29 B7
Road U SE
Grant Co WA 29 B7
Grant Co WA 39 B1
Road V NE
Grant Co WA 29 B1
Road W NE
Grant Co WA 29 C1
E Roanoke St
Seattle WA 128 D2
Seattle WA 129 A2
Robal Rd
Bend OR 190 A2
Deschutes Co OR 190 A2
Roberts Dr
Black Diamond WA 25 E5
Robertson St
Victoria BC 112 B7
Robertson Bridge Rd
Josephine Co OR 86 E5
S Robinson Rd
Canyon Co ID 83 D2
Rock Creek Dam Rd
Wasco Co OR 56 D2
Rock Hill Dr
Linn Co OR 64 D1
Rocking Horse Rd
Deschutes Co OR 191 D6
S Rock Lake Rd
Spokane Co WA 31 A5
W Rockland Rd
N Vancouver Dist BC 108 D2
Rocklyn Rd
Lincoln Co WA 30 B3
Rocky Point Rd
Metchosin BC 14 A3
Rodeo Ln
Canyon Co ID 83 A1
Roeder Av
Bellingham WA 113 B3
Rogue River Hwy
Grants Pass OR 87 A5
Grants Pass OR 197 D6
Josephine Co OR 197 D6
Rogue River Hwy SR-99
Grants Pass OR 87 A5
Grants Pass OR 197 D6
Josephine Co OR 197 D6
E Roosevelt Av
Nampa ID 220 D5
Roosevelt Blvd
Eugene OR 64 B5
Eugene OR 180 D7
Eugene OR 181 A7
N Roosevelt Dr
Clatsop Co OR 154 D3
Gearhart OR 154 D3
Seaside OR 154 C4
N Roosevelt Dr US-26
Clatsop Co OR 154 D3
Gearhart OR 154 D3
Seaside OR 154 C4
N Roosevelt Dr US-101
Clatsop Co OR 154 D3
Gearhart OR 154 D3
Seaside OR 154 C4
S Roosevelt Dr
Clatsop Co OR 154 B7
Seaside OR 154 C6
S Roosevelt Dr US-26
Clatsop Co OR 154 B7
Seaside OR 154 B7
S Roosevelt Dr US-101
Clatsop Co OR 154 B7
Seaside OR 154 B7
Roosevelt St
Port Townsend WA 119 E3
N Roosevelt St
Walla Walla WA 208 C3
S Roosevelt St
Walla Walla WA 208 C3
Roosevelt Wy NE
Seattle WA 124 E4
Seattle WA 128 D1
Roosevelt Grade Rd
Klickitat Co WA 48 A4
N Rosa Parks Wy
Portland OR 161 E4
Portland OR 162 A4
NE Rosa Parks Wy
Portland OR 162 A4
Rosario Rd
Skagit Co WA 15 A2
Rose Av
Columbia Co OR 44 C4
Vernonia OR 44 C4
Rose Av SR-47
Columbia Co OR 44 C4
Vernonia OR 44 C4
Rose Av SR-202
Columbia Co OR 44 C4
Vernonia OR 44 C4
E Rose St
Walla Walla WA 207 E3
Walla Walla WA 208 A3
N Rose St
Walla Walla WA 208 A2
W Rose St
College Place WA 207 C4
Walla Walla WA 50 B2
Walla Walla WA 207 D4
W Rose Hill St
Boise ID 223 E2
Boise ID 224 A2
Rosemont Rd
Clackamas Co OR 55 A1
West Linn OR 55 A1
E Rosenoff Rd
Adams Co WA 29 E7
Adams Co WA 30 A7
W Rosenoff Rd
Adams Co WA 29 C7
Ross Ln
Jackson Co OR 87 C6
Ross Ln N
Jackson Co OR 87 C6
Medford OR 87 C6
Ross Rd
Abbotsford BC 5 C4
Ross St
Victoria BC 112 B7
Rossanley Dr
Jackson Co OR 87 C6
Jackson Co OR 198 A4
Medford OR 87 C6
Medford OR 198 A4
Rossanley Dr SR-238
Jackson Co OR 87 C6
Jackson Co OR 198 A4
Medford OR 87 C6
Medford OR 198 A4
Ross Island Br
Portland OR 165 E4
Portland OR 166 A4
Ross Island Br US-26
Portland OR 165 E4
Portland OR 166 A4
N Ross Point Rd
Kootenai Co ID 216 C5
Post Falls ID 216 C5
S Ross Point Rd
Kootenai Co ID 216 C5
Post Falls ID 216 C5
Ross Point-Rathdrum Hwy
Kootenai Co ID 216 B3
Post Falls ID 216 B3
Ross Point-Rathdrum Hwy SR-41
Kootenai Co ID 216 B3
Post Falls ID 216 B3
SW Roxbury St
King Co WA 135 E2
King Co WA 136 B2
Seattle WA 25 C3
Seattle WA 135 E2
Seattle WA 136 B2
Roy St
Seattle WA 128 B4
E Roy St
Seattle WA 128 D4
Royal Av
Eugene OR 64 B5
Royal Av
Eugene OR 180 C6
Eugene OR 181 A6
Lane Co OR 180 A6
New Westminster BC 4 E3
S Royal Brougham Wy
Seattle WA 132 C1
N Ruby St
Spokane WA 210 A6
N Ruby St US-2
Spokane WA 210 A6
N Ruby St US-395
Spokane WA 210 A6
Rucker Av
Everett WA 120 C3
SE Rupert Dr
Clackamas Co OR 170 B7
Rupert Rd E
Nanaimo BC 3 B1
Nanaimo District BC 3 B1
Rush Rd
Lewis Co WA 34 E4
Russell Rd
Kent WA 140 C7
N Russell St
Portland OR 161 E7
N Ruston Wy
Ruston WA 25 B5
Tacoma WA 25 B5
Tacoma WA 141 D1
Rutland Rd
Oak Bay BC 112 E3
Rutledge Ln
Sherman Co OR 57 B1
Rw Johnson Blvd SW
Olympia WA 145 B7
Tumwater WA 145 B7
Tumwater WA 147 B1
S Ryan Wy
Seattle WA 137 B3
Tukwila WA 137 B3

S

S-507
Wasco Co OR 56 B3
Saanich Rd
Saanich BC 111 D2
W Saanich Rd
North Saanich BC 14 B1
W Saanich Rd PROV-17A
North Saanich BC 14 B1
Sage Rd
Jackson Co OR 87 C6
Jackson Co OR 198 A4
Medford OR 198 A4
Sagehill Rd
Franklin Co WA 39 B4
St. Charles St
Victoria BC 112 B6
St. Helens Av
Tacoma WA 142 A4
Vancouver WA 159 B6
NW St. Helens Rd
Portland OR 44 E6
Portland OR 161 A6
NW St. Helens Rd US-30
Portland OR 44 E6
Portland OR 161 A5
NE St. James Rd
Clark Co WA 158 C2
Vancouver WA 158 C1
St. Johns Blvd
Vancouver WA 158 B3
NE St. Johns Rd
Clark Co WA 158 C1
Vancouver WA 158 C1
St. Lawrence St
Victoria BC 111 D5
St. Louis Rd NE
Marion Co OR 54 D3
St. Paul Av
Tacoma WA 142 B5
St. Paul Hwy NE
Marion Co OR 54 D2
Salem Av SE
Albany OR 176 B2
Linn Co OR 176 C2
Salem Hwy
Salem OR 171 D7
Salem Hwy SR-99E BUS
Salem OR 171 D7
Salem Pkwy
Keizer OR 172 B2
Salem OR 54 C4
Salem OR 171 E4
Salem OR 172 B2
Salem Pkwy SR-99E BUS
Keizer OR 172 B2
Salem OR 54 C4
Salem OR 171 E4
Salem OR 172 B2
Salem Dallas Hwy NW
Salem OR 173 A1
Salem Dallas Hwy NW SR-22
Salem OR 173 A1
Sales Rd S
Lakewood WA 143 D7
Pierce Co WA 143 D7
SW Salmon St
Portland OR 165 D2
Salmon la Sac Rd
Kittitas Co WA 26 E5
Salmon la Sac Rd SR-903
Kittitas Co WA 26 E5
Salmon River Hwy
McMinnville OR 54 B3
Yamhill Co OR 54 B3
Salmon River Hwy SR-18
McMinnville OR 54 B3
Yamhill Co OR 54 B3
S Salnave Rd
Medical Lake WA 30 E3
S Salnave Rd
Spokane Co WA 30 E3
S Salnave Rd SR-902
Medical Lake WA 30 E3
Spokane Co WA 30 E3
W Salnave Rd
Cheney WA 31 A3
E Saltese Av
Spokane Valley WA 214 A6
Samish Wy
Bellingham WA 5 C7
Bellingham WA 113 D6
N Samish Wy
Bellingham WA 113 D5
S Samish Wy
Bellingham WA 113 D6
Sam Orcutt Wy NE
Keizer OR 171 E3
Sams Valley Hwy
Jackson Co OR 87 C5
Sams Valley Hwy SR-234
Jackson Co OR 87 C5
Sandlake Rd
Tillamook Co OR 53 C2
Sand Point Wy NE
Seattle WA 125 C6
Sand Point Wy NE SR-513
Seattle WA 125 C6
Sand Ridge Rd
Linn Co OR 64 C1
Sandridge Rd
Pacific Co WA 33 C6
NE Sandy Blvd
Gresham OR 164 D6
Maywood Park OR 163 C5
Portland OR 45 A6
Portland OR 162 D7
Portland OR 163 A7
Portland OR 164 A5
Portland OR 166 B2
NE Sandy Blvd US-30 BYP
Gresham OR 164 D6
Portland OR 45 A6
Portland OR 163 D5
Portland OR 164 A5
SE Sandy Blvd
Portland OR 166 A2
San Francisco Av NE
Olympia WA 146 A3
San Juan Av
Port Townsend WA 119 C2
Santiam Hwy
Jefferson Co OR 66 A2
Linn Co OR 54 D7
Linn Co OR 64 D1
Linn Co OR 65 E2
Santiam Hwy SR-126
Jefferson Co OR 66 A2
Linn Co OR 65 D2
Santiam Hwy US-20
Jefferson Co OR 66 A2
Linn Co OR 54 D7
Linn Co OR 64 E2
Linn Co OR 65 D2
Santiam Hwy SE
Albany OR 54 C7
Albany OR 176 E3
Linn Co OR 176 C3
Santiam Hwy SE US-20
Albany OR 54 C7
Albany OR 176 E3
Linn Co OR 176 C3
N Santiam Hwy
Linn Co OR 65 E1
Marion Co OR 174 E5
Salem OR 54 D5
Salem OR 174 C4
N Santiam Hwy SR-22
Linn Co OR 65 E1
Marion Co OR 174 E5
Salem OR 54 D5
Salem OR 174 B4
N Santiam Hwy SR-99E BUS
Salem OR 54 D5
Salem OR 174 B4
N Santiam Hwy SE
Marion Co OR 54 D5
Marion Co OR 55 A6
Sublimity OR 54 D5
N Santiam Hwy SE SR-22
Marion Co OR 54 D5
Marion Co OR 55 A6
Sublimity OR 54 D5
S Santiam Hwy
Linn Co OR 64 D1
Linn Co OR 65 D2
S Santiam Hwy US-20
Linn Co OR 64 D1
Linn Co OR 65 D2
Santiam Wy
Albany OR 176 A3
Santiam Wy US-20
Albany OR 176 A3
Sapp Rd SW
Thurston Co WA 147 A1
Tumwater WA 147 A1
Saratoga Rd
Island Co WA 15 B6
Langley WA 15 B6
Sauk Valley Rd
Skagit Co WA 16 C3
Sauk Valley Rd SR-530
Skagit Co WA 16 C3
NE Savage St
Grants Pass OR 197 D3
NW Savage St
Grants Pass OR 197 C3
Sawyers Bar Rd
Siskiyou Co CA 98 C7
Scappoose Vernonia Hwy
Columbia Co OR 44 D4
Scenic Dr
Yakima WA 37 C4
Yakima Co WA 37 C4
Scenic Wy
Asotin Co WA 41 D6
Scenic Wy SR-128
Asotin Co WA 41 D6
Schaupp Rd
Klamath Co OR 100 B1
Scholz Rd
Whitman Co WA 41 B1
School Av
Walla Walla WA 208 D3
Walla Walla Co WA 208 D5
W Schrag Rd
Adams Co WA 29 C7
Schuster Pkwy
Tacoma WA 141 E2
Tacoma WA 142 A3
Scoon Rd
Sunnyside WA 38 B7
E Scootney St
Othello WA 39 B2
Scott Rd
Surrey BC 4 E3
S Scott St
Spokane WA 212 B6
SE Scott St
Bend OR 192 A1
Scott Canyon Rd
Rufus OR 47 C5
NE Scoville Rd
Grants Pass OR 197 D2
Scravel Hill Rd NE
Linn Co OR 54 C7
Scravel Hill Rd SE
Linn Co OR 176 E3
Seabeck Hwy NW
Kitsap Co WA 24 E2
NW Seabeck Holly Rd
Kitsap Co WA 24 E3
Seahurst Av
Everett WA 120 A5
Sea to Sky Hwy
Greater Vancouver BC 4 C1
West Vancouver BC 4 C1
Sea to Sky Hwy PROV-99
Greater Vancouver BC 4 C1
West Vancouver BC 4 C1
W Seattle Br
Seattle WA 131 E3
Seattle WA 132 C3
Seaview Av NW
Seattle WA 123 C6
Seaview Pl NW
Seattle WA 123 C4
E Section St
Mt Vernon WA 116 D5
SE Sedgwick Rd
Kitsap Co WA 25 B3
SE Sedgwick Rd SR-160
Kitsap Co WA 25 B3
Sehmel Dr NW
Pierce Co WA 25 A5
Selah Loop Rd
Yakima Co WA 37 C4
Sellards Rd
Benton Co WA 48 E2
Benton Co WA 49 A1
Sellwood Br
Portland OR 169 E1
Portland OR 170 A1
E Seltice Wy
Kootenai Co ID 216 D5
Post Falls ID 31 E1
Post Falls ID 215 D4
Post Falls ID 216 C5
E Seltice Wy I-90 BUS
Post Falls ID 215 D4
W Seltice Wy
Coeur d'Alene ID 218 A4
Kootenai Co ID 215 A4
Post Falls ID 215 C4
N Seneca Dr
Burns OR 80 C2
N Seneca Dr US-20
Burns OR 80 C2
N Seneca Dr US-395
Burns OR 80 C2
Seneca Rd
Eugene OR 181 A7
Eugene OR 185 A1
N Seneca Rd
Eugene OR 181 A7
Seneca St
Seattle WA 128 C6
N Sequim Av
Clallam Co WA 118 D4
Sequim WA 118 D5
S Sequim Av
Sequim WA 118 D5
Sequim-Dungeness Wy
Clallam Co WA 118 D2
N Sequim-Dungeness Wy
Clallam Co WA 118 D4
Sequim WA 118 D4
Service Creek-Mitchell Hwy
Wheeler Co OR 58 A7
Service Cr-Mitchell Hy SR-207
Wheeler Co OR 58 A7
Sevenmile Rd
Klamath Co OR 88 D3
W Seven Mile Rd
Spokane Co WA 31 A1
Seward Park Av S
Seattle WA 133 C6
Seattle WA 137 C2
Seymour St
Vancouver BC 109 E2
Vancouver BC 110 A2
Seymour St PROV-99
Vancouver BC 109 E2
Vancouver BC 110 A2
Seymour St PROV-99A
Vancouver BC 110 A2

19 INDEX

INDEX 19

Street Index

NW Shadybrook Rd — Tennant Wy

STREET / City State / Map# / Grid

NW Shadybrook Rd
North Plains OR 44 D6
Washington Co OR 44 D6
Shaniko-Fossil Hwy
Wheeler Co OR 57 E5
Wheeler Co OR 58 A5
Shaniko-Fossil Hwy SR-218
Wheeler Co OR 57 E5
Wheeler Co OR 58 A5
N Shasta Lp
Eugene OR 186 A6
Shasta Wy
Klamath Co OR 89 A7
Klamath Co OR 202 C7
Klamath Falls OR 201 E7
Klamath Falls OR 202 A7
Shaw Rd E
Puyallup WA 25 C7
Shawnigan Lake Rd
Cowichan Valley BC 4 A7
Cowichan Valley BC 14 A1
Shelbourne St
Saanich BC 112 B3
Victoria BC 112 B3
Shell Rock Rd
Clackamas Co OR 55 E3
W Shelton-Matlock Rd
Mason Co WA 24 B6
Sherars Bridge Hwy
Sherman Co OR 57 A2
Sherars Bridge Hwy SR-216
Sherman Co OR 57 A2
Sheridan Av
North Bend OR 194 A2
Port Townsend WA 15 A5
Port Townsend WA 119 B5
Sheridan Av US-101
North Bend OR 194 A2
E Sheridan Av
Nampa ID 220 C5
S Sheridan Av
Tacoma WA 143 E4
SW Sheridan St
Portland OR 165 D4
SW Sheridan St US-26
Portland OR 165 D4
Sherman Av
North Bend OR 194 A1
Sherman Av US-101
North Bend OR 194 A1
E Sherman Av
Coeur d'Alene ID 218 D6
E Sherman Av I-90 BUS
Coeur d'Alene ID 218 D6
Sherman Rd
Cowichan Valley BC 3 E6
N Sherman Rd
Spokane Co WA 21 A6
S Sherman St
Spokane WA 212 A2
NW Shevlin Park Rd
Bend OR 189 B6
Shincke Rd NE
Thurston Co WA 146 D1
Shoestring Rd
Lane Co OR 75 B2
W Shore Dr
Whatcom Co WA 5 A7
N Shore Rd
Cowichan Valley BC 3 C6
NE Shore Rd
Mason Co WA 24 E4
S Shore Rd
Cowichan Valley BC 3 C6
S Shore Rd PROV-18
Cowichan Valley BC 3 C6
SW Shorebrook Dr
Normandy Park WA 139 B3
SE Shoreland Dr
Bellevue WA 130 C7
Shoreline Dr
Boise ID 222 A7
SE Shorewood Dr
Vancouver WA 158 E5
NW Shute Rd
Hillsboro OR 44 D6
Washington Co OR 44 D6
N Side Dr
Linn Co OR 64 E2
S Side Rd
Josephine Co OR 86 E6
Josephine Co OR 87 A6
W Side Rd
Klamath Co OR 88 D4
Sidney Rd SW
Kitsap Co WA 25 A4
Sievers Duecy Blvd
Everett WA 120 A7
Siletz Hwy
Lincoln Co OR 53 C7
Toledo OR 53 C7
Siletz Hwy SR-229
Lincoln Co OR 53 C7
Toledo OR 53 C7
Siletz Hwy US-20 BUS
Lincoln Co OR 53 C7
Toledo OR 53 C7
Silica Rd SW
Grant Co WA 28 B7
Grant Co WA 38 B1
Sills Rd
Island Co WA 15 C7
Silvercreek Rd
Lewis Co WA 35 A5
Silvercreek Rd SR-122
Lewis Co WA 35 A5
Silver Falls Hwy SE
Marion Co OR 54 E5
Silver Falls Hwy SE SR-214
Marion Co OR 54 E5
Silver Lake Rd
Klamath Co OR 77 C7
Lake Co OR 77 C7
Silverton Rd NE
Marion Co OR 54 D4
Marion Co OR 172 E4
Salem OR 172 B5
Silverton Rd NE SR-213
Marion Co OR 54 D4
Marion Co OR 172 E5
Simnasho Rd
Wasco Co OR 56 C5
Simnasho Rd B-9
Wasco Co OR 56 C4
Simplot Blvd
Caldwell ID 219 A3
Canyon Co ID 83 B1
Canyon Co ID 219 A3
Simplot Blvd SR-19
Caldwell ID 219 A3
Canyon Co ID 83 B1
Canyon Co ID 219 A3
E Simplot Blvd
Caldwell ID 219 B3
E Simplot Blvd SR-19
Caldwell ID 219 B3
W Simplot Blvd
Caldwell ID 219 A3
Canyon Co ID 219 A3
W Simplot Blvd SR-19
Caldwell ID 219 A3
Canyon Co ID 219 A3
Simpson Av
Vancouver WA 157 D3
SW Simpson Av
Bend OR 191 C1
E Sims Wy
Port Townsend WA 119 D4
E Sims Wy SR-20
Port Townsend WA 119 D4
W Sims Wy
Jefferson Co WA 119 A5
Port Townsend WA 119 B5
W Sims Wy SR-20
Jefferson Co WA 119 A5
Port Townsend WA 119 B5
Sinclair Rd
Saanich BC 112 D1
Siskiyou Blvd
Ashland OR 87 E7
Ashland OR 199 E4
Ashland OR 200 B5
Jackson Co OR 200 C6
Siskiyou Blvd SR-99
Ashland OR 87 E7
Ashland OR 199 E4
Ashland OR 200 B5
Jackson Co OR 200 C6
NE Skidmore St
Portland OR 164 A6
Skilift Rd
West Vancouver BC 107 B2
Skinner St
Victoria BC 111 D4
NW Skyline Blvd
Multnomah Co OR 44 E6
Portland OR 44 E6
SW Skyline Blvd
Multnomah Co OR 165 A2
Portland OR 165 A3
Skyline Rd
Clackamas Co OR 56 A4
NW Skyliners Rd
Bend OR 189 C7
Bend OR 191 B1
Slater Av NE
Kirkland WA 126 E2
Slavin Rd
Yakima Co WA 37 B5
Sleater Kinney Rd NE
Lacey WA 146 E4
Olympia WA 146 E4
Thurston Co WA 24 E7
Thurston Co WA 146 E3
Sleater Kinney Rd SE
Lacey WA 146 E6
Olympia WA 146 E4
Slocan St
Vancouver BC 110 E7
E Smith Rd
Whatcom Co WA 5 C6
W Smith Rd
Ferndale WA 5 B6
Whatcom Co WA 5 B6
Smith St
Seattle WA 128 B2
Smithe St
Vancouver BC 109 E2
Vancouver BC 110 A3
NE Smith Rock Wy
Deschutes Co OR 66 E3
S Smugglers Cove Rd
Island Co WA 15 B6
Soap Hill Rd
Umatilla Co OR 59 C3
Social Ridge Ln
Morrow Co OR 58 C1
Sommers Rd
Whitman Co WA 41 B2
Sooke Rd
Langford BC 14 A3
Sooke Rd PROV-14
Langford BC 14 A3
E Sooke Rd
Capital BC 14 A3
NE Sorenson Rd
Clark Co WA 45 A3
Southbay Rd NE
Olympia WA 146 C4
Thurston Co WA 146 D1
Southborough Dr
West Vancouver BC 107 E1
Southcenter Blvd
Seatac WA 140 A1
Tukwila WA 140 C1
Southcenter Pkwy
Tukwila WA 140 C3
E Southeast Blvd
Spokane WA 212 C3
S Southeast Blvd
Spokane WA 212 B3
South Entrance Rd
Klamath Co OR 88 C1
South Fork Rd
Benton Co OR 63 E3
Southgate St
Victoria BC 111 E6
Southside Blvd
Nampa ID 83 D3
Southside Expwy
Klamath Co OR 100 A1
Klamath Falls OR 100 A1
Southside Expwy SR-140
Klamath Co OR 100 A1
Klamath Falls OR 100 A1
Southwood Ln
Eugene OR 181 E7
Eugene OR 182 A7
Spanaway McKenna Hwy
Pierce Co WA 35 B1
Spanaway McKenna Hwy SR-507
Pierce Co WA 35 B1
S Spangler Rd
Clackamas Co OR 55 A2
SE Sparrow St
Milwaukie OR 170 B5
Speyers Rd
Yakima Co WA 37 C4
Spicer Dr
Linn Co OR 64 D1
Spirit Lake Hwy
Cowlitz Co WA 34 E7
Cowlitz Co WA 35 A7
Spirit Lake Hwy SR-504
Cowlitz Co WA 34 E7
Cowlitz Co WA 35 A7
N Spokane St
Post Falls ID 215 D3
N Spokane St I-90 BUS
Post Falls ID 215 D5
S Spokane St
Seattle WA 132 E3
SW Spokane St
Seattle WA 131 C3
Seattle WA 132 B3
NE Spokane Wy
Vancouver WA 159 C1
W Spokane Falls Blvd
Spokane WA 211 E1
Spokane WA 212 A1
S Spotted Rd
Spokane Co WA 31 A2
E Sprague Av
Spokane WA 212 D1
Spokane Valley WA 212 E1
Spokane Valley WA 213 A4
Spokane Valley WA 214 A4
E Sprague Av I-90 BUS
Spokane WA 212 D1
Spokane Valley WA 212 E1
Spokane Valley WA 213 A4
Spokane Valley WA 214 A4
S Sprague Av
Tacoma WA 141 E5
Tacoma WA 143 D1
W Sprague Av
Spokane WA 211 E1
Spokane WA 212 A1
E Sprague Avenue Access 1
Spokane WA 212 B2
E Sprague Av Acc 1 I-90 BUS
Spokane WA 212 B1
E Sprague Avenue Access 3
Spokane WA 212 B1
E Sprague Av Acc 3 I-90 BUS
Spokane WA 212 B1
Sprague Highway Rd
Lincoln Co WA 30 D5
Sprague River Rd
Chiloquin OR 88 E4
Sprauge St
Wilson Creek WA 29 B4
Spring Blvd
Eugene OR 186 B5
Lane Co OR 186 B5
Spring St
Friday Harbor WA 14 D2
Seattle WA 128 C6
Springbrook Rd
Medford OR 198 D3
Springdale-Hunters Rd
Stevens Co WA 20 C5
NW Springhill Dr
Benton Co OR 54 B6
Spring Valley Rd
Spokane Co WA 31 C5
S Springwater Rd
Clackamas Co OR 55 B1
Spruce St
Florence OR 63 A6
Myrtle Point OR 74 A6
Port Townsend WA 119 D2
Squalicum Wy
Bellingham WA 113 B1
Stackpole Rd
Pacific Co WA 33 C4
Stackpole Rd SR-103
Pacific Co WA 33 C4
Stadium Frwy
Portland OR 161 D7
Portland OR 165 D3
Stadium Frwy I-405
Portland OR 161 D7
Portland OR 165 D3
Stadium Frwy US-30
Portland OR 161 E7
Stadium Wy S
Tacoma WA 142 A3
Stage Rd S
Jackson Co OR 87 C6
Medford OR 87 C6
W Staley Rd
Spokane Co WA 21 A7
Stanley Park Cswy
Vancouver BC 107 D6
Stanley Park Cswy PROV-1A
Vancouver BC 107 D6
Stanley Park Cswy PROV-99
Vancouver BC 107 D6
NE Stapleton Rd
Clark Co WA 158 E2
Vancouver WA 158 E3
Star Rd
Canyon Co ID 83 D2
Nampa ID 83 D2
N Star Rd
Star ID 83 D1
Stark St N
Salem OR 171 E4
SE Stark St
Gresham OR 45 B7
Gresham OR 168 D3
Portland OR 166 E2
Portland OR 167 D3
Portland OR 168 B3
Troutdale OR 45 B7
SW Stark St
Portland OR 165 E2
State Av
Marysville WA 15 D5
State Av NE
Olympia WA 145 E5
Olympia WA 146 A4
State Av NW
Olympia WA 145 E5
State St
Lostine OR 51 B7
Marion Co OR 54 D5
Marion Co OR 174 E2
Salem OR 173 E1
Salem OR 174 A1
State St SR-82
Lostine OR 51 B7
N State St
Bellingham WA 113 C4
Clackamas Co OR 170 A6
Lake Oswego OR 170 A6
N State St SR-43
Clackamas Co OR 170 A6
Lake Oswego OR 170 A6
S State St
Bellingham WA 113 A6
Lake Oswego OR 169 E7
Lake Oswego OR 170 A7
Tacoma WA 141 D6
S State St SR-43
Lake Oswego OR 169 E7
Lake Oswego OR 170 A7
W State St
Ada Co ID 221 A1
Boise ID 83 E1
Boise ID 221 A2
Boise ID 222 A5
Garden City ID 83 E1
Garden City ID 221 A2
Star ID 83 D1
W State St SR-44
Ada Co ID 221 A1
Boise ID 221 A1
Garden City ID 221 A1
Star ID 83 D1
State Highway 3
Nez Perce Co ID 42 A5
State Highway 3 SR-3
Nez Perce Co ID 42 A5
State Line Rd
Klamath Co OR 100 A2
Siskiyou Co CA 99 E2
Siskiyou Co CA 100 A2
State Line Rd SR-161
Klamath Co OR 100 A2
Siskiyou Co CA 99 E2
Siskiyou Co CA 100 A2
State Route 105
Grays Harbor Co WA 150 C7
State Route 105 SR-105
Grays Harbor Co WA 150 C7
W Stayton Rd SE
Marion Co OR 54 D6
Steamboat Island Rd NW
Thurston Co WA 24 D7
Stearns Ln
Douglas Co OR 75 A4
Steel Br
Portland OR 165 E1
Portland OR 166 A1
Steele St S
Lakewood WA 25 B7
Pierce Co WA 25 B7
Pierce Co WA 143 D7
S Steele St
Pierce Co WA 143 D7
Tacoma WA 143 D7
Steens Hwy
Harney Co OR 80 C2
Harney Co OR 81 A5
Steens Hwy SR-78
Harney Co OR 80 C2
Harney Co OR 81 A5
Steilacoom Blvd SW
Lakewood WA 143 A6
Stein Rd
Yakima Co WA 37 C5
Stenkamp Rd
Deschutes Co OR 66 E5
NE Stephens St
Douglas Co OR 196 A1
Roseburg OR 196 A3
NE Stephens St SR-99
Douglas Co OR 196 A1
Roseburg OR 196 A3
SE Stephens St
Douglas Co OR 195 E7
Roseburg OR 195 E7
Roseburg OR 196 A5
SE Stephens St SR-42
Douglas Co OR 195 E7
Roseburg OR 195 E7
SE Stephens St SR-99
Douglas Co OR 195 E7
Roseburg OR 195 E7
Roseburg OR 196 A5
SE Stephens St SR-138
Roseburg OR 196 A5
SW Stephenson St
Lake Oswego OR 169 B4
Portland OR 169 C4
E Steuben St
Bingen WA 46 C5
E Steuben St SR-14
Bingen WA 46 C5
Stevens Dr
Benton Co WA 39 A7
Richland WA 39 A7
Richland WA 203 C1
West Vancouver BC 107 E2
West Vancouver BC 108 A1
Stevens Dr SR-240 BUS
Richland WA 203 C2
Stevens Rd
Bend OR 192 E3
Deschutes Co OR 192 E3
N Stevens St
Spokane WA 211 E1
Tacoma WA 141 B1
S Stevens St
Spokane WA 211 E2
Tacoma WA 141 B5
Stevens Canyon Rd
Lewis Co WA 36 B3
Stevens Pass Hwy
Monroe WA 15 E7
Snohomish Co WA 15 E7
Snohomish Co WA 26 B1
Stevens Pass Hwy US-2
Monroe WA 15 E7
Snohomish Co WA 15 E7
Snohomish Co WA 26 B1
Steveston Hwy
Richmond BC 4 D3
Stewart Av
Nanaimo BC 3 D3
Stewart Av TCH-1
Nanaimo BC 3 D3
E Stewart Av
Medford OR 198 C7
W Stewart Av
Medford OR 198 B7
NW Stewart Pkwy
Roseburg OR 195 E2
Stewart Rd
Sunshine Coast BC 4 B1
Stewart Rd PROV-101
Sunshine Coast BC 4 B1
Stewart St
Seattle WA 128 C6
Stone Rd
Yakima Co WA 37 B5
Stone Wy N
Seattle WA 124 C7
Seattle WA 128 C2
N Strahorn Rd
Hayden ID 32 A1
Hayden ID 217 C3
Hayden Lake ID 32 A1
Hayden Lake ID 217 C4
Kootenai Co ID 32 A1
Kootenai Co ID 217 C2
Strander Blvd
Tukwila WA 140 D2
Succor Creek Hwy
Malheur Co OR 71 E7
Malheur Co OR 82 E1
Succor Creek Hwy SR-201
Malheur Co OR 71 E7
Malheur Co OR 82 E1
N Sullivan Rd
Spokane Valley WA 214 D1
S Sullivan Rd
Spokane Co WA 214 E7
Spokane Valley WA 31 C2
Spokane Valley WA 214 E5
Sullivan Creek Rd
Pend Oreille Co WA 11 B6
E Sumach St
Walla Walla WA 208 A2
S Sumas Rd
Chilliwack BC 5 E4
Sumas Wy
Abbotsford BC 5 D5
Sumas Wy PROV-11
Abbotsford BC 5 D5
E Summa St
Centralia WA 151 D6
Lewis Co WA 151 D6
W Summa St
Centralia WA 151 C6
Summer St
Bellingham WA 113 C2
Summer St NE
Salem OR 171 E7
Salem OR 173 E1
Summers Ln
Klamath Co OR 202 B7
Summerville Rd
Imbler OR 50 D7
Union Co OR 50 D7
Summit Av
Everett WA 120 E2
Summit Dr
Hood River Co OR 46 B6
NW Summit Dr
Bend OR 189 D5
Summit Grade
Nez Perce Co ID 42 B5
Summit Ridge Rd
Wasco Co OR 47 A7
Summitview Av
Yakima WA 37 C4
Summitview Rd
Tieton WA 37 B4
Summitview-Cowiche Rd
Yakima Co WA 37 C4
Sumpter Stage Hwy
Baker Co OR 60 E7
Sumpter Stage Hwy SR-7
Baker Co OR 60 E7
Sunnyridge Rd
Nampa ID 220 C7
Sunnyside Rd
Umatilla Co OR 50 A3
Sunnyside Rd SR-332
Umatilla Co OR 50 A3
SE Sunnyside Rd
Clackamas Co OR 45 A7
Sunnyslope Ln
Baker Co OR 61 A5
Sunnyslope Rd
Canyon Co ID 83 B2
Sunnyslope Rd SR-55
Canyon Co ID 83 B2
Sunnyview Rd NE
Marion Co OR 54 D4
Marion Co OR 172 E6
Salem OR 172 D6
Sunrise Av
Medford OR 198 D5
Sunrise Dr NE
Bainbridge Island WA 25 B2
Sunset Blvd N
Renton WA 138 C6
Sunset Blvd N SR-900
Renton WA 138 C6
Sunset Blvd NE
Renton WA 138 D5
Sunset Blvd NE SR-900
Renton WA 138 C6
NE Sunset Blvd
Renton WA 138 D4
NE Sunset Blvd SR-900
Renton WA 138 D4
SW Sunset Blvd
Renton WA 137 E7
Renton WA 138 A7
SW Sunset Blvd SR-900
Renton WA 137 E7
Renton WA 138 A7
W Sunset Blvd
Spokane WA 211 C2
Spokane Co WA 211 A3
W Sunset Blvd I-90 BUS
Spokane WA 211 C2
Spokane Co WA 211 A3
Sunset Dr
Bellingham WA 113 C2
E Sunset Dr
Bellingham WA 113 E1
E Sunset Dr SR-542
Bellingham WA 113 E1
S Sunset Dr
Island Co WA 15 B4
Sunset Hwy
Chelan Co WA 27 D4
Clatsop Co OR 43 C3
Clatsop Co OR 44 A4
Multnomah Co OR 165 A3
Portland OR 165 A3
Washington Co OR 44 D6
Sunset Hwy US-2
Chelan Co WA 27 D4
Sunset Hwy US-26
Clatsop Co OR 43 C3
Clatsop Co OR 44 A4
Multnomah Co OR 165 A3
Portland OR 165 A3
Washington Co OR 44 D6
Sunset Hwy US-97
Chelan Co WA 27 D4
NW Sunset Hwy
Washington Co OR 44 C5
NW Sunset Hwy SR-47
Washington Co OR 44 C5
NW Sunset Hwy US-26
Washington Co OR 44 C5
W Sunset Hwy
Spokane WA 211 A3
Spokane Co WA 211 A3
W Sunset Hwy I-90 BUS
Spokane WA 211 A3
Spokane Co WA 211 A3
Sunset Rd
Whitman Co WA 31 B7
Sunshine Coast Hwy
Sunshine Coast BC 1 E7
Sunshine Coast BC 4 A1
Sunshine Coast Hwy PROV-101
Sunshine Coast BC 1 E7
Sunshine Coast BC 4 A1
Superior St
Victoria BC 111 D6
Surber Dr NE
Seattle WA 129 B1
NE Surber Dr
Seattle WA 129 B1
Sutherlin-Umpqua Rd
Douglas Co OR 75 A4
Suver Rd
Polk Co OR 54 B6
S Swan Falls Rd
Kuna ID 83 E4
Swantown Rd
Island Co WA 15 A3
Sweet Rd
Whatcom Co WA 5 A5
Swenson Rd
Stevens Co WA 21 A7
S Swenson Rd
Stevens Co WA 21 A7
Swift Av S
Seattle WA 132 E6
Seattle WA 133 A7
Swift Blvd
Richland WA 203 B5
Sylvan Wy
Bremerton WA 122 C2
Kitsap Co WA 25 A3
Kitsap Co WA 122 C2
Sylvan Wy SR-306
Bremerton WA 122 C2
Kitsap Co WA 25 A3
Kitsap Co WA 122 C2
Sylvan Wy SW
Seattle WA 131 E7
Seattle WA 132 A7
NE Sylvan Wy
Kitsap Co WA 122 E2
NE Sylvan Wy SR-306
Kitsap Co WA 122 D2
Sylvester Rd SW
Burien WA 139 B3
Normandy Park WA 139 B2
W Sylvester St
Pasco WA 49 B1
Pasco WA 204 B6

T

Table Rock Rd
Central Point OR 87 D6
Central Point OR 198 A1
Jackson Co OR 87 D6
Jackson Co OR 198 A2
Medford OR 87 D6
Medford OR 198 A2
W Table Rock Rd
Medford OR 198 A3
Tacoma Av N
Tacoma WA 141 E3
Tacoma WA 142 A3
Tacoma Av S
Tacoma WA 142 A6
Tacoma WA 144 A1
SE Tacoma St
Portland OR 170 C2
S Tacoma Wy
Lakewood WA 143 C6
Tacoma WA 25 B6
Tacoma WA 141 E7
Tacoma WA 142 A6
Tacoma WA 143 C1
Tacoma Mall Blvd
Lakewood WA 143 D5
Tacoma WA 143 D1
Tacoma Mall Blvd S
Lakewood WA 143 D5
Tacoma WA 143 D6
Taft St
Elk River ID 42 D2
Taft St SR-8
Elk River ID 42 D2
Talbot Rd S
Marion Co OR 54 C6
Renton WA 138 B7
Talbot Rd S SR-515
Renton WA 138 B7
Talbot Rd SE
Marion Co OR 54 C6
Talley Wy
Cowlitz Co WA 156 C6
Kelso WA 156 C6
Tammany Creek Rd
Nez Perce Co ID 41 E6
Tanner Av
Powell River BC 1 A4
S Tapps Dr E
Pierce Co WA 25 D6
Tattersall Dr
Saanich BC 111 E1
Saanich BC 112 A1
Taumarson Rd
College Place WA 207 C7
Walla Walla Co WA 207 D7
Tausick Wy
Walla Walla WA 208 D2
Walla Walla Co WA 208 D2
Taylor
Pierce Co WA 144 D7
Taylor Av N
Seattle WA 128 B4
SE Taylor St
Portland OR 166 A3
SW Taylor St
Portland OR 165 D2
Taylor Wy
West Vancouver BC 107 D3
Taylor Wy PROV-1A
West Vancouver BC 107 D3
Taylor Wy PROV-99
West Vancouver BC 107 D3
Taylor Flats Rd
Franklin Co WA 39 B6
SW Taylors Ferry Rd
Portland OR 165 E7
Portland OR 169 C2
Tekoa-Farmington Rd
Tekoa WA 31 D6
Whitman Co WA 31 D6
Ten Barr Rd
Deschutes Co OR 66 E5
N Ten Mile Rd
Meridian ID 83 D1
S Ten Mile Rd
Ada Co ID 83 D2
Tennant Wy
Cowlitz Co WA 44 D1
Cowlitz Co WA 155 E6

20 INDEX

INDEX 20

Tennant Wy

Westview Dr

Street Index

STREET City State Map# Grid

Tennant Wy
Cowlitz Co WA 156 B7
Kelso WA 156 C7
Longview WA 155 D5
Tennant Wy SR-432
Cowlitz Co WA 44 D1
Cowlitz Co WA 155 E6
Cowlitz Co WA 156 B7
Kelso WA 156 C7
Longview WA 155 D5
Tennant Way Frontage Rd
Cowlitz Co WA 155 E5
Longview WA 155 E5
Terminal Av
Vancouver BC 110 B3
Territorial Hwy
Lane Co OR 64 A5
Terry Av
Seattle WA 128 C5
N Terry St
Eugene OR 64 B5
Eugene OR 180 B6
Lane Co OR 180 B5
Terry Fox Wy
Vancouver BC 110 A3
SW Terwilliger Blvd
Clackamas Co OR 169 E5
Clackamas Co OR 170 A5
Lake Oswego OR 169 E5
Lake Oswego OR 170 A5
Multnomah Co OR 169 E4
Portland OR 165 D4
Portland OR 169 D2
Thain Rd
Lewiston ID 41 E6
Thayer Dr
Richland WA 39 A7
Richland WA 203 C4
The Dalles-California Hwy
Deschutes Co OR 77 B2
Klamath Co OR 76 E7
Klamath Co OR 99 E1
Klamath Co OR 201 B1
Klamath Falls OR 201 C7
The Dalles-California Hy SR-39
Klamath Falls OR 201 B2
The Dalles-California Hy US-97
Deschutes Co OR 77 B3
Klamath Co OR 76 E7
Klamath Co OR 99 E2
Klamath Co OR 201 B1
Klamath Falls OR 201 C7
SE Thiessen Rd
Clackamas Co OR 170 E7
SW Thistle St
Seattle WA 25 C3
Seattle WA 135 D1
Seattle WA 136 A1
E Thomas St
Seattle WA 128 E5
Thompson Av
Vancouver WA 157 D4
S Thompson Av
Tacoma WA 142 A7
Tacoma WA 144 A1
NW Thompson Rd
Multnomah Co OR 44 E6
Washington Co OR 44 E6
Thompson Creek Rd
Jackson Co OR 87 A7
Josephine Co OR 87 A7
Thompson Yakima Transition
Tacoma WA 144 A2
S Thor Pl
Spokane WA 212 E1
S Thor St
Spokane WA 212 D1
SE Thorburn St
Portland OR 167 A2
Thorndyke Av W
Seattle WA 127 D3
Thrall Rd
Kittitas Co WA 37 D2
Three Lakes Rd
Snohomish Co WA 15 E7
Threemile Rd
Wasco Co OR 46 E7
Three Rivers Hwy
Tillamook Co OR 53 C2
Three Rivers Hwy SR-22
Tillamook Co OR 53 C2
NW Thurman St
Portland OR 161 D7
Thurston Rd
Springfield OR 188 C1
NE Thurston Wy
Vancouver WA 159 B1
E Tietan St
Walla Walla WA 208 B5
W Tietan St
Walla Walla WA 207 E5
Walla Walla WA 208 A5
Tieton Dr
Yakima WA 37 C4
W Tilden St
Seattle WA 127 D1
NE Tillamook St
Portland OR 162 B7
Tiller Trail Hwy
Canyonville OR 87 A1
Douglas Co OR 75 B7
Tiller-Trail Hwy
Jackson Co OR 87 D3
Tiller Trail Hwy SR-227
Canyonville OR 87 A1
Douglas Co OR 75 B7
Tiller-Trail Hwy SR-227
Jackson Co OR 87 D3
Tilley Rd S
Thurston Co WA 34 D2
Thurston Co WA 147 D7

Tilley Rd S
Tumwater WA 147 D7
Tillicum Rd
Esquimalt BC 111 B3
Saanich BC 111 C1
SE Tillstrom Rd
Clackamas Co OR 45 B7
Damascus OR 45 B7
Timberline Dr
Eugene OR 184 E4
Timothy Lake Rd
Clackamas Co OR 55 E3
Tollgate Rd
Elmore Co ID 84 D4
SE Tolman St
Portland OR 166 C7
Tonasket-Havillah Rd
Okanogan Co WA 8 E7
Okanogan Co WA 9 A7
Tonasket WA 8 E7
Tonquin Av SW
Ocean Shores WA 149 C4
Totem Lake Blvd NE
King Co WA 126 D1
Kirkland WA 126 E1
N Tower Av
Centralia WA 151 D4
N Tower Av SR-507
Centralia WA 151 D5
S Tower Av
Centralia WA 151 D5
Lewis Co WA 151 D6
S Tower Av SR-507
Centralia WA 151 D5
S Township Rd
Clackamas Co OR 55 A2
Tracyton Beach Rd NW
Bremerton WA 122 A3
Kitsap Co WA 122 A2
Trade St SE
Salem OR 173 D1
Trade St SE SR-22
Salem OR 173 D1
Trade St SE SR-99E BUS
Salem OR 173 D1
S Trafton St
Tacoma WA 141 D5
Trail Av
Sunshine Coast BC 1 E7
Trans Canada Hwy
Coquitlam BC 5 B4
Cowichan Valley BC 4 A7
Fraser Valley BC 6 D1
Hope BC 6 C1
Langford BC 14 A1
Nanaimo BC 3 E4
North Vancouver BC 108 E4
N Vancouver Dist BC 108 C3
Saanich BC 111 C1
Surrey BC 5 B4
Victoria BC 111 D7
West Vancouver BC 107 D3
West Vancouver BC 108 A3
Trans Canada Hwy PROV-19A
Nanaimo BC 3 E4
Trans Canada Hwy PROV-99
West Vancouver BC 107 D3
Trans Canada Hwy TCH-1
Coquitlam BC 5 B4
Cowichan Valley BC 4 A7
Fraser Valley BC 6 C1
Hope BC 6 C1
Langford BC 14 A1
Nanaimo BC 3 E4
North Vancouver BC 108 C3
N Vancouver Dist BC 108 E4
Saanich BC 111 C1
Surrey BC 5 B4
Victoria BC 111 E6
West Vancouver BC 107 D3
West Vancouver BC 108 A3
Travis Rd
Benton Co WA 48 E1
Trelstad Av SE
Salem OR 174 B7
Tremont St
Coos Bay OR 194 A4
North Bend OR 194 A3
Tremont St US-101
Coos Bay OR 194 A4
North Bend OR 194 A3
E Trent Av
Millwood WA 213 B2
Spokane WA 210 C7
Spokane WA 212 A1
Spokane Co WA 31 C2
Spokane Valley WA 31 C2
Spokane Valley WA 213 A2
Spokane Valley WA 214 A1
E Trent Av SR-290
Millwood WA 213 B2
Spokane WA 210 C7
Spokane WA 212 A1
Spokane Co WA 31 C2
Spokane Valley WA 31 C2
Spokane Valley WA 213 A2
Spokane Valley WA 214 A1
Trenton Av
Bremerton WA 122 D5
Kitsap Co WA 122 D5
Trenton Av NE
Kitsap Co WA 122 D2
NW Trenton Av
Bend OR 189 D6
S Trenton St
Seattle WA 136 D1
Triton Dr NW
Seattle WA 123 D3
Trosper Rd SW
Thurston Co WA 147 C3
Tumwater WA 147 C3
Trout Lake Hwy
Klickitat Co WA 46 D3

SE Truman Av
Bend OR 192 A2
SW Truman Av
Bend OR 192 A2
Tualatin Valley Hwy
Yamhill Co OR 54 C1
Tualatin Valley Hwy SR-47
Yamhill Co OR 54 C1
Tucker Rd
Lewis Co WA 34 E5
Tukwila Pkwy
Tukwila WA 140 D2
Tukwila International Blvd
King Co WA 137 A5
Seatac WA 140 A1
Tukwila WA 137 A5
Tukwila WA 140 A2
Tukwila Int'l Blvd SR-99
King Co WA 137 A5
Seatac WA 140 A1
Tukwila WA 137 A5
Tukwila WA 140 A2
NW Tumalo Av
Bend OR 189 E7
Tumalo Rd
Deschutes Co OR 66 D4
Tumwater Blvd SE
Thurston Co WA 147 E4
Thurston Co WA 148 A4
Tumwater WA 147 E4
Tumwater Blvd SW
Thurston Co WA 147 B4
Tumwater WA 147 D5
Tumwater Access Rd
Clallam Co WA 117 A5
Port Angeles WA 117 A5
S Tumwater Access Rd
Clallam Co WA 117 A5
Port Angeles WA 117 B3
S Tumwater Access Rd SR-117
Clallam Co WA 117 A5
Port Angeles WA 117 B3
Turner Rd SE
Salem OR 174 B4
Turner Wy E
Seattle WA 129 A4
Twin Lakes Rd
Ferry Co WA 20 A4
Tyee Dr
Whatcom Co WA 4 D5
Tyee Rd
Douglas Co OR 74 E4
Tyee Rd CO-33
Douglas Co OR 74 E4
Tygh Ridge Rd
Wasco Co OR 56 E1
Tyler St
Port Townsend WA 119 D4
S Tyler St
Tacoma WA 141 B6
Tacoma WA 143 B2
Tyndell Rd NE
Grant Co WA 29 A6
Tzouhalem Rd
Cowichan Valley BC 4 A6

U

Ukiah-Hilgard Hwy
Umatilla Co OR 59 C3
Ukiah-Hilgard Hwy SR-244
Umatilla Co OR 59 C3
Umpqua Hwy
Douglas Co OR 74 E2
Douglas Co OR 75 A1
Umpqua Hwy SR-38
Douglas Co OR 74 E2
Douglas Co OR 75 A1
N Umpqua Hwy
Douglas Co OR 76 C5
Douglas Co OR 196 D5
Roseburg OR 196 D5
N Umpqua Hwy SR-138
Douglas Co OR 76 C5
Douglas Co OR 196 D5
Roseburg OR 196 D5
N Union Av
Tacoma WA 141 C3
S Union Av
Tacoma WA 141 C5
Tacoma WA 143 C1
Union St
Seattle WA 128 C6
Vancouver BC 110 B2
E Union St
Seattle WA 128 E6
Seattle WA 129 A6
N Union St
Kennewick WA 205 C2
S Union St
Kennewick WA 205 C3
W Union St
Boise ID 222 C6
Union Bay Pl NE
Seattle WA 125 A7
Union-Cove Hwy
Union Co OR 60 E2
Union-Cove Hwy SR-237
Union Co OR 60 E2
NE Union Hill Rd
King Co WA 25 E2
University Br
Seattle WA 128 D1
W University Dr
Boise ID 224 B1
N University Rd
Spokane Valley WA 213 E3
S University Rd
Spokane Valley WA 213 E7
University St
Seattle WA 128 C6
University Wy NE
Seattle WA 124 E7

University Wy NE
Seattle WA 128 E1
Upham St
Klamath Falls OR 201 C5
Upper Dr
Lake Oswego OR 169 B7
Upper Applegate Rd
Jackson Co OR 87 B7
S Upper Highland Rd
Clackamas Co OR 55 B2
Upper Nestucca Rd
Tillamook Co OR 53 D2
E Upriver Dr
Spokane WA 210 E6
Spokane Co WA 31 B2
Spokane Co WA 210 E6
Urquhart
Krupp WA 29 C4
E Urquhart Rd
Adams Co WA 30 B7
US Highway 12
Nez Perce Co ID 42 C5
US Highway 12 US-12
Nez Perce Co ID 42 C5
US Highway 95
Nez Perce Co ID 41 E5
Nez Perce Co ID 42 A6
US Highway 95 US-95
Nez Perce Co ID 41 E5
Nez Perce Co ID 42 A6
US Highway 95 N
Lewiston ID 41 E5
Nez Perce Co ID 41 E5
US Highway 95 N US-12
Lewiston ID 41 E5
Nez Perce Co ID 41 E5
US Highway 95 N US-95
Lewiston ID 41 E5
Nez Perce Co ID 41 E5
US Highway 128
Lewiston ID 41 E5
US Highway 128 SR-128
Lewiston ID 41 D5
Ustick Rd
Caldwell ID 83 C1
Canyon Co ID 83 B2
Canyon Co ID 219 A7
E Ustick Rd
Caldwell ID 83 C2
Caldwell ID 219 D7
Canyon Co ID 83 C2
Canyon Co ID 219 D7
W Ustick Rd
Ada Co ID 83 D1
Boise ID 221 C5
Caldwell ID 219 A7
Canyon Co ID 83 D1
Canyon Co ID 219 A7
Garden City ID 221 C5

V

Vail Cto SE
Thurston Co WA 35 A2
Vail Rd SE
Thurston Co WA 35 B2
Valley Av E
Fife WA 25 C6
Valley Hwy
Whatcom Co WA 5 D7
Valley Hwy SR-9
Whatcom Co WA 5 D7
E Valley Hwy E
Sumner WA 25 D6
W Valley Hwy
Kent WA 25 D4
Kent WA 140 E3
Tukwila WA 140 E3
W Valley Hwy SR-181
Kent WA 25 D4
Kent WA 140 D5
Tukwila WA 140 E3
Valley St
Seattle WA 128 C4
Valley River Dr
Eugene OR 181 C6
Valley View Rd
Whatcom Co WA 5 B5
S Valley View Rd
Jackson Co OR 199 B1
Vanbelle Rd
Yakima Co WA 38 A7
NW Van Buren Av
Corvallis OR 178 B5
Linn Co OR 178 B5
NW Van Buren Av SR-34
Corvallis OR 178 B5
Linn Co OR 178 B5
NW Van Buren Av US-20
Corvallis OR 178 B5
Van Buren Rd
Whatcom Co WA 5 C5
N Vancouver Av
Portland OR 162 A2
Portland OR 166 A1
N Vancouver Wy
Portland OR 157 E7
Portland OR 161 E1
Portland OR 162 A1
NE Vancouver Wy
Portland OR 162 A1
NE Vancouver Mall Dr
Clark Co WA 159 A1
Vancouver WA 159 B1
Van Giesen St
Richland WA 203 C3
Van Giesen St SR-224
Richland WA 203 A3
Vangilder Rd
Moro OR 47 B7
Sherman Co OR 47 B7
Vashon Hwy SW
King Co WA 25 B4

Vaughn Rd
Lane Co OR 63 E5
Lane Co OR 64 A5
NW Vaughn St
Portland OR 161 C7
Vedder Mountain Rd
Chilliwack BC 5 E4
Venables St
Vancouver BC 110 C3
Verda Ln NE
Keizer OR 172 A2
Salem OR 172 A3
SW Vermont St
Portland OR 165 A7
Vernon Av
Pacific Co WA 33 C5
Saanich BC 111 D1
Vernon Av PROV-17
Saanich BC 111 D1
Vernon Av SR-103
Pacific Co WA 33 C5
E Veterans Memorial Pkwy
Boise ID 221 D5
Garden City ID 221 D5
N Veterans Memorial Pkwy
Boise ID 221 E5
Garden City ID 221 D5
S Viaduc
Centralia WA 151 D6
NE Victoria Av
Portland OR 162 A7
Victoria Dr
Coquitlam BC 5 A2
Port Coquitlam BC 5 A2
Vancouver BC 110 D6
Victoria Diversion
Vancouver BC 110 D5
W Victory Ln
Ada Co ID 83 D4
E Victory Rd
Ada Co ID 83 E2
Meridian ID 83 E2
W Victory Rd
Ada Co ID 83 E2
Ada Co ID 223 D5
Boise ID 83 E2
Boise ID 223 D5
Vilas Rd E
Jackson Co OR 87 D6
Medford OR 87 D6
SE Village Lp
Vancouver WA 160 C7
Vancouver WA 164 C1
W Vineyard Dr
Kennewick WA 206 B2
Virginia Av
North Bend OR 73 E3
North Bend OR 193 E2
North Bend OR 194 A2
Virginia St
Seattle WA 128 C5
Virginia Wy
Longview WA 155 D1
S Vista Av
Boise ID 84 A2
Boise ID 224 B4
SW Vista Av
Portland OR 165 C4
Vista Dr
Ferndale WA 5 B6
Island Co WA 15 B4
Vista Wy
Kennewick WA 205 D2
Vye Rd
Abbotsford BC 5 D4

W

W St
Port Townsend WA 119 D2
WA-302 KP N
Pierce Co WA 25 A5
N Wahanna Rd
Clatsop Co OR 154 D3
Seaside OR 154 D4
S Wahanna Rd
Seaside OR 154 C6
Waldrick Rd SE
Thurston Co WA 34 E2
Walker Av
Ashland OR 200 A5
SW Walker Rd
Beaverton OR 44 E7
Walker St
Port Townsend WA 119 D4
Wall St
Seattle WA 128 B5
N Wall St
Spokane Co WA 31 B1
Spokane Co WA 209 E1
NW Wall St
Bend OR 189 E7
Bend OR 190 A7
Bend OR 191 E1
SW Wall St
Bend OR 191 E1
Wallace Rd
Coos Bay OR 193 C4
Wallace Rd NW
Polk Co OR 54 C4
Polk Co OR 171 B5
Salem OR 171 C5
Wallace Rd NW SR-221
Polk Co OR 54 C4
Polk Co OR 171 B5
Salem OR 171 C5
SE Wallace Rd
Yamhill Co OR 54 C3
SE Wallace Rd SR-221
Yamhill Co OR 54 C3
Waller Rd E
Pierce Co WA 25 C6
Pierce Co WA 142 E7
Pierce Co WA 144 E1

Wallingford Av N
Seattle WA 124 C3
Seattle WA 128 C1
Wallowa Lake Hwy
Union Co OR 50 E6
Union Co OR 60 D1
Wallowa Co OR 51 C7
Wallowa Lake Hwy SR-82
Union Co OR 50 E6
Union Co OR 60 D1
Wallowa Co OR 51 A6
W Walnut Av
Coeur d'Alene ID 218 B5
W Walnut Av US-95
Coeur d'Alene ID 218 B5
NW Walnut Blvd
Benton Co OR 177 C4
Corvallis OR 54 B7
Corvallis OR 177 C3
Corvallis OR 178 B2
S Walnut Pl
Spokane WA 211 D2
Walnut Rd NW
Olympia WA 145 C3
Walnut St
Everett WA 120 E3
Port Townsend WA 119 D2
S Walnut St
Spokane WA 211 D2
Wamic Mkt Rd
Wasco Co OR 56 D2
W Wanamaker Rd
Island Co WA 15 A5
W Wanamaker Rd SR-20
Island Co WA 15 A5
W Wapato Rd
Wapato WA 37 D6
Yakima Co WA 37 D6
Wapato Wy
Chelan Co WA 18 A7
Wapato Wy SR-150
Chelan Co WA 18 A7
Wapinitia Rd
Wasco Co OR 56 D4
Wapinitia Rd B-3
Wasco Co OR 56 D4
Ward Rd
Deschutes Co OR 66 D6
NW Wardway St
Portland OR 161 B7
E Warm Springs Av
Boise ID 222 C7
Boise ID 224 D1
Warm Springs Hwy
Jefferson Co OR 56 D6
Warm Springs Hwy US-26
Jefferson Co OR 56 D6
Warner Hwy
Lake Co OR 90 E7
Warner Hwy SR-140
Lake Co OR 90 E7
S Warner St
Tacoma WA 141 C7
Tacoma WA 143 C1
Warren Av
Bremerton WA 122 B6
Kitsap Co WA 122 B6
Warren Av SR-303
Bremerton WA 122 B6
Kitsap Co WA 122 B6
Warren St
Eugene OR 184 E3
Warren Av Br
Bremerton WA 122 B4
Warren Av Br SR-303
Bremerton WA 122 B4
Warrenton-Astoria Hwy
Astoria OR 153 C3
Clatsop Co OR 153 B5
Warrenton OR 153 A5
Warrenton-Astoria Hy US-101 BU
Astoria OR 153 C3
Clatsop Co OR 153 B5
Warrenton OR 153 A5
NE Wasco St
Portland OR 166 C1
Wasco-Heppner Hwy
Gilliam Co OR 57 E1
Wasco-Heppner Hwy SR-206
Gilliam Co OR 57 E1
Washburn Wy
Klamath Co OR 202 A7
Klamath Falls OR 202 A5
Washington Av
Bremerton WA 122 C6
Washington Av SR-304
Bremerton WA 122 C6
E Washington Av
Sequim WA 118 E5
SE Washington Av
Roseburg OR 196 A5
SE Washington Av SR-138
Roseburg OR 196 A5
Washington St
Cheney WA 31 A3
Cowlitz Co WA 156 A3
Eugene OR 185 D1
Kelso WA 156 A3
Port Townsend WA 119 D4
Vancouver WA 157 E4
E Washington St
Sequim WA 118 D5
N Washington St
Kennewick WA 206 B2
Spokane WA 209 E7
Spokane WA 211 E1
S Washington St
Benton Co WA 206 B4
Kennewick WA 206 C4
Spokane WA 211 E2
SE Washington St
Portland OR 167 B3

SE Washington St
Roseburg OR 196 A5
SE Washington St SR-138
Roseburg OR 196 A5
SW Washington St
Portland OR 165 E2
Roseburg OR 196 A5
SW Washington St SR-138
Roseburg OR 196 A5
W Washington St
Sequim WA 118 B5
Washington Wy
Cowlitz Co WA 155 A4
Cowlitz Co WA 156 A3
Kelso WA 156 A3
Longview WA 155 B5
Longview WA 156 A3
N Wasson St
Coos Bay OR 193 B4
SE Water Av
Portland OR 166 A3
Water St
Port Townsend WA 119 D4
Water St SR-20
Port Townsend WA 119 D4
Water St NW
Olympia WA 145 E5
S Water St
Silverton OR 54 E4
S Water St SR-214
Silverton OR 54 E4
Water Gap Rd
Josephine Co OR 87 A7
Watson Br
Burlington WA 116 B1
Mt Vernon WA 116 B1
N Waugh Rd
Mt Vernon WA 116 E2
Wauncher Gulch Rd
Nez Perce Co ID 42 B4
Waverly Dr SE
Albany OR 176 B4
Linn Co OR 176 A7
Wawawai Rd
Whitman Co WA 41 C4
Wawawai Grade Rd
Whitman Co WA 41 B4
Wawawai River Rd
Whitman Co WA 41 C4
Wawawai River Rd SR-193
Whitman Co WA 41 D6
Webb Rd
Nez Perce Co ID 42 A6
Weed Rd E
Klamath Co OR 88 D3
Weedin Pl NE
Seattle WA 124 D5
N Weidler St
Portland OR 165 E1
Portland OR 166 A1
NE Weidler St
Portland OR 166 B1
Portland OR 167 E1
Welch Rd
Snohomish Co WA 25 E1
E Wellesley Av
Spokane WA 31 B2
Spokane WA 210 B3
Spokane Co WA 31 D2
W Wellesley Av
Spokane WA 209 C4
Wells Rd
Whitman Co WA 31 A5
E Wellsandt Rd
Ritzville WA 30 B7
Wellsian Wy
Richland WA 203 C6
West Blvd
Vancouver BC 109 C7
N West St
Modoc Co CA 101 C7
N West St CO-60
Modoc Co CA 101 C7
Western Av
Seattle WA 128 B5
Western Av W
Seattle WA 128 A5
N Western Av
Chelan Co WA 27 E4
Wenatchee WA 27 E4
SW Western Blvd
Corvallis OR 177 C6
SW Western Blvd SR-34
Corvallis OR 177 C6
SW Western Blvd US-20
Corvallis OR 177 C6
Western Raite Ln
Morrow Co OR 59 A3
N Westgate Blvd
Tacoma WA 141 A3
Westhill Dr
West Vancouver BC 107 B2
Westlake Av
Seattle WA 128 C5
Westlake Av N
Seattle WA 128 B2
West Side Hwy
Cowlitz Co WA 156 A3
Kelso WA 156 A3
Longview WA 156 A3
Westside Hwy
Cowlitz Co WA 156 A2
Kelso WA 156 A3
Longview WA 156 A2
West Side Hwy SR-411
Cowlitz Co WA 156 A3
Kelso WA 156 A3
Longview WA 156 A3
Westside Hwy SR-411
Cowlitz Co WA 156 A2
Kelso WA 156 A3
Longview WA 156 A2
Westview Dr
North Vancouver BC 108 C3

21 INDEX

INDEX 21

Westview Dr

E 6th Av SR-126 BUS

Street Index

STREET City State Map# Grid

Westview Dr
N Vancouver Dist BC 108 C3
Westwick Rd
Snohomish Co WA 15 E7
Wetmore Av
Everett WA 120 C7
Wharf St
Victoria BC 111 D5
Wheatland Rd N
Marion Co OR 54 C4
Wheaton Wy
Bremerton WA 122 C2
Kitsap Co WA 122 C1
Wheaton Wy SR-303
Bremerton WA 122 C2
Kitsap Co WA 122 C1
N Wheeler Av
Portland OR 166 A1
E Whidbey Av
Oak Harbor WA 15 A4
Whiskey Creek Rd
Tillamook Co OR 43 C7
SW White Center Cto
King Co WA 136 A3
Whiteman Rd KP S
Pierce Co WA 24 E6
Whitman Pl N
Seattle WA 124 B6
Whitman St
Walla Walla WA 208 B3
Wiggins Rd SE
Olympia WA 146 D7
Olympia WA 148 D1
N Wilbur Av
Walla Walla WA 208 C2
S Wilbur Av
Walla Walla WA 208 C3
Wilbur Gulch Rd
Whitman Co WA 41 C3
Wilbur Gulch Rd SR-194
Whitman Co WA 41 C3
Wilco Hwy NE
Marion Co OR 54 E3
Woodburn OR 54 E3
Wilco Hwy NE SR-214
Marion Co OR 54 E3
Woodburn OR 54 E3
SW Wildwood Pl
Seattle WA 135 D2
Wildwood Rd
Lewis Co WA 34 C6
Willagillespie Rd
Eugene OR 181 D6
N Willamette Blvd
Portland OR 161 C3
Willamette Dr
West Linn OR 55 A1
Willamette Dr SR-43
West Linn OR 55 A1
Willamette Hwy
Klamath Co OR 77 A4
Lane Co OR 64 E7
Lane Co OR 65 A7
Lane Co OR 187 A7
Willamette Hwy SR-58
Klamath Co OR 77 A4
Lane Co OR 64 E7
Lane Co OR 65 A7
Lane Co OR 187 A7
Willamette Hwy SR-99
Lane Co OR 187 A7
Willamette St
Eugene OR 64 C5
Eugene OR 185 D5
Willamina Creek Rd
Willamina OR 54 A3
Yamhill Co OR 54 A3
Willamina-Salem Hwy
Polk Co OR 54 B5
Salem OR 171 C7
Salem OR 173 A1
Willamina-Salem Hwy SR-22
Polk Co OR 54 B5
Salem OR 171 C7
Salem OR 173 B1
SW William Av
Chehalis WA 152 C5
N Williams Av
Portland OR 162 A5
Williams Hwy
Grants Pass OR 87 A6
Grants Pass OR 197 B7
Josephine Co OR 197 B7
Williams Hwy SR-238
Grants Pass OR 87 A6
Grants Pass OR 197 C6
Josephine Co OR 197 B7
Williams Hwy US-199
Grants Pass OR 197 C6
Williams Lake Rd
Lincoln Co WA 30 D5
Stevens Co WA 20 D1
N Williams Valley Rd
Stevens Co WA 21 A7
N Willis Blvd
Portland OR 161 B2
Willow St
Spray OR 58 C5
Willow St SR-19
Spray OR 58 C5
Willow St SR-207
Spray OR 58 C5
NE Willow St
Portland OR 167 A1
Willow Creek Rd
Eugene OR 184 B2
Morrow Co OR 58 E1
Wilson Av S
Seattle WA 133 C5
SE Wilson Av
Bend OR 192 A2
SW Wilson Av
Bend OR 192 A2
Wilson St
Mission BC 5 C3
Wilson River Hwy
Tillamook Co OR 44 A6
Wilson River Hwy SR-6
Tillamook Co OR 44 A6
NE Wilsonville Rd
Newberg OR 54 D2
Yamhill Co OR 54 D2
SW Wilsonville Rd
Wilsonville OR 54 E2
Wind River Rd
Skamania Co WA 46 A4
Windsor Rd
Oak Bay BC 112 D5
N Wing Rd
Ada Co ID 83 D1
Winlock-Vader Rd
Lewis Co WA 34 D6
Winona Av N
Seattle WA 124 C5
Wintercreek Dr
Eugene OR 184 E4
Eugene OR 185 A4
Wisconsin St
Priest River ID 21 E5
NE Wistaria Dr
Portland OR 162 D7
NW Witham Hill Dr
Benton Co OR 177 D3
Corvallis OR 177 D3
Woburn St
Bellingham WA 113 E4
N Wolverton Ct
Spokane WA 210 B5
Woodburn-Estacada Hwy
Estacada OR 55 B3
Woodburn-Estacada Hwy SR-211
Estacada OR 55 B3
Woodburn-Sandy Hwy
Clackamas Co OR 55 C1
Sandy OR 55 C1
Woodburn-Sandy Hwy SR-211
Clackamas Co OR 55 C1
Sandy OR 55 C1
Woodland Av
Centralia WA 151 C6
Woodland Av E
Pierce Co WA 25 C7
Woodland Dr
Coos Bay OR 193 E5
North Bend OR 193 E4
Woodland Pl N
Seattle WA 124 B6
Woodlawn Av N
Seattle WA 124 D6
Woodlawn Av NE
Seattle WA 124 D5
Woods Rd E
Kitsap Co WA 25 B3
SE Woodstock Blvd
Portland OR 166 D7
Portland OR 167 B7
S Wycoff Av
Bremerton WA 122 A6
S Wycoff Av SR-304
Bremerton WA 122 A6
Wyoming St
Deary ID 42 B2
Wyoming St SR-3
Deary ID 42 B2

Y

Y Av
La Grande OR 60 C1
Yakima Av S
Pierce Co WA 144 A7
Tacoma WA 144 A7
N Yakima Av
Tacoma WA 141 E3
Tacoma WA 142 A3
S Yakima Av
Pierce Co WA 144 A7
Tacoma WA 25 B6
Tacoma WA 142 A7
Tacoma WA 144 A2
Yakima Valley Hwy
Sunnyside WA 38 B7
Yakima Co WA 38 A6
Yale Av
Seattle WA 128 C5
Yale Rd E
Chilliwack BC 6 A3
Yale Rd W
Chilliwack BC 5 E4
N Yale St
Nampa ID 220 B3
SE Yamhill St
Portland OR 166 A3
SW Yamhill St
Portland OR 165 E2
Yamhill-Newberg Hwy
Yamhill Co OR 54 C1
Yamhill-Newberg Hwy SR-240
Yamhill Co OR 54 C1
Yarrow Point Rd
Clyde Hill WA 130 B3
Yarrow Point WA 130 B3
Yellow Point Rd
Nanaimo District BC 3 E4
Yelm Hwy SE
Lacey WA 148 E3
Thurston Co WA 35 A1
Thurston Co WA 148 A2
Tumwater WA 148 A2
Yeoman Rd
Bend OR 190 D3
Deschutes Co OR 190 D3
NW Yeon Av
Portland OR 161 C6
NW Yeon Av US-30
Portland OR 161 C6
Yesler Wy
King Co WA 128 C7
Seattle WA 128 D7
E Yesler Wy
Seattle WA 128 E7
Seattle WA 129 A7
Yew St
Centralia WA 151 C5
Yokum Rd
Douglas Co OR 87 A1
Riddle OR 87 A1
Yolanda Av
Lane Co OR 64 C5
Lane Co OR 183 C6
Springfield OR 64 C5
Springfield OR 183 C6
York St
Bellingham WA 113 D3
Youngs Bay Br
Astoria OR 153 A2
Youngs Bay Br US-26
Astoria OR 153 A2
Youngs Bay Br US-101
Astoria OR 153 A2
Youngs River Rd
Clatsop Co OR 43 D1
Clatsop Co OR 153 C6

Z

Zena Rd
Polk Co OR 54 B4
Zena Rd NW
Polk Co OR 54 C4

#

1 Av
Delta BC 4 D4
1st Av
Cowlitz Co WA 156 A4
Kelso WA 156 A4
Longview WA 156 A4
Riddle OR 87 A1
Seattle WA 128 B5
1st Av SR-411
Cowlitz Co WA 156 A4
Kelso WA 156 A4
Longview WA 156 A4
1st Av E
Albany OR 175 E2
Albany OR 176 A2
1st Av N
Seattle WA 128 B5
1st Av NE
Seattle WA 124 D2
1st Av NW
Cowlitz Co WA 156 A3
Kelso WA 156 A3
1st Av NW SR-411
Cowlitz Co WA 156 A3
Kelso WA 156 A3
1st Av S
Burien WA 136 C7
Burien WA 139 C4
Des Moines WA 139 C7
Federal Way WA 25 C5
King Co WA 25 C4
King Co WA 136 C5
Normandy Park WA 139 C7
Seattle WA 128 C7
Seattle WA 132 C2
Seattle WA 136 C2
1st Av S SR-509
Burien WA 139 C4
Des Moines WA 139 C7
Normandy Park WA 139 C7
1st Av W
Albany OR 175 E2
E 1st Av
Vancouver BC 4 D2
Vancouver BC 110 D3
N 1st Av
Baker Co OR 70 C2
Unity OR 70 C2
N 1st Av US-26
Baker Co OR 70 C2
Unity OR 70 C2
NE 1st Av
Portland OR 166 A1
SW 1st Av
Portland OR 165 E3
W 1st Av
Kennewick WA 206 B2
Spokane WA 211 E1
1st Pl S
Des Moines WA 139 C7
Normandy Park WA 139 C7
1st Pl S SR-509
Des Moines WA 139 C7
Normandy Park WA 139 C7
1st St
Asotin WA 41 D6
Benton City WA 38 E7
Bremerton WA 25 A3
Bremerton WA 122 C6
Cheney WA 31 A4
Clearwater Co ID 42 D2
Elk River ID 42 D2
Kitsap Co WA 122 C6
Lane Co OR 64 C6
Lane Co OR 187 A7
Linn Co OR 64 D1
Oakesdale WA 31 C7
Waterloo OR 64 D1
1st St SR-8
Clearwater Co ID 42 D2
Elk River ID 42 D2
1st St SR-27
Oakesdale WA 31 C7
1st St SR-99
Lane Co OR 64 C6
Lane Co OR 187 A7
1st St SR-129
Asotin WA 41 D6
1st St SR-225
Benton City WA 38 E7
1st St SR-304
Bremerton WA 25 A3
Bremerton WA 122 C6
Kitsap Co WA 122 C6
1st St SR-904
Cheney WA 31 A4
E 1st St
Dorris CA 99 E2
Island City OR 60 D1
Port Angeles WA 14 B5
Port Angeles WA 117 E5
E 1st St SR-237
Island City OR 60 D1
E 1st St US-97
Dorris CA 99 E2
E 1st St US-101
Port Angeles WA 14 B5
Port Angeles WA 117 E4
N 1st St
Aumsville OR 54 D5
Hermiston OR 49 A4
Marion Co OR 54 D5
Mt Vernon WA 116 B4
Oakland OR 75 A4
Tacoma WA 142 A3
Yakima WA 37 D4
N 1st St SR-32
Hermiston OR 49 A4
N 1st St SR-99
Oakland OR 75 A4
N 1st St US-395
Hermiston OR 49 A4
NE 1st St
Bellevue WA 130 B5
Medina WA 130 B5
S 1st St
Benton Co OR 63 E2
Coos Bay OR 194 B7
Mt Vernon WA 116 B4
Roslyn WA 27 A6
St. Helens OR 44 E4
Yakima WA 37 D5
S 1st St SR-536
Mt Vernon WA 116 B4
S 1st St SR-903
Roslyn WA 27 A6
S 1st St US-101
Coos Bay OR 194 B7
SE 1st St
Clark Co WA 45 B6
Clark Co WA 160 E5
Vancouver WA 45 B6
Vancouver WA 160 E5
W 1st St
Centralia WA 151 C4
Port Angeles WA 117 C3
Rufus OR 47 B5
Wapato WA 37 D6
1st Av Br S
Seattle WA 132 C6
1st Av Br S SR-99
Seattle WA 132 C6
1st Av Br S SR-509
Seattle WA 132 C7
2nd Av
Gold Hill OR 87 C5
Seattle WA 128 B5
Zillah WA 37 E6
2nd Av SR-99
Gold Hill OR 87 C5
2nd Av SR-234
Gold Hill OR 87 C5
2nd Av N
Okanogan WA 18 D3
2nd Av N SR-215
Okanogan WA 18 D3
2nd Av N US-97 BUS
Okanogan WA 18 D3
2nd Av S
Payette ID 72 A5
2nd Av S SR-52
Payette ID 72 A5
2nd Av SE
Albany OR 175 E2
Albany OR 176 A2
2nd Av SW
Albany OR 175 E2
Seattle WA 132 C7
2nd Av W
Seattle WA 128 A4
E 2nd Av
Spokane WA 212 B2
Vancouver BC 110 A3
E 2nd Av I-90 BUS
Spokane WA 212 A2
N 2nd Av
Walla Walla WA 207 E3
N 2nd Av US-12 BUS
Walla Walla WA 207 E3
N 2nd Av SW
Tumwater WA 147 E1
NW 2nd Av
Portland OR 165 E2
S 2nd Av
Everett WA 120 D7
Walla Walla WA 208 A4
S 2nd Av SW
Tumwater WA 147 D2
SW 2nd Av
Portland OR 165 E2
W 2nd Av
Spokane WA 211 E2
Spokane WA 212 A1
Vancouver BC 110 A3
W 2nd Av I-90 BUS
Spokane WA 211 E2
Spokane WA 212 A1
2nd St
La Grande OR 60 C1
Morton WA 35 C5
Snohomish WA 15 E7
2nd St SR-7
Morton WA 35 C5
2nd St S
Nampa ID 83 D2
Nampa ID 220 D4
2nd St S I-84 BUS
Nampa ID 220 C3
2nd St S SR-45
Nampa ID 220 C4
2nd St S SR-55
Nampa ID 220 C3
E 2nd St
The Dalles OR 46 E6
E 2nd St US-30
The Dalles OR 46 E6
NE 2nd St
Benton Co OR 178 B4
Corvallis OR 178 B4
NE 2nd St US-20
Benton Co OR 178 B4
Corvallis OR 178 B4
NW 2nd St
Corvallis OR 178 B5
Grants Pass OR 197 C4
McMinnville OR 54 B2
NW 2nd St US-20
Corvallis OR 178 B5
S 2nd St
Almira WA 29 C2
Lincoln Co WA 29 C2
Mt Vernon WA 116 B4
Renton WA 138 B6
Skagit Co WA 116 B5
Springfield OR 186 E2
S 2nd St SR-900
Renton WA 138 B6
SE 2nd St
Bend OR 192 A1
2nd Av Ext S
Seattle WA 128 C7
3rd Av
Cowlitz Co WA 44 D1
Cowlitz Co WA 155 E5
Cowlitz Co WA 156 A4
Longview WA 44 D1
Longview WA 155 E5
Longview WA 156 A4
3rd Av SR-411
Cowlitz Co WA 44 D1
Cowlitz Co WA 155 E6
Cowlitz Co WA 156 A4
Longview WA 44 D1
Longview WA 155 E6
Longview WA 156 A4
3rd Av SR-432
Cowlitz Co WA 155 E5
Longview WA 155 E5
3rd Av NW
Seattle WA 25 C2
Seattle WA 124 A4
3rd Av SW
Burien WA 139 C1
3rd Av W
Seattle WA 128 A2
E 3rd Av
Post Falls ID 31 E1
Post Falls ID 215 E5
Post Falls ID 216 A5
Spokane WA 212 D2
E 3rd Av I-90 BUS
Spokane WA 212 A2
NE 3rd Av
Camas WA 45 B6
Washougal WA 45 B6
NW 3rd Av
Portland OR 165 E2
S 3rd Av
Clallam Co WA 118 C6
Everett WA 120 D5
Sequim WA 14 D6
Sequim WA 118 C6
Walla Walla Co WA 208 A6
Yakima WA 37 D5
SW 3rd Av
Portland OR 165 E2
SW 3rd Av US-26
Portland OR 165 D4
W 3rd Av
Spokane WA 211 D2
Spokane WA 212 A2
W 3rd Av I-90 BUS
Spokane WA 211 D2
Spokane WA 212 A2
3rd St
Castlegar BC 10 E2
Gervais OR 54 D3
Nanaimo BC 3 D3
Pacific Co WA 33 C6
Sedro-Woolley WA 15 D2
Tillamook OR 43 C7
Tillamook Co OR 43 C7
3rd St US-101
Pacific Co WA 33 C6
3rd St E
North Vancouver BC 108 D6
3rd St N
Nampa ID 220 D4
3rd St W
North Vancouver BC 108 C5
E 3rd St
Prineville OR 67 B3
E 3rd St US-26
Prineville OR 67 B3
E 3rd St S
Nampa ID 220 C3
E 3rd St S I-84 BUS
Nampa ID 220 C3
E 3rd St S SR-45
Nampa ID 220 C4
N 3rd St
Coeur d'Alene ID 218 C5
Renton WA 138 B6
Turner OR 54 D5
NE 3rd St
Bend OR 66 D5
Bend OR 190 A7
Bend OR 192 A1
McMinnville OR 54 B2
Renton WA 138 C6
NE 3rd St US-20
Bend OR 66 D5
Bend OR 190 A7
NE 3rd St US-97 BUS
Bend OR 66 D5
Bend OR 190 A7
Bend OR 192 A1
NW 3rd St
Corvallis OR 178 B5
NW 3rd St SR-34
Corvallis OR 178 B5
NW 3rd St SR-99W
Corvallis OR 178 B5
NW 3rd St US-20
Corvallis OR 178 B5
S 3rd St
Elma WA 34 B1
Mt Vernon WA 116 B4
Renton WA 138 B7
S 3rd St SR-900
Renton WA 138 B7
SE 3rd St
Bend OR 191 E5
Bend OR 192 A1
Dayton OR 54 C2
Yamhill Co OR 54 C2
SE 3rd St SR-221
Dayton OR 54 C2
Yamhill Co OR 54 C2
SE 3rd St US-97 BUS
Bend OR 191 E5
Bend OR 192 A1
SW 3rd St
Corvallis OR 178 A5
SW 3rd St SR-34
Corvallis OR 178 A6
SW 3rd St SR-99W
Corvallis OR 178 A6
SW 3rd St US-20
Corvallis OR 178 A6
W 3rd St S
Nampa ID 220 B3
W 3rd St S I-84 BUS
Nampa ID 220 B3
W 3rd St S SR-55
Nampa ID 220 B3
4th Av
Gold Hill OR 87 C5
Omak WA 18 D3
Seattle WA 128 B5
4th Av SR-215
Omak WA 18 D3
4th Av SR-234
Gold Hill OR 87 C5
4th Av US-97 BUS
Omak WA 18 D3
4th Av E
Olympia WA 145 E5
Olympia WA 146 A5
4th Av N
Kelso WA 156 B3
Seattle WA 128 B5
4th Av N SR-4
Kelso WA 156 B3
4th Av S
Kelso WA 156 B3
Seattle WA 128 D7
Seattle WA 132 C6
4th Av SW
Burien WA 136 B5
King Co WA 136 C4
Seattle WA 136 B2
4th Av W
Bothell WA 25 D1
Olympia WA 145 D5
E 4th Av
Post Falls ID 215 D5
N 4th Av
Franklin Co WA 204 C1
Pasco WA 39 B7
Pasco WA 204 C2
Walla Walla WA 207 E2
NW 4th Av
Portland OR 165 E1
SW 4th Av
Portland OR 165 D4
W 4th Av
Kennewick WA 206 A2
Spokane WA 211 D2
Vancouver BC 4 D2
Vancouver BC 109 B3
4th St
Canyon Co ID 83 D4
Klamath Co OR 88 D3
Melba ID 83 D4
Okanogan Co WA 8 E7
Shaniko OR 57 B4
St. Maries ID 32 B5
Tonasket WA 8 E7
Wasco Co OR 57 B4
4th St SR-5
St. Maries ID 32 B5
4th St SR-62
Klamath Co OR 88 D3
4th St US-97
Shaniko OR 57 B4
Wasco Co OR 57 B4
4th St N
Wilson Creek WA 29 B4
4th St SE
Douglas Co WA 28 A5
E 4th St
Medford OR 198 B5
N 4th St
Coeur d'Alene ID 32 A2
Coeur d'Alene ID 218 C3
Coos Bay OR 194 B6
Mt Vernon WA 116 B3
Renton WA 138 C6
NE 4th St
Bellevue WA 130 C6
Renton WA 25 D4
Renton WA 138 D6
NW 4th St
Corvallis OR 178 B5
NW 4th St SR-34
Corvallis OR 178 B5
NW 4th St SR-99W
Corvallis OR 178 B5
NW 4th St US-20
Corvallis OR 178 B5
S 4th St
Coos Bay OR 73 E4
Coos Bay OR 194 B7
SW 4th St
Corvallis OR 178 A5
SW 4th St SR-34
Corvallis OR 178 A6
SW 4th St SR-99W
Corvallis OR 178 A6
SW 4th St US-20
Corvallis OR 178 A6
5th Av
Castlegar BC 10 E2
Seattle WA 128 C6
5th Av N
Kelso WA 156 B3
Seattle WA 128 B4
5th Av N SR-4
Kelso WA 156 B3
5th Av NE
Seattle WA 124 D7
5th Av NW
Cowlitz Co WA 156 A3
Kelso WA 156 A3
5th Av S
Kelso WA 156 B3
King Co WA 136 C4
Seattle WA 128 D7
Seattle WA 136 C1
5th Av SW
Cowlitz Co WA 156 A3
Kelso WA 156 A3
Olympia WA 145 D5
5th Av W
Seattle WA 128 A2
N 5th Av
Sandpoint ID 22 B3
Spirit Lake ID 21 E6
N 5th Av SR-41
Spirit Lake ID 21 E6
N 5th Av SR-200
Sandpoint ID 22 B4
N 5th Av US-2
Sandpoint ID 22 B4
N 5th Av US-95
Sandpoint ID 22 B4
SW 5th Av
Portland OR 165 D4
SW 5th Av US-26
Portland OR 165 D4
W 5th Av
Vancouver BC 109 D3
5th St
Astoria OR 153 C3
Hoquiam WA 33 D1
Lane Co OR 182 E6
Lyons OR 55 A6
Springfield OR 64 C5
Springfield OR 182 E6
Springfield OR 186 E2
Wenatchee WA 27 E4
Zillah WA 37 E6
5th St SR-226
Lyons OR 55 A6
5th St W
Toledo WA 34 E6
5th St W SR-505
Toledo WA 34 E6
E 5th St
Port Angeles WA 117 D5
N 5th St
Jacksonville OR 87 C6
N 5th St SR-238
Jacksonville OR 87 C6
S 5th St
Klamath Falls OR 201 D6
Springfield OR 186 E2
S 5th St SR-39
Klamath Falls OR 201 D6
SE 5th St
Bellevue WA 130 C7
W 5th St
Grandview WA 38 B7
Port Angeles WA 117 A3
6th Av
Asotin Co WA 41 D6
Coos Bay OR 194 C7
Hope BC 6 D1
New Westminster BC 4 E3
Seattle WA 128 D7
Tacoma WA 25 B6
Tacoma WA 141 A4
Tacoma WA 142 A4
6th Av SR-128
Asotin Co WA 41 D6
6th Av N
Seattle WA 128 B2
6th Av NE
Seattle WA 124 D5
6th Av S
King Co WA 136 C3
E 6th Av
Eugene OR 185 E1
Junction City OR 64 B4
E 6th Av SR-99
Eugene OR 185 D1
E 6th Av SR-126 BUS
Eugene OR 185 D1

22 INDEX
INDEX 22
SW 6th Av
NE 24th St

Street Index

STREET City State Map# Grid

SW 6th Av
Portland OR 165 D4
W 6th Av
Eugene OR 185 D1
Vancouver BC 109 D4
Vancouver BC 110 A4
W 6th Av SR-99
Eugene OR 185 C1
W 6th Av SR-126
Eugene OR 185 D1
W 6th Av SR-126 BUS
Eugene OR 185 D1
NE 6th Dr
Portland OR 158 A7
Portland OR 162 A1
6th St
Bremerton WA 122 A5
Castlegar BC 10 E2
Curry Co OR 85 C2
Klamath Falls OR 201 D6
Port Orford OR 85 C2
Potlatch ID 41 E1
Tonasket WA 8 E7
6th St SR-6
Potlatch ID 41 E1
6th St SR-20
Tonasket WA 8 E7
6th St SR-39
Klamath Falls OR 201 D6
6th St SR-310
Bremerton WA 122 A5
6th St US-101
Curry Co OR 85 C2
Port Orford OR 85 C2
E 6th St
Vancouver WA 158 A4
N 6th St
Cheney WA 31 A3
Renton WA 138 C5
Yakima WA 37 D4
NW 6th St
Grants Pass OR 197 C3
NW 6th St SR-99
Grants Pass OR 197 C3
NW 6th St US-199
Grants Pass OR 197 C3
S 6th St
Klamath Co OR 89 A7
Klamath Co OR 202 A7
Klamath Falls OR 201 E7
Klamath Falls OR 202 A7
S 6th St SR-39
Klamath Co OR 89 A7
Klamath Co OR 202 A7
Klamath Falls OR 201 E7
Klamath Falls OR 202 A7
SW 6th St
Grants Pass OR 197 C5
SW 6th St SR-99
Grants Pass OR 197 C5
SW 6th St US-199
Grants Pass OR 197 C5
W 6th St
Aberdeen WA 33 D1
Centralia WA 151 D4
The Dalles OR 46 D6
Vancouver WA 157 E4
Vancouver WA 158 A4
W 6th St SR-507
Centralia WA 151 D4
W 6th St US-30
The Dalles OR 46 D6
7th Av
Cowlitz Co WA 155 E4
Cowlitz Co WA 156 A3
Kelso WA 156 A3
Longview WA 155 E5
Longview WA 156 A4
Mission BC 5 C3
Seattle WA 128 D6
7th Av N
Kelso WA 156 B2
7th Av NE
Seattle WA 124 D7
Seattle WA 128 D1
7th Av S
Nampa ID 220 C3
Seattle WA 136 D1
7th Av SE
Albany OR 175 E3
7th Av SW
Cowlitz Co WA 156 A3
Kelso WA 156 A3
E 7th Av
Eugene OR 185 E1
E 7th Av SR-99
Eugene OR 185 E1
E 7th Av SR-126 BUS
Eugene OR 185 E1
NE 7th Av
Island Co WA 15 A4
Oak Harbor WA 15 A4
S 7th Av SW
Tumwater WA 147 D1
SE 7th Av
Portland OR 166 A3
W 7th Av
Eugene OR 64 C5
Eugene OR 185 C1
Spokane WA 211 E2
W 7th Av SR-99
Eugene OR 64 C5
Eugene OR 185 C1
W 7th Av SR-126
Eugene OR 185 D1
W 7th Av SR-126 BUS
Eugene OR 185 D1
7th Pl S
Des Moines WA 139 C7
7th St
Astoria OR 153 C3
Lewis Co WA 34 D6
Vader WA 34 D6
7th St SR-506
Lewis Co WA 34 D6
Vader WA 34 D6
7th St N
Nampa ID 220 D3
7th St S
Nampa ID 220 B4
E 7th St
Weiser ID 72 A3
E 7th St US-95
Weiser ID 72 A3
N 7th St
Coos Bay OR 194 B6
NE 7th St
Grants Pass OR 87 A5
Grants Pass OR 197 D3
NE 7th St SR-99
Grants Pass OR 87 A5
Grants Pass OR 197 D3
NE 7th St US-199
Grants Pass OR 87 A5
Grants Pass OR 197 D3
S 7th St
Coos Bay OR 194 A6
Tacoma WA 142 A4
SE 7th St
Grants Pass OR 197 C5
SE 7th St SR-99
Grants Pass OR 197 C5
SE 7th St US-199
Grants Pass OR 197 C5
8 Av
Langley Township BC 5 C4
8th Av
New Westminster BC 4 E3
Seattle WA 128 D6
8th Av NE
Seattle WA 124 D6
8th Av NW
Seattle WA 124 A3
Shoreline WA 25 C1
8th Av S
Burien WA 136 D5
Burien WA 139 D1
King Co WA 136 D5
Pierce Co WA 25 B7
Pierce Co WA 35 B1
Seattle WA 136 D1
8th Av SW
King Co WA 136 B2
Seattle WA 136 B2
8th Av W
Seattle WA 128 A2
E 8th Av
Spokane WA 212 E2
Spokane Co WA 213 B5
Spokane Valley WA 31 B2
Spokane Valley WA 212 E2
Spokane Valley WA 213 A5
S 8th Av
Elgin OR 50 D6
S 8th Av SR-82
Elgin OR 50 D6
W 8th Av
Spokane WA 211 E2
8th St
Astoria OR 43 D1
Astoria OR 153 C1
Castlegar BC 10 E2
Lewiston ID 41 E6
Myrtle Point OR 74 A7
8th St SR-42
Myrtle Point OR 74 A7
8th St US-30
Astoria OR 153 C1
8th St E
Edgewood WA 25 C6
Milton WA 25 C6
8th St NE
Auburn WA 25 D5
King Co WA 25 D5
8th St SE
Douglas Co WA 27 E5
E 8th St
Medford OR 198 B5
Port Angeles WA 117 C4
N 8th St
Boise ID 222 C7
NE 8th St
Bellevue WA 25 D3
Bellevue WA 130 B5
Bend OR 190 B6
Bend OR 192 B1
SE 8th St
Bellevue WA 25 D3
Bellevue WA 130 D7
W 8th St
Medford OR 198 A6
Port Angeles WA 14 B5
Port Angeles WA 117 B3
Vancouver WA 157 E4
9th Av
Seattle WA 128 C5
9th Av N
Seattle WA 128 C5
9th Av NE
Seattle WA 124 E5
9th Av SE
Albany OR 175 E3
Albany OR 176 A3
9th Av SE SR-99E
Albany OR 175 E3
Albany OR 176 A3
9th Av SE US-20
Albany OR 175 E3
Albany OR 176 A3
9th Av SW
Albany OR 175 E3
Seattle WA 136 B1
9th Av SW US-20
Albany OR 175 E3
9th Av W
Seattle WA 128 A2
N 9th Av
Walla Walla WA 207 E3
N 9th Av SR-125
Walla Walla WA 207 E3
S 9th Av
Walla Walla WA 207 E4
S 9th Av SR-125
Walla Walla WA 207 E4
SW 9th Av
Portland OR 165 E2
W 9th Av
Spokane WA 211 E2
Spokane WA 212 A2
9th St
Castlegar BC 10 E2
Nespelem WA 19 C5
Okanogan Co WA 19 C5
Priest River ID 21 E4
9th St SR-57
Priest River ID 21 E4
E 9th St
Wapato WA 37 D6
Yakima Co WA 37 D6
N 9th St
Boise ID 222 C7
Coeur d'Alene ID 218 C4
Cottage Grove OR 64 C7
Klamath Falls OR 201 D5
Tacoma WA 141 C4
N 9th St SR-99
Cottage Grove OR 64 C7
NE 9th St
Bend OR 192 B1
NW 9th St
Bend OR 189 E7
S 9th St
Boise ID 222 B7
Boise ID 224 B1
Klamath Falls OR 201 D5
Tacoma WA 142 A4
SE 9th St
Bend OR 192 B2
10th Av E
Seattle WA 128 D3
10th Av SW
Albany OR 175 E3
10th Av W
Seattle WA 128 A3
E 10th Av
Benton Co WA 206 C3
Kennewick WA 206 C3
Spokane WA 212 A2
N 10th Av
Caldwell ID 219 C3
Pasco WA 204 C6
NE 10th Av
Clark Co WA 45 A4
NW 10th Av
Portland OR 165 E1
S 10th Av
Caldwell ID 83 C1
Caldwell ID 219 B5
Canyon Co ID 219 B7
Pasco WA 204 C7
S 10th Av SR-397
Pasco WA 204 C7
SW 10th Av
Portland OR 165 D2
W 10th Av
Kennewick WA 49 A1
Kennewick WA 205 E3
Kennewick WA 206 B3
Vancouver BC 109 A4
10th St
Baker City OR 60 E6
Bellingham WA 113 A7
Castlegar BC 10 E2
Nanaimo BC 3 D3
10th St US-30
Baker City OR 60 E6
N 10th St
Coos Bay OR 194 A6
Klamath Falls OR 201 C5
NE 10th St
Bend OR 190 B7
Bend OR 192 B1
Grants Pass OR 197 D3
Hermiston OR 49 A4
NE 10th St CO-1219
Hermiston OR 49 A4
S 10th St
Coos Bay OR 194 A6
SE 10th St
Vancouver WA 159 D6
11th Av
Lewiston ID 41 E6
11th Av N
Nampa ID 220 D3
11th Av N I-84 BUS
Nampa ID 220 D3
11th Av NE
Seattle WA 124 E7
Seattle WA 128 E1
11th Av S
Nampa ID 220 C4
11th Av S I-84 BUS
Nampa ID 220 C4
11th Av W
Seattle WA 127 E3
E 11th Av
Eugene OR 185 E2
Eugene OR 186 A2
NE 11th Av
Portland OR 162 B3
Portland OR 166 B1
NW 11th Av
Portland OR 165 D1
SE 11th Av
Portland OR 166 A3
SW 11th Av
Portland OR 165 D3
W 11th Av
Eugene OR 184 C1
Eugene OR 185 D2
W 11th Av
Lane Co OR 64 B5
Lane Co OR 184 B1
W 11th Av SR-126
Eugene OR 184 C1
Eugene OR 185 B2
Lane Co OR 64 B5
Lane Co OR 184 B1
11th St
Bellingham WA 113 A6
Bremerton WA 122 A5
E 11th St
Bremerton WA 122 D5
Tacoma WA 142 C4
N 11th St
Coeur d'Alene ID 32 A2
Coeur d'Alene ID 218 C6
Klamath Falls OR 201 D5
S 11th St
Klamath Falls OR 201 D5
Tacoma WA 141 E5
Tacoma WA 142 A5
12 Av
Delta BC 4 D4
12th Av
Seaside OR 43 C2
Seaside OR 154 C4
Seattle WA 128 E5
12th Av E
Seattle WA 128 D5
12th Av NE
Seattle WA 124 E5
12th Av S
Nampa ID 220 C4
Seattle WA 128 D7
Seattle WA 132 D1
12th Av S SR-45
Nampa ID 220 C4
12th Av SW
Normandy Park WA 139 A3
E 12th Av
Vancouver BC 4 D2
Vancouver BC 110 B4
NE 12th Av
Portland OR 166 B2
NW 12th Av
Portland OR 165 D2
SE 12th Av
Portland OR 166 B4
SW 12th Av
Portland OR 165 D2
W 12th Av
Vancouver BC 109 D4
Vancouver BC 110 A4
12th Pl SW
Normandy Park WA 139 A3
12th St
Anacortes WA 15 B2
Anacortes WA 114 D2
Bellingham WA 113 A7
Davenport WA 30 B2
Port Townsend WA 119 C5
12th St SR-11
Bellingham WA 113 A7
12th St SR-20 SPUR
Anacortes WA 15 B2
Anacortes WA 114 D2
12th St SR-28
Davenport WA 30 B2
12th St NE
Salem OR 173 E1
12th St SE
Salem OR 173 D5
NE 12th St
Bellevue WA 130 D5
Clyde Hill WA 130 A5
Medina WA 130 A5
Renton WA 138 E4
NW 12th St
Bend OR 189 D6
S 12th St
Klamath Falls OR 201 D5
Lebanon OR 64 D1
Tacoma WA 25 B6
Tacoma WA 141 A5
Tacoma WA 142 B5
S 12th St SR-39
Klamath Falls OR 201 D5
S 12th St US-97 BUS
Klamath Falls OR 201 D5
SE 12th St
College Place WA 207 B6
12th Av Rd
Nampa ID 83 C2
Nampa ID 220 B5
12th Av Rd SR-45
Nampa ID 83 C2
Nampa ID 220 B5
12th St Cto SE
Salem OR 173 D6
13th Av
Seattle WA 128 E6
13th Av N
Walla Walla WA 50 B2
Walla Walla WA 207 D2
Walla Walla Co WA 207 D2
13th Av N SR-125
Walla Walla WA 50 B2
Walla Walla WA 207 D2
Walla Walla Co WA 207 D2
13th Av S
Kelso WA 156 B4
Seattle WA 132 D6
13th Av SW
Normandy Park WA 139 A3
E 13th Av
Eugene OR 185 D2
NE 13th Av
Portland OR 166 B1
SE 13th Av
Portland OR 166 B7
Portland OR 170 A1
SW 13th Av
Portland OR 165 D2
W 13th Av
Eugene OR 185 C2
13th St
Chehalis WA 34 D4
Chehalis WA 152 C6
13th St E
North Vancouver BC 108 D5
13th St NE
Salem OR 173 E1
13th St SE
Salem OR 173 D2
13th St W
North Vancouver BC 108 C5
N 13th St
Shelton WA 24 D6
S 13th St
Benton Co OR 64 A1
Philomath OR 64 A1
Tacoma WA 142 A5
SW 13th St
Chehalis WA 152 D5
14th Av
Mission BC 5 C3
Seattle WA 128 E7
14th Av NW
Olympia WA 145 A3
Thurston Co WA 145 A3
14th Av S
King Co WA 136 D2
Seattle WA 128 E7
Seattle WA 136 D1
14th Av SE
Lacey WA 146 E6
Olympia WA 145 E6
Olympia WA 146 A6
E 14th Av
Spokane WA 212 A3
NW 14th Av
Portland OR 161 D7
Portland OR 165 D1
SW 14th Av
Portland OR 165 D2
W 14th Av
Ellensburg WA 37 D1
Spokane WA 211 E3
Spokane WA 212 A3
14th St
Lewiston ID 41 E6
Springfield OR 187 A2
14th St S
Nampa ID 220 B5
NE 14th St
Lincoln City OR 53 B4
NW 14th St
Bend OR 189 D7
Bend OR 191 D1
S 14th St
Springfield OR 187 A2
15th Av
Longview WA 155 D5
Seattle WA 128 E5
15th Av E
Seattle WA 128 E5
15th Av NE
Lacey WA 24 E7
Lacey WA 146 E3
Olympia WA 146 E3
Seattle WA 25 C2
Seattle WA 124 E3
Seattle WA 128 E1
Thurston Co WA 24 E7
Thurston Co WA 146 E3
15th Av NW
Seattle WA 25 C2
Seattle WA 123 E5
15th Av S
Seattle WA 132 E2
15th Av W
Seattle WA 127 E3
E 15th Av
Kootenai Co ID 215 D3
Post Falls ID 31 D1
Post Falls ID 215 C4
NE 15th Av
Portland OR 162 B5
Portland OR 166 B1
Vancouver WA 158 B2
NW 15th Av
Portland OR 161 D7
Portland OR 165 D2
SW 15th Av
Portland OR 165 D2
15th St
Garfield Co WA 41 A5
West Vancouver BC 107 C3
15th St SR-128
Garfield Co WA 41 A5
15th St SW
Auburn WA 25 D5
E 15th St
Tacoma WA 142 B5
Vancouver WA 158 A4
E 15th St SR-501
Vancouver WA 158 A4
N 15th St
Boise ID 222 B6
Coeur d'Alene ID 32 A1
Coeur d'Alene ID 218 D3
Kootenai Co ID 32 A1
Kootenai Co ID 218 D2
Mt Vernon WA 116 C3
NE 15th St
Bend OR 190 C7
Bend OR 192 C1
S 15th St
Boise ID 222 B7
Mt Vernon WA 116 C5
Tacoma WA 142 A5
SE 15th St
Bend OR 66 D6
Bend OR 192 C5
Deschutes Co OR 192 C5
Vancouver WA 160 D6
W 15th St
Vancouver WA 157 E4
Vancouver WA 158 A4
W 15th St SR-501
Vancouver WA 157 E4
Vancouver WA 158 A4
16 Av
Surrey BC 4 E4
Surrey BC 5 B4
16th Av
Lewiston ID 41 E6
Longview WA 155 E4
16th Av N
Nampa ID 220 D4
16th Av S
Des Moines WA 25 C5
King Co WA 136 E1
Nampa ID 220 D4
Seattle WA 132 E7
Seattle WA 136 E1
Tukwila WA 136 E1
16th Av SW
Burien WA 136 A4
Burien WA 139 A2
King Co WA 136 A4
Normandy Park WA 139 A2
Seattle WA 132 A7
Seattle WA 136 A2
E 16th Av
Spokane Valley WA 31 C2
Spokane Valley WA 213 E6
Spokane Valley WA 214 D6
NE 16th Av
Portland OR 166 B1
NW 16th Av
Portland OR 161 D7
Portland OR 165 D2
S 16th Av
Yakima WA 37 D5
W 16th Av
Vancouver BC 4 D2
Vancouver BC 109 C5
16th St
Everett WA 120 D1
North Bend OR 193 D3
16th St W
North Vancouver BC 108 B4
N 16th St
Boise ID 222 B6
S 16th St
Boise ID 222 B7
SE 16th St
Bellevue WA 25 D3
W 16th St
Port Angeles WA 117 A4
Vancouver WA 157 D4
17th Av
Longview WA 155 D4
17th Av SW
King Co WA 136 A2
Seattle WA 136 A2
SE 17th Av
Clackamas Co OR 170 B2
Milwaukie OR 170 B3
Portland OR 170 B2
Portland OR 166 B5
Portland OR 170 B2
17th St
Baker City OR 60 E6
North Bend OR 193 E3
Washougal WA 45 C6
17th St NE
Salem OR 172 A7
Salem OR 173 E1
Salem OR 174 A1
17th St SE
Salem OR 173 E1
S 17th St
Tacoma WA 142 A5
18th Av SE
Olympia WA 146 D6
E 18th Av
Eugene OR 185 E3
Eugene OR 186 A2
S 18th Av
Caldwell ID 219 C4
SW 18th Av
Portland OR 165 D2
W 18th Av
Eugene OR 64 B5
Eugene OR 184 E2
Eugene OR 185 C2
18th St
Bend OR 190 C2
Deschutes Co OR 190 C2
E 18th St
Vancouver WA 158 E4
Vancouver WA 159 A3
NE 18th St
Bend OR 190 C2
Clark Co WA 160 C4
Deschutes Co OR 190 C2
Vancouver WA 45 B6
Vancouver WA 159 E4
Vancouver WA 160 A4
S 18th St
St. Helens OR 44 E4
19th Av
Seattle WA 128 E5
19th Av E
Seattle WA 128 E4
19th Av SW
Burien WA 139 A2
E 19th Av
Eugene OR 185 E3
SW 19th Av
Portland OR 165 D2
19th St
Everett WA 15 D6
Everett WA 120 D2
Lane Co OR 183 B6
Port Townsend WA 119 C4
Springfield OR 183 B6
19th St E
North Vancouver BC 108 E4
NW 19th St
Redmond OR 66 E3
S 19th St
Fircrest WA 141 A6
Tacoma WA 25 B6
Tacoma WA 141 B6
Tacoma WA 142 A5
20th Av NE
Seattle WA 124 E5
20th Av W
Seattle WA 127 E2
E 20th Av
Eugene OR 185 D3
N 20th Av
Pasco WA 204 B4
NE 20th Av
Portland OR 166 B2
SE 20th Av
Portland OR 166 B2
20th St E
Fife WA 25 C6
Fife WA 142 E6
20th St SE
Snohomish Co WA 15 E6
E 20th St
Vancouver WA 158 C3
SE 20th St
Vancouver WA 160 D7
SW 20th St
Chehalis WA 152 E6
Lewis Co WA 152 E6
W 20th St
Vancouver WA 157 D3
20th St Dr E
Fife WA 142 E6
Tacoma WA 142 E6
21st Av S
Seattle WA 132 E3
21st Av SW
Burien WA 136 A7
Burien WA 139 A1
Federal Way WA 25 C5
N 21st Av
Caldwell ID 219 D4
NE 21st Av
Portland OR 162 B6
Portland OR 166 B1
S 21st Av
Caldwell ID 219 D4
SE 21st Av
Portland OR 166 B4
21st St
Bellingham WA 113 B6
West Vancouver BC 4 D2
West Vancouver BC 107 B3
N 21st St
Tacoma WA 25 B6
Tacoma WA 141 C3
S 21st St
Tacoma WA 142 A6
S 21st St SR-509
Tacoma WA 142 B6
22nd Av E
Pierce Co WA 25 C7
22nd Av S
Nampa ID 220 D4
22nd Av SE
Olympia WA 146 B6
NE 22nd Av
Portland OR 166 B1
SE 22nd Av
Milwaukie OR 170 B5
23rd Av
Seattle WA 25 C3
Seattle WA 128 E6
Seattle WA 129 A6
23rd Av E
Seattle WA 129 A5
23rd Av S
Seattle WA 129 A7
Seattle WA 132 E3
Seattle WA 133 A1
E 23rd Av
Eugene OR 185 E3
NW 23rd Av
Portland OR 161 C7
Portland OR 165 C1
23rd St E
North Vancouver BC 108 D4
23rd St W
North Vancouver BC 108 C4
N 23rd St
Coeur d'Alene ID 218 E6
24 Av
Surrey BC 4 E4
Surrey BC 5 A4
24-SW Rd
Grant Co WA 38 C3
24th Av E
Pierce Co WA 144 D7
Seattle WA 129 A4
24th Av NE
Seattle WA 125 A2
24th Av NW
Seattle WA 25 C2
Seattle WA 123 D3
24th Av S
King Co WA 136 E5
Seatac WA 136 E7
Seatac WA 139 E1
E 24th Av
Eugene OR 185 E3
Eugene OR 186 A3
NE 24th Av
Portland OR 166 C1
S 24th Av
Caldwell ID 219 D4
24th St E
Edgewood WA 25 C6
NE 24th St
Bellevue WA 25 D2
Bellevue WA 130 E4
Clyde Hill WA 130 B4
Medina WA 130 A4

23 INDEX

INDEX 23

S 24th St

SW 92nd Av

Street Index

STREET / City State	Map#	Grid
S 24th St		
Tacoma WA	142	B6
25th Av NE		
Seattle WA	125	A6
E 25th Av		
Benton Co WA	206	E5
SE 25th Av		
Portland OR	166	C3
25th St		
West Vancouver BC	4	D2
West Vancouver BC	107	A3
25th St E		
North Vancouver BC	108	D3
25th St SE		
Salem OR	174	A3
25th St W		
North Vancouver BC	108	D3
NE 25th St		
Vancouver WA	159	A3
S 25th St		
Tacoma WA	141	E6
Tacoma WA	142	A6
SE 25th St		
Bellevue WA	134	C2
26th Av		
Cowlitz Co WA	155	C5
Longview WA	155	C5
26th Av E		
Seattle WA	129	A2
26th Av NE		
Olympia WA	146	D2
Thurston Co WA	146	A2
26th Av S		
Lakewood WA	143	D7
Pierce Co WA	143	D7
Seatac WA	139	E6
W 26th Pl		
Kennewick WA	206	B5
E 26th St		
Tacoma WA	142	B6
N 26th St		
Tacoma WA	141	A2
S 26th St		
Tacoma WA	142	B6
27th Av SE		
Olympia WA	146	D7
E 27th Av		
Benton Co WA	49	B1
Benton Co WA	206	D5
Kennewick WA	206	C5
NE 27th Av		
Portland OR	166	C1
W 27th Av		
Benton Co WA	206	B5
Kennewick WA	205	D5
Kennewick WA	206	A5
27th St		
Bend OR	66	D6
Bend OR	192	E5
Deschutes Co OR	66	D6
Deschutes Co OR	192	E5
27th St W		
University Place WA	25	B6
E 27th St		
Tacoma WA	142	C6
N 27th St		
Boise ID	222	A6
NE 27th St		
Bend OR	66	D5
Bend OR	190	D5
Bend OR	192	D1
Renton WA	138	D3
S 27th St		
Boise ID	222	A7
Tacoma WA	142	B6
SW 27th St		
Redmond OR	66	E4
28 Av		
Delta BC	4	D4
28th Av NW		
Olympia WA	145	B2
Seattle WA	123	D4
Thurston Co WA	145	B2
28th Av S		
Seatac WA	139	E5
28th Av W		
Seattle WA	25	C2
Seattle WA	127	D3
NE 28th Av		
Portland OR	166	C1
SE 28th Av		
Portland OR	166	C6
W 28th Av		
Eugene OR	185	C4
28th St		
Springfield OR	64	C5
Springfield OR	183	C7
Springfield OR	187	C1
E 28th St		
Tacoma WA	142	D6
E 28th St SR-167		
Tacoma WA	142	D6
N 28th St		
Boise ID	84	A1
Boise ID	222	A4
NE 28th St		
Clark Co WA	160	E3
Vancouver WA	45	B6
Vancouver WA	159	E3
Vancouver WA	160	A3
S 28th St		
Tacoma WA	142	A6
E 29th Av		
Eugene OR	185	E4
Spokane WA	31	B2
Spokane WA	212	B4
Vancouver BC	4	D2
Vancouver BC	110	E6
NE 29th Av		
Portland OR	162	C3
W 29th Av		
Eugene OR	185	D4
Spokane WA	211	E4
Spokane WA	212	A4
W 29th Av		
Vancouver BC	110	A6
29th St E		
North Vancouver BC	108	E3
N Vancouver Dist BC	108	E3
29th St SE		
Auburn WA	25	D5
30th Av		
Longview WA	155	C3
30th Av NE		
Seattle WA	125	A7
30th Av SW		
Seattle WA	131	E6
30th Av W		
Seattle WA	127	D1
E 30th Av		
Eugene OR	64	C5
Eugene OR	185	E4
Eugene OR	186	A4
Lane Co OR	186	C5
SW 30th Av		
Portland OR	165	B7
N 30th St		
Renton WA	138	C2
Tacoma WA	25	B5
Tacoma WA	141	A2
NE 30th St		
Renton WA	138	C2
NW 31st Av		
Clark Co WA	45	A4
31st St		
Lane Co OR	183	C7
Springfield OR	183	C7
West Vancouver BC	4	D2
32 Av		
Langley Township BC	5	A4
Surrey BC	5	A4
32nd Av		
Seattle WA	129	A7
32nd Av NW		
Seattle WA	25	C2
Seattle WA	123	D4
32nd Av SE		
Salem OR	174	B7
E 32nd Av		
Spokane Co WA	214	D7
Spokane Valley WA	31	C2
Spokane Valley WA	213	E7
Spokane Valley WA	214	C7
SE 32nd Av		
Milwaukie OR	170	C2
Portland OR	170	C2
32nd St		
Anacortes WA	114	C3
S 32nd St		
Lane Co OR	187	C3
Springfield OR	187	C2
E 33rd Av		
Vancouver BC	110	B7
NE 33rd Av		
Portland OR	162	C5
Portland OR	166	C1
NE 33rd Dr		
Portland OR	158	C7
Portland OR	162	C2
33rd St		
Astoria OR	153	E1
E 33rd St		
Vancouver WA	158	C2
NE 33rd St		
Deschutes Co OR	66	E3
S 33rd St		
Yakima Co WA	37	D4
34th Av		
Seattle WA	129	B6
34th Av SE		
Albany OR	175	E5
Albany OR	176	A5
34th Av SW		
Albany OR	175	D5
34th Av W		
Seattle WA	25	C2
Seattle WA	123	C7
Seattle WA	127	C1
SE 34th Av		
Milwaukie OR	170	C3
E 34th St		
Tacoma WA	142	B7
N 34th St		
Seattle WA	128	C2
S 34th St		
Tacoma WA	142	B7
SE 34th St		
Vancouver WA	45	B6
Vancouver WA	164	D1
35th Av NE		
Seattle WA	125	B7
35th Av S		
Seatac WA	140	A7
Tukwila WA	137	A6
35th Av SE		
Snohomish Co WA	15	D7
35th Av SW		
Seattle WA	25	C3
Seattle WA	131	E6
Seattle WA	135	E4
SW 35th Av		
Portland OR	169	B3
SW 35th Dr		
Portland OR	169	B2
35th St		
Astoria OR	153	E1
N 35th St		
Seattle WA	128	B1
NW 35th St		
Corvallis OR	177	D5
S 35th St		
Tacoma WA	141	C7
SW 35th St		
Benton Co OR	177	D5
Corvallis OR	177	D5
36th Av NE		
Thurston Co WA	24	E7
36th Av SE		
Salem OR	174	C7
36th St		
Anacortes WA	15	B2
Anacortes WA	114	D4
Bellingham WA	113	D6
36th St SR-20 SPUR		
Anacortes WA	15	B2
Anacortes WA	114	D4
N 36th St		
Boise ID	84	A1
Boise ID	221	E3
Seattle WA	128	B1
Tacoma WA	141	C1
NW 36th St		
Corvallis OR	177	D4
Seattle WA	128	A1
S 36th St		
Tacoma WA	141	C7
SE 36th St		
Bellevue WA	134	E3
37th Av SE		
Lacey WA	148	E1
Olympia WA	148	E1
37th Av SW		
Seattle WA	131	E3
NE 37th Av		
Portland OR	162	D5
Portland OR	166	D1
37th Pl S		
Kent WA	140	A7
Seatac WA	140	A7
37th St		
Anacortes WA	15	A2
Anacortes WA	114	C4
N 37th St		
Tacoma WA	141	B1
S 37th St		
Tacoma WA	143	C1
38th Av		
Longview WA	44	D1
Longview WA	155	A2
38th Av E		
Pierce Co WA	25	C7
NW 38th Av		
Camas WA	45	B6
E 38th St		
Tacoma WA	25	C6
Tacoma WA	144	C1
E 38th St SR-7		
Tacoma WA	144	B1
N 38th St		
Seattle WA	128	B1
S 38th St		
Tacoma WA	25	B6
Tacoma WA	143	E1
Tacoma WA	144	A1
S 38th St SR-7		
Tacoma WA	144	B1
39th Av S		
Seattle WA	137	B2
NE 39th Av		
Portland OR	162	D7
Portland OR	166	D1
SE 39th Av		
Portland OR	166	D3
E 39th St		
Vancouver WA	158	B2
N 39th St		
Seattle WA	128	B1
NE 39th St		
Clark Co WA	45	B5
Clark Co WA	160	D2
Vancouver WA	160	D2
NW 39th St		
Seattle WA	128	A1
W 39th St		
Vancouver WA	45	A5
Vancouver WA	157	E2
Vancouver WA	158	A2
40 Av		
Langley Township BC	5	B4
40th Av SW		
Lakewood WA	143	B7
E 40th Av		
Eugene OR	64	C6
Eugene OR	185	D6
S 40th Av		
Yakima WA	37	D5
SW 40th Av		
Portland OR	169	A1
40th Pl S		
Kent WA	140	B7
Seatac WA	140	A7
40th St NW		
Pierce Co WA	25	A5
40th St W		
Fircrest WA	143	A1
Tacoma WA	143	A1
University Place WA	25	B6
University Place WA	143	A1
N 40th St		
Seattle WA	128	C1
NE 40th St		
Clark Co WA	158	E2
Clark Co WA	159	A2
Seattle WA	128	D1
Vancouver WA	159	A2
S 40th St		
Tacoma WA	143	D1
SE 40th St		
Mercer Island WA	133	E3
Mercer Island WA	134	A3
41 B St		
Delta BC	4	D4
E 41st Av		
Vancouver BC	4	D3
Vancouver BC	110	B7
NE 41st Av		
Portland OR	162	D6
NW 41st Av		
Clark Co WA	44	E5
W 41st Av		
Vancouver BC	4	D2
W 41st Av		
Vancouver BC	109	E7
Vancouver BC	110	A7
W 41st Av PROV-99		
Vancouver BC	109	D7
41st St		
Anacortes WA	15	B2
Anacortes WA	114	C4
Everett WA	120	C5
NE 41st St		
Seattle WA	129	B1
42nd Av NE		
Seattle WA	129	B1
42nd Av S		
Kent WA	140	B7
Seatac WA	140	B7
Tukwila WA	137	B5
42nd Av SW		
Seattle WA	131	D6
NE 42nd Av		
Clark Co WA	158	D2
Portland OR	162	D6
42nd St		
Springfield OR	183	D7
Springfield OR	187	D1
S 42nd St		
Lane Co OR	187	E3
Springfield OR	187	E2
43rd Av NE		
Seattle WA	125	B7
Seattle WA	129	B1
E 43rd Av		
Eugene OR	186	A6
Spokane WA	212	B6
E 43rd St		
Tacoma WA	144	B1
S 43rd St		
Tacoma WA	144	B1
SW 43rd St		
Kent WA	140	E4
Renton WA	140	E4
Tukwila WA	140	E4
44th Av W		
Lynnwood WA	25	C1
NE 44th St		
Clark Co WA	158	D1
Renton WA	138	C1
Vancouver WA	158	C1
45th Av SE		
Lacey WA	34	E1
45th Av SW		
Seattle WA	135	D2
SW 45th Av		
Portland OR	165	A6
Portland OR	169	A1
W 45th Av		
Benton Co WA	206	A6
Kennewick WA	49	B1
Kennewick WA	205	E6
Kennewick WA	206	A6
SW 45th Dr		
Portland OR	169	A2
NE 45th Pl		
Seattle WA	125	A7
SE 45th Pl		
Milwaukie OR	170	D2
Portland OR	170	D2
N 45th St		
Seattle WA	124	C7
NE 45th St		
Seattle WA	124	D7
Seattle WA	125	B7
NE 45th St SR-513		
Seattle WA	125	A7
46th Av		
Longview WA	44	D1
N 46th St		
Seattle WA	124	B7
Tacoma WA	25	B5
47th Av SW		
Seattle WA	131	D7
NE 47th Av		
Portland OR	162	E7
Portland OR	166	E1
S 47th St		
Tacoma WA	143	C2
48th Av		
Longview WA	44	D1
48th Av SW		
Seattle WA	131	C7
SW 48th Av		
Portland OR	169	A2
48th St		
Springfield OR	188	A2
48th St E		
Pierce Co WA	144	E2
E 48th St		
Tacoma WA	144	C2
NE 48th St		
Vancouver WA	160	C1
S 48th St		
Tacoma WA	143	E2
Tacoma WA	144	A2
49		
Boise ID	223	A2
49th Av SW		
Seattle WA	131	D4
Thurston Co WA	147	A2
SW 49th Av		
Lake Oswego OR	169	A4
Portland OR	169	A4
49th St		
Port Townsend WA	119	B2
NE 49th St		
Vancouver WA	159	E1
Vancouver WA	160	A1
50th Av S		
Seattle WA	133	C5
NE 50th Av		
Clark Co WA	45	A5
SE 50th Av		
Portland OR	45	A7
Portland OR	166	E4
50th Pl S		
Tukwila WA	137	C5
N 50th St		
Seattle WA	124	C7
NE 50th St		
Seattle WA	124	E7
51st Av S		
King Co WA	25	C5
Seattle WA	137	C4
Tukwila WA	137	C4
Tukwila WA	140	C1
51st St W		
Fircrest WA	141	A7
Fircrest WA	143	A1
Tacoma WA	141	A6
Tacoma WA	143	A3
University Place WA	143	A3
N 51st St		
Ruston WA	25	B5
S 51st St W		
Fircrest WA	141	A6
Fircrest WA	143	A1
Tacoma WA	141	A6
Tacoma WA	143	A2
University Place WA	143	A2
52nd Av W		
Snohomish Co WA	15	C7
SE 52nd Av		
Portland OR	45	A7
Portland OR	166	E5
Portland OR	170	E1
52nd St		
Springfield OR	188	A1
52nd St SE		
Everett WA	120	C6
53rd St		
Port Townsend WA	119	B1
NE 53rd St		
Clark Co WA	45	B5
NW 53rd St		
Benton Co OR	177	C5
SW 53rd St		
Benton Co OR	177	C6
Corvallis OR	64	B1
Corvallis OR	177	C6
54th Av SW		
Thurston Co WA	34	D1
Thurston Co WA	147	B2
Tumwater WA	34	D1
Tumwater WA	147	A2
NE 54th Av		
Clark Co WA	158	E2
Vancouver WA	158	E2
NW 54th St		
Seattle WA	123	D6
55th Av NE		
Seattle WA	125	C5
NW 55th Pl		
Seattle WA	124	A6
NE 55th St		
Seattle WA	125	B6
NW 55th St		
Seattle WA	124	A6
56 St		
Delta BC	4	D4
56th Av		
Abbotsford BC	5	C4
Langley Township BC	5	C4
E 56th St		
Tacoma WA	25	C6
Tacoma WA	144	C3
S 56th St		
Tacoma WA	25	B6
Tacoma WA	143	B3
Tacoma WA	144	B3
University Place WA	143	A3
N 57		
Priest River ID	21	E4
N 57 SR-57		
Priest River ID	21	E4
E 57th Av		
Spokane WA	212	B7
Spokane Co WA	31	B2
Spokane Co WA	212	C7
NE 57th Av		
Portland OR	162	E7
S 57th St		
Lane Co OR	64	D5
Lane Co OR	188	B3
Springfield OR	64	D5
Springfield OR	188	B3
58 Av		
Surrey BC	4	E4
58 Av PROV-10		
Surrey BC	4	E4
58th Av		
Abbotsford BC	5	C4
58th Av E		
Pierce Co WA	25	C7
58th Av S		
Tukwila WA	137	C7
58th Av SW		
Seattle WA	131	C3
58th St		
Springfield OR	64	D5
Springfield OR	188	C2
NE 58th St		
Clark Co WA	45	B5
NE 58th St SR-500		
Clark Co WA	45	B5
59th Av SW		
Seattle WA	131	C3
59th Pl S		
Kent WA	140	C6
NE 60th Av		
Portland OR	163	A4
Portland OR	167	A2
SE 60th Av		
Portland OR	167	A3
NE 60th St		
King Co WA	126	E7
Kirkland WA	126	E7
Kirkland WA	130	E1
SE 60th St		
Issaquah WA	25	D3
King Co WA	25	D3
61st Av S		
Tukwila WA	140	C2
61st St		
Deschutes Co OR	66	D4
SW 61st St		
Deschutes Co OR	66	D4
62 B St		
Delta BC	4	D3
62nd Av S		
Kent WA	140	C6
63rd Av NE		
Thurston Co WA	24	E7
63rd Av SW		
Seattle WA	131	B3
N 63rd St		
Seattle WA	124	B6
64 Av		
Delta BC	4	E3
Surrey BC	5	A4
64th Av S		
Kent WA	140	D7
King Co WA	137	D6
S 64th Av		
Yakima Co WA	37	C5
64th Pl S		
King Co WA	137	D5
64th St E		
Pierce Co WA	144	E4
64th St NE		
Marysville WA	15	D6
64th St NE SR-528		
Marysville WA	15	D6
E 64th St		
Pierce Co WA	144	E4
Tacoma WA	144	B4
N 64th St		
Seattle WA	124	C6
S 64th St		
Tacoma WA	143	E4
Tacoma WA	144	A4
SW 65th Av		
Clackamas Co OR	54	E1
Washington Co OR	54	E1
N 65th St		
Seattle WA	124	B6
NE 65th St		
Seattle WA	25	D2
Seattle WA	124	D6
Seattle WA	125	C6
NW 65th St		
Seattle WA	25	C2
Seattle WA	123	E5
Seattle WA	124	A6
66th Av E		
Pierce Co WA	25	C7
66th Av S		
Tukwila WA	140	D1
N 66th Av		
Yakima Co WA	37	C4
66th St		
Springfield OR	64	D5
Springfield OR	188	D2
66th St W		
Pierce Co WA	143	A4
Tacoma WA	143	A4
N 66th St		
Seattle WA	124	C5
S 66th St		
Tacoma WA	143	C4
67th Av NE		
Marysville WA	15	D5
N 67th St		
Seattle WA	124	B5
68th Av NE		
King Co WA	125	D1
68th Av S		
King Co WA	137	D5
Renton WA	137	D6
NE 68th Av		
Portland OR	167	A1
NE 68th St		
Kirkland WA	126	D7
SE 68th St		
Mercer Island WA	134	A7
70th Av E		
Pierce Co WA	35	C1
NE 70th Pl		
Kirkland WA	126	D7
NE 70th St		
Seattle WA	124	D5
Seattle WA	125	C5
NE 71st St		
Seattle WA	124	D5
72 Av		
Delta BC	4	E3
Langley Township BC	5	A3
NE 72nd Av		
Clark Co WA	45	A5
S 72nd Av		
Yakima WA	37	C5
NE 72nd Pl		
Kirkland WA	126	D7
72nd St E		
Pierce Co WA	25	C6
Pierce Co WA	144	C4
Tacoma WA	144	C4
E 72nd St		
Pierce Co WA	144	B4
Tacoma WA	144	B4
S 72nd St		
Tacoma WA	143	E4
Tacoma WA	144	A4
SE 72nd St		
Mercer Island WA	25	D3
Mercer Island WA	133	E7
Mercer Island WA	134	A7
NE 73rd St		
Seattle WA	124	E5
74th Av S		
King Co WA	137	E5
Seattle WA	137	E5
74th St W		
Lakewood WA	143	A4
Tacoma WA	143	A4
S 74th St		
Lakewood WA	143	A4
Tacoma WA	25	B6
Tacoma WA	143	D5
NE 75th St		
Seattle WA	25	C2
Seattle WA	124	E5
Seattle WA	125	B5
76th Pl NE		
King Co WA	125	E3
King Co WA	126	A2
78th Av E		
Pierce Co WA	25	C7
NE 78th St		
Clark Co WA	45	A5
80 Av		
Delta BC	4	E3
Surrey BC	5	B3
80th Av S		
Kent WA	140	E4
Renton WA	140	E4
S 80th Av		
Yakima WA	37	C5
Yakima Co WA	37	C5
80th Pl S		
Kent WA	140	E4
80th St E		
Pierce Co WA	144	D5
N 80th St		
Seattle WA	124	C4
NE 80th St		
Seattle WA	124	D4
NW 80th St		
Seattle WA	25	C2
Seattle WA	123	D4
Seattle WA	124	A4
NE 82nd Av		
Portland OR	163	C5
Portland OR	167	B1
NE 82nd Av SR-213		
Portland OR	163	B6
Portland OR	167	B1
SE 82nd Av		
Portland OR	45	A7
Portland OR	167	B3
SE 82nd Av SR-213		
Portland OR	45	A7
Portland OR	167	B4
84 Av		
Abbotsford BC	5	C3
Langley Township BC	5	C3
84th Av NE		
Clyde Hill WA	130	A4
Hunts Point WA	130	A3
Kenmore WA	25	D2
King Co WA	126	A2
Medina WA	130	A4
84th Av S		
Kent WA	25	D4
84th Av SE		
Mercer Island WA	134	A7
84th St E		
Pierce Co WA	144	D6
84th St NE		
Snohomish Co WA	15	E6
84th St S		
Lakewood WA	143	C5
Tacoma WA	143	D5
S 84th St		
Lakewood WA	143	D6
Tacoma WA	143	E5
Tacoma WA	144	A6
85th St E		
Pierce Co WA	144	C6
N 85th St		
Seattle WA	124	B4
NE 85th St		
Kirkland WA	126	D5
NE 85th St SR-908		
Kirkland WA	126	E5
NW 85th St		
Seattle WA	123	D4
Seattle WA	124	A4
NE 86th Av		
Vancouver WA	159	B3
NE 87th Av		
Vancouver WA	159	B4
88 Av		
Langley Township BC	5	B3
Surrey BC	4	E3
Surrey BC	5	A3
88th Av SE		
Thurston Co WA	34	E1
Thurston Co WA	147	E7
Thurston Co WA	148	A7
Tumwater WA	34	E1
Tumwater WA	147	E7
Tumwater WA	148	A7
SE 88th Pl		
Newcastle WA	138	E2
SE 88th St		
Newcastle WA	138	D2
SE 89th Pl		
Newcastle WA	138	E2
89th St SW		
Lakewood WA	143	B6
90 Av		
Delta BC	4	E3
NW 90th St		
Seattle WA	123	E3
92nd Av NE		
Clyde Hill WA	130	B4
Yarrow Point WA	130	B3
NE 92nd Av		
Vancouver WA	159	C5
SE 92nd Av		
Portland OR	167	C7
Vancouver WA	159	C5
SW 92nd Av		
Washington Co OR	44	E7

Points of Interest Index

Points of Interest Index

Points of Interest Index

Points of Interest Index

Points of Interest Index

Points of Interest Index

Colleges & Universities

FEATURE NAME Address City State	MAP#	GRID
British Columbia Institute of Technology, 555 Seymour St - Vancouver, BC	110	A2
Camosun College-Interurban, Saanich, BC	14	B2
Camosun College-Lansdowne, 3100 Foul Bay Rd, Saanich, BC	112	C3
Capilano College, North Vancouver District, BC	4	E2
Cascade College, 9101 E Burnside St, Portland, OR	167	C2
Centralia College, 600 W Locust St, Centralia, WA	151	C5
Central Oregon Community College, Bend, OR	189	C6
Central Washington University, Ellensburg, WA	37	D1
Chemeketa Community College, 4000 Lancaster Dr NE - Marion Co, OR	172	C4
Chemeketa Community College, McMinnville, OR	54	B2
City University, 789 W Pender St, Vancouver, BC	110	A1
City University, 12500 SE 126th Av, Vancouver, WA	160	A5
City University-Bellevue, 11900 NE 1st St, Bellevue, WA	130	D6
City University-North Seattle, 2150 N 107th St, Seattle, WA	124	C2
Clackamas Community College, Oregon City, OR	55	A1
Clark College, 1800 E McLoughlin Blvd, Vancouver, WA	158	B4
Clatsop Community College, 1653 Jerome Av, Astoria, OR	153	D2
Clover Park Technical College, 4500 Steilacoom Blvd SW - Lakewood, WA	143	B6
Columbia Basin College, 2600 N 20th Av, Pasco, WA	204	B4
Columbia Basin College-Richland, 1011 Northgate Dr, Richland - WA	203	C5
Concordia University, 2811 NE Holman St, Portland, OR	162	C4
Corban College, Salem, OR	174	E7
Cornish College of the Arts, 1000 Lenora St, Seattle, WA	128	C5
Eastern Oregon University, La Grande, OR	60	D1
Eastern Washington University, Cheney, WA	31	A3
Eastern Washington University-Spokane, 705 W 1st Av - Spokane, WA	211	E1
Edmonds Community College, Lynnwood, WA	25	C1
Embry-Riddle Aeronautical Univ Seattle Ctr - 1000 Oakesdale Av SW, Renton, WA	137	E7
Erickson College, 2021 Columbia St, Vancouver, BC	110	A4
Eugene Bible College, 2155 Bailey Hill Rd, Lane Co, OR	184	D3
Everest College, 425 SW Washington St, Portland, OR	165	E2
Everest College-Vancouver, 120 NE 136th Av, Vancouver, WA	160	A5
Everett Community College, Everett, WA	15	D6
Evergreen State College, Thurston Co, WA	145	A1
Evergreen State College-Tacoma, 1210 6th Av, Tacoma, WA	141	E4
George Fox University, Newberg, OR	54	D1
Golden Gate University, 1425 4th Av, Seattle, WA	128	C6
Gonzaga University, 502 N Addison St, Spokane, WA	210	A7
Grays Harbor College, Aberdeen, WA	33	D1
Heald College Sch of Bus & Tech-Portland, 625 SW Broadway - Portland, OR	165	E2
Henry Cogswell College, 3002 Colby Av, Everett, WA	120	C3
International Air Academy, 2901 Grand Blvd, Vancouver, WA	158	C4
Kwantlen University College-Langley, Langley, BC	5	B4
Kwantlen University Col-Richmond, Richmond, BC	4	C3
Lane Community College, Gonyea Rd, Lane Co, OR	186	D6
Langara College, Vancouver, BC	4	D3
Lasalle College International, 535 Howe St, Vancouver, BC	110	A2
Lewis & Clark College, 615 SW Palatine Hill Rd, Portland, OR	169	E3
Lewis & Clark Law School, 10015 SW Terwilliger Blvd, Portland - OR	169	D3
Lewis-Clark State College, W Hubbard Av, Coeur d'Alene, ID	218	A5
Lewis-Clark State College, Lewiston, ID	41	E6
Linfield College-McMinnville, McMinnville, OR	54	B2
Linfield College-Portland, 2255 NW Northrup St, Portland, OR	165	C1
Lower Columbia College, 1600 Maple St, Longview, WA	155	E4
Mars Hill Graduate School, 2501 Elliott Av, Seattle, WA	128	B6
Marylhurst University, Lake Oswego, OR	55	A1
Mt Hood Community College, Gresham, OR	45	B7
Mt Hood Community College-Maywood Campus - 10100 NE Prescott St, Maywood Park, OR	163	D5
Multnomah Bible College, 8435 NE Glisan St, Portland, OR	167	C2
National College of Naturopathic Medicine, 049 SW Porter St - Portland, OR	165	E4
North Idaho College, 1000 W Garden Av, Coeur d'Alene, ID	218	A6
North Seattle Community College, 9600 College Wy N, Seattle - WA	124	C3
Northwest Christian College, Eugene, OR	185	E2
Northwest Nazarene University, Nampa, ID	220	C5
Northwest University, 5520 108th Av NE, Kirkland, WA	130	C1
Olympic College, 1600 Chester Av, Bremerton, WA	122	B4
Oregon College of Oriental Medicine - 10525 SE Cherry Blossom Dr, Portland, OR	167	D3
Oregon Graduate Institute, Hillsboro, OR	44	D7
Oregon Health & Science University - 3181 SW Sam Jackson Park Rd, Portland, OR	165	D4
Oregon Institute of Technology, 3201 Campus Dr - Klamath Falls, OR	201	D2
Oregon State Health University, 3303 SW Moody Av, Portland - OR	165	E4
Oregon State University, 1500 SW Jefferson Wy, Corvallis, OR	178	A5
Oregon State University-Cascades, 2600 NW College Wy - Bend, OR	189	C6
Pacific Bible College, 670 Superior Ct, Medford, OR	198	B4
Pacific Gateway International Col-Victoria, 1012 Douglas St - Victoria, BC	111	E5
Pacific Lutheran University, Pierce Co, WA	25	B7
Pacific Northwest College of Art, 1241 NW Kearney St - Portland, OR	165	D1
Pacific University, Forest Grove, OR	44	C7
Pacific University-Eugene, 40 E Broadway, Eugene, OR	185	D1
Pattison College Language Centre, 981 Nelson St, Vancouver - BC	109	E2
Pierce College-Fort Steilacoom, Lakewood, WA	25	B6
Portland Community College-Cascade, 705 N Killingsworth St - Portland, OR	161	E4
Portland Community College-Rock Creek, Washington Co, OR	44	E6
Portland Community College-SE Center, Portland, OR	45	A7
Portland Community College-Southeast Center - 2305 SE 82nd Av, Portland, OR	167	B4
Portland Community College-Sylvania, Portland, OR	169	A4
Portland State University, 1633 SW Park Av, Portland, OR	165	D3
Puget Sound Christian College, 2610 Wetmore Av, Everett - WA	120	C2
Reed College, 3203 SE Woodstock Blvd, Portland, OR	166	C7
Renton Technical College, 3000 NE 4th St, Renton, WA	138	E6
Rhodes Career College, 1125 Howe St, Vancouver, BC	109	E2
Rogue Community College-Medford, 202 S Riverside Av - Medford, OR	198	B6
Royal Oak College, 1130 Alberni St, Vancouver, BC	109	E1
Royal Roads University, Colwood, BC	14	A2
St. Michaels University School, 3400 Richmond Rd, Saanich - BC	112	C2
Seattle Central Community College, 1701 Broadway, Seattle - WA	128	D5
Seattle Pacific University, 3307 3rd Av W, Seattle, WA	128	A1
Seattle University, 901 12th Av, Seattle, WA	128	D6
Shoreline Community College, Shoreline, WA	25	B1
Simon Fraser University, Burnaby, BC	4	E2
Simon Fraser University-Harbour Center, 515 W Hastings St - Vancouver, BC	110	A2
Skagit Valley College-Mt Vernon, Mt Vernon, WA	116	D2
Southern Oregon University, 1250 Siskiyou Blvd, Ashland, OR	200	A5
South Puget Sound Community College, 2011 Mottman Rd SW - Olympia, WA	145	C7
South Seattle Community College, 6000 16th Av SW, Seattle - WA	132	B6
Southwestern Oregon Community Col, 1988 Newmark Av - Coos Bay, OR	193	D4
Spokane Community College, 1810 N Greene St, Spokane, WA	210	D6
Spokane Falls Community College - 3410 W Fort George Wright Dr, Spokane, WA	209	B6
Sprott-Shaw Community Col-Vancouver, 885 Dunsmuir St - Vancouver, BC	110	A2
Sprott-Shaw Community Col-Victoria, 2621 Douglas St - Victoria, BC	111	E4
Stenberg College-Vancouver, 1111 Melville St, Vancouver, BC	109	E1
Stevens-Henager College, 730 S Americana Blvd, Boise, ID	222	A7
Treasure Valley Community College, Ontario, OR	72	A5
Trinity Western University, Langley Township, BC	5	B3
Umpqua Community College, Douglas Co, OR	75	A5
University College of Fraser Valley, Abbotsford, BC	5	D4
University of British Columbia, Vancouver, BC	4	C2
University of Idaho-Boise, 322 E Front St, Boise, ID	224	C1
University of Idaho-Coeur d'Alene, W Hubbard St - Coeur d'Alene, ID	218	A6
University of Oregon, 1217 E 13th Av, Eugene, OR	186	A2
University of Oregon-Portland Center, 722 SW 2nd Av - Portland, OR	165	E2
University of Phoenix-Spokane-Rock Pointe - 1330 N Washington St, Spokane, WA	209	E7
University of Portland, 5000 N Willamette Blvd, Portland, OR	161	A3
University of Puget Sound, 1500 N Warner St, Tacoma, WA	141	C3
University of Victoria, 3749 Finnerty Rd, Saanich, BC	112	D1
University of Washington, 4098 15th Av NE, Seattle, WA	128	E1
University of Washington-Bothell, Bothell, WA	25	D1
University of Washington-Tacoma, 1900 Commerce St - Tacoma, WA	142	A6
Valley Medical College, 4707 Silverton Rd NE, Marion Co, OR	172	E4
Vancouver Career College-Vancouver, 570 Dunsmuir St - Vancouver, BC	110	A2
Vancouver Career College-Victoria, 1483 Douglas St, Victoria - BC	111	E5
Vancouver Cmty College-City Center, 250 W Pender St - Vancouver, BC	110	A2
Vancouver Community Col-King Edward, 1155 E Broadway - Vancouver, BC	110	C4
Vancouver Comm College-International Ctr, 1080 Alberni St - Vancouver, BC	109	E2
Vancouver Premier College, 1338 W Broadway, Vancouver, BC	109	D4
Vincennes University-Washington, 2255 Cole Av, Kitsap Co - WA	122	A6
Walla Walla College, 204 S College Av, College Place, WA	207	B5
Warner Pacific College, 2219 SE 68th Av, Portland, OR	167	A4
Washington Baptist Teachers College, 2500 S 66th St, Tacoma - WA	143	D4
Washington State University-Prosser, Benton Co, WA	38	C7
Washington State University-Pullman, Pullman, WA	41	D3
Washington State University-Spokane, 310 N Riverpoint Blvd - Spokane, WA	212	A1
Washington State University-Tri-Cities, Richland, WA	39	A7
Washington State University-Vancouver, Clark Co, WA	45	A5
Wenatchee Valley College, Wenatchee, WA	27	D4
West Coast Col of Massage Therapy, 637 Bay St, Victoria, BC	111	E4
Western Business College, 120 SE 136th Av, Vancouver, WA	160	A5
Western Oregon University, Monmouth, OR	54	B5
Western Seminary, 5511 SE Hawthorne Blvd, Portland, OR	166	E3
Western States Chiropractic College, 2900 NE 132nd Av - Portland, OR	164	A7
Western Town College, 626 W Pender St, Vancouver, BC	110	A2
Western Washington University, 516 High St, Bellingham, WA	113	B5
Whatcom Community College, Bellingham, WA	5	B6
Whitman College, 345 Boyer Av, Walla Walla, WA	208	A3
Whitworth College, Spokane Co, WA	31	A1
Willamette University, Salem, OR	173	D1
Yakima Valley Cmty Col-Grandview, Grandview, WA	38	B7
Yakima Valley Community College, Yakima, WA	37	D5

Entertainment & Sports

FEATURE NAME Address City State	MAP#	GRID
2nd St Theatre, 220 NE Lafayette Av, Bend, OR	190	A7
Academy of Children's Theater, 213 Wellsian Wy, Richland - WA	203	C7
A Contemporary Theater, 100 W Roy St, Seattle, WA	128	A4
ACT, 700 Union St, Seattle, WA	128	C6
Aladdin Theatre & Performance Center, 3017 SE 11th Av - Portland, OR	166	A4
Ambridge Event Center, 300 NE Multnomah St, Portland, OR	166	A1
Anacortes Community Theatre, 918 M Av, Anacortes, WA	114	D1
Annex Theatre, 1017 E Pike St, Seattle, WA	128	D5
Arlene Schnitzer Concert Hall, 1037 SW Broadway, Portland - OR	165	D2
Artists Repertory Theater, 1516 SW Alder St, Portland, OR	165	D2
Arts Club Theatre, 1585 Johnston St, Vancouver, BC	109	D3
Ashland Community Theater, 2305 Ashland St, Ashland, OR	200	C5
Autzen Stadium, 2727 Leo Harris Pkwy, Eugene, OR	186	A1
Avista Stadium, 602 N Havana St, Spokane Valley, WA	210	E7
Baker Stadium, 1500 N Warner St, Tacoma, WA	141	C4
Ballard Locks & Botanical Garden, 3015 NW 54th St, Seattle - WA	123	D6
Ballet Arts Center, 204 100th Av NE, Bellevue, WA	130	C6
Bank of Amer Arena at Hec Edmundson Pavilion - 3858 Montlake Blvd NE, Seattle, WA	129	A1
Bathhouse Theater, 7312 W Green Lake Dr N, Seattle, WA	124	C5
BC Place Stadium, 777 Pacific Blvd, Vancouver, BC	110	A2
Belfry Theatre, 1291 Gladstone Av, Victoria, BC	112	A4
Bellevue Botanical Garden, 12001 Main St, Bellevue, WA	130	E6
Bell Harbor International Conference Center - 2211 Alaskan Wy, Seattle, WA	128	B6
Benaroya Symphony Hall, 200 University St, Seattle, WA	128	C6
Berry Botanic Garden, 11505 SW Summerville Av - Multnomah Co, OR	170	A4
Blue Monkey Theater, 6922 SE Mall St, Portland, OR	167	A6
Bohler Gymnasium, NE Colorado St, Pullman, WA	41	D3
Boise Contemporary Theater, 854 W Fulton St, Boise, ID	222	B7
Boise Little Theatre, 100 E Fort St, Boise, ID	222	D7
Borleske Stadium, 409 E Rees Av, Walla Walla, WA	208	A2
Broadway Performance Hall, 1625 Broadway, Seattle, WA	128	D5
Brody Theater, 1904 NW 27th Av, Portland, OR	161	C7
Bronco Stadium, W Bronco Cir, Boise, ID	224	C2
Bug Lab Invertebrate Zoo, 616 Columbia St, New Westminster - BC	4	E3
Camelot Theatre Company, 295 E Main St, Ashland, OR	199	E4
Capital Playhouse, 612 4th Av E, Olympia, WA	146	A5
Carco Theatre, 1717 SE Maple Valley Hwy, Renton, WA	138	C6
Carousel Theatre Company, 1411 Cartwright St, Vancouver, BC	109	D3
Cat Tales Zoological Park, 17020 N Newport Hwy, Spokane Co - WA	31	B1
Centennial Theatre, 2300 Lonsdale Av, North Vancouver, BC	108	D4
Center Stage Theatre, 1017 W 1st Av, Spokane, WA	211	E1
Charlotte Y Martin Centre, 710 E Lower Kennedy Dr, Spokane - WA	210	A7
Cheney Stadium, 2502 S Tyler St, Tacoma, WA	141	B6
Chiles Center, 5000 N Willamette Blvd, Portland, OR	161	A3
Christian Youth Theatre, 708 W Nora Av, Spokane, WA	209	E6
Civic Field Complex, 1225 Civic Field Wy, Bellingham, WA	113	E4
Civic Light Opera, 7110 62nd Av NE, Seattle, WA	125	D5
Civic Stadium, 2077 Willamette St, Eugene, OR	185	D3
Clarence D Martin Stadium, NE Stadium Wy, Pullman, WA	41	D3
Classic Greek Theatre, 3131 NE Glisan St, Portland, OR	166	C1
Cleman's View Park & Sports Complex, Yakima Co, WA	37	B3
Clinton Street Theatre, 2522 SE Clinton St, Portland, OR	166	B4
Columbia Arts Center, 400 W Evergreen Blvd, Vancouver, WA	157	E4
Community Theatre, 599 Lebo Blvd, Bremerton, WA	122	C4
Community Theatre of the Cascades, 148 NW Greenwood Av - Bend, OR	190	A7
Cougar Mountain Zoological Park, 19525 SE 54th St, Issaquah - WA	25	E3
Craterian Ginger Rogers Theater, 23 S Central Av, Medford - OR	198	B5
Crystal Springs Rhododendron Garden, 6001 SE 28th Av - Portland, OR	166	C7
Cuthbert Amphitheatre, 601 Day Island Rd, Eugene, OR	186	A1
Debut Theater, 2320 California St, Everett, WA	120	D3
Dust Devils Stadium, Pasco, WA	39	B7
Echo Theatre, 1515 SE 37th Av, Portland, OR	166	C3
Edgar Brown Memorial Stadium, W Octave St, Pasco, WA	204	C6
Elsinore Theater, 170 High St SE, Salem, OR	173	D1
Empty Space Theatre, 3509 E Marion St, Seattle, WA	128	D6
Envoy Theatre Company, 902 N State St, Bellingham, WA	113	C4
Eugene Civic Stadium, Eugene, OR	185	E3
Everett Events Center, 2000 Hewitt Av, Everett, WA	120	C3
Everett Memorial Stadium, 3900 Broadway, Everett, WA	120	C4
Everett Performing Arts Center, 2710 Wetmore Av, Everett - WA	120	C3
Evergreen Playhouse, 226 W Center St, Centralia, WA	151	D5
Express Theatre Northwest, 2136 W Riverside Av, Spokane - WA	211	C1
Fifth Avenue Theatre, 1308 5th Av, Seattle, WA	128	C6
Firehall Arts Centre, 280 E Cordova St, Vancouver, BC	110	B2
Firehouse Theatre, 1436 SW Montgomery St, Portland, OR	165	D3
Gill Coliseum, 2003 NW Monroe Av, Corvallis, OR	177	E5
Grays Harbor County Fairgrounds, Grays Harbor Co, WA	34	A1
Greater Tacoma Convention & Trade Center, 1500 Broadway - Tacoma, WA	142	A5
Greater Vancouver Zoological Centre, 5048 264 St - Langley Township, BC	5	C4
Green Thumb Theatre, 1885 Venables St, Vancouver, BC	110	D3
Greyhound Park & Event Center, 5100 W Riverbend Av - Kootenai Co, ID	31	D2
Grinning Dragon Theatre, 1616 McLean Dr, Vancouver, BC	110	D3
Hastings Park Racecourse, Vancouver, BC	4	D2
Hillsboro Stadium, Hillsboro, OR	44	D6
Hollywood Theatre, 4122 NE Sandy Blvd, Portland, OR	166	D1
Horn Rapids Athletic Complex, Snyder St, Richland, WA	203	B1
Hoyt Arboretum, 4000 SW Fairview Blvd, Portland, OR	165	B3
Hult Center for Performing Arts, 1 E 7th Av, Eugene, OR	185	D1
Husky Stadium, 3800 Montlake Blvd NE, Seattle, WA	129	A1
Idaho Center, 16200 Can Ada Rd, Nampa, ID	83	D2
Imago Theatre, 17 SE 8th Av, Portland, OR	166	A2
Impact Theatre, 2520 Harris St, Eugene, OR	185	E3
Impromaniacs Theatre Company, 50 Montreal St, Victoria, BC	111	C6
INB Performing Arts Center, 334 W Spokane Falls Blvd - Spokane, WA	211	E1
Interstate Firehouse Cultural Center, 5340 N Interstate Av - Portland, OR	161	E5
Intiman Theatre, 201 Mercer St, Seattle, WA	128	B4
Japanese Garden, 1501 Lake Washington Blvd E, Seattle, WA	129	A3
Japanese Gardens, 611 SW Kingston Av, Portland, OR	165	B2
Japanese Garden-Wash Park Arboretum - 1075 Lake Washington Blvd E, Seattle, WA	129	A4
Joe Albi Stadium, Spokane, WA	209	A3
John A Finch Arboretum, Spokane, WA	211	B3
Kay Meek Centre, 1750 Mathers Av, West Vancouver, BC	107	C3
Keller Auditorium, 222 SW Clay St, Portland, OR	165	E3
Key Arena, 400 1st Av N, Seattle, WA	128	B4
Keystone Center for the Arts, 619 Commercial Av, Anacortes - WA	114	D1
Kiggins Bowl, 800 E 40th St, Vancouver, WA	158	A1
King County Aquatic Center, 650 SW Campus Dr, Federal Way - WA	25	C5
Kirkland Performance Center, 350 Kirkland Av, Kirkland, WA	126	C6
Kitsilano Showboat Society, 2300 Cornwall Av, Vancouver, BC	109	C3
Knock 'em Dead Dinner Theater, 333 S 9th St, Boise, ID	222	B7
Koerner Recital Hall, 1270 Chestnut St, Vancouver, BC	109	C3
Ladybug Theatre, 2315 SE Grant St, Portland, OR	166	C4
Lake City Playhouse, 1320 E Garden Av, Coeur d'Alene, ID	218	D6
Lakewood Playhouse, 5729 Lakewood Towne Center Blvd - Lakewood, WA	143	A7
Lakewood Theatre, 368 S State St, Lake Oswego, OR	169	E7
Langston Hughes Performing Arts Center, 104 17th Av S - Seattle, WA	128	E7
Legacy Sports Centre, 32470 Haida Dr, Abbotsford, BC	5	C4
Les Bois Park, N Kent Ln, Ada Co, ID	221	B4
Les Schwab Amphitheater, 344 SW Shevlin-Hixon Dr, Bend, OR	191	E2
Lincoln Theatre Center, 712 S 1st St, Mt Vernon, WA	116	B4
Linkville Playhouse, 201 Main St, Klamath Falls, OR	201	C6
Little Wheels, 21800 Meridian Av E, Pierce Co, WA	25	C7
Lord Leebrick Theatre Company, 540 Charnelton St, Eugene - OR	185	D1
Main Street Playhouse, 904 SW Main St, Portland, OR	165	D2
Majestic Bay Theater, 2044 NW Market St, Seattle, WA	123	D6
Marine View Banquet Center, 404 14th St, Everett, WA	120	B1
Marion Oliver McCaw Hall, 321 Mercer St, Seattle, WA	128	B4
McCarthey Athletic Center, 801 N Cincinnati St, Spokane, WA	210	B7
McIntyre Hall, 2401 E College Wy, Mt Vernon, WA	116	D2
McPherson Playhouse, 3 Government St, Victoria, BC	111	E4
Meany Theatre-University of Washington, 4000 15th Av NE - Seattle, WA	128	E1
Memorial Coliseum, 300 N Winning Wy, Portland, OR	165	E1
Memorial Stadium, 5600 N Glenwood St, Garden City, ID	221	A3
Memorial Stadium, 300 Republican St, Seattle, WA	128	B4
Metropolitan Performing Arts Center, 901 W Sprague Av - Spokane, WA	211	E1
Meydenbauer Center, 11100 NE 6th St, Bellevue, WA	130	C5
Miracle Theatre, 525 SE Stark St, Portland, OR	166	A2
Moore Theatre, 1932 2nd Av, Seattle, WA	128	C6
Morrison Center, 2201 W Campus Ln, Boise, ID	224	B1
Mountaineers Forest Theater, 300 3rd Av W, Seattle, WA	128	A5
Mount Baker Theatre, 104 N Commercial St, Bellingham, WA	113	C3
Music Theatre of Idaho, 203 9th Av S, Nampa, ID	220	C3
Nat Bailey Stadium, Vancouver, BC	110	A6
Nautilus Inc., Vancouver, WA	45	B6
New City Theater & Art Center, 1634 11th Av, Seattle, WA	128	D5
New Heritage Theatre Company, 106 N 6th St, Boise, ID	222	C7
Norman Rothstein Theatre, 950 W 41st Av, Vancouver, BC	109	E7
Old Slocum House Theatre Company, 605 Esther St, Vancouver - WA	157	E4

Points of Interest Index

Points of Interest Index

Points of Interest Index

Historic Sites

FEATURE NAME Address City State	MAP#	GRID
American Legion Hall, 219 Legion Wy SW, Olympia, WA	145	E5
Beaver Dick's Ferry, E Warm Springs Av, Ada Co, ID	84	A2
Beekman House, W California St, Jacksonville, OR	87	C6
Black Lake School, 6000 Black Lake Blvd SW, Thurston Co, WA	34	D1
Bonneville Point, S Upper Blacks Creek Rd, Ada Co, ID	84	B2
Burnaby Lake Nature House, 4519 Piper Av, Burnaby, BC	4	E2
Calvin & Pamela Hale House, 902 Tullis St NE, Olympia, WA	146	A4
Camp Polk, Cemetery Rd, Deschutes Co, OR	66	C3
Capitol Boulevard Crossing Historic Bridge, Capitol Blvd SW - Tumwater, WA	147	E1
Captain Vancouver Monument, Esther St, Vancouver, WA	157	E4
Celebration Park, 5000 Victory Ln, Canyon Co, ID	83	D4
Charbonneau Grave Site, Old Ion Hwy, Malheur Co, OR	94	D1
Cloverfields, 1100 Carlyon Av SE, Olympia, WA	146	A7
Colvin House, 16828 Old Highway 99 SE, Thurston Co, WA	34	E2
Commanding Officer's House, Pershing Av, Port Townsend - WA	119	D2
Covington House, 4201 Main St, Vancouver, WA	158	A1
Craigdarroch Castle, 1050 Joan Cres, Victoria, BC	112	A5
Craigflower Manor, 2709 Shoreline Dr, View Royal, BC	111	A2
Delphi School, 7601 Delphi Rd SW, Thurston Co, WA	34	D1
Diversion Dam-New York Canal, Ada Co, ID	84	A2
Dofflemyer Point Light, 211 73rd Av NE, Thurston Co, WA	24	E7
Dominion Astrophysical Observatory, 5071 W Saanich Rd - Saanich, BC	14	B2
Earthquake Point, Chelan Co, WA	27	E2
Elbe Church National Historic Site, 542nd St E, Pierce Co, WA	35	D3
Elks Building, 607 Capitol Wy S, Olympia, WA	145	E5
Ewald House, 5829 Gull Harbor Dr NE, Thurston Co, WA	24	E7
Flavel House, 441 8th St, Astoria, OR	153	C1
Fort Astoria, 15th St, Astoria, OR	153	D1
Fort Boise-Original Site, Canyon Co, ID	72	A7
Fort Boise-Replica, Parma, ID	72	A7
Fort Henness Site, 6600 183rd Av SW, Thurston Co, WA	34	D2
Fort Klamath Historical Frontier Post, Crater Lake Hwy - Klamath Co, OR	88	D3
Fort Langley National Historic Site, 23433 Mavis Av - Langley Township, BC	5	B3
Fort Nisqually Historic Site, Fort Nisqually By-Pass Rd, Tacoma - WA	25	B5
Fort to Sea Trail North Entrance, Fort Clatsop Rd, Clatsop Co - OR	43	D1
Fort to Sea Trail South Entrance, Sunset Beach Rd, Clatsop Co - OR	43	C1
Fort Vancouver National Historic Site, 612 E Reserve St - Vancouver, WA	158	A4
Fort Victoria, 1000 Government St, Victoria, BC	111	E5
Fort Walla Walla Heritage Marker, Walla Walla Co, WA	49	C2
Frank Rudkin House, 1005 Olympia Av NE, Olympia, WA	146	A4
Funk House, 1202 Olympia Av NE, Olympia, WA	146	A4
FW Schmidt House, 2831 Orange St SE, Olympia, WA	146	A7
Gate School, 16925 Moon Rd SW, Thurston Co, WA	34	C2
George Washington Rutledge House, 13425 Littlerock Rd SW - Thurston Co, WA	34	D2
Good Shepard Center, 4649 Sunnyside Av N, Seattle, WA	124	C7
Government House, 1401 Rockland Av, Victoria, BC	112	A6
Grays Harbor Historical Seaport, 813 E Heron St, Aberdeen - WA	33	D1
Gulf of Georgia Cannery National Site, 11999 4th Av - Richmond, BC	4	D3
Helmcken House, 10 Elliot Street Sq, Victoria, BC	111	E5
Henry J Kaiser Shipyard Memorial, SE Marine Park Wy - Vancouver, WA	158	D6
Henry McCleary House, 111 21st Av SW, Olympia, WA	145	E6
Historical Flippin Castle, 620 SW Tichenor St, Clatskanie, OR	44	C1
Historical Salt Works, Lewis & Clark Wy, Seaside, OR	154	B6
Historic Columbia River Highway, 500 E Columbia River Hwy - Troutdale, OR	45	B6
Historic Fort Steilacoom, 9601 Steilacoom Blvd SW, Lakewood - WA	25	B6
Historic Hughes House, Cape Blanco Hwy, Curry Co, OR	85	C1
History Highlights, 315 N Stadium Wy, Tacoma, WA	142	A3
Holy Trinity Orthodox Church, 433 Long St, Wilkeson, WA	25	E7
Hotel Olympian, 519 Washington St SE, Olympia, WA	145	E5
Hovander Homestead, 5299 Nielsen Av, Whatcom Co, WA	5	B6
Howard House, 750 Anderson St, Vancouver, WA	158	A4
Indian Shaker Church, 1801 Shaker Church Rd NW, Thurston Co - WA	24	D7
Initial Point, Initial Point Rd, Ada Co, ID	83	E4
Jaaska House & Warehouse, 11300 Independence Rd SW - Thurston Co, WA	34	C2
Jackson Hall Memorial Hall, 9161 Washington Av NW - Kitsap Co, WA	25	A2
James F Bybee House, 13901 NW Howell Park Rd - Multnomah Co, OR	44	E6
Japanese-American Historical Plaza, 2 NW Naito Pkwy - Portland, OR	165	E2
Jason Lee Manor, 1551 Center St NE, Salem, OR	173	E1
Jean Baptiste Charbonneau, Danner Loop Rd, Malheur Co, OR	94	D1
Jeffers Studio, 500 Washington St SE, Olympia, WA	145	E5
J Gary Fenton Historical Marker, Skookumchuck Rd SE - Thurston Co, WA	35	A3
Jimi Hendrix's Grave Site, 350 Monroe Av NE, Renton, WA	138	E6
Joaquin Miller's Cabin, S Canyon City Blvd, Canyon City, OR	69	C2
John R Jackson House Historic Site, Jackson Hwy, Lewis Co - WA	34	E5
Johnson House, 19540 Johnson Rd SE, Thurston Co, WA	35	B3
Jonas Erickson Farmstead, 13121 Independence Rd SW - Thurston Co, WA	34	C3
Klondike Gold Rush National Historical Park, 117 S Main St - Seattle, WA	128	C7
L.N. Rice House, 12247 Vail Rd SE, Thurston Co, WA	35	B2
Lackamas School, 16240 Bald Hill Rd SE, Thurston Co, WA	35	B2
Leir House Cultural Center, 220 Manor Park Av, Penticton, BC	8	D1
Log House Museum-Birthplace, 3003 61st Av SW, Seattle, WA	25	C3
Long Lake Recreation Hall, 3054 Carpenter Rd SE, Thurston Co - WA	34	E1
Lost Creek Covered Bridge, Lost Creek Rd, Jackson Co, OR	88	A6
McConnell Mansion, 327 E 2nd St, Moscow, ID	41	E3
Meyer House, 1136 Eastbay Dr NE, Olympia, WA	146	A4
Miller-Brewer House, 17915 Guava St SW, Thurston Co, WA	34	D2
Mima Mounds Natural Area Preserve, Thurston Co, WA	34	D2
Monte Cristo, Monte Cristo Tr, Snohomish Co, WA	16	C6
Mother Joseph Monument, 400 NE Mother Joseph Pl - Vancouver, WA	159	C5
Mottman Building, 101 Capitol Wy N, Olympia, WA	145	E4
Mt St Helens National Volcanic Monument - 3029 Spirit Lake Hwy, Cowlitz Co, WA	34	E7
Naches Basket Fort, Yakima Co, WA	37	C4
Neely Mansion, SE Auburn Black Diamond Rd, King Co, WA	25	D5
Nisqually School, 341 Nisqually Cut Off Rd SE, Thurston Co, WA	25	A7
Nye Books House, 727 NW 3rd St, Newport, OR	53	B7
O'Farrell Cabin, W Fort St, Boise, ID	222	C7
Officers Row-Marshall House, 1301 Officers Row, Vancouver - WA	158	B4
Old Capitol Building, 600 Washington St NE, Olympia, WA	145	E4
Olympia Knitting Mills, 514 Jefferson St SE, Olympia, WA	146	A5
Olympia National Bank, 422 Capitol Wy S, Olympia, WA	145	E5
Oregon Holocaust Memorial, SW Washington Wy, Portland - OR	165	C2
Oregon Korean War Memorial, 29600 SW Park Pl, Wilsonville - OR	54	E1
Oregon Trail Centennial Greenway, Fountain Pth, Caldwell, ID	219	B2
Oregon Trail Historic Reserve, 4500 E Lake Forest Dr, Boise, ID	84	A2
Overlook House, 3839 N Melrose Dr, Portland, OR	161	D6
Parkersville Site, Washougal, WA	45	B6
Pelota Court-Jordan Valley, Bassett St, Jordan Valley, OR	83	A7
Pettygrove House, 2287 NW Pettygrove St, Portland, OR	45	A6
Philip Foster Farm, 29912 Woodburn-Sandy Hwy, Clackamas Co - OR	55	C1
Pioneer Square Historic District, 600 1st Av, Seattle, WA	128	C7
Pittock Mansion, 3229 NW Pittock Dr, Portland, OR	44	E7
Quarry House, Howard St S, Tenino, WA	34	E2
Queen Anne Victorian Mansion, 1441 N McClellan St, Portland - OR	161	E2
Queen of Angels Monastery, 840 S Main St, Mt Angel, OR	54	E4
Rochester Elementary School, 10140 183rd Av SW - Thurston Co, WA	34	C2
Roeder Home, 2600 Sunset Dr, Bellingham, WA	113	C2
Saint Joseph's Mission at Ahtanum, Yakima Co, WA	37	B5
St. Peter's Landmark, Lincoln St, The Dalles, OR	46	E6
Salsich Lumber Co Superintendent's House, 10808 Vail Rd SE - Thurston Co, WA	35	B1
Schmidt House Museum, 512 SW 5th St, Grants Pass, OR	197	C5
Seatco Prison Site, 720 S Factory St, Bucoda, WA	34	E3
Seattle Birthplace Monument, 2800 Alki Av SW, Seattle, WA	131	B2
Security Building, 203 4th Av E, Olympia, WA	145	E5
Settlemeier House, 355 N Settlemeir Av, Woodburn, OR	54	D3
Spalding Site, US Highway 95, Nez Perce Co, ID	42	A5
Sprague-Marshall-Bowie House, 2234 NW Johnson St, Portland - OR	165	C1
Steunenberg Memorial, W Jefferson St, Boise, ID	222	C7
Stimson-Green Mansion, 1204 Minor Av, Seattle, WA	128	D6
Summit House, Pierce Co, WA	35	E3
Tetherow Crossing, 5810 NW Tetherow Rd, Deschutes Co, OR	66	D3
The Brewery Blocks, 1137 W Burnside St, Portland, OR	165	D2
The Good Shepard Center, 4649 Sunnyside Av N, Seattle, WA	25	C2
The Sage House, 821 NW Wall St, Bend, OR	189	E7
Ticknor School, 7212 Skookumchuck Rd SE, Thurston Co, WA	34	E3
Trevett-Nunn House, 2347 NW Flanders St, Portland, OR	165	C1
Tumwater Methodist Church, 219 B St SW, Tumwater, WA	147	E1
Union Mills Superintendent's House, 7716 Union Mills Rd SE - Thurston Co, WA	34	E1
US Post Office, 801 Capitol Wy S, Olympia, WA	145	E5
Vietnam Veterans of Oregon Memorial, Portland, OR	165	B3
Wilkeson Arch, 201 Church St, Wilkeson, WA	25	E7
William Owen Bush Monument, 1398 85th Av SE, Thurston Co - WA	148	A7
Winters House, 2102 Bellevue Wy SE, Bellevue, WA	134	D2
Women's Club of Olympia, 1002 Washington St SE, Olympia - WA	145	E5
Woolrey-Koehler Hop Kiln, 17212 159th Av E, Pierce Co, WA	25	D7

Hospitals

FEATURE NAME Address City State	MAP#	GRID
Adventist Med Ctr, 10123 SE Market St, Portland, OR	167	D3
Allenmore Community Hosp, Tacoma, WA	25	B6
Allenmore Hosp, 1901 S Union Av, Tacoma, WA	141	C6
Ashland Community Hosp, Ashland, OR	199	C2
Auburn Regional Med Ctr, Auburn, WA	25	D5
Bay Area Hosp, Coos Bay, OR	193	E5
BC Children & Women's Hosp, Vancouver, BC	109	E6
Benewah Community Hosp, 229 S 7th St, St. Maries, ID	32	B5
Blue Mountain Hosp, John Day, OR	69	C2
Bonner General Hosp, Sandpoint, ID	22	B3
Burnaby General Hosp, Burnaby, BC	4	E2
Capital Med Ctr, Olympia, WA	145	A5
Cascade Med Ctr, 817 Commercial St, Leavenworth, WA	27	C3
Cascade Valley Hosp, Arlington, WA	15	D5
Central Washington Hosp, Wenatchee, WA	27	E4
Children's Hosp & Med Ctr, 4800 Sand Point Wy NE, Seattle - WA	125	B7
Chilliwack General Hosp, Menholm Rd, Chilliwack, BC	6	A3
Clearwater Valley Hosp, Orofino, ID	42	D5
Columbia Basin Hosp, Ephrata, WA	28	D5
Columbia Memorial Hosp, Astoria, OR	153	D1
Coquille Valley Hosp, Coquille, OR	74	A5
Cottage Grove Community Hosp, Cottage Grove, OR	64	C7
Coulee Community Hosp, Grand Coulee, WA	19	B7
Cowichan District Hosp, 3045 Gibbins Rd, Cowichan Valley, BC	3	E6
Curry General Hosp, 94220 E 4th St, Gold Beach, OR	85	D5
Dayton General Hosp, Dayton, WA	40	D7
Deaconess Med Ctr-Spokane, 800 W 5th Av, Spokane, WA	211	E2
Deer Park Hosp, Deer Park, WA	21	A6
Delta Hosp, Delta, BC	4	D4
Doernbecher Children's Hosp, 3181 SW Campus Dr, Portland - OR	165	D5
Eagle Ridge Hosp, Port Moody, BC	5	A2
East Adams Rural Hosp, 903 S Adams St, Ritzville, WA	30	A7
Eastmoreland Hosp, 2900 SE Steele St, Portland, OR	166	C6
Eastside Hosp, Redmond, WA	25	D2
Elmore Med Ctr, Mountain Home, ID	84	D5
Enumclaw Regional Hosp, Cinkovich St, Enumclaw, WA	25	E6
Evergreen Healthcare, 12040 NE 128th St, Kirkland, WA	126	E1
Evergreen Hosp Med Ctr, Kirkland, WA	25	D2
Fairchild Med Ctr, Yreka, CA	98	E4
Fairfax Hosp, 10200 NE 132nd St, King Co, WA	126	C1
Ferry County Memorial Hosp, Republic, WA	19	D1
Forks Community Hosp, Forks, WA	13	A6
Garfield County Memorial Hosp, 66 N 6th St, Pomeroy, WA	41	A5
Good Samaritan Hosp, Puyallup, WA	25	C6
Good Samaritan Regional Med Ctr, Corvallis, OR	178	C1
Good Shepherd Med Ctr, Hermiston, OR	49	A4
Grande Ronde Hosp, La Grande, OR	60	C1
Grays Harbor Community Hosp, Aberdeen, WA	33	D1
Gritman Med Ctr, Moscow, ID	41	E3
Group Health Central Hosp, 201 16th Av E, Seattle, WA	128	E5
Harborview Med Ctr, 325 9th Av, Seattle, WA	128	D7
Harney District Hosp, 557 W Washington St, Burns, OR	80	C2
Harrison Hosp, Bremerton, WA	122	C4
Highline Community Hosp, 16251 Sylvester Rd SW, Burien, WA	139	B2
Highline Community Hosp, Tukwila, WA	25	C4
Highline Med Ctr, Tukwila, WA	137	A6
Holy Family Hosp, Spokane, WA	210	A2
Holy Rosary Med Ctr, Ontario, OR	72	A5
Intermountain Hosp, Boise, ID	223	C1
Island Hosp, Anacortes, WA	114	D3
Jefferson Healthcare, Port Townsend, WA	119	B5
JM Wainwright Memorial VA Med Ctr, Walla Walla, WA	207	D5
Kadlec Med Ctr, Richland, WA	203	C5
Kaiser Permanente-Sunnyside, Clackamas Co, OR	45	A7
Kennewick General Hosp, 900 S Auburn St, Kennewick, WA	206	B3
Kindred Hosp Seattle, 10560 5th Av NE, Seattle, WA	124	D2
Kittitas Valley Community Hosp, Ellensburg, WA	37	D1
Klickitat Valley Hosp, Goldendale, WA	47	B4
Kootenai Med Ctr, Coeur d'Alene, ID	218	A4
Lake Chelan Community Hosp, Chelan, WA	28	B1
Lake District Hosp, Lakeview, OR	101	E1
Langley Memorial Hosp, Langley Township, BC	5	B4
Legacy Emanuel Hosp, 2801 N Gantenbein Av, Portland, OR	161	E6
Legacy Good Samaritan Hosp, 1015 NW 22nd Av, Portland - OR	165	C1
Legacy Meridian Park Hosp, Tualatin, OR	54	E1
Legacy Mt Hood Med Ctr, Gresham, OR	45	B7
Legacy Salmon Creek Hosp, Clark Co, WA	45	A5
Lincoln Hosp, Davenport, WA	30	C2
Lions Gate Hosp, North Vancouver, BC	108	D5
Lourdes Med Ctr, N 4th Av, Pasco, WA	204	D6
Lower Umpqua Hosp, Regents Pl, Reedsport, OR	74	A1
Mark Reed Hosp, McCleary, WA	24	C7
Mary Bridge Children's Hosp & Health Center - 317 Martin Luther King Jr Wy, Tacoma, WA	141	E4
Mason General Hosp, Shelton, WA	24	C6
McKenzie-Willamette Med Ctr, Springfield, OR	187	A1
Mercy Med Ctr, Nampa, ID	220	C6
Mercy Med Ctr, NW Medical Lp, Roseburg, OR	195	D2
Merle West Med Ctr, Klamath Falls, OR	201	C2
Mid-Columbia Med Ctr, The Dalles, OR	46	E6
Mid-Valley Hosp, Okanogan Co, WA	18	D3
Mission Memorial Hosp, Mission, BC	5	C3
Modoc Med Ctr, Modoc Co, CA	101	D7
Morton General Hosp, Morton, WA	35	C5
Mountain View Hosp District, Madras, OR	56	E7
Mt Carmel Hosp, Colville, WA	20	D1
Mt St Joseph Hosp, 3080 Prince Edward St, Vancouver, BC	110	B5
MSA General Hosp, Abbotsford, BC	5	D4
Nanaimo Regional General Hosp, Nanaimo, BC	3	D3
Newport Community Hosp, Newport, WA	21	D4
North Valley Hosp, 2nd St W, Tonasket, WA	8	E7
Northwest Hosp, Seattle, WA	25	C2
Northwest Hosp & Med Ctr, 1550 N 115th St, Seattle, WA	124	C1
Ocean Beach Hosp, Ilwaco, WA	33	C6
Odessa Memorial Hosp, Odessa, WA	29	D5
OHSU Hosp, SW Sam Jackson Park Rd, Portland, OR	45	A7
Okanogan Douglas District Hosp, Brewster, WA	18	C5
Olympic Med Ctr, Port Angeles, WA	117	D4
Oregon Health & Science University Hosp - 3181 SW Sam Jackson Park Rd, Portland, OR	165	D4
Othello Community Hosp, Othello, WA	39	B2
Overlake Hosp Med Ctr, 1035 116th Av NE, Bellevue, WA	130	D5
Peace Arch District Hosp, White Rock, BC	5	A4
Peace Harbor Hosp, Florence, OR	63	A6
Penticton Regional Hosp, Penticton, BC	8	D1
Physicians Hosp, 10300 NE Hancock St, Portland, OR	167	D1
Pioneer Memorial Hosp, Heppner, OR	58	E1
Pioneer Memorial Hosp, Prineville, OR	67	B3
Powell River General Hosp, 5000 Joyce Av, Powell River, BC	1	A4
Prosser Memorial Hosp, 723 Memorial St, Prosser, WA	48	C1
Providence Centralia Hosp, Centralia, WA	151	A5
Providence Everett Med Ctr-Colby, 1321 Colby Av, Everett - WA	120	C1
Providence Everett Med Ctr-Pacific, 916 Pacific Av, Everett - WA	120	B3
Providence Medford Med Ctr, Medford, OR	198	C4
Providence Milwaukie Hosp, 10150 SE 32nd Av, Milwaukie - OR	170	C3
Providence Newberg Hosp, Newberg, OR	54	D1
Providence Portland Med Ctr, 4805 NE Glisan St, Portland, OR	166	E1
Providence Seaside Hosp, Seaside, OR	154	D6
Providence St Peter Hosp, Olympia, WA	146	D4
Providence St Vincent Med Ctr, Washington Co, OR	44	E7
Providence Toppenish Hosp, 502 W 4th Av, Toppenish, WA	37	E6
Pullman Regional Hosp, Pullman, WA	41	D3
Quincy Valley Med Ctr, Quincy, WA	28	C6
Richmond Hosp, Richmond, BC	4	D3
Ridge Meadows Hosp, Maple Ridge, BC	5	B3
Rogue Valley Med Ctr, Medford, OR	198	E6
Royal Columbian Hosp, New Westminster, BC	4	E3
Royal Jubilee Hosp, Victoria, BC	112	C4
Saanich Peninsula Hosp, Central Saanich, BC	14	B1
Sacred Heart Med Ctr, 1255 Hilyard St, Eugene, OR	185	E2
Sacred Heart Med Ctr, 101 W 8th Av, Spokane, WA	212	A2
St. Alphonsus Regional Med Ctr, Boise, ID	221	D7
St. Anthony Hosp, Pendleton, OR	49	D5
St. Charles Med Ctr-Bend, Bend, OR	190	D6
St. Charles Med Ctr-Redmond, Redmond, OR	66	E3
St. Clare Hosp, Lakewood, WA	25	B7
St. Elizabeth Health Services, Baker City, OR	60	E6
St. Francis Hosp, Federal Way, WA	25	C5
St. John's Med Ctr, Longview, WA	155	D5
St. Joseph Hosp, Bellingham, WA	113	C1
St. Joseph Hosp, 1717 S J St, Tacoma, WA	25	B6
St. Joseph Med Ctr, 1717 S J St, Tacoma, WA	142	A5
St. Joseph Regional Med Ctr, Lewiston, ID	41	E6
St. Joseph's Hosp, 500 E Webster Av, Chewelah, WA	20	E4
St. Luke's Meridian Med Ctr, E Promenade St, Meridian, ID	83	E2
St. Luke's Regional Med Ctr, 190 E Bannock St, Boise, ID	222	D7
St. Mary Med Ctr, Walla Walla, WA	207	E4
St. Mary's Hosp, Cottonwood, ID	52	D2
St. Mary's Hosp, 5544 Wharf Rd, Sunshine Coast, BC	2	A7
St. Paul's Hosp, 1081 Burrard St, Vancouver, BC	109	E2
Salem Memorial Hosp, 665 Winter St SE, Salem, OR	173	D2
Samaritan Albany General Hosp, 1046 6th Av SW, Albany, OR	175	D3
Samaritan Hosp, Moses Lake, WA	29	A7
Samaritan Lebanon Community Hosp, Lebanon, OR	64	D1
Samaritan North Lincoln Hosp, Lincoln City, OR	53	B4
Samaritan Pacific Communities Hosp, Newport, OR	53	B7
Santiam Memorial Hosp, Stayton, OR	54	E6
Shoshone Med Ctr, Kellogg, ID	32	D3
Shriners Hosp for Children, 3101 SW Sam Jackson Park Rd - Portland, OR	165	D4
Silverton Hosp, Silverton, OR	54	E4
Skagit Valley Hosp, 1415 E Kincaid St, Mt Vernon, WA	116	C4
Skyline Hosp, White Salmon, WA	46	C5
Snoqualmie Valley Hosp, 9575 Ethan Wade Wy SE, Snoqualmie - WA	26	A3
Southern Coos Hosp, Bandon, OR	73	D6
Southwest Washington Med Ctr, 400 NE Mother Joseph Pl - Vancouver, WA	159	C5
Southwest Washington Med Ctr-Memorial Campus - 3400 Main St, Vancouver, WA	158	A2
Squamish General Hosp, Squamish, BC	2	D5
Stevens Hosp, Edmonds, WA	25	C1
Sunnyside Community Hosp, Sunnyside, WA	38	B7
Surprise Valley Community Hosp, Modoc Co, CA	102	A6
Surrey Memorial Hosp, Surrey, BC	5	A3
Sutter Coast Hosp, Del Norte Co, CA	96	E4
Swedish Med Ctr-Ballard, 5300 Tallman Av NW, Seattle, WA	123	E6
Swedish Med Ctr-Cherry Hill Campus, 500 17th Av, Seattle - WA	128	E6
Swedish Med Ctr-First Hill, 747 Broadway, Seattle, WA	128	D6
Swedish Med Ctr-Providence, 500 17th Av, Seattle, WA	25	C3
Syringa General Hosp, 607 W Main St, Grangeville, ID	52	E3

Points of Interest Index

Hospitals | Museums

Points of Interest Index

Points of Interest Index

INDEX 37

Points of Interest Index

Parks & Recreation

FEATURE NAME Address City State	MAP#	GRID
Fort Clatsop National Memorial, Clatsop Co, OR	43	D1
Fort Columbia State Pk, Pacific Co, WA	33	C7
Fort Dent Pk, Tukwila, WA	140	D1
Fort Ebey State Pk, Island Co, WA	15	A4
Fort Flagler State Pk, Jefferson Co, WA	15	A5
Fort Okanogan State Pk, Okanogan Co, WA	18	D5
Fort Rock State Pk, Lake Co, OR	77	E4
Fort Rodd Hill & Fisgard Lighthouse, Colwood, BC	14	B2
Fort Simcoe State Pk, Yakima Co, WA	37	B7
Fort Stevens State Pk, Clatsop Co, OR	33	C7
Fort Vancouver National Historic Site, Vancouver, WA	45	A6
Fort Ward State Pk, Bainbridge Island, WA	25	B3
Fort Worden State Pk, Port Townsend, WA	119	D1
Foss Waterway Pk, Tacoma, WA	142	B6
Four Seasons Pk, Vancouver, WA	159	E3
Frank Kinney Pk, Eugene, OR	185	E7
Franklin Pk, Eugene, OR	186	B2
Franklin Pk, Spokane, WA	209	E3
Franklin Pk, Tacoma, WA	141	C5
Franklin Place, Seattle, WA	128	A4
Fraser Pk, Portland, OR	166	E1
Freeway Pk, Seattle, WA	128	C6
Fremont Canal Pk, Seattle, WA	128	B1
Friendly Pk, Eugene, OR	185	C4
Friendship Pk, Spokane, WA	210	A1
Frink Pk, Seattle, WA	129	A7
Fruitland Pk, Kennewick, WA	206	B1
Fruit Valley Pk, Vancouver, WA	157	D2
Fulton Pk, Portland, OR	169	D1
Gabiola Fields, Caldwell, ID	219	D4
Gabriel Pk, Portland, OR	165	A7
Gabriel Pk, Walla Walla, WA	208	A3
Gaddis Pk, Roseburg, OR	195	E4
Galloping Goose Regional Trail, Saanich, BC	111	D1
Gamebird Pk, Springfield, OR	188	D1
Gammans Pk, Portland, OR	161	D3
Garden Pk, Vancouver, BC	110	E4
Garden Way Pk, Ashland, OR	200	B5
Garfield Landing Pk, Mercer Island, WA	133	D2
Garfield Pk, Ashland, OR	200	A4
Garfield Pk, Eugene, OR	185	B2
Garfield Pk, Everett, WA	120	E2
Garfield Pk, Tacoma, WA	141	E3
Garfield Playfield, Seattle, WA	129	A6
Garibaldi Provincial Pk, Squamish-Lillooet, BC	2	E1
Gas Works Pk, Seattle, WA	128	C2
Gateway State Wayside, Josephine Co, OR	97	C2
Gene Coulon Memorial Beach Pk, Renton, WA	138	C4
General Anderson Pk, Vancouver, WA	158	E5
General Brock Pk, Vancouver, BC	110	E6
Genesee Pk & Playfield, Seattle, WA	133	B4
George H Eckstein Pk, Grants Pass, OR	197	E6
George Himes Pk, Portland, OR	165	D7
George Rogers Pk, Lake Oswego, OR	170	A7
Georgetown Playfield, Seattle, WA	132	D5
George Wainborn Pk, Vancouver, BC	109	E3
George W Joseph State Pk, Multnomah Co, OR	45	C7
Gilbert Heights Pk, Portland, OR	168	A6
Gilbert Primary Pk, Portland, OR	168	A7
Gilham Pk, Eugene, OR	182	A3
Gilmore Field, Salem, OR	173	D3
Glass Pk, Spokane, WA	210	A4
Glenfair Pk, Portland, OR	168	C2
Glenhaven Pk, Portland, OR	163	B7
Glen Pk, Vancouver, BC	110	C6
Glenwood Pk, Ashland, OR	199	E5
Glenwood Pk, Portland, OR	167	C7
Goddard Pk, Bellevue, WA	130	C5
Golden & Silver Falls State Pk, Coos Co, OR	74	B3
Golden Ears Provincial Pk, Mission, BC	5	C1
Golden Gardens Pk, Lane Co, OR	180	C3
Golden Gardens Pk, Seattle, WA	123	C4
Goldstream Provincial Pk, Langford, BC	14	A2
Gonzales Hill Regional Pk, Victoria, BC	112	C6
Gorge Pk, Saanich, BC	111	B2
Governor Patterson Memorial State Ranger Sta, Lincoln Co - OR	179	A6
Governors Pk, Portland, OR	165	D3
Governor Tom McCall Waterfront Pk, Portland, OR	165	E3
Gowlland Tod Provincial Pk, Capital, BC	14	A1
Gracemont Pk, Salem, OR	173	C4
Grand Avenue Pk, Everett, WA	120	C1
Grandview Pk, Vancouver, BC	110	D3
Grant Pk, Salem, OR	171	E7
Grant Pk, Spokane, WA	212	B2
Granville Pk, Vancouver, BC	109	D4
Grass Lake Pk, Olympia, WA	145	A3
Grayland Beach State Pk, Pacific Co, WA	33	B2
Green Lake Pk, Seattle, WA	124	C5
Green River Trail, Tukwila, WA	137	B4
Greenwood Pk, North Vancouver, BC	108	E4
Greenwood Pk, Seattle, WA	124	B4
Gretchen Fraser Pk, Vancouver, WA	160	C6
Griffiths Pk, Caldwell, ID	219	E5
Griffiths-Priday Ocean State Pk, Grays Harbor Co, WA	23	B6
Groveland Pk, Mercer Island, WA	134	A6
Guelph Pk, Vancouver, BC	110	B4
Guy Lee Pk, Springfield, OR	182	D7
Guy W Talbot State Pk, Multnomah Co, OR	45	C7
Haagen Pk, Vancouver, WA	160	A4
Hadden Pk, Vancouver, BC	109	C2
Hald Strawberry Pk, Ashland, OR	199	C3
Hamilton Pk, Portland, OR	165	A5
Hamilton Viewpoint Pk, Seattle, WA	131	D1
Hampton Pk, Saanich, BC	111	C1
Hancock Pk, Portland, OR	167	C1
Hanging Gardens State Pk, King Co, WA	25	E5
Harborview Pk, Seattle, WA	128	D7
Hares Canyon State Pk, Washington Co, OR	44	C5
Harmon Pk, Bend, OR	189	E7
Harmon Pk, Spokane, WA	210	D2
Harmon Pk, Tacoma, WA	144	A5
Harris Beach State Pk, Brookings, OR	96	D1
Harrison Pk, Portland, OR	167	C4
Harvest Landing Pk, Lane Co, OR	183	B5
Hastings Mill Pk, Vancouver, BC	109	A3
Hatfield Pk, Kennewick, WA	206	A2
Hat Rock State Pk, Umatilla Co, OR	49	B3
Hawkins Heights Pk, Eugene, OR	185	A3
Hawthorne Pk, Kennewick, WA	205	D1
Hawthorne Pk, Medford, OR	198	B5
Hay Pk, West Vancouver, BC	107	B3
Hays Pk, Spokane, WA	210	C4
Hazelnut Pk, Tukwila, WA	137	C7
Hazel Valley Pk, King Co, WA	136	C5
Hazelwood Pk, Newcastle, WA	134	D7
Healy Heights Pk, Portland, OR	165	C5
Hearthwood Pk, Vancouver, WA	160	B5

FEATURE NAME Address City State	MAP#	GRID
Heather Pk, Vancouver, BC	109	E5
Heidelberg Davis Pk, Tacoma, WA	141	B6
Hells Canyon National Rec Area, Wallowa Co, OR	52	B5
Hells Gate State Pk, Nez Perce Co, ID	41	D6
Henderson Pk, Oak Bay, BC	112	D2
Hendricks Pk, Eugene, OR	186	B3
Heritage Pk, Vancouver, WA	164	D1
Heyburn State Pk, Benewah Co, ID	32	A4
Heywood Pk, North Vancouver, BC	108	B4
Hiawatha Playfield, Seattle, WA	131	D2
Hidden Pk, Vancouver, WA	157	E2
Hidden Valley Sports Pk, Bellevue, WA	130	D4
High Bridge Pk, Spokane, WA	211	C2
Highland Pk, Pasco, WA	204	E6
Highland Pk, Salem, OR	171	E6
Highland Pk Playfield, Seattle, WA	136	B1
Highlands Pk, Renton, WA	138	D5
High Point Playfield, Seattle, WA	131	E7
Highrock Pk, Esquimalt, BC	111	B4
Hilgard Junction State Pk, Union Co, OR	60	C1
Hillcrest Pk, Vancouver, BC	110	A6
Hillsdale Pk, Bend, OR	189	D6
Hillsdale Pk, Portland, OR	165	C6
Hillside Community Center, Portland, OR	165	B1
Hillside Pk, Bend, OR	189	D6
Hillside Pk, Boise, ID	221	E2
Hillside Pk, Victoria, BC	112	A3
Hilltop Pk, King Co, WA	136	E5
Hillview Pk, Salem, OR	173	C5
Hing Hay Pk, Seattle, WA	128	D7
Hiram M Chittenden Locks, Seattle, WA	123	D6
Hixon Pk, Bend, OR	191	E1
Hj Morton Memorial State Pk, Lane Co, OR	65	B5
Hoffman Memorial State Pk, Coos Co, OR	74	A7
Holladay East Pk, Portland, OR	168	A1
Holladay Pk, Portland, OR	166	B1
Holland Point Pk, Victoria, BC	111	D7
Hollinshead Pk, Bend, OR	190	B6
Hollman State Wayside, Polk Co, OR	54	C5
Hollygrape Pk, Bend, OR	191	C5
Hollywood Pk, Victoria, BC	112	B6
Holman Pk, Portland, OR	165	B1
Holmes Pk, Medford, OR	198	E6
Homestead Field, Mercer Island, WA	134	A3
Homestead Pk, Vancouver, WA	160	C7
Honeydew Pk, King Co, WA	138	E3
Hoover Pk, Salem, OR	172	B7
Horner Pk, Saanich, BC	112	C1
Horse Heaven Hills Pk, Kennewick, WA	205	E5
Horsethief Lake State Pk, Klickitat Co, WA	46	E6
Houghton Neighborhood Pk, Kirkland, WA	130	D1
Houghton Pk, Kirkland, WA	130	C1
Howard Amon Pk, Richland, WA	203	D5
Howarth Pk, Everett, WA	120	A5
Howell Pk, Seattle, WA	129	B5
Hugo Ray Pk, West Vancouver, BC	107	E3
Hug Point State Pk, Clatsop Co, OR	43	C4
Hulls Gulch Pk, Boise, ID	222	D4
Humbug Mountain State Pk, Curry Co, OR	85	C3
Hunter Pk, Ashland, OR	200	B4
Hunter Pk, North Vancouver District, BC	108	E2
Hunts Point Pk, Hunts Point, WA	130	A3
Idaho Anne Frank Human Rights Memorial, Boise, ID	224	B1
Ikawa Pk, Tukwila, WA	140	D1
Ike Kinswa State Pk, Lewis Co, WA	35	B4
Illahee State Pk, Kitsap Co, WA	122	E2
Illinois River State Pk, Josephine Co, OR	86	C7
Indian Trail Pk, Spokane, WA	209	A1
Interlaken Pk, Seattle, WA	128	E3
International Childrens Pk, Seattle, WA	128	D7
Iron Horse State Pk, Kittitas Co, WA	26	E6
Iron Mountain Pk, Lake Oswego, OR	169	C7
Irving Pk, Portland, OR	162	A6
Irving Pk, Tacoma, WA	141	E6
Irwin Pk, Eugene, OR	180	B4
Irwin Pk, West Vancouver, BC	107	A3
Island Crest Pk, Mercer Island, WA	134	A6
Island Pk, Springfield, OR	186	E2
Ivywild Pk, Boise, ID	224	D4
Jack B Lively Memorial Pk, Springfield, OR	188	C1
Jack Hyde Pk, Tacoma, WA	141	E2
Jackson F Kimball State Pk, Klamath Co, OR	88	D3
Jackson Pk, Bremerton, WA	121	C4
Jackson Pk, Medford, OR	198	A5
Jaggy Road Pk, Vancouver, WA	159	A1
James Island State Pk, San Juan Co, WA	15	A2
James J Hill Pk, Spokane, WA	210	C2
James Pk, Lane Co, OR	186	D3
Jamison Square, Portland, OR	165	D1
Jane Clark Playfield, Tacoma, WA	141	B1
Jarrell Cove State Pk, Mason Co, WA	24	E5
Jason Lee Pk, Richland, WA	203	B3
Jasper State Pk, Lane Co, OR	64	D6
Jaycee Pk, Bend, OR	192	B1
Jaycee Pk, Caldwell, ID	219	C2
Jedediah Smith Redwoods State Pk, Del Norte Co, CA	97	A4
Jefferson Pk, Eugene, OR	185	C2
Jefferson Pk, Tacoma, WA	141	B4
Jefferson Pk, Walla Walla, WA	207	E5
Jenne Butte Pk, Gresham, OR	168	E7
Jennie B Harris State Wayside, Lane Co, OR	65	D4
Jesse Maine Memorial Pk, Springfield, OR	188	D3
Jessie M Honeyman Memorial St Pk, Lane Co, OR	63	A6
JJ Hill Pk, Everett, WA	120	D3
Joemma Beach State Pk, Pierce Co, WA	24	E6
John Ball Pk, Vancouver, WA	157	E3
John B Yeon State Pk, Multnomah Co, OR	45	E6
John C Little Senior Pk, Seattle, WA	133	B7
John Day Fossil Beds National Monument, Grant Co, OR	68	D1
John Day Fossil Beds National Monument, Wheeler Co, OR	57	D5
John Day Pk, Kennewick, WA	205	C1
John Dean Provincial Pk, North Saanich, BC	14	B1
John Dobson Pk, Chehalis, WA	152	C4
John Hendry Pk, Vancouver, BC	110	D5
John Luby Pk, Portland, OR	164	A7
John R Jackson House, Lewis Co, WA	34	E5
Johnson Creek Pk, Portland, OR	170	B2
Jonathan Rogers Pk, Vancouver, BC	110	A4
Jones Island State Pk, San Juan Co, WA	14	D1
Jones Pk, Renton, WA	138	B6
Jones Pk, Vancouver, BC	110	D7
Joseph Foster Memorial Pk, Tukwila, WA	137	C7
Joseph Stewart State Pk, Jackson Co, OR	87	E3
Joseph Whidbey State Pk, Island Co, WA	15	A4
Joseph Wood Hill Pk, Portland, OR	163	C6
Js Burres State Pk, Gilliam Co, OR	47	D7
Juanita Bay Pk, Kirkland, WA	126	C3
Juanita Beach Pk, Kirkland, WA	126	B3

FEATURE NAME Address City State	MAP#	GRID
Juanita Heights Pk, King Co, WA	126	B2
Juanita Triangle Pk, King Co, WA	126	A2
Juanita Woodlands Pk, King Co, WA	126	A2
Judkins Pk, Seattle, WA	132	E1
Julia Davis Pk, Boise, ID	224	C1
Julia's Gulch, Tacoma, WA	142	E1
Juniper Pk, Bend, OR	190	B7
Kanasket Palmer State Pk, King Co, WA	26	A5
Kandle Pk, Tacoma, WA	141	A3
Kathryn Albertson Pk, Boise, ID	222	A7
Keewaydin Pk, Kennewick, WA	206	B2
Keith-Lynn Pk, North Vancouver, BC	108	E4
Keizer Little League Pk, Keizer, OR	172	B1
Keller Pk, Milwaukie, OR	170	B5
Kelly Butte Pk, Portland, OR	167	D5
Kelly Butte Pk, Springfield, OR	186	D1
Kelsey Creek Community Pk, Bellevue, WA	130	E7
Kenilworth Pk, Portland, OR	166	C5
Kennydale Beach Pk, Renton, WA	138	B2
Kennydale Lions Pk, Renton, WA	138	D3
Kensington Pk, Vancouver, BC	110	C7
Kenton Pk, Portland, OR	161	D2
Kenwood Pk, Kennewick, WA	206	B4
Kern Pk, Portland, OR	167	A5
Kerrisdale Centennial Pk, Vancouver, BC	109	B7
Kerrisdale Pk, Vancouver, BC	109	C7
Kerry Pk, Seattle, WA	128	A4
Kevanna Pk, Vancouver, WA	159	D1
Kilbourne Pk, Seattle, WA	135	D2
Killarney Glen Pk, Bellevue, WA	134	C1
Kincaid Pk, Eugene, OR	186	A6
King County Pk, Renton, WA	138	C1
Kingcrest Pk, Vancouver, BC	110	C6
King School Pk, Portland, OR	162	A6
Kinnear Pk, Seattle, WA	128	A4
Kinsmen Gorge Pk, Esquimalt, BC	111	B3
Kitsap Lake Pk, Kitsap Co, WA	121	B6
Kitsap Memorial State Pk, Kitsap Co, WA	25	A1
Kitsilano Beach, Vancouver, BC	109	C3
Kiwanis Memorial Pk, Seattle, WA	123	C7
Kiwanis Pk, Bend, OR	192	B2
Kiwanis Pk, College Place, WA	207	B5
Kiwanis Pk, Everett, WA	120	C4
Kiwanis Pk, Kirkland, WA	126	B4
Kiwanis-Schonwald Memorial Pk, Burien, WA	139	C2
Klahanie Pk, West Vancouver, BC	107	E4
Klamath Falls Lakeview Wayside, Klamath Co, OR	89	C6
Knott Pk, Portland, OR	163	E7
Koberg Beach State Pk, Hood River Co, OR	46	C5
Kobe Terrace Pk, Seattle, WA	128	D7
Kopachuck State Pk, Pierce Co, WA	25	A5
Kroeger Pk, Boise, ID	224	D4
Kubota Gardens, Seattle, WA	137	C3
Ladds Circle & Squares Pk, Portland, OR	166	B3
Ladybird Pk, Garden City, ID	221	B4
Lafferty Pk, Eugene, OR	185	D5
Lair Hill Pk, Portland, OR	165	D4
Lake Boren Pk, Newcastle, WA	138	E1
Lake Burien School Memorial Pk, Burien, WA	136	A7
Lake Chelan State Pk, Chelan Co, WA	18	A7
Lake City Pk, Seattle, WA	125	A1
Lake Cushman State Pk, Mason Co, WA	24	C4
Lake Easton State Pk, Kittitas Co, WA	26	D6
Lake Heights Pk, Bellevue, WA	134	E5
Lake Lenore Caves State Pk, Grant Co, WA	28	E4
Lake Newport State Pk, Pend Oreille Co, WA	21	C4
Lake Owyhee State Pk, Malheur Co, OR	82	D2
Lakeridge Pk, Seattle, WA	137	D3
Lake Sakajawea Pk, Longview, WA	155	D4
Lake Sammamish State Pk, King Co, WA	25	E3
Lake Sylvia State Pk, Montesano, WA	34	A1
Lake Terrell Wildlife Area, Whatcom Co, WA	5	A6
Lakeview Pk, Burien, WA	139	B1
Lakeview Pk, Nampa, ID	220	D3
Lake View Pk, Seattle, WA	129	B5
Lake Wenatchee State Pk, Chelan Co, WA	27	B1
Lakewood Active Pk, Lakewood, WA	143	A7
Lakewood Pk, King Co, WA	136	B4
Langus Riverfront Pk, Everett, WA	120	E1
Larkspur Pk, Bend, OR	192	C3
Larrabee State Pk, Whatcom Co, WA	15	C1
Larry Frost Pk, Tacoma, WA	142	A4
Laurel Hill Pk, Eugene, OR	186	C4
Laurelhurst Pk, Portland, OR	166	D2
Laurelhurst Pk, Seattle, WA	125	B7
Laurelhurst Pk Theatre Annex, Portland, OR	166	D2
Laurel Point Pk, Victoria, BC	111	D5
Laurelwood Pk, Portland, OR	167	A6
Laurelwood Pk, Roseburg, OR	196	A5
Lava Beds National Monument, Siskiyou Co, CA	100	B4
Lave Cast Forest, Deschutes Co, OR	77	D1
Lawton Pk, Seattle, WA	127	D1
Layton Pk, Kennewick, WA	206	C3
Lba Pk, Olympia, WA	148	C1
Leach Botanical Garden, Portland, OR	168	A7
Leach Creek Conservation Pk, University Place, WA	143	A3
Leach Pk, Vancouver, WA	158	A3
Leadbetter Point State Pk, Pacific Co, WA	33	C4
Lee Pk, Salem, OR	173	E2
Lents Pk, Portland, OR	167	C6
Leschi Pk, Seattle, WA	129	B7
Leverich Pk, Vancouver, WA	158	B2
Lewis & Clark Campsite State Pk, Pacific Co, WA	33	C7
Lewis & Clark National Historical Pk, Clatsop Co, OR	43	C1
Lewis & Clark Pk, Bend, OR	189	B7
Lewis & Clark State Pk, Lewis Co, WA	34	E5
Lewis & Clark State Pk, Multnomah Co, OR	45	B6
Lewis & Clark Trail State Pk, Columbia Co, WA	40	C7
Lewisville, Clark Co, WA	45	B4
Lexington Pk, Albany, OR	176	B4
Leyland Pk, West Vancouver, BC	107	D3
Liberty Pk, Boise, ID	223	C1
Liberty Pk, Nampa, ID	220	C6
Liberty Pk, Renton, WA	138	C6
Liberty Pk, Spokane, WA	212	C2
Liberty Ship Memorial Pk, Portland, OR	165	E1
Licton Springs Pk, Seattle, WA	124	C3
Lieser Crest Pk, Vancouver, WA	159	B5
Lillis-Albina Pk, Portland, OR	161	E7
Lime Kiln State Pk, San Juan Co, WA	14	D2
Lincoln-Eldridge Pk, Tacoma, WA	142	A7
Lincoln Heights Pk, Tacoma, WA	141	D7
Lincoln Pk, Portland, OR	168	A4
Lincoln Pk, Seattle, WA	135	C1
Lincoln Pk, Spokane, WA	212	C3
Lincoln Rock State Pk, Douglas Co, WA	27	E3
Lindsey Creek State Pk, Hood River Co, OR	46	B5
Linwood Pk, Spokane Co, WA	209	D1

Points of Interest Index

Parks & Recreation

FEATURE NAME Address City State	MAP#	GRID
Lions Community Playfield, Bremerton, WA	122	B3
Lions Pk, Nampa, ID	220	A3
Lions Pk, Olympia, WA	146	B5
Lithia Pk, Ashland, OR	199	D4
Little Squalicum Pk, Whatcom Co, WA	113	A1
Livingston Pk, Salem, OR	172	C6
Logan Pk, Centralia, WA	151	C5
Loma Vista Pk, Spokane, WA	209	C2
Loomis Lake State Pk, Pacific Co, WA	33	C5
Loren Kondo Pk, Spokane, WA	210	E3
Lotus Isle Pk, Portland, OR	157	E6
Louisa Boren Pk, Seattle, WA	128	E3
Louis P Aldrich Pk, Salem, OR	173	E2
Lovejoy Pk, Portland, OR	165	D3
Lowell Pk, Everett, WA	120	D5
Lowell State Pk, Lowell, OR	64	E6
Lowman Beach Pk, Seattle, WA	131	C7
Lownsdale Square, Portland, OR	165	E3
Loyal Heights Playfield, Seattle, WA	123	E5
Luby Pk, Caldwell, ID	219	D2
Lucas Pk, Pasco, WA	204	C4
Lucky Peak State Pk, Ada Co, ID	84	B2
Luther Burbank Pk, Mercer Island, WA	134	A2
Lynchview Pk, Portland, OR	168	D3
Lynchwood Pk, Portland, OR	168	D5
Lynwood Loop Pk, Richland, WA	203	C1
Lyons Ferry State Pk, Franklin Co, WA	40	C4
Macaulay Point Pk, Esquimalt, BC	111	B5
MacDonald Pk, Victoria, BC	111	D6
Mackay Creek Pk, North Vancouver District, BC	108	B2
Mackay Pk, North Vancouver District, BC	108	B5
Maclean Pk, Vancouver, BC	110	C2
Madison Pk, Seattle, WA	129	B3
Madrona Pk, Portland, OR	161	D5
Madrona Pk, Seattle, WA	129	B6
Magnolia Pk, Seattle, WA	127	C2
Mahon Pk, North Vancouver, BC	108	C4
Malkin Pk, Vancouver, BC	109	A7
Manchester State Pk, Kitsap Co, WA	25	B3
Mangan Pk, Eugene, OR	180	D4
Manito Pk, Spokane, WA	212	A4
Manitou Pk, Boise, ID	224	C3
Manitou Pk, Tacoma, WA	143	B4
Manning Provincial Pk, Okanagan-Similkameen, BC	7	B3
Maplecrest Pk, Clark Co, WA	160	E3
Maplewood Pk, Renton, WA	138	E7
Maplewood Playfield, Seattle, WA	132	D4
Maplewood Roadside Pk, Renton, WA	138	E7
Marathon Pk, Olympia, WA	145	D6
Maria C Jackson State Pk, Coos Co, OR	74	C6
Maricara Pk, Portland, OR	169	B3
Marina Pk, Kirkland, WA	126	C6
Marine Pk, Tacoma, WA	141	C1
Marine Pk, Vancouver, WA	158	D6
Marine View Pk, Normandy Park, WA	139	B7
Marion Square Pk, Salem, OR	171	D7
Maritime Heritage Pk, Bellingham, WA	113	C3
Marquam Nature Pk, Portland, OR	165	C4
Marshall Community Pk, Vancouver, WA	158	A4
Marshall Pk, Portland, OR	169	C2
Marsh Pk, Kirkland, WA	126	C7
Martha Washington School Pk, Seattle, WA	133	C7
Martin Luther King Jr Pk, Seattle, WA	133	A2
Mar Vista Pk, Normandy Park, WA	139	B6
Maryhill State Pk, Klickitat Co, WA	47	B5
Mary Minerva McCroskey Memorial St Pk, Benewah Co, ID	31	E7
Mary Minerva McCroskey Memorial St Pk, Latah Co, ID	31	D7
Mary S Young State Pk, West Linn, OR	55	A1
Masko Pk, Fircrest, WA	141	A7
Matia Island State Pk, San Juan Co, WA	4	E7
Matilda Jackson State Pk, Lewis Co, WA	34	E5
Matthews Beach Pk, Seattle, WA	125	C3
Maud Williamson State Pk, Yamhill Co, OR	54	C3
Maurie Jacobs Pk, Eugene, OR	181	C7
May Creek Pk, Newcastle, WA	138	E2
Mayer State Pk, Wasco Co, OR	46	D5
Maynard Pk, Saanich, BC	112	E1
Mcauliffe Pk, Kirkland, WA	126	D3
McBride Pk, Vancouver, BC	109	A3
McCarver Pk, Tacoma, WA	142	A6
McCormick Pk, Bellevue, WA	130	C5
McCoy Pk, Portland, OR	161	B1
McCurdy Pk, Seattle, WA	129	A2
McDonald Provincial Pk, North Saanich, BC	4	B7
McDonald State Pk, Benton Co, OR	177	A1
McKay Pk, Bend, OR	191	E1
McKay Pk, Salem, OR	172	D6
McKenna Pk, Portland, OR	161	A2
McKinley Pk, Tacoma, WA	142	C7
McLoughlin State Pk, Multnomah Co, OR	45	E6
McMicken Heights Pk, Seatac, WA	140	B2
McMicken Island State Pk, Mason Co, WA	24	E6
McRea Pk, Salem, OR	174	A1
McSpadden Pk, Vancouver, BC	110	D4
Meadowbrook Marsh Pk, Vancouver, WA	159	B3
Meadowbrook North Pk, Vancouver, WA	159	C3
Meadowbrook Playfield, Seattle, WA	125	A2
Meadow Homes Pk, Vancouver, WA	158	D3
Meadow Pk, Saanich, BC	111	B1
Meadow Pk, Springfield, OR	186	E1
Medina Beach Pk, Medina, WA	129	E5
Medina Pk, Medina, WA	130	A5
Mee-Kwa-Mooks Pk, Seattle, WA	131	C4
Meldrum Bar State Pk, Gladstone, OR	55	A1
Melvin Miller Pk, Eugene, OR	185	A3
Memaloose State Pk, Wasco Co, OR	46	D5
Memorial Pk, Bellingham, WA	113	D2
Memorial Pk, Boise, ID	222	C6
Memorial Pk, Caldwell, ID	219	B4
Memorial Pk, Esquimalt, BC	111	A4
Memorial Pk, Pasco, WA	204	C6
Memorial Pk, West Vancouver, BC	107	B3
Memorial South Pk, Vancouver, BC	110	C7
Memory Mill Plain Pk, Vancouver, WA	158	B4
Mercerdale Hillside Pk, Mercer Island, WA	133	E3
Mercerdale Pk, Mercer Island, WA	133	E2
Mercer Slough Pk, Bellevue, WA	134	D3
Mercier Pk, Pasco, WA	204	D7
Merrifield Pk, Portland, OR	163	E7
Meydenbauer Pk, Bellevue, WA	130	B6
Midland Pk, Portland, OR	167	E3
Mike Whittam Pk, Keizer, OR	172	B1
Millcoma Myrtle Grove State Pk, Coos Co, OR	74	B3
Millenium Plaza Pk, Lake Oswego, OR	169	E7
Millersylvania State Pk, Thurston Co, WA	34	E2
Mill Pk, Portland, OR	167	E4
Mill Plain One Pk, Vancouver, WA	159	E5
Mill Race Pk, Salem, OR	173	E1
Millwood Pk, Millwood, WA	213	C1
Milo McIver State Pk, Clackamas Co, OR	55	B1
Milwaukee Pk, Boise, ID	221	A5
Minnehaha Pk, Spokane, WA	210	E5
Minnitti Recreational Pk, Tacoma, WA	141	A5
Minto-Brown Island Pk, Salem, OR	173	A2
Mirabeau Pk, Spokane Valley, WA	214	B1
Mission Pk, Spokane, WA	210	B7
Mitchell Pk, Grants Pass, OR	197	B5
Molalla River State Pk, Clackamas Co, OR	54	E2
Monroe Pk, Eugene, OR	185	C1
Montavilla Pk, Portland, OR	167	B1
Montgomery Pk, Vancouver, BC	109	D7
Montlake Playfield, Seattle, WA	128	E2
Moodyville Pk, North Vancouver, BC	108	E6
Moore Pk, Klamath Falls, OR	201	A5
Moran State Pk, San Juan Co, WA	5	A7
Morningside Pk, Salem, OR	173	E5
Morningside Pk, Yarrow Point, WA	130	B2
Morse Ranch Pk, Eugene, OR	185	D4
Moses Lake State Pk, Moses Lake, WA	29	A7
Mosquito Creek Pk, North Vancouver, BC	108	C4
Moulton Falls State Pk, Clark Co, WA	45	B4
Mountain View Pk, Boise, ID	221	B5
Mt Baker Pk, Seattle, WA	133	C4
Mt Pleasant Pk, Vancouver, BC	110	A5
Mt Rainier National Pk, Pierce Co, WA	36	A2
Mt Scott Pk, Portland, OR	167	B7
Mt Seymour Provincial Pk, North Vancouver District, BC	4	E1
Mt Spokane State Pk, Spokane Co, WA	21	C7
Mt St Helens National Monument, Skamania Co, WA	35	D7
Mt Tabor Pk, Portland, OR	167	A3
Mt Tolmie Pk, Saanich, BC	112	C1
Mukilteo State Pk, Mukilteo, WA	15	C7
Municipal Pk, Boise, ID	224	D1
Munson Creek Falls State Pk, Tillamook Co, OR	53	D1
Murdo Frazer Pk, North Vancouver District, BC	108	B3
Muriel O Ponsler Memorial St Wayside, Lane Co, OR	63	A4
Myrtle Edwards Pk, Seattle, WA	128	A5
Nathan Hale Playfield, Seattle, WA	125	B2
Nature Trails Pk, Normandy Park, WA	139	B5
Nehalem Bay State Pk, Tillamook Co, OR	43	C5
Nehalem Pk, Portland, OR	170	E1
Neighbors Pk, Tacoma, WA	142	A4
Nelson Pk, Salem, OR	173	A5
Nelson Pk, Vancouver, BC	109	E2
Neptune State Pk, Lane Co, OR	63	B3
Neskowin Beach State Wayside, Tillamook Co, OR	53	C3
Nestucca Spit State Pk, Tillamook Co, OR	53	C2
Nevada Playfield, Spokane, WA	210	B2
Newberry National Volcanic Monument, Deschutes Co, OR	77	D2
Newcastle Beach Pk, Bellevue, WA	134	D4
Newport Hills Pk, Bellevue, WA	134	D6
Nez Perce National Historical Pk, Nez Perce Co, ID	42	C6
Nolte State Pk, King Co, WA	25	E6
Norgate Pk, North Vancouver District, BC	108	A4
Normandale Pk, Portland, OR	166	E1
Norquay Pk, Vancouver, BC	110	E7
North Acres Pk, Seattle, WA	124	D1
North Cascades National Pk, Chelan Co, WA	17	A2
North Clackamas City Pk, Milwaukie, OR	170	E6
Northgate Pk, Portland, OR	161	A1
Northgate Pk, Salem, OR	172	B4
Northgate Pk, Seattle, WA	124	D2
North Highlands Pk, Renton, WA	138	D4
North Kirkland Community Center, Kirkland, WA	126	C2
North Mercerdale Hillside Pk, Mercer Island, WA	133	E2
North Mountain Pk, Ashland, OR	200	A3
North Passage Point Pk, Seattle, WA	128	D1
North Pk Blocks, Portland, OR	165	E2
North Powellhurst Pk, Portland, OR	168	B3
North Rose Hill Pk, Kirkland, WA	126	E4
North Santiam State Pk, Marion Co, OR	55	A6
North Seatac Pk, Seatac, WA	136	E6
North Seattle Pk, Seattle, WA	124	C2
North Shorewood Pk, King Co, WA	136	A3
North Slope Historic District Pk, Tacoma, WA	141	E3
Northtowne Pk, Bellevue, WA	130	C3
Northview Terrace Pk, Keizer, OR	172	A2
North Westmoreland Pk, Eugene, OR	185	C2
Norwood Village Pk, Bellevue, WA	134	E1
NW Paradise Pk State Pk, Clark Co, WA	45	A4
Oakbrook Pk, Vancouver, WA	159	D2
Oakland Pk, Tacoma, WA	141	B7
Oaklands Pk, Victoria, BC	112	B3
Oakmont Pk, Eugene, OR	182	A6
Oak Pk, Richland, WA	203	C2
Oaks Pioneer Pk, Portland, OR	170	A1
Oak Tree Pk, Tacoma, WA	143	C5
Occidental Square Pk, Seattle, WA	128	C7
Ocean City State Pk, Grays Harbor Co, WA	23	B7
Ochoco Lake State Pk, Crook Co, OR	67	C3
Ochoco State Pk, Prineville, OR	67	B3
Ohde Avenue Pk, Kirkland, WA	126	D6
Olallie State Pk, King Co, WA	26	B4
Old Apple Tree Pk, Vancouver, WA	158	A5
Old Fort Townsend State Pk, Jefferson Co, WA	15	A6
Old Man House State Pk, Kitsap Co, WA	25	B2
Old Mission State Pk, Kootenai Co, ID	32	C3
Old Town Pk, Tacoma, WA	141	D2
Olmstead Place State Pk, Kittitas Co, WA	37	D1
Olympia City Pk, Olympia, WA	146	A5
Olympic National Pk, Jefferson Co, WA	23	D2
Olympic National Pk, Port Angeles, WA	117	C6
Olympic Sculpture Pk, Seattle, WA	128	B5
Ona Beach State Pk, Lincoln Co, OR	63	B1
Ontario State Pk, Ontario, OR	72	A5
Oppenheimer Pk, Vancouver, BC	110	B2
Orchard Heights Pk, Salem, OR	171	B6
Orchards Pk, Clark Co, WA	159	C1
Oredson Todd Woods, Jackson Co, OR	200	B7
Oregon Cascades Rec Area, Klamath Co, OR	76	D4
Oregon Caves National Monument, Josephine Co, OR	97	E1
Oregon Dunes National Rec Area, Coos Co, OR	73	E3
Oregon Dunes National Rec Area, Lane Co, OR	63	A6
Oregon Pk, Portland, OR	166	C1
Osoyoos State Pk, Okanogan Co, WA	8	E5
Oswald Pk, Victoria, BC	112	A3
Oswald West State Pk, Tillamook Co, OR	43	C4
Otter Crest State Pk, Lincoln Co, OR	53	B6
Overlook Pk, Portland, OR	161	D6
Owen Rose Garden, Eugene, OR	181	D7
Owens Pk, Boise, ID	221	E3
Owyhee Pk, Boise, ID	224	A5
Oyhut Wildlife Rec Area, Ocean Shores, WA	149	B6
Pacific Beach State Pk, Grays Harbor Co, WA	23	B6
Pacific Community Pk, Clark Co, WA	160	D4
Pacific Pines State Pk, Pacific Co, WA	33	C5
Pacific Pk, Bend, OR	189	E7
Pacific Rim National Pk, Cowichan Valley, BC	12	E1
Packer Johns Cabin State Pk, Adams Co, ID	62	E4
Page Pk, Lane Co, OR	183	A6
Painted Hills State Pk, Wheeler Co, OR	57	E7
Palma Ciea Pk, Keizer, OR	171	D2
Palouse Falls State Pk, Franklin Co, WA	40	B4
Pandora Pk, Vancouver, BC	110	E2
Park Blocks, Eugene, OR	185	E1
Parkcenter Pk, Boise, ID	224	D2
Parkdale Pk, Marion Co, OR	172	E3
Parklane Pk, Portland, OR	168	C3
Park on the Lid, Mercer Island, WA	133	E1
Pasco Youth Baseball Complex, Pasco, WA	204	C7
Patos Island State Pk, San Juan Co, WA	4	E6
Pat Pfeifer Barrier-Free Pk, Gresham, OR	168	E2
Patrick S Byrne Pk, Spokane, WA	210	A4
Patton Square, Portland, OR	161	E5
Peace Arch Provincial Pk, White Rock, BC	5	A5
Peace Arch State Pk, Blaine, WA	5	A5
Pearrygin Lake State Pk, Okanogan Co, WA	18	A2
Peck Field, Tacoma, WA	141	D5
Pemberton Pk, Victoria, BC	112	C6
Pendleton Miller Playfield, Seattle, WA	128	E5
Pendleton Pk, Portland, OR	165	A6
Peninsula Pk Rose Garden, Portland, OR	161	E4
Penrose Point State Pk, Pierce Co, WA	25	A6
People's Pk, Tacoma, WA	141	E4
Peter Kerr Pk, Multnomah Co, OR	170	A5
Peter Kirk Pk, Kirkland, WA	126	C6
Petersen Pk, Eugene, OR	180	D6
Peter Skene Ogden State Pk, Jefferson Co, OR	66	E2
Peter S Ogden Pk, Vancouver, WA	159	B3
Pettygrove Pk, Portland, OR	165	E3
Philip Arnold Pk, Renton, WA	138	C7
Philip Foster Farm, Clackamas Co, OR	55	C1
Phillippi Pk, Boise, ID	223	D4
Piccolo Pk, Portland, OR	166	C4
Pierce Pk, Springfield, OR	183	C6
Pikes Peak Greenbelt, Bellevue, WA	130	E2
Pilot Butte State Pk, Bend, OR	190	C7
Pioneer Pk, Bend, OR	190	A6
Pioneer Pk, Corvallis, OR	178	A6
Pioneer Pk, Mercer Island, WA	134	A7
Pioneer Pk, Tumwater, WA	148	A3
Pioneer Pk, Walla Walla, WA	208	B3
Pioneer Square, Portland, OR	165	E2
Pioneer Square Pk, Seattle, WA	128	C7
Pistol River State Pk, Curry Co, OR	85	D6
Pittock Acres Pk, Portland, OR	165	B2
Platt Gardens, Boise, ID	224	B2
Playfair Pk, Saanich, BC	112	A1
Pleasant Harbor State Pk, Jefferson Co, WA	24	E2
Plum Tree Pk, Seattle, WA	129	A5
Ponderosa Pk, Bend, OR	192	C1
Porteau Cove Provincial Pk, Squamish-Lillooet, BC	2	C7
Portland Avenue Pk, Tacoma, WA	142	D7
Portland Classical Chinese Garden, Portland, OR	165	E2
Portland Heights Pk, Portland, OR	165	B4
Portland Women's Forum State Pk, Multnomah Co, OR	45	C7
Port Orford Heads State Pk, Curry Co, OR	85	C2
Portside Pk, Vancouver, BC	110	B2
Portsmouth Pk, Portland, OR	161	A2
Posey Island State Pk, San Juan Co, WA	14	D1
Potholes State Pk, Grant Co, WA	39	A1
Potlatch State Pk, Mason Co, WA	24	C5
Powell Butte Nature Pk, Portland, OR	168	C6
Powell Pk, Portland, OR	166	B5
Powers Marine Pk, Portland, OR	170	A2
Prairie Creek Redwoods State Pk, Humboldt Co, CA	97	A7
Pratt Pk, Seattle, WA	128	E7
Prentis I Frazier Pk, Seattle, WA	129	A5
Pride Pk, Springfield, OR	187	C2
Priest Lake St Park-Indian Creek Unit, Bonner Co, ID	21	E1
Priest Point Pk, Olympia, WA	146	A2
Prince Edward Pk, Vancouver, BC	110	B5
Prince of Wales Pk, Vancouver, BC	109	C6
Princess Pk, North Vancouver District, BC	108	E2
Prineville Reservoir State Pk, Crook Co, OR	67	B5
Pringle Creek Pk, Salem, OR	173	D1
Pritchard Island Beach, Seattle, WA	137	C1
Private Pk, Normandy Park, WA	139	A3
Private Pk Kingsgate, King Co, WA	126	E1
Prospect State Wayside, Jackson Co, OR	88	A3
Providence Pk, Bend, OR	190	E7
Puget Gardens Pk, Tacoma, WA	141	C2
Puget Pk, Seattle, WA	132	A5
Puget Pk, Tacoma, WA	141	C2
Puget Sound Pk, King Co, WA	136	C5
Quail Ridge Pk, Eugene, OR	180	D1
Quarnberg Pk, Vancouver, WA	158	B4
Queen Anne Bowl, Seattle, WA	128	A2
Queen Elizabeth Pk, Vancouver, BC	110	A6
Quilchena Pk, Vancouver, BC	109	C6
Quintus Pk, Roseburg, OR	195	D4
Racine Pk, Bellingham, WA	113	E1
Railroad District Pk, Ashland, OR	199	E3
Rainbow Falls State Pk, Lewis Co, WA	34	C4
Rainbow Pk, Victoria, BC	111	C4
Rainier Beach Playfield, Seattle, WA	137	C1
Rainier Playfield, Seattle, WA	133	B4
Raven-Eckstein Pk, Seattle, WA	125	A6
Ravenna Pk, Seattle, WA	124	E6
Ravine Pk, Vancouver, BC	109	C6
Raymond Pk, Portland, OR	167	E6
Recreation Pk, Chehalis, WA	152	C5
Red Bridge State Pk, Union Co, OR	60	B2
Redwood National Pk, Del Norte Co, CA	96	E4
Redwood National Pk, Humboldt Co, CA	97	A7
Reservoir Park-Kirkland, Kirkland, WA	126	C4
Rey Sargent Pk, North Vancouver, BC	108	D4
Rhododendron State Pk, Island Co, WA	15	A4
Richardson Pk, Pasco, WA	204	B5
Riley Pk, Vancouver, BC	110	A6
River Front Pk, Roseburg, OR	195	E4
Riverfront Pk, Salem, OR	173	C1
Riverfront Pk, Spokane, WA	211	E1
River Road Pk, Salem, OR	171	D4
River's Edge Pk, Keizer, OR	171	D4
Riverside Pk, Boise, ID	222	A7
Riverside Pk, Centralia, WA	151	C4
Riverside Pk, Portland, OR	166	A5
Riverside State Pk, Spokane Co, WA	209	A5
Riverview Pk, Bend, OR	190	A5
Riverview Playfield, Seattle, WA	132	B7
River Villa Pk, Clackamas Co, OR	170	A6
Roanoke Pk, Seattle, WA	128	D2
Robert J Porter Pk, Victoria, BC	112	A6

Points of Interest Index

Parks & Recreation

FEATURE NAME Address City State	MAP# GRID
Robert Morris Earthworks Pk, Seatac, WA	140 A7
Robert W Sawyer River Pk, Bend, OR	190 A4
Robson Pk, Vancouver, BC	110 B5
Robson Square, Vancouver, BC	109 E2
Rochester Heights Pk, Spokane, WA	210 C3
Rockcrest Pk, Esquimalt, BC	111 A4
Rock Island State Pk, Douglas Co, WA	28 A5
Rockport State Pk, Skagit Co, WA	16 B2
Rockwood Central Pk, Gresham, OR	168 E3
Rocky Butte State Pk, Portland, OR	163 D7
Rocky Creek State Scenic Viewpoint, Lincoln Co, OR	53 B6
Roehr Pk, Lake Oswego, OR	170 A6
Rogers Pk, Tacoma, WA	142 C7
Rolley Lake Provincial Pk, Mission, BC	5 C2
Roosevelt Field, Bremerton, WA	122 B4
Roosevelt Pk, Bellingham, WA	113 E2
Roosevelt Pk, Tacoma, WA	144 D1
Rooster Rock State Pk, Multnomah Co, OR	45 D6
Rose City Pk, Portland, OR	163 A7
Roselawn Pk, Portland, OR	162 B5
Ross Lake National Rec Area, Whatcom Co, WA	7 A5
Rossman Pk, Lake Oswego, OR	169 E6
Ross Playfield, Seattle, WA	124 A7
Rotary Pk, Everett, WA	120 E7
Rotary Pk, Mercer Island, WA	134 B4
Rotary Pond Pk, Caldwell, ID	219 B1
Rough & Ready Creek State Pk, Josephine Co, OR	97 C1
Round Butte State Pk, Jefferson Co, OR	66 D1
Round Lake State Pk, Bonner Co, ID	22 A4
Roxhill Pk, Seattle, WA	135 E2
Royal Athletic Pk, Victoria, BC	112 A4
Royal Delle Pk, Lane Co, OR	182 E6
Royal Oaks Pk, Salem, OR	172 E7
Rudd Pk, Saanich, BC	111 D2
Ruhl Pk, Medford, OR	198 E5
Ruth Pk, Spokane, WA	209 E2
Sacajawea Pk, Portland, OR	163 B5
Sacajawea State Pk, Pasco, WA	49 C1
Saddle Mountain State Pk, Clatsop Co, OR	43 E3
St. Alban's Pk, North Vancouver District, BC	108 D1
St. Ann's Academy Grounds, Victoria, BC	111 E6
Saint Edward State Pk, Kenmore, WA	25 C2
St. Francis Pk, Portland, OR	166 B2
St. Helens Pk, Vancouver, WA	158 D4
Salmon Bay Pk, Seattle, WA	123 E5
Salmon Creek Pk, King Co, WA	136 B4
Salmon Creek Ravine, Burien, WA	136 A5
Salmon Creek Waterway, Burien, WA	136 A5
Saltwater State Pk, Des Moines, WA	25 C5
Sam Brown Pk, Vancouver, WA	158 E4
Samuel H Boardman State Pk, Curry Co, OR	85 D7
San Juan Isl National Hist Park-Amr Cmp, San Juan Co, WA	14 D2
San Juan Isl National Hist Park-Engl Cmp, San Juan Co, WA	14 D1
San Salvador State Pk, Marion Co, OR	54 C2
Santana County Pk, Marion Co, OR	174 E3
Santiam State Forest, Clackamas Co, OR	55 B5
Santiam State Forest, Linn Co, OR	55 B7
Santiam State Forest, Marion Co, OR	55 B5
Sarah Helmick State Pk, Polk Co, OR	54 B6
Sather Pk, Port Townsend, WA	119 D3
Saxe Point Pk, Esquimalt, BC	111 A5
Scenic Beach State Pk, Kitsap Co, WA	24 E2
Scenic Pk, Ashland, OR	199 D2
Schafer State Pk, Mason Co, WA	24 A7
Schlagel Pk, Pasco, WA	206 D1
Schmitz Pk, Seattle, WA	131 C3
School District Playfield, Seattle, WA	123 E6
Schrunk Plaza, Portland, OR	165 E3
Scott Pk, Milwaukie, OR	170 B3
Seacrest Marina Pk, Seattle, WA	131 E1
Seaforth Peace Pk, Vancouver, BC	109 C3
Seahurst Pk, Burien, WA	136 A6
Seaquest State Pk, Cowlitz Co, WA	34 E7
Sebree Pk, Caldwell, ID	219 C4
Secret Pk, Mercer Island, WA	133 D2
Seeley Lake Pk, Lakewood, WA	143 A7
Sellwood Pk, Portland, OR	170 A1
Sellwood Riverfront Pk, Portland, OR	170 A1
Senator Henry M Jackson Pk, Everett, WA	120 E1
Seneca Fouts Memorial State Pk, Hood River Co, OR	46 B5
Seola Pk, Seattle, WA	135 E4
Sequim Bay State Pk, Clallam Co, WA	14 D6
Sewallcrest Pk, Portland, OR	166 C3
Seward Pk, Seattle, WA	133 D5
Shadle Pk, Spokane, WA	209 C4
Shaughnessy Pk, Vancouver, BC	109 D5
Sheldon Pk, Eugene, OR	182 A5
Shelton Wayside, Wheeler Co, OR	58 A5
Shepperd's Dell State Pk, Multnomah Co, OR	45 D6
Sheridan Pk, Tacoma, WA	141 E6
Sherwood Pk, Ashland, OR	200 B5
Shevlin Regional Pk, Bend, OR	189 A4
Shively Pk, Astoria, OR	153 D3
Shore Acres State Pk, Coos Co, OR	73 D4
Shoreline Pk, Boise, ID	222 A7
Shorewood Pk, Burien, WA	135 E4
Shoshone Pk, Boise, ID	224 B4
Sierra Heights Pk, King Co, WA	138 E3
Silver Falls State Pk, Marion Co, OR	55 A5
Siskiyou Mountain Pk, Jackson Co, OR	200 A7
Skagit Valley Provincial Pk, Fraser Valley, BC	6 E4
Skinner Butte Pk, Eugene, OR	181 D7
Skyline Pk, Salem, OR	173 A7
Skyliner Summit Pk, Bend, OR	191 C1
Skyline Sports Complex, Bend, OR	191 C2
Skyway Pk, King Co, WA	137 E5
Sladden Pk, Eugene, OR	181 C7
Slater Pk, Mercer Island, WA	133 D2
S Leslie Groves Pk, Richland, WA	203 D4
Slocan Pk, Vancouver, BC	110 E6
Smith Cove Pk, Seattle, WA	127 D3
Smith River National Rec Area, Del Norte Co, CA	97 B3
Smith Rock State Pk, Deschutes Co, OR	66 E3
Snake Lake Pk, Tacoma, WA	141 B6
Soccer Field, Salem, OR	174 A1
Sorrel Way Pk, Eugene, OR	182 A7
Soundview Playfield, Seattle, WA	123 E3
South 23rd and Alaska Pk, Tacoma, WA	141 E6
South Beach State Pk, Newport, OR	53 B7
South Beach State Pk, Pacific Co, WA	33 B2
South Cliff Pk, Vancouver, WA	158 D5
South End Rec Area, Tacoma, WA	143 B3
Southern Heights Pk, King Co, WA	136 D5
Southgate Pk, Tukwila, WA	137 B6
South Lake Union Pk, Seattle, WA	128 C4
South Mercer Playfield, Mercer Island, WA	134 A7
South Passage Point Pk, Seattle, WA	128 D1
South Pk, Tacoma, WA	143 C2
South Pk Blocks, Portland, OR	165 D3
South Village Pk, Salem, OR	173 D5
South Waterfront Pk, Portland, OR	165 E5
South Whidbey State Pk, Island Co, WA	15 B6
Sowden Pk, North Vancouver District, BC	108 B3
Spencer Spit State Pk, San Juan Co, WA	14 E2
Spinney Homestead Pk, Kirkland, WA	126 E4
Spokane Battlefield State Pk, Spokane Co, WA	30 E2
Springbrook Pk, Lake Oswego, OR	169 B6
Spring Garden Pk, Portland, OR	169 B1
Spring Pk, Milwaukie, OR	170 B5
Spring Street Pk, Seattle, WA	128 E6
Springwater Trail Corridor, Portland, OR	168 B7
Spruce Pk, Seattle, WA	128 E7
Squak Mountain State Pk, King Co, WA	25 E4
Squaw Creek State Wayside, Lane Co, OR	63 A4
Squaxin Island State Pk, Mason Co, WA	24 E6
Squilchuck State Pk, Chelan Co, WA	27 E5
Stadacona Pk, Victoria, BC	112 B5
Stan Hedwall Pk, Chehalis, WA	152 C6
Stanley Pk, Milwaukie, OR	170 E4
Stanley Pk, Vancouver, BC	107 D6
Stanley Playfield, Tacoma, WA	141 E6
Stan Sayres Memorial Pk, Seattle, WA	133 B3
Starvation Creek State Pk, Hood River Co, OR	46 B5
State Street Pk, Eugene, OR	180 A4
Station Camp Pk, Pacific Co, WA	33 C7
Stawamus Chief Provincial Pk, Squamish, BC	2 D6
Steamboat Rock State Pk, Grant Co, WA	29 B1
Steptoe Butte State Pk, Whitman Co, WA	31 C7
Steptoe Memorial State Pk, Whitman Co, WA	31 B6
Steven J Underwood Memorial Pk, Des Moines, WA	139 E7
Stevens Canyon Pk, Bremerton, WA	122 B3
Stevens Field Pk, Olympia, WA	145 E6
Stewart Heights Pk, Tacoma, WA	144 B3
Stewart Park-Fir Grove Section, Roseburg, OR	195 D5
Stonefield Beach State Wayside, Lane Co, OR	63 A3
Strathcona Pk, Vancouver, BC	110 C3
Stretch Point State Pk, Mason Co, WA	24 E5
Stuart Island State Pk, San Juan Co, WA	4 C7
Sturgus Pk, Seattle, WA	132 E1
Sucia Island State Pk, San Juan Co, WA	4 E6
Sullivan Pk, Spokane Valley, WA	214 D2
Summer Falls State Pk, Grant Co, WA	29 A4
Summer's Walk Pk, Vancouver, WA	160 E7
Summit Pk, Bend, OR	189 D5
Summit Pk, Everett, WA	120 E2
Summit Pk, Victoria, BC	112 A3
Sun Lakes State Pk, Grant Co, WA	28 E3
Sun Meadow Pk, Bend, OR	192 B4
Sunnyside Pk, Vancouver, BC	110 C5
Sunnyslope Pk, Salem, OR	173 A6
Sunset Bay State Pk, Coos Co, OR	73 D4
Sunset Beach, Vancouver, BC	109 D2
Sunset Court Pk, Renton, WA	138 D4
Sunset Hill Viewpoint Pk, Seattle, WA	123 C5
Sunset Pk, Boise, ID	221 E4
Sunset Pk, Keizer, OR	171 D3
Sunset Pk, Seatac, WA	136 E6
Sunset View Pk, Bend, OR	189 C7
Swan Creek Pk, Tacoma, WA	144 D3
Swan Lake Pk, Saanich, BC	111 D1
Sylvan Pk, Bend, OR	189 D5
Sylvester Pk, Pasco, WA	204 D6
Tam-O-Shanter Pk, Kelso, WA	156 C4
Tanner Springs Pk, Portland, OR	165 D1
Tapiola Pk, Astoria, OR	153 B3
Tatlow Pk, Vancouver, BC	109 B3
Templeton Pk, Vancouver, BC	110 E2
Terrace Pk, Kirkland, WA	126 C7
Terrace View Pk, Spokane Valley, WA	214 C6
Terry Pettus Pk, Seattle, WA	128 D3
Terwilliger Pk, Portland, OR	165 D6
Thea's Pk, Tacoma, WA	142 A4
The Cove Palisades State Pk, Jefferson Co, OR	66 D1
The Grotto, Portland, OR	163 C6
Thomas Kay Historical Pk, Salem, OR	173 E1
Thompson Pk, Portland, OR	164 B7
Thorndyke Pk, Seattle, WA	127 D3
Thornton Creek Natural Area, Seattle, WA	125 A3
Thornton Creek Pk, Seattle, WA	125 A1
Thornton Creek Pk 2, Seattle, WA	124 E3
Thornton Creek Pk 6, Seattle, WA	124 D2
Thornton Murphy Pk, Spokane, WA	212 D4
Thornton Pk, Vancouver, BC	110 B3
Thurston Pk, Springfield, OR	188 C2
Tideman Johnson Pk, Portland, OR	170 D2
Tietan Pk, Walla Walla, WA	208 B5
Tillamook State Forest, Clatsop Co, OR	43 D6
Tillamook State Forest, Tillamook Co, OR	43 D6
Tillicum Pk, Saanich, BC	111 B1
Timber-Linn Memorial Pk, Albany, OR	176 D3
Tolmie State Pk, Thurston Co, WA	24 E7
Topaz Pk, Victoria, BC	111 E3
Tou Velle State Pk, Jackson Co, OR	87 D5
Tower Crest Pk, Clark Co, WA	159 A1
Trafalgar Pk, Vancouver, BC	109 B5
Trainsong Pk, Eugene, OR	181 A6
Trenton Pk, Portland, OR	161 C2
Triangle Pk, Ashland, OR	199 E4
Tryon Creek State Pk, Lake Oswego, OR	169 E5
Tryon Creek State Pk, Portland, OR	169 D3
TT Minor Pk, Seattle, WA	128 E6
Tub Springs State Wayside, Jackson Co, OR	99 A1
Tugman Pk, Eugene, OR	185 E5
Tukwila Community Center Pk, Tukwila, WA	137 B5
Tukwila Pk, Tukwila, WA	140 D1
Tukwila Pond Pk, Tukwila, WA	140 D2
Tumalo State Pk, Deschutes Co, OR	66 D5
Turn Island State Pk, San Juan Co, WA	14 E2
Twanoh State Pk, Mason Co, WA	24 D5
Twenty Five Mile Creek State Pk, Chelan Co, WA	17 E6
Twin Falls State Pk, King Co, WA	26 B4
Twin Harbors State Pk, Grays Harbor Co, WA	150 C7
Tygh Valley State Wayside, Wasco Co, OR	56 E2
Tyson Pk, Springfield, OR	187 D2
Umpqua Lighthouse State Pk, Douglas Co, OR	74 A1
Underhill Playfield, Spokane, WA	212 D2
Underwood Pk, Kennewick, WA	205 E3
Union Pk, Medford, OR	198 A6
US Grant Pk, Portland, OR	162 D7
Ustick Pk, Caldwell, ID	219 C7
Unity Lake State Pk, Baker Co, OR	70 C1
University Pk, Eugene, OR	186 A3
University Pk, Portland, OR	161 B2
Unthank Pk, Portland, OR	161 E6
Uplands Pk, Oak Bay, BC	112 E3
Upper Macleay Pk, Portland, OR	165 A1
Ursich Gulch Pk, Tacoma, WA	141 D2
Valdez Pk, Vancouver, BC	109 A5
Valley of the Rogue State Pk, Jackson Co, OR	87 B5
Valley Ridge Pk, Seatac, WA	140 B4
Van Aalst Pk, Kirkland, WA	126 C5
Van Asselt Playfield, Seattle, WA	133 A7
Vance Pk, Gresham, OR	168 E3
Vancouver Lake Lowlands, Vancouver, WA	157 C1
Vancouver Lake Pk, Clark Co, WA	157 A1
Vandusen Botanical Garden, Vancouver, BC	109 D7
Van Fleet Pk, Vancouver, WA	159 A4
Vanier Pk, Vancouver, BC	109 D2
Vassault Playfield, Tacoma, WA	141 A1
Ventura Pk, Portland, OR	167 E2
Veterans Memorial Pk, Boise, ID	221 E5
Veterans Memorial Pk, Medford, OR	198 C7
Veterans Pk, Klamath Falls, OR	201 C6
Victoria Pk, North Vancouver, BC	108 D5
Victoria West Pk, Victoria, BC	111 D4
Victor Steinbrueck Pk, Seattle, WA	128 B6
Viento State Pk, Hood River Co, OR	46 B5
Vietnam Veterans Memorial Pk, Portland, OR	165 B3
View Point Pk, Medina, WA	130 A6
Viewpoint Pk, Seattle, WA	132 D3
View Point Playfield, Seattle, WA	125 B5
Village Pk, Vancouver, BC	109 C5
Vinzenz Lausmann Memorial St Pk, Hood River Co, OR	46 B5
Viretta Pk, Seattle, WA	129 B5
Virginia Vogel Pk, Medford, OR	198 B3
Vogel Pk, Ashland, OR	199 E3
Volunteer Pk, Pasco, WA	204 D6
Volunteer Pk, Seattle, WA	128 E4
Volunteer Pk, Springfield, OR	187 E3
Volunteer Pk, Vancouver, BC	109 B3
Walbran Pk, Oak Bay, BC	112 C6
Waldo J Dahl Playfield, Seattle, WA	125 A5
Wallace Falls State Pk, Snohomish Co, WA	16 B7
Wallace M Ruff Jr Memorial Pk, Lane Co, OR	188 D1
Wallace Pk, Portland, OR	165 C1
Wallace Pk, Salem, OR	171 D6
Walla Walla Pk, Walla Walla, WA	207 D5
Wallingford Playfield, Seattle, WA	124 C7
Wallowa Lake State Pk, Wallowa Co, OR	61 D1
Waluga Pk, Lake Oswego, OR	169 A7
Wanapum State Pk, Kittitas Co, WA	38 B2
Wapato Hills Pk, Tacoma, WA	143 D3
Wapato Pk, Tacoma, WA	143 E4
Ward Lake Pk, Olympia, WA	148 B2
Wards Lake Pk, Lakewood, WA	143 D6
Warm Springs Pk, Boise, ID	224 E2
Warren G Magnuson Pk, Seattle, WA	125 D5
Washburn Pk, Eugene, OR	186 A3
Washington/Jefferson Pk, Eugene, OR	181 D7
Washington Pk, Eugene, OR	185 D3
Washington Pk, Portland, OR	165 B3
Washington Pk, Seattle, WA	129 A3
Washington Pk, Walla Walla, WA	207 E3
Washington School Pk, Vancouver, WA	158 B2
Waterfront Pk, Seattle, WA	128 C6
Waterfront Pk, Vancouver, WA	158 A5
Waterfront Trails, North Vancouver, BC	108 B5
Watershed Pk, Kirkland, WA	130 D2
Watershed Pk, Olympia, WA	146 A7
Water Tower Pk, Des Moines, WA	139 C6
Water Tower Pk, Milwaukie, OR	170 D3
Waterworks Gardens, Renton, WA	137 E7
Waterworks Pk, Vancouver, WA	158 B3
Waverly Beach Pk, Kirkland, WA	126 B5
Waverly Pk, Kirkland, WA	126 B6
Wb Nelson State Recreation Site, Lincoln Co, OR	179 E5
Webster Pk, Port Angeles, WA	117 D4
Webster Pk, Seattle, WA	123 D5
Webster Pk, Spokane, WA	209 A4
We Johnson Pk, Richland, WA	203 A5
Welch Pk, North Vancouver District, BC	108 A5
Wellington Pk, Portland, OR	163 A6
Wenatchee Confluence State Pk, Chelan Co, WA	27 D4
Wenberg State Pk, Snohomish Co, WA	15 D5
West Bank Pk, Eugene, OR	181 C5
Westcrest Pk, Seattle, WA	136 B1
West D Street Greenway, Springfield, OR	186 D2
West Ewing Pk, Seattle, WA	128 A1
Westhaven State Pk, Westport, WA	150 B2
Westholm Pk, Grants Pass, OR	197 B4
Westlake Pk, Lake Oswego, OR	169 A6
West Magnolia Pk, Seattle, WA	127 C2
West Montlake Pk, Seattle, WA	128 E2
Westmoreland Pk, Eugene, OR	185 C3
Westmoreland Pk, Portland, OR	170 B1
West Pk, Nampa, ID	220 A4
Westport Light State Pk, Westport, WA	150 B4
West Powellhurst Pk, Portland, OR	167 E4
West Queen Anne Playfield, Seattle, WA	128 A3
West Salem Pk, Salem, OR	173 B1
West Spencer Butte Pk, Lane Co, OR	185 D7
Westwood Pk, Des Moines, WA	139 C5
Whalen Island State Pk, Tillamook Co, OR	53 C1
White Center Heights Pk, King Co, WA	136 B3
White Center Pk, King Co, WA	136 B3
White River Falls State Pk, Wasco Co, OR	56 E3
Whitman Mission National Historical Site, Walla Walla Co - WA	50 A2
Whittenberger Pk, Caldwell, ID	219 B2
Whittier Pk, Fircrest, WA	141 A7
Whittier Pk, Spokane, WA	211 B2
Wichita Pk, Milwaukie, OR	170 E4
Wiggums Hollow Pk, Everett, WA	120 D1
Wilburton Hill Pk, Bellevue, WA	130 E6
Wildflower Neighborhood Pk, Bend, OR	190 E6
Wildflower Pk, Bend, OR	191 B5
Wildwood Pk, Mercer Island, WA	134 A7
Wilkes Pk, Portland, OR	164 C6
Willamalane Pk, Springfield, OR	187 A1
Willamette Greenway State Pk, Yamhill Co, OR	54 D2
Willamette Heights Pk, Springfield, OR	186 E3
Willamette Manor Pk, Keizer, OR	171 E3
Willamette Mission State Pk, Marion Co, OR	54 C3
Willamette Pk, Portland, OR	165 E7
William A Bush Pk, Lacey, WA	148 E3
William E Moshier Memorial Pk, Burien, WA	139 C1
William Griffin Pk, North Vancouver District, BC	108 B3
William Grose Pk, Seattle, WA	129 A5
William M Tugman State Pk, Coos Co, OR	74 A2
William M Tugman State Pk, Douglas Co, OR	74 A2
William S Fort Memorial Pk, Springfield, OR	188 C2
Williams Pk, Boise, ID	224 D3
William T Wooten State Pk, Columbia Co, WA	40 E7
Willow Lane Pk, Boise, ID	221 D4

Points of Interest Index

Visitor Information

FEATURE NAME Address City State	MAP# GRID

Note Page

Note Page

Note Page